3D Computer Vision and Smart Building and City, 2nd Edition–Volume I

3D Computer Vision and Smart Building and City, 2nd Edition–Volume I

Topic Editors

Junxing Zheng
Peng Cao

MDPI

Basel • Beijing • Wuhan • Barcelona • Belgrade • Novi Sad • Cluj • Manchester

Topic Editors
Junxing Zheng
School of Civil and Hydraulic Engineering
Huazhong University of Science and Technology
Wuhan
China

Peng Cao
College of Architecture and Civil Engineering
Beijing University of Technology
Beijing
Chin

Editorial Office
MDPI AG
Grosspeteranlage 5
4052 Basel, Switzerland

This is a reprint of the Topic, published open access by the journals *Buildings* (ISSN 2075-5309), *Drones* (ISSN 2504-446X), *Energies* (ISSN 1996-1073), *Sensors* (ISSN 1424-8220), *Sustainability* (ISSN 2071-1050) and *ISPRS International Journal of Geo-Information* (ISSN 2220-9964), freely accessible at: https://www.mdpi.com/topics/0J25AOPO4H.

For citation purposes, cite each article independently as indicated on the article page online and as indicated below:

Lastname, A.A.; Lastname, B.B. Article Title. *Journal Name* **Year**, *Volume Number*, Page Range.

Volume I
ISBN 978-3-7258-6542-0 (Hbk)
ISBN 978-3-7258-6543-7 (PDF)
https://doi.org/10.3390/books978-3-7258-6543-7

Set
ISBN 978-3-7258-6540-6 (Hbk)
ISBN 978-3-7258-6541-3 (PDF)

Contents

sensors

MDPI

Article

Enhanced 3D Pose Estimation in Multi-Person, Multi-View Scenarios through Unsupervised Domain Adaptation with Dropout Discriminator

Junli Deng, Haoyuan Yao and Ping Shi *

School of Information and Communication Engineering, Communication University of China, Beijing 100024, China; dengjunliok@cuc.edu.cn (J.D.); tinsleyyao@cuc.edu.cn (H.Y.)
* Correspondence: shiping@cuc.edu.cn

Abstract: Data-driven pose estimation methods often assume equal distributions between training and test data. However, in reality, this assumption does not always hold true, leading to significant performance degradation due to distribution mismatches. In this study, our objective is to enhance the cross-domain robustness of multi-view, multi-person 3D pose estimation. We tackle the domain shift challenge through three key approaches: (1) A domain adaptation component is introduced to improve estimation accuracy for specific target domains. (2) By incorporating a dropout mechanism, we train a more reliable model tailored to the target domain. (3) Transferable Parameter Learning is employed to retain crucial parameters for learning domain-invariant data. The foundation for these approaches lies in the H-divergence theory and the lottery ticket hypothesis, which are realized through adversarial training by learning domain classifiers. Our proposed methodology is evaluated using three datasets: Panoptic, Shelf, and Campus, allowing us to assess its efficacy in addressing domain shifts in multi-view, multi-person pose estimation. Both qualitative and quantitative experiments demonstrate that our algorithm performs well in two different domain shift scenarios.

Keywords: domain adaptation; 3D pose estimation; transfer learning

1. Introduction

Due to the numerous real-world applications of 3D multi-view multi-person human pose estimation, such as human-computer interaction [1], virtual and augmented reality [2,3], etc., the field of computer vision has seen significant research in this area [4–7], which has been driven by deep neural networks and large-scale human-annotated datasets [8,9]. These multi-view pose estimation methods have achieved excellent performance on the benchmark datasets [8,9], but still face challenges because of the wide variation in viewpoints, personal appearance, backgrounds, illumination, image quality, and so on. Due to unavoidable domain shifts, pose estimators developed for one particular domain (i.e., the source domain) may not generalize well to novel testing domains (i.e., the target domains). For example, a 3D pose estimator trained on the Panoptic [9] dataset suffers a severe performance drop when evaluated on the Campus [10] and Shelf [10] datasets. In Figure 1, which shows several datasets used for 3D human pose estimation, we can see a considerable domain shift.

Even if more training data from various domains could solve this problem, it may be impractical due to the complexity of real-world scenarios and the high cost of 3D annotation. As a result, methods for successfully transferring a 3D pose estimator trained on a labeled source domain to a new unlabeled target domain are in high demand.

Even if gathering more training data from diverse domains could solve this issue, it may be impractical due to the complexity of real-world scenarios and the high expense of 3D annotation. For this reason, there is a great need for methods that can successfully transfer a 3D pose estimator trained on a labeled source domain to a new unlabeled target domain.

Figure 1. Depiction of various datasets utilized for multi-view, multi-person 3D pose estimation. Image examples are sourced from Panoptic [9], Campus [10], and Shelf [10], respectively. While all datasets feature scenes with clean backgrounds, they differ in aspects such as clothing, resolution, lighting, body size, and more. These visual disparities among the datasets complicate the task of applying pose estimation models across different domains.

Our research focuses on domain adaptation for multi-view, multi-person 3D pose estimation with covariate shift. We develop an end-to-end deep learning model called "Domain Adaptive VoxelPose" that is based on the cutting-edge VoxelPose model [11]. An unsupervised domain adaptation case occurs when full supervision is available in the source domain but none in the target domain. As a result, there should be no additional annotation costs in the target domain to obtain better 3D pose estimation.

We add three elements to the VoxelPose model to minimize the domain divergence between two domains in order to correct the domain shift. First, we train a domain classifier [12] using adversarial training to learn domain-invariant, reliable features. Second, we apply dropout to multiple discriminators by missing or dropping out each discriminator's feedback with a specific probability at the end of each batch. This makes the feature extractor more domain-invariant by requiring its output to satisfy a dynamic ensemble of discriminators as opposed to a singular discriminator. Thirdly, we present Transferable Parameter Learning (TransPar) [13] to eliminate the side effects of domain-specific information and enhance domain-invariant learning. TransPar divides all parameters into two categories: transferable parameters and non-transferable parameters. Consequently, TransPar provides distinct update rules for these two categories of parameters.

In conclusion, the following are the principal contributions of our work: (1) We provide domain adaptation components to reduce domain disparity between the selected target domain and the respective source domain. (2) To train a more domain-invariant feature extractor, we propose a novel method that applies an ensemble of dynamic dropout domain discriminators. (3) We employ Transferable Parameter Learning (TransPar) to reduce the negative effects of domain-specific knowledge throughout the learning process as well as to enhance the retention of domain-independent knowledge. (4) The suggested components are incorporated into the VoxelPose model, and the resulting system is capable of end-to-end training. Our method was evaluated on three datasets, and the results suggested that it could enhance the accuracy of cross-domain multi-view multi-person 3D pose estimation.

The paper is organized as follows. Section 2 discusses related works of the methods, including 3D human pose estimation and unsupervised domain adaptation. Section 3 introduces the main baseline, theory, hypothesis, and datasets used in the paper. Section 4 details the proposed methodology for unsupervised multi-view, multi-person 3D pose estimation. Section 5 verifies the feasibility of the proposed model. Section 6 concludes the paper, points out the limitations of the research, and proposes some future work.

2. Related Work

2.1. 3D Human Pose Estimation

3D pose estimation from monocular inputs [14–22] presents an ill-posed problem, as multiple 3D predictions can correspond to the same 2D projection. Multi-view approaches have been developed to alleviate such projective ambiguity. Some methods aggregate data from multiple cameras, utilizing camera settings to identify matching epipolar lines between various views [23]. Additionally, existing camera parameters can be leveraged to generalize new camera setups not present in the training data [24,25].

However, the complexity increases significantly when approaching multi-person scenarios. For multi-person tasks, current approaches mostly use a multi-stage pipeline, including reconstruction-based [10,26–30], volumetric paradigms [11,31], and regression-based approaches [6]. Using a combination of geometric and appearance signals as well as the cycle-consistency constraint, [26] matches 2D postures across several views. Ref. [11] proposes a two-stage volumetric paradigm that circumvents the cross-view matching problem, thereby decreasing the impact of erroneously created cross-view correspondences. Ref. [6] shows skeleton joints as learnable query embeddings and lets them gradually attend to and reason over the multi-view information from the input images to directly regress the actual 3D joint location.

Nevertheless, those efforts focused on the traditional context without taking domain adaptation into account. In this work, we adopt VoxelPose [11] as our foundational pose estimator and augment its generalization capabilities for multi-view, multi-person 3D pose estimation through domain adaptation.

2.2. Unsupervised Domain Adaptation

Deep learning algorithms are impacted by the domain-shift problem [32–34], which manifests as networks trained on one distribution of data performing poorly on another distribution. This issue typically arises when models are deployed in circumstances that are marginally different from those in the training set. The data from various domains is aligned so that the resulting models have strong generalization performance, which is how unsupervised domain adaptation approaches are typically used to solve this problem. Existing theoretical works can be broadly classified into two types: distance measurement methods and adversarial learning methods. (1) Method based on distance measurement. By reducing the Maximum Mean Discrepancy [35,36], investigate domain-invariant feature learning. (2) Method based on adversarial learning. Inspired by GANs [37], adversarial learning was used to align feature distributions across several domains on various 2D vision tasks [12,38–41]. Applying dropout to each discriminator's feedback [42] allows the generator to satisfy a dynamic ensemble of discriminators rather than a static single discriminator, which motivates us to include dropout mechanisms in our domain adaptation component.

Additionally, [43,44] attempts to translate images to close the domain gap at the pixel level. To lessen the $\mathcal{H}\Delta\mathcal{H}$ discrepancy, [45] adopted a two-branch classifier. Refs. [46,47] use curriculum learning [48] and sort cases based on how hard it is for them to realize the local sample-level curriculum. Ref. [49] suggests a way of gradually extending the feature norm to close the domain gap. Ref. [13] separates the parameters of a deep unsupervised domain adaptive network into two sections to reduce the impact of domain-specific information, as opposed to previous approaches that depended on learning domain-invariant feature representations. Pose estimators based on volumetric paradigms suffer from computation-intensive 3D convolutions, including many domain-specific parameters. It is suitable to use this Transferable Parameter Learning technique to better utilize domain-invariant parameters.

On par with the developments on domain adaptation for image recognition tasks, some recent works also aim to address the domain shift in regression tasks [31,50–54].

However, despite extensive research on the multi-view, multi-person 3D pose estimation task [6,26,55–59], there are very few jobs that focus on the domain shift problem of multi-view multi-person 3D pose estimation. We propose a novel adversarial training pipeline for domain-adaptive 3D human pose estimation that achieves superior performance in evaluated settings.

3. Preliminaries

3.1. VoxelPose

We present a brief overview of the VoxelPose model, which serves as the baseline for our research. VoxelPose projects 2D joint heatmaps from various viewpoints into a voxelized 3D space, enabling the direct detection and prediction of 3D human poses. The process begins with the estimation of 2D heatmaps for each view, encoding the per-pixel likelihood of all joints. Features from all camera views are aggregated in the 3D voxel space and processed by the Cuboid Proposal Network to localize individuals. This projection into a common 3D space results in a more comprehensive feature volume, allowing for an accurate estimation of 3D joint positions. Furthermore, the Pose Regression Network is used to estimate a full 3D pose for each proposal. All camera views' noisy and incomplete information is warped to a common 3D space to create a feature volume that may be used for 3D estimation.

3.2. Fundamental Conceptual Framework

The $\mathcal{H}\Delta\mathcal{H}$-Divergence is an influential construct within unsupervised domain adaptation (UDA). In UDA scenarios, we are presented with a labeled source domain, $\widehat{\mathcal{S}}$, and an unlabeled target domain, $\widehat{\mathcal{T}}$. The overarching aim is to develop a hypothesis capable of proficiently predicting within the target domain, notwithstanding the lack of its labels.

The groundwork for understanding this theory lies in the theorem titled "Bound with Disparity" [34]. According to this theorem, given a symmetric loss function ℓ that adheres to the triangle inequality, the disparity between any two hypotheses h and h' on a distribution $\mathcal{D}$ can be defined as:

$$\epsilon_{\mathcal{D}}(h,h') = \mathbb{E}_{(\mathbf{x},\mathbf{y})\sim\mathcal{D}}[\ell(h(\mathbf{x}),h'(\mathbf{x}))] \tag{1}$$

Subsequently, the target risk $\epsilon_{\mathcal{T}}(h)$ can be constrained by:

$$\epsilon_{\mathcal{T}}(h) \leq \epsilon_{\mathcal{S}}(h) + [\epsilon_{\mathcal{S}}(h^*) + \epsilon_{\mathcal{T}}(h^*)] + |\epsilon_{\mathcal{S}}(h,h^*) - \epsilon_{\mathcal{T}}(h,h^*)| \tag{2}$$

Here, h^* denotes the optimal joint hypothesis.

Building upon this premise, the essence of the $\mathcal{H}\Delta\mathcal{H}$-Divergence is to provide an upper boundary for the disparity difference. The core merit of this divergence, as highlighted in our work, is its capability to be estimated using finite, unlabeled samples from both the source and target domains. However, the direct computation of this divergence is notably intricate and challenging to optimize. Thus, it is approximated by training a domain discriminator D that separates the source and target samples. To accomplish this, we employ a dropout discriminator, which not only prevents mode collapse but also enhances the robustness of our algorithm.

The lottery ticket hypothesis refers to a hypothesis in deep learning that suggests finding sparse subnetworks, known as "winning tickets", within over-parameterized neural networks. These winning tickets can achieve comparable or even better performance than the original large network when trained in isolation under suitable conditions.

In the context of domain adaptation, the lottery ticket hypothesis can be applied to transfer learning scenarios. By identifying winning tickets or subnetworks that generalize well to both the source and target domains, we can effectively adapt the model from the source domain to the target domain. This can help in mitigating the issue of distribution shift between the two domains and improving the performance of the model on the target domain with limited labeled data. This is also the theoretical basis for transferable parameter learning.

3.3. Dataset

As shown in Table 1, our evaluation employs three datasets:

Campus [10]: It is a dataset of three people conversing with one another in the outdoor environment, recorded by three calibrated cameras. To assess the precision of the 3D location of the body parts, we utilize the percentage of correctly estimated parts (3D PCP) [10]. We adjust our pose estimator using the dataset's unlabeled images as the target domain.

Shelf [10]: The Shelf Dataset includes a scenario of ordinary social interactions. In contrast to Campus, this is a more complex dataset, which consists of four individuals deconstructing a shelf at close range. Around them, there are five calibrated cameras, but each view is severely obstructed. 3D PCP [10] is also used as the assessment metric. This dataset's unlabeled images serve as our target domain.

CMU Panoptic [9]: This dataset was recorded in a lab setting, which contains multiple people engaging in social activities. With hundreds of cameras, it is able to obtain compelling motion capture findings. It is a sizable dataset of social interactions with numerous and various natural interactions. We use it as our source domain.

Table 1. Overview of the datasets used in our study, emphasizing their characteristics and intended application domains.

Datasets	Duration	Views	Characteristics	Application
Campus	3–4 min	3	3 people on campus grounds.	Target Domain
Shelf	6–7 min	5	4 people disassembling a shelf	Target Domain
Panoptic	60 h	30	Lab-based multi-player interactions	Source Domain

4. Method: Domain Adaptation for Multi-View Multi-Person 3D Pose Estimation

In this section, we detail our proposed methodology for supervised multi-view multi-person 3D pose estimation. In supervised multi-view multi-person 3D pose estimation, we have n labeled samples $\{(x_i, y_i)\}_{i=1}^{n}$ from $\mathcal{X} \times \mathcal{Y}^K$, where $\mathcal{X} \in R^{H \times W \times 3}$ represents the input space, $\mathcal{Y} \in R^3$ the output space and K the number of keypoints for each input. The samples randomly selected from distribution D are denoted as $\widehat{D}$. The objective is to identify a regressor $f \in \mathcal{F}$ that yields the lowest error rate $\text{err}_D = \mathbb{E}_{(x,y)\sim D} L(f(x), y)$ on D, where L is a loss function we shall explain later. In unsupervised domain adaptation, there exists a labeled source domain $\widehat{P} = \{(x_i^s, y_i^s)\}_{i=1}^{n}$ and an unlabeled target domain $\widehat{Q} = \{x_i^t\}_{i=1}^{m}$. The objective is to minimize err_Q.

4.1. Domain Adaptation Component

In the VoxelPose model, the feature representation refers to the feature map outputs of the base convolutional layers (as depicted by the green parallelogram in Figure 2). Specifically, we train a domain classifier to mitigate the domain distribution discrepancy on feature maps. The domain classifier predicts the domain label for each feature map, which corresponds to input images I_i from the source or target domain.

This decision has two advantages: (1) Aligning representations at the image level often reduces the shift caused by variations in the images, such as image style, human body scale, illumination, etc. (2) The batch size is typically quite small while training a pose estimation network due to the utilization of high-resolution input. This approach allows more data to be employed in training the domain classifier.

Let's represent the domain label of the i-th training image by H_i, where $H_i = 0$ for the source domain and $H_i = 1$ for the target domain. The feature map of the i-th image after the base 2D convolutional layers is denoted by F_i. Using the cross entropy loss and denoting the output of the domain classifier $D(F_i)$, the domain adaptation loss can be written as:

$$\mathcal{L}_D = -\sum_i [H_i \log D(F_i) + (1 - H_i) \log(1 - D(F_i))] \tag{3}$$

To align the domain distributions, we need to simultaneously optimize the parameters of the base 2D network to maximize the above domain classification loss and minimize the keypoint regression loss. In order to optimize the base network used to maximize the domain classifier, we adopt the gradient reverse layer [12], as opposed to regular gradient descent. To maximize the domain classifier loss, the gradient must first pass through a gradient reverse layer, where its sign is inverted.

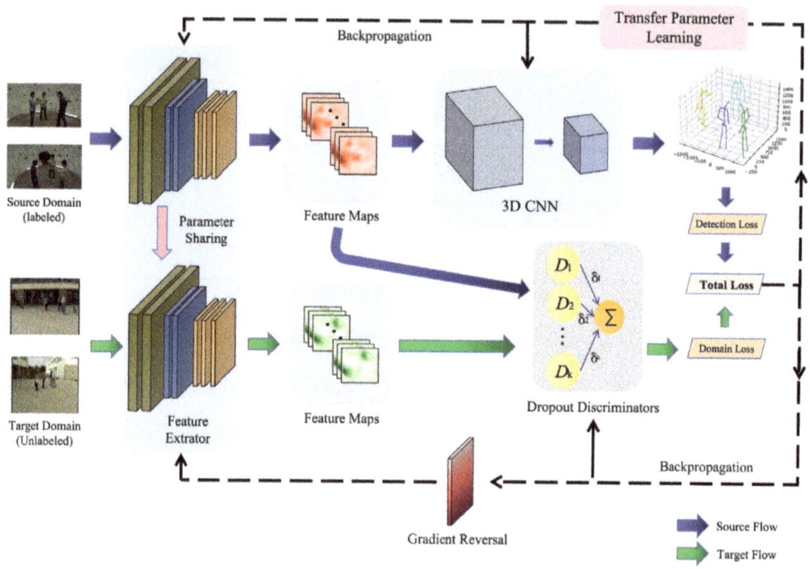

Figure 2. An overview of our Domain Adaptive VoxelPose model. An adversarial training method is used to train the domain classifier. The selection of certain discriminators is determined by a probability δ_k. The network performs a robust positive update for the transferable parameters and performs a negative update for the untransferable parameters.

4.2. Dropout Domain Adaptation Component

In order to force the pose estimator to learn from a dynamic ensemble of discriminators, we propose the integration of adversarial feedback dropout in adversarial networks. The feedback of each discriminator is randomly excluded from the ensemble with a specific probability d at the end of each batch. This indicates that the pose estimator considers only the loss of the remaining discriminators when updating its parameters.

Figure 2 illustrates our proposed framework, including our initial modification to the adversarial training loss function L, as shown in Equation (2). In this equation, δ_k is a Bernoulli variable ($\delta_k \sim Bern(1-d)$), and $\{D_k\}$ is the set of K total discriminators. When $\delta_k = 1$, with $P(\delta_k = 1) = 1 - d$, the gradients derived from the loss of the supplied discriminator $\{D_k\}$, are exclusively employed to produce the final gradient updates for the pose estimator. Otherwise, this discrimination-related information is ignored:

$$\mathcal{L}_D = -\sum_i \sum_{k=1}^{K} \delta_k [H_i \log D_k(F_i) + (1 - H_i) \log(1 - D_k(F_i))] \quad (4)$$

Each discriminator trains independently, i.e., is unaware of the others, since no changes are made to their individual gradient updates. Figure 3 depicts the proposed solution's algorithm in detail.

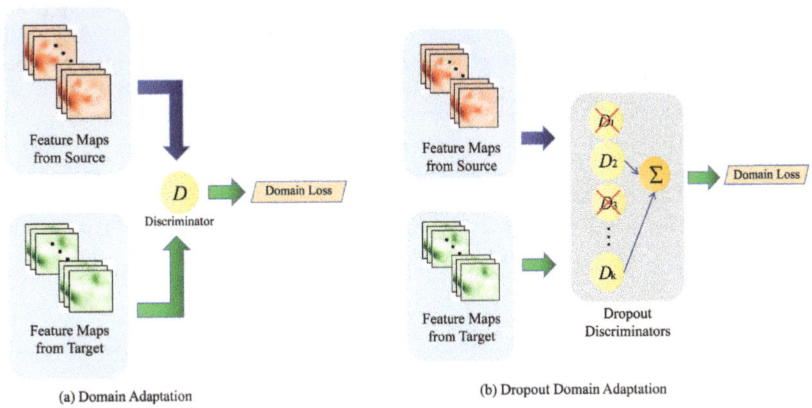

Figure 3. The original adversarial framework (**a**) is extended to incorporate multiple adversaries. In this enhancement, certain discriminators are probabilistically omitted (**b**), resulting in only a random subset of feedback (depicted by the arrows) being utilized by the feature extractor at the end of each batch.

4.3. Transferable Parameter Learning Component

The Transferable Parameter Learning Component is designed to distinguish between transferable and non-transferable parameters, enabling robust unsupervised domain adaptation. To minimize the model's ability to retain domain-specific information, distinct updating rules are used for different types of parameters [13]. Consider a parameter, denoted by $\mathrm{w}_i(t) \in \mathcal{W}_*(t)$, its gradient is $\nabla \mathcal{L}_D(\mathrm{w}_i(t))$ at the t-th iteration. The identifying criterion is defined by

$$\mathcal{T}_i(t) = |\nabla \mathcal{L}_D(\mathrm{w}_i(t)) \times \mathrm{w}_i(t)|, i \in [m_*] \tag{5}$$

where m_* is the parameter number of a module in a deep unsupervised domain adaptation network. If the value of $\mathcal{T}_i(t)$ is large, $\mathrm{w}_i(t)$ is viewed as a transferable parameter. On the contrary, if the value of $\mathcal{T}_i(t)$ is small, e.g., zero or very close to zero, $\mathrm{w}_i(t)$ is regarded as an untransferable parameter. It is not important for fitting domain-invariant information. If we update it, it will tend to fit domain-specific information. By utilizing objective function gradients and weight decay on the transferable parameters $\mathcal{W}^{\mathrm{tr}}$, a robust positive update is executed.

$$\mathcal{W}^{\mathrm{tr}}(t+1) \rightarrow \mathcal{W}^{\mathrm{r}}(t) - \eta\left(\frac{\partial(\mathcal{L}_D(\mathcal{W}^{\mathrm{tr}}(t)))}{\partial \mathcal{W}_*^{\mathrm{r}}(t)} - \lambda \mathcal{W}^{\mathrm{rr}}(t)\right) \tag{6}$$

Furthermore, the non-transferable parameters $\mathcal{W}^{\mathrm{utr}}$, which tend to over-adapt to domain-specific details, are negatively updated.

$$\mathcal{W}^{\mathrm{utr}}(t+1) \rightarrow \mathcal{W}^{\mathrm{utr}}(t) - \eta(\lambda \mathcal{W}_*^{\mathrm{utr}}(t)) \tag{7}$$

where $\eta > 0$ refers to the learning rate and $\mathcal{W}(t)$ stands for the set of parameters at the t-th iteration. The term $\lambda \mathcal{W}(t)$ refers to the common weight decay method, which can avoid overfitting by keeping the parameters from being too big. λ is the weight decay coefficient. This method for domain adaptation is straightforward and independent of other approaches.

4.4. Network Overview

Figure 2 offers a detailed portrayal of our Domain Adaptive VoxelPose model, an enhancement of the baseline VoxelPose framework with three added components. Primarily, we have incorporated a domain classifier subsequent to the final 2D base convolution layer.

Additionally, we have integrated a dropout mechanism that probabilistically neglects the feedback from each discriminator at the end of every batch. Finally, we apply transferable parameter learning to enforce distinct update rules for transferable and non-transferable parameters. The cumulative loss incurred during the training of our proposed network encompasses both the human pose estimation segment as well as the domain adaptation segment. Algorithm 1 provides a comprehensive overview of our approach, which optimizes two kinds of parameters using distinct update rules. It is important to note that our method preserves the architecture of the existing multi-view, multi-person 3D estimation networks. Consequently, both the time complexity and space complexity remain consistent with those of the original networks.

$$L = L_{\text{hm}} + \lambda(L_D) \tag{8}$$

Algorithm 1: Voxelpose with dropout discriminator and transfer parameter learning

```
Input: Camera Views of source domain, Camera views of target domain
Output: 3D human poses for all cuboids
begin
    Initialize a 3D voxel space, V
    foreach camera view in Camera Views do
        Estimate 2D heatmap, H_s, for the source domain
        Estimate 2D heatmap, H_t, for the target domain
        Domain loss = Dropout Discriminator (H_s or H_t)
        Project H_s into the 3D voxel space, V
    Aggregate features from all views in V
    Cuboids = Cuboid Proposal Network(V)
    foreach cuboid in Cuboids do
        Get 3D pose using the Pose Regression Network
    Detection loss = mpjpe(3D human poses for all cuboids, ground truth)
    /*identify transferable parameters*/
    Divide W into W_tr and W_utr with Equation (5)
    Update W_trf, W_trc, and W_trd with Equation (6)
    Update W_utr, W_utr, and W_utrd with Equation (7)
    Return 3D human poses for all cuboids
```

5. Experiments

In this section, we verify the feasibility of the proposed Domain Adaptive VoxelPose model. Utilizing the Panoptic [9] dataset as the source domain, the performance of the technique is examined in two distinct scenarios of domain shift: (1) An outdoor environment, where the Campus [10] test dataset captures three individuals interacting outdoors through three calibrated cameras. (2) An indoor social interaction setting, where the Shelf [10] test dataset, which is more complex, features four individuals closely deconstructing a shelf. There are five calibrated cameras surrounding them, but each view has severe occlusion. Due to differences in annotation formats between the source and target domains, a conversion measure is employed to align the model's output with the target domain annotations (e.g., in a model trained on Panoptic outputs, the position of the nose can be viewed as the head-center position of the Campus dataset).

5.1. Experiment Setup

In our experiments, we use the unsupervised domain adaptation approach. The training set is divided into two parts: the source training set, which includes photos and their pose annotations, and the target training set, which only includes unlabeled images. In order to demonstrate the efficacy of the proposed approach, we present not only the conclusive results of our model but also the findings obtained by using each component.

This is done for two common domain shift scenarios. We use the original VoxelPose model as a baseline. It was trained using training data from the source domain without taking domain adaptation into account. To assess the accuracy of the estimated 3D poses, we present the Percentage of Correct Parts (PCP3D) across all tests. We use Mean Per Joint Position Error (MPJPE) on the training set.

We conducted our experiments on a computer equipped with an NVIDIA Tesla V100 GPU and implemented our algorithm using PyTorch. For the task of multi-view image feature extraction, we employed a pose estimation model built upon ResNet-50 [11]. The backbone of this model was specifically initialized using weights pre-trained on the COCO dataset. During the model training phase, we utilized the AdamW optimizer [60] with an initial learning rate of 0.001, a batch size of 4, and a total of 20 training epochs. The 2D backbone and the remaining components of the model were trained jointly. Each training batch consisted of two images: one from the source domain and another from the target domain. For training on the Panoptic dataset, which serves as our source domain, we employed three camera views (03, 12, and 23).

5.2. Outdoor Environment Experimental Results

With the rapid advancement of 3D human pose estimation, the motion capture (mocap) system is emerging as an effective means to augment datasets. However, the Mocap system, originally designed for laboratory use, poses challenges for implementation in natural settings. A discernible visual disparity exists between laboratory data and outdoor scenarios, often leading to a performance gap between models trained in these different environments. Our initial experiment seeks to ascertain the applicability of the proposed method in this context.

Results: The results of the different methods are summarized in Table 2. Specifically, using the dropout domain adaptation component alone, we achieve a +5.9% performance gain over VoxelPose. Using the dropout domain adaptation component embedded with transfer parameter learning yields an improvement of 6.9%, validating our hypothesis regarding the necessity of reducing domain shifts. This demonstrates that the domain shift between a lab and an outdoor environment can be effectively reduced by the components we proposed.

Table 2. Quantitative analysis of adaptation results on Campus as a validation set, models are trained on the Panoptic training set. Ours(a) represents the VoxelPose method solely augmented with the domain adaptation module. Ours(b) builds upon the Ours(a) approach by incorporating a dropout mechanism into the discriminator. Ours(c) extends the Ours(a) method by integrating the Transferable Parameter Learning mechanism. Ours(d) represents the optimal approach that amalgamates both the dropout discriminator method and the Transferable Parameter Learning mechanism.

P → C	DA	Dropout DA	TranPar	Actor 1	Actor 2	Actor 3	Average
VoxelPose				78.8	82.8	67.4	76.3
Ours(a)	√			78.6	86.8	79.6	81.7
Ours(b)	√	√		79.3	85.5	78.2	82.2
Ours(c)	√		√	84.3	86.0	78.0	82.8
Ours(d)	√	√	√	85.1	86.3	78.4	83.2

Note: All values are in PCP3D.

As illustrated in Figure 4, the qualitative metrics reveal that our method effectively minimizes false detections. Table 3 demonstrates a significant improvement in performance for joint locations with substantial variations, such as the lower arms and lower legs. We evaluated the generalization performance of our method in comparison to other domain adaptation techniques applied to this scenario, and the results are detailed in Table 4. Based on the results presented in Figure 5, a qualitative comparison is provided between our proposed method and other state-of-the-art algorithms. The results clearly demonstrate that our algorithm exhibits enhanced robustness in cross-domain scenarios.

Figure 4. Estimated 3D poses and their corresponding images in an outdoor environment (Campus Dataset). Different colors represent different people detected. The penultimate column is the output result of the original voxelpose, which has misestimated the person. The last column shows the estimated 3D poses by our algorithm.

Table 3. Quantitative analysis of the algorithm's performance improvement on different keypoints, using Campus as a validation set.

Methods	Voxelpose				Ours(d)			
Bone Group	**Actor 1**	**Actor 2**	**Actor 3**	**Average**	**Actor 1**	**Actor 2**	**Actor 3**	**Average**
Head	90.8	68.5	71.4	76.9	91.8	69.7	83.8	81.8
Torso	89.7	95.1	74.7	86.5	90.5	96.2	89.7	92.1
Upper arms	73.5	92.3	71.2	79	82.5	93.1	73.8	83.1
Lower arms	65.9	73.4	58.7	66	78.5	82.3	73.7	78.2
Upper legs	86	92.3	65.1	81.1	85.3	93.4	75.8	84.8
Lower legs	66.9	75.1	63.3	68.4	81.8	83.1	73.3	79.4
Total	78.8	82.8	67.4	76.3	85.1	86.3	78.4	83.2

Note: All values are in PCP3D.

Table 4. The Average Percentage of Correct Parts(PCP3D) of Campus and Shelf dataset. Ours(a,b,c,d) represents the different settings of our algorithm, which is explained in Table 2.

Methods	P $\rightarrow$ C	P $\rightarrow$ S
VoxelPose [11]	76.3	93.4
VoxelPose-DDC [61]	76.4	90.1
VoxelPose-JAN [62]	81.1	91.2
VoxelPose-DAN [36]	78.7	88.9
VoxelPose-DeepCoral [63]	80.3	87.8
VoxelPose-MMD [61]	74.6	82.5
VoxelPose-RSD [52]	82.2	95.3
Ours(a)	81.7	95.0
Ours(b)	82.8	95.5
Ours(c)	82.5	94.9
Ours(d)	83.2	96.1

Note: All values are in PCP3D.

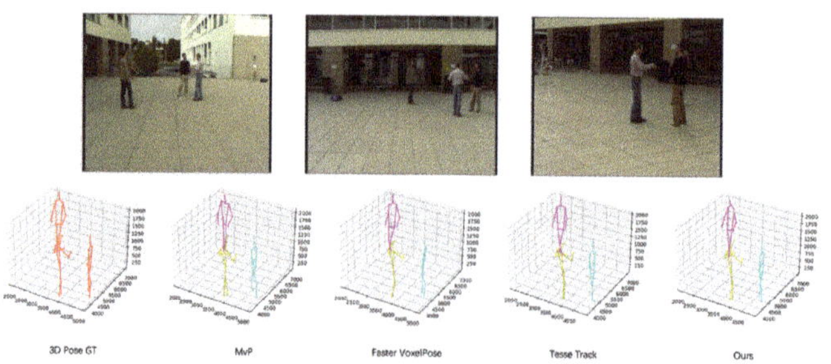

Figure 5. Cross-domain qualitative comparison between our method and other state-of-the-art multi-view multi-person 3D pose estimation algorithms. The evaluated methods were trained on the Panoptic dataset and validated on the Campus dataset. Different colors represent different people detected, with red indicating the ground truth.

5.3. Indoor Social Interaction Environment Experimental Results

Despite considerable advancements in multi-person 3D human pose estimation, numerous challenging scenarios persist, including obscured keypoints, invisible keypoints, and crowded backgrounds that hinder accurate keypoint localization. For a generalized 3D human position estimation system, precise operation in diverse social interaction environments is vital. This subsection examines the efficacy of 3D pose estimation in the context of group interactions.

Results: Our findings, as well as those of other baselines, are included in Table 5. Similar observations apply in the outdoor environment. When all the parts are put together, our complete adaptive Voxelpose model is 2.7% better than the baseline Voxelpose model. In addition, we can see that the improvement generalizes well across different actors, indicating that the proposed method can also reduce domain discrepancies between different individuals.

Table 5. Quantitative analysis of adaptation results on Shelf as a validation set, models are trained on the Panoptic training set.

P → S	DA	Dropout DA	TranPar	Actor 1	Actor 2	Actor 3	Average
VoxelPose				93.2	90.5	96.5	93.4
Ours(a)	√			95.1	92.4	97.4	95.0
Ours(b)	√	√		95.2	94.5	96.2	95.6
Ours(c)	√		√	96.0	93.8	97.1	95.1
Ours(d)	√	√	√	96.5	94.1	97.7	96.1

Note: All values are in PCP3D.

Figure 6 illustrates the qualitative results of our algorithm, highlighting its capability to not only avoid false detection but also to yield more realistic and natural pose estimation outcomes. In Table 6, notable improvements are evident in joint localizations, particularly for the lower arms and lower legs. In Table 4, we present the results, comparing the generalization performance of our method with other unsupervised domain adaptation techniques applied to this scenario. In Figure 7, we compared our proposed method with other advanced algorithms and found that our approach performs better in cross-domain scenarios. These results indicate that our algorithm is more robust than others.

In Table 7, we evaluate the generalization performance of several state-of-the-art algorithms, including MvP [6], Faster VoxelPose [31], and TesseTrack [57], as detailed in Section 2.2 of the article. Our results demonstrate that in cross-domain scenarios, our method outperforms these other approaches while maintaining the model's performance on the original dataset.

Figure 6. Estimated 3D poses and their corresponding images in an indoor social interaction environment (Shelf Dataset). The penultimate column is the output result of the original voxelpose, which has misestimated person. The last column shows the estimated 3D poses by our algorithm.

Table 6. Quantitative analysis of the algorithm's performance improvement on different keypoints, using Shelf as a validation set.

Methods	Voxelpose				Ours(d)			
Bone Group	Actor 1	Actor 2	Actor 3	Average	Actor 1	Actor 2	Actor 3	Average
Head	78.2	94.6	92.1	88.3	87.2	95.3	94.3	92.3
Torso	98.5	96.1	99	97.9	99.5	96.6	99	98.4
Upper arms	94.3	93.2	96.3	94.6	95.6	93.9	96.8	95.4
Lower arms	93.5	64.9	94	84.1	98.5	81.3	97.2	92.3
Upper legs	96.7	97.4	98.7	97.6	98.3	97.4	98.7	98.1
Lower legs	97.9	96.6	98.5	97.7	99.9	100	100	100
Total	93.2	90.5	96.4	93.4	96.5	94.1	97.7	96.1

Note: All values are in PCP3D.

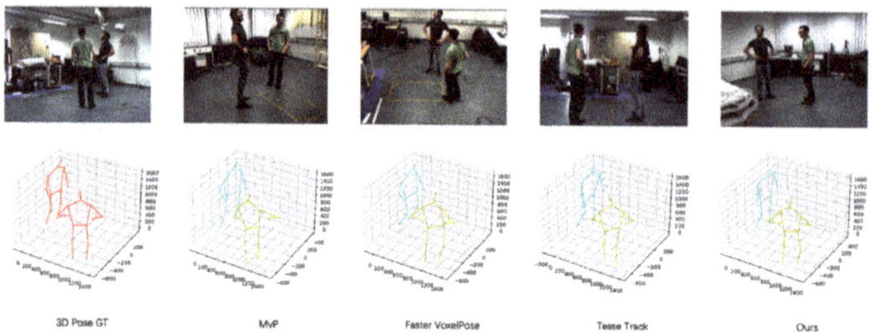

Figure 7. Cross-domain qualitative comparison between our method and other state-of-the-art multi-view multi-person 3D pose estimation algorithms in the Shelf dataset. the evaluated methods were trained on the Panoptic dataset and validated on the Shelf dataset.

Table 7. Quantitative Comparative Experiments with other State-of-the-Art Methods in Cross-Domain Scenarios. P represents the original performance of Other State-of-the-Art Methods on the panoptic dataset. For our approach, the performance metric of P signifies the retained performance on the original panoptic dataset after undergoing domain adaptation processes. The unit of measurement for P is MPJPE, while others are measured in PCP3D.

Methods	**P → C**	**P → S**	**P**
MvP [6]	80.3	92.6	15.8
Faster Voxelpose [31]	77.1	94.0	18.26
TesseTrack [57]	79.8	92.6	18.7
Ours(a)	81.7	95.0	20.61
Ours(b)	82.8	95.5	19.88
Ours(c)	82.5	94.9	19.56
Ours(d)	83.2	96.1	19.37

5.4. Ablation Studies and Discussions

5.4.1. Domain Adaptation Component

The training process of the adversarial domain adaptation component is characterized as a zero-sum, non-cooperative contest between the base feature extractor and the domain discriminator. As the domain discriminator learns to distinguish between source and target domain features, the feature extractor simultaneously learns domain-invariant feature representation to confound the domain discriminator, thereby enhancing cross-domain adaptation capability.

Due to the single-adversarial method's limited distribution alignment ability, the improvement is small and erratic. Mode collapse, as a consequence of overfitting to the feedback of a single discriminator, shows up as difficulties with convergence.

5.4.2. Dropout Domain Adaptation Component

The multi-adversarial domain adaptation method has been empirically validated as an efficacious technique for improving domain adaptation capabilities [41,64]. This method involves dynamically altering the adversarial ensemble at each batch, stimulating the generator to cultivate domain-invariant representations that can deceive the remaining discriminators. The dynamic alteration not only encourages the generator to master domain-invariant representation but also amplifies the probability of successfully misleading any residual discriminators. By aligning the feature representation across diverse feature dimensions, complementary features are learned. This alignment facilitates a more efficient reduction of domain discrepancies with unlabeled target data, thereby bolstering the model's generalization prowess. The efficacy of the dropout domain adaptive component is further illustrated in Figure 8.

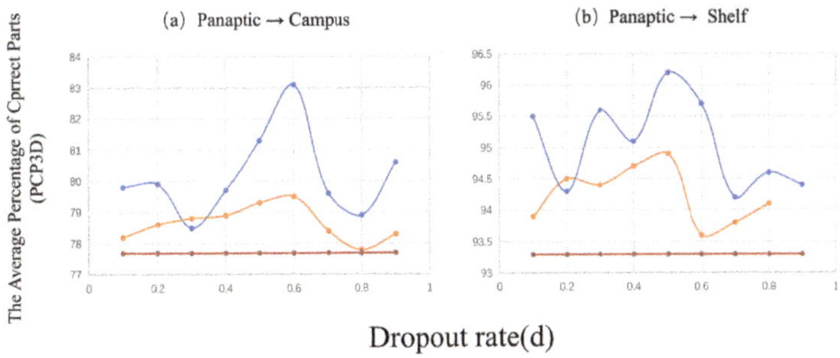

Figure 8. An illustration of the Average Percentage of Correct Parts (PCP3D) on the Campus and Shelf datasets, with the Dropout Rate (d) plotted on the horizontal axis and PCP3D on the vertical axis. The methods are distinguished by color: the red line for the DA baseline method, the yellow line for the dropout DA method, and the blue line for our proposed full method with TransPar.

Figure 8 illustrates the relationship between the dropout rate and the generalization ability of the feature representation. This figure emphasizes that selecting an excessively large or small ratio for Parameter d can complicate training. By striving to enhance the generalizability of the feature representations created by the base feature extractor, this type of dropout can be seen as a form of regularization. We found that employing any dropout rate within the range ($0 < d \leq 1$) consistently outperformed a static ensemble of adversaries ($d = 0$). Specifically, utilizing a moderate dropout rate often led to superior results, as previously noted in [42,65].

5.4.3. Transferable Parameter Learning Component

The central concept of the aforementioned components is to acquire transferable feature representations by confusing a domain discriminator in a two-player game, leading to state-of-the-art results in various visual tasks [12,41,64]. Deep Unsupervised Domain Adaptation (UDA) research expects precise feature representations, and insights derived from the source domain can be effectively applied to the target domain. However, during the learning process of domain-invariant features and source hypotheses, unnecessary domain-specific information is inevitably incorporated, hindering generalization to the target domain. The lottery ticket hypothesis [66] reveals that only certain parameters are crucial for generalization. Thus, by eliminating the adverse effects of domain-specific information prior to testing, deep UDA networks can become more resilient and adaptable.

Voxelpose utilizes a 3D-CNN to estimate the 3D locations of the body joints based on the feature volume. This method suffers from a large number of domain-specific parameters. We believe that only partial "transferable parameters" are essential for learning domain-invariant information and generalizing well in UDA; on the other hand, "untransferable parameters" tend to suit domain-specific information and rarely generalize.

In order to lessen the negative impacts of domain-specific knowledge during the learning process, we introduce Transferable Parameter Learning (TransPar) into our network, providing unique update rules for these two categories of parameters.

While Tables 2 and 5 have shown the benefits of the introduced Learning Transferable Parameters, Figure 9 demonstrates that the performance achieved by medium-to-high ratios is relatively important.

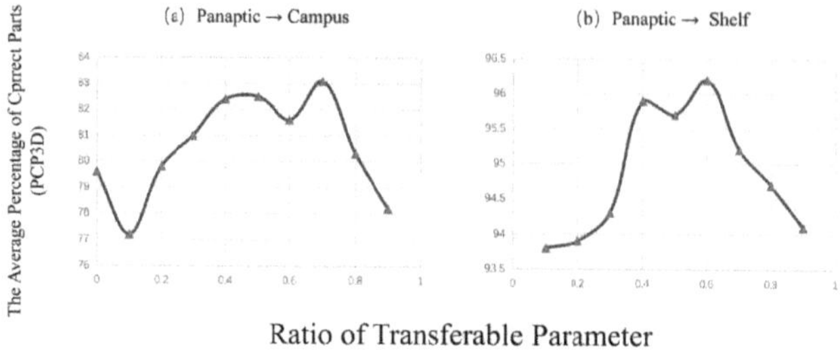

Figure 9. The Average Percentage of Correct Parts (PCP3D), based on Wider Ratios of Transferable Parameters, on Campus and Shelf dataset.

6. Conclusions and Outlook

In this research, we present the Domain Adaptive VoxelPose model, which is an efficient method for cross-domain multi-view multi-person 3D pose estimation. Without needing any extra labeled data, one can build a robust pose estimator for a new domain using our method. Our strategy is based on the state-of-the-art VoxelPose model. We introduced a domain adaptation component and the dropout mechanism for our network based on the theoretical analysis that we did for cross-domain pose estimation. A collection of dropout discriminators is used to learn a robust model for the domain. We also introduced transfer parameter learning into our network, which used distinct updating rules for two types of parameters. These components are meant to alleviate the performance drop that is caused by domain shifting. Our methodology is validated on several different domain shift scenarios, and the adaptive method relatively outperforms the baseline VoxelPose method. This demonstrates the approach's efficiency for cross-domain, multi-view, multi-person 3D pose estimation. In summary, our approach offers industrial advantages by strengthening the robustness of multi-view, multi-person estimation models in real-world conditions, minimizing errors and false positives, increasing operational efficiency, enhancing safety, and alleviating the burden of manual data labeling. However, it's important to address some inherent limitations in the methodology that could potentially affect its precision and scalability.

6.1. Limitations

Primarily, our model confronts the challenge of quantization errors during the transition from 2D to 3D representations. This issue is particularly crucial as it may lead to discernible inaccuracies, undermining the algorithm's efficacy. Secondly, the computational expenses for training our algorithm escalate with an increasing number of views. This scalability issue limits its applicability in contexts requiring large-scale, high-throughput processing. Moreover, our model currently lacks the incorporation of spatial-temporal data, despite the inherent correlation of human body postures over time. This limitation is especially poignant when the model needs to discern closely intertwined joints or intricate inter-human interactions.

6.2. Future Directions

The limitations of the current model naturally guide our future research. One promising direction is the development of an end-to-end framework aiming to mitigate the cumulative effects of quantization errors. Furthermore, we recognize the urgent need for the seamless integration of spatial-temporal data to improve the model's precision in capturing human interactions and movements over time.

Author Contributions: Conceptualization, J.D.; Methodology, J.D.; Software, H.Y.; Validation, J.D., H.Y. and P.S.; Formal analysis, J.D. and H.Y.; Investigation, J.D.; Resources, H.Y.; Data curation, H.Y.; Writing—original draft preparation, J.D.; Writing—review and editing, H.Y.; Visualization, J.D. and

H.Y.; Supervision, P.S.; Project administration, P.S. All authors have read and agreed to the published version of the manuscript.

Funding: This research received no external funding.

Institutional Review Board Statement: Not applicable.

Informed Consent Statement: Not applicable.

Data Availability Statement: The Shelf and Campus datasets are available at https://campar.in.tum.de/Chair/MultiHumanPose (accessed on 28 September 2022). The Panoptic datasets are available at http://domedb.perception.cs.cmu.edu (accessed on 28 September 2022).

Conflicts of Interest: The authors declare no conflict of interest.

References

1. Song, L.; Yu, G.; Yuan, J.; Liu, Z. Human pose estimation and its application to action recognition: A survey. *J. Vis. Commun. Image Represent.* **2021**, *76*, 103055. [CrossRef]
2. Bagautdinov, T.; Wu, C.; Simon, T.; Prada, F.; Shiratori, T.; Wei, S.; Xu, W.; Sheikh, Y.; Saragih, J. Driving-signal aware full-body avatars. *ACM Trans. Graph.* **2021**, *40*, 1–17. [CrossRef]
3. Wang, J.; Yan, S.; Dai, B.; Lin, D. Scene-aware generative network for human motion synthesis. In Proceedings of the IEEE/CVF Conference on Computer Vision and Pattern Recognition, Nashville, TN, USA, 20–25 June 2021; pp. 12206–12215.
4. Moon, G.; Chang, J.Y.; Lee, K.M. Camera distance-aware top-down approach for 3d multi-person pose estimation from a single rgb image. In Proceedings of the IEEE/CVF International Conference on Computer Vision, Seoul, Republic of Korea, 27 October–2 November 2019; pp. 10133–10142.
5. Zeng, A.; Ju, X.; Yang, L.; Gao, R.; Zhu, X.; Dai, B.; Xu, Q. Deciwatch: A simple baseline for 10x efficient 2d and 3d pose estimation. *arXiv* **2022**, arXiv:2203.08713.
6. Zhang, J.; Cai, Y.; Yan, S.; Feng, J. Direct multi-view multi-person 3d pose estimation. *Adv. Neural Inf. Process. Syst.* **2021**, *34*, 13153–13164.
7. Cheng, Y.; Wang, B.; Tan, R. Dual networks based 3d multi-person pose estimation from monocular video. *IEEE Trans. Pattern Anal. Mach. Intell.* **2022**, *42*, 1636–1651. [CrossRef]
8. Belagiannis, V.; Amin, S.; Andriluka, M.; Schiele, B.; Navab, N.; Ilic, S. 3d pictorial structures for multiple human pose estimation. In Proceedings of the IEEE Conference on Computer Vision and Pattern Recognition, Columbus, OH, USA, 23–28 June 2014; pp. 1669–1676.
9. Joo, H.; Liu, H.; Tan, L.; Gui, L.; Nabbe, B.; Matthews, I.; Kanade, T.; Nobuhara, S.; Sheikh, Y. Panoptic studio: A massively multiview system for social motion capture. In Proceedings of the IEEE International Conference on Computer Vision, Santiago, Chile, 7–13 December 2015; pp. 3334–3342.
10. Belagiannis, V.; Amin, S.; Andriluka, M.; Schiele, B.; Navab, N.; Ilic, S. 3d pictorial structures revisited: Multiple human pose estimation. *IEEE Trans. Pattern Anal. Mach. Intell.* **2015**, *38*, 1929–1942. [CrossRef]
11. Tu, H.; Wang, C.; Zeng, W. Voxelpose: Towards multi-camera 3d human pose estimation in wild environment. In *Computer Vision—ECCV 2020, Proceedings of the 16th European Conference, Glasgow, UK, 23–28 August 2020*; Springer: Cham, Switzerland, 2020; pp. 197–212.
12. Ganin, Y.; Lempitsky, V. Unsupervised domain adaptation by backpropagation. In Proceedings of the International Conference on Machine Learning, Lille, France, 6–11 July 2015; pp. 1180–1189.
13. Han, Z.; Sun, H.; Yin, Y. Learning transferable parameters for unsupervised domain adaptation. *IEEE Trans. Image Process.* **2022**, *31*, 6424–6439. [CrossRef]
14. Wang, Z.; Nie, X.; Qu, X.; Chen, Y.; Liu, S. Distribution-aware single-stage models for multi-person 3d pose estimation. In Proceedings of the IEEE/CVF Conference on Computer Vision and Pattern Recognition, New Orleans, LA, USA, 19–20 June 2022; pp. 13096–13105.
15. Hua, G.; Liu, H.; Li, W.; Zhang, Q.; Ding, R.; Xu, X. Weakly-supervised 3d human pose estimation with cross-view u-shaped graph convolutional network. *IEEE Trans. Multimed.* **2022**, *25*, 1832–1843. [CrossRef]
16. Zhang, J.; Tu, Z.; Yang, J.; Chen, Y.; Yuan, J. Mixste: Seq2seq mixed spatio-temporal encoder for 3d human pose estimation in video. *arXiv* **2022**, arXiv:2203.00859.
17. Sun, Y.; Liu, W.; Bao, Q.; Fu, Y.; Mei, T.; Black, M.J. Putting people in their place: Monocular regression of 3d people in depth. *arXiv* **2021**, arXiv:2112.08274.
18. Mahmood, B.; Han, S.; Seo, J. Implementation experiments on convolutional neural network training using synthetic images for 3d pose estimation of an excavator on real images. *Autom. Constr.* **2022**, *133*, 103996. [CrossRef]
19. Wu, Y.; Kong, D.; Wang, S.; Li, J.; Yin, B. Hpgcn: Hierarchical poselet-guided graph convolutional network for 3d pose estimation. *Neurocomputing* **2022**, *487*, 243–256. [CrossRef]

20. Jin, L.; Xu, C.; Wang, X.; Xiao, Y.; Guo, Y.; Nie, X.; Zhao, J. Single-stage is enough: Multi-person absolute 3d pose estimation. In Proceedings of the IEEE/CVF Conference on Computer Vision and Pattern Recognition, New Orleans, LA, USA, 18–24 June 2022; pp. 13086–13095.
21. Park, C.; Lee, H.S.; Kim, W.J.; Bae, H.B.; Lee, J.; Lee, S. An Efficient Approach Using Knowledge Distillation Methods to Stabilize Performance in a Lightweight Top-Down Posture Estimation Network. *Sensors* **2021**, *21*, 7640. [CrossRef]
22. Nguyen, H.-C.; Nguyen, T.-H.; Scherer, R.; Le, V.-H. Unified End-to-End YOLOv5-HR-TCM Framework for Automatic 2D/3D Human Pose Estimation for Real-Time Applications. *Sensors* **2022**, *22*, 5419. [CrossRef]
23. Qiu, H.; Wang, C.; Wang, J.; Wang, N.; Zeng, W. Cross view fusion for 3d human pose estimation. In Proceedings of the IEEE/CVF International Conference on Computer Vision, Seoul, Republic of Korea, 27 October–2 November 2019; pp. 4342–4351.
24. He, Y.; Yan, R.; Fragkiadaki, K.; Yu, S. Epipolar transformers. In Proceedings of the IEEE/CVF Conference on Computer Vision and Pattern Recognition, Seattle, WA, USA, 13–19 June 2020; pp. 7779–7788.
25. Chen, X.; Lin, K.-Y.; Liu, W.; Qian, C.; Lin, L. Weakly-supervised discovery of geometry-aware representation for 3d human pose estimation. In Proceedings of the IEEE/CVF Conference on Computer Vision and Pattern Recognition, Seoul, Republic of Korea, 27 October–2 November 2019; pp. 10895–10904.
26. Dong, J.; Fang, Q.; Jiang, W.; Yang, Y.; Huang, Q.; Bao, H.; Zhou, X. Fast and robust multi-person 3d pose estimation and tracking from multiple views. *IEEE Trans. Pattern Anal. Mach. Intell.* **2021**, *44*, 6981–6992. [CrossRef] [PubMed]
27. Burenius, M.; Sullivan, J.; Carlsson, S. 3d pictorial structures for multiple view articulated pose estimation. In Proceedings of the IEEE Conference on Computer Vision and Pattern Recognition, Portland, OR, USA, 23–28 June 2013; pp. 3618–3625.
28. Chu, H.; Lee, J.H.; Lee, Y.G.; Hsu, C.H.; Li, J.D.; Chen, C.S. Part-aware measurement for robust multi-view multi-human 3d pose estimation and tracking. In Proceedings of the IEEE/CVF Conference on Computer Vision and Pattern Recognition, Nashville, TN, USA, 20–25 June 2021; pp. 1472–1481.
29. Habermann, M.; Xu, W.; Zollhofer, M.; Pons-Moll, G.; Theobalt, C. Deepcap: Monocular human performance capture using weak supervision. In Proceedings of the IEEE/CVF Conference on Computer Vision and Pattern Recognition, Seattle, WA, USA, 13–19 June 2020; pp. 5052–5063.
30. Hu, W.; Zhang, C.; Zhan, F.; Zhang, L.; Wong, T.T. Conditional directed graph convolution for 3d human pose estimation. In Proceedings of the 29th ACM International Conference on Multimedia, Virtual, 20–24 October 2021; pp. 602–611.
31. Ye, H.; Zhu, W.; Wang, C.; Wu, R.; Wang, Y. Faster voxelpose: Real-time 3d human pose estimation by orthographic projection. In Proceedings of the European Conference on Computer Vision (ECCV), Tel Aviv, Israel, 25–27 October 2022.
32. Wang, M.; Deng, W. Deep visual domain adaptation: A survey. *Neurocomputing* **2018**, *312*, 135–153. [CrossRef]
33. Wang, J.; Lan, C.; Liu, C.; Ouyang, Y.; Zeng, W.; Qin, T. Generalizing to unseen domains: A survey on domain generalization. *arXiv* **2021**, arXiv:2103.03097.
34. Jiang, J.; Shu, Y.; Wang, J.; Long, M. Transferability in deep learning: A survey. *arXiv* **2022**, arXiv:2201.05867.
35. David, S.B.; Lu, T.; Luu, T.; Pál, D. Impossibility theorems for domain adaptation. In Proceedings of the Thirteenth International Conference on Artificial Intelligence and Statistics, Sardinia, Italy, 13–15 May 2010; pp. 129–136.
36. Long, M.; Cao, Y.; Wang, J.; Jordan, M. Learning transferable features with deep adaptation networks. In Proceedings of the International Conference on Machine Learning, Lille, France, 6–11 July 2015; pp. 97–105.
37. Goodfellow, I.J.; Pouget-Abadie, J.; Mirza, M.; Xu, B.; Warde-Farley, D.; Ozair, S.; Courville, A.; Bengio, Y. Generative adversarial nets. *arXiv* **2014**, arXiv:1406.2661.
38. Chen, Y.; Li, W.; Sakaridis, C.; Dai, D.; Gool, L.V. Domain adaptive faster r-cnn for object detection in the wild. In Proceedings of the IEEE Conference on Computer Vision and Pattern Recognition, Salt Lake City, UT, USA, 18–23 June 2018; pp. 3339–3348.
39. Saito, K.; Ushiku, Y.; Harada, T.; Saenko, K. Strong-weak distribution alignment for adaptive object detection. In Proceedings of the IEEE/CVF Conference on Computer Vision and Pattern Recognition, Long Beach, CA, USA, 15–20 June 2019; pp. 6956–6965.
40. Zhu, L.; She, Q.; Chen, Q.; You, Y.; Wang, B.; Lu, Y. Weakly supervised object localization as domain adaption. *arXiv* **2022**, arXiv:2203.01714.
41. Tzeng, E.; Hoffman, J.; Saenko, K.; Darrell, T. Adversarial discriminative domain adaptation. In Proceedings of the IEEE Conference on Computer Vision and Pattern Recognition, Honolulu, HI, USA, 21–26 July 2017; pp. 7167–7176.
42. Mordido, G.; Yang, H.; Meinel, C. Dropout-gan: Learning from a dynamic ensemble of discriminators. *arXiv* **2018**, arXiv:1807.11346.
43. Hoffman, J.; Tzeng, E.; Park, T.; Zhu, J.-Y.; Isola, P.; Saenko, K.; Efros, A.; Darrell, T. Cycada: Cycle-consistent adversarial domain adaptation. In Proceedings of the International Conference on Machine Learning, Stockholm, Sweden, 10–15 July 2018; pp. 1989–1998.
44. Zhang, Y.; Qiu, Z.; Yao, T.; Liu, D.; Mei, T. Fully convolutional adaptation networks for semantic segmentation. In Proceedings of the IEEE Conference on Computer Vision and Pattern Recognition, Salt Lake City, UT, USA, 18–23 June 2018; pp. 6810–6818.
45. Saito, K.; Watanabe, K.; Ushiku, Y.; Harada, T. Maximum classifier discrepancy for unsupervised domain adaptation. In Proceedings of the IEEE Conference on Computer Vision and Pattern Recognition, Salt Lake City, UT, USA, 17–23 June 2018; pp. 3723–3732.
46. Supancic, J.S.; Ramanan, D. Self-paced learning for long-term tracking. In Proceedings of the IEEE Conference on Computer Vision and Pattern Recognition, Portland, OR, USA, 23–28 June 2013; pp. 2379–2386.
47. Choi, J.; Jeong, M.; Kim, T.; Kim, C. Pseudo-labeling curriculum for unsupervised domain adaptation. *arXiv* **2019**, arXiv:1908.00262.
48. Bengio, Y.; Louradour, J.; Collobert, R.; Weston, J. Curriculum learning. In Proceedings of the 26th Annual International Conference on Machine Learning, Montreal, QC, Canada, 14–18 June 2009; pp. 41–48.

49. Xu, R.; Li, G.; Yang, J.; Lin, L. Larger norm more transferable: An adaptive feature norm approach for unsupervised domain adaptation. In Proceedings of the IEEE/CVF International Conference on Computer Vision, Seoul, Republic of Korea, 27 October–2 November 2019; pp. 1426–1435.
50. Cao, J.; Tang, H.; Fang, H.-S.; Shen, X.; Lu, C.; Tai, Y.-W. Cross-domain adaptation for animal pose estimation. In Proceedings of the IEEE/CVF International Conference on Computer Vision, Seoul, Republic of Korea, 27 October–2 November 2019; pp. 9498–9507.
51. Li, C.; Lee, G.H. From synthetic to real: Unsupervised domain adaptation for animal pose estimation. In Proceedings of the IEEE/CVF Conference on Computer Vision and Pattern Recognition, Nashville, TN, USA, 20–25 June 2021; pp. 1482–1491.
52. Jiang, J.; Ji, Y.; Wang, X.; Liu, Y.; Wang, J.; Long, M. Regressive domain adaptation for unsupervised keypoint detection. In Proceedings of the IEEE/CVF Conference on Computer Vision and Pattern Recognition, Nashville, TN, USA, 20–25 June 2021; pp. 6780–6789.
53. Zhou, X.; Karpur, A.; Gan, C.; Luo, L.; Huang, Q. Unsupervised domain adaptation for 3d keypoint estimation via view consistency. In Proceedings of the European Conference on Computer Vision (ECCV), Munich, Germany, 8–14 September 2018; pp. 137–153.
54. Zhang, X.; Wong, Y.; Kankanhalli, M.S.; Geng, W. Unsupervised domain adaptation for 3d human pose estimation. In Proceedings of the 27th ACM International Conference on Multimedia, Nice, France, 21–25 October 2019; pp. 926–934.
55. Chen, H.; Guo, P.; Li, P.; Lee, G.H.; Chirikjian, G. Multi-person 3d pose estimation in crowded scenes based on multi-view geometry. In *Computer Vision—ECCV 2020, Proceedings of the 16th European Conference, Glasgow, UK, 23–28 August 2020*; Springer: Cham, Switzerland, 2020.
56. Huang, C.; Jiang, S.; Li, Y.; Zhang, Z.; Traish, J.; Deng, C.; Ferguson, S.; Xu, R.Y.D. End-to-end dynamic matching network for multi-view multi-person 3d pose estimation. In *Computer Vision—ECCV 2020, Proceedings of the 16th European Conference, Glasgow, UK, 23–28 August 2020*; Springer: Cham, Switzerland, 2020; pp. 477–493.
57. Reddy, N.D.; Guigues, L.; Pishchulin, L.; Eledath, J.; Narasimhan, S.G. Tessetrack: End-to-end learnable multi-person articulated 3d pose tracking. In Proceedings of the IEEE/CVF Conference on Computer Vision and Pattern Recognition, Nashville, TN, USA, 20–25 June 2021; pp. 15190–15200.
58. Saini, N.; Bonetto, E.; Price, E.; Ahmad, A.; Black, M.J. Airpose: Multi-view fusion network for aerial 3d human pose and shape estimation. *IEEE Robot. Autom. Lett.* **2022**, *7*, 4805–4812. [CrossRef]
59. Chen, Y.; Gu, R.; Huang, O.; Jia, G. Vtp: Volumetric transformer for multi-view multi-person 3d pose estimation. *arXiv* **2022**, arXiv:2205.12602.
60. Loshchilov, I.; Hutter, F. Decoupled weight decay regularization. *arXiv* **2017**, arXiv:1711.05101.
61. Tzeng, E.; Hoffman, J.; Zhang, N.; Saenko, K.; Darrell, T. Deep domain confusion: Maximizing for domain invariance. *arXiv* **2014**, arXiv:1412.3474.
62. Long, M.; Zhu, H.; Wang, J.; Jordan, M.I. Deep transfer learning with joint adaptation networks. In Proceedings of the International Conference on Machine Learning, Sydney, Australia, 6–11 August 2017; pp. 2208–2217.
63. Sun, B.; Saenko, K. Deep coral: Correlation alignment for deep domain adaptation. In *Computer Vision, Proceedings of the ECCV 2016 Workshops, Amsterdam, The Netherlands, 8–10. 15–16 October 2016*; Springer: Cham, Switzerland, 2016; pp. 443–450.
64. Long, M.; Cao, Z.; Wang, J.; Jordan, M.I. Conditional Adversarial Domain Adaptation. *arXiv* **2017**, arXiv:1705.10667.
65. Hinton, G.E.; Srivastava, N.; Krizhevsky, A.; Sutskever, I.; Salakhutdinov, R.R. Improving neural networks by preventing co-adaptation of feature detectors. *arXiv* **2012**, arXiv:1207.0580.
66. Frankle, J.; Carbin, M. The lottery ticket hypothesis: Finding sparse, trainable neural networks. *arXiv* **2018**, arXiv:1803.03635.

sensors

MDPI

Article

The Spatio-Temporal Patterns of Regional Development in Shandong Province of China from 2012 to 2021 Based on Nighttime Light Remote Sensing

Hongli Zhang [1], Quanzhou Yu [1,2,*], Yujie Liu [3], Jie Jiang [1], Junjie Chen [1] and Ruyun Liu [1]

[1] School of Geography and Environment, Liaocheng University, Liaocheng 252059, China; zhang304279228@163.com (H.Z.); jiangjie1592020@163.com (J.J.); chenjunjie0103@163.com (J.C.); liuruyun0414@126.com (R.L.)

[2] Yellow River Research Institute, Liaocheng University, Liaocheng 252000, China

[3] Research Center for Ecological Civilization, Chinese Research Academy of Environmental Sciences, Beijing 100012, China; liuyj@craes.org.cn

* Correspondence: yuquanzhou2008@126.com

Abstract: As a major coastal economic province in the east of China, it is of great significance to clarify the temporal and spatial patterns of regional development in Shandong Province in recent years to support regional high-quality development. Nightlight remote sensing data can reveal the spatio-temporal patterns of social and economic activities on a fine pixel scale. We based the nighttime light patterns at three spatial scales in three geographical regions on monthly nighttime light remote sensing data and social statistics. Different cities and different counties in Shandong Province in the last 10 years were studied by using the methods of trend analysis, stability analysis and correlation analysis. The results show that: (1) The nighttime light pattern was generally consistent with the spatial pattern of construction land. The nighttime light intensity of most urban, built-up areas showed an increasing trend, while the old urban areas of Qingdao and Yantai showed a weakening trend. (2) At the geographical unit scale, the total nighttime light in south-central Shandong was significantly higher than that in eastern and northwest Shandong, while the nighttime light growth rate in northwest Shandong was significantly highest. At the urban scale, Liaocheng had the highest nighttime light growth rate. At the county scale, the nighttime light growth rate of counties with a better economy was lower, while that of counties with a backward economy was higher. (3) The nighttime light growth was significantly correlated with Gross Domestic Product (GDP) and population growth, indicating that regional economic development and population growth were the main causes of nighttime light change.

Keywords: nighttime light remote sensing; Shandong Province; regional development; difference analysis; temporal and spatial pattern

1. Introduction

Under the background of high-quality economic development in China, the study of regional development differences has become a hot issue in the study of human geography. Fan et al. [1] analyzed the evolution of China's regional development pattern since the reform and opening up and discussed the key points for the regulation and control of China's regional development pattern in the next 30 years. Deng et al. [2] summarized the patterns of China's regional balanced development in different periods, discussed the scientific connotation of regional balanced development and put forward some suggestions for China's regional balanced development. Cao et al. [3] quantitatively measured the comprehensive development level of the Huaihe River economic belt based on the four dimensions, economy, society, ecological environment and sustainable development, and analyzed the spatio-temporal differentiation patterns and regional differences of regional development. Li studied the urban economic development of the Guangdong Province and put forward some feasible suggestions on how to solve the differences in regional social and economic development [4]. Entering the period of 'The 14th five-year Plan', China has begun a new journey of building a modern socialist country in every respect. In addition, people pay increasing attention to regional openness and inter-regional interaction. A regionally coordinated development strategy has been a dominant strategy to enhance and deepen inter-regional economic and social relations, which can solve the problem of imbalance and inadequacy in China's economic development [5,6].

Most of these studies are based on the traditional methods of panel data analysis, which are highly dependent on statistical data [7]. On the one hand, statistical data are easily affected by people, and the accuracy and objectivity of them are affected. In addition, most of the statistical data are investigated by administrative units and lack more detailed analysis in space. As a special remote sensing image data, Nighttime Light data is closely related to patterns of urban economic development, which can comprehensively characterize the breadth and intensity of human activities. The recorded luminance value of light radiation has a unique effect in explaining the phenomenon of human activities and social and economic development, and can analyze economic and social activities on a relatively fine spatial scale [8]. For example, Meng estimated carbon emissions from 2000 to 2019 based on Defense Meteorological Satellite Program/Operational Linescan System (DMSP/OLS) Nighttime Light images of Jiangsu Province in China [9]. Using the Nighttime Light remote sensing time series data from 1992 to 2013, Martin quantitatively extracted and analyzed the information, and revealed the spatio-temporal patterns of China's urbanization [10]. Zhang et al. [11] studied the variation of Nighttime Light in Pakistan from 2012 to 2019 at different geographical scales based on Visible Infrared Imager Radiometer Suite (VIIRS) monthly Nighttime Light remote sensing images. Ding et al. [12] studied the spatio-temporal patterns of county economic development in Shandong Province based on DMSP/OLS Nighttime Light data, using the method of spatial statistical analysis.

In the past 10 years, the economic and social development of Shandong Province has entered a new era, showing new patterns. There is an urgent need to clarify the temporal and spatial patterns and evolution laws of Shandong's regional development, so as to provide a guarantee for the high-quality development of the Yellow River basin and realize the goal of "The peak of carbon emissions, carbon neutrality". Therefore, aimed at the problem of regional development in Shandong Province, this study analyzes the distribution patterns and changing trend of Nighttime Light in Shandong Province by using pixel-based statistical analysis, trend analysis, stability analysis and spatial regional statistics and correlation analysis based on the monthly visible infrared imaging radiometer (National Polar-orbiting Partnership, Visible and Infrared Imaging Radiometer Suite, NPP/VIIRS) Nighttime Light remote sensing data from the past 10 years. From this perspective, clarifying the temporal and spatial patterns of the regional development of Shandong Province in the past 10 years allows us to provide some support for the high-quality development of Shandong Province.

With the rapid development of economic globalization and urbanization, cities are showing a trend for rapid development and competitive development, especially the development and growth of some large and medium-sized cities, which can not only be supported by national policies. In addition, they can absorb the resources of the surrounding areas and the scale of expansion is rapid. However, the development and expansion of many cities in the Shandong Province are not carried out according to the unified model, and each city has its own particularity. The form of urban spatial development will be affected by the direction and topography of the surrounding urban agglomeration integration, and will form its own unique development model. Since the beginning of new century, the external expansion and internal reconstruction of urban structures are the main patterns in China's urban spatial development. Against this background, multi-core structures appear in big cities, commercial plots gather, and new commercial districts are gradually formed. Industrial development has gradually gathered into industrial zones and economic development zones, and urban space tends to be regionalized.

This study is of great significance to the research on the exploration of regional social and economic development based on Nighttime Light data, which can reflect the regional social and economic situation of Shandong Province to a considerable extent, and help to explore the law of temporal and spatial changes of social and economic activities. It can provide a scientific basis for relevant government departments to scientifically and reasonably formulate regional macro development strategy decisions, so as to quickly promote the coordinated development of urban agglomeration, and city and county integration in Shandong Province. It is beneficial for Shandong Province to become a demonstration area for the development of international urban agglomeration.

2. Data and Methods

2.1. General Situation of the Study Area

Shandong Province is located on the eastern coast of China and the lower reaches of the Yellow River. The province has a land area of about 155,800 km^2 and a marine area of 159,600 km^2. According to the seventh national census, the resident population of the province is 101.527 million. The regional GDP in 2021 was 8.30959 trillion ¥, an increase of 8.3% compared to the previous year. Shandong Province ranks third in GDP and second in population in the country. It is the largest economic and populous province in China. By the end of 2020, Shandong Province had jurisdiction over 16 prefecture-level cities, 136 county-level administrative districts (58 municipal districts, 26 county-level cities and 52 counties) and 1822 township-level administrative districts. Shandong Province belongs to the warm, temperate monsoon climate, with the same season of rain and heat, an annual average temperature of 11–14 (Celsius temperature) and an average annual precipitation of 550–590 mm [13]. The precipitation gradually decreases from the southeast coast to the northwest inland. The proportion of crop planting area is large; this is an important major grain producing area in China. The distribution characteristics of vegetation have obvious spatial differences. Shandong Province is a fast-growing economic province along the eastern coast of China, which plays an important role for the whole country. However, there are still issues of spatial imbalance and incoordination in the regional economic and social development of Shandong Province [14,15]. Shandong Peninsula urban agglomeration as a whole is more developed than central and western Shandong, and the development speed here is the fastest [12].

2.2. Data

2.2.1. NPP/VIIRS Nighttime Light Data

This study used the monthly NPP/VIIRS (National Polar-orbiting Partnership, Visible and Infrared Imaging Radiometer Suite) Nighttime Light remote sensing data from April 2012 to October 2021. A total of 115 images were used. The data sensor, carried by the Suomi NPP satellite from the United States, was launched and put into use in 2011. Its specific parameters are shown in Table 1. The NPP/VIIRS Nighttime Light data unit is nW/cm^2/sr. Before the monthly average image is released, the NPP/VIIRS data are processed by stray light, moonlight, cloud and other factors.

Table 1. Satellite and sensor parameters involved [16].

Data Type	NPP/VIIRS
Strip width	~3000 km
Night transit time (local time)	~01:30
Low light imaging bandpass	Panchromatic 0.5–0.9 μm
Value	Absolute radiation value
Spatial resolution	15 arc seconds (500 m)
Calibration	Satellite calibration
Saturation	None
Product cycle	Month
Time series	Daily data: 20120201 to present Monthly composite data: 201204 to present

2.2.2. Auxiliary Data for Regional Development Analysis

In addition, the study uses Shandong statistical yearbook data, such as GDP, population and annual carbon emissions from various prefecture-level cities in Shandong Province, as relevant indicators of regional development, and analyzes the correlation with Nighttime Light data. Meanwhile, it uses the boundary vector data of Shandong Province and its prefecture-level cities provided by the National basic Geographic Information Center [17], and the land use type data of Shandong Province provided by the Resource and Environmental Science and data Center of the Chinese Academy of Sciences [18]. The multi-source data used in this paper are publicly available, and the dataset information is shown in Table 2.

Table 2. Auxiliary data used in this study.

Data Name	Year	Source	Resolution
GDP	2020	Shandong statistical yearbook	
Population	2020	Shandong statistical yearbook	
Carbon emissions	2020	Shandong statistical yearbook	
City boundary vector layers	2020	National basic Geographic Information Center	
Land use type data	2020	Resource and Environmental Science and data Center of the Chinese Academy of Sciences	30 M
NPP-VIIRS of monthly	April 2012–October 2021	Earth Observation Group [19]	500 M

2.3. *Methods*

2.3.1. Nighttime Light Data Preprocessing

The noctilucent data preprocessing, downloaded from the EOG (Earth Observation Group) website, includes data denoising, data interpolation and projection conversion [16] to convert the processed image projection into an equal area projection coordinate system [20]. Due to the influence of stray light, the "vcmcfg" product of NPP/VIIRS data has a serious numerical deficiency in the middle and high latitudes of summer [21], and the officially revised "vcmslcfg" product still lacks June data for 2012 and 2013, so it is interpolated with the May and July averages of 2012 and 2013, respectively. After filling up the missing data, the vector boundary of Shandong Province is used to clip the monthly Nighttime Light images of Shandong Province. Data flow processing is shown in Figure 1.

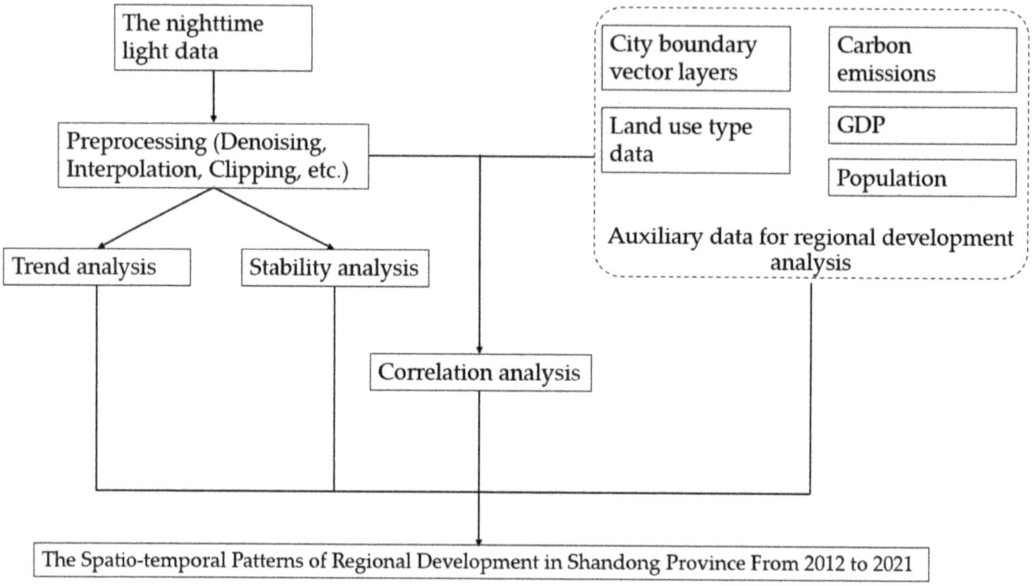

Figure 1. Data processing flow chart.

2.3.2. Statistical Analysis Based on Pixels

The univariate linear regression method was used to fit and analyze the changing trend. The DN value of Nighttime Light data and the change rate of related socio-economic elements are defined as the slope of a linear regression equation that changes month by month during the study period expressed by a slope; the formula is as follows:

$$\text{Slope} = \frac{n* \sum_{i=1}^{n}(i * DN_i) - \sum_{i=1}^{n} i * \sum_{i=1}^{n} DN_i}{\text{n}* \sum_{i=1}^{n} t_i^2 - (\sum_{i=1}^{n} t_i)^2} \tag{1}$$

In the formula, the variable i is the sequence number of the monthly synthetic image according to time, and the value of i is 1,2, . . ., 115; n is the number of samples, n = 115; DN_i is the DN value of the i scene image; t_i is the corresponding time of the i scene image (t_i = YEARi + MONTHi/12, in which YEAR_i and MONTH_i are the year and month of the I scene image, respectively); and Slope is the slope of the regression equation during the study period, if slope > 0, it indicates that the Nighttime Light or some element index of the pixel in this period shows an upward trend, otherwise it decreases. The slope of the equation is regarded as the trend of Nighttime Light change.

For stability analysis of Nighttime Light change in the past 10 years, this study uses Formulas (2) and (3) to calculate the coefficient of variation of Nighttime Light value per pixel from 2012 to 2021, so as to reflect the degree of Nighttime Light fluctuation on different pixels in the study area in the past 10 years. The large fluctuation value indicates that the disturbance intensity is large and unstable; the small fluctuation value means that the state is stable.

$$\text{S} = \sqrt{\frac{\sum_{i=1}^{n}\left(DN_i - \overline{DN}\right)^2}{n-1}} \tag{2}$$

$$Cv = \frac{S}{\overline{DN}} \tag{3}$$

In the formula: Cv is the coefficient of variation, S is the standard deviation, (DN) is the average value of DN for many years and the variable i is the sequence number of the monthly synthetic image according to time.

2.3.3. Spatial Regional Statistics and Correlation Analysis

After downloading the data on land use types in Shandong Province in 2020, the built area is extracted to study the statistical patterns and changes of Nighttime Light in Shandong Province over the past 10 years. The land use types in Shandong Province in 2020 are shown in Figure 1. Pearson correlation analysis was carried out between the Nighttime Light statistics and the corresponding data for GDP, population and carbon emissions in each city and built-up area, in order to make clear the reason for the change in Nighttime Light and its effect in indicating regional development.

3. Results and Discussion

3.1. Spatio-Temporal Pattern of Nighttime Light in Shandong Province

3.1.1. Present Situation of Land Use and Average Nighttime Light Pattern

Figures 2 and 3 show that in the past 10 years, there has been obvious spatial consistency between the Nighttime Light mean distribution and the land use pattern in Shandong Province, especially with the urban construction land distribution. The areas with higher lighting at night are concentrated in the area of construction land, and emphasize a trend of gradually decreasing from the center to the edge of the construction land. In particular, it shows the patterns of the bipolar leadership of Qingdao and Jinan, and the multi-point scattered development of Weifang, Linyi, Zibo and Yantai. As far as each prefecture-level city is concerned, it shows the distribution patterns of one core plus multiple points, and the lighting has a good consistency with the resident distribution pattern of cities and counties. The Nighttime Light of other land types is generally low.

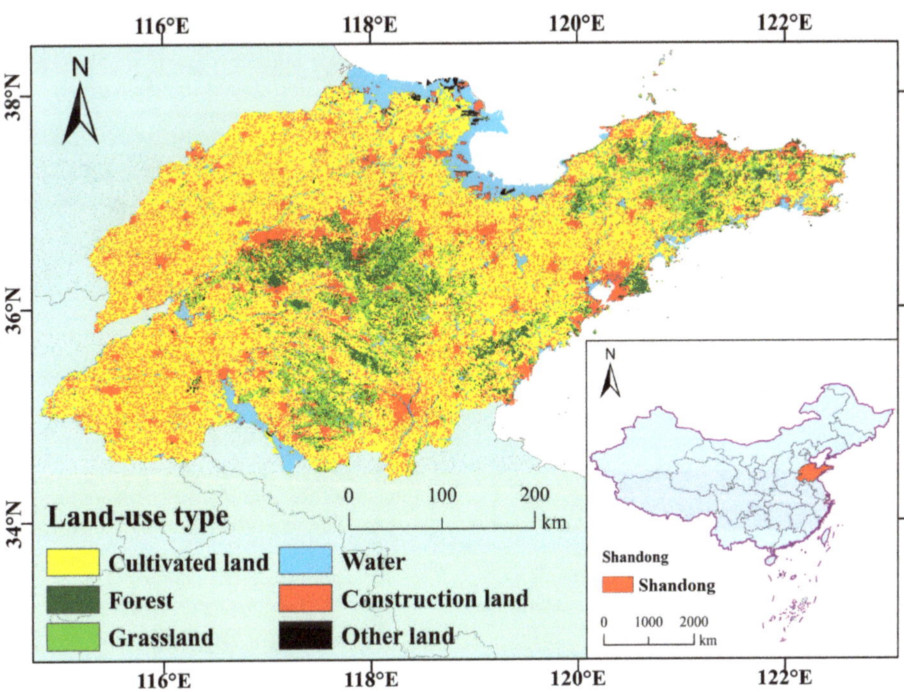

Figure 2. Land cover in Shandong province in 2020.

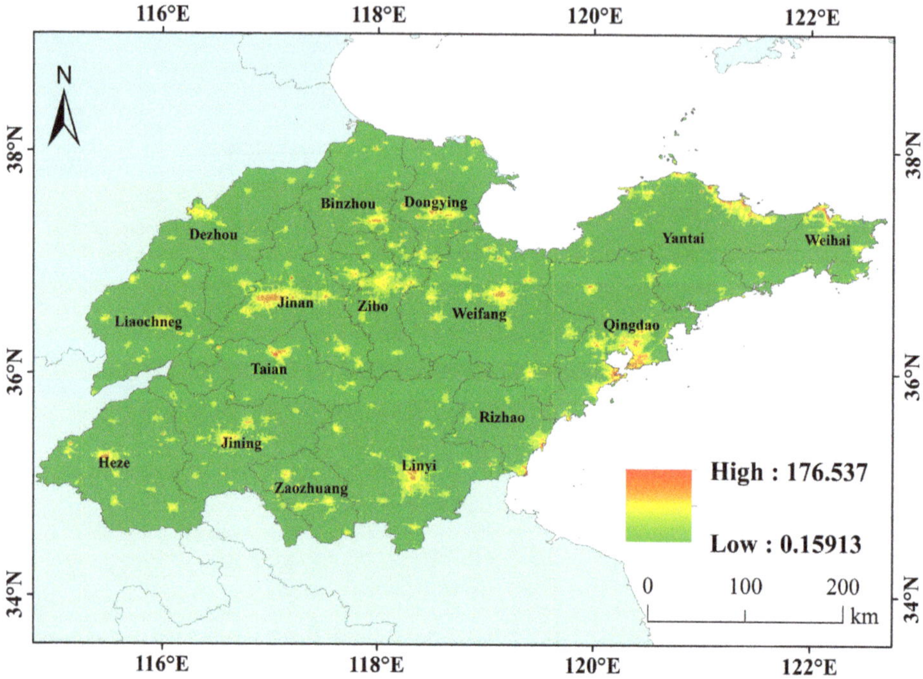

Figure 3. Spatial pattern of mean Nighttime Light in Shandong province from April 2012 to October 2021.

In terms of Nighttime Light intensity, the Nighttime Light intensity of prefecture-level cities is significantly higher than that of county-level cities, and that of the main urban areas is higher than that of suburbs and rural areas. The coastal Nighttime Light is higher than inland; the coastal areas of Shandong Peninsula are economically developed, and the Nighttime Light of towns here is generally high. At the same time, Dongying oil field and coastal ports have large-scale infrastructure and continuous operation, and the Nighttime Light brightness is also significant. Nighttime light is mainly distributed in economic and densely populated spot areas such as Jinan and Qingdao, but also shows a zonal distribution along the traffic line and coastline.

3.1.2. Spatio-Temporal Variation in Nighttime Lights in the Past Ten Years

The changing trends in Nighttime Light can be seen from Figures 4 and 5. Figure 4 displays the slope of Nighttime Light growth over the past decade. Red represents a rapid increase and blue represents a decrease. In Figure 5, red means more than 100% compared to its own growth, green means a reduction of 100%. The Nighttime Light changes slowly in most areas in Shandong Province, but there is also obvious spatial heterogeneity of Nighttime Light changes in some areas. The changing areas are mainly distributed in the coastal areas of the Shandong Peninsula, along the Jinan-Weifang section of Jiaoji Railway, along the Shandong section of the east line of The South-to-North Water Diversion Project and in urban areas in western Shandong. Specifically, the administrative stations of most prefecture-level cities and some surrounding counties have an obvious increasing trend in Nighttime Light, and the intensity of growth weakens from the city center to the periphery, indicating that, in the past 10 years, urbanization has developed rapidly, and the urban infrastructure has been gradually improved. However, the Nighttime Light in Qingdao, Yantai and Weihai in Shandong Peninsula has unique patterns. The Nighttime Light in the core urban areas decreases or does not obviously change, while the Nighttime Light in the new urban areas around it clearly increases. This feature is most obvious in Qingdao, where there is a downward trend in Nighttime Light in the old urban area of the east coast, and there is an obvious growth trend in the new area of the west coast. This may also imply that the urban economy of Jiaodong Peninsula has entered a stage of high-quality development.

The decline in Nighttime Light in Taian City is mainly in Dongping County, especially near Dongping Lake; there is a similar decline near Nansi Lake in Jining. This may be due to the local closure of many industrial and mining enterprises in order to prevent the impact of pollution on the fishery of Dongping Lake [22], and the establishment of closed fishing periods and areas in the lake area to prevent overfishing [23]. At the same time, the county government actively guided fishermen to return to the lake and to change production, but a large number of fishermen joined other industries [24]. Zaozhuang is listed as one of the second batch of resource-exhausted city transformation pilot cities under the State Council, and the reduction in coal mine output has to some extent affected the Nighttime Light [25,26]. Jining is one of the thirteen coal energy bases in China, and the local coal mining subsidence is controlled according to local conditions [25]. This may also lead to a downward trend in its Nighttime Light.

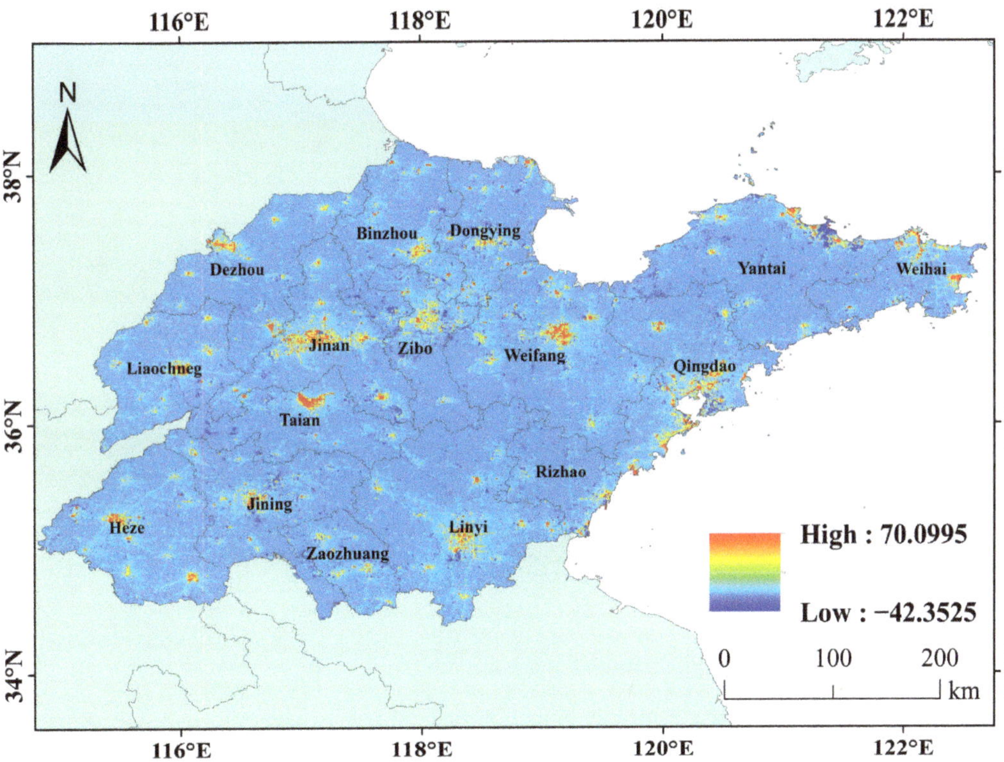

Figure 4. Spatio-temporal changes in Nighttime Light in Shandong province from April 2012 to October 2021.

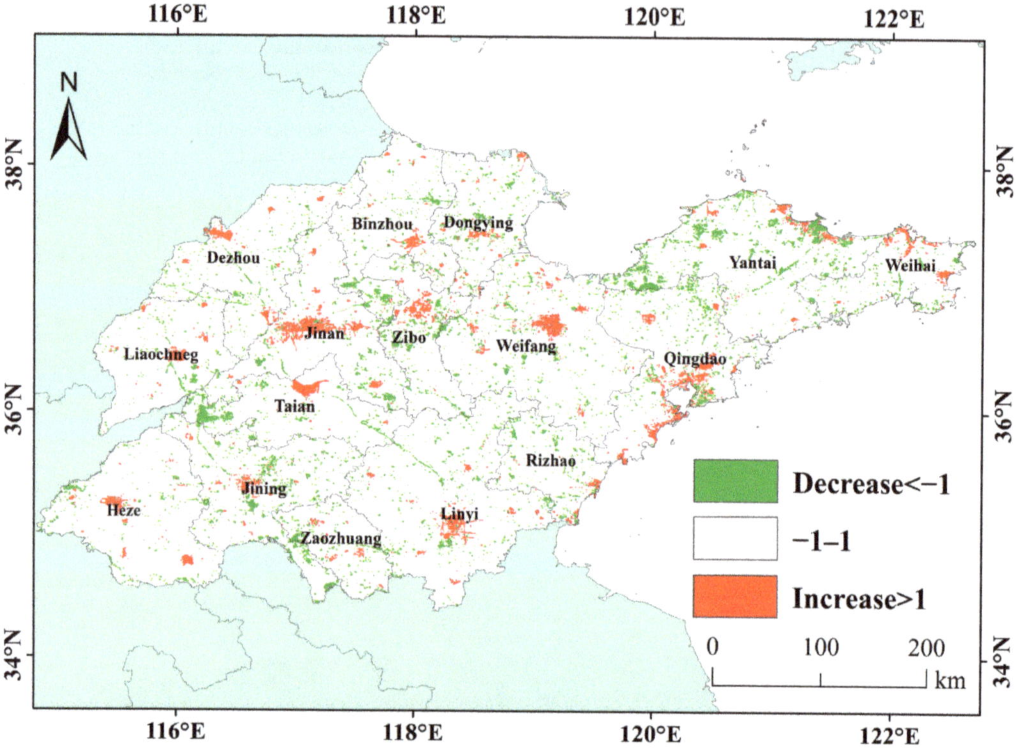

Figure 5. Key areas of Nighttime Light change in Shandong province from April 2012 to October 2021.

We divide the Nighttime light stability level into five levels, as shown in Figure 6; this picture shows stability, which means the absolute value of change. The most stable area of Nighttime Light in Shandong Province in the past 10 years ($Cv < 0.2$) is located in the old urban areas of Qingdao and Jinan, indicating that the changes in urban lighting in the old urban areas of big cities have been relatively gentle in the past 10 years, and the infrastructure in the old urban areas may not have changed significantly, or it may imply that the relationship between deep economic development and Nighttime Light growth is not significant. The most unstable areas ($Cv > 0.8$) are scattered across the whole province, among which the more concentrated areas are the central and eastern part of Weihai, the estuary of the Yellow River Delta, the provincial capital, metropolitan area and the periphery of related cities in southern Shandong and the north of Jiaozhou Bay in Qingdao. On the one hand, the instability of Nighttime Light in these areas may be due to drastic changes in infrastructure in the periphery of cities due to the intensification and expansion of cities. On the other hand, the construction and operation of new infrastructure may also lead to Nighttime Light instability in these areas. For example, the construction of Qingdao Jiaodong International Airport [27], the traffic trunk road, the construction of oil industry facilities in the Yellow River Delta [28] and the construction of Huangdao and the Huangdao national oil storage caverns [29]. In short, drastic changes in land use, especially those related to infrastructure land, lead to drastic changes in Nighttime Light.

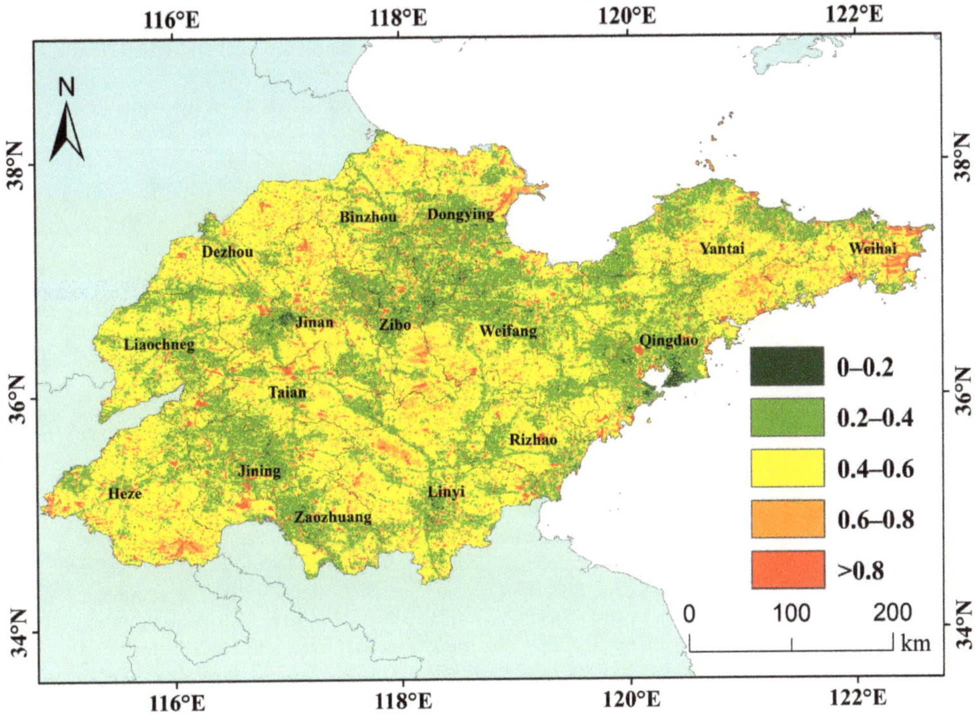

Figure 6. Stability pattern of Nighttime Light in Shandong province from April 2012 to October 2021.

3.2. Nighttime Light Differences on Different Spatial Scales

3.2.1. Nighttime Light Differences of Three Geographic Units in Shandong Province

According to previous data, Shandong Province is divided into three geographical regions: northwest Shandong, south-central Shandong and eastern Shandong [30]. The northwest of Shandong includes Dongying, Binzhou, Dezhou, Liaocheng, Heze, Liangshan County, Wenshang County, Jiaxiang County, Jinxiang County, Yutai County, Weishan County and Liangshan County in Jining, as well as Shouguang City in Weifang, Gaoqing County in Zibo, Dongping County in Taian, Jiyang District and Shanghe County in Jinan. South-central Shandong includes all counties in Jinan except Jiyang District and Shanghe County, all of Zibo County except Gaoqing County, all of Weifang County except Shouguang City, Gaomi City and Zhucheng City, all of Tai'an County except Dongping County, the Jining City area, Zoucheng City, Qufu City, Sishui County, Zaozhuang and Linyi. Eastern Shandong mainly includes Weihai, Yantai, Qingdao, Rizhao and Gaomi City and cities in Weifang.

In Table 3 it can be seen that the total amount of Nighttime Light in each region has increased significantly from 2012 to 2021, which means that the overall economy of Shandong Province has developed to a great extent in these 10 years. Among them, the Nighttime Light growth rate in the northwest of Shandong is the highest, reaching 245.95%, which is almost twice that of the eastern Shandong. The Nighttime Light growth rate in the central and southern parts of Shandong is in the middle, and the Nighttime Light growth rate gradually increases from the eastern Shandong through central and southern Shandong to the northwest of Shandong. It shows that, although the level of economic development in northwest Shandong is relatively backward, the society has developed rapidly in recent years, and even the degree of relative growth in this decade has greatly exceeded that of the economically developed eastern Shandong region. At the same time, it also implies that the economic development stages of the three major geographical units in

Shandong Province are not synchronized, that is, they are in different stages of high-quality development; the development of northwest Shandong tends towards the traditional extensive economic development model. The consumption of energy and electricity may be greater, while the development of eastern Shandong tends towards an intensive and high-quality development model.

Table 3. Nighttime Light change data from three geographical units in Shandong province from April 2012 to October 2021.

Region	Total Amount of Regional Nighttime Light/(nW/cm^2/sr)		Nighttime-Light Growth-Scale /(nW/cm^2/sr)	Nighttime Light Growth Rate /%	Total Amount of Nighttime Light Slope/(nW/cm^2/sr)
	Year 2012	Year 2021			
Northwest Shandong	173,355.01	599,725.90	426,370.89	245.95%	16,055.57
South-central Shandong	311,984.31	781,625.68	469,641.37	150.53%	6204.76
Eastern Shandong	208,258.41	467,140.42	258,882.01	124.31%	4655.77
Total	693,597.73	1,848,492.00	1,154,894.27	166.51%	26,916.10

3.2.2. Nighttime Light Patterns at the Urban Scale in Shandong Province

According to Table 4, the total amount of Nighttime Light in all prefecture-level cities in Shandong Province showed an increasing trend from 2012 to 2021. Liaocheng had the largest Nighttime Light growth rate of 309.54%, followed by Dezhou City (199.20%), Linyi City (191.27%), Heze City (186.45%) and so on. Although the level of economic development of Liaocheng, Dezhou and Heze is relatively backward in Shandong Province, they have grown rapidly in the past 10 years, indicating that the relative development of these three cities is very fast, and the gap between these three cities and developed cities is narrowing. The cities with the lowest increase in total Nighttime Light volume from 2012 to 2021 were Yantai (80.02%), Zibo (91.17%), Dongying (92.82%) and Jinan (95.57%). The level of social development in these cities is relatively high, and the dependence of their economic development on resources and electricity may be relatively low, so the lighting growth rate is relatively low.

Table 4. Nighttime Light change data of 16 prefecture-level cities in Shandong province from April 2012 to October 2021.

Region	Total Amount of Regional Nighttime Light/(nW/cm^2/sr)		Nighttime-Light Growth-Scale/(nW/cm^2/sr)	Nighttime Light Growth Rate/%	Total Amount of Nighttime Light Slope/(nW/cm^2/sr)
	Year 2012	Year 2021			
Binzhou	44,650.55	105,405.01	60,754.47	136.07%	3930.26
Dongying	52,951.51	102,103.42	49,151.92	92.82%	3281.23
Dezhou	32,894.84	98,421.34	65,526.50	199.20%	6172.03
Heze	49,310.93	141,253.51	91,942.58	186.45%	6581.39
Jinan	104,759.04	204,873.39	100,114.35	95.57%	9012.95
Jining	55,779.22	142,984.11	87,204.89	156.34%	3524.73
Liaocheng	24,811.57	101,606.38	76,794.81	309.51%	5025.86
Linyi	59,740.39	174,008.03	114,267.65	191.27%	−397.83
Qingdao	113,954.34	257,093.59	143,139.25	125.61%	11,365.05
Rizhao	24,306.46	56,928.44	32,621.99	134.21%	1855.87
Taian	32,926.04	84,017.92	51,091.88	155.17%	3225.36
Weifang	85,184.51	198,850.53	113,666.02	133.44%	8814.29
Weihai	29,399.35	78,879.87	49,480.52	168.30%	5310.10
Yantai	80,574.92	145,051.16	64,476.25	80.02%	−207.45
Zibo	55,354.61	105,823.48	50,468.88	91.17%	4229.70
Zaozhuang	27,161.18	60,815.65	33,654.47	123.91%	2186.87
Total	873,759.46	205,8115.86	1184,356.40	135.55%	73,910.42

Nearly 10 years of Nighttime Light growth slope (slope) data show that the urban Nighttime Light total slope is the highest in Qingdao, Jinan and Weifang, while Linyi and Yantai's Nighttime Light slopes are negative. On the one hand, this may be related to the overall economic development model and speed of the city, and it also has a lot to do with the degree of coordinated development in urban and rural areas. The total value of the growth slopes for urban and rural areas with well coordinated development is generally higher.

3.2.3. Nighttime Light Patterns at Counties Scale in Shandong Province

There are 136 districts and counties in Shandong Province, and they are ranked according to their GDP; Table 5 shows the top five districts in terms of GDP. The total amount of GDP and the Nighttime Light slope in Jinan is far ahead than the rest of the province. But in terms of nighttime light growth rate, Huangdao District is far higher than other areas, which was 163.57%. The growth rate and change in the Yantai district are ranked low among the five districts and counties. The districts and counties in the bottom five in terms of GDP are shown in Table 6. As can be seen from Table 6, the total amount of Nighttime Light in Chengwu County in Heze increased rapidly from 2012 to 2021, with a growth rate of 229.18%. This was followed by Gaotang County in Liaocheng (167.25%), Qingyun County in Dezhou (156.73%), Zhanhua County in Binzhou (95.44%) and Dong'e County in Liaocheng (81.51%). The total-amount-of-Nighttime-Light slope also proves this point; the change rate for total Nighttime Light amount corresponds to the Nighttime Light slope, and the districts and counties with high rates of change in Nighttime Light area also have high Nighttime Light slopes. Overall, the Nighttime Light growth rate of economically backward districts and counties is relatively high, while that of better economic districts and counties is the opposite.

Table 5. Data for Nighttime Light changes in the top five economic districts and counties of Shandong Province from April 2012 to October 2021.

Region	GDP in 2020/RMB100 Million	Total Amount of Regional Nighttime Light/(nW/cm^2/sr)		Nighttime-Light Growth-Scale/(nW/cm^2/sr)	Nighttime Light Growth Rate/%	Total Amount of Nighttime Light Slope/(nW/cm^2/sr)
		Year 2012	Year 2021			
Central urban area of Jinan	7533.1	57,930.91	112,657.13	54,726.22	94.47%	5522.16
Central urban area of Qingdao	4876.4	53,441.99	88,023.37	34,581.37	64.71%	2150.36
Huangdao District	3721.7	15,614.12	41,153.98	25,539.86	163.57%	2599.66
Central urban area of Yantai	3467.3	24,491.77	34,625.67	10,133.90	41.38%	284.05
Central urban area of Zibo	2633.7	41,671.64	72,272.46	30,600.82	73.43%	2406.66
Total	22,232.2	193,150.44	348,732.61	155,582.17	80.55%	12,962.88

Table 6. Nighttime Light change data of five districts and counties in Shandong Province from April 2012 to October 2021.

Region	GDP in 2020/RMB100 Million	Total Amount of Regional Nighttime Light/(nW/cm^2/sr)		Nighttime-Light Growth-Scale/(nW/cm^2/sr)	Nighttime Light Growth Rate/%	Total Amount of Nighttime Light Slope/(nW/cm^2/sr)
		Year 2012	Year 2021			
Dong'e County	147.2	4185.12	7596.63	3411.50	81.51%	141.27
Gaotang County	151.2	3194.49	8537.23	5342.74	167.25%	477.22
Chengwu County	155.4	2407.41	7924.80	5517.39	229.18%	527.43
Zhanhua County	162.6	4384.32	8568.94	4184.61	95.44%	269.07
Qingyun County	165.5	1566.77	4022.39	2455.62	156.73%	282.32
Total	781.9	15,738.12	36,649.98	20,911.86	132.87%	1697.32

3.3. *Correlation Analysis of Light Change at Nighttime Light*

3.3.1. The Relationship between the Total Amount of Nighttime Light and Economic Indicators in Various Prefecture-Level Cities

Using the built-up area range of land use extraction in Shandong Province in 2020, bivariate Pearson correlation analysis was carried out between the mean Nighttime Light for each city region and urban core area from April 2012 to October 2021 and the mean ten-year GDP value, the ten-year population average value and the average carbon emission value for each city (six years' worth of data from 2012 to 2017). The results are shown in Table 7.

Table 7. Correlation analysis between ten-year Nighttime Light average and GDP, population and carbon emissions in Shandong province.

		Average GDP	Average Population	Average Carbon Emission
The average Nighttime Light value of each prefecture-level city	Pearson correlation	0.600 *	0.350	0.379
	Significant (double tail)	0.014	0.184	0.148
	Number of cases	16	16	16
Average Nighttime Light value of urban core area	Pearson correlation	0.748 **	0.013	0.403
	Significant (double tail)	0.001	0.963	0.122
	Number of cases	16	16	16

* at level 0.05 (double tail), the correlation was significant. ** at level 0.01 (double tail), the correlation was significant.

It is found that there is a significant correlation between the mean Nighttime Light intensity and GDP in both the urban unit and the urban core area, especially in the core area. There is a very significant positive correlation between the Nighttime Light mean and its GDP ($p < 0.01$), indicating that the Nighttime Light intensity in the core urban area is closely related to economic development. The correlation between average Nighttime Light and population and carbon emissions is not significant; however,, it may imply that the increase in population can not be directly reflected in energy and electricity consumption. In addition, carbon emission data may lead to insignificant patterns due to time scale mismatch. In short, it can be explained that the average Nighttime Light value can be used as an effective index to measure regional economic development.

3.3.2. The Correlation between Nighttime Light Growth and Economic Index Growth in Cities at Each Prefecture Level

In order to further analyze the relationship between the Nighttime Light index and regional development, the relationship between Nighttime Light index growth and economic index growth is studied and calculated. Based on the annual growth (slope) of mean Nighttime Light from April 2012 to October 2021 in 16 prefecture-level cities in Shandong Province, and the slope of GDP, the slope of population and the slope of carbon emissions (2012–2017), the Pearson correlation is calculated. It can be seen from Table 8 that there is a significant positive correlation between the Nighttime Light slope and slope of GDP in 16 prefecture-level cities, and there is also a significant correlation between the urban Nighttime Light slope and the population slope, indicating that the growth of urban Nighttime Light intensity is closely related to local human, social and economic activities.

Table 8. Correlation analysis between nighttime light emission and slope of GDP, population and carbon emissions in Shandong.

		Slope of GDP	Slope of Population	Slope of Carbon Emission
Urban Nighttime Light slope	Pearson correlation	0.570 *	0.531 *	~0.177
	Significant (double tail)	0.021	0.034	0.513
	Number of cases	16	16	16
Nighttime Light slope in the core area of the city	Pearson correlation	0.45	0.378	~0.185
	Significant (double tail)	0.08	0.149	0.493
	Number of cases	16	16	16

* at level 0.05 (double tail), the correlation was significant.

However, the Nighttime Light slope in the core areas of 16 prefecture-level cities was not correlated with the slope of population, the slope and carbon emission or the slope of GDP. Further comparing the data in the table, it is found that the correlation between the GDP slope and the population slope has decreased, indicating that the social and economic activities in urban non-core areas (rural areas) of 16 prefecture-level cities in Shandong Province are also factors affecting Nighttime Light slope.

3.4. Limitations and Prospects

Although this study has made some breakthroughs in describing the regional development pattern of Shandong Province, due to the limitations of data acquisition and workload, there are still some shortcomings. The Night Light remote sensing sensor used was disturbed by cloud, fog, terrain and other factors in the imaging process, and the available multi-temporal data in the study area is limited. The method models used are too few and have not been cross verified with other remote sensing data.

The spatio-temporal resolution is not fine enough and can be analyzed by combining a variety of Nighttime Light satellites in the future.

At the same time, Nighttime Light remote sensing data can not only be combined with GDP and population data to study urban economic development, but also can be used for the urban belt and urban agglomeration development trajectory monitoring, urban land use scale prediction, poverty index and other related research.

Models can be built to make Nighttime Light data better reflect regional economic activities.

4. Conclusions

In this study, the spatio-temporal variation patterns and reasons for Nighttime Light in Shandong Province are analyzed on the basis of three geographical units, city scale, county scale and pixel scale. There were different regional development models used on different scales, among which the most obvious one is at the city scale. The main results are as follows:

(1) The average Nighttime Light in Shandong Province in the past 10 years decreases from the center of the urban built-up area to the edge. From the spatio-temporal patterns of provincial Nighttime Light, the average Nighttime Light distribution is consistent with that of construction land. In the past 10 years, the change pattern for Nighttime Light showed a certain spatial heterogeneity, the Nighttime Light in the built-up areas of most cities showed an increasing trend, while in the old urban areas of Qingdao and Yantai and other non-urban areas, the Nighttime Light showed a weakening trend. This may be related to different stages of regional social development.

(2) There are differences in the total Nighttime Light amount and mean value of the three geographical units in Shandong Province, and the Nighttime Light growth rate is higher in the northwest of Shandong Province (246%), which has a lower level of economic development. The growth rate of Nighttime Light in eastern Shandong, which has a higher level of economic development, is lower. The Nighttime Light growth rate increases sequentially from the eastern part of Shandong through the central and southern parts of Shandong and into the northwest of Shandong. It implies that the level of regional development in eastern Shandong, south-central Shandong and northwest Shandong is becoming increasingly balanced.

(3) At the urban scale, Nighttime Light growth does not completely match its level of economic development. The economic development level of Liaocheng, Dezhou and Heze is relatively backward, but Nighttime Light has increased rapidly in the past 10 years, by 309.51%, 199.20% and 186.45%. While the peninsula cities, such as Yantai and Qingdao, have a high economic output, the Nighttime Light growth is slow, at 80.02% and 125.61%, and some built-up areas have declined. At the same time, in areas like Zaozhuang City, the growth rate of Nighttime Light is slow due to the influence of the South-to-North Water

Diversion Project and the reduction in local coal mine production. This shows that different cities may be in different stages of regional high-quality development.

(4) At the county and district scale, except in Huangdao District, the Nighttime Light growth rate of the top five counties in 2020 is relatively slow, especially in Yantai City. The Nighttime Light growth rate of the counties in the bottom five in 2020 is relatively high, especially in Chengwu County in Heze. This implies that the regional consumption of resources and electricity is different at different stages of economic development.

(5) The correlation analysis at the city level showed that there was a significant positive correlation between the mean Nighttime Light and GDP (R = 0.60, $p < 0.05$), especially in the urban area (R = 0.60, $p < 0.01$). In terms of growth, there is a significant correlation between Nighttime Light growth and GDP and population growth ($p < 0.05$). This shows that the main factors affecting Nighttime Light growth are economic development and population growth, and it also shows that Nighttime Light data can better reflect regional development.

Author Contributions: H.Z., Y.L. and Q.Y. conceived this study, analyzed the data and wrote the paper; Y.L. and J.J. revised the paper and carried out the paper analysis; R.L. and J.C. participated in the data analysis. All authors have read and agreed to the published version of the manuscript.

Funding: This research was funded by the National Natural Science Foundation of China, grant number 31800367, the Natural Science Foundation of Shandong Province, grant number ZR2023MD129 and Shandong Province college student innovation and entrepreneurship training program, grant number S202210447048.

Data Availability Statement: The multi-source data used in this paper are publicly available, and the dataset information is shown in Table 2.

Acknowledgments: Over the course of my researching and writing this paper, I would like to express my thanks to all those who have helped me, especially Xianxian Zhao, Feng Li and Tianzhu Li.

Conflicts of Interest: The authors declare no conflict of interest.

References

1. Fan, J.; Wang, Y.; Liang, B. The evolution process and regulation of China's regional development pattern. *Acta Geogr. Sin.* **2019**, *74*, 2437–2454.
2. Deng, X.; Liang, L.; Wu, F. Balanced regional development in China from the perspective of development geography. *Acta Geogr. Sin.* **2021**, *76*, 261–276.
3. Cao, Y.; Xia, Y.; Mao, G. Regional development differences and coordinated development strategies of Huaihe River eco-economic belt. *Econ. Geogr.* **2019**, *39*, 213–221.
4. Li, Z. Analysis of Urban Economic Development in Guangdong Province. *China Mark.* **2018**, *12*, 25.
5. Wang, P.; Ji, C. An Analysis of the Mechanism of resolving the contradiction between the imbalance of Economic Development and Social Stability in China—Based on the interpretation of people's Longitudinal Achievement. *Political Sci. Res.* **2019**, *1*, 63–76.
6. Sun, J.; Hu, J. Exploration of China's Regional coordinated Development Strategy towards Modernization. *Reform* **2022**, *343*, 1–10.
7. Zyphur, M.; Voelkle, M. From Data to Causes II: Comparing Approaches to Panel Data Analysis. *Organ. Res. Methods* **2020**, *23*, 688–716. [CrossRef]
8. Rybnikova, N. Everynight Accounting: Nighttime Lights as a Proxy for Economic Performance of Regions. *Remote Sens.* **2022**, *14*, 825. [CrossRef]
9. Meng, H.; Zhang, X.; Du, X. Spatiotemporal Heterogeneity of the Characteristics and Influencing Factors of Energy-Consumption-Related Carbon Emissions in Jiangsu Province Based on DMSP-OLS and NPP-VIIRS. *Land* **2023**, *12*, 1369. [CrossRef]
10. Ma, T. The Spatio-temporal characteristics of China's urbanization from the Perspective of Nighttime Light remote Sensing big data. *J. Geo-Inf. Sci.* **2019**, *21*, 59–67.
11. Zhang, L.; Li, X. Analysis of regional development differences in Pakistan from the perspective of Nighttime Light remote sensing. *J. Wuhan Univ. (Inf. Sci. Ed.)* **2022**, *47*, 269–279.
12. Ding, Y.; Yu, Q.; Lin, Y. Study on the Spatio-temporal pattern of County economy Development in Shandong Province based on Nighttime Light data. *Surv. Mapp. Spat. Geogr. Inf.* **2019**, *42*, 71–73+77.
13. Shan, B.; Zhang, Q.; Ren, Q.; Yu, X.; Chen, Y. Spatial heterogeneity of urban–rural integration and its influencing factors in Shandong province of China. *Sci. Rep.* **2022**, *12*, 14317. [CrossRef] [PubMed]
14. Wang, M.; Zhao, X.; Gong, Q. Measurement of Regional Green Economy Sustainable Development Ability Based on Entropy Weight-Topsis-Coupling Coordination Degree—A Case Study in Shandong Province, China. *Sustainability* **2019**, *11*, 280. [CrossRef]
15. Wang, M.; Yang, S.; Gao, H. The Characteristics, Influencing Factors, and Push-Pull Mechanism of Shrinking Counties: A Case Study of Shandong Province, China. *Sustainability* **2021**, *13*, 2402. [CrossRef]

16. Nighttime Light, Earth Observation Group [DB/OL]. Available online: https://eogdata.mines.edu/products/vnl/ (accessed on 1 October 2021).
17. National Basic Geographic Information Center [DB/OL]. Available online: https://www.ngcc.cn/ngcc/html/1/index.html (accessed on 15 September 2021).
18. Shandong Bureau of Statistics. *Shandong Statistical Yearbook*; China Bureau of Statistics and Publication: Beijing, China, 2020.
19. Elvidge, C.D.; Zhizhin, M.; Ghosh, T. Annual Time Series of Global VIIRS Nighttime Lights Derived from Monthly Averages: 2012 to 2019. *Remote Sens.* **2021**, *13*, 922. [CrossRef]
20. Li, G.; Fan, J.; Zhou, Y. Study on Development characteristics of Shandong Peninsula Urban agglomeration based on VIIRS Nighttime Light data. *Remote Sens. Technol. Appl.* **2020**, *35*, 1348–1359.
21. Chen, M.; Cai, H. Comparison of monthly product interpolation methods for VIIRS/DNB Nighttime Light—A case study of Beijing. *Adv. Geogr.* **2019**, *38*, 126–138.
22. Zhang, X.; Wang, G.; Tan, Z.; Wang, Y.; Li, Q. Effects of ecological protection and restoration on phytoplankton diversity in impounded lakes along the eastern route of China's South-to-North Water Diversion Project. *Sci. Total Environ.* **2021**, *795*, 148870. [CrossRef]
23. Fang, J.; Yang, R.; Cao, Q. Differences of the microbial community structures and predicted metabolic potentials in the lake, river, and wetland sediments in Dongping Lake Basin. *Environ. Sci. Pollut. Res.* **2020**, *27*, 19661–19677. [CrossRef]
24. Sun, X. Dongping Lake aquaculture high-quality development to promote rural revitalization. *Guide Get. Rich Fish.* **2021**, *5*, 21–24.
25. Sun, H. The path of transformation and upgrading of resource-based cities in Shandong Province. *J. Shandong Inst. Ind. Technol.* **2019**, *33*, 96–105.
26. Liu, H.; Di, Q. Analysis of the influence of the first phase of the eastern route of the South-to-North Water transfer Project on the economic development of cities along the Beijing-Hangzhou Grand Canal—An empirical study based on synthetic control method. *Resour. Dev. Mark.* **2020**, *36*, 1185–1191.
27. Qingdao Jiaodong International Airport, Officially Launched, CCTV Network [DB/OL]. Available online: https://news.cctv.com/2021/08/13/ARTIBsPyZiungdRihbvZxpCz210813.shtml (accessed on 13 August 2021).
28. Shale Oil in Sheng Li Oilfield Has Achieved a Strategic Breakthrough in the First Batch of Predicted Reserves of 458 Million Tons, CCTV Network [DB/OL]. Available online: https://news.cctv.com/2021/11/02/ARTIPlP26tt699HgHK4EiOUb211102.shtml (accessed on 2 November 2021).
29. Bureau of Statistics: Important Progress Has Been Made in the Construction of National Oil Reserves, CCTV Network [DB/OL]. Available online: http://news.cctv.com/2016/09/02/ARTIFabippEj0PyeKPv1OpME160902.shtml (accessed on 2 September 2016).
30. Zhang, Z.; Jiang, L.; Li, Z. *Geography of Shandong*; Beijing Normal University Press: Beijing, China, 2014.

buildings

MDPI

Article

Image-Enhanced U-Net: Optimizing Defect Detection in Window Frames for Construction Quality Inspection

Jorge Vasquez *, Tomotake Furuhata and Kenji Shimada

Mechanical Engineering Department, College of Engineering, Carnegie Mellon University, Pittsburgh, PA 15215, USA; tomotake@cmu.edu (T.F.); shimada@cmu.edu (K.S.)
* Correspondence: jivasque@andrew.cmu.edu; Tel.: +1-1412-996-9738

Abstract: Ensuring the structural integrity of window frames and detecting subtle defects, such as dents and scratches, is crucial for maintaining product quality. Traditional machine vision systems face challenges in defect identification, especially with reflective materials and varied environments. Modern machine and deep learning (DL) systems hold promise for post-installation inspections but face limitations due to data scarcity and environmental variability. Our study introduces an innovative approach to enhance DL-based defect detection, even with limited data. We present a comprehensive window frame defect detection framework incorporating optimized image enhancement, data augmentation, and a core U-Net model. We constructed five datasets using cell phones and the Spot Robot for autonomous inspection, evaluating our approach across various scenarios and lighting conditions in real-world window frame inspections. Our results demonstrate significant performance improvements over the standard U-Net model, with a notable 7.43% increase in the F1 score and 15.1% in IoU. Our approach enhances defect detection capabilities, even in challenging real-world conditions. To enhance the generalizability of this study, it would be advantageous to apply its methodology across a broader range of diverse construction sites.

Keywords: surface detection; image enhancement; image processing techniques; segmentation networks

1. Introduction

The construction industry stands at a pivotal juncture, grappling with the dual challenge of escalating demand for quality inspection and a diminishing pool of available inspectors. Traditional inspection mechanisms, long reliable in controlled manufacturing environments, face redefinition in response to evolving industry dynamics, particularly in construction.

This transformation stems from a growing emphasis on post-installation quality assessments, notably in uncontrolled environments like bustling construction sites. Traditional machine vision systems, foundational to industrial processes, reveal their limitations in these dynamic settings, characterized by unpredictable variables and ceaseless activity. These systems often require extensive parameter tuning and can falter, especially in uncontrolled environments marked by fluctuating lighting conditions and unexpected defects [1–3].

In parallel, the allure of machine and deep learning (ML/DL) promises to overcome these challenges by offering a more adaptable approach to defect detection. However, the effectiveness of ML/DL critically hinges on the availability of extensive, high-quality datasets, a rarity in the context of construction quality inspection. Even advanced DL models can underperform due to the scarcity of comprehensive training data and the influence of unpredictable external factors, as exemplified by notable studies [1,2,4–6].

To bridge this critical gap, the integration of data augmentation surfaces as the initial solution [7,8]. Furthermore, image enhancement techniques aim to bolster DL models by enhancing image clarity, mitigating shadows, and accentuating defects. The synergistic fusion of DL with a judicious image enhancement (IE) strategy can revolutionize defect identification and reshape the industrial landscape [9]. Recent research, exemplified by Wu et al. [10] and Tang et al. [11], has effectively utilized these strategies to improve segmentation networks. Wu et al. notably enhanced crack segmentation accuracy using MobileNetV2_DeepLabV3, while Tang employed image refinement post-processing with U-Net for similar gains. These studies showcase the applicability of these strategies in current research. Alongside technological challenges, the construction sector faces an escalating demand for rigorous quality inspections and a diminishing pool of human inspectors. Even seemingly minor defects can tarnish a brand's reputation and compromise functional aesthetics [3].

This paper introduces a novel amalgamation of advanced image processing, data augmentation techniques, and DL methodologies to address the challenges posed by intricate lighting conditions and limited data availability on construction sites. We aim to ensure consistent inspections in uncontrolled domains and establish a benchmark for construction quality assessments. Additionally, through a rigorous comparison with a sophisticated segmentation model, we underscore the potential of our proposed methodology, particularly in the burgeoning domain of automated building inspection [7,8].

Our primary research objective is to develop an advanced defect detection method utilizing deep learning (DL). Specifically, we present an innovative DL-based framework for detecting defects in window frames. This framework combines data augmentation, customized image enhancement techniques, and a detection model designed to enhance the quality of defect detection.

In this context, we operate under the assumption that construction sites often present intricate lighting conditions and suffer from limited data availability. These inherent challenges in uncontrolled environments require a more robust defect detection solution. Our research addresses these assumptions by establishing a new benchmark for quality inspections in construction sites.

The subsequent sections of this paper are structured as follows: Section 2 delves into the relevant literature, Section 3 outlines our approach, Section 4 unveils our experimental design and findings, and Section 5 offers conclusions and insights from our research.

2. Related Work

This section provides a comprehensive overview of prior research and methodologies in defect detection, tracking the historical evolution of techniques and highlighting recent advancements.

2.1. Traditional Computer Vision Approaches

Defect detection in construction and manufacturing has been a prominent research focus. Traditional machine vision systems, relying on predefined algorithms, have played a pivotal role in quality control across diverse industries [12].

- Threshold Techniques: Automatic thresholding has been crucial in industries such as glass manufacturing [13,14] and textiles [15]. Dynamic thresholding has found applications in road crack segmentation [16]. The Retinex Algorithm has been used for edge detection [17,18], and innovative approaches like combining morphological processing with genetic algorithms have introduced new dimensions to defect detection strategies [19].
- Edge Detection and Morphological Processing: The Retinex Algorithm has been prominent in edge detection for defect identification. The fusion of morphological processing with genetic algorithms has also introduced innovative dimensions to defect detection strategies.
- Fourier and Texture Analysis: Fourier series is useful in line defect detection [20], while texture analysis proves reliable in labs [18,21–23]. Combining impulse/response

testing with statistical pattern recognition has helped to detect defects in concrete plates [24].

- Innovative Approaches: Recent innovations, such as impulse/response testing and statistical pattern recognition, have effectively detected defects in concrete plates. However, traditional machine vision systems have limitations in complex, dynamic settings like construction sites, where unpredictable variables like complex lighting challenge their efficacy.

2.2. Challenges in Conventional Machine Vision Methods

Traditional machine vision methods excel in controlled environments but face significant hurdles in complex settings like construction sites. Key challenges include the following:

- Variable Lighting: Fluctuating natural and artificial lighting conditions impact system performance [1–3].
- Dynamic Environments: Rapid changes in construction sites challenge machine vision adaptability, reducing accuracy.
- Noise and Interference: Visual noise and electromagnetic interference disrupt defect detection [1].
- Scale and Perspective Variations: Varying object sizes and perspectives require extensive system adjustments.
- Real-Time Demands: Meeting real-time requirements can be challenging for traditional methods.
- Data Annotation: Creating and maintaining labeled datasets is labor-intensive and complex in dynamic environments.

Innovative approaches, including deep learning and adaptive algorithms, are needed to enhance defect detection in construction.

2.3. Machine Learning and Deep Learning-Based Methods

This subsection explores recent advancements in machine learning, particularly deep learning (DL) models, for defect detection. With increased computing power and data availability, DL, particularly convolutional neural networks (CNNs), has gained popularity in quality inspection.

- Supervised object detection supervised defect detection relies on labeled datasets with defect-free and defective samples, resulting in high detection rates. This approach annotates each object with its class label and bounding box coordinates during training. Various datasets are used in supervised learning, including fabric defect datasets [25] and rail defect datasets [26,27].
- Unsupervised object detection unsupervised methods aim to overcome the limitations of supervised learning by leveraging inherent data characteristics for classification. These approaches detect defects and objects in images without using labeled training data. Instead, they rely on patterns, structures, or anomalies in the data to identify objects. Techniques like clustering, anomaly detection, and feature extraction are commonly used for unsupervised defect detection.
- Object detection model current object detection in deep learning falls into two main categories. The first encompasses two-stage object detection models, which include R-CNNs [28], Fast R-CNNs [29], and Faster R-CNNs [30]. For example, U-Net for defect segmentation using synthetic data was used by Boikov et al. [31]. The second category features one-stage models like YOLO [32] and SSD [33].

2.4. Challenges in DL-Based Defect Detection

In the realm of deep learning-based defect detection in construction, formidable challenges persist despite significant advancements in computer vision for monitoring structural health and identifying unsafe behaviors [34]. These challenges encompass a range of issues, including identifying multiple defects or concurrent unsafe behaviors, which remain problematic due to the high noise levels inherent in construction settings. Balancing datasets for deep learning training poses difficulties, particularly when certain defects or behaviors occur infrequently, leading to unbalanced data [35]. Moreover, the scarcity of labeled data, especially for rare defects, hampers the development of robust models. Pursuing real-time performance without compromising accuracy is an ongoing challenge, and the issue of inaccurate or inconsistent labeling adversely affects model precision. Furthermore, the variability in inspection standards hinders integrating deep learning models with human inspectors. At the same time, environmental factors like changing lighting conditions introduce variability in model accuracy in the dynamic construction environment.

2.5. Hybrid Models for Defect Detection

Hybrid models for defect detection represent a compelling approach by integrating image processing techniques (IPTs) and image enhancement techniques (IETs) with machine learning (ML) and deep learning (DL) methodologies. This fusion has demonstrated significant advantages across various domains, including defect identification. This section delves into such hybrid models' underlying principles and practical applications. One avenue of exploration involves the integration of IPTs with ML techniques, offering a robust framework for defect detection. For instance, combining edge detection algorithms with convolutional neural networks (CNNs) has yielded substantial improvements in tasks like weld segmentation, resulting in enhanced accuracy and efficiency in defect identification processes. Additionally, the domain of deep learning has witnessed a transformative impact on defect detection, particularly through models like CNNs. However, integrating image enhancement techniques can further elevate their performance, making them increasingly applicable in industries such as construction. Techniques like data augmentation, which generates diverse training data, and image enhancement algorithms that enhance image clarity, reduce shadows, and accentuate defects, contribute to fine-tuning DL models for more effective defect identification tasks, ultimately facilitating their integration into real-world applications such as construction [36].

These hybrid models find applications across industries, from manufacturing to construction, demonstrating their ability to handle complex image data and enhance defect identification in challenging settings. However, challenges remain, including parameter optimization and dataset availability. Some recent research used image enhancement and refinement to improve crack segmentation [10,11]. Our research addresses these challenges, focusing on the domain-specific context of cosmetic quality inspection for window frames. We aim to uncover the most effective image enhancement strategies and data augmentation techniques to enhance defect detection systems' precision, robustness, and real-world applicability.

3. Proposed Method

The demand for robust defect detection becomes paramount in industrial environments marked by unpredictable lighting conditions. Our proposed method is a comprehensive solution that integrates an image quality assessment tool, a sophisticated image enhancement strategy, advanced data augmentation processes, and a deep learning-based defect detection model. The framework of our approach, illustrated in Figure 1, visually represents the various components and their interplay.

Our system begins with inputting RGB images captured by the Spot Robot. Subsequently, the data augmentation module comes into play, employing a combination of geometric operations and a range of image enhancement techniques to generate vast enhanced data.

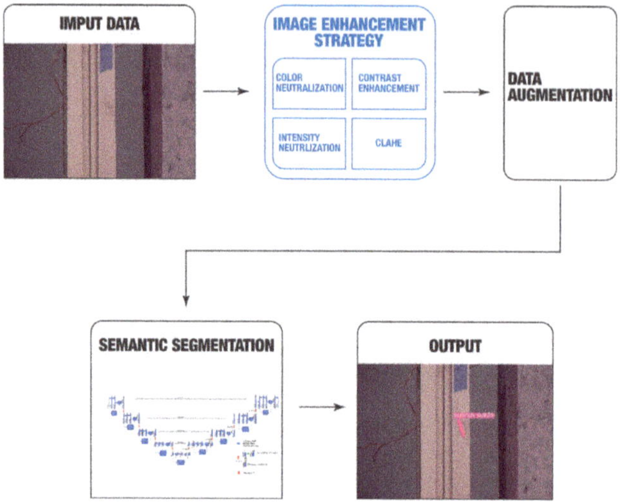

Figure 1. The framework of the window frame defect detection system (WFDD). The input comprises RGB images captured by the Spot Robot. The data augmentation module employs geometric operations and applies different image enhancement techniques. The preprocessing module is then employed to enhance the performance of the defect detection model. Within the detection module, defects are identified among all detected window frames, with the output showcasing U-Net-generated segmentation blobs.

The preprocessing module further enhances the defect detection model's performance, ensuring optimal results. Finally, within the detection module, defects are identified among all detected window frames, with the output showcasing U-Net-generated segmentation blobs, ultimately providing a comprehensive overview of detected defects within the industrial setting. This holistic approach empowers the system to operate effectively in dynamic and challenging environments, setting new standards for defect detection accuracy and reliability.

3.1. Data Collection

Our dataset consists of 1356 original images sourced from five distinct datasets:

- Cellphone Dataset (441 Images): This dataset comprises color images capturing non-installed window frames both indoors and outdoors (see Figure 2).
- Construction Site Dataset (235 Images): Captured on a real-world construction site using inspector cellphone cameras, this dataset includes various installed window frame types and diverse conditions (see Figure 3).
- Lab-1 Dataset (100 Images): Collected in a controlled lab environment using the Spot Robot's PTZ camera, this dataset features a range of window frame samples with variations in colors, lighting conditions and angles (see Figure 4).
- Lab-2 Dataset (80 Images): Focused on a single window frame within a cluttered lab setting, this dataset offers images captured at different zoom levels (see Figure 5).
- Demo Site Dataset (500 Images): Captured at a construction site using the Spot Robot, this dataset encompasses multiple window frame types and a variety of lighting conditions (see Figure 6).

Figure 2. Example from Cellphone Dataset.

Figure 3. Samples of Construction Site Dataset.

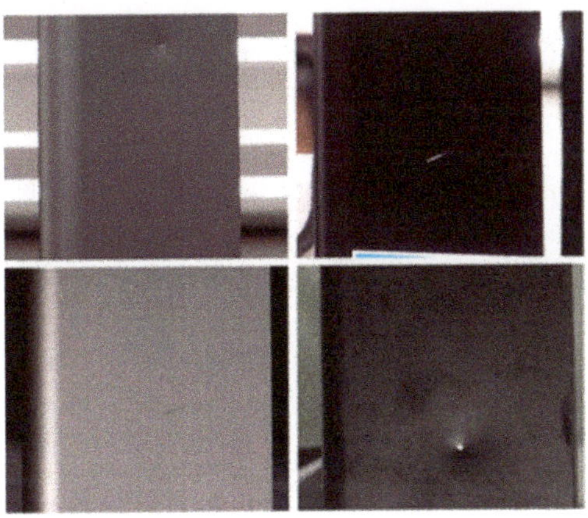

Figure 4. Example from Lab-1 Dataset.

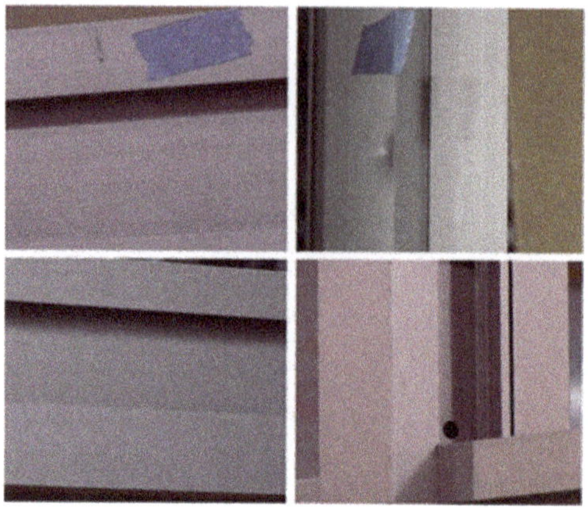

Figure 5. Example from Lab-2 Dataset.

Figure 6. Samples of Demo Site Dataset.

3.2. Data Labeling

Our data labeling process was meticulously designed to accurately identify defects within the images. The manual labeling of images was conducted using the Roboflow Platform [37]. Examples of labeled defects, including dents and scratches, are visually depicted in Figures 5 and 6.

The labeling process is visualized in Figure 7. Following the meticulous labeling procedure, images were stored in COCO format at a resolution of 500 $\times$ 500 pixels. This curated labeled image dataset was an invaluable reference standard for our defect detection methodology.

3.3. Geometric Data Augmentation

In the first stage, we leveraged geometric data augmentation techniques to enhance dataset diversity and size. This process involved applying three geometric transformations: anti-clockwise rotation, clockwise rotation, and horizontal flipping. By incorporating these transformations, we expanded our dataset threefold, enriching the variety of samples available for training and validation.

Figure 7. Example of labeling.

3.4. *Image Enhancement Techniques (IETs)*

Our defect detection methodology incorporates a range of image enhancement techniques (IETs) carefully selected to enhance the quality of input images before input into the segmentation network. These techniques are pivotal in accentuating object details, reducing noise, and optimizing overall image quality, thus facilitating more precise detection. Below is an overview of the IETs employed in our approach:

- Shadow Removal (SR): To address shadow removal, we adopted the pre-trained dual hierarchical aggregation network (DHAN) developed by Cun et al. [38], which is based on VGG16 with the context aggregation network (CAN). This approach effectively mitigates shadows, a common challenge in image quality.
- Color Neutralization (CN): CN plays a crucial role in ensuring a consistent foundation for subsequent processing by harmonizing color variations across images, promoting uniformity.
- Contrast Enhancement (CE): CE significantly enhances image clarity, making even subtle defects more discernible. This enhancement aids in the accurate identification of defects.
- Intensity Level Neutralization (IN): IN standardizes intensity levels across the dataset, reducing disparities that could otherwise affect the analysis. This step contributes to data consistency.
- CLAHE (Contrast-Limited Adaptive Histogram Equalization): CLAHE, a localized contrast enhancement technique, enhances small-scale details while preserving overall image contrast. It improves the visibility of fine details without oversaturating the image.

The choice of these five image enhancement techniques and our data augmentation strategy was informed by extensive experimentation, explained in Section 4. We rigorously assessed various combinations of techniques to ensure they collectively enhanced image quality without introducing noise or misleading information. This careful selection process ensures the reliability and effectiveness of our approach in the context of defect detection.

3.4.1. Shadow Removal (SR) Process

Harnessing the capabilities of the pre-trained dual hierarchical aggregation network (DHAN) proposed by Cun et al. [38], we adeptly addressed the challenge of shadow removal. The DHAN network, underpinned by the esteemed VGG16 architecture—a convolutional neural network archetype—employs the context aggregation network (CAN) for encoding.

The DHAN network pinpoints and eliminates shadows from the imagery by orchestrating dilation convolutions and leveraging hierarchical aggregation of multi-contextual features. With weights furnished by the original authors, our application of the network inference method effectively expunged shadows from the entire dataset, as elucidated in Figure 8.

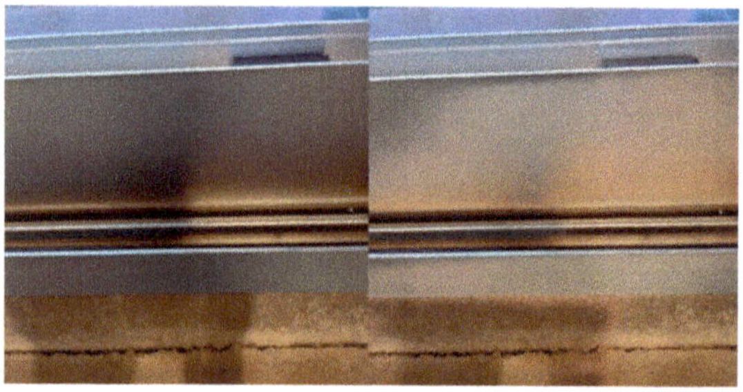

Figure 8. Comparative sample using the shadow removal technique.

3.4.2. Color Neutralization (CN)

It was imperative to refine the color definition within the dataset. Our approach pivoted on the Von Kries chromatic adaptation transformation [39], a robust chromatic adaptation methodology. This technique seamlessly transitions from source to target colors within the LMS (long, medium, short) color spectrum. By adapting the RGB illuminant color of dataset samples to varied illuminates, it preserves the pristine white color. This equates to enhanced color consistency and bolsters feature extraction, as illustrated in Figure 9.

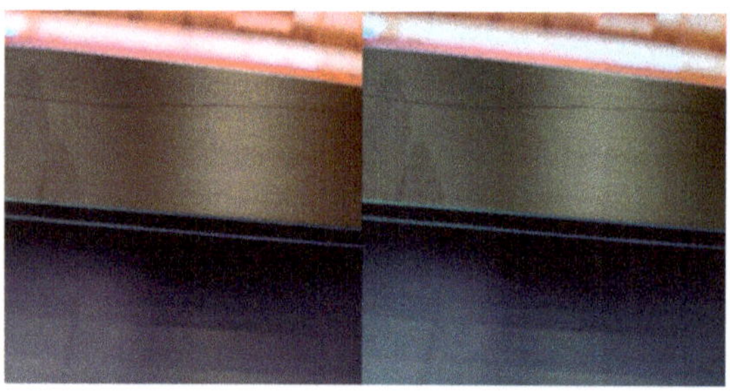

Figure 9. Comparative sample using the color neutralization technique.

3.4.3. Contrast Enhancement (CE)

Our image processing strategy concluded with a pivotal step—contrast enhancement. By transmuting dataset samples into RGB channels, we embraced a histogram equalization approach [40]. This technique magnifies the visual fidelity of the image, making defect spotting significantly more intuitive. The overall image contrast is augmented by streamlining the histogram, translating it to an enriched feature representation, and consequently enhancing it in the deep-learning phase, as showcased in Figure 10.

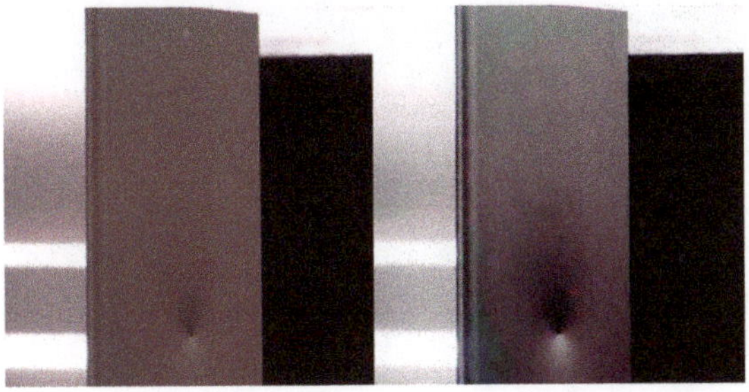

Figure 10. Comparative sample using the contrast enhancement technique.

3.4.4. Intensity Level Neutralization (IN)

The multi-scale Retinex (MSR) algorithm was brought to refine the intensity channel. The outcome colors were fine-tuned such that the chromaticity mirrored the original snapshot. This meticulous filtration aids in preserving relative lightness, ensuring a harmonized image intensity without any distortion to chromaticity and color composition.

Land and Maccan's research [41] laid the groundwork for this approach. They postulated that the visual cortex discerns relative, not absolute, lightness—nuances in localized image segments.

Our adherence to this philosophy culminated in negating intensity variations that might otherwise hamper feature extraction and image data processing, as captured in Figure 11.

Figure 11. Comparative sample using the intensity neutralization technique.

3.4.5. Contrast-Limited Adaptive Histogram Equalization or CLAHE (CLAHE)

CLAHE plays a pivotal role in our novel strategy, enhancing image contrast by equalizing the histogram for each contextual region or tile in an image. This technique effectively limits histogram amplification via clipping at a predefined limit. The crucial steps of the CLAHE algorithm are as follows:

1. Divide the input image into non-overlapping tiles of size $m \times n$, resulting in $M \times N$ tiles.
2. Perform histogram equalization on each tile, using the probability density function (PDF) and cumulative distribution function (CDF) to distribute pixel intensities effectively.
3. Apply contrast limiting by clipping the histogram at a predefined limit, CL, to prevent excessive amplification.
4. Conduct bilinear interpolation to eliminate artificial boundaries between tiles, resulting in a smoothly enhanced output image.

Our study applied the contrast-limited adaptive histogram equalization (CLAHE) method to the luminance (L) channel within the lab color space. Results are shown in Figure 12.

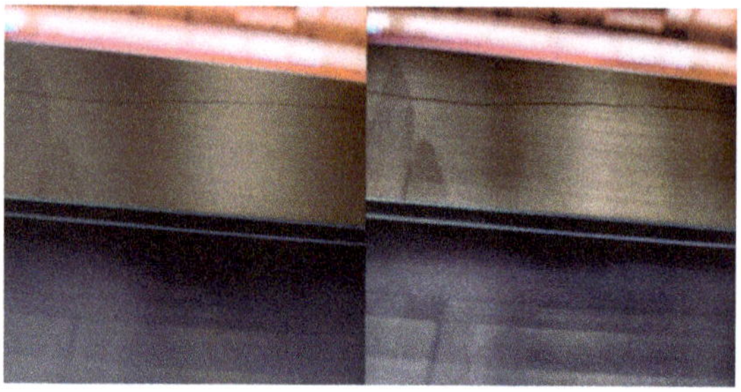

Figure 12. Comparative sample using the CLAHE technique.

3.5. IE-Enhanced Data Augmentation

We implemented an advanced data augmentation process involving an IE-enhanced augmentation. For the second stage of data augmentation, we harnessed the power of 40 IE combinations, including the 'Normal' dataset and results from five image enhancement techniques (IETs) where the order of application was irrelevant. This comprehensive approach created 40 distinct datasets, each representing a unique IE combination. These augmented datasets played a vital role in training our model, enabling it to learn from various enhanced variations, ultimately enhancing its defect detection capabilities. Notably, this 40 included the 4! (4 factorial) combinations from the five IEs, and 16 additional datasets were created by inserting CLAHE into the best-performing ones.

3.6. Defect Detection Model

Our defect detection model is a culmination of data augmentation and image enhancement techniques strategies, meticulously designed to enhance its performance. The model leverages a U-Net neural network architecture to segment defects within the input images effectively. A detailed breakdown of our defect detection process is described as follows:

1. Data Preprocessing: Following data augmentation and IPT application, we preprocess the images to prepare them for defect detection. These preprocessed images, post-IPT, were resized to a standardized 500×500 pixel format.
2. Ground Truth-Guided Learning: During the training phase, our U-Net neural network relied on ground truth masks. These masks serve as invaluable references, guiding the network to detect defects with exceptional precision.
3. Intersection of Classes: Our defect detection is specifically tailored to identify defects within window frames. We utilize the concept of the intersection of classes, ensuring that our results exclusively represent defects inside the window frames.
4. Neural Network Architecture: Our neural network architecture is a fusion of two powerful components: ResNet152 and U-Net. We employ transfer learning to harness the feature extraction capabilities of ResNet152. Its encoder is utilized, with the last layer discarded and then integrated with a decoder. This fusion results in an expansive feature map that excels in defect localization.
5. Semantic Segmentation Model: The architecture of our deep learning-based semantic segmentation model. This model combines the robustness of ResNet152 with the precision of U-Net, providing an ideal balance between feature extraction and localization.

Integrating U-Net with the feature-rich ResNet152 encoder enhances the model's ability to accurately detect defects within window frames, making it a formidable tool for defect detection in industrial environments.

4. Experiments and Results

In this section, we delve into the practical aspects of our experiments, which aimed to optimize defect detection in window frames through the strategic deployment of image enhancement techniques (IETs). Our objective was to evaluate the performance enhancements achieved by these strategies, comparing them against a baseline machine learning (ML) model. To quantitatively assess the efficacy of our approach, we employed two key metrics: the F1-score and IoU (intersection over union). The F1 score provides a balanced measure of precision and recall, allowing us to gauge the accuracy of our defect detection model. Additionally, IoU quantifies the overlap between predicted and ground truth defect regions, offering insights into the model's localization precision. Together, these metrics enable us to comprehensively evaluate and present the results of our defect detection system.

4.1. Data Collection

To assess the efficacy of our IET-enhanced deep learning-based defect detection model, we utilized the Spot Robot using Boston Dynamics in our experiments. This robotic platform allowed us to capture high-resolution images of window frames under various lighting conditions, enabling a comprehensive examination of defect detection in complex real-world environments.

4.2. Experimental Setup

At the heart of our defect detection model lies the integration of image enhancement techniques (IETs). Informed by insights from our experiments, we devised four distinct methods and their synergistic combinations tailored for robust industrial-scale deployment. These strategies draw from our findings in Experiments 1 and 2, wherein specialized techniques and IET-based data augmentation played pivotal roles in improving the defect detection accuracy.

4.3. Experiment 1: Integration of Image Enhancement Techniques

This experiment enhanced defect detection accuracy by optimizing our preprocessing pipeline's sequence of image enhancement techniques (IETs). We evaluated IETs individually and in various combinations.

The best strategies are summarized in Tables 1 and 2.

Table 1. Comparison of F1 scores for bend, dent, and scratch detection.

Process/Test Metrics	Bend	Dent	Scratch
	F1-Score	**F1-Score**	**F1-Score**
Normal	0.857	0.648	0.529
Best IET Strategy	0.906	0.713	0.572
Improvement	5.70%	9.92%	8.11%

Table 2. Comparison of IoU scores for bend, dent, and scratch detection.

Process/Test Metrics	Bend	Dent	Scratch
	IoU	**IoU**	**IoU**
Normal	0.848	0.627	0.473
Best IET Strategy	0.903	0.6945	0.518
Improvement	6.49%	10.70%	9.60%

4.3.1. Experiment 1 Results

In our pursuit of elucidating the factors behind our results, particularly concerning performance disparities across different defect detection categories, we comprehensively explored over 40 image enhancement (IE) combinations. The derivation of this extensive set of combinations involved a meticulous examination of 24 permutations of the 4 enhancement techniques, each applied in varying orders—a total of 24 of the 4 factorials. Additionally, we introduced the "CLAHE" (contrast-limited adaptive histogram equalization) enhancement technique to the best 16 combinations, further enriching our analysis.

We present the top 10 image enhancement (IE) combinations for each defect out of the over 40 combinations tested.

Bend Detection Results

Table 3 shows the top 10 IE combinations with the highest F1 scores for bend detection.

Table 3. Bend F1 scores for IE combinations.

IE Combination	Bend F1 Score
CLAHE + SR + CN + IN	0.9065
CLAHE + SR + IN + CE	0.8780
CLAHE + CE	0.8779
CLAHE + CE + IN	0.8734
CLAHE + SR + CE + IN + CN	0.8716
CLAHE + SR + IN	0.8702
CLAHE + SR	0.8663
CLAHE + SR + CE + CN + IN	0.8661
CE + IN + CN + SR	0.8661
CLAHE + SR + IN + CN	0.8575

Dent Detection Results

Table 4 presents the top 10 IE combinations with the highest F1 scores for dent detection.

Table 4. Dent F1 scores for IE combinations.

IE Combination	Dent F1 Score
CLAHE + SR + IN + CE	0.7130
CLAHE + CN	0.7022
CLAHE + IN	0.6773
CE + CN + IN	0.6749
SR + IN + CE	0.6699
CLAHE + IN + CE	0.6719
CLAHE + CN + IN + CE	0.6706
CE + CN	0.6683
CLAHE + SR + CN + IN	0.6633
SR + IN + CE + CN	0.6696

Scratch Detection Results

Table 5 displays the top 10 IE combinations with the highest F1 scores for scratch detection.

Table 5. Scratch F1 scores for IE combinations.

IE Combination	Scratch F1 Score
CE + CN + IN	0.5721
CLAHE + IN	0.5721
IN + CE	0.5703
SR + IN	0.5696
CLAHE + SR + IN + CE	0.5689
CE + CN	0.5672
IN + CE + CN	0.5672
CN	0.5672
CLAHE + IN + CE	0.5664
SR + IN + CE + CN	0.5662

4.3.2. Experiment 1 Insights

This thorough exploration allowed us to systematically evaluate a broad spectrum of enhancement strategies and their influence on defect detection performance. From this exhaustive analysis, the following key insights emerged:

- IE Strategy Effectiveness: The most notable discovery revolves around the substantial enhancements observed in F1 and IoU scores across all defect categories (bend, dent, and scratch) when implementing the 'Best IE Strategy'. The improvement in dent detection is particularly striking, showcasing a remarkable 9.92% increase in the F1 score and an impressive 10.70% surge in the IoU score. This underscores the pivotal role of tailored image enhancement strategies in effectively addressing specific defect characteristics, particularly those highly susceptible to lighting conditions, as exemplified by the dent defects.

- Overall Improvement: On average, our model featuring the "Best IE Strategy" consistently outperformed the baseline U-Net model, achieving a noteworthy 7.67% improvement in F1 scores and an impressive 8.60% enhancement in IoU scores. This serves as compelling evidence for the efficacy of integrating IE techniques into the defect detection pipeline.
- Performance Variability: It is crucial to acknowledge that the magnitude of improvement varied across defect categories. This variability emphasizes the need for adaptable defect detection systems capable of accommodating the diverse characteristics and challenges associated with different defect types.
- Enhancement Strategies: A consistent trend emerges in our findings, revealing that the combination of image enhancement techniques consistently enhances F1 scores and precision. This underscores the intrinsic value of systematic experimentation in optimizing image enhancement for defect detection.
- CLAHE Success: The "CLAHE" technique consistently played a pivotal role in enhancing F1 scores and precision across various defect categories. This reaffirms its significance in improving detection accuracy and highlights its effectiveness.
- Trade-offs and Context: It is essential to strike a balance between accuracy and localization precision, as certain enhancements may influence IoU values differently. This trade-off consideration underscores the need for a nuanced approach in selecting and fine-tuning enhancement techniques based on specific detection requirements.
- Fine-tuning Opportunities: The results underscore the potential for further customization by exploring enhancement combinations and adjustments to model architectures. This fine-tuning process holds the key to optimizing defect detection systems for specific application contexts.

In summary, our meticulous exploration of over 40 IE combinations, driven by 24 permutations of the 4 enhancement techniques and incorporating "CLAHE" into the best 16 combinations, provides a robust foundation for understanding the intricate relationship between image enhancement strategies and defect detection performance. These findings offer valuable insights into the dynamic interplay of enhancement techniques in optimizing the accuracy and precision across diverse defect categories.

4.4. *Experiment 2: IE-Data Augmentation and Results*

In Experiment 2, we investigated the impact of IE (image enhancement) as a data augmentation technique on object detection performance across various categories, including bend, dent, and scratch. IE-based data augmentation involves enhancing the quality and features of input images before applying object detection algorithms.

4.4.1. Experiment 2 Results

This subsection discusses the findings and insights gained from this experiment. These results are visualized in Tables 6 and 7.

We exhaustively explored 30 IE combinations to identify the most effective strategies. The outcomes of the top 10 IE combinations are presented in Tables 8–10. Our approach resulted in over 30 combinations tested, as we initially generated 24 combinations using the permutations of 4 enhancement techniques (4 factorial) and subsequently inserted CLAHE into the 6 best-performing combinations. This approach ensured a thorough evaluation of enhancement strategies, considering their individual and collective impact on defect detection performance. Table 8 presents the top 10 combinations of Image Enhancement (IE) techniques that yield the highest F1 scores for detecting bends. Similarly, Table 9 continues this analysis, showcasing the top 10 IE combinations with the highest F1 scores specifically for scratch detection. Meanwhile, Table 10 focuses on the top 10 IE combinations that have achieved the best F1 scores for detecting dents.

Table 6. Comparison of F1 scores for bend, dent, and scratch detection in Experiment 2.

Process/Test Metrics	Bend F1	Dent F1	Scratch F1
Normal	0.877	0.706	0.570
Best IE	0.980	0.7122	0.626
Improvement	11.65%	0.83%	9.82%

Table 7. Comparison of IoU scores for bend, dent, and scratch detection in Experiment 2.

Process/Test Metrics	Bend IoU	Dent IoU	Scratch IoU
Normal	0.872	0.683	0.507
Best IE	0.980	0.691	0.669
Improvement	12.33%	1.13%	31.84%

Table 8. Top 10 image enhancement combinations for bend defect.

IE Combination	Bend F1 Score
CE	0.98
CN + IN + CE	0.95855
SR	0.936037
SR + CE	0.926856
SR + CN + CE	0.913967
SR + IN + CE	0.882706
SR + CN + IN + CE	0.889351
CN + CLAHE	0.883122385
CN + CE + CLAHE	0.855731428
IN + CLAHE	0.860007882

Table 9. Top 10 image enhancement combinations for the scratch defect.

IE Combination	Scratch F1 Score
CN	0.547862
SR + CE	0.494919
CN + CE	0.480775
CE + CLAHE	0.453691274
SR + IN + CE + CLAHE	0.54746002
SR + CN + IN + CE + CLAHE	0.564718306
SR + CN + CE + CLAHE	0.538104832
SR + CN + IN + CLAHE	0.577393591
IN + CLAHE	0.585907996
CN + IN + CE + CLAHE	0.590137661

Table 10. Top 10 image enhancement combinations for the dent defect.

IE Combination	Dent F1 Score
CLAHE + SR + IN + CE	0.7130
CLAHE + CN	0.7022
CLAHE + IN	0.6773
CE + CN + IN	0.6749
SR + IN + CE	0.6699
CLAHE + IN + CE	0.6719
CLAHE + CN + IN + CE	0.6706
CE + CN	0.6683
CLAHE + SR + CN + IN	0.6633
SR + IN + CE + CN	0.6696

4.4.2. Experiment 2 Insights

Experiment 2 introduced a distinct dimension to our exploration by employing image enhancement (IE) techniques not only to enhance the quality of the existing data but also to create new data samples through augmentation. This innovative approach provided valuable insights into the interplay between IE techniques and defect detection performance, particularly in the context of industrial applications.

- Impact of Image Enhancement Techniques: We assessed the influence of individual image enhancement techniques (e.g., CE, IN, CN, SR, and CLAHE) on object detection accuracy. These techniques exhibited varying effects on IoU scores, highlighting trade-offs between localization accuracy and detection precision.
- Combination Strategies: Combinations of enhancement techniques, such as "CN + CE" and "SR + IN", were explored to evaluate their impact on detection performance. Different combinations produced diverse outcomes, emphasizing the complexity of selecting the right strategy.
- CLAHE Effectiveness: CLAHE consistently improved IoU values across multiple detection categories, underscoring its importance in enhancing accuracy and precision.
- Comprehensive Combinations: Comprehensive combinations like "SR + CN + IN + CE + CLAHE" were investigated to identify strategies with strong overall performance regarding IoU scores, but their complexity warrants careful evaluation.
- Balancing Trade-offs: IE-based data augmentation involves balancing improved IoU scores and detection accuracies. Some techniques may favor one aspect, requiring thoughtful adaptations to specific detection needs.
- Comparison of F1 and IoU Scores: We compared F1 and IoU scores for bend, dent, and scratch detection under "Normal" and "Best IE" strategies. Our strategy consistently improved both scores, enhancing detection accuracy.

In summary, IE-based data augmentation significantly enhances object detection accuracy and precision. The enhancement techniques and combinations should align with the specific detection goals and trade-offs that are set. Experiment 2 highlights the importance of IE-based data augmentation and its potential to improve object detection performance substantially.

4.5. Experiment 1 vs. Experiment 2: A Comparison

4.5.1. Experiment 1 Insights

- Category-Specific Improvement: Experiment 1 showed significant F1 score improvements for bend (5.70%), dent (9.92%), and scratch (8.11%) detection, highlighting the importance of tailored enhancement strategies.
- IoU Improvement: IoU scores were improved, with bend IoU and dent IoU increasing by 6.49% and 10.70%, respectively, and scratch IoU improving by 9.60%.
- Model Architecture Impact: Our model consistently outperformed U-Net, emphasizing the role of the model's architecture.

4.5.2. Experiment 2 Insights

- IE-Based Data Augmentation: Experiment 2 introduced IE-based data augmentation, resulting in substantial F1 and IoU score improvements across all defect categories. Notably, the scratch detection F1 score improved by 9.82%.
- Category-Specific Improvement: Category specific enhancement, with bend F1 and dent F1 scores showing notable increases (11.65% and 0.83%, respectively).
- IoU Improvement: IoU scores were improved, with bend IoU and dent IoU increasing by 12.33% and 1.13%, respectively, and scratch IoU showing a remarkable 31.84% improvement.
- Overall Model Performance: Our model enhanced with IE-based data augmentation outperformed the baseline U-Net model, with a 7.43% improvement in the F1 score and a substantial 15.10% improvement in IoU scores.

4.5.3. Comparative Insights

Both experiments emphasize the importance of tailored strategies and model architecture choices in defect detection. Experiment 2's IE-based data augmentation approach demonstrated superior results, particularly in improving IoU scores, making it a promising avenue for enhancing defect detection accuracy in complex environments. The insights from both experiments contribute to the understanding of how image enhancement techniques can be seamlessly integrated into deep learning architectures for defect detection.

5. Discussion

Our extensive experiments have underscored the significant impact of image enhancement (IE) techniques on enhancing defect detection accuracy and offered crucial insights for their application in industrial contexts. Our findings' implications extend to industrial quality control, where precise defect identification is paramount.

In Experiment 1, we unequivocally demonstrated the effectiveness of tailored enhancement strategies. These strategies led to substantial improvements in both F1 and IoU scores across all defect categories. The marked enhancement in dent detection, with a notable 9.92% increase in the F1 score and a 10.70% surge in the IoU score, emphasizes the value of personalized enhancement techniques. These findings underscore the importance of making informed choices when selecting enhancement methods, thereby optimizing defect detection accuracy.

Building on the insights from Experiment 1, Experiment 2 introduced an innovative concept—IE-based data augmentation. This novel approach further elevated detection performance, particularly in improving IoU scores. The implications of this experiment are profound, as they suggest a promising avenue for substantially enhancing defect detection accuracy in complex industrial environments. In industrial settings where precise localization of defects is critical, the improved IoU scores offer a compelling advantage.

The practical implications of these insights for industrial applications are significant. Our research highlights the transformative potential of seamlessly integrating IE techniques into deep learning architectures for defect detection. By doing so, we not only enhance the accuracy of defect detection but also open valuable opportunities for fine-tuning and optimizing industrial quality control processes. Our findings offer a path to more reliable and effective quality control in the industrial sector, where even minor defects can compromise product quality, reputation, and safety. The ability to detect defects accurately, particularly in challenging environments with varying lighting conditions and defect types, is essential for ensuring product excellence and safety.

In conclusion, our experiments provide valuable guidance for implementing IE techniques in industrial defect detection, showcasing their potential to revolutionize the field. These insights promise to enhance the accuracy and efficiency of quality control processes, ultimately benefiting industrial applications and contributing to improved product quality and safety.

6. Conclusions

In conclusion, our study has illuminated a path of profound significance in industrial defect detection by integrating image enhancement (IE) techniques with deep learning. Our research is not just a scientific endeavor; it is a practical solution that holds transformative implications for industries relying on precise defect identification in challenging operational environments.

Across two comprehensive experiments, we have emphasized the critical importance of customization, underlining the necessity of tailoring enhancement strategies to specific defect categories. Furthermore, we have highlighted the pivotal role played by the selection of model architecture, showcasing how it can influence the accuracy and precision of defect detection. Experiment 2, introducing IE-based data augmentation, has emerged as an innovative development. It has yielded remarkable improvements in F1 and IoU scores, offering a novel method for enhancing detection accuracy in complex industrial settings.

This innovative approach unlocks the potential for industries to significantly elevate their product quality and bolster their production efficiency by ensuring precise defect detection.

Our research is not confined to theoretical insights; it provides practical solutions for real-world challenges. We have demonstrated that industries can achieve more accurate and reliable defect detection with the right combination of enhancement techniques and thoughtful adaptations. As computer vision continues to evolve, our findings offer a clear roadmap for implementing advanced defect detection systems, ultimately enhancing product quality, safety, and operational efficiency within industrial settings. There are numerous avenues for future research, including expanding datasets to encompass a broader range of defect types and operational conditions, exploring adaptive strategies for automatic technique selection, and integrating our enhanced defect detection approach into real-time industrial quality inspection using mobile robots.

In summary, our research signifies a pivotal moment in the domain of image enhancement techniques for industrial defect detection. It provides practical solutions and novel insights that empower industries to embrace cutting-edge technology, ensuring product excellence, reputation protection, and efficient production processes. Our journey has just begun, and we look forward to further advancing the field and driving excellence in industrial quality control.

Author Contributions: Methodology, J.V. and T.F.; investigation, J.V.; data curation, J.V.; writing—original draft preparation, J.V.; writing—review and editing, J.V.; supervision, T.F. and K.S.; project administration, K.S.; funding acquisition, K.S. All authors have read and agreed to the published version of the manuscript.

Funding: This research received no external funding.

Data Availability Statement: We published our data publicly at https://github.com/jvasqueza/Inspection (accessed on 1 November 2023).

Conflicts of Interest: The authors declare no conflict of interest.

References

1. Silva, W.R.; Lucena, D.S. Concrete Cracks Detection Based on Deep Learning Image Classification. *Proceedings* **2018**, *2*, 489. [CrossRef]
2. Dung, C.V.; Anh, L.D. Autonomous concrete crack detection using deep fully convolutional neural network. *Autom. Constr.* **2019**, *99*, 52–58. [CrossRef]
3. Garcia, J.; Villavicencio, G.; Altamirano, F.; Crawford, B.; Soto, R.; Minatogawa, V.; Franco, M.; Martínez-Muñoz, D.; Yepes, V. Machine learning techniques applied to construction: A hybrid bibliometric analysis of advances and future directions. *Autom. Constr.* **2022**, *142*, 104532. [CrossRef]
4. Zhao, Z.Q.; Zheng, P.; Xu, S.T.; Wu, X. Object Detection with Deep Learning: A Review. *IEEE Trans. Neural Netw. Learn. Syst.* **2019**, *30*, 3212–3232. [CrossRef] [PubMed]
5. Bang, H.; Min, J.; Jeon, H. Deep learning-based concrete surface damage monitoring method using structured lights and depth camera. *Sensors* **2021**, *21*, 2759. [CrossRef]
6. Yang, J.; Li, S.; Wang, Z.; Dong, H.; Wang, J.; Tang, S. Using deep learning to detect defects in manufacturing: A comprehensive survey and current challenges. *Materials* **2020**, *13*, 5755. [CrossRef]
7. Wang, J.; Perez, L. The Effectiveness of Data Augmentation in Image Classification using Deep Learning. *arXiv* **2017**, arXiv:1712.04621. Available online: https://arxiv.org/abs/1712.04621 (accessed on 1 November 2023).
8. Saberironaghi, A.; Ren, J.; El-Gindy, M. Defect Detection Methods for Industrial Products Using Deep Learning Techniques: A Review. *Algorithms* **2023**, *16*, 95. [CrossRef]
9. Shorten, C.; Khoshgoftaar, T.M. A survey on Image Data Augmentation for Deep Learning. *J. Big Data* **2019**, *6*, 60. [CrossRef]
10. Wu, Z.; Tang, Y.; Hong, B.; Liang, B.; Liu, Y. Enhanced Precision in Dam Crack Width Measurement: Leveraging Advanced Lightweight Network Identification for Pixel-Level Accuracy. *Int. J. Intell. Syst.* **2023**, *2023*, 9940881. [CrossRef]
11. Tang, Y.; Huang, Z.; Chen, Z.; Chen, M.; Zhou, H.; Zhang, H.; Sun, J. Novel visual crack width measurement based on backbone double-scale features for improved detection automation. *Eng. Struct.* **2023**, *274*, 115158. [CrossRef]
12. Einizinab, S.; Khoshelham, K.; Winter, S.; Christopher, P.; Fang, Y.; Windholz, E.; Radanovic, M.; Hu, S. Enabling technologies for remote and virtual inspection of building work. *Autom. Constr.* **2023**, *156*, 105096. [CrossRef]
13. Ng, H.F. Automatic thresholding for defect detection. *Pattern Recognit. Lett.* **2006**, *27*, 1644–1649. [CrossRef]
14. Bandyopadhyay, Y. Glass Defect Detection and Sorting Using Computational Image Processing. *Int. J. Emerg. Technol. Innov. Res.* **2015**, *2*, 73–75.

15. Wakaf, Z.; Jalab, H.A. Defect detection based on extreme edge of defective region histogram. *J. King Saud. Univ. Comput. Inf. Sci.* **2018**, *30*, 33–40. [CrossRef]
16. Oliveira, H.; Correia, P.L. Automatic road crack segmentation using entropy and image dynamic thresholding. In Proceedings of the European Signal Processing Conference (EUSIPCO), Glasgow, UK, 24–28 August 2009.
17. Pan, Y.; Lu, Y.; Dong, S.; Zhao, Z.; Zhao, Z. Defect detection based on edge detection and connected region filtering algorithm. In Proceedings of the 2019 International Conference on Communications, Information System, and Computer Engineering, (CISCE), Haikou, China, 5–7 July 2019.
18. Zhao, H.; Qin, G.; Wang, X. Improvement of canny algorithm based on pavement edge detection. In Proceedings of the 3rd International Congress on Image and Signal Processing (CISP), Yantai, China, 16–18 October 2010.
19. Zheng, H.; Kong, L.X.; Nahavandi, S. Automated visual inspection of metallic surface defects using genetic algorithms. *J. Mater. Process Technol.* **2002**, *125–126*, 427–433. [CrossRef]
20. Altantsetseg, E.; Muraki, Y.; Matsuyama, K.; Konno, K. Feature line extraction from unorganized noisy point clouds using truncated Fourier series. *Vis. Comput.* **2013**, *29*, 617–626. [CrossRef]
21. Hocenski, Z.; Vasilic, S.; Hocenski, V. Improved Canny Edge Detector in Ceramic Tiles Defect Detection. In Proceedings of the 32nd Annual Conference on IEEE Industrial Electronics (IECON), Paris, France, 6–10 November 2006.
22. Shi, T.; Kong, J.Y.; Wang, X.D.; Liu, Z.; Zheng, G. Improved Sobel algorithm for defect detection of rail surfaces with enhanced efficiency and accuracy. *J. Cent. South. Univ.* **2016**, *23*, 2867–2875. [CrossRef]
23. Fleyeh, H.; Roch, J. *Benchmark Evaluation of HOG Descriptors as Features for Classification of Traffic Signs*; Högskolan Dalarna: Borlänge, Sweden, 2013.
24. Sajid, S.; Taras, A.; Chouinard, L. Defect detection in concrete plates with impulse-response test and statistical pattern recognition. *Mech. Syst. Signal Process.* **2021**, *161*, 107948. [CrossRef]
25. Silvestre-Blanes, J.; Albero-Albero, T.; Miralles, I.; Pérez-Llorens, R.; Moreno, J. A Public Fabric Database for Defect Detection Methods and Results. *Autex Res. J.* **2019**, *19*, 363–374. [CrossRef]
26. Gan, J.; Li, Q.; Wang, J.; Yu, H. A Hierarchical Extractor- Based Visual Rail Surface Inspection System. *IEEE Sens. J.* **2017**, *17*, 7935–7944. [CrossRef]
27. Shim, S.; Kim, J.; Lee, S.W.; Cho, G.C. Road surface damage detection based on hierarchical architecture using lightweight auto-encoder network. *Autom. Constr.* **2021**, *130*, 103833. [CrossRef]
28. Girshick, R.; Donahue, J.; Darrell, T.; Malik, J. Rich feature hierarchies for accurate object detection and semantic segmentation. In Proceedings of the IEEE Conference on Computer Vision and Pattern Recognition (CVPR), Columbus, OH, USA, 23–28 June 2014.
29. Girshick, R. Fast R-CNN. In Proceedings of the IEEE International Conference on Computer Vision (ICCV), Santiago, Chile, 7–13 December 2015.
30. Ren, S.; He, K.; Girshick, R.; Sun, J. Faster R-CNN: Towards Real-Time Object Detection with Region Proposal Networks. In Proceedings of the Advances in Neural Information Processing Systems (NIPS), Montreal, QC, Canada, 7–12 December 2015.
31. Boikov, A.; Payor, V.; Savelev, R.; Kolesnikov, A. Synthetic data generation for steel defect detection and classification using deep learning. *Symmetry* **2021**, *13*, 1176. [CrossRef]
32. Redmon, J.; Divvala, S.; Girshick, R.; Farhadi, A. You Only Look Once: Unified, Real-Time Object Detection. In Proceedings of the IEEE Conference on Computer Vision and Pattern Recognition (CVPR), Las Vegas, NV, USA, 27–30 June 2016.
33. Liu, W.; Anguelov, D.; Erhan, D.; Szegedy, C.; Reed, S.; Fu, C.Y.; Berg, A.C. SSD: Single Shot MultiBox Detector. In Proceedings of the European Conference on Computer Vision (ECCV), Amsterdam, The Netherlands, 11–14 October 2016.
34. Liu, J.; Luo, H.; Liu, H. Deep learning-based data analytics for safety in construction. *Autom. Constr.* **2022**, *140*, 104302. [CrossRef]
35. Panella, F.; Lipani, A.; Boehm, J. Semantic segmentation of cracks: Data challenges and architecture. *Autom. Constr.* **2022**, *135*, 104110. [CrossRef]
36. Panella, F.; Boehm, J.; Loo, Y.; Kaushik, A.; Gonzalez, D. Deep learning and image processing for automated crack detection and defect measurement in underground structures. *Int. Arch. Photogramm. Remote Sens. Spatial Inf. Sci.* **2018**, *42*, 829–835. [CrossRef]
37. Lin, Q.; Ye, G.; Wang, J.; Liu, H. RoboFlow: A Data-centric Workflow Management System for Developing AI- enhanced Robots. In Proceedings of the 5th Conference on Robot Learning, London, UK, 8–11 November 2022.
38. Cun, X.; Pun, C.M.; Shi, C. Towards Ghost-free Shadow Removal via Dual Hierarchical Aggregation Network and Shadow Matting GAN. In Proceedings of the AAAI Conference on Artificial Intelligence, New York, NY, USA, 7–12 February 2020.
39. Lecca, M.; Messelodi, S. Computing von Kries Illuminant Changes by Piecewise Inversion of Cumulative Color Histograms. *ELCVIA Electron. Lett. Comput. Vis. Image Anal.* **2009**, *8*, 1–17. [CrossRef]
40. Mustafa, W.A.; Kader, M.M. A Review of Histogram Equalization Techniques in Image Enhancement Application. *J. Phys. Conf. Ser.* **2018**, *1019*, 012026. [CrossRef]
41. Land, E.H.; Mccann, J.J. Lightness and Retinex Theory. *J. Opt. Soc. Am.* **1971**, *61*, 1–11. [CrossRef]

sensors

MDPI

Article

Research on Pedestrian Crossing Decision Models and Predictions Based on Machine Learning

Jun Cai, Mengjia Wang * and Yishuang Wu

School of Architecture & Fine Art, Dalian University of Technology, Dalian 116024, China;
caimans@dlut.edu.cn (J.C.); wuyishuang@mail.dlut.edu.cn (Y.W.)
* Correspondence: wangmengjia@mail.dlut.edu.cn

Abstract: Systematically and comprehensively enhancing road traffic safety using artificial intelligence (AI) is of paramount importance, and it is gradually becoming a crucial framework in smart cities. Within this context of heightened attention, we propose to utilize machine learning (ML) to optimize and ameliorate pedestrian crossing predictions in intelligent transportation systems, where the crossing process is vital to pedestrian crossing behavior. Compared with traditional analytical models, the application of OpenCV image recognition and machine learning methods can analyze the mechanisms of pedestrian crossing behaviors with greater accuracy, thereby more precisely judging and simulating pedestrian violations in crossing. Authentic pedestrian crossing behavior data were extracted from signalized intersection scenarios in Chinese cities, and several machine learning models, including decision trees, multilayer perceptrons, Bayesian algorithms, and support vector machines, were trained and tested. In comparing the various models, the results indicate that the support vector machine (SVM) model exhibited optimal accuracy in predicting pedestrian crossing probabilities and speeds, and it can be applied in pedestrian crossing prediction and traffic simulation systems in intelligent transportation.

Keywords: intelligent traffic safety; machine learning; pedestrian crossing; characteristics of crossing behavior; available crossing gaps

1. Introduction

The current paradigm in road design significantly prioritizes motor vehicles, rendering pedestrians in a vulnerable position and maintaining a high rate of pedestrian accidents. As per the *2021 China Traffic Accident Statistical Yearbook*, motorized, non-motorized, and pedestrian accidents were recorded at 2.67 million, 390,000, and 140,000 incidents, respectively. Hence, understanding pedestrian crossing behaviors and decision-making processes is crucial. Although several methods such as the Harders, Ashworth, and Raff methods, as well as the Logit process calculation and the maximum likelihood estimation method, have been widely researched for investigating vehicle crossing gaps, there is a notable deficit in studies focusing on pedestrian crossing decision making. Some scholars have suggested calculating critical gaps using the average single-lane pedestrian crossing time. However, the randomness in pedestrian crossings introduces errors to this method. Furthermore, pedestrian crossing resembles a dynamic game, where both vehicles and pedestrians aim to traverse with minimum delays and the utmost safety, but due to the unpredictability of choices, not all pedestrians choose to cross even with ample gaps. A dynamic game theory perspective has revealed that a pedestrian's decision to cross is influenced by the interacting vehicle's speed and distance or the headway time. Presently, research on pedestrian crossing decision making primarily revolves around two aspects, which are discussed below.

The first facet involves exploring pedestrians' permissible crossing gaps. Early research, such as that by Wilson and Grayson [1], primarily analyzed the proportion of acceptable gaps for various demographic groups, revealing, for instance, that 11.1% of pedestrians accepted a crossing gap of less than 2 s. Chae et al. [2] discerned an acceptable pedestrian crossing gap of approximately 5.1 s using data from American roundabouts. Meanwhile, subsequent gap research, such as the studies by Himanen [3] and Cavallo [4], have primarily concentrated on formulating crossable gap models and dissecting influencing factors, such as vehicle speed, distance, and pedestrian age, all of which are pivotal in determining gap acceptance. Further studies have explored various pedestrian behaviors. Kadali and Rathi [5] illustrated the notable impacts of pedestrian crossing speed and conflicting vehicle speed and distance on gap acceptance. Shabban and Mohammed [6] developed models for two street-crossing methods, revealing that factors such as crossing distance and pedestrian crossing speed significantly influenced both. A distinct relationship between young pedestrians and accident proneness was identified by Niaz et al. [7], while Granié [8] and Ezzati Amini [9] highlighted that younger pedestrians often engage in riskier crossing behaviors and accept smaller gaps. Contrarily, Dommes et al. [10] emphasized elderly pedestrians' higher collision risks due to attention and physical limitations. Zafri et al. [11] showcased that elderly individuals exhibit fewer rolling gap crossings, underlining varied findings across studies on different age demographics and their crossing behaviors.

The second domain involves researching pedestrian crossing speeds, a critical parameter in intersection design that ensures both safety and traffic efficiency. The initial studies on this subject predominantly analyzed the influences of age and gender on crossing speeds. Govinda L. and Abhigna D. [12] demonstrated that young individuals generally traverse faster than the elderly, with gender presenting no substantial impact on crossing speed. Moore [13] identified that smaller accepted gaps were correlated with faster crossing speeds (i.e., 1.2 m/s for gaps of > 7 s and 1.5 m/s for those of < 3 s). In subsequent research, Lam and Lee [14] found that the average speed during red-light crossings was 1.5 m/s, which exceeded the 1.27 m/s observed during green-light crossings. Similarly, Gates and Noyce [15] found a higher average speed during non-green-light crossings (1.57 m/s) compared with green-light crossing speeds (1.37 m/s). Recent findings by Koh and Wong [16] have highlighted significant differences between walking and cycling crossing speeds. Feng Shumin and Wu Yuexin [17] deduced an average pedestrian crossing speed of 1.47 m/s, with an 85th percentile of 1.74 m/s, using data from Harbin. By examining data from Nanjing's Xinjiekou area, Lu Jian and Ye Huiqiong [18] established elderly and young people's average crossing speeds as 1.17 m/s and 1.29 m/s, respectively. Figueroa-Medina et al. [19] pinpointed age and acceptable gap as the significant determinants of pedestrian crossing speed. Ku et al. [20] employed a discriminative algorithm based on deep image learning to conduct a quantitative analysis of the safety and economic issues arising from traffic vulnerability. Their study did not consider the exact number of dispatchers required for certain aspects of deep learning and the data collection process. Alver et al. [21] proposed a comprehensive AHP-FL (analytic hierarchy process–fuzzy logic) method to address the issue of how pedestrians assess the safety of available gaps. However, this method is susceptible to individual subjective biases. Li et al. [22] introduced a method combining foreground detection with deep learning to detect moving pedestrians, effectively utilizing the invariant background of video images.

However, the existing research faces the following issues: (1) traditional models, primarily those using non-trajectory data, inadequately illustrate the dynamic and mobile characteristics impacting pedestrian crossing decisions; (2) most studies on pedestrian crossing gaps have focused on predicting the psychological thresholds for crossing without adequately simulating actual behaviors. Using image recognition and machine learning can address these problems, enabling more accurate analysis of factors affecting unlawful pedestrian crossings, thereby optimizing decision models and precisely simulating crossing behaviors. Machine learning methods offer the ability to efficiently process and analyze large volumes of complex data, adapt and improve over time, automate decision-making processes, and provide powerful predictive and personalization capabilities across various domains. One's suggestions make the logic more standardized. This study first synthesized the existing research, and the first chapter of this paper discusses the OpenCV-based data collection and extraction, which we applied to five Dalian City intersections. The second chapter presents our methodology, which used various predictive methods. The third part validates and compares each method, and it conducts a feature analysis. The fourth part outlines our conclusions and projections.

2. Transportation Surveys and Data Processing

2.1. Survey and Sampling

To ensure sample diversity, this study selected four representative intersections in Dalian, China. Intersection 1 was in an aging residential area with many elderly residents. Intersection 2 was surrounded by modern commercial complexes. Intersection 3 was near primary and secondary schools. Intersection 4 was near a newly developed residential area with nearby amenities such as a small plaza and kindergarten. These four intersections were chosen to guarantee the data comprehensiveness and accuracy.

2.1.1. Location

Data were gathered using wide-angle cameras, with a total of four wide-angle cameras and four roadside cameras strategically installed across four collection sites, as shown in Figure 1. This setup ensured that the pedestrian and vehicle data collected at these locations were sufficiently clear and abundant for analysis.

Figure 1. Camera angles at four data collection sites: (**a**) Shandong Road–Songjiang Road; (**b**) Hongyun Road–Zhelin Street; (**c**) Zhangqian Road–Hongjin Road; and (**d**) Huadong Road–Qianshan Road.

2.1.2. Collection Time

Video data for this study were collected during busy morning and evening peak hours, characterized by high vehicle flow and low speeds, alongside increased pedestrian crossing demands. Additionally, data were gathered during less busy off-peak periods with lower vehicle flow and higher speeds, resulting in fewer pedestrian crossings. This method ensured data accuracy and completeness. Collection dates and durations are detailed in the accompanying table. Cameras were discreetly set up to avoid influencing pedestrian behavior, thus maintaining the accuracy and authenticity of the data. The video collection times and durations for each surveyed road section are listed in the Table 1 below.

Table 1. Statistics.

Type	Date	Location	Collection Time	Duration
8-lane roadway	14 November 2022	Zhangqian Road–Hongjin Road	6:45–9:45 12:00–15:00	180 min 180 min
	15 November 2022	Huadong Road–Qianshan Road	7:00–10:00 12:00–15:00	180 min 150 min
6-lane roadway	15 November 2022	Shandong Road–Songjiang Road	6:45–9:45 11:30–2:00	180 min 150 min
	14 November 2022	Hongyun Road–Zhelin Street	7:00–10:00 16:00–19:00	180 min 180 min

The lengthy and high-resolution videos collected consumed substantial memory. To protect pedestrian and driver privacy and manage memory use, the resolution was reduced, ensuring that vehicle and pedestrian data remained identifiable. Cameras were suspended at an elevated position on electric iron poles on both sides of the road using pulleys. They were secured in place via magnetic attachment, as shown in Figure 2. The collection team remotely controlled the camera's shooting direction and tilt angle using a motorized pan-tilt head, ensuring that the camera's field of view adequately covered the required areas.

Figure 2. Installation process of cameras for data collection.

2.2. Data Collection Methods and Numerical Statistics Based on OpenCV

Surface traffic data surveys fundamentally inform our understanding of pedestrian crossing and vehicular driving behaviors and serve as data sources for establishing pedestrian red-light violation and crossing accident models. Currently, there are the following two main categories of traffic data collection: traditional manual surveys, which can acquire data on vehicle and pedestrian behaviors at intersections via designed questionnaires and data statistics but are time-, resource-, and accuracy-limited, and technologically driven methods, which have gained traction with the advancements in computer and communication technologies, notably, image recognition and processing technologies that automatically recognize video data via computer programs. OpenCV enables the intuitive recognition of road environments and traffic entities, processing data such as traffic flows and entities via visual detection and enhancing traffic management and safety by analyzing and visually presenting the detected data. The OpenCV runtime interface is shown in the following Figure 3.

In OpenCV, the following steps are performed for data processing: A video is input for processing, whereby a recorded 24 h video is loaded into YOLO-v5 sequentially and vehicle, pedestrian, and traffic light detection is carried out. The YOLO-v5 network is utilized, and it is trained using the COCO dataset to detect and label targets. For traffic light recognition (i.e., determining the currently illuminated type), a self-designed classification network is employed to detect red, green, and blue in the input traffic light images, and subsequently, target tracking is performed. The target-tracking frame is input, the detected targets are numbered, and then the target speed measurements and distance measurements are carried out. The pixel difference between the tracked targets' prior and subsequent target frames is selected to calculate the target speed. Finally, data visualization is performed. This process enabled us to recognize and determine intersection vehicle driving behaviors, pedestrian crossing behaviors, and violations. Ultimately, we were able to save the pedestrian crossing features and vehicle driving data results in a CSV table and display the data in the CSV table. A total of 1904 sets of data were collected. To ensure the accuracy of the research results, certain samples were excluded, such as those where age could not be discerned in the video, samples involving patients with disabilities or illnesses, and samples of infants. Consequently, we obtained 1644 valid samples, and the partial numerical statistical results are shown in Table 2 and Figure 4. In the pedestrian age column in Table 2, 0 represents the elderly, 1 represents the middle-aged, and 2 represents children. In the pedestrian crossing choice in Table 2, 0 indicates that traversal was selected, and 1 indicates that traversal was not selected.

Figure 3. Image recognition interface.

Table 2. Statistics on vehicle speed (x), vehicle distance (y), pedestrian age (z), pedestrian crossing choice (p), and crossing speed (v).

x (km/h)	y (m)	z	p	v (m/s)
13	37	1	1	0
82	58	2	1	0
49	29	2	1	0
5	23	0	1	0
86	48	1	1	0
115	15	1	0	1.26
109	26	2	0	1.18
		...		

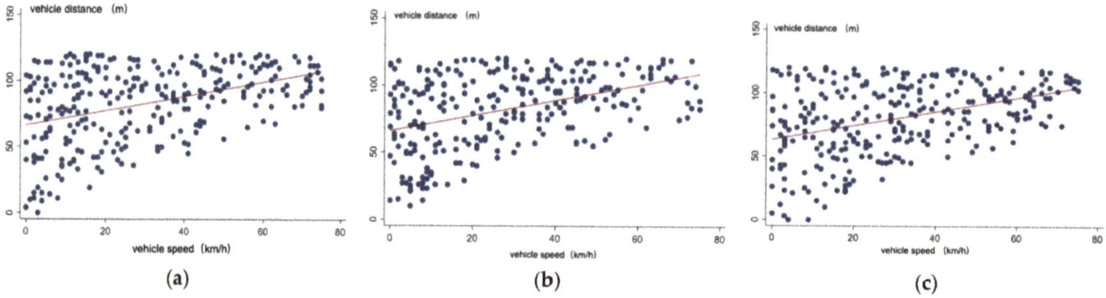

Figure 4. Vehicle speed and distance statistics. (**a**) Statistics of the elderly; (**b**) statistics of middle-aged people; (**c**) statistics of children.

3. Method

This study implemented a machine learning approach to predict pedestrian crossing probability and speed during street crossings, and it proposes a research method that is divided into the following parts: the previous chapter discussed the data collection for the pedestrian crossing features and vehicle driving data results, which led to the acquired dataset. Subsequently, four different machine learning models are established, and each model's experimental results are displayed herein. The most suitable machine learning model for this research is determined via analysis and comparison. The factors influencing the results are also discussed herein. Figure 5 depicts a schematic diagram of the proposed research method.

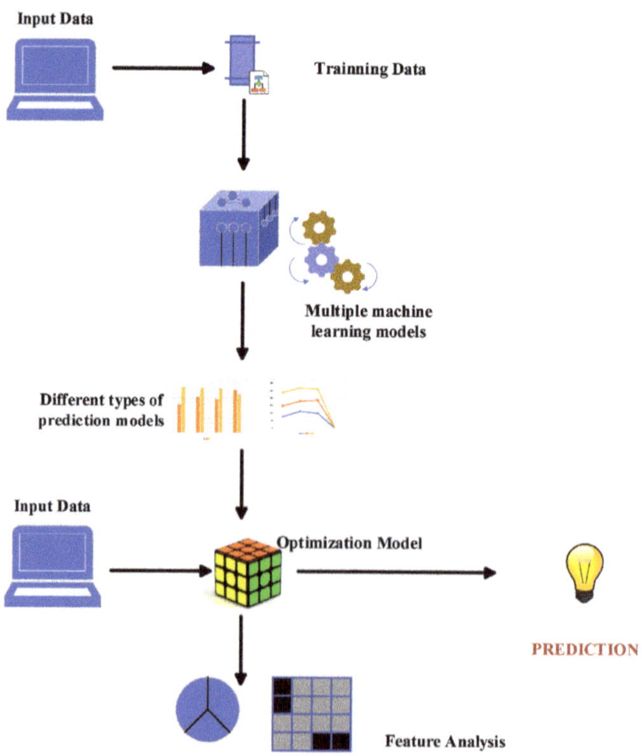

Figure 5. Pedestrian crossing prediction methods and procedures.

3.1. Data Preprocessing

After completing the data collection, label encoding was applied to the categorical feature 'z' in the obtained dataset, converting it into a numerical representation. The categorical column 'p' was transformed into a binary categorical column for the model training. The dataset was then subjected to z-score standardization.

3.2. Selection of Machine Learning Models

After appropriate data processing, this study employed four algorithms, namely, decision trees, the Bayesian algorithm, the BP neural network, and a support vector machine, to separately predict crossing probability and crossing speed.

3.2.1. Decision Tree

Decision trees formulate models utilizing tree structures, and they strive to predict numerical outputs via the adoption of straightforward decision rules. A dataset is progressively broken down into smaller subsets while concurrently constructing associated decision trees, as depicted in Figure 6. The end product is a tree featuring decision nodes and leaf nodes, with leaves symbolizing the outcomes, while the decision nodes indicate the points at which the data were partitioned [23]. This model is characterized by its simplicity, ease of interpretation, and ease of implementation.

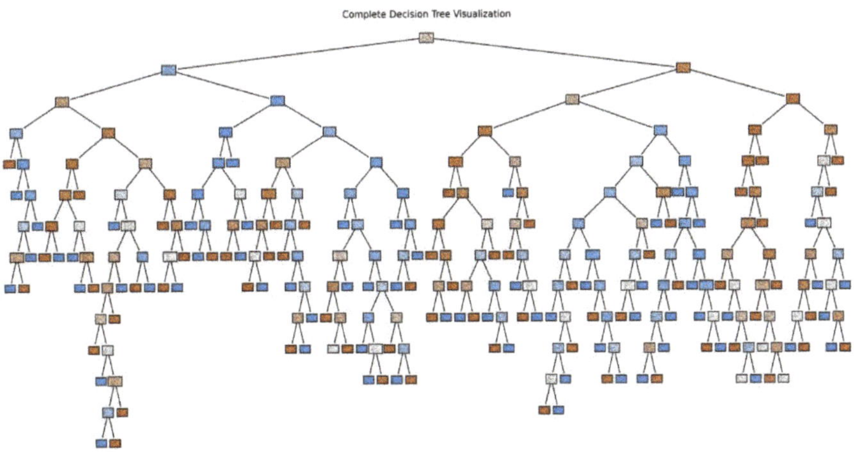

Figure 6. Structure diagram of decision tree.

3.2.2. Bayesian Algorithm

The Bayesian algorithm exhibits a remarkable ability to handle uncertainty and noise, and hence, it is frequently utilized in classification and regression problems, especially in scenarios with limited data. Grounded in Bayesian probability theory, the algorithm is capable of providing explicit estimates of uncertainty. Furthermore, Bayesian models are conveniently able to be updated, and they can progressively assimilate new data to refine the model, proving to be particularly applicable in dynamic environments such as pedestrian street crossings [24,25].

3.2.3. Support Vector Machines

Support vector machines (SVMs) are supervised learning algorithms developed by Vapnik et al. [26] that are founded on statistical learning theory, and they are widely utilized for addressing classification and regression problems. Moreover, they can make accurate predictions even with limited sample data, making them suitable for resolving the issues discussed in this paper. In this type of algorithm, data points are separated with a hyperplane, and kernel functions are utilized to map the data from the input space to a higher-dimensional feature space where it is easier to locate the optimal separating hyperplane. The hyperplane can be represented with the following linear equation:

$$f(x) = w \cdot x + b \tag{1}$$

where w is the weight vector, and b is the bias term. The objective of an SVM is to minimize the following objective function to find the maximum margin:

$$\min_{w,b} \frac{1}{2} \|w\|^2 \tag{2}$$

where $||\cdot||$ represents the norm, which is subject to the following constraints for each data point i:

$$y_i(w \cdot x_i + b) \geq 1 \tag{3}$$

Herein, y_i represents the class label of the data point x_i. In practical problems, data are often not linearly separable. To handle non-linearly separable data, an SVM employs the so-called 'kernel trick', namely, mapping the original data to a higher-dimensional feature space where they are linearly separable via the kernel function $K(x,x')$. Common kernel functions include the radial basis function (RBF), polynomial kernels, and multilayer perceptron kernels, among others [27]. This study adopted the radial basis function, which is expressed as follows:

$$K(x, x') = \exp\left(-\gamma \|x - x'\|^2\right) \tag{4}$$

3.2.4. Multi-Layer Perceptron Neural Network

The structural principle of multi-layer perceptrons (MLPs) is illustrated in Figure 7, and they constitute a type of feedforward neural network that encompasses an input layer, hidden layers, and an output layer, with each layer being composed of several neurons that are connected to other layers via weighted connections. An MLP utilizes non-linear activation functions, such as Sigmoid or ReLU, to introduce non-linear properties. Trained via optimization algorithms such as backpropagation and gradient descent, an MLP is capable of learning complex mapping relationships between input data and output labels. Owing to their high flexibility and wide applicability, MLPs are extensively used for classification, regression, and other machine learning tasks.

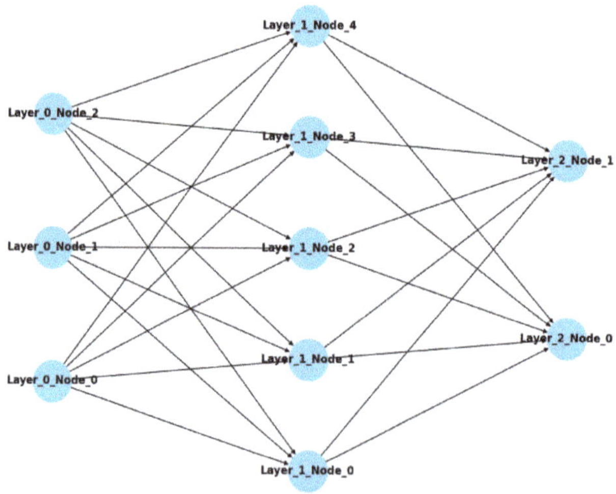

Figure 7. The structure of multi-layer perceptron.

3.3. Parameter Settings

This research employed k-fold cross-validation (k = 5) as the primary hyperparameter-tuning strategy to prevent overfitting. Among various complexity parameters (cp) in the decision tree model, cp = 0.1 outperformed the other values, achieving the highest average performance during the cross-validation process. For the Naïve Bayes algorithm, cross-validation was utilized to select the optimal smoothing parameter α and other parameters. In the support vector machine model (Gaussian kernel), the parameters sigma = 0.01 and C = 0.01 demonstrated superior generalization capabilities during the cross-validation process. In the training of the multi-layer perceptron model, a grid search revealed that a single hidden layer containing 10 neurons exhibited an optimal performance in the model. Sensitivity analysis was also conducted, and although certain parameters (such as the C value in the support vector machine) exhibited relative sensitivities, these sensitivities did not significantly impact the model's performance within the scope of the current study.

4. Results and Discussion

4.1. Prediction Results for Crossing Probability

For the prediction of crossing probability, the four aforementioned machine learning models were utilized, with the accuracy, Kappa coefficient, sensitivity, and specificity employed as the evaluation metrics for the models. The results are presented in Table 3.

Table 3. Prediction results for the machine learning models.

Technique	Accuracy (%)	Kappa Coefficient	Sensitivity (%)	Specificity (%)
Decision tree	92	0.637	81.7	82.4
Bayesian	94.3	0.788	96.4	83.2
MLP	92	0.717	98.4	77.0
SVR	92	0.813	92.4	88.8

Based on the results presented, it was observable that the decision tree model exhibited a mediocre predictive performance, with relatively low accuracy and Kappa coefficient. The Naive Bayes model demonstrated moderate performances on both the training and test sets, and despite exhibiting high sensitivity on the training set, it showed lower specificity. The MLP model performed well on both the training and test sets, achieving a higher accuracy and Kappa coefficient. The support vector machine model outperformed the others, offering the highest accuracy and Kappa coefficient, with balanced sensitivity and specificity.

This study also employed techniques such as McNemar's test for accuracy to statistically test the significance of differences between models. Using a random seed of 42, the results of McNemar's test for single prediction outcomes among various models are as shown in Table 4.

Table 4. Model comparison in single experiment.

Model Comparison	Statistical Data	*p*-Value	Significance Analysis
Decision tree vs. SVM	0.696	0.404	No significant difference
Decision tree vs. MLP	1.44	0.230	No significant difference
Decision tree vs. Naïve Bayes	0.121	0.728	No significant difference
SVM vs. MLP	0.167	0.683	No significant difference
SVM vs. Naïve Bayes	2.722	0.099	There is no significant difference, but it tends to be significant, which is worth further exploration
MLP vs. Naïve Bayes	4.5	0.034	There is a significant difference, indicating that the performance of the two models is significantly different

It can be concluded that there is a significant difference in performance between the MLP and Naïve Bayes models (*p*-value of less than 0.05). This indicates that in this specific scenario, the performances of these two models significantly differ. The p-values between some models did not reach the traditional level of significance, but they tended toward significance, for example, "SVM vs. Naive Bayes" and "KNN vs. Naive Bayes".

To minimize randomness, multiple experiments (20 times) were conducted, each time using a different random seed. The average of the obtained statistical data and p-values was then calculated, yielding the following results as shown in Table 5.

Table 5. Model comparison across multiple experiments.

Model Comparison	Average Statistical Data	Average p-Value	Significance Analysis
Decision tree vs. SVM	2.694	0.331	No significant difference
Decision tree vs. MLP	2.177	0.318	No significant difference
Decision tree vs. Naive Bayes	0.816	0.537	No significant difference
SVM vs. MLP	1.064	0.502	No significant difference
SVM vs. Naive Bayes	4.820	0.126	There is no significant difference, but it tends to be significant, which may indicate that there are performance differences between models
MLP vs. Naive Bayes	3.009	0.284	There is no significant difference, but it tends to be significant and may need more data verification

It can be inferred that the average p-values for most model comparisons are greater than 0.05, indicating no statistically significant difference in performance between the models. However, there is a trend toward significance in the comparisons of "Decision Tree vs. Random Forest", "SVM vs. Naive Bayes", "MLP vs. Naive Bayes", "KNN vs. Naive Bayes", and "Naive Bayes vs. Random Forest".

The ROC curves for each machine learning model are illustrated in Figure 8, where multiple ROC curves, each corresponding to a different cross-validation fold, are plotted in each subplot. The x-axis represents the "False Positive Rate (FPR)" while the y-axis depicts the "True Positive Rate (TPR)". The ROC curves were generated by translating the model-predicted probabilities into class labels using varying thresholds. The AUC (area under the curve) is a metric utilized to quantify a model's performance. Each fold provides an AUC value, which is also displayed on the label of each ROC curve. The average ROC curve, represented in blue, is the mean of the ROC curves across all the folds. The average AUC is the mean value of the AUCs across all the folds. The gray shaded area denotes the standard deviation range of the average ROC curve, providing an indication of the uncertainty in the model's performance. The red diagonal line illustrates the performance of the random classifier (i.e., a classifier without predictive capabilities), where the true positive rate (TPR) was equal to the false positive rate (FPR). All models used a consistent split ratio (1200:300) to ensure fairness in the comparison of the training and validation set sizes. The variation in the AUC for the same model under different seeds highlights the impacts of the initial conditions and randomness in the model training and validation process.

The Table 6 below shows the dataset split ratios and random seed parameters for each of the four models in different fold tests, along with their corresponding AUC values.

Table 6. AUC values of each model.

Model	Fold	Seed	Split Ratio	AUC
Decision tree	1	596	1200:300	0.881764
	2	977	1200:300	0.882486
	3	565	1200:300	0.880411
	4	90	1200:300	0.873843
	5	513	1200:300	0.865351

Table 6. *Cont.*

Model	Fold	Seed	Split Ratio	AUC
SVM	1	51	1200:300	0.975063
	2	379	1200:300	0.980226
	3	924	1200:300	0.976258
	4	558	1200:300	0.969963
	5	397	1200:300	0.973170
MLP	1	206	1200:300	0.973259
	2	424	1200:300	0.968795
	3	261	1200:300	0.980294
	4	77	1200:300	0.968291
	5	879	1200:300	0.971182
Naive Bayes	1	545	1200:300	0.958243
	2	541	1200:300	0.971884
	3	788	1200:300	0.973530
	4	995	1200:300	0.962103
	5	631	1200:300	0.977370

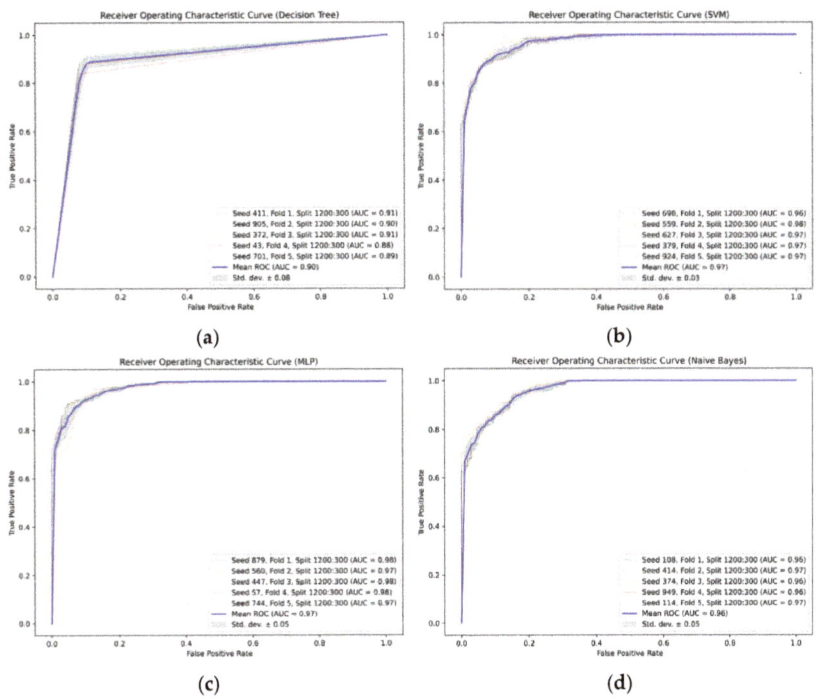

Figure 8. ROC curves for each machine learning model. (**a**) Decision tree; (**b**) SVM; (**c**) MLP; and (**d**) Naïve Bayes.

It can be observed that the support vector machine (SVM) and multilayer perceptron (MLP) models consistently exhibit higher AUC values across all folds, indicating superior performance in this specific task. However, considering the other metrics where SVM excels, it is the most suitable model when evaluated comprehensively.

4.2. Prediction Results for Crossing Speed

For the prediction of crossing speed, the aforementioned four machine learning models were employed, and we utilized MSE, RMSE, R^2, and MAD as the evaluation metrics. The performance metrics for each fold are presented in Table 7.

Table 7. The performance metrics for each fold.

Model	Fold	Random Seed	Train Ratio	Test Ratio	MSE	RMSE	MAD	R^2
Decision tree	1	6132	0.8	0.2	0.225215	0.474568	0.430690	0.478519
	2	7321	0.8	0.2	0.199337	0.446472	0.410487	0.510846
	3	5204	0.8	0.2	0.190829	0.436840	0.397907	0.531904
	4	43	0.8	0.2	0.209782	0.458020	0.411726	0.512356
	5	1975	0.8	0.2	0.176267	0.419842	0.392056	0.577930
Bayesian Ridge	1	114	0.8	0.2	0.212515	0.460993	0.377595	0.462405
	2	3610	0.8	0.2	0.246985	0.496975	0.397476	0.410508
	3	7240	0.8	0.2	0.260120	0.510020	0.413945	0.388587
	4	5365	0.8	0.2	0.255769	0.505736	0.399616	0.393398
	5	2144	0.8	0.2	0.280739	0.529848	0.426510	0.348115
SVR	1	7544	0.8	0.2	0.210965	0.457642	0.423549	0.516097
	2	9700	0.8	0.2	0.202718	0.450198	0.439083	0.529888
	3	4056	0.8	0.2	0.124318	0.473622	0.375354	0.639779
	4	6671	0.8	0.2	0.200251	0.447952	0.374838	0.496490
	5	7528	0.8	0.2	0.228423	0.373082	0.401708	0.483284
MLP	1	4934	0.8	0.2	0.195281	0.441907	0.395040	0.547751
	2	3821	0.8	0.2	0.179646	0.423847	0.389555	0.555520
	3	90	0.8	0.2	0.207948	0.456013	0.403807	0.509789
	4	9156	0.8	0.2	0.189576	0.435404	0.390474	0.519733
	5	9706	0.8	0.2	0.245861	0.495844	0.419475	0.437373

The average performance metrics of the four machine learning models are shown in Table 8.

Table 8. The average performance of each model.

Model	MSE	RMSE	MAD	R^2
Bayesian Ridge	0.251226	0.500715	0.403028	0.400602
Decision tree	0.200286	0.447148	0.408573	0.522311
MLP	0.203663	0.450603	0.397670	0.514033
SVM	0.193335	0.440499	0.402906	0.533108

Based on the aforementioned results, the following conclusions can be drawn: The decision tree model exhibited an average performance on both the training and testing sets, characterized by a higher R^2, but also a higher MSE, RMSE, and MAD. The naive Bayes model demonstrated the poorest performance on both sets, characterized by the highest MSE, the highest RMSE, the lowest R^2, and a higher MAD. The MLP neural network model also showed general performance on both sets, associated with its higher MSE, higher RMSE, lower R^2, and higher MAD. The support vector machine model performed the best, boasting the lowest mean squared error (MSE) and root mean squared error (RMSE), as well as the highest coefficient of determination (R^2) and a lower mean absolute deviation (MAD).

Overall, the support vector machine model showcased superior performance on this dataset, having the smallest mean squared error and root mean squared error, and it was able to fit the data well, with a relatively high coefficient of determination (R^2). It can be concluded that the support vector machine algorithm emerges as the most apt model for predicting the probability and speed of pedestrian crossings.

4.3. Feature Analysis

4.3.1. Analysis of Pedestrian Crossing Probability

To investigate the impacts of various features on prediction outcomes, a feature importance ranking analysis was conducted using permutation importance. Permutation importance is a method to assess the impacts of features on the performance of prediction models, primarily based on the idea of shuffling the values of each feature and observing the effect of this disruption on the model performance. Unlike other feature importance methods, Permutation importance is model-agnostic, meaning it can be used with any model. Initially, the model is trained using the original dataset, and its performance is evaluated. Then, for each feature, the values in that feature column are randomly shuffled, keeping other features unchanged, and the performance is reassessed to record the change in the model performance. The permutation importance of a feature is typically defined as the difference between the original performance and the performance after shuffling that feature. If shuffling a particular feature significantly decreases model performance, this implies that the feature is very important for model predictions. To minimize the impact of randomness, this process is repeated multiple times, and the average change in performance is taken as the permutation importance of that feature. Upon analyzing the permutation importance of each feature in the best-performing SVM model, the results are as follows: the importance of feature x is 0.299, y is 0.151, and z is 0.002. Hence, it can be concluded that x has the most significant impact on the model, followed by y, while the impact of feature z is relatively minor.

After evaluating the feature importance for the entire model, we conducted a Shapley additive explanations (SHAP) analysis on the SVM-based cross-probability prediction model for a deeper analysis of individual predictions, as shown in Figure 9.

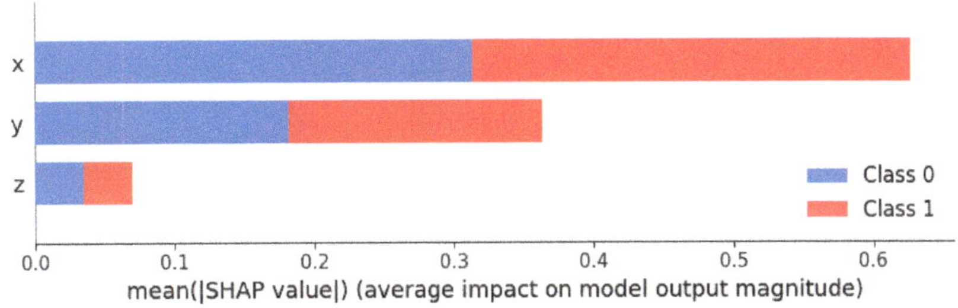

Figure 9. SHAP analysis conducted on the crossing probability prediction model based on the SVM.

From the graphical analysis, it is evident that the 'x' feature exerted the most substantial impact on the predictive outcomes, where an increase in its value inclined the model toward predicting p. The influence of the 'y' feature was secondary, with its value increase also biasing the model toward a p prediction. The 'z' feature exhibited a relatively minimal impact on the classification results. Consequently, the vehicle speed surface was the paramount factor affecting a pedestrian's decision to cross, followed by the vehicle distance. Although the age factor held a relatively modest influence, it still imparted a discernible impact on the predictive values.

To explore the impact patterns of various factors across different age groups on the predictive outcomes, this study separately visualized the output results of the SVM-based crossing probability prediction model for different age segments. Figure 10 illustrates a three-dimensional scatter plot established based on vehicle speed, vehicle distance, and pedestrian crossing probability. The points in the graphs represent the probabilities of pedestrians opting to jaywalk with different vehicle distances and speeds. Distances are categorized into 24 groups, ranging from 0–5 m to 115–120 m, while speeds are divided into 15 groups, from 0–5 km/h to 70–75 km/h. Each increment in distance or speed represents an increase to the next interval in its respective range. The graph reveals that the probability of a pedestrian choosing to cross increased with the enlargement of the nearest vehicle's distance, and it decreased with an escalation in the nearest vehicle's speed.

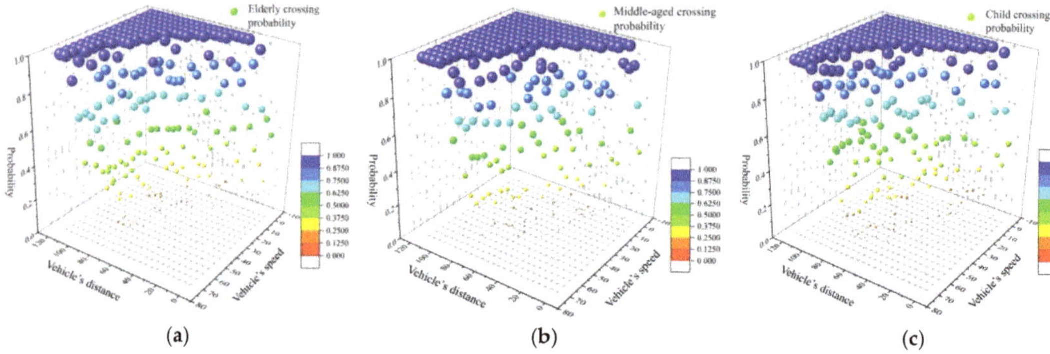

Figure 10. Probability model of pedestrians' crossing behaviors. (**a**) Crossing probability model for the elderly; (**b**) crossing probability model for middle−aged adult pedestrians; (**c**) crossing probability model for children.

The crossing probability model for the elderly is illustrated in Figure 8a. As the vehicle speed increased, the likelihood of an elderly pedestrian choosing to cross decreased, and conversely, as the vehicle distance increased, an elderly pedestrian's crossing probability increased. When the nearest vehicle on the roadway was more than 95 m away, the elderly were nearly 100% likely to choose to cross, regardless of the vehicle's speed. The mapping distribution of the elderly pedestrians' crossing probabilities with respect to vehicle distance leaned left compared with those of middle-aged adult and child pedestrians, indicating that the overall vehicle distance was greater when an elderly pedestrian chose to cross. The crossing probability model for middle-aged adult pedestrians is depicted in Figure 8b. With an acceleration in vehicle speed, the probability of a middle-aged individual jaywalking diminished, while with an extension in vehicle distance, their jaywalking probability was augmented. When the distance to the nearest vehicle on the lane exceeded 75 m, the likelihood of a middle-aged individual choosing to cross was approximately 100%, regardless of the vehicle's speed. The distribution of the middle-aged adult pedestrians' crossing probability model, in relation to vehicle distance, was generally right-aligned compared with those of elderly and child pedestrians, implying that middle-aged adults were willing to cross at larger vehicle distances. Adults, having a heightened perception of vehicle speed and distance, along with abundant street-crossing experience, tended to take more risks when crossing. The children's crossing probability model, as shown in Figure 8c, demonstrated a decrease in the likelihood of running a red light with an increase in vehicle speed, whereas an augmentation in the crossing probability occurred as vehicle distances grew. Once the vehicle in the closest lane was more than 80 m away, regardless of its speed, a child was nearly 100% likely to opt to cross. The mapping distribution of the crossing probability model for children concerning vehicle distance presented considerable variability, indicating a substantial discreteness in crossing probability. Children, with their relatively limited cognition of vehicle speed and distance and their lack of street-crossing experience, exhibited a more scattered mapping for speed and distance.

4.3.2. Analysis of Pedestrian Crossing Speed

To iIn the regression analysis, the SVR model exhibited the most favorable performance. Feature importance was ranked within this model, revealing that the 'x' feature holds the highest importance with a score of 1.03, followed by 'y' with a score of 0.81, while the importance of 'z' is comparatively lower at 0.16.

After evaluating the feature importance for the entire model, we conducted a Shapley additive explanations (SHAP) analysis on the SVM-based cross-probability prediction model for a deeper analysis of individual predictions, as shown in Figure 11.

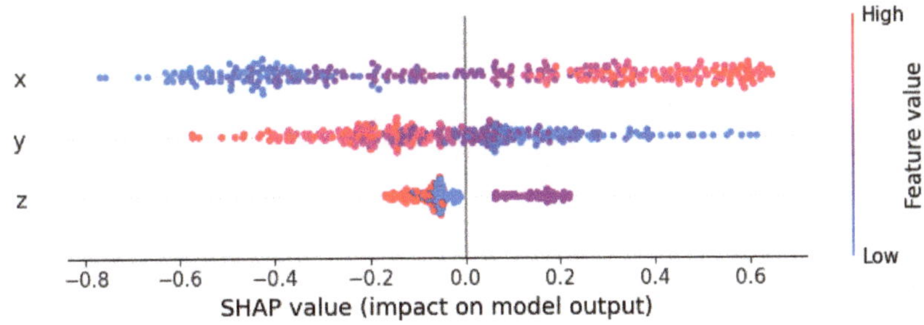

Figure 11. SHAP analysis based on the support vector regression (SVR) model.

In the SHAP plot, red indicates the higher feature values, while blue denotes the lower ones. The diagram reveals that the x feature was the most crucial, y was the second most vital, and z had a comparatively minor impact. For the x feature, higher values (shown in red) were associated with larger positive SHAP values, while lower values (shown in blue) correlated with more significant negative SHAP values, indicating a positive correlation between the x values and the predictions. Higher values for y (shown in red) correlated with negative SHAP values, signifying that the y values were inversely related to the predictions. The SHAP values for the z feature were relatively evenly distributed, with many colors mixed together (i.e., a blend of red and blue points), which could imply that the relationship between this feature and the prediction outcome was non-linear or more complex.

Upon analyzing the influence of each feature on the predictive model, this study further visualized the output results of the crossing speed model for the different age groups, as depicted in Figure 12. Here, the deeper red areas represent faster pedestrian crossing speeds while the deeper blue areas indicate slower speeds.

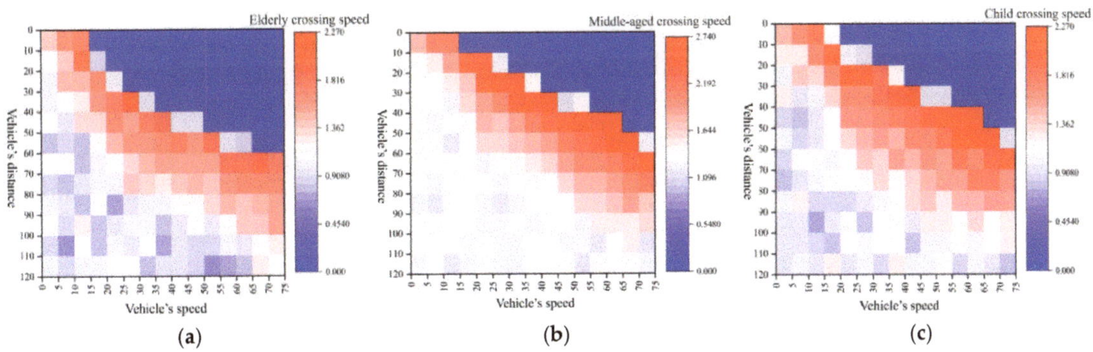

Figure 12. Crossing speed model of the pedestrians. (**a**) Crossing speeds of elderly individuals; (**b**) crossing speeds of middle-aged individuals; (**c**) crossing speeds of children.

Figure 10a illustrates the crossing speeds of elderly individuals. The points (15, 0), (75, 60), and (75, 0) generated a dark blue, triangular-like region for the elderly, wherein the probability of crossing within this interval was zero, and thus the speed was also zero. The red area denotes scenarios where the elderly had limited time to cross, necessitating a swifter crossing speed. The white area represents scenarios where pedestrians had ample time to cross, and thus, they opted to traverse at normal speeds. Due to the physical constraints that align with age, the crossing speeds of the elderly were slower than those of younger adults. Figure 10b presents the speed distributions of the young and middle-aged individuals choosing to cross at different vehicle speeds and distances. The young and middle-aged individuals formed a dark blue, triangular-like region at points (15, 0), (75, 50), and (75, 0). Due to excessively high vehicle speeds or minimal vehicle distances, the probability of crossing within these intervals was zero for young and middle-aged individuals. With a more pronounced inclination toward risk taking, the overall deep red area was more prevalent, signifying a general preference amongst young and middle-aged individuals to engage in riskier, faster crossings. Figure 10c depicts the crossing speed distributions for children based on varying vehicle speeds and distances. At points (15, 0), (75, 50), and (75, 0), the children formed a dark blue, triangular-like area, wherein the crossing probability was zero due to either overly high vehicle speeds or insufficient vehicle distances. Previous analyses have illuminated that children due to inaccurate judgments about vehicle speeds and distances and limited crossing experience, exhibit dispersed crossing probabilities. Coupled with the widespread red area in the current speed distribution depiction, it was evident that even when the vehicle distance and speed would permit crossing at regular speeds, children were predisposed to choose faster crossing speeds during traversal.

4.4. Application Method

Simulating realistic pedestrian crossing decisions enhances the pedestrian module's application in traffic simulation software. PTV−VISSIM2020, a leading microsimulation software, facilitates the construction of complex traffic environments. In Vissim, pedestrian simulation is crucial for assessing the pedestrian flow capacity and infrastructure service levels, yet it overlooks pedestrian safety evaluation. The pedestrian module in Vissim, operating in a social force model, is 'repulsive' to the vehicle module and assumes strict adherence to traffic signals by both pedestrians and vehicles, limiting the evaluation of safety in current traffic environments and the 'realistic' simulation of traffic entities. Future developments in the Vissim platform could involve modifying the pedestrian module for a more authentic simulation of pedestrian crossing behaviors, considering varied pedestrian and vehicle characteristics.

5. Conclusions and Future Prospects

This study, conducted using real-world data collected from four signal-controlled intersections in Dalian, China, uniquely applied a variety of machine learning methods to evaluate, analyze, and predict jaywalking behaviors at pedestrian crosswalks. The methods included Bayesian models, decision trees (DTs), support vector machines (SVMs), and multilayer perceptrons (MLPs). Precise pedestrian crosswalk and vehicle motion data were extracted using OpenCV technology, providing high-quality inputs for the machine learning models. This study highlighted the compensatory nature of the SVM model in predicting crossing probabilities, exhibiting outstanding performance in metrics such as accuracy, Kappa coefficient, sensitivity, and specificity. Additionally, techniques like McNemar's test for accuracy were employed to statistically test the significance of differences between models. Feature importance ranking, SHAP analysis, and feature quantity visualization were used to analyze the SVM model from different aspects. This work provides significant technical support for pedestrian safety in the intelligent vehicle domain, especially in terms of predicting pedestrian behavior and devising accident prevention measures.

However, the data in this study are from major cities in China, and the results may not fully apply to traffic environments under different national regulations or settings. Moreover, the study only addressed conflicts between motor vehicles and pedestrians in predicting pedestrian crossing behavior and did not investigate the specific impacts of non-motor vehicles and public buses on such behaviors.

Future work could expand the scope of the data collection to include various types of vehicles (like buses, bicycles, trucks, etc.) and more diverse urban environments. A deeper investigation into other factors influencing pedestrian crosswalk behavior, integrating these as machine learning features, could further enhance model accuracy and practicality. Our plans are to apply these findings to existing traffic simulation systems, such as VISSIM, SUMO, and the Transportation Modeling Platform, for a more realistic simulation of pedestrian behaviors, thereby enhancing their roles in intelligent transportation systems. Additionally, the development of a machine learning model capable of real-time prediction of pedestrian jaywalking behavior, to be implemented in intelligent vehicles, is also underway.

Author Contributions: Conceptualization, J.C.; Methodology, M.W.; Software, M.W.; Validation, Y.W.; Formal analysis, M.W.; Investigation, M.W.; Resources, Y.W.; Data curation, Y.W.; Writing—original draft, M.W.; Writing—review & editing, J.C.; Visualization, M.W.; Supervision, J.C.; Project administration, J.C.; Funding acquisition, J.C. All authors have read and agreed to the published version of the manuscript.

Funding: This research was funded by the National Natural Science Foundation of China grant number [52278048] project name Research on Theory and Intelligent Method of Road Network Quality Improving Planning from the Perspective of Dual Motive of City and Block. And the APC was funded by the National Natural Science Foundation of China.

Institutional Review Board Statement: Not applicable.

Informed Consent Statement: Not applicable.

Data Availability Statement: Data are contained within the article.

Conflicts of Interest: The authors declare no conflict of interest.

References

1. Wilson, D.; Grayson, G. *Age-Related Differences in the Road Crossing Behaviour of Adult Pedestrians*; National Technical Information Service: Springfield, VA, USA, 1980.
2. Chae, K. Simulation of Pedestrian-Vehicle Interactions at Roundabouts. Ph.D. Thesis, North Carolina State University, Raleigh, NC, USA, 2005.
3. Himanen, V.; Kulmala, R. An application of Logistic models in analysing the behaviour of pedestrians and car drivers on pedestrian crossings. *Accid. Anal. Prev.* **1988**, *20*, 187–197. [CrossRef] [PubMed]
4. Lobjois, R.; Cavallo, V. The effects of aging on street-crossing behavior: From estimation to actual crossing. *Accid. Anal. Prev.* **2009**, *41*, 259–267. [CrossRef] [PubMed]
5. Kadali, B.; Rathi, N.; Perumal, V. Evaluation of pedestrian mid-block road crossing behaviour using artificial neural network. *J. Traffic Transp. Eng.* **2014**, *1*, 111–119. [CrossRef]
6. Shaaban, K.; Muley, D.; Mohammed, A. Analysis of illegal pedestrian crossing behavior on a major divided arterial road. *Transp. Res. Part F Traffic Psychol. Behav.* **2018**, *54*, 124–137. [CrossRef]
7. Zafri, N. Walk or run? An observational study to explore pedestrian crossing decision-making at intersections in Dhaka, Bangladesh applying rules mining technique. Transportation research. *Transp. Res. Part F Traffic Psychol. Behav.* **2023**, *94*, 83–98. [CrossRef]
8. Marie-Axelle, G.; Pannetier, M.; Ludivine, G. Developing a self-reporting method to measure pedestrian behaviors at all ages. *Accid. Anal. Prev.* **2013**, *50*, 830–839. [CrossRef]
9. Amini, R.; Katrakazas, C.; Antoniou, C. Negotiation and Decision-Making for a Pedestrian Roadway Crossing: A Literature Review. *Sustainability* **2019**, *11*, 6713. [CrossRef]
10. Dommes, A.; Cavallo, V.; Oxley, J. Functional declines as predictors of risky street-crossing decisions in older pedestrians. *Accid. Anal. Prev.* **2013**, *59*, 135–143. [CrossRef]
11. Zafri, N.M.; Sultana, R.; Himal, M.R.H.; Tabassum, T. Factors influencing pedestrians' decision to cross the road by risky rolling gap crossing strategy at intersections in Dhaka, Bangladesh. *Accid. Anal. Prev.* **2023**, *142*, 105564. [CrossRef]
12. Govinda, L.; Abhigna, D.; Nair, P.M.; Shankar, K. Comparative Study of Pedestrian Crossing Behaviour at Uncontrolled Intersection and Midblock Locations. *Transp. Res. Procedia* **2020**, *48*, 698–706. [CrossRef]
13. Zhang, H.L.; Ge, P. Analyzing on the Relationship between the Pedestrian Speed and the Ratio of the Older Pedestrian at the Signalized Intersection. *Sci. Technol. Eng.* **2018**, *18*, 287–292.
14. Lam, W.; Lee, J.; Cheung, C.Y. Study of the bi-directional pedestrian flow characteristics at Hong Kong signalized crosswalk facilities. *Transportation* **2002**, *29*, 169–192. [CrossRef]

15. Gates, T.; Noyce, D.A.; Bill, A.; Van, N. Recommended Walking Speeds for Timing of Pedestrian Clearance Intervals Based on Characteristics of the Pedestrian Population. *Transp. Res. Rec. J. Transp. Res. Board* **2006**, *1982*, 38–47. [CrossRef]
16. Koh, P.P.; Wong, Y.D.; Chandrasekar, P. Safety evaluation of pedestrian behaviour and violations at signalised pedestrian crossings. *Saf. Sci.* **2014**, *70*, 143–152. [CrossRef]
17. Feng, X.S.; Wu, X. Crossing speed analysis for pedestrian at signalized intersection. *J. Harbin Inst. Technol.* **2004**, *36*, 76–78. [CrossRef]
18. Lu, J.; Ye, H.Q.; Yao, D.L. Reasonable distance of pedestrian crossing facilities. *J. Traffic Transp. Eng.* **2002**, *2*, 63–67.
19. Figueroa-Medina, A.M.; Valdés-Díaz, D.; Colucci-Ríos, B.; Cardona-Rodriguez, N.; Chamorro-Parejo, A. Analysis of walking speeds and success rates on mid-block crossings using virtual reality simulation. *Accid. Anal. Prev.* **2023**, *183*, 106987. [CrossRef] [PubMed]
20. Ku, D.; Choi, M.; Oh, H. Assessment of the resilience of pedestrian roads based on image deep learning models. *Proc. Inst. Civ. Eng. Munic. Eng.* **2022**, *3*, 135–147. [CrossRef]
21. Alver, Y.; Katanalp, B.Y. Evaluating the Pedestrian Gap Acceptance in Semicontrolled Midblock Crosswalks with an Integrated AHP-FL Approach. *J. Transp. Eng. Part A. Syst.* **2022**, *9*, 04022066. [CrossRef]
22. Li, M.; Xie, W. Pedestrian Motion Path Detection Method Based on Deep Learning and Foreground Detection. *Complexity* **2021**, *2021*, 5596135. [CrossRef]
23. Carrizosa, E.; Molero-Río, C.; Romero, M.D. Mathematical optimization in classification and regression trees. *TOP* **2021**, *29*, 5–33. [CrossRef]
24. Zhou, S.; Xu, A.; Tang, Y. Fast Bayesian Inference of Reparameterized Gamma Process with Random Effects. *IEEE Trans. Reliab.* **2023**, 1–14. [CrossRef]
25. Luo, C.; Shen, L.; Xu, A. Modelling and estimation of system reliability under dynamic operating environments and lifetime ordering constraints. *Reliab. Eng. Syst. Saf.* **2022**, *218*, 108136. [CrossRef]
26. Cortes, C.; Vapnik, V. Support-vector networks. *Mach. Learn.* **1995**, *20*, 273–297. [CrossRef]
27. Xuegong, Z. Introduction to statistical learning theory and support vector machines. *Acta Autom. Sin.* **2000**, *26*, 32–42.

sensors

MDPI

Article

Ship-Fire Net: An Improved YOLOv8 Algorithm for Ship Fire Detection

Ziyang Zhang, Lingye Tan * and Robert Lee Kong Tiong

School of Civil and Environmental Engineering, Nanyang Technological University, Singapore 639798, Singapore; ziyang004@e.ntu.edu.sg (Z.Z.); clktiong@ntu.edu.sg (R.L.K.T.)
* Correspondence: lingye001@e.ntu.edu.sg

Abstract: Ship fire may result in significant damage to its structure and large economic loss. Hence, the prompt identification of fires is essential in order to provide prompt reactions and effective mitigation strategies. However, conventional detection systems exhibit limited efficacy and accuracy in detecting targets, which has been mostly attributed to limitations imposed by distance constraints and the motion of ships. Although the development of deep learning algorithms provides a potential solution, the computational complexity of ship fire detection algorithm pose significant challenges. To solve this, this paper proposes a lightweight ship fire detection algorithm based on YOLOv8n. Initially, a dataset, including more than 4000 unduplicated images and their labels, is established before training. In order to ensure the performance of algorithms, both fire inside ship rooms and also fire on board are considered. Then after tests, YOLOv8n is selected as the model with the best performance and fastest speed from among several advanced object detection algorithms. GhostnetV2-C2F is then inserted in the backbone of the algorithm for long-range attention with inexpensive operation. In addition, spatial and channel reconstruction convolution (SCConv) is used to reduce redundant features with significantly lower complexity and computational costs for real-time ship fire detection. For the neck part, omni-dimensional dynamic convolution is used for the multi-dimensional attention mechanism, which also lowers the parameters. After these improvements, a lighter and more accurate YOLOv8n algorithm, called Ship-Fire Net, was proposed. The proposed method exceeds 0.93, both in precision and recall for fire and smoke detection in ships. In addition, the mAP@0.5 reaches about 0.9. Despite the improvement in accuracy, Ship-Fire Net also has fewer parameters and lower FLOPs compared to the original, which accelerates its detection speed. The FPS of Ship-Fire Net also reaches 286, which is helpful for real-time ship fire monitoring.

Keywords: ship-fire detection; YOLOv8n; deep learning; GhostnetV2; ODConv; SCConv

1. Introduction

Oceans encompass approximately 71% of the Earth's surface, giving rise to extensive water bodies that serve as natural channels. Since the 15th century, the rapid growth of maritime transportation has facilitated intercontinental mobility for humans, leading to extensive exchanges of people and goods that have had profound impacts on both social and natural environments. Historically, the majority of international trade, approximately 80–90%, has been facilitated through maritime transportation. Ships play a pivotal role in the domain of maritime transportation, serving as crucial facilitators for the transportation of commodities, people, and assets over the vast expanse of the Earth's oceans, seas, rivers, and other aquatic passages. Although shipping is often regarded as an efficient mode of transportation, it poses significant risks to the safety and well-being of all ships aboard. A common occurrence in the shipping industry is the potential hazard of fire, which poses a significant risk. A ship fire disaster is a highly consequential incident that poses a significant risk to the safety of maritime transportation, and may result in the loss of the ship, damage to cargo, environmental contamination, human injuries, and even fatalities [1].

According to the Safety and Shipping Review 2023 conducted by Allianz [2], the world's most well-known and largest insurer and financial services group, fire was as the second most prevalent factor contributing to the loss of shipping vessels in the previous year. There are about a total of 250,000 claims within the maritime insurance market, and it has been shown that fire was the costliest source of loss, representing 18% of the total value of all claims that were examined. However, with the development of technology and training for safety awareness and the professional skills crew members have shown on encountering risks, there has been a significant decline in shipping loss in the previous decade (eight vessels in 2022 compared with over 100 in 2013). However, the number of fire accidents in ships does not follow this trend. In 2022, there were a total of 209 recorded fire occurrences, which is the highest number in a decade. In the previous five years, a total of 64 ships were lost due to fires. There have been large numbers of devastating ship fire accidents in recent years. For instance, in January 2022, one ship carrying more than 4000 cars, including Porsche, Audi, Bentley, and Lamborghini models, caught fire in the mid-Atlantic. The projected economic impact of this unfortunate event was approximately USD 438 million worth of goods. In addition to economic losses, fire-in-fire may also threaten human lives and safety. According to CNN, two firemen perished while engaged in combat against conflagration, and a minimum of at least six other individuals sustained injuries. Almost 1200 vehicles and 157 containers burst onto the ground, resulting in significant economic losses. Moreover, ship fires can have a significant environmental impact, as the combustion of fuel, cargo, and other ship components results in the emission of pollutants into both atmospheric and aquatic environments. In addition, ships can transfer hazardous and toxic chemicals, resulting in severe damage to the environment. For instance, on 20 May 2021, a cargo ship carrying tons of hazardous and toxic chemicals caught fire near Colombo's commercial harbor, resulting in hazardous poisonous substances discharged into the ocean. These examples prove that fire accidents in ships may result in economic loss and threaten health and environmental hazards. Early detection of fire and smoke can both give time for crew members and passengers to evacuate or put out the fire to lower the loss. A 10-min delay in extinguishing a fire in the engine room might potentially incur a financial loss of USD 200,000; however, a 20-min delay could result in a tenfold increase in the loss [3].

Currently, there are three fundamental approaches for fire identification: human inspection, sensor-based detection, and image processing technology. Human inspectors who have received formal training possess specialized knowledge and practical skills that are useful for carrying out their duties. They can discern tiny indications of potential fire risks and demonstrate proficiency in evaluating intricate circumstances. However, there is a remarkable shortage of human inspections. Assessments conducted by human inspectors may be influenced by subjective factors, resulting in the uneven rating of fire safety measures. The accuracy and dependability of inspections may also be influenced by several factors, including human prejudice and judgment. Additionally, inspectors may experience weariness while engaging in extended and repeated inspection activities, thereby increasing the probability they will overlook or fail to identify crucial safety concerns. Manual inspections are also susceptible to the inherent dangers of human error. These shortcomings result in high economic costs.

With regard to sensor-based detection, sensor-based systems can identify fires during their first phases, often before the emergence of visible flames or smoke. The provision of an early warning system enables expedited reaction durations and heightened fire-suppression probabilities before fire propagation. In addition, sophisticated sensor technologies have been developed to reduce the occurrence of false alarms by effectively differentiating between genuine fire incidents and other extraneous elements, such as cooking smoke or dust present in the environment. Although sensor-based detection has these advantages, it also has some shortcomings: sensors have restricted coverage ranges, resulting in diminished efficacy in expansive, unenclosed environments or locales characterized by blocked sightlines. In order to provide sufficient coverage over large regions, it may be necessary to use many sensors, resulting in higher costs. Moreover, regular maintenance and calibration of sensors are necessary to guarantee their accuracy and dependability. Failure to prioritize maintenance may result in inaccurate alerts or, even more concerning, a failure to identify critical events. Compared with the first two methods of fire detection, image processing has the advantages of cost-effectiveness and efficiency, and its accuracy has shown consistent improvement with the development of improved processing power and the availability of specialized hardware, such as GPUs. Consequently, some researchers have used image-processing methodologies to identify and classify flames. In being applied to fire detection, conventional image processing methods often rely on manually selected characteristics, such as color [4,5], texture [6,7], and geometric features [8,9], to effectively partition fire instances. These segmented fires are then subjected to classification and matching procedures that are facilitated by machine learning algorithms, such as support vector machines (SVMs) [10], random forests [11], and K-means [12], to accomplish the task of fire detection. Nevertheless, standard image-processing approaches are inadequate for meeting the requirements of model generalization capability and durability in actual engineering situations via manually created feature extraction, which is mostly due to the complex nature of the fire environment.

Compared to traditional machine learning, where feature extraction is performed by humans, deep learning models can autonomously acquire pertinent characteristics from unprocessed inputs. The use of deep learning obviates the need for human feature engineering, enabling the model to autonomously uncover complicated patterns and representations. In addition, deep learning models, and artificial neural networks in particular, use non-linear activation functions inside their layers. The presence of nonlinearity enables models to effectively capture complex connections within the data, which is a task that linear models frequently used in conventional machine learning sometimes struggle with. Fire detection systems that use deep learning for fire identification are more effective than standard image-processing-based approaches. As a result, there is growing interest in fire detection systems that employ deep learning techniques instead of relying on feature descriptions [13,14].

However, the majority of deep-learning video fire detection systems available on the market require the use of high-performance central processing units (CPUs) and graphics processing units (GPUs) to enhance computational efficiency. Additionally, several embedded platforms are required for picture recognition from cloud-based sources, which may be attributed to the prioritization of real-time recognition in target identification and the substantial computational requirements associated with deep learning. The detection targets of most detection algorithms are normal or forest fires, and not ship fires, which have unique characteristics, when compared to other fires. In normal forest fires, the background is always land or forest, whereas in the case of ship fires, it is always water or the ocean. Different backgrounds may result in the former fire detection algorithm losing its accuracy, because the features of fire with a land background are significantly different from those with a sea background. Although a large number of algorithms use computer vision or deep learning for fire detection [15–18], most are aimed at fire or smoke detection for forests, rather than ships. The ship fire possesses a different background compared with fire in forests, and this may result in bad performance when using forest fire detection algorithms to detect ship fire. In addition, algorithms for forest fire detection are not sufficiently lightweight to be arranged on ships. And there are only a limited number of deep algorithms that can be used to detect ship fire [19–22], and all of them possess disadvantages. Park et al. [19] use yolo to detect engine room fires in ships with a high degree of accuracy. However, their detection targets are only fires in engine rooms, meaning that fires on board or in the living rooms are not considered. Xu et al. [20] design a multi-layer convolutional neural network to classify the fire hazard levels in ship cabins. However, all the data are not real data and are simulated by software, which may account for the algorithm not being applicable in the real world. Wu et al. [21] propose an improved YOLOv4-tiny algorithm for ship fire detection. Although the precision and recall increase after modification, both detection time and FPS decrease. Avazov et al.

propose an improved YOLOv7 algorithm for ship fire detection. Although the precision and recall improve after modification, the proposed dataset for training may have some shortcomings. About 2400 images are cut from videos, which account for more than half of the dataset: the video frames also have a similar background, which may result in the usage of the trained algorithm being limited. Above all, the existing algorithm has some disadvantages in detecting fire, including the fact they can only detect fire, and not smoke which is an important derivative of fire that can also be detected. In this study, we propose an improved YOLOv8 algorithm that considers both fire and smoke, and which provides a better performance (in terms of both detection speed and accuracy), when compared with other advanced algorithms after experiments. In addition, other improvements are also made to Ship-Fire Net to make it more accurate and faster. The specific work follows:

1. We created a dataset for ship fire detection that contained images of fires in both rooms and boards. After excluding similar images, we created labels manually to ensure the quality of fire and smoke.
2. We broadened the backbone network of YOLOv8n by adding a GhostnetV2-C2F module for long-range attention with an inexpensive operation.
3. We used spatial and channel reconstruction convolution (SCConv) to reduce redundant features with significantly lower complexity and computational costs for real-time ship fire detection.
4. We used omni-dimensional dynamic convolution is the multi-dimensional attention mechanism; on the one hand, this lowers the parameters, and on the other, it improves the models' capacity to comprehend contextual information and then improve precision.
5. We proposed a lighter and more accurate YOLOv8n algorithm, and named it "Ship-Fire net". Compared to the original YOLOv8n, it has fewer parameters, fewer FLOPs, and higher FPS when its accuracy is increased.
6. Ship fire nets can also detect smoke, which other ship fire-detection algorithms ignore.

The remainder of the paper is structured as follows: Section 2 discusses the present development status of fire detection technologies and target detection techniques in the areas of machine learning and deep learning. Section 3 presents the improved lightweight convolutional neural method for ship fire detection ("Ship-Fire Net") in detail. Section 4 illustrates the details of how the datasets were built, and also outlines the establishment of the experimental environment settings and the evaluation index. Section 5 discusses the selection of the original algorithms and ablation tests, and also offers a comparison that considers ship fire nets against ship fire detection algorithms proposed by other researchers. Finally, Section 6 concludes the paper, discusses its limitations and outlines future research directions.

2. Literature Review

There are two primary classifications of fire detection strategies for visual recognition: conventional detection approaches that rely on picture characteristics, and detection methods based on deep learning principles. Previous studies in the field of visual identification have primarily used feature extraction techniques, including flame-specific chromatograms, forms, textures, and flame motion. A significant issue associated with these conventional approaches is the intricate nature of the manual feature extraction process. Deep learning-based detection approaches can automatically extract intricate picture details and features, thus efficiently addressing the issues of duplication and interference associated with human image feature extraction. Hence, recent scholarly investigations have primarily focused on the utilization of deep-learning techniques for fire detection, and their outcomes have consistently shown enhanced precision rates and reduced false alarm rates. Fire-detection methods based on color features have also been widely studied.

2.1. Machine Learning

In previous research, scientists have used color, texture, flame shape, and flame motion features to identify or detect features. Celik et al. used the [5] YC_bC_r color rather than RGB to separate luminance from chrominance, and found that YC_bC_r was more effective. Khalil et al. [23] proposed a novel fire-detection method based on a combination of RGB and CIL $L*a*b$ color models. Poobalan et al. [24] used RGB and HSL filters to detect the color of a fire with bag-of-features (BoF), in order to ascertain the classification and calculation of the rate. Vipin [25] presented a new algorithm that uses the RGB and YC_bC_r color space and tests two sets of images. The Lucas–Kanade optical flow algorithm was proposed to calculate the optical flow of candidate fire and smoke [26], and the determination of potential smoke areas was achieved by using a background estimate and a color-based decision procedure.

Flame-texture feature extraction is often used in the detection and identification of fires, including by Cui et al. [27], who presented a method for analyzing the texture of fire smoke by combining two innovative texture analysis tools: wavelet analysis and gray-level co-occurrence matrices (GLCM). Yu et al. [28] proposed a method for real-time fire smoke detection based on the GLCM, which featured a neural network that could be used to classify smoke texture features from non-smoke texture features. Chino et al. [29] provided an innovative approach for detecting fires in static images, and introduced an approach that used color feature classification in conjunction with texture classification in superpixel areas. Ye et al. [30] proposed a novel dynamic texture descriptor by putting forward a surface transform and hidden Markov tree (HTM) model.

In addition to the extant research that has examined color and texture characteristics, fire detection algorithms that rely on flame shape features and flame motion data have also been used. Foggia et al. [7] applied complementary information based on color, shape variation, and motion analysis, and then combined it with a multi-expert system. Subsequently, a novel descriptor based on the bag-of-words approach was proposed to represent motion. Chi et al. [31] built fire detection systems based on chromatic, dynamic, textural, and contour features by using a novel algorithm to extract moving regions and analyze the frequency of flickers.

As described above, many techniques have been proposed for extracting flame characteristics that have significantly contributed to the progress of visual fire detection and improved its accuracy. However, the detection accuracy has been negatively affected by the human extraction of features under fire conditions, because of their inherent complexity.

2.2. Deep Learning

In recent years, the advent of powerful GPUs and TPUs that can handle the intense computational demands of deep learning algorithms has significantly accelerated the development of deep learning. Such developments have also accelerated research into the use of deep learning algorithms for fire detection or motivation. In general, deep learning algorithms can be divided into two categories: one-stage detectors, such as the single-shot multibox detector (SSD) [32], including You Only Looking Once (YOLO) [33], and RetinaNet [34]; and two-stage detectors, such as R-CNN [35], Fast R-CNN [36], Faster R-CNN [37], and Mask R-CNN [38]. The two-stage algorithms operate in two steps: first, regions of interest (ROIs) where objects might be located are proposed, before the bounding boxes of regions are classified, refined and widely used for fire detection. Zhang et al. [39] employed a Faster R-CNN to detect wildland forest fires, and, in seekingto address the scarcity of training data (whose deficiency hampers the development of robust models), generated synthetic smoke pictures, in a process that involves the incorporation of (authentic or simulated) smoke into the forest backdrop. Chaoxia et al. [40] presented an improved and Faster R-CNN method to detect flames, which included a color-guided anchoring strategy and embedded global information-guided flame detection; and Barmpoutis et al. [41] presented a method that combined a Faster R-CNN network with linear dynamic systems (LDS) to locate fire regions.

In addition to two-stage algorithms, one-stage algorithms are also widely used in fire detection, and this is because of their elegant pose structure and faster detection speed. For example, Li et al. [42] tested the fire detection performance of advanced object detection CNN models (Faster-RCNN, R–FCN, SSD, and YOLO v3), and found that YOLO v3 had the highest FPS and precision. Zhao et al. [15] proposed an improved YOLO algorithm, Fire-YOLO, that could be used to detect fires, and particularly small targets, in fire scenarios; Dou et al. [43] used YOLOv5s, in cooperation with a convolutional block attention module (CBAM), along with MobileNetV3, ShuffleNetV2, and GhostNet, to achieve the goal of a lightweight algorithm; and Talaat presented the smart fire detection system (SFDS), which uses the improved YOLOv8 to monitor fires in smart cities.

The research mentioned above was not specifically aimed at ship fires, and mostly concentrated on forest fires or fires in cities. Few studies have focused on ship fires. Kim et al. [44] proposed an innovative method that integrates composite channel data, namely, RGB and IR channels, to enhance the effectiveness of fire detection in image-based systems by using convolutional neural networks (CNNs); Park et al. [19] used YOLO to detect fires in the engine room of a ship. Xu et al. [20] proposed an evaluation model based on a CNN that could determine the hazard levels of different cabins in a real-time fire; Wu et al. [21] proposed a modified YOLOv4-tiny algorithm for detecting ship fires; Avazov et al. [22] used YOLOv7 with an improved E-ELAN (extended efficient layer aggregation network) for fire detection and monitoring; and Zhu et al. [45] improved the YOLOv7-tiny model to enhance fire detection performance in a ship engine room. However, these studies have several limitations, which are shown in Table 1. In this study, we created better datasets and used a lighter algorithm (Ship-Fire Net) than the one applied in the other studies. FPS means frames per second, which is always regarded as an important measure for objection detection. The fire spreads fast in ships and needs to be monitored in real-time, and high FPS ensures that a timely response is forthcoming. In addition, a high frame rate per second (FPS) in surveillance and monitoring systems facilitates the real-time processing of video feeds, allowing prompt identification of fire or smoke as they occur. In our research, we have managed to build a lighter weight algorithm and achieve a higher FPS than preceding studies, and we are confident this will contribute to timely fire detection that will reduce response time when ship fires occur.

Table 1. Summary of research that used CNN for ship fire detection.

Name	Based Algorithm	Datasets	Advantages	Disadvantages	FPS
Park et al. [19]	YOLOv2-tiny	5259 images	High accuracy	Only detects fire; smoke is ignored; it focuses on the fire in the engine room.	117
Wu et al. [21]	YOLOv4-tiny	2160 images	Use land dataset to train the model and transfer the weights	Small datasets for ship fire; data augmentation is used to enlarge datasets.	138
Avazov et al. [22]	YOLOv7	4622 images	Both fire inside and outside vessels are used	Data augmentation is used to enlarge datasets; some data are video frames and may possess high similarity.	175
Zhu et al. [45]	YOLOv7-tiny	12,986 images	Large datasets	The fire is simulated; the algorithm ignores the fire in other rooms and the deck.	189
Ours	YOLOv8n	4227 images	Both fire and smoke are detected. All images are checked for similarity. Fast detection speed.	Inside and outside fire images for ships show quantity variance	286

3. Materials and Methods

3.1. Model Structure of the YOLOv8n Network

The YOLOv8 model is a sophisticated iteration that integrates the fundamental design ideas of YOLOv5 and YOLOv7 ELAN, its predecessorsYOLOv5 and YOLOv7 ELAN, as shown in Figure 1. The proposed model maintains the essential structure of YOLOv5 while integrating new features and improvements to boost its effectiveness and adaptability. The YOLOv8 model integrates innovative elements, including a redesigned backbone network architecture, an anchor-free detection head, and a revolutionary loss function. The product line offers a diverse range of models of different sizes, including N/S/M/L/X scales that were calibrated by using scaling factors.

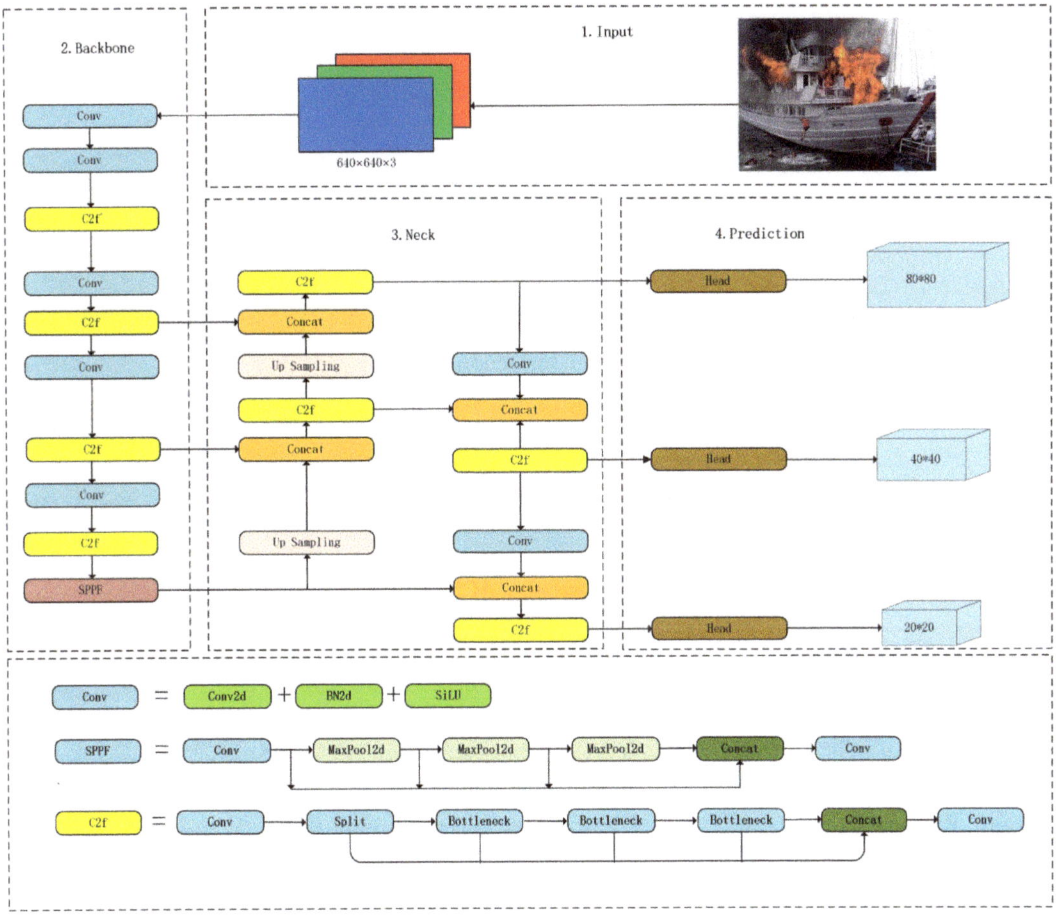

Figure 1. Structure of the YOLOv8n network.

The head of YOLOv8 underwent significant modifications, and a decoupled head structure was used to separate the classification and detection heads, before the detection head was converted from an anchor-based to an anchor-free approach. The Loss computation in this study utilized the task-aligned-assignment method to allocate positive samples and distribute focal losses. In addition, a data enhancement component was used by employing the mosaic enhancement strategy during the last ten epochs of the YOLOX model. This methodology has been shown to substantially improve the accuracy of the model. In summary, YOLOv8 is an advanced model that improves the achievements of its predecessor (YOLO), and achieves this by introducing innovative features and enhancements. The product line offers various models of different sizes and incorporates various design adjustments to improve performance and flexibility.

3.2. Using GhostNetv2 for Cheap Operation with Long-Range Attention

In YOLOv8, conventional convolution and C2F modules were employed to effectively perform feature extraction and image downsampling, resulting in superior quality outcomes. Nevertheless, the inclusion of an upsampling procedure in the neck component and the utilization of the Bi-PAN–FPN resulted in a notable augmentation of both the model parameters and its overall complexity. To reduce the number of parameters and complexity of the backbone, this study incorporates the Ghostblock and double-fully-connected DFC attention idea from Ghostnetv2 [46] into the backbone and uses this structure to replace some C2f modules, in order to achieve cheap operation with long-range attention. GhostNetV2 [29] introduced a hardware-friendly attention mechanism known as DFC attention. This mechanism aims to enhance the long-distance dependence of feature maps by incorporating them after regular convolution and cheapening operations. The goal is to increase the expressiveness and diversity of the feature maps, thereby enhancing the detection performance of the model. The lightweight feature extraction structure C2F-GhostNetV2 was designed by using the benefits of the GhostNetV2Bottleneck, as shown in Figure 2.

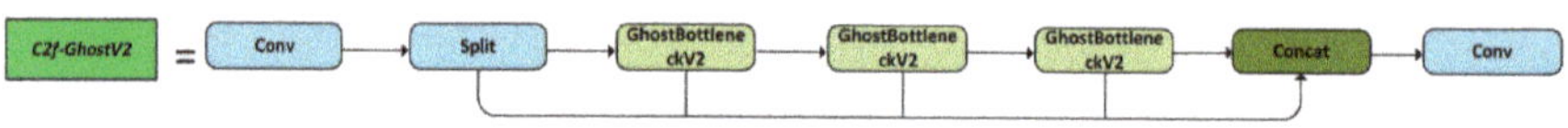

Figure 2. The architecture of the C2F-GhostNetV2 block.

The GhostNetV2Bottleneck is a type of inverse residual bottleneck comprising two ghost modules, as shown in Figure 3. The primary ghost module augments the number of feature channels, whereas the secondary ghost module decreases the channel count to provide output features. The present strategy successfully mitigates the issue of excessive interdependence between model expressiveness and capacity [30], thereby addressing the problem of overfitting during training and inadequate generalization ability during testing. The attention branch of the DFC model is designed to capture the long-range correlation between pixels located at distinct spatial locations. The use of the DFC attention branch in conjunction with the first ghost module augmented the feature characteristics. Subsequently, the improved features are received by the second host module, which generates the output features, thereby improving the performance of the model.

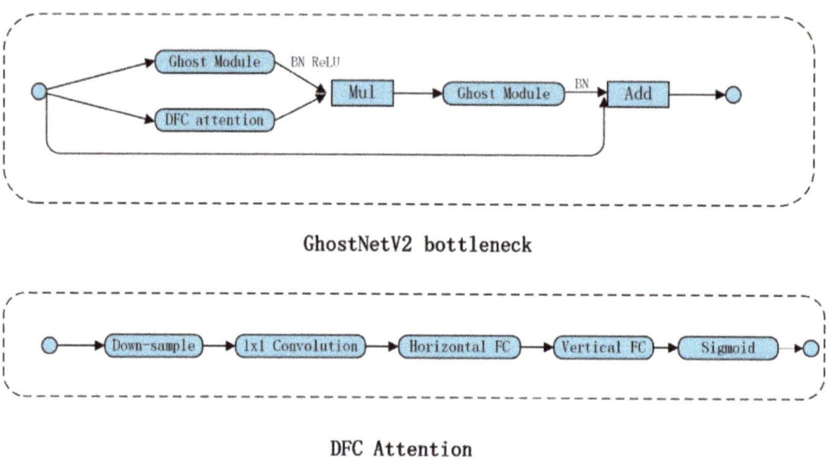

Figure 3. The architecture of the GhostNetV2 bottleneck and DFC attention.

3.3. Using SCConv for Feature Redundancy Reduction

CNNs have been widely used in various computer vision tasks because they can obtain representative features [24]. Nevertheless, achieving such success is strongly dependent on the availability of extensive computational and storage capabilities, which presents significant hurdles to the efficient deployment of these technologies in contexts with limited resources. To address these issues, researchers have investigated many approaches, such as model compression methodologies and network designs, with the aim of enhancing network efficiency. The former includes network pruning, weight quantization, low-rank factorization, and knowledge distillation. While such strategies are useful for compressing the model size, they do not always result in reduced accuracy. The latter includes ResNet [10] and DenseNet [14], which minimize the inherent redundancy in dense model parameters and advance the development of a more lightweight network mode. Nevertheless, the aforementioned approaches mostly concentrate on reducing redundancy, whether in the channel or spatial dimensions, with the consequence that networks continue to encounter challenges associated with feature redundancy. SCConv appears to be a good solution to problems of this kind, as it exploits the redundancy of intermediate feature maps and reduces the parameters and computation without performance loss. SCConv uses a two-step procedure, spatial reconstruction unit (SRU) and channel reconstruction unit (CRU), to reduce the number of parameters and FLOPs (see Figure 4).

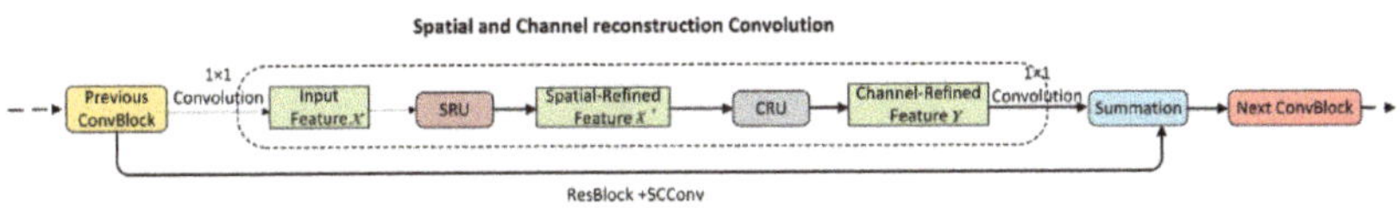

Figure 4. The architecture of SCConv integrated with a SRU and a CRU.

Through these two procedures, the feature representation capability was also strengthened. The SRU can be considered a process of Separate-and-Reconstruct operation, as shown in Figure 5.

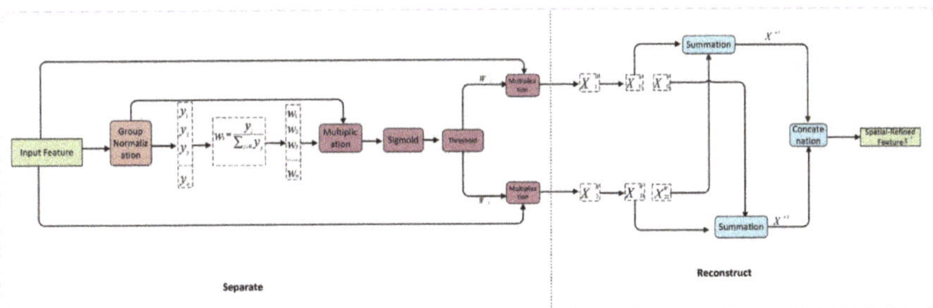

Figure 5. The architecture of the Spatial Reconstruction Unit (SRU).

The objective of the separate operation is to distinguish and isolate relevant feature maps from less informative counterparts that correspond to the spatial content. The informative content of various feature maps was evaluated by using scaling factors in the group normalization (GN) layers [29]. The trainable parameters of the GN layers were used to quantify the spatial variation in the pixels within each batch and channel. The increased richness of spatial information is indicative of greater diversity in spatial pixels, which in turn contributes to the enlargement of the parameters. The weight values of the feature maps were subsequently adjusted and used to map the range between 0 and 1 by applying a sigmoid function. These values were then subjected to a gating threshold. Finally, the feature maps were given multiple informative and non-informative weights. The outcomes of the feature map times the noninformative weights were regarded as redundant. For the reconstruction operation, rather than directly including these two components, a cross-reconstruction process was used to effectively merge the weighted informative features and enhance the information exchange between them. Subsequently, the cross-reconstructed features were concatenated to obtain spatially refined feature maps.

Subsequently, the CRU method uses a split-transform-and-use approach (shown in Figure 6), and this was done to further reduce the duplication present in the spatially refined feature maps throughout the channel dimension. In addition, the CRU algorithm utilizes lightweight convolutional operations to extract valuable representative features, while efficiently eliminating redundant features by using inexpensive operations and feature-reuse techniques. Generally, CRU can be used alone or in conjunction with SRU operations. The proposed SCConv was established by organizing the SRU and CRU sequentially, resulting in a highly efficient convolution operation with the potential to replace ordinary convolutions.

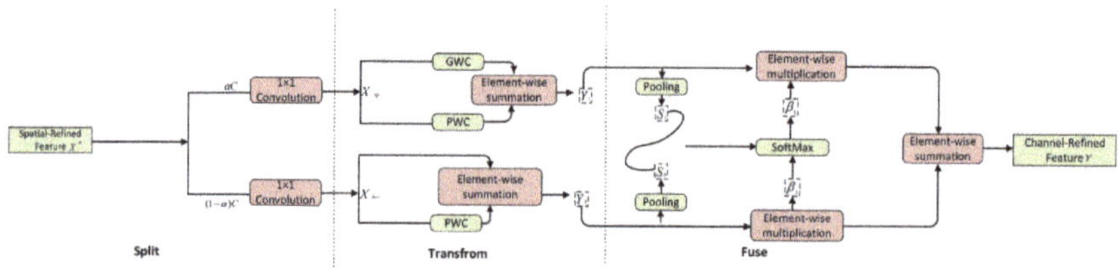

Figure 6. The architecture of the channel reconstruction unit (CRU).

3.4. Omin-Dimensional Dynamic Convolution for Multi-Dimensional Attention Mechanism

Traditional approaches to dynamic convolution often use attention techniques to dynamically adjust the weights of the convolution kernels in a single dimension of the kernel space. As shown in Figure 7, input variable x is subjected to an initial global average pooling (GAP) operation, and subsequently it undergoes further processing via fully connected (FC) layers and activation functions, namely, the Rectified Linear Unit (ReLU). Unlike traditional dynamic convolutions, ODConv has four separate header branches, which are each equipped with a fully connected layer and a Softmax or Sigmoid activation function. A mathematical representation of this process can be described by using (1): by integrating dynamic convolutions, the model acquires the capacity to flexibly modify the weights of the convolution kernels in response to the distinctive characteristics of the input data. This enhances the ability of the model to combine and integrate features. Consequently, the ability of the model to perceive and capture high-frequency information, such as intricate visual features and textures, was strengthened, resulting in improved performance and accuracy.

$$y = \left(\alpha_{\omega 1} \odot \alpha_{f1} \odot \alpha_{c1} \odot \alpha_{s1} \odot W_1 + \cdots + \odot \alpha_{\omega n} \odot \alpha_{fn} \odot \alpha_{cn} \odot \alpha_{sn} \odot W_{1n}\right) * x. \quad (1)$$

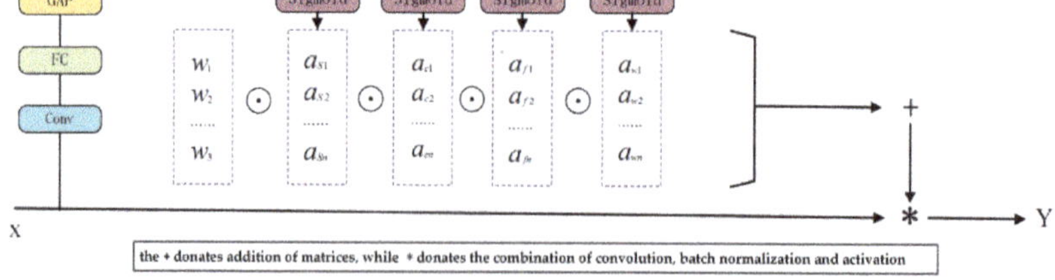

Figure 7. Schematic of an omni-dimensional dynamic convolution.

The attention mechanism in the ODConv framework was designed to function across four dimensions of kernel space: location, channel, filter, and kernel. The use of complementary attention mechanisms in a convolution operation allows the integration of varying attention at each stage, resulting in diverse influences acting on each dimension of the input. This methodology enables more efficient use of geographical data and produces better results when collecting complex contextual information. The integration of ODConv into the slim-neck design successfully mitigated the negative consequences associated with the significant use of lightweight convolution kernels and depth-wise convolutions. This improved the capacity of the model to comprehend contextual information and spatial dimensions, which in turn improved the precision and resilience of job detection.

3.5. Structure of the Ship-Fire Net

Figure 8 shows the structure of the improved YOLOv8n (Ship-Fire Net) for ship fire and smoke detection. In the case of the backbone part, spatial and reconstruction convolution were used to replace the traditional convolution part in the first C2F module reduction of feature redundancy, which created a new C2F-SCConv module. The GhostNetV2 bottleneck was then used to replace the original bottleneck in the fourth C2F part, in order to achieve cheap operation with long-range attention. In the case of the neck part, omni-dimensional dynamic convolution was used for the multidimensional attention mechanism, which improved the precision and resilience of detection.

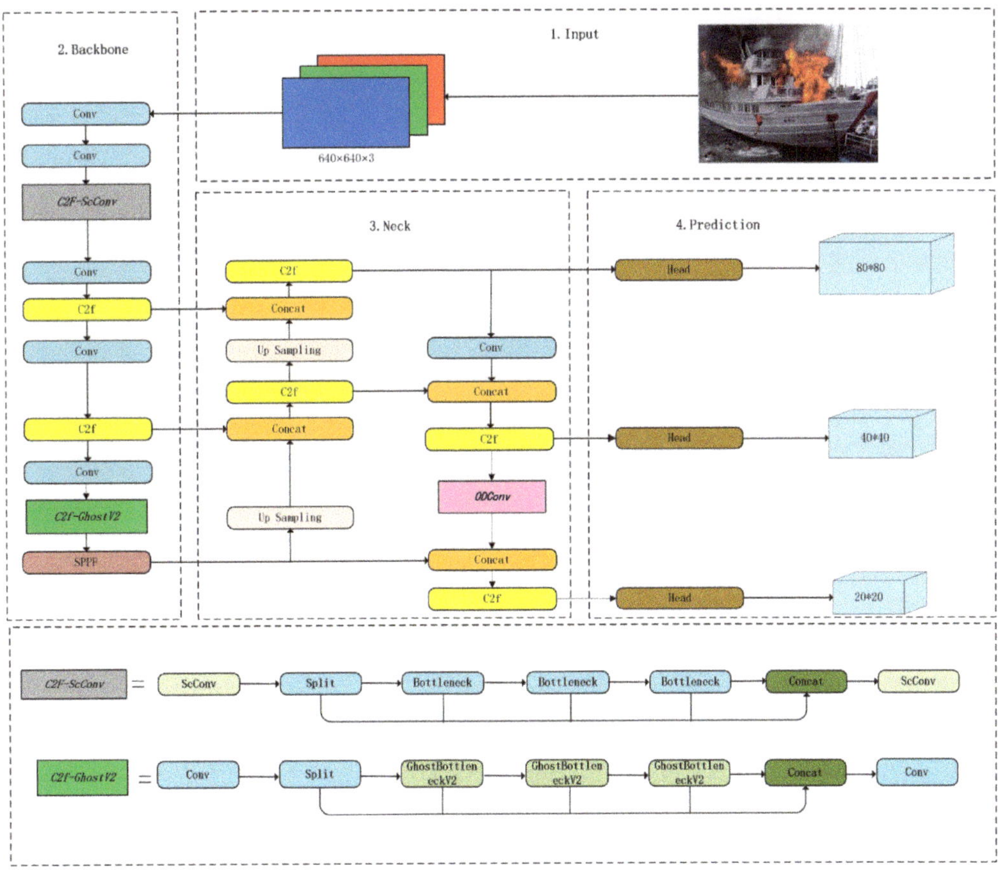

Figure 8. The architecture of proposed model (Ship-Fire Net).

4. Data Collection and Experimental Setting

4.1. Ship Fire Data Set Collection

Ship fires may occur inside ships, such as in cargo control rooms, fire control and storage rooms, or stevedore cabins. When these fires occur, the background is dissimilar to fires that occur on the deck. Therefore, to simulate fire in the vessels, we considered two types of datasets: fire inside vessels and fire outside vessels. When a fire occurs inside vessels, the first reaction of passengers or sailors is to put out the fire rather than record it with a camera, making the fire inside the ship slightly harder to find. The foundation of the dataset consists of two parts of the main job: searching the ship fire images and using labeling tools to locate the position of fire and smoke in the images. To achieve the first goal, large search engines like Baidu and Google are used to search keywords such as 'ship + fire', 'ship + fire + rooms', 'ship + smoke', and so on. Then, in order to save the time that would otherwise need to be committed to downloading the images one by one, python was used as the web crawler to download the images. All the images were checked for copyright for academic purposes. One problem in the collection of datasets is image repetition, as different websites may possess the same images, which may be downloaded by web crawlers. To improve the diversity of the dataset, all images are pre-processed before being labeled by using the Visual Similarity Duplicate Image Finder software (Figure 9). The version of it is 8.3.0.1. This software can change the score of similarity from 0–100 percent, and scan the whole folder to find and list similar images. Images with a similarity higher than 90 percent will be regarded as duplicates and will be deleted to ensure the quality of the datasets and performance of the algorithm.

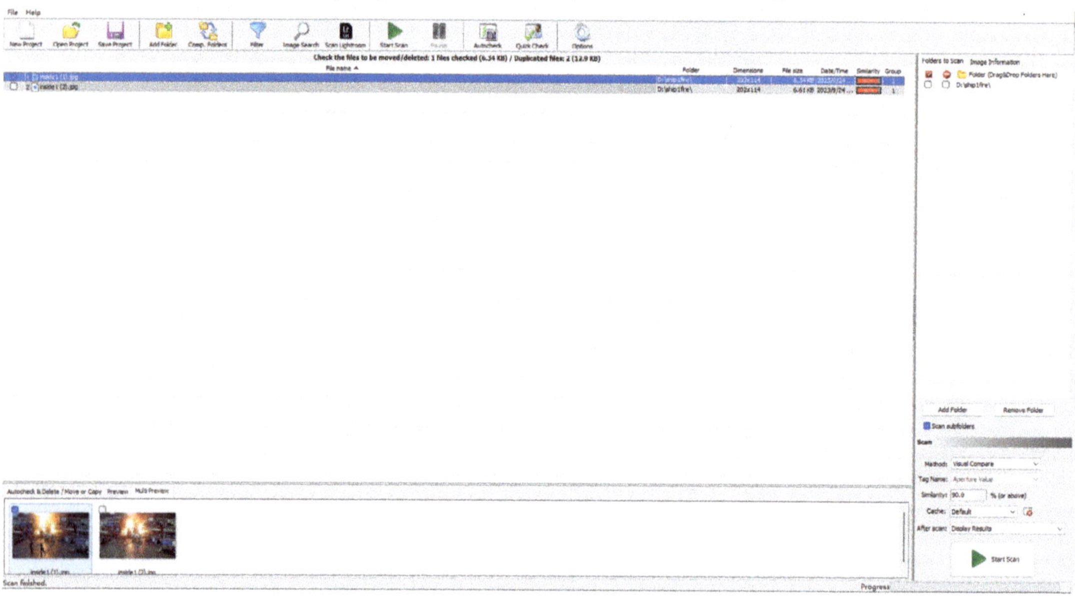

Figure 9. The pre-process before labeling using Visual Similarity Duplicate Image Finder.

After these processes, 576 'inside' and 3651 'outside' fire images were selected. Samples of onboard fires are shown in Figure 10, and samples of fires inside rooms are shown in Figure 11.

After the collection of datasets, researchers then used 'LabelMe' to label fire and smoke in the images. All fires and smoke use a rectangular box to indicate their location and can then be extracted as feature maps for the CNN network. All labels were written in TXT format. The labels are made and located by researchers, and so the theme and content of images can be guaranteed to be ship fire. The labels and images were renamed as a one-to-one correspondence, and each image had its corresponding label. When compared to the other datasets of ship fire, our datasets are distinguished by the fact that they divide ship fire images into two categories: ship fire inside rooms and ship fire on board—this is done to ensure the algorithm can be used in the whole ship. In addition, the other datasets just consider the fire, while our dataset, in considering fire detection, considers both fire and smoke, which is important because smoke is an important signal of fire. All the datasets were uploaded to Google Drive, which is shown here: https://drive.google.com/drive/folders/118jiofV1EVOwY715T_zeCdk6zpkLErlp?usp=drive_link (accessed on 11 November 2023). There are two subfolders entitled 'inside_' and 'outside_', which respectively relate to onboard fire inside rooms and fire outside rooms. The images and labels are also numbered, and correspond to each other in 'inside' and 'outside' subfolders.

Figure 10. Example of the ship fire and smoke datasets (outside).

Figure 11. Example of the ship fire and smoke datasets (inside).

The images were folder images, and their corresponding labels were folder labels. They were divided as follows: 70% for training, 10% for testing, and 20% for validation, as shown in Table 2. The visualization results of the dataset analysis are presented in Figure 12. In Figure 12a, the distribution of the object centroid positions is depicted, with the abscissa and ordinate representing the centroid positions. Figure 12b illustrates the distribution of the object sizes, with the abscissa and ordinate representing the width and height of the object, respectively. The data revealed a higher concentration of targets in the middle area, and a majority of these targets were small. This observation aligns with real-world fire situations and substantiates the claim that our algorithm is effective in detecting fires during their early stages, when they have smaller dimensions.

Table 2. Distribution of fire images in the dataset.

Dataset	Training Images	Testing Images	Validation Images	Total
Fire in ship room	2556	730	365	3651
Fire on board	403	115	58	576

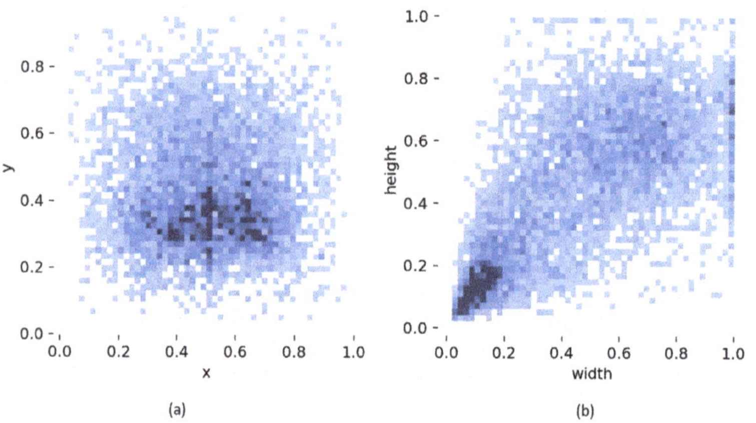

Figure 12. Visualization results of the analysis of the dataset. (**a**) Distribution of object centroid locations; (**b**) distribution of object sizes.

4.2. Experimental Environment

The present study was carried out with an Ubuntu 20.04 operating system, employing an 11th Generation Intel i9-11950H central processing unit and an RTX A5000 graphics processing unit in Intel, Singapore. The GPU acceleration environment was established by using CUDA 11.3, and the network architecture was constructed by employing Python 3.9 and PyTorch 1.11.1. The study's development platform was Visual Studio Code version 1.75.0.

4.3. Hyperparameter Setting

All experiments were performed by using the same listed hyperparameters to demonstrate the effectiveness of the proposed method, as shown in in Table 3.

Table 3. Training parameters of the ship fire detection model.

Training Parameters	Details
Epochs	300
batch-size	16
image-size (pixels)	640 × 640
Initial learning rate	0.01
Optimization algorithm	SGD
Pre-training weights	None

4.4. Model Evaluation Metrics

The evaluation of model performance often involves the use of two criteria to assess its strengths and limitations. Recall, accuracy, and mean average precision (MAP) are typically used as measures for assessing a model's detection capabilities. The metrics used to assess the detection speed and computational complexity of the model include parameters such as the floating point operations (FLOPS) and frames per second (FPS). In this study, the precision was used as a determinant to assess the accuracy of the model. Accuracy was defined as the ratio of correct positive predictions (TP) to the overall number of positive outcomes (TP + FP) projected by the model, and was significantly affected by the presence of a significant number of false positives (forest fire [26]). The range 0–1 was calculated with precision by using the following methodology:

$$\mathbf{P(Precision)} = \frac{\mathbf{TP}}{\mathbf{TP + FP}}. \tag{2}$$

Recall is defined as the proportion of correctly identified positive instances (true positives) relative to the sum of true positives and false negatives. The recall can be determined by using the following mathematical expression:

$$\mathbf{R(Recall)} = \frac{\mathbf{TP}}{\mathbf{TP + FN}}. \tag{3}$$

The F1-score is defined as the harmonic mean of Precision and Recall. The definition can be stated as follows:

$$\mathbf{F_1} = \mathbf{2} \times \frac{\mathbf{Precison \times Recall}}{\mathbf{Precison + Recall}}. \tag{4}$$

The concept of average precision (AP) refers to a measure of precision that encompasses all elements within a specific category of pills, as outlined in Equation (5):

$$\mathbf{AP} = \int_0^1 \mathbf{P(R)dR}. \tag{5}$$

The MAP was calculated as the arithmetic mean of the average precision (AP) values obtained for each category in the dataset. This metric was used to assess the overall model performance. This definition is illustrated in Equation (6):

$$\mathbf{mAP} = \frac{\mathbf{1}}{\mathbf{N}} \sum\nolimits_{i=1}^{N} \mathbf{AP_i} \tag{6}$$

The complexity of each model was assessed by using characteristics such as FLOPs and FPS. The parameters of the CNN model refer to the variables obtained and modified by the network during training. The number of parameters in a CNN model is determined by its architectural configuration, which includes variables such as the number of layers, dimensions of filters, and number of neurons in each layer. Models with more layers and neurons often demonstrate a corresponding increase in the number of parameters. The total number of parameters in a CNN model is a crucial factor that significantly influences the complexity of the model, memory requirements, and training time. Models that are more complex and have a larger number of layers and neurons tend to have more parameters, and consequently require longer training times. In addition to these characteristics, the computational efficiency of the model is influenced by the number of floating-point operations per second. Floating-point operations are mathematical calculations that involve actual numbers with fractional components, and they play a crucial role in CNNs for various computational tasks that include convolutions, matrix multiplications, element-wise operations, and nonlinear activations. In the CNN context, standard procedures include the application of operations to the input data and the learnable parameters of the network, namely weights and biases. The results of these procedures include the generation of forecasts and the creation of characteristic representations. The use of floating-point operations is crucial for facilitating the effective processing and manipulation of numerical information inside CNNs, and these procedures enable precise and sophisticated calculations that are necessary for a range of activities, such as picture categorization, object recognition, and image synthesis. FLOPS pertains to the investigation of floating-point operations in CNNs within the wider context of scholarly inquiry, which involves scrutinizing the computing demands linked to the different layers and operations. This study provides an examination of optimization approaches to reduce computational complexity, and also gives insight into research into hardware accelerators and parallelization methodologies. A significant emphasis in this field of research is the development of algorithms and models that can effectively balance accuracy and computing efficiency. The acronym "FPS" refers to the measurement of the frequency at which frames, or visual representations, are processed or created inside a CNN model or computer vision system. The FPS measure is of great significance within the domain of CNNs because it plays a crucial role in assessing the computational efficiency and real-time capabilities of jobs related to image or video processing, which are both useful to assessments of the performance of the ship-fire networks.

5. Results and Discussion

5.1. Based Algorithms Selection

The training procedure for each experiment involved the utilization of six well-established object detection algorithms: Faster R-CNN ResNet50 [29], SSD MobileNet_V1 [30], SSD Inception_V2 [31], swin transformer [47], Densenet [48], YOLOv3-tiny [33], YOLOv5s [49], YOLOv7-tiny [50], and YOLOv8n [51]. These algorithms were specifically trained for fire detection by using internally generated datasets. The findings of these studies and their corresponding comparisons are summarized in Table 4.

Table 4. Results of classical advanced deep learning algorithms.

Models	Precision	Recall	F1	mAP@50	Parameters (m)	FLOPS (G)	FPS
ResNet50	0.524	0.531	0.53	0.494	42.25	430.9	30
MbileNet_V1	0.675	0.542	0.60	0.581	5.53	13.2	72
Inception_V2	0.689	0.701	0.69	0.644	13.32	7.6	53
swin transformer	0.741	0.681	0.71	0.623	28	47.1	45
densenet	0.671	0.612	0.64	0.563	66.76	32.7	35
YOLOv3-Tiny	0.797	0.821	0.81	0.745	8.7	12.9	140
YOLOv5s	0.901	0.855	0.88	0.814	7.02	16	114
YOLOv7-tiny	0.857	0.7921	0.82	0.758	6.02	13.2	143
YOLOv8n	0.897	0.907	0.90	0.856	3.01	8.2	192

YOLOv5s has superior recall compared to the other models; however, its accuracy, recall, F1, and map metrics are not as efficient as YOLOv8n. Both the precision and recall of yolov8n reached about 0.9 and the mAP@50 attained arrives 0.856. Taking into account the primary objective of this research, namely to develop a lighter and faster detection model, the speed of detection should be considered in conjunction with accuracy metrics. The weight of the model was then assessed by using the FLOPs and parameters. YOLOv8n's parameters are only 3.01 million, the lowest among the algorithms. YOLOv8n can also detect 192 frames per second on average, which is faster than the others. While Inception_V2 may exhibit some benefits in terms of FLOPs, it falls far short of YOLOv8n in terms of parameters and FPS. In addition, YOLOv8n's precision, recall and mAP@50 all exceed the Inception_V2 counterparts. The experimental findings for the five widely used detection algorithms indicate that YOLOv8n has notable benefits, in terms of both accuracy and efficiency. We therefore chose YOLOv8n as the initial model for future enhancements and improvements.

5.2. Ablation Tests Results

Eight ablation experiments were conducted to examine the impact of the various approaches. All experimental groups used identical datasets, training settings, and methodologies for training. The empirical findings are presented in Table 5.

The first row in Table 5 shows the results of the original YOLOv8n network without any improvement measures. Compared to the original YOLOV8n, all three new models became lighter and faster after the GhostNetV2, ODConv, or SCConv modules were inserted to replace the original part. Especially when GhostNetV2 was used in the algorithm, the FLOPS reduced to 7.85 (G) and FPS reached above 220. In addition, map@0.5, ODConv, and SCConv increased by 1.1% and 2.0%, respectively. After all three different improvements to the algorithm, a ship-fire net was formed. Compared to the original, it improves exponentially by approximately 3.4%, 3.1%, 3.2%, and 4.1% in terms of precision, recall, F1, and map@0.5%, respectively. In addition, the parameter flops were the lowest in the three models, while its FPS exceeded 280. In summary, after the improvements and modifications, the Ship-Fire Net's precision and recall both reached about 0.93 and the detection speed also improved, as reflected by the decrease in the parameters and Flops and the increase of FPS.

The precision–epoch and recall-epoch curves are shown in Figure 13. As the number of training epochs increases, both the precision and recall curves become larger for the two algorithms. When the number of epochs exceeds 200, the proposed model is significantly different from the original YOLOv8n model.

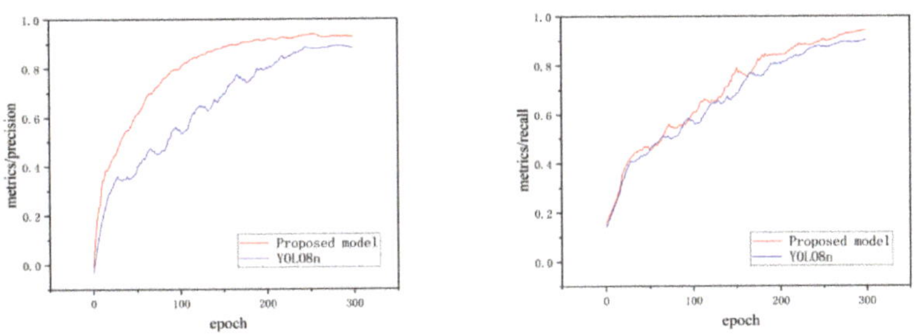

Figure 13. Precision–epoch and recall-epoch curve.

This system was tested in real-world scenarios with rooms inside the vessels and vessels. Figures 14 and 15 illustrate fire detection under different conditions.

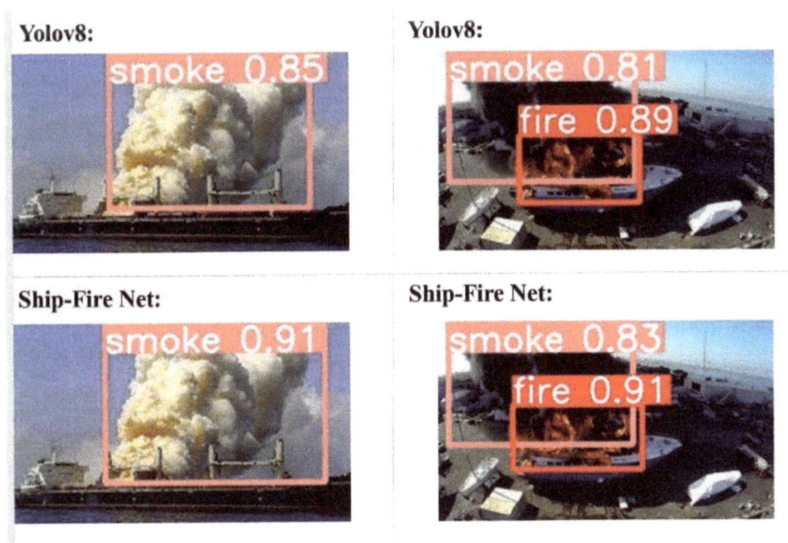

Figure 14. Results of Ship-Fire Net and YOLOv8n for outside images.

Figure 15. Results of Ship-Fire Net and YOLOv8n for inside images.

Table 5. Results of ablation experiments.

Models	Precision	Recall	F1	mAP@0.5	Parameters (m)	FLOPS (G)	FPS
YOLOv8n	0.897	0.907	0.902	0.856	3.01	8.2	192
YOLOv8n + ODConv	0.913	0.912	0.912	0.867	3	8.1	213
YOLOv8n + GhostNetV2	0.908	0.916	0.912	0.859	2.72	7.85	222
YOLOv8n + SCConv	0.915	0.914	0.914	0.876	3	8.1	217
YOLOv8n + GhostNetV2 + ODConv	0.926	0.929	0.927	0.862	2.71	7.75	263
YOLOv8n + GhostNetV2 + SCConv	0.924	0.932	0.928	0.887	2.71	7.75	278
YOLOv8n + ODCONV + SCConv	0.928	0.933	0.930	0.841	2.99	8	270
YOLOv8n + GhostNetV2 + ODConc + SCConv (Ship-Fire Net)	0.931	0.938	0.934	0.897	2.69	7.65	286

6. Discussions and Limitations

The success of the novel system can be attributed to the ability of the YOLOv8 model to localize fires and smoke, both in rooms and onboard. The efficiency and performance of a system may vary under various conditions, such as lighting variations, smoke, variable sensitive environmental factors, and obstructions. The foundation of the two categories of datasets and the labeling work of smoke and fire helped to achieve this, and ensure that the algorithm could be strongly implemented after the training process for fire and smoke detection purposes. When compared to other advanced object detection algorithms, YOLOv8 was found to provide higher-class results in detecting fires in bright and dark lighting, recognizing small fires and flames, and distinguishing between fire and non-fire scenarios. To make it lightweight, several improvements to GhostnetV2, SCConv, and ODConv were implemented. After these improvements, the parameters and FLOPs significantly improved, which also accounted for the higher FPS. We have also searched relevant studies about ship fire detection by using CNNs, and tried to use their algorithms for training on our datasets. Table 6 records recently published fire detection methods and compares them with the proposed method.

The results in Table 6 confirm that Ship-Fire Net showed great performance in both accuracy and detection speed. Compared to the Tiny-YOLOv2 model, YOLOv4-tiny model, YOLOv7 model, and YOLOv7-tiny model, the mAP@0.5 Of the Ship-Fire Net increased by 10.8%, 9.3%, 8.4% and 5.2%, respectively. Precision increased by 11.8%,6.8%,6.3%, and 5.9%, while recall enhanced by 13.9%, 10.2%, 8.6%, and 6.9%, respectively. In addition to flame detection, Ship-Fire Net also achieved a high detection accuracy rate for smoke, as shown by a mAP@0.5 that reached 0.884. The detection speed was also guaranteed to beabove 200 FPS, and our model is also the fastest one of the five. In conclusion, Ship-Fire Net outperforms the other algorithms that seek to achieve ship fire detection in mAP@0.5, accuracy, and recall, and also don't manage to achieve lightweight real-time ship fire detection.

Table 6. Comparison of detection consequence of the ship fire detection algorithms proposed by others and Ship-Fire Net.

Name	Based Algorithm	FPS	Precision	Recall	F1	mAP@0.5
Park et al. [19]	Tiny-YOLOv2	117	0.813	0.799	0.806	0.789
Wu et al. [21]	YOLOv4-tiny	138	0.863	0.836	0.849	0.804
Avazov et al. [22]	YOLOv7	175	0.868	0.852	0.860	0.813
Zhu et al. [45]	YOLOv7-tiny	189	0.872	0.869	0.870	0.845
Ship-Fire Net	YOLOv8n	286	0.931	0.938	0.934	0.897 (fire at 0.911 while smoke at 0.884)

However, our dataset and algorithm still have some limitations. Firstly, our study only focused on the presence or absence of fire, without considering its extent and progression. This study is also confined to the realm of algorithms, and therefore neglects practical applications. During the course of the trial, several photos, including objects resembling fire, were correctly identified as fire. If a picture exhibits the presence of luminous sunshine, highly saturated yellowish-red lights, or incandescent bulbs such as fire, it may be identified as a depiction of fire. In addition, ships, and especially large cargo ships or large cruise ships, may have a large number of cameras to capture fire or smoke images from different angles for detection. However, on small ships the lack of cameras or detection systems may result in the algorithm not being applicable and useful. Last but not least, there is a significant category disproportion between the 576 interior ship fire images and the 3651 exterior ship fire images. This is because, when a ship fire happens, passengers or sailors who observe the fire will always try to first extinguish the fire rather than record it on phones or cameras. When a fire happens on board, passengers, whether on other ships or on land, may help to record the fire.

To deal with such limitations, we must not only focus on the occurrence of a fire but also conduct comprehensive investigations of post-fire circumstances, including by examining the progression of the fire and analyzing the crew's evacuation routes. In addition, we intend to integrate the established techniques and algorithms to enhance the performance of the model. For instance, we may include long short-term memory (LSTM), a widely used approach in the domain of natural language processing, as well as the temporal difference method, which is often used in conventional moving object identification research. For fire-like objects, we will expand the datasets and create labels for fire-like objects to train the model, thereby reducing the false alarm rate. And in seeking t deal with the concern of long-distance fire or blocked fire in small ships, we will to combine our fire detection system with traditional temperature sensors and smoke sensors; with the help of traditional sensors, even long-distance fire or blocked fire can be detected in the early stage. And finally, in engaging the category disproportion problem, we will try to arrange drills about ship fire inside rooms and record them for further studies, as this will balance the category disproportion.

7. Conclusions

In conclusion, we propose an improved and faster version of a fire detection system for ships using the YOLOv8n architecture. Thorough experiments and system evaluation, we demonstrated that the proposed system is highly efficient in detecting real-time fires and smoke in challenging environments. To achieve this goal, we first attempted to create a dataset that contained both fire in the rooms of a ship and fire onboard, which ensures that the algorithm can be used and works well both onboard and in rooms. All images were checked for similarity and labeled manually. After comparing the performance of several selected advanced objections, we found that, although YOLOv5s had the best performance in precision, YOLOv8n had a better detection consequence for index recall, F1, and mAP@.5.

In addition, YOLOv8n has the fastest detection speed of all advanced models, which enables it to achieve real-time ship fire detection. After improvements under the same settings, we trained and evaluated the 'YOLOv8n + Ghostnetv2 + SCConv + ODConv' (Ship-Fire Net) and other competitors in ablation tests. The results indicate that the proposed algorithm exhibits the best performance for accuracy and speed. The accuracy and recall of our proposed Ship-Fire net are 0.931 and 0.938 respectively, and its F1 score is 0. 934. When compared to the original YOLOV8n, the modified algorithm was found to outperform it in terms of precision, recall, F1, and exponentially, by 3.4%, 3.1%, and 3.25% respectively, which underlined it would be able to detect and locate fire and smoke more accurately. In addition, the proposed model had lower FLOPs and parameters, and its FPS reached 280, which satisfied the requirements for real-time ship fire detection. After comparison with the other algorithms proposed for ships, our algorithm was found to have a wide usage range, the highest FPS, and to be the lightest. Finally, our algorithm can detect both fire and smoke, and its mAP@50 reaches 0.911 and 0.884 respectively, which proves that our model can effectively detect fire and its derivative(smoke). The detection of smoke can facilitate the detection of flame and improve the reliability of the detection system.

Author Contributions: Methodology, Z.Z.; Software, Z.Z.; Validation, L.T.; Formal analysis, L.T.; Data curation, Z.Z. and L.T.; Writing—original draft, Z.Z.; Writing—review & editing, R.L.K.T.; Supervision, R.L.K.T. All authors have read and agreed to the published version of the manuscript.

Funding: This research received no external funding.

Institutional Review Board Statement: Not applicable.

Informed Consent Statement: Not applicable.

Data Availability Statement: Data are contained within the article.

Conflicts of Interest: The authors declare no conflict of interest.

References

1. Luo, M.; Shin, S.-H. Half-century research developments in maritime accidents: Future directions. *Accid. Anal. Prev.* **2019**, *123*, 448–460. [CrossRef] [PubMed]
2. Allianz Global Corporate & Specialty. *Safety and Shipping Review 2023*; Allianz Global Corporate & Specialty SE: Hong Kong, China, 2023.
3. Truong, C.T.; Nguyen, T.H.; Vu, V.Q.; Do, V.H.; Nguyen, D.T. Enhancing Fire Detection Technology: A UV-Based System Utilizing Fourier Spectrum Analysis for Reliable and Accurate Fire Detection. *Appl. Sci.* **2023**, *13*, 7845. [CrossRef]
4. Marbach, G.; Loepfe, M.; Brupbacher, T. An image processing technique for fire detection in video images. *Fire Saf. J.* **2006**, *41*, 285–289. [CrossRef]
5. Çelik, T.; Demirel, H. Fire detection in video sequences using a generic color model. *Fire Saf. J.* **2009**, *44*, 147–158. [CrossRef]
6. Chenebert, A.; Breckon, T.P.; Gaszczak, A. A non-temporal texture driven approach to real-time fire detection. In Proceedings of the 2011 18th IEEE International Conference on Image Processing, Brussels, Belgium, 11–14 September 2011; IEEE: New York, NY, USA, 2011.
7. Foggia, P.; Saggese, A.; Vento, M. Real-time fire detection for video-surveillance applications using a combination of experts based on color, shape, and motion. *IEEE Trans. Circuits Syst. Video Technol.* **2015**, *25*, 1545–1556. [CrossRef]
8. Mueller, M.; Karasev, P.; Kolesov, I.; Tannenbaum, A. Optical Flow Estimation for Flame Detection in Videos. *IEEE Trans. Image Process.* **2013**, *22*, 2786–2797. [CrossRef]
9. Wang, S.; He, Y.; Yang, H.; Wang, K.; Wang, J. Video smoke detection using shape, color and dynamic features. *J. Intell. Fuzzy Syst.* **2017**, *33*, 305–313. [CrossRef]
10. Zhao, J.; Zhang, Z.; Han, S.; Qu, C.; Yuan, Z.; Zhang, D. SVM based forest fire detection using static and dynamic features. *Comput. Sci. Inf. Syst.* **2011**, *8*, 821–841. [CrossRef]
11. Ko, B.; Kwak, J.-Y.; Nam, J.-Y. Wildfire smoke detection using temporospatial features and random forest classifiers. *Opt. Eng.* **2012**, *51*, 017208-1–017208-10. [CrossRef]
12. Khatami, A.; Mirghasemi, S.; Khosravi, A.; Lim, C.P.; Nahavandi, S. A new PSO-based approach to fire flame detection using K-Medoids clustering. *Expert Syst. Appl.* **2017**, *68*, 69–80. [CrossRef]
13. Dunnings, A.J.; Breckon, T.P. Experimentally defined convolutional neural network architecture variants for non-temporal real-time fire detection. In Proceedings of the 2018 25th IEEE International Conference on Image Processing (ICIP), Athens, Greece, 7–10 October 2018; IEEE: New York, NY, USA, 2018.

14. Shen, D.; Chen, X.; Nguyen, M.; Yan, W.Q. Flame Detection Using Deep Learning. In Proceedings of the 2018 4th International Conference on Control, Automation and Robotics (ICCAR), Auckland, New Zealand, 20–23 April 2018; IEEE: New York, NY, USA, 2018.
15. Zhao, L.; Zhi, L.; Zhao, C.; Zheng, W. Fire-YOLO: A Small Target Object Detection Method for Fire Inspection. *Sustainability* **2022**, *14*, 4930. [CrossRef]
16. Xu, R.; Lin, H.; Lu, K.; Cao, L.; Liu, Y. A Forest Fire Detection System Based on Ensemble Learning. *Forests* **2021**, *12*, 217. [CrossRef]
17. Talaat, F.M.; ZainEldin, H. An improved fire detection approach based on YOLO-v8 for smart cities. *Neural Comput. Appl.* **2023**, *35*, 20939–20954. [CrossRef]
18. Xiao, Z.; Wan, F.; Lei, G.; Xiong, Y.; Xu, L.; Ye, Z.; Liu, W.; Zhou, W.; Xu, C. FL-YOLOv7: A Lightweight Small Object Detection Algorithm in Forest Fire Detection. *Forests* **2023**, *14*, 1812. [CrossRef]
19. Park, K.-M.; Bae, C.-O. A Study on Fire Detection in Ship Engine Rooms Using Convolutional Neural Network. *J. Korean Soc. Mar. Environ. Saf.* **2019**, *25*, 476–481. [CrossRef]
20. Xu, H.; Yuan, W.; Yu, M. Real-time Classification of Ship Cabins Fire Hazard Levels Based on CNN. In Proceedings of the 2019 Chinese Automation Congress (CAC), Hangzhou, China, 22–24 November 2019; IEEE: New York, NY, USA, 2019.
21. Wu, H.; Hu, Y.; Wang, W.; Mei, X.; Xian, J. Ship Fire Detection Based on an Improved YOLO Algorithm with a Lightweight Convolutional Neural Network Model. *Sensors* **2022**, *22*, 7420. [CrossRef] [PubMed]
22. Avazov, K.; Jamil, M.K.; Muminov, B.; Abdusalomov, A.B.; Cho, Y.-I. Fire Detection and Notification Method in Ship Areas Using Deep Learning and Computer Vision Approaches. *Sensors* **2023**, *23*, 7078. [CrossRef] [PubMed]
23. Khalil, A.; Rahman, S.U.; Alam, F.; Ahmad, I.; Khalil, I. Fire Detection Using Multi Color Space and Background Modeling. *Fire Technol.* **2020**, *57*, 1221–1239. [CrossRef]
24. Poobalan, K.; Liew, S.-C. Fire detection based on color filters and Bag-of-Features classification. In Proceedings of the 2015 IEEE Student Conference on Research and Development (SCOReD), Kuala Lumpur, Malaysia, 13–14 December 2015; IEEE: New York, NY, USA, 2015.
25. Vipin, V. Image processing based forest fire detection. *Int. J. Emerg. Technol. Adv. Eng.* **2012**, *2*, 87–95.
26. Chunyu, Y.; Jun, F.; Jinjun, W.; Yongming, Z. Video Fire Smoke Detection Using Motion and Color Features. *Fire Technol.* **2010**, *46*, 651–663. [CrossRef]
27. Cui, Y.; Dong, H.; Zhou, E. An early fire detection method based on smoke texture analysis and discrimination. In Proceedings of the 2008 Congress on Image and Signal Processing, Sanya, China, 27–30 May 2008; IEEE: New York, NY, USA, 2008.
28. Chunyu, Y.; Yongming, Z.; Jun, F.; Jinjun, W. Texture analysis of smoke for real-time fire detection. In Proceedings of the 2009 Second International Workshop on Computer Science and Engineering, Qingdao, China, 28–30 October 2009; IEEE: New York, NY, USA, 2009.
29. Chino, D.Y.T.; Avalhais, L.P.S.; Rodrigues, J.F.; Traina, A.J.M. Bowfire: Detection of fire in still images by integrating pixel color and texture analysis. In Proceedings of the 2015 28th SIBGRAPI conference on Graphics, Patterns and Images, Salvador, Brazil, 26–29 August 2015; IEEE: New York, NY, USA, 2015.
30. Ye, W.; Zhao, J.; Wang, S.; Wang, Y.; Zhang, D.; Yuan, Z. Dynamic texture based smoke detection using Surfacelet transform and HMT model. *Fire Saf. J.* **2015**, *73*, 91–101. [CrossRef]
31. Chi, R.; Lu, Z.M.; Ji, Q.G. Real-time multi-feature based fire flame detection in video. *IET Image Process.* **2017**, *11*, 31–37. [CrossRef]
32. Liu, W.; Anguelov, D.; Erhan, D.; Szegedy, C.; Reed, S.; Fu, C.Y.; Berg, A.C. Ssd: Single shot multibox detector. In Proceedings of the Computer Vision–ECCV 2016: 14th European Conference, Amsterdam, The Netherlands, 11–14 October 2016; Proceedings, Part I 14. Springer: Berlin/Heidelberg, Germany, 2016.
33. Redmon, J.; Divvala, S.; Girshick, R.; Farhadi, A. You only look once: Unified, real-time object detection. In Proceedings of the IEEE Conference on Computer Vision and Pattern Recognition, Las Vegas, NV, USA, 27–30 June 2016.
34. Lin, T.-Y.; Goyal, P.; Girshick, R.; He, K.; Dollár, P. Focal loss for dense object detection. In Proceedings of the IEEE International Conference on Computer Vision, Venice, Italy, 22–29 October 2017.
35. Girshick, R.; Donahue, J.; Darrell, T.; Malik, J. Rich Feature Hierarchies for Accurate Object Detection and Semantic Segmentation. In Proceedings of the IEEE Conference on Computer Vision and Pattern Recognition, Columbus, OH, USA, 23–28 June 2014.
36. Girshick, R. Fast r-cnn. In Proceedings of the IEEE International Conference on Computer Vision, Santiago, Chile, 7–13 December 2015.
37. Ren, S.; He, K.; Girshick, R.; Sun, J. Faster R-CNN: Towards real-time object detection with region proposal networks. In Proceedings of the Advances in Neural Information Processing Systems 28 (NIPS 2015), Montreal, QC, Canada, 7–12 December 2015; Volume 28.
38. He, K.; Gkioxari, G.; Dollár, P.; Girshick, R. Mask r-cnn. In Proceedings of the IEEE International Conference on Computer Vision, Venice, Italy, 22–29 October 2017.
39. Zhang, Q.-X.; Lin, G.-H.; Zhang, Y.-M.; Xu, G.; Wang, J.-J. Wildland Forest Fire Smoke Detection Based on Faster R-CNN using Synthetic Smoke Images. *Procedia Eng.* **2018**, *211*, 441–446. [CrossRef]
40. Chaoxia, C.; Shang, W.; Zhang, F. Information-Guided Flame Detection Based on Faster R-CNN. *IEEE Access* **2020**, *8*, 58923–58932. [CrossRef]

41. Barmpoutis, P.; Dimitropoulos, K.; Kaza, K.; Grammalidis, N. Fire detection from images using faster R-CNN and multidimensional texture analysis. In Proceedings of the ICASSP 2019—2019 IEEE International Conference on Acoustics, Speech and Signal Processing (ICASSP), Brighton, UK, 12–17 May 2019; IEEE: New York, NY, USA, 2019.
42. Li, P.; Zhao, W. Image fire detection algorithms based on convolutional neural networks. *Case Stud. Therm. Eng.* **2020**, *19*, 100625. [CrossRef]
43. Dou, Z.; Zhou, H.; Liu, Z.; Hu, Y.; Wang, P.; Zhang, J.; Wang, Q.; Chen, L.; Diao, X.; Li, J. An Improved YOLOv5s Fire Detection Model. *Fire Technol.* **2023**, 1–32. [CrossRef]
44. Kim, D.; Ruy, W. CNN-based fire detection method on autonomous ships using composite channels composed of RGB and IR data. *Int. J. Nav. Arch. Ocean Eng.* **2022**, *14*, 100489. [CrossRef]
45. Zhu, J.; Zhang, J.; Wang, Y.; Ge, Y.; Zhang, Z.; Zhang, S. Fire Detection in Ship Engine Rooms Based on Deep Learning. *Sensors* **2023**, *23*, 6552. [CrossRef]
46. Tang, Y.; Han, K.; Guo, J.; Xu, C.; Xu, C.; Wang, Y. GhostNetv2: Enhance cheap operation with long-range attention. *Adv. Neural Inf. Process. Syst.* **2022**, *35*, 9969–9982.
47. Liu, Z.; Lin, Y.; Cao, Y.; Hu, H.; Wei, Y.; Zhang, Z.; Lin, S.; Guo, B. Swin transformer: Hierarchical vision transformer using shifted windows. In Proceedings of the IEEE/CVF International Conference on Computer Vision, Montreal, BC, Canada, 11–17 October 2021.
48. Huang, G.; Liu, Z.; Van Der Maaten, L.; Weinberger, K.Q. Densely connected convolutional networks. In Proceedings of the IEEE Conference on Computer Vision and Pattern Recognition, Honolulu, HI, USA, 21–26 July 2017.
49. ultralytics, YOLOv5. Available online: https://github.com/ultralytics/yolov5 (accessed on 11 November 2023).
50. Wang, C.-Y.; Bochkovskiy, A.; Liao, H.-Y.M. YOLOv7: Trainable bag-of-freebies sets new state-of-the-art for real-time object detectors. In Proceedings of the IEEE/CVF Conference on Computer Vision and Pattern Recognition, Vancouver, BC, Canada, 18–22 June 2023.
51. ultralytics, YOLOv8. Available online: https://github.com/ultralytics/ultralytics (accessed on 11 November 2023).

sensors

MDPI

Article

Model-Based 3D Gaze Estimation Using a TOF Camera

Kuanxin Shen [1,†], Yingshun Li [2,*,†], Zhannan Guo [2], Jintao Gao [1] and Yingjian Wu [1]

1 School of Chemical Process Automation, Shenyang University of Technology, Liaoyang 111003, China; skx13188644041@smail.sut.edu.cn (K.S.); jintao.sut.edu.cn@smail.sut.edu.cn (J.G.); yingjianwu@smail.sut.edu.cn (Y.W.)
2 School of Control Science and Engineering, Dalian University of Technology, Dalian 116024, China; guozhannan@mail.dlut.edu.cn
* Correspondence: yingshun_li@smail.sut.edu.cn; Tel.: +86-13188644041
† These authors contributed equally to this work.

Abstract: Among the numerous gaze-estimation methods currently available, appearance-based methods predominantly use RGB images as input and employ convolutional neural networks (CNNs) to detect facial images to regressively obtain gaze angles or gaze points. Model-based methods require high-resolution images to obtain a clear eyeball geometric model. These methods face significant challenges in outdoor environments and practical application scenarios. This paper proposes a model-based gaze-estimation algorithm using a low-resolution 3D TOF camera. This study uses infrared images instead of RGB images as input to overcome the impact of varying illumination intensity in the environment on gaze estimation. We utilized a trained YOLOv8 neural network model to detect eye landmarks in captured facial images. Combined with the depth map from a time-of-flight (TOF) camera, we calculated the 3D coordinates of the canthus points of a single eye of the subject. Based on this, we fitted a 3D geometric model of the eyeball to determine the subject's gaze angle. Experimental validation showed that our method achieved a root mean square error of 6.03° and 4.83° in the horizontal and vertical directions, respectively, for the detection of the subject's gaze angle. We also tested the proposed method in a real car driving environment, achieving stable driver gaze detection at various locations inside the car, such as the dashboard, driver mirror, and the in-vehicle screen.

Keywords: model-based gaze estimation; TOF camera; YOLOv8 neural network; eye tracking on driver; low-resolution infrared image

1. Introduction

Gaze-estimation technology has been receiving increasing attention due to its significant application value. This technology has been applied in numerous fields such as computer communication and text input [1], human–computer interaction [2], virtual reality (VR) [3], psychological research [4], advertising and entertainment gaming [5], animation creation [6], and driver distraction monitoring [7]. Eyeball gazing is a form of non-verbal communication. By observing the gaze points of people in images or scenes, key information hidden in the images can be revealed. Before the application of convolutional neural networks (CNNs) in gaze estimation, the primary research methods for gaze estimation were traditional machine learning and methods based on eyeball geometric models. Mora et al. [8] used gaze appearance images as ground truth images, from which they built appearance models and used regression and KNN machine-learning methods to determine the gaze angle of the subjects. Wood [9] used 3D head scans and realistic rendering methods to create a synthetic eye image dataset and trained a gaze-estimation model on this dataset using machine-learning methods. Chen et al. [10] and Li et al. [11] created realistic 3D eyeball models through facial landmarks detection, allowing for 3D gaze estimation with just a single calibration from the subject. Their 3D eye model does not employ the corneal reflection points of external light sources mentioned by Guestrin et al. [12], a method which is capable of estimating the point of gaze only when the head is held completely still. Furthermore, 3D eye-modeling techniques that utilize corneal reflection points are often considered to be intrusive and unfriendly to the subject, as they constitute an invasive approach to gaze estimation.

Following the rapid advancements in the research and application of convolutional neural networks (CNNs) in the fields of computer vision and deep learning, numerous scientists have begun to incorporate CNNs into the domain of gaze estimation. Zhang et al. [13] proposed the first appearance-based deep gaze-estimation method, and MPIIGaze [14] has become a commonly used dataset for gaze estimation among researchers. Subsequently, Zhang et al. introduced a gaze-estimation method based on the full-face images of subjects [15]. Unlike Ref. [13], which only used the eye region images of the subjects as the model input, Ref. [15] used the entire face image as input, achieving more accurate gaze estimation on the MPIIGaze dataset than [13]. Park et al. [16] proposed a novel 3D gaze image representation method. They used a deep convolutional neural network architecture to handle the projections of the eyeball and iris in 3D space onto a two-dimensional map, and regressed on the map to obtain the gaze angle. Bâce et al. [17] combined appearance-based gaze estimation with optical flow in the eye region to jointly analyze single-channel eye movement dynamics.

In the current landscape of appearance-based gaze estimation, the most advanced model on the MPIIGaze dataset is FAZE [18], while the L2CS [19] model achieved the second-highest global performance ranking on both the Gaze360 and MPIIGaze datasets. These models perform exceptionally well in scenarios using visible light cameras. However, in situations such as nighttime driving tasks, models trained on RGB images prove to be ineffective. As Murthy et al. [20] noted, existing appearance-based gaze-estimation models lack generalization in driving tasks and have not been evaluated for deployment in real-world applications. Vasli et al. [21] proposed a geometry-based gaze-estimation method for drivers, utilizing the physical constraints of the automotive cockpit environment. However, their model, like that of Vora et al. [22], focuses on determining the gaze region of the driver rather than providing a specific and precise gaze angle. Shah et al. [23] believe that using visual area analysis to determine whether a driver is distracted is a fundamental concept. Their work achieved high precision in detecting the gaze angle of drivers in both vertical and horizontal directions. However, it is regrettable that they still only used visible light cameras. Vicente et al. [24] conducted commendable early research. They used a near-infrared camera and a visible light camera to track the driver's line of sight and evaluated the effects during both day and night. They particularly considered obstructions from sunglasses and extreme head pose. Their work was meticulous and reliable.

In contrast to the aforementioned studies, our proposed method for 3D gaze estimation, suitable for automobile drivers, exclusively utilizes infrared images. This approach is instrumental in overcoming the challenges posed by variations in lighting intensity in practical application scenarios, particularly enhancing its utility during nighttime. Considering economic factors in real-world applications, unlike [24], we do not employ multiple cameras, rather, we utilize a single time-of-flight (TOF) camera equipped with an infrared sensor. This study aims to explore a method for implementing 3D gaze estimation on low-resolution TOF cameras (see Figure 1) and to evaluate its accuracy and feasibility in real automotive driving situations. We trained a model using YOLOv8 to detect eye regions and landmarks to obtain the positions of eye landmarks including the pupils and left and right eye corners of the subjects. Then, we performed image distortion correction, followed by the calculation of the 3D coordinates of these eye landmarks using the depth image captured by the TOF camera. We then fit a 3D eyeball model in both horizontal and vertical directions, and on this basis, calculated the final gaze angle. Our primary contributions include:

- We propose a novel method for fitting a 3D eye model. This approach calculates the 3D center of the eyeball using just two eye corners of a single eye. By employing fewer constraint conditions, it reduces computational burden;
- We propose an infrared image dataset for gaze estimation, named "Infrared Gaze Dataset (IRGD)", created using a TOF camera with a low resolution of 300,000 (640 × 480) pixels and a precision of 1% within a working range of 1 m. This dataset features a larger gaze angle range than MPIIGaze, with participants freely moving their heads during the recording process. Our work aims to achieve gaze estimation under natural conditions;
- Using mean absolute error (MAE) and root mean square error (RMSE) as performance evaluation metrics, we assessed the gaze-estimation method presented in this paper on the benchmark dataset IRGD. We verified that the maximum absolute deviation in gaze angle detection of the proposed model is less than 9 degrees. Furthermore, the model's reliability in detecting the driver's line of sight angles was validated in real driving tasks with Toyota commercial vehicles.

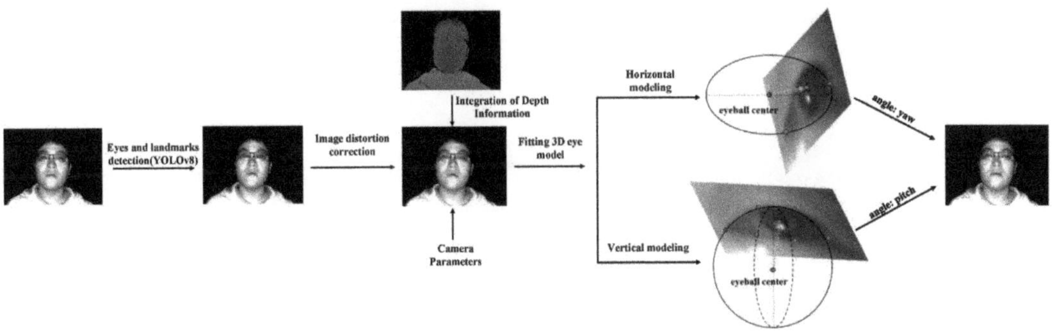

Figure 1. The overall process of the proposed model-based 3D gaze estimation using a TOF camera method. The green arrow represents the subject's gaze direction.

The remainder of this paper is organized as follows: Section 2 reviews existing gaze-estimation techniques. Section 3 provides a detailed introduction to our proposed IRGD dataset, comparing it with other publicly available gaze-estimation datasets. Section 4 elaborates on our gaze-estimation method using a TOF camera, including the computation for image distortion correction and detailed modeling of the eyeball model when subjects gaze in horizontal and vertical directions. Section 5 presents the accuracy and evaluation results of the gaze-estimation method proposed in this paper. We also ran five existing state-of-the-art gaze-estimation models on the benchmark dataset IRGD and compared their results with our work. Finally, we collected images of driver gaze during real driving tasks in a Toyota commercial SUV, and evaluated the detection results of the proposed model on these images. Section 6 concludes our work and provides prospects for further research.

2. Related Works

In this chapter, we briefly reviewed existing gaze-estimation methods and works related to the method or content of this paper, especially the facial landmarks detection and eyeball center localization methods.

2.1. Appearance-Based Gaze Estimation

Different classifications of existing gaze-estimation methods will yield different results when viewed from different angles. From the principle of gaze-estimation models, existing methods can be divided into model-based methods and regression-based methods [25], and regression-based methods can be further subdivided into feature-based methods and appearance-based methods. Feature-based methods learn the mapping function from eye features to gaze direction, with the offset vector between the inner eye corner and the pupil center being the most commonly used feature mapping. However, researchers have discovered a fact: when the tester looks in different directions, the inner eye corner will move [26]. Therefore, the inner eye corner cannot serve as a stable anchor point. Some researchers use the nostril position as the feature vector for regression, but thus far no researchers have confirmed which set of facial feature points is the most ideal [9]. Appearance-based methods learn the mapping relationship from the appearance of the eye to the gaze point or gaze angle, avoiding feature tracking. Park et al. [27] believe that there is a strong relationship between what the user is looking at and the appearance of the user's eyes. At present, the latest appearance-based methods are almost all implemented based on CNNs. Another study by Park et al. used a CNN architecture to train a stacked hourglass network on the synthetic image dataset UnityEyes to estimate eye area feature points, and on this basis, the gaze direction was obtained through regression [28]. However, as they stated, the most effective appearance-based methods are black-box solutions and understanding why and when they work may be a challenge. Furthermore, although the human eye indeed has three degrees of freedom of motion, due to the physiological relationship between the human eye and the head, people always turn their heads before moving their eyes when they gaze in a certain direction. Therefore, appearance-based gaze estimation is easily affected by head pose.

2.2. Model-Based Gaze Estimation

Compared with appearance-based methods, model-based methods can obtain more accurate gaze estimates, but they rely on high-resolution images to fit and track local features used to estimate geometric parameters [29]. A common practice is to use a high-resolution infrared camera to capture the corneal reflection points (Purkinje images) of the subject because the pupil of the eyeball can reflect infrared light well and thus the pupil position can be easily identified on infrared images [30]. By fitting the eyeball with the pupil and corneal reflection points, the direction of the subject's gaze can be detected with high accuracy on high-resolution infrared images.

Scientists introduced the concepts of visual axis and optical axis to analyze the gaze direction of the human eye. The angle between the visual axis and the optical axis is called the kappa angle, which is approximately 5°. Traditional model-based gaze-estimation methods need to use this physical relationship between the optical axis and the visual axis to solve for the visual axis. Chen et al. [10] proposed a model-based 3D gaze-estimation eyeball modeling method. They used a generic 3D face model composed of six rigid facial points to obtain the 3D coordinates of the subject's facial landmarks and then calculated the 3D coordinates of the canthus midpoint, eyeball center point, pupil point, and corneal center point of the subject's single eye in order to calculate the optical axis, and then calculate the 3D visual axis and gaze point position. LI et al. [11] used a research method similar to [10]. Although this traditional model-based gaze-estimation method avoids the intrusion on the subjects as in [12], their solution process is very complex and computationally intensive. Taking the work of [10] as an example, in the calibration process of the subject, for N calibration points, there are 7N equations, with 6N+5 unknowns. Compared with these previous works, we only use the two canthus points of the subject's single eye to approximate the position of the center of the 3D eyeball. This simple solution method is feasible in our research.

In subsequent model-based gaze-estimation methods, the gaze vector is defined as a line passing through the center of the eyeball to the iris [31]. This definition ignores the kappa angle between the optical axis and the visual axis, omits the calculation of deriving the visual axis from the optical axis, and is equally effective in detecting the gaze direction of the subject. The advantage of the model-based method is that it can consider changes in head pose more effectively than appearance-based methods [30]. This paper, like [8], uses a camera with depth information for gaze estimation under free head movement. The difference is that the depth camera we use also has infrared images.

2.3. Facial Landmarks Detection

In the current research, a commonality between model-based methods and appearance-based methods is the need for facial landmarks detection on the subject before gaze estimation. The purpose of detecting facial landmarks in appearance-based gaze-estimation methods is to calculate the head pose of the subject [30] and to standardize the image in conjunction with the head pose before inputting the subject's gaze image into the neural network [13,15,32,33], to reduce the negative impact of head pose on gaze estimation. Ref. [15] used Alexnet to perform appearance-based full-face gaze estimation on 37,667 images with facial landmarks, Ref. [30] used the open-source model of OpenFace [34] to detect the facial landmarks of the subjects, and ref. [28] used the Tensorflow framework to train a stacked hourglass network for detecting eye region feature points on the annotated synthetic dataset UnityEyes.

The purpose of facial landmarks detection in model-based gaze-estimation methods is to fit and solve the positions of each eye component. Ref. [24] uses the SDM tracker to detect the positions of seven eye landmarks, including the pupil point, on a single-eye image of the subject and calculates the 3D coordinates of the pupil based on this. In existing research methods for estimating the gaze of car drivers, Ref. [23] uses an improved YOLOv4 face detector to detect the driver's face. The YOLO series of neural networks are one-stage object-detection models, which are widely used in the field of artificial intelligence due to their fast detection speed, high accuracy, and ease of deployment. Unlike [23], this paper uses the open-source YOLOv8-pose [35] module to train a model for detecting the eye area and landmarks of the subject in infrared images on the IRGD dataset labeled with eye corner points, pupil points, etc.

YOLOv8 is an open-source convolutional neural network encompassing functionalities for object detection, instance segmentation, and landmark detection. By default, it utilizes the SiLU (sigmoid linear unit) activation function. The architecture of YOLOv8 comprises two primary components: the backbone and the head. The backbone, a modified version of CSPDarknet53, primarily serves as a feature extractor, responsible for deriving features from the input images. The head, consisting of multiple convolutional layers followed by a series of fully connected layers, is tasked with predicting the bounding boxes, object detection scores, and class probabilities for detected objects within the image. YOLOv8 employs CIoU (complete intersection over union) and DFL (distance-IoU front-end loss) for bounding box location loss, alongside BCE (binary cross-entropy) for classification loss. The network is standardly configured with 53 layers. In this study, the YOLOv8s neural network was utilized to train a subject's eye landmark detection model. The images input into the network were of a default size of 640 × 480 pixels. Upon invoking the trained landmark detection model for inference on single-subject gaze images within the test set, the model outputs a tensor of dimensions [2,27], where 2 corresponds to the detected left and right eyes of the subject, while 27 represents the detected attributes of a single eye. These attributes include the bounding box's position (x, y, w, h), the confidence of the bounding box, the probabilities associated with the categories, and the 2D coordinates and confidences of seven landmark points.

Data Augmentation

Data augmentation is an effective method to prevent overfitting in eye landmark detection models. As illustrated in Figure 2, we augment the images from the IRGD dataset using computer vision methods such as Gaussian filtering, mean filtering, median filtering, brightness enhancement, contrast enhancement, adding salt and pepper noise, horizontal flipping, rotation, and scaling. Through this approach, the amount of data used to train the eye landmark detection model in this study was increased by a factor of six from the original 75,000 images in the IRGD dataset, resulting in a total of 525,000 images. Furthermore, this paper divides the dataset into a training set and a testing set in a 4:1 ratio. These data augmentation techniques serve as a regularization mechanism for training neural network models in facial landmark detection. During the training process, data augmentation introduces randomness into the data fed into the network. This randomness is then mitigated in the test set to enhance the network's generalization ability. Implementing this practice is expected to improve the robustness of the facial landmark detection model in complex scenarios with variable lighting conditions.

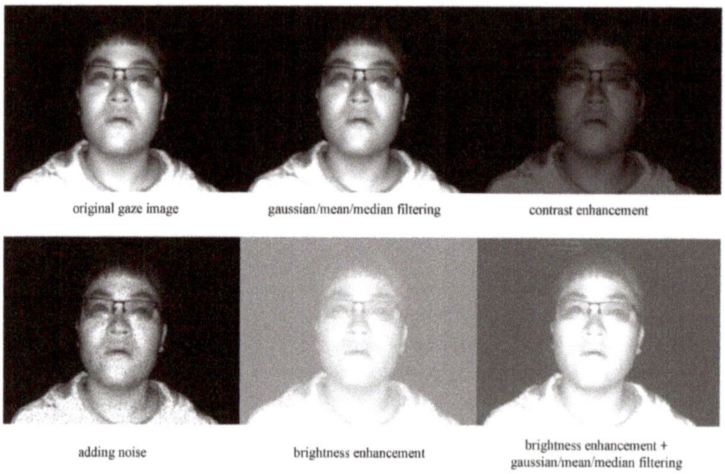

Figure 2. The partial effectiveness of data augmentation.

The eye landmarks detection model we trained, based on YOLOv8, outputs the coordinates of seven eye landmarks for a single eye image of the subject, including the left and right eye corners, the pupil, and the upper and lower eyelid points (see Figure 3). To improve work efficiency, we annotate the eye landmarks of participants on the IRGD dataset in a semi-automatic manner to quickly obtain training set data.

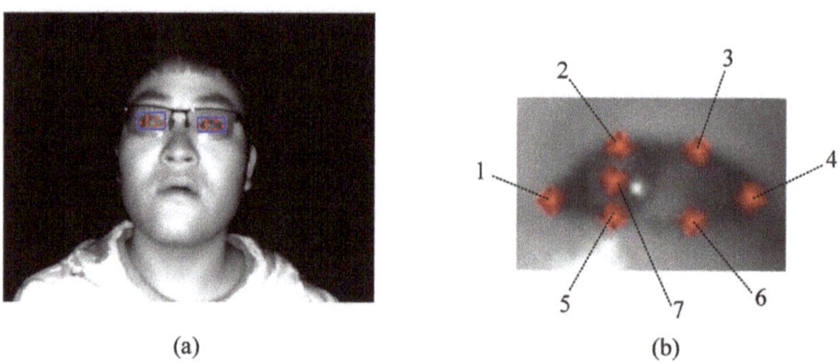

Figure 3. The eye region and landmark detection model trained on the IRGD dataset using YOLOv8 shows the detection effect on the subject's gaze image (**a**). The landmark detection model outputs 7 target points for a single-eye image of the subject (**b**): 1—Left eye corner point; 2—First upper eyelid point; 3—Second upper eyelid point; 4—Right eye corner point; 5—First lower eyelid point; 6—Second lower eyelid point; 7—Pupil point.

2.4. 3D Eyeball Center Positioning Method

The center of the eyeball is an eye component hidden outside the image, which cannot be directly observed in the gaze image like the eyelids and pupils. Existing model-based gaze-estimation literature varies in their computation and fitting methods for the 3D center of the eyeball. Refs. [10,11] detect the head pose angle and sequentially calculate the 3D pupil point coordinates and 3D corneal center point coordinates in the facial landmarks, then obtain the 3D coordinates of the eyeball through individual calibration of the subject. Their calculation method is quite complex. Vicente et al. [24] assumed that the eyeball is spherical and is at a rigid point relative to the head model, thereby approximating the 3D coordinate position of the eyeball. However, this is merely an approximate estimation method and unfortunately, they have not proven the effectiveness of their method.

2.4.1. Localization Method Based on Eye Corners and Eyeball Radius

Modern medical data on human eyeball anatomy indicate that the average radius of the human eye is 12 mm. In model-based gaze estimation, a novel method for locating the eyeball center involves obtaining the 3D coordinates of the left and right eye corners to compute the 3D midpoint of the eye corners. The eyeball center is then defined as the position 12 mm away from the eye corner midpoint in the Z-axis direction of the camera coordinate system, thereby transforming the model-based method into a calibration-free gaze-estimation method. Ref. [30] used the open-source OpenFace model to detect the head pose of the subject, combined with the 3D coordinates of the left and right eye corners and the constant value of the 12 mm eyeball radius to calculate the 3D coordinates of the subject's eyeball center. The subject's gaze angle is then computed based on this.

We replicated the eyeball center localization method mentioned in [30]. To eliminate the interference of head pose on the eyeball center localization method mentioned in [30], we calculated the horizontal gaze angle (yaw) on the gaze images of the subject's lizard movement collected by the TOF camera (see Figure 4). The feasibility of this 3D eyeball center localization method was judged by the absolute deviation size between the calculated gaze angle and the ground-truth angle. We manually annotated the left and right eye corner points and pupil points of these six images and strictly calculated the 3D eyeball center coordinates according to the eyeball center localization method of [30]. We found that within $\pm 30^\circ$ of small gaze angle calculation, the eyeball center localization method mentioned in [30] can obtain very accurate gaze estimation, with an absolute deviation angle value within 5°. However, this eyeball center localization method fails in gaze estimation at large angles greater than 30°.

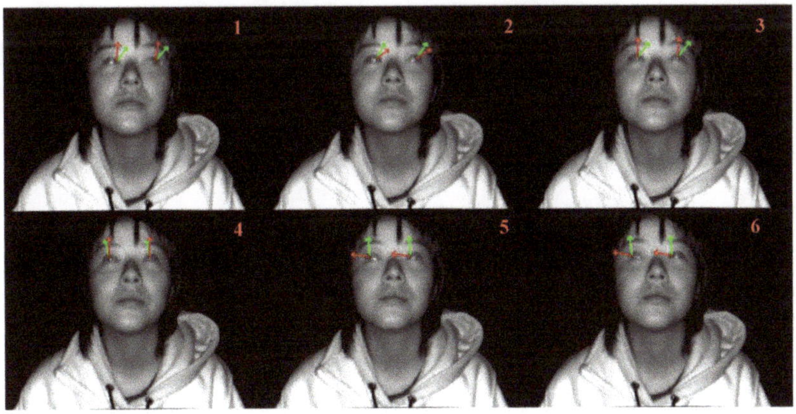

Figure 4. The subject maintained a head pose angle of 0° in both the horizontal and vertical directions and performed a series of coherent lizard movements. The green arrow indicates the ground-truth gaze direction, while the red arrow represents the final gaze direction obtained using the eyeball center calculation method proposed in [30]. As the subject's gaze angle gradually increased, the deviation between the gaze angle calculated by this eyeball center localization method and the ground-truth gaze angle began to increase. Table 1 shows the results of our calculations.

Table 1. The angle calculation results of gaze estimation based on the 3D eyeball center localization method mentioned in [30].

Number	Ground-Truth Yaw Angle [Degree]	Distance from Pupil to TOF Camera [mm]	Calculated Yaw Angle Value [Degree]	Absolute Deviation [Degree]
1	41.6	495.29	30.7	**10.9**
2	27.01	502.35	33.19	6.18
3	8.39	495.29	9.83	1.44
4	−12.3	498.82	−12.93	0.63
5	−30.39	498.82	−24.13	6.26
6	−43.54	502.35	−52.93	9.39

2.4.2. 3D Eyeball Fitting Based on Nonlinear Least Square Method

In the many methods of fitting the 3D eyeballs, we noticed a type of nonlinear least squares method. Like most studies [21,24], we assume that the eyeball is spherical. We replicated the method of fitting the eyeball in [36], solving for the coordinate values of the 3D eyeball center through eight marked points on a single-eye image (see Figure 5), with the number of marked points satisfying the condition of array size ≥ 5 required for the solving process. We collected images at approximate distances of 200 mm, 300 mm, and 400 mm from the TOF camera to the subject's head, and the radius values of the fitted 3D eyeball models are shown in Table 2.

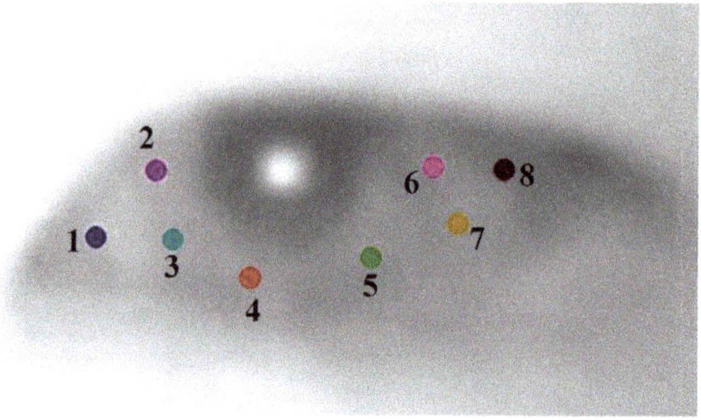

Figure 5. Eight marked points are manually annotated on the image of the subject's single eye. These points are randomly distributed on the sclera of the eye, not the cornea. We use these eight 3D coordinate points to fit the eyeball model and solve for the 3D coordinates of the eyeball center and the radius of the eyeball.

The nonlinear least squares method has demonstrated highly accurate fitting results in fitting the 3D eyeball model. As shown in Table 2 the fitted eyeball radius is very close to the average value of 12 mm of the human eye. However, it relies on high-resolution eye images and a large number of marked points. The more marked points involved in fitting the eyeball and the more dispersed the distribution of marked points on the sclera, the more accurate the solved eyeball model. However, obtaining as many marked points as possible on low-resolution images is a challenge. We collected detailed images of the eyes of subjects wearing glasses and not wearing glasses at different distances between 200 mm and 500 mm from a 300,000-pixel TOF camera (see Figure 6). When the distance between the subject's eyes and the TOF camera exceeds 300 mm, the contrast between the sclera and cornea severely decreases, and the only easily observable details in the subject's eye area are the corners of the eyes and the pupils. Therefore, the eyeball center locating method based on nonlinear least squares does not apply to the low-resolution infrared images used in this study. We propose a method to fit the 3D eyeball center using only the left and right corner points of a single eye (see Section 4.3). The subject only needs to undergo one calibration to complete the solution calculation.

Table 2. The radius value of the 3D eyeball model fitted using the method from [36].

The Distance from the Subject's Head to the TOF Camera [mm]	The Depth Values of Each Marked Point on the Depth Image [mm]								The Radius Value of the Eyeball [mm]
	1	2	3	4	5	6	7	8	
≈200	184.3	184.3	184.6	188.2	183.7	188.2	184.3	185.6	11.8
≈300	274.5	274.5	273.2	274.4	278.4	279.1	278.4	274.5	12.5
≈400	360.8	360.8	361.2	362.2	356.9	361.2	356.9	360.8	11.5

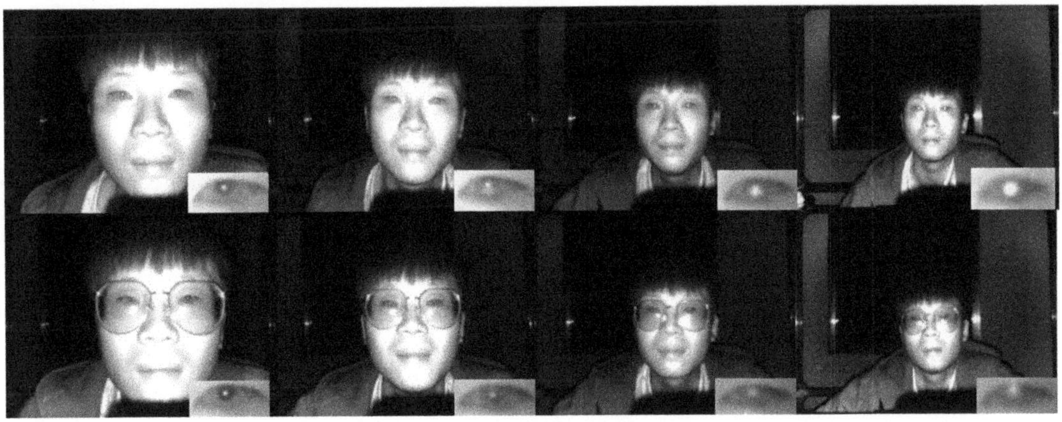

Figure 6. Eye detail images taken by the TOF camera at a distance of 200 mm–500 mm from the subject. The experiment is divided into two scenarios: the subject not wearing myopia glasses (**top**) and wearing glasses (**bottom**). The occlusion of glasses reduces some of the clarity and contrast of the subject's eyes, but it is much less than the impact of a longer distance. When the distance between the subject and the TOF camera exceeds 300 mm, the only observable details in the eye area are the corners of the eyes and the pupil points.

3. Dataset

To achieve stable 3D gaze estimation under various complex backgrounds and lighting conditions, we used a TOF camera equipped with an infrared sensor to record the benchmark dataset IRGD for gaze estimation. The use of an infrared camera can overcome the negative impact of uneven changes in lighting intensity on gaze estimation. The gaze-estimation model based on infrared images can operate in two different scenarios, day and night, which is extremely beneficial for the gaze estimation of car drivers and has been reflected in the work of [24].

3.1. Existing Dataset

Currently, many public datasets for gaze estimation have been generated in previous studies. Due to the different purposes and focuses of these studies, the characteristics of their public datasets also vary. Siegfried et al. [37] researched gaze estimation in conversation and operation scenarios and recorded the Gaze_VFOA dataset, which is a video dataset including three sub-datasets such as ManiGaze [38]. The ManiGaze dataset is especially used for assessing the gaze estimation of subjects during human–computer interaction. Other video datasets include EYEDIAP [39] and EVE [27], of which EVE was recorded on a computer monitor using a network port camera, aiming to estimate the gaze of subjects watching videos. Kellnhofer et al. recorded the large-scale gaze tracking dataset Gaze360 [40] which includes indoor and outdoor environments. They used the AprilTag image that was also used in the ManiGaze dataset during the recording process, which is convenient for marking target locations in 3D space. Similar to Gaze360, the MPIIGaze dataset is also used for gaze estimation in outdoor environments. This dataset is collected from subjects gazing at laptop screens in daily life. Due to the limitations of the recording scenario, the gaze angle range of the MPIIGaze dataset is relatively small. Due to the privacy protection set by the authors, researchers can only access the images of the eye area in the MPIIGaze dataset. If researchers want to explore the role of information from other parts of the face in gaze estimation, they can access the MPIIFaceGaze dataset, which comes from the same source as MPIIGaze. The latter is based on the former and provides complete facial area images and facial feature point annotations. For research on gaze estimation in extreme head poses, the ETH-XGaze dataset is often used. This dataset provides high-resolution images under extreme head pose and gaze directions with over a million samples [32]. The ETH-XGaze dataset contains images with a resolution of 24 MP (6000 $\times$ 4000 pixels). Another dataset with high-resolution images is Columbia [41], with an image resolution of 18 MP (5184 $\times$ 3456). However, the Columbia dataset only has 5880 images, and compared to the MPIIGaze dataset, Columbia has a smaller gaze angle range. Krafka et al. proposed a large-scale dataset, GazeCapture [42], for eye-tracking on mobile phones and tablets. The gaze-estimation model, iTracker, they developed based on the GazeCapture dataset was used in a commercial mobile phone software. Because this work is based on gaze estimation on small planes such as mobile phones or tablets, GazeCapture, like MPIIGaze, has the disadvantage of a smaller gaze angle range.

Synthetic datasets are another type of dataset commonly used in gaze-estimation work. Unlike real human eye gaze images, synthetic datasets are based on the scanning and reconstruction of real human eyes using 3D rendering models. However, this does not mean that synthetic datasets are not practical. In fact, synthetic datasets avoid the angle errors in the recording process of real eye datasets. For example, in our research experience, due to physiological factors, the subjects' eyes inevitably become tired during the long data-recording process, leading to errors in gaze angle. The recording process of real human eye datasets requires the subjective cooperation of the subjects. Sugano et al. [33] proposed a synthetic dataset, UT Multi-view, which contains multi-view gaze images reconstructed from real human eyes. Other synthetic datasets include SynthesEyes and UnityEyes. SynthesEyes contains 11,382 synthesized close-up eye images and 10 dynamic eye area models; these synthesized images have achieved photo-realistic quality [43]. The UnityEyes dataset is generated by rendering 3D eye area models, capturing a large number of eye appearance variations, and can estimate challenging eye gaze images [44]. Wood has created open-source software to generate the UnityEyes dataset, and researchers can use this software to generate synthetic eye images with custom resolutions.

Most existing popular gaze datasets are RGB images with high resolution. However, image blur is a factor that leads to inaccuracies in the analysis of human social interactions involving gaze [45]. Therefore, it is particularly necessary to explore gaze estimation on low-resolution images. The low-resolution IR image dataset proposed in this paper addresses the challenge of RGB images in existing public datasets being easily affected by lighting conditions. A summary and comparison of the popular open-source datasets and the IRGD dataset proposed in this study can be seen in Table 3.

Table 3. Comparison and summary of current open-source datasets and our proposed IRGD dataset.

Datasets	With Face	Total	Gaze Pitch	Gaze Yaw	Image Types
MPIIGaze	No	213 K images	±20°	±20°	RGB
MPIIFaceGaze	Yes	213 K images	±20°	±20°	RGB
EYEDIAP	Yes	94 Videos	±30°	±40°	RGB and RGBD
UnityEyes	No	User defined	User defined	User defined	RGB
ETH-XGaze	Yes	Over 1 M images	±70°	±120°	RGB
ManiGaze	Yes	11 K images (from videos)	±40°	±50°	RGB and RGBD
Gaze360	Yes	172 K images	−50°	±140°	RGB
Columbia	Yes	5 K	±10°	±15°	RGB
EVE	Yes	Over 12 M images (from videos)	±50°	±60°	RGB
GazeCapture	Yes	Over 2 M images	±20°	±20°	RGB
UT Multi-view	No	64 K	±36°	±50°	RGB
SynthesEyes	No	11 K	±25°	±35°	RGB
IRGD	Yes	150 K	±50°	±50°	IR and Depth

3.2. Data Collection Procedure

The TOF camera can simultaneously capture infrared images and depth images. The infrared images provide 2D information about the human eye during the gaze process, while the depth images provide 3D information about the 2D eye landmarks in the camera coordinate system. TOF cameras have been widely used in the automotive intelligent cockpit industry for driver behavior detection such as smoking and phone calling. To save economic costs for car manufacturers, we perform model-based 3D gaze estimation based on the automotive-grade TOF camera with a resolution of 300,000 pixels and an accuracy of 1% (1 m), which is widely used in cars.

Before officially recording the IRGD dataset, we created and calibrated a standard plane for gaze estimation using a level, based on a standard wall (see Figure 7a). This standard plane consists of a grid of squares with a side length of 200 mm, arranged in 17 columns and 11 rows. We ordered the grid, and the intersections of the grid on the standard plane are the gaze points, which are located in the coordinate system of the standard plane. To increase the diversity of lighting conditions during data recording, we chose the location of the standard plane at the indoor doorway to approach the lighting changes in the external environment and organized participants to record data at three different times: morning, noon, and evening. The TOF camera is fixed on the standard plane and does not change its position during data recording. The size of the standard plane is 3.4 m × 2.2 m, which is sufficient to meet the recording of gaze data at extreme angles. We created a standard plane coordinate system $X_w - Y_w - Z_w$ and camera coordinate system $X_c - Y_c - Z_c$ (see Figure 7b). Since the fixed position of the camera on the standard plane is known, the 3D coordinate values of each gaze point in the camera coordinate system can be obtained through the transformation relationship between the two coordinate systems. The specific transformation calculation is as follows:

$$P_x = -\left(s \times \left(num - \left(col \times \left\lfloor \frac{num}{col} \right\rfloor\right) - 1\right) - camera_x\right) \quad (1)$$

$$P_y = s \times \left\lfloor \frac{num}{col} \right\rfloor - camera_y \quad (2)$$

$$P_z = -camera_z \quad (3)$$

where (P_x, P_y, P_z) represents the 3D coordinates of the gaze point on the standard plane in the coordinate system of the TOF camera. $(camera_x, camera_y, camera_z)$ denotes the fixed position of the TOF camera in the coordinate system of the standard plane. s represents the size of the regular quadrilateral grid on the standard plane, which is set to 200 mm in this study. num represents the gaze point number, and col represents the number of regular quadrilateral grids per row on the standard plane.

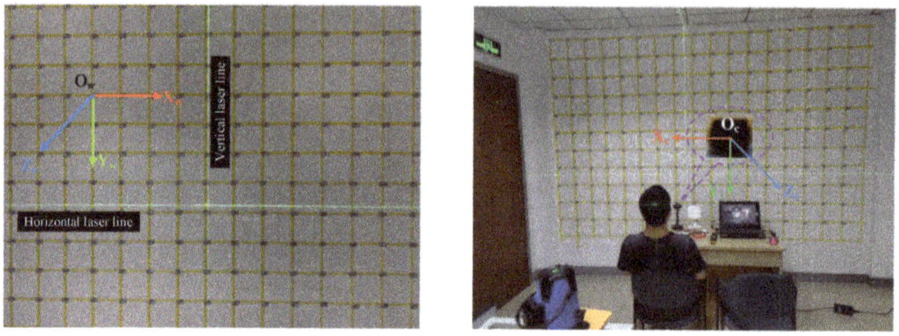

(a) (b)

Figure 7. Creating a standard plane with multiple gaze points using a level's laser line (**a**) and fixing a TOF camera on the plane (**b**).

To establish a tacit understanding with the participants during the data-recording process, we developed a camera acquisition software and ran it on a laptop. Unlike Columbia and UT Multi-view, we did not use a head fixation device, allowing participants in the data recording to perform natural eye movements as described in the EVE dataset, without any constraints. Participants freely gaze at the gaze points on the standard plane and inform the camera acquisition software of the current gaze point number via voice commands. The camera acquisition software captures the participant's gaze image 0.5 s later. Figure 8 shows some examples from the IRGD dataset we recorded.

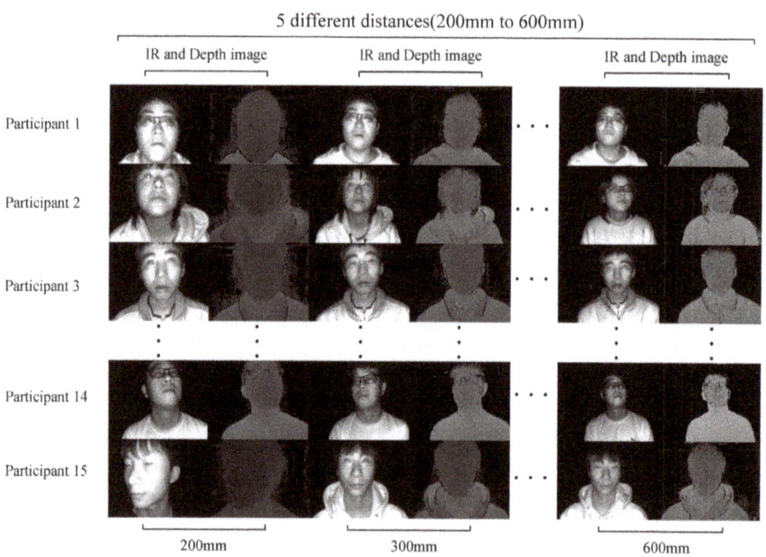

Figure 8. Sample pictures of the IRGD dataset proposed in this paper. We recorded gaze data at five different distances from the participant to the TOF camera, ranging from 200 mm to 600 mm. The TOF camera simultaneously collected IR images and depth images of the participant gazing at the gaze points on the standard plane. All participants performed natural eye movements and coherent head movements.

3.3. Dataset Characteristics

The process of recording the dataset was quite laborious [28], and the creation of the IRGD dataset proposed in this paper took a considerable amount of time. We ultimately organized 15 participants to join this work, including 7 individuals wearing nearsighted glasses, 9 males, and 6 females, all of whom were Asian. Each participant recorded data at five different distances from the TOF camera: 200 mm, 300 mm, 400 mm, 500 mm, and 600 mm (see Figure 8). The TOF camera had a sampling frame rate of 30 fps and a sampling interval of 4, capturing 1000 IR images and 1000 depth images for each participant at each distance, resulting in a total of 75K IR images and their corresponding 75K depth images in the IRGD dataset. These ample data laid a solid foundation for training the eye landmarks detection model using YOLOv8. To provide a comprehensive description of the characteristics of the IRGD dataset, we discuss it in detail from the following aspects.

3.3.1. Image Resolution

The IRGD dataset proposed in this paper includes both IR and depth images. These two types of images were captured by an automotive-grade TOF camera with 300,000 pixels, both of which have a low resolution of 640 × 480.

3.3.2. Gaze Direction

The IRGD dataset is composed of gaze images from 15 participants, each of whom sequentially gazed at 35 target gaze points on a standard plane. These gaze points form a gaze area of 1.4 m × 0.8 m on the standard plane, with the participants' gaze angles in the horizontal and vertical directions within this gaze area being $\pm 50^\circ$.

3.3.3. Light Condition

In this study, a lux meter was used to record the ambient illumination levels during data acquisition. To enhance the adaptability of the gaze-estimation model to variations in illumination intensity, the benchmark dataset IRGD was recorded under a wide range of lighting conditions, from complete darkness (0 lux) to illumination levels nearing outdoor sunlight exposure (170,000 lux). The automotive-grade TOF camera utilized in this work demonstrated stable performance across this spectrum of illumination intensities.

3.3.4. Head Pose

Existing work on head pose handling can be divided into two categories: one is to normalize the images using the detected head pose angles before training the network to reduce the impact of head pose on gaze estimation [15], and the other is to use head pose to compensate for the estimated gaze angle [24]. The head pose handling approach Mora et al. mentioned is more ingenious than that of [15]; they use an RGBD camera and rigid ICP algorithm to track the subject's head pose frame by frame to generate the subject's frontal gaze image. This method has the advantage of decoupling the gaze angle from the head pose, significantly reducing the complexity of gaze-estimation problems caused by the head pose [8]. However, for cases where the subject's eyes are self-occluded at larger gaze angles, it is not possible to restore the subject's frontal gaze image from the gaze image with the head pose. The gaze-estimation method proposed in this paper calculates the subject's eyes in 3D space, so it is not disturbed by head pose like traditional 2D-image-based gaze-estimation methods. Our work does not directly regress gaze angles from gaze images, so there is no need to normalize the images like [33]. Since head pose detection is not the goal of this study, we only use existing head pose detection methods to statistically analyze the head pose angles of the IRGD dataset. We use the 6-point facial method [46] and the 12-point method [47] to detect the head poses of participants in the manually annotated IRGD dataset, but the detected results have significant deviations in both direction and angle. Subsequently, we used the state-of-the-art head pose estimation model 6DRepNet [48] on the BIWI dataset to detect and calculate the absolute values of the average head pose angles of participants gazing at 35 gaze points in the IRGD dataset (see Figure 9).

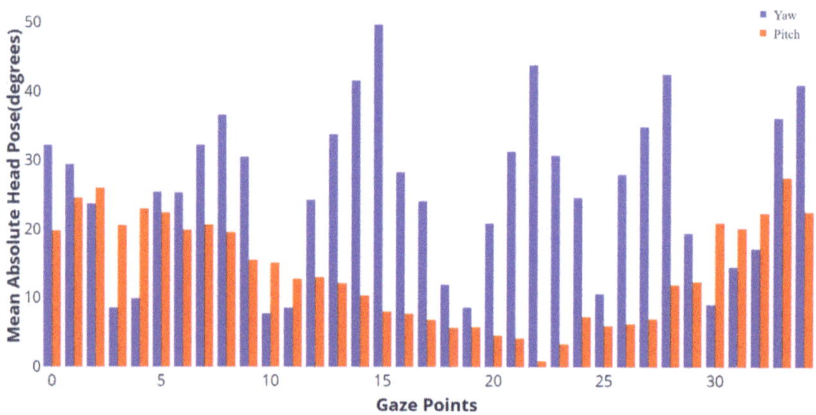

Figure 9. The absolute values of the average head pose angles of the participants at 35 gaze points in the IRGD dataset. The maximum absolute angle of the participants' head pose in the horizontal direction (yaw) is approximately 50°, while in the vertical direction (pitch), it is approximately 30°.

4. Method

In this chapter, we will focus on the distortion correction calculations on the IR gaze images taken by the TOF camera and the methods of fitting the 3D eyeball center in the horizontal and vertical directions. We will discuss the drawbacks of using the TOF camera directly for gaze estimation and the methods to address this issue.

4.1. Image Distortion Correction

Distortion refers to the degree of distortion of the image formed by an optical system relative to the object itself. It is an inherent characteristic of optical lenses, directly caused by the inconsistent magnification between the edge and the center of the lens. Radial distortion is caused by the shape of the lens, while tangential distortion is caused by the tilt of the lens and the imaging plane during the camera assembly process [49]. Thanks to the improvement of camera assembly and production technology, the distortion values of current industrial cameras and network cameras are relatively small, with the former generally having a distortion value of only 1–2 pixels, and the latter only a few pixels. The average distortion value of the TOF camera used in this study is 7 pixels, with different distortion sizes at different positions on the image, and the smallest distortion value in the central area. For gaze-estimation methods on 2D images, image distortion may not affect the accuracy of gaze estimation like other factors. However, our work requires extracting the depth value at the pixel coordinates of the target point on the depth image, and the depth values of different target points may not be the same. Before correcting the distortion of the eye landmarks on the subject's gaze image, we use OpenCV's camera calibration tool [50] to obtain the intrinsic matrix and distortion coefficients of the TOF camera:

$$Intrinsic\ Matrix = \begin{bmatrix} f_x & 0 & c_x \\ 0 & f_y & c_y \\ 0 & 0 & 1 \end{bmatrix} \tag{4}$$

$$Distortion\ Coefficient = (k_1, k_2, p_1, p_2, k_3) \tag{5}$$

where (k_1, k_2, k_3) represents the radial distortion coefficient, and (p_1, p_2) denotes the tangential distortion coefficient.

In Section 2.3, we presented the output results of the eye landmarks detection model trained using YOLOv8. For the 7 landmarks obtained on the single-eye image of the subject shown in Figure 3b, the calculation methods for radial and tangential distortion correction are as follows:

$$r_i^2 = u_i^2 + v_i^2 \tag{6}$$

$$\acute{u}_i = u_i * \left(1 + k_1 r_i^2 + k_2 r_i^4 + k_3 r_i^6\right) + 2p_1 u_i v_i + p_2\left(r_i^2 + 2u_i^2\right) + u_i \tag{7}$$

$$\acute{v}_i = v_i * \left(1 + k_1 r_i^2 + k_2 r_i^4 + k_3 r_i^6\right) + 2p_1\left(r_i^2 + 2v_i^2\right) + 2p_2 u_i v_i + v_i \tag{8}$$

where (u_i, v_i) represents the 2D pixel coordinates of the i-th target point among the 7 landmarks detected on the original gaze image, and $(\acute{u}_i, \acute{v}_i)$ denotes the pixel coordinates of the i-th landmarks point after distortion correction. We only correct the distortion of the eye landmarks in the subject's gaze image, rather than every pixel of the image. This approach is beneficial for improving the computational efficiency of gaze estimation.

4.2. Integration of Depth Information

After eye landmarks detection and distortion correction on the IR gaze images captured by the TOF camera, we utilize the depth information from the TOF camera to convert the coordinates of the landmarks in the 2D image coordinate system into 3D coordinates in the camera coordinate system. The detailed calculation method is as follows:

$$X_i = \frac{Z_i * \left(\acute{u}_i - \frac{w}{2}\right)}{f_x} \tag{9}$$

$$Y_i = \frac{Z_i * \left(\acute{v}_i - \frac{h}{2}\right)}{f_y} \tag{10}$$

$$Z_i = \frac{g_i}{255} * (f - n) + n \tag{11}$$

where (X_i, Y_i, Z_i) is the 3D coordinate value corresponding to the 2D pixel coordinate $(\acute{u}_i, \acute{v}_i)$ of the i-th eye landmark, f_x and f_y are the intrinsic parameters of the TOF camera. w and h are the width and height of the image, which are 640 and 480, respectively, in this study. g_i is the grayscale value at point $(\acute{u}_i, \acute{v}_i)$ on the depth image, f is the maximum distance value of the TOF camera's range measurement, and n is the minimum distance value of the TOF camera's range.

4.3. Fitting of Eyeball

In this study, we fit the center of the eyeball using the left and right canthus points on the image of a single eye of the subject. We draw inspiration from Abdelrahman et al. [19] who used two fully connected layers to independently regress each gaze angle (yaw and pitch) to improve the prediction accuracy of gaze estimation. We model the eyeball in the horizontal (yaw) and vertical (pitch) directions when the subject is gazing (see Figure 10). We use the coordinates of the subject's eyeball center fitted in the horizontal and vertical directions to calculate the gaze angles in the two directions, respectively. This study assumes that the left and right canthus points of the subject are on the spherical surface with the eyeball center as the center and the distance to the surface of the eyeball is dif. For the center of the eyeball in the horizontal direction, its Y-coordinate value is set as the average of the left and right canthus points. Assuming that the radius of the eyeball model in the horizontal direction R_1 and dif are known, the detailed calculation of the center of the eyeball is as follows:

$$y_{eye} = \frac{Y_1 + Y_2}{2} \tag{12}$$

$$\left(x_{eye} - X_1\right)^2 + \left(y_{eye} - Y_1\right)^2 + \left(z_{eye} - Z_1\right)^2 = (R_1 + dif)^2 \tag{13}$$

$$\left(x_{eye} - X_4\right)^2 + \left(y_{eye} - Y_4\right)^2 + \left(z_{eye} - Z_4\right)^2 = (R_1 + dif)^2 \tag{14}$$

where (X_1, Y_1, Z_1) and (X_4, Y_4, Z_4) are the 3D coordinates of the left and right canthus points of the subject after distortion correction, respectively. $(x_{eye}, y_{eye}, z_{eye})$ is the calculated center coordinate of the subject's eyeball in the horizontal gaze direction in the TOF camera coordinate system, and z_{eye} is taken as the maximum value solution in the calculation.

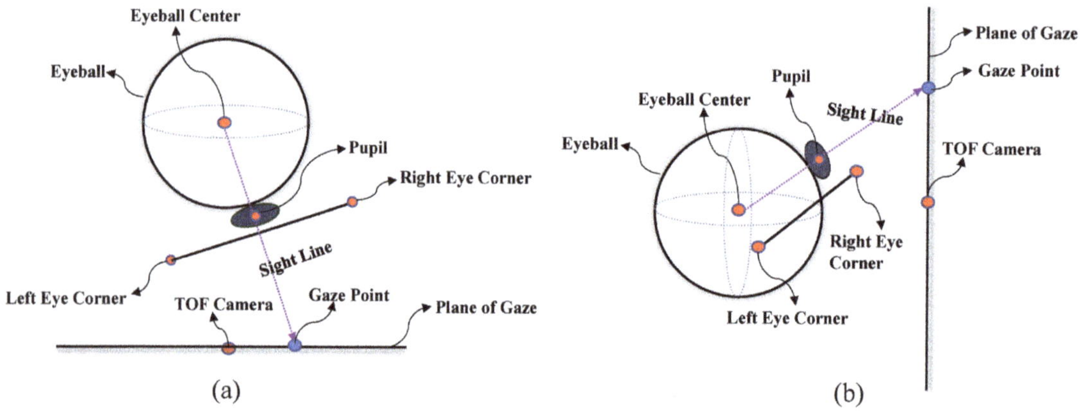

Figure 10. Independent modeling and solution of eyeball center coordinates in horizontal (**a**) and vertical (**b**) gaze directions of subjects.

For the vertical direction of the eyeball model, the X-coordinate value of the eyeball center is set as the average of the left and right eye corner points. The following method is used to solve for the position of the eyeball center:

$$x_{\acute{eye}} = \frac{X_1 + X_4}{2} \tag{15}$$

$$\left(x_{\acute{eye}} - X_1\right)^2 + \left(y_{eye} - Y_1\right)^2 + \left(z_{\acute{eye}} - Z_1\right)^2 = (R_2 + dif)^2 \tag{16}$$

$$\left(x_{\acute{eye}} - X_4\right)^2 + \left(y_{\acute{eye}} - Y_4\right)^2 + \left(z_{\acute{eye}} - Z_4\right)^2 = (R_2 + dif)^2 \tag{17}$$

where R_2 represents the radius value of the participant's eyeball when gazing in the vertical direction. Assuming R_2 is known, the vertical coordinate $(x_{\acute{eye}}, y_{\acute{eye}}, z_{\acute{eye}})$ of the eyeball center can be calculated. In fact, in the specific calculation process, the value of $y_{\acute{eye}}$ depends on the participant's vertical eyeball pitch state. If the coordinate axis direction of the TOF camera coordinate system $X_c - Y_c - Z_c$ in Figure 7b is used to define the positive and negative values of the gaze angles in horizontal and vertical directions, then $y_{\acute{eye}}$ takes the minimum value solution when the participant is looking down (pitch in the positive direction), and $y_{\acute{eye}}$ takes the maximum value solution when the participant is looking up. This study uses the aspect ratio of the participant's eye appearance to determine the pitch state of the eyeball. We randomly selected participants for experiments to explore the trend of changes between the vertical gaze angle *pitch* of the eyeball and the aspect ratio p of the participant's eye appearance. Figure 11 presents our experimental results.

From the research results of Baltrušaitis [51], we find that for gaze-estimation tasks, the accuracy of gaze angle detection in the vertical direction of the participants is lower than that in the horizontal direction, which is a typical phenomenon in gaze estimation. The reason for this phenomenon is that there are fewer pixels on the iris used for Y-axis estimation, and the pupil being covered by the upper and lower eyelids is also a significant factor. Therefore, it is highly meaningful to study the gaze angles of the participants in the horizontal and vertical directions separately. The work of predecessors has validated the value of our research.

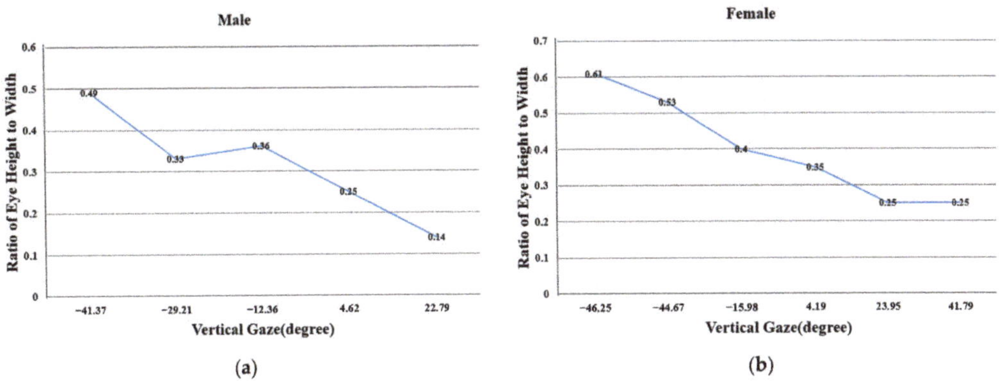

Figure 11. Variation trends of the aspect ratio of eye appearance with vertical gaze angle in male (**a**) and female (**b**) participants. In male participants, the aspect ratio of eye appearance is less than 0.3 when the eyeball is looking down, while in female participants, the aspect ratio of eye appearance is less than 0.4 when the eyeball is looking down.

4.4. Compute the Aspect Ratio of Eye Appearance

The purpose of calculating and statistically analyzing the aspect ratio of the eye appearance of the participant's eyes before gaze estimation is to determine the pitch state of the participant's eyeball in the vertical direction, to obtain the correct solution for the participant's eyeball center in the vertical direction. This work is primarily accomplished in the calibration phase of Section 4.6. Section 2.3 presents the results of the participant's eye landmark detection. This paper uses the 2 upper eyelid points and 2 lower eyelid points output from the participant's single-eye gaze image to calculate the aspect ratio of the participant's eye appearance. It is worth noting that when manually annotating the training set images for landmark detection, the first upper eyelid point is annotated at 1/3 of the participant's upper eyelid contour, and the second upper eyelid point is annotated at 2/3 of the upper eyelid contour. Similarly, the first lower eyelid point is annotated at 1/3 of the lower eyelid contour, and the second lower eyelid point is annotated at 2/3 of the lower eyelid contour (see Figure 3b). The eye landmark detection model trained under these annotation position constraints can output 4 eyelid point coordinates that also satisfy the position relationship. This constraint calculates the aspect ratio of the participant's eye appearance more accurately. The calculation of the aspect ratio of the participant's eye appearance is as follows:

$$\begin{cases} u_a = \frac{\acute{u}_2+\acute{u}_3}{2}, v_a = \frac{\acute{v}_2+\acute{v}_3}{2}, Z_a = \frac{g_a}{255} * (f-n) + n \\ u_b = \frac{\acute{u}_5+\acute{u}_6}{2}, v_b = \frac{\acute{v}_5+\acute{v}_6}{2}, Z_b = \frac{g_b}{255} * (f-n) + n \\ X_a = \frac{Z_a * \left(u_a - \frac{w}{2}\right)}{f_x}, Y_a = \frac{Z_a * \left(v_a - \frac{h}{2}\right)}{f_y} \\ X_b = \frac{Z_b * \left(u_b - \frac{w}{2}\right)}{f_x}, Y_b = \frac{Z_b * \left(v_b - \frac{h}{2}\right)}{f_y} \\ p = \frac{\sqrt{(X_a-X_b)^2+(Y_a-Y_b)^2+(Z_a-Z_b)^2}}{\sqrt{(X_1-X_4)^2+(Y_1-Y_4)^2+(Z_1-Z_4)^2}} \end{cases} \quad (18)$$

where $(\acute{u}_2,\acute{v}_2)$ represents the pixel coordinates of the first upper eyelid point on the distortion-corrected gaze image of the participant, and $(\acute{u}_3,\acute{v}_3)$ represents the pixel coordinates of the second upper eyelid point after distortion correction. (u_a, v_a) is the pixel coordinates of the midpoint of the two upper eyelid points. Similarly, $(\acute{u}_5,\acute{v}_5)$ and $(\acute{u}_6,\acute{v}_6)$ are the pixel coordinates of the first lower eyelid point and the second lower eyelid point after distortion correction, respectively, and (u_b, v_b) is their midpoint. g_a and g_b are the grayscale values of (u_a, v_a) and (u_b, v_b) on the depth image of the TOF camera, respectively. (X_a, Y_a, Z_a) and (X_b, Y_b, Z_b) are the 3D coordinates in the TOF camera coordinate system corresponding to (u_a, v_a) and (u_b, v_b), respectively. p is the calculated aspect ratio of the participant's eye appearance.

4.5. Drawbacks of TOF Cameras in Operation

The infrared light emitted by the TOF camera has strong penetration and can directly illuminate the pupil area. In addition, the pupil reflects infrared light more than the cornea and lens; hence, the pupil presents higher contrast and brightness in the infrared image, making it easy to detect on the infrared image. The TOF camera relies on the infrared pulse light reflected by the object under test to measure the distance from the object to the camera, but at certain special gaze angles, the subject's pupil will absorb the infrared pulse light from the TOF camera. This results in the pupil being easy to detect on the 2D infrared image but unable to extract depth information from on the depth image (see Figure 12).

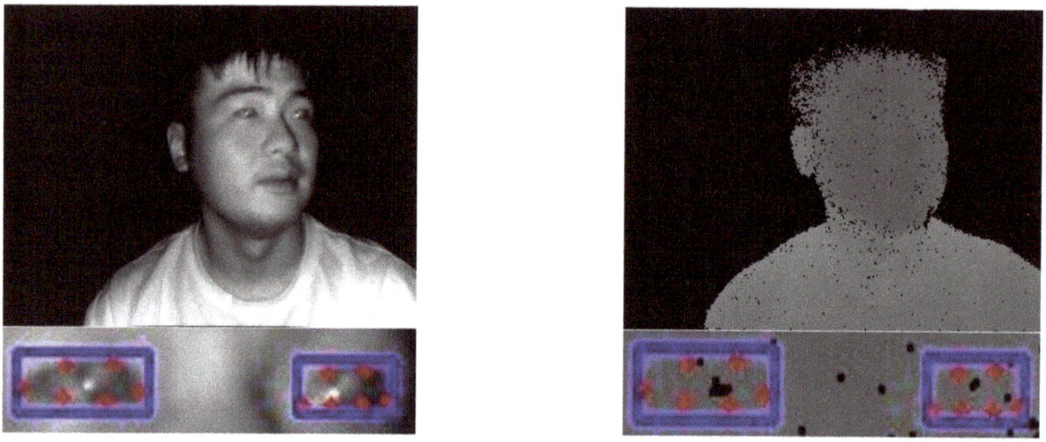

(a) (b)

Figure 12. The drawback of the inability to extract pupil point depth values from the depth image of the TOF camera. For gaze images at certain special angles, the pupil point can be observed on its IR image (**a**), but due to the absorption of infrared light by the pupil, a 'black hole' appears at the position of the pupil point on the corresponding depth image (**b**) of the IR image.

This study does not use the method of obtaining distance information of landmarks on the subject's face using a 3D face model [10,13,15,32], but calculates the depth value under the TOF camera coordinate system for each eye landmark using the grayscale value on the depth image. We found that the depth values of the left and right eye corners of the subject can always be stably obtained. However, in certain special head poses or gaze angles, due to the pupil absorbing the infrared light from the TOF camera, a 'black hole' appears at the corresponding position on its depth image. This results in a grayscale value of 0 for the pupil point on the depth image, thereby making it impossible to solve for the 3D coordinate value of the pupil point.

In response to the operational drawback of the TOF camera being unable to extract the depth information of the pupil point in some subjects' gaze images, we use the constraint relationship that the distance between the subject's pupil point and the center of the eyeball is a certain value, combined with the 2D pixel coordinates of the pupil point detected on the IR gaze image, to solve for the 3D coordinates of the pupil. Since we model the subject's horizontal and vertical gaze directions separately, the distance between the pupil point and the center of the eyeball in these two directions is two different values for the subject.

Assuming that the distance in 3D space between the pupil point and the center of the eyeball in the horizontal gaze direction of the subject is d_1, then:

$$\begin{cases} X_7 = \frac{Z_7 * \left(u_7 - \frac{w}{2}\right)}{f_x} \\ Y_7 = \frac{Z_7 * \left(v_7 - \frac{h}{2}\right)}{f_y} \\ \left(x_{eye} - X_7\right)^2 + \left(y_{eye} - Y_7\right)^2 + \left(z_{eye} - Z_7\right)^2 = d_1^2 \end{cases} \tag{19}$$

where (u_7, v_7) represents the pixel coordinate values of the pupil outputted from the eye landmark detection model after distortion correction on the subject's IR gaze image. (X_7, Y_7, Z_7) signifies the calculated 3D coordinate values of the pupil point in the TOF camera coordinate system when the subject gazes in the horizontal direction. The value of Z_7 is obtained by taking the minimum solution.

Assuming that the distance between the pupil point and the center of the eyeball in the vertical gaze direction of the subject is d_2, we then have:

$$\begin{cases} \acute{X}_7 = \frac{\acute{Z}_7 * \left(u_7 - \frac{w}{2}\right)}{f_x} \\ \acute{Y}_7 = \frac{\acute{Z}_7 * \left(v_7 - \frac{h}{2}\right)}{f_y} \\ \left(x\acute{_{eye}} - \acute{X}_7\right)^2 + \left(y\acute{_{eye}} - \acute{Y}_7\right)^2 + \left(z\acute{_{eye}} - \acute{Z}_7\right)^2 = d_2^2 \end{cases} \tag{20}$$

where $(\acute{X}_7, \acute{Y}_7, \acute{Z}_7)$ represents the calculated 3D coordinate values of the pupil point when the subject gazes in the vertical direction, and $\acute{Z}_7$ is obtained by taking the minimum solution.

After addressing the operational drawbacks of the TOF camera and obtaining the 3D coordinate values of the pupil points under the camera coordinate system, the coordinates of the eyeball center from Section 4.3 can be used to determine the gaze angles yaw and $pitch$ of the subject in the horizontal and vertical directions, respectively:

$$yaw = \frac{180}{\pi} * \tan^{-1}\left(\frac{X_7 - x_{eye}}{z_{eye} - Z_7}\right) \tag{21}$$

$$pitch = \frac{180}{\pi} * \tan^{-1}\left(\frac{\acute{Y}_7 - y\acute{_{eye}}}{z\acute{_{eye}} - \acute{Z}_7}\right) \tag{22}$$

4.6. Person-Dependent Calibration

The average value of the human eyeball radius is 12 mm, and the distance from the center of the eyeball to the pupil is 13.1 mm [11]. Through our measurements, the average value of dif among different subjects is 5 mm. Using these constants to assign values to the above variables and calculate the final gaze angles in the horizontal and vertical directions, we found that precise calculation results can be obtained at the gaze points of individual subjects, but these constants do not apply to most subjects, and the deviation of the calculated gaze angles far exceeds 10°. The calculation of the subject's eyeball center and pupil in this paper is based on the known conditions of R_1, R_2, d_1, d_2, and dif. These subject-specific parameters need to be obtained through calibration. The research results of Zhang et al. [13] show that among the various challenges faced by unconstrained gaze, the performance gap in gaze estimation caused by individual differences is 40%, which is higher than the 25% of gaze range and 35% of lighting conditions. Therefore, in model-based gaze estimation, individual calibration is also an important task, which can significantly improve the accuracy of gaze estimation.

Chen et al. [10] proposed a 9-point method for calibrating individual-specific eyeball parameters of subjects, while Shah et al. [23] suggested that users could be instructed to look at specific points on the screen to adjust the intrinsic parameters of the eye model to avoid time-consuming calibration procedures. In the experimental results of [25], the more calibration samples there are, the smaller the average deviation of the gaze angles calculated by the algorithm, and as the number of samples increases, the calibrated eyeball parameters approach the ground-truth parameters. Our work combines their calibration approaches:

1. Assuming there is a calibration screen in the subject's gaze space and as many gaze points as possible are spread across the calibration screen (see Figure 13). The number of gaze points is denoted as M, and the position relationship of each gaze point with the TOF camera is recorded. The ground-truth gaze angle of the eyeball when the subject gazes at the gaze point in the r-th row and c-th column on the calibration screen in the horizontal direction is denoted as α_{rc}, and the ground-truth gaze angle of the eyeball when gazing at the gaze point in the r-th row and c-th column in the vertical direction is denoted as β_{rc};
2. Constraining the values of R_1, R_2, d_1, and d_2 within a certain range and traversing these parameters with a step size of 0.1 within this range, we calculate the absolute deviation between the gaze angle values obtained by each set of parameters at each gaze point and the ground-truth angle values, using the aforementioned gaze-estimation calculation method;
3. Computing the average absolute gaze angle deviation corresponding to each set of parameters at M gaze points in N calibrations. The set of R_1, R_2, d_1, and d_2 parameters that yield the smallest average absolute deviation is outputted and denoted as the ground-truth parameters of the subject's eyeball.

In the specific experiment, since the influence of the dif value on the gaze angle is consistent with R_1 and R_2, it can be considered that the calibration effect of dif is included in the calibration effect of R_1 and R_2. Therefore, we set dif as a fixed value of 5 mm and only calibrate R_1 and R_2. From the perspective of human eye anatomy, the parameters of the human eye must have reasonable values [25]. After fully considering the prior values of the structural parameters of the human eye in medicine, we set the values of R_1, R_2, d_1, and d_2 to [5,40].

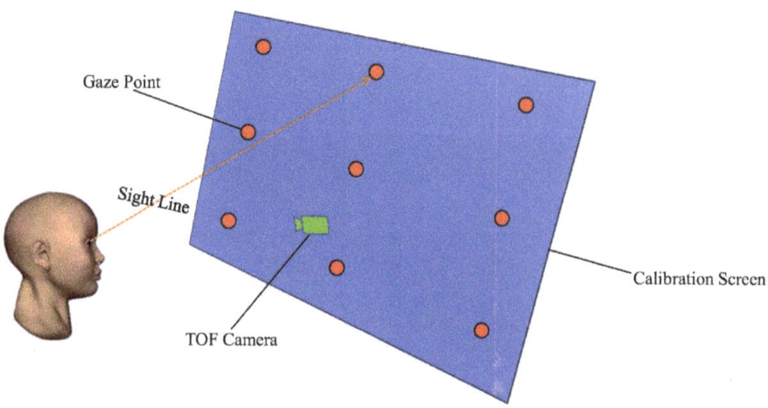

Figure 13. Schematic diagram of the calibration process for individual-specific eyeball parameters of the subject.

In the calibration process, the calculation of the absolute deviation between the gaze angle of the subject's eyeball obtained by the gaze-estimation method in this paper and the ground-truth angle corresponding to the gaze point on the calibration screen is as follows:

$$e = |\alpha_{rc} - yaw_{rc}(R_1 d_1)|, R_1 \in [5,\ 40], d_1 \in [5,\ 40] \tag{23}$$

$$\acute{e} = |\beta_{rc} - pitch_{rc}(R_2 d_2)|, R_2 \in [5, 40], d_2 \in [5,\ 40] \tag{24}$$

where $yaw_{rc}(R_1 d_1)$ represents, within the range of [5,40] when the horizontal radius of the subject's eyeball is R_1 and the distance from the center of the eyeball to the pupil is d_1, the horizontal gaze angle calculated by the gaze-estimation method proposed in this paper when the subject gazes at the gaze point at the r-th row and c-th column on the calibration screen. Similarly, $pitch_{rc}(R_2 d_2)$ represents, within the range of [5,40] when the vertical radius of the subject's eyeball is R_2 and the distance from the center of the eyeball to the pupil is d_2, the vertical gaze angle calculated by the gaze-estimation method in this paper when the subject gazes at the gaze point at the r-th row and c-th column. e represents the absolute deviation between the horizontal gaze angle calculated under the current set of (R_1, d_1) parameters and the ground-truth angle, while $\acute{e}$ represents the absolute deviation between the vertical gaze angle of the subject calculated under the current set of (R_2, d_2) parameters and the ground-truth angle.

The calculation method for the average gaze-estimation angle deviation of M gaze points on the calibration screen in N calibrations is as follows:

$$\overline{e(yaw)} = \frac{\sum_{i=1}^{N}\sum_{j=1}^{M} e_{ij}}{N * M} \quad (25)$$

$$\overline{e(pitch)} = \frac{\sum_{i=1}^{N}\sum_{j=1}^{M} \acute{e}_{ij}}{N * M} \quad (26)$$

where $\overline{e(yaw)}$ represents the average angle deviation in the horizontal direction, $\overline{e(pitch)}$ represents the average angle deviation in the vertical direction, e_{ij} represents the absolute deviation between the gaze angle value corresponding to the j-th gaze point on the calibration screen and the ground-truth angle during the i-th calibration by the subject in the horizontal direction, and $\acute{e}_{ij}$ represents the absolute deviation between the gaze angle value corresponding to the j-th gaze point on the calibration screen and the ground-truth angle during the i-th calibration by the subject in the vertical direction.

In this study, the calibration screen used for calibrating the subject-specific eye structure parameters is not a fixed scene. The subject should choose an appropriate calibration screen based on the actual application of gaze estimation. For example, when implementing gaze estimation for drivers in a car, the car's central control screen can be used as the calibration screen. When performing eye tracking for gamers on a computer, the computer monitor can be used as the calibration screen. The selection of the calibration screen should be combined with the subject's work environment, and the subject should perform complete and as many gaze point calibrations as possible. Figure 14 shows the calibration results of the eye structure parameters for three randomly selected subjects.

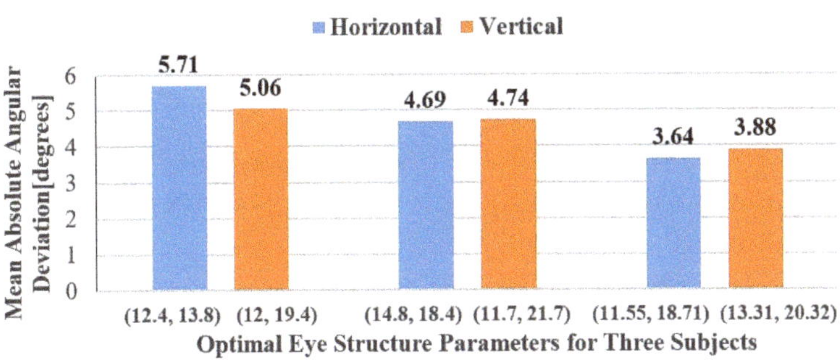

Figure 14. Calibration results of eyeball parameters for three subjects. We obtained the optimal eyeball structure parameters (R_1, d_1) and (R_2, d_2) for 3 subjects through 10 calibrations, each involving gazing at 20 gaze points. At the same time, we calculated the mean absolute deviation between the gaze angles in the horizontal direction (blue) and vertical direction (orange) computed from this set of parameters and the ground-truth angles.

5. Experiment

For the model-based 3D gaze-estimation method presented in this paper, we demonstrate its accuracy and effectiveness in detecting the gaze of subjects through several experiments. Following existing experimental approaches, we evaluate the method using a leave-one-out strategy on one subject from the IRGD dataset, while the data from the remaining 13 subjects are used for training the eye landmark detection model based on YOLOv8. We apply the trained model to detect facial images of the evaluation subject at different distances and calculate the detection deviation of the seven landmarks on the subject's single-eye image by comparing the Euclidean distance between the detected landmarks' pixel coordinates and the ground-truth landmarks' pixel coordinates. The final calculated mean deviation is 7.42 pixels. Since four of the seven landmarks (eyelid points) are only used for determining the subject's eyeball pitch state, when disregarding the eyelid points detection deviation, the model's average detection deviation for the two eye corner points and the pupil point used to calculate the gaze angle is 1.86 pixels. Therefore, we believe that a YOLOv8 landmark detection model with a good detection accuracy has been trained on the IRGD dataset.

5.1. Pupil Depth Error

We conducted experiments on the IRGD dataset by dividing it into two different groups, male and female, to test the accuracy of the pupil depth calculation method proposed in this paper. In total, nine male subjects participated in 28 experimental sessions within a range of 500 mm–600 mm from the TOF camera, while six female subjects participated in 23 sessions within a range of 400 mm–500 mm. We intentionally aimed to verify the accuracy of pupil depth calculation at different distances. Figure 15 shows the results of the calculated pupil depth values and the ground-truth pupil depth values obtained during the experiments.

For the male subject group, the mean absolute error between the calculated pupil depth values and the ground-truth pupil depth in the horizontal gaze direction was 9.23 mm, and in the vertical gaze direction, it was 17.81 mm. For the female subject group, the mean absolute error in the horizontal gaze direction was 6.73 mm, and in the vertical gaze direction, it was 14.39 mm. Overall, the pupil depth calculation method proposed in this study has a greater accuracy in the horizontal direction than in the vertical direction.

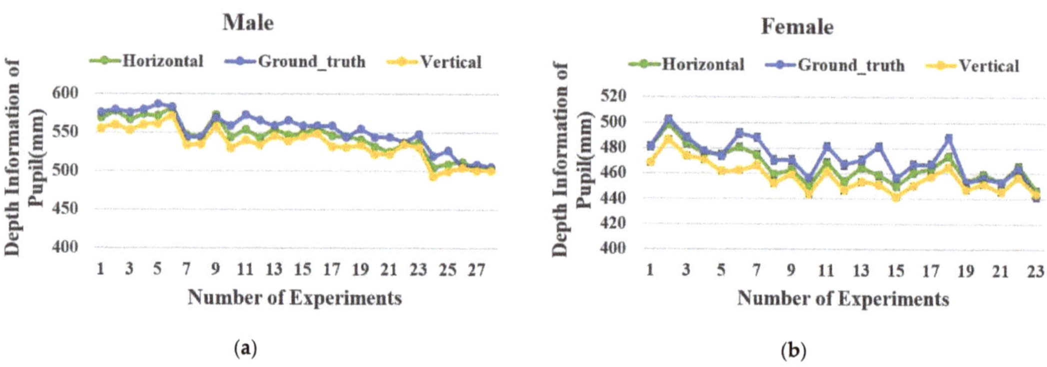

Figure 15. Experiment results on calculating the average pupil depth information and corresponding ground-truth values in horizontal and vertical gaze directions for the male group (**a**) and female group (**b**).

5.2. Deviation of Gaze Angle

Figure 16 presents the results of the gaze-estimation method proposed in this paper for the subjects' eye tracking. The results in Section 2 indicate that when the subjects are closer to the TOF camera, the clarity of the eye region is higher. To evaluate the gaze-estimation model's detection results at greater distances, we maintained the nine male subjects at a distance of 500 mm–600 mm from the TOF camera and the six female subjects at a distance of 400 mm–500 mm. These test ranges closely approximate the typical distances between drivers and the common camera installation locations in real driving scenarios. Figure 17 shows the comparison between the estimated gaze angles and the ground-truth angles for male subjects targeting 8 uniformly distributed points within the gaze space and female subjects targeting 16 points in the test environment. To evaluate the accuracy of our method in detecting the subjects' gaze angles, we used the mean absolute error (MAE) as the performance evaluation criterion to calculate the average deviation between the model's detection results and the ground-truth gaze angles for both male and female subject groups. Ultimately, the average deviation for the male subjects was 4.51° in the horizontal direction and 4.43° in the vertical direction. For the female subjects, the average deviation was 5.71° in the horizontal direction and 5.07° in the vertical direction.

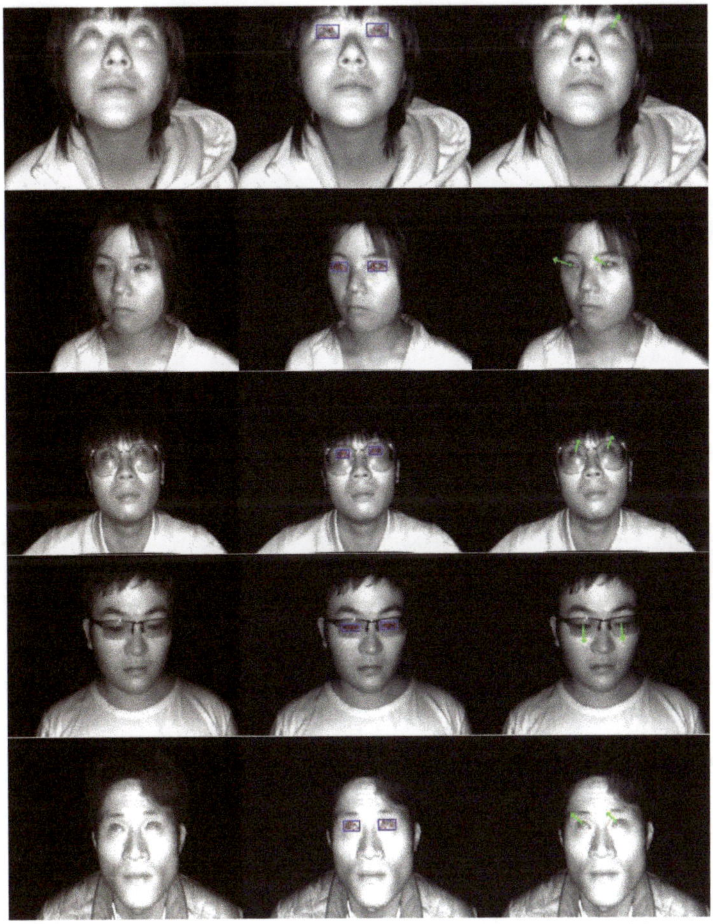

(a) (b) (c)

Figure 16. Results of the subject's gaze detection. Column (**a**) presents the original gaze images of the subject, column (**b**) shows the results of eye landmark detection based on YOLOv8, and column (**c**) visualizes the subject's gaze direction. The green arrow indicates the gaze direction detected by our model.

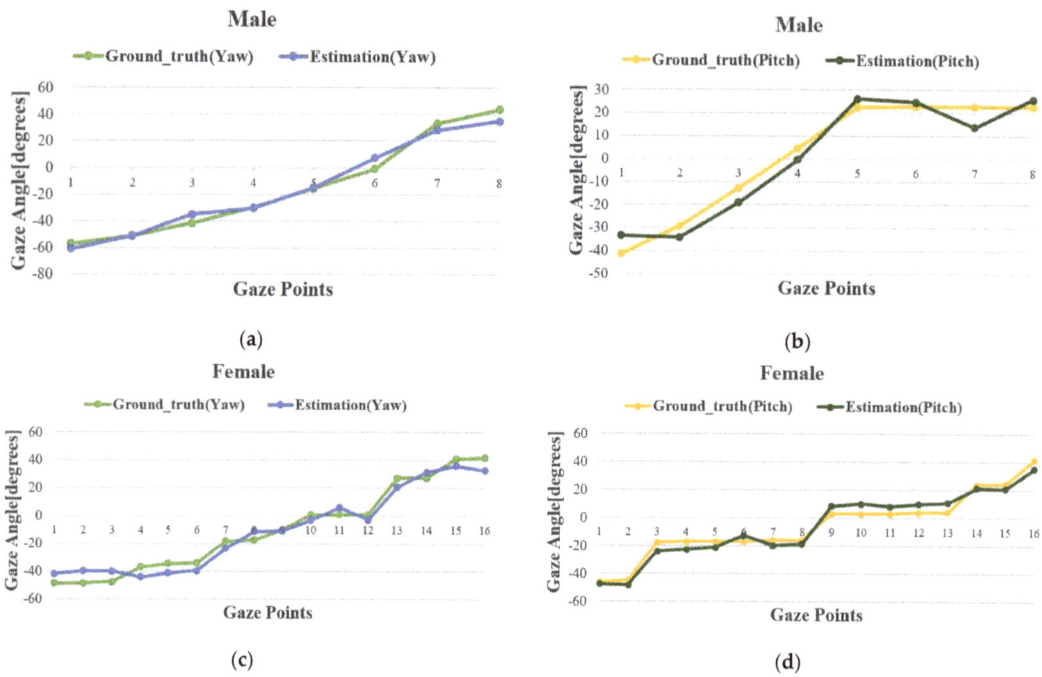

Figure 17. Gaze angle detection results of male and female subject groups using the gaze-estimation method proposed in this study. Specifically, (**a**) represents the horizontal gaze results of the male group, (**b**) shows the vertical gaze results of the male group. (**c**) illustrates the horizontal gaze results of the female group, and (**d**) presents the vertical gaze results of the female subjects.

5.3. Comparison with Other State-of-the-Art Methods

In this subsection, we combined the test data from both male and female groups and set up a testing environment for state-of-the-art gaze-estimation models such as OpenFace2.2, ETH-XGaze, MPIIGaze (also known as GazeNet), MPIIFaceGaze (also referred to as Spatial Weights CNN), and L2CS on local computer devices. These state-of-the-art models are all trained on RGB images. Kendrick et al. [52] showed that RGB images perform best in facial landmark detection before gaze estimation, and the model converges the fastest. However, when predicting a wide range of landmarks, grayscale images are superior to RGB images. RGB images are sensitive to lighting and partial occlusion, which lack feature points [53]. In our experiments, we found that these state-of-the-art models have issues with infrared image data, as they are unable to detect the facial landmarks of the subjects and thus cannot output gaze angles. OpenFace2.2 performs better in detecting infrared gaze images of subjects than ETH-XGaze, MPIIFaceGaze, and MPIIGaze, as the latter three often fail to output gaze angles. L2CS significantly deviates from the ground-truth size in the angle values detected from some infrared gaze images. We calculated the accuracy of these five state-of-the-art models and the gaze-estimation model proposed in this study based on RMSE (see Figure 18). The gaze-estimation method proposed in this study has a root mean square error of 6.03° in the horizontal direction (yaw) and 4.83° in the vertical direction (pitch). The method for calculating the root mean square error (RMSE) between the gaze angle values detected by the model for the subjects and the ground-truth gaze angle values is as follows:

$$RMSE(yaw) = \sqrt{\frac{1}{Q}\sum_{i=1}^{Q}(yaw_i - yaw_{t,i})^2} \tag{27}$$

$$RMSE(pitch) = \sqrt{\frac{1}{Q}\sum_{i=1}^{Q}(pitch_i - pitch_{t,i})^2} \tag{28}$$

where $RMSE(yaw)$ represents the root mean square error (RMSE) between the model-predicted gaze angle and the ground-truth gaze angle in the horizontal direction, while $RMSE(pitch)$ denotes the RMSE for the vertical direction. Q signifies the number of experimental samples. yaw_i refers to the model-predicted gaze angle of the subject in the horizontal direction during the i-th experiment, and $yaw_{t,i}$ is the ground-truth gaze angle of the subject in the horizontal direction. Similarly, $pitch_i$ represents the model-predicted gaze angle in the vertical direction for the i-th experiment, and $pitch_{t,i}$ indicates the ground-truth gaze angle of the subject in the vertical direction.

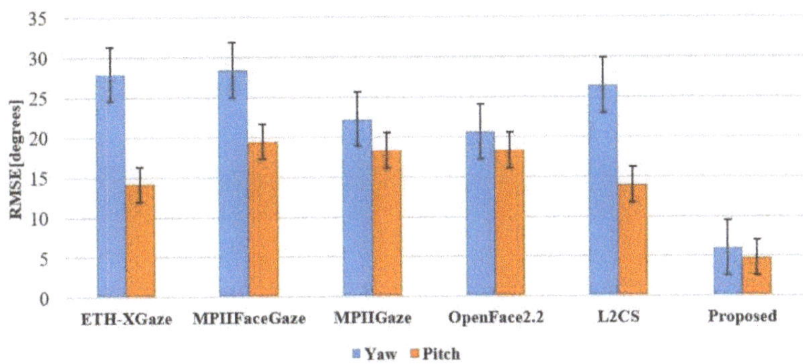

Figure 18. Comparative accuracy results of our proposed gaze-estimation model with other state-of-the-art models in infrared gaze test images.

5.4. *Experiments in Real Driving Scenarios for Automobile*

To validate the performance of our gaze-estimation model in real-world application scenarios, we conducted driver gaze detection in a real driving environment within a full-scale car cabin. We organized 15 subjects to gaze at five target points during car driving, including the dashboard, back mirror, in-vehicle screen, driver mirror, and driver window (see Figure 19). Before recording these gaze data, we first calibrated the five gaze points and the TOF camera fixed points in the Toyota business SUV used, to measure the ground-truth gaze angles of the 15 drivers. The subjects performed free driving tasks in the experiment, with the TOF camera fixed in front of the car steering wheel and at a distance of 450 mm–600 mm from the subjects. Figure 20 shows the mean absolute error between the detection results of our gaze-estimation model for these target points and the ground-truth gaze angles. In normal car driving, the distance from the driver to the dashboard is about 600 mm. Moreover, adjusting the installation position of the TOF camera and maintaining a closer distance between the camera and the driver can appropriately improve the accuracy of driver gaze detection.

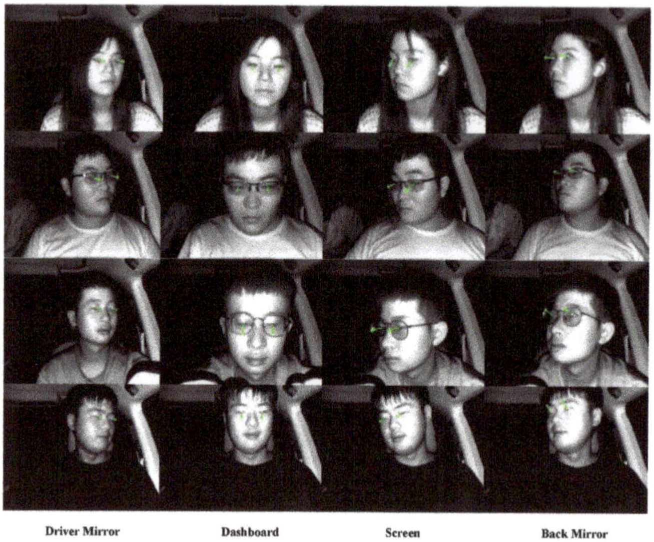

Figure 19. Detection results of driver's partial gaze points in the interior of a Toyota business SUV. Green arrows indicate the driver's gaze direction detected by our gaze-estimation model.

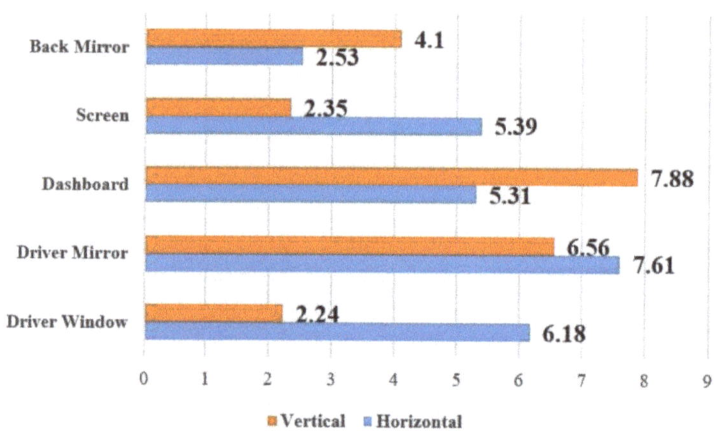

Figure 20. Mean absolute error between the detected driver's gaze angles and ground-truth angles at various gaze points inside the car.

5.5. Discussion

Calibration of the subject's eyeball parameters is a very important task for our model-based gaze-estimation method. In the experiment, setting individual subjects' eyeball radius and the distance from the center of the eyeball to the pupil as medical constants of 12 mm and 13.1 mm, respectively, can also achieve a good gaze angle detection accuracy, but not all subjects' eyeball parameters are close to these two constants. Therefore, it is imperative to calibrate individual-specific eyeball parameters. Since we approximate the position of the subject's eyeball center separately in the horizontal and vertical directions, the eyeball structure parameters estimated in these two gaze directions are also different. Summarizing the overall computational process, the implementation steps of the gaze-estimation method proposed in this paper are as follows:

1. Utilizing the YOLOv8s neural network, a model for eye landmark detection is trained. This landmark detection model is then employed to perform inference on the gaze images of subjects, yielding 2D coordinates of seven landmark points on the image of a single eye of the subject, including points at the corners of the eye and the pupil;
2. Distortion correction is applied to the gaze images of the subjects, resulting in the acquisition of the 2D coordinates of the seven eye landmarks after distortion correction;
3. By integrating the depth images captured simultaneously by the TOF camera during the subject's gaze, the 3D coordinates of the seven landmark points are computed within the coordinate system of the TOF camera;
4. An eyeball model in the horizontal and vertical directions is constructed using the left and right corner points of a single eye of the subject. The aspect ratio of the eye's appearance during the subject's gaze is calculated. Based on this aspect ratio value, the solution for the eyeball's center point in the horizontal and vertical gaze directions of the subject is determined;
5. Based on the distance constraint between the center of the eyeball and the pupil point, combined with the 2D coordinates of the pupil on the gaze image of the subject, the 3D coordinates of the pupil in the horizontal and vertical directions within the TOF camera coordinate system are calculated;
6. Calibration of the subject-specific parameters of the eyeball structure is conducted to ascertain the optimal structural parameters of the eyeball and the range of the subject's eye appearance aspect ratio variation with the vertical gaze angle. Based on these optimal parameters, the gaze angles of the subject in the horizontal and vertical directions, specifically yaw and pitch, are calculated.

In this study, we evaluate the performance of five state-of-the-art gaze-estimation models, namely ETH-XGaze, L2CS, MPIIFaceGaze (also referred to as Spatial Weights CNN), MPIIGaze (also known as GazeNet), and OpenFace 2.2, on our proposed IRGD benchmark dataset for subject gaze detection. These state-of-the-art models were assessed on a local PC, and their effectiveness in detecting the gaze direction of subjects is illustrated in Figure 21. Compared to these state-of-the-art models, the gaze-estimation method proposed in this paper demonstrates the highest accuracy in subject gaze detection. The superior performance is attributed to the proposed method's robust detection capabilities on low-resolution gaze images and images where the subject is situated at a greater distance from the camera. In gaze images characterized by low resolution, large head pose angles, and a substantial distance between the subject and the camera ($\geq$500 mm), existing state-of-the-art gaze-estimation methods often yield significant discrepancies between the estimated and ground-truth gaze angles due to the blurriness of the image and the limited availability of extractable information from the subject's eye region. In some instances, the estimated gaze direction may even be the opposite of the subject's ground-truth line of sight. The gaze-estimation method proposed in this paper overcomes these limitations by utilizing only two eye corner points of a single eye to model the eyeball and employing easily observable pupil points to calculate the gaze angle. Remarkably, even on low-resolution images of 300,000 pixels, our method accurately computes the subject's gaze angle, maintaining its precision at a distance of 600 mm between the subject and the camera. Our proposed method computes the subject's gaze angle within the 3D coordinate system of a TOF camera, which significantly mitigates the influence of the head pose on gaze angle estimation. In contrast, existing state-of-the-art gaze-estimation approaches predict the subject's gaze angle based on 2D images and are highly susceptible to perturbations caused by the subject's head pose.

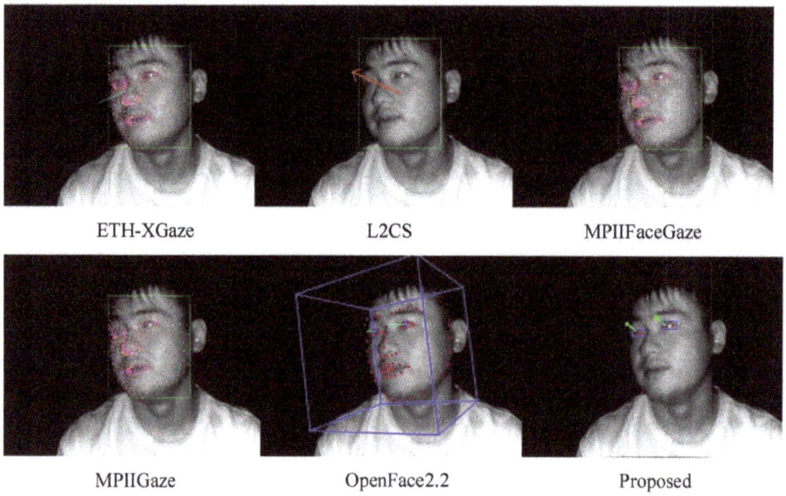

Figure 21. Detection effect of existing state-of-the-art gaze-estimation methods on the IRGD dataset proposed in this study, with arrows and lines indicating the predicted gaze direction of the subject by each model.

In this study, subjects were divided into male and female groups to conduct cross-gender research, aiming to investigate the influence of gender factors on gaze estimation. We found that the aspect ratio of female subjects' eyes was slightly larger than that of males, but the average gaze angle deviation calculated was close to that of males. The driver gaze detection experiment was conducted within the normal driving distance of 450 mm–600 mm from the dashboard, and the final results confirmed that our proposed gaze-estimation method has stable detection capabilities at different distances. In all experimental results, the maximum gaze angle deviation of the subjects did not exceed 9°, which means that within a driving distance of 600 mm, the maximum detection deviation of our gaze-estimation model in the horizontal and vertical directions is 95 mm. In our Toyota SUV, the distances between various gaze target points inside the car are much greater than this deviation value. Therefore, the detection deviation of the gaze-estimation model proposed in this study is sufficient to distinguish and recognize the driver's gaze fixation points within the car.

6. Conclusions

This paper presents a model-based 3D gaze estimation method using a TOF camera. Unlike most gaze-estimation methods that use RGB images, our gaze-estimation work is completed on low-resolution infrared images, which is extremely advantageous for applications with varying lighting conditions and complex environments, particularly suitable for driver gaze detection in night-time scenarios.

Our main contributions include proposing an infrared gaze dataset (IRGD) for a wide range of free head and eyeball movements and training an eye landmark detection model for the subject's eye area on the IRGD dataset using YOLOv8. In addition, this study proposes a method to fit a 3D eyeball model using only two corner points of the subject's single-eye image, enabling our gaze-estimation method to work stably in images where the subject is far from the camera or in low resolution. To address the drawback of the TOF camera not being able to capture the depth information of the subject's pupil at certain special gaze angles, we solve for the 3D coordinates of the pupil point using the constraint relationship between the subject's pupil and the center of the eyeball. This paper analyzes the subject's gaze angle in two directions, horizontal and vertical, and the subject only needs to be calibrated once to calculate the centers of the eyeball and pupil under the horizontal and vertical gaze directions.

Through experimental comparison with other state-of-the-art gaze-estimation models, we have confirmed the effectiveness and advancement of our proposed gaze-estimation method. By comparing with the ground truth gaze angle, the maximum detection deviation of the gaze-estimation method proposed in this paper is less than 9° for the subjects. Using RMSE as the performance evaluation standard, our gaze-estimation method has detection deviations of 6.03° and 4.83° in the horizontal and vertical directions, respectively. We employed the proposed gaze-estimation method to detect gaze angles in subject images with a resolution of 640 × 480. The model proposed in this paper achieved a detection speed of 7.8 frames per second (FPS) when implemented on a local PC equipped with an Intel Core i7-11800H @ 2.30GHz CPU. We also evaluated the accuracy of our gaze-estimation method for driver gaze detection in real car driving scenarios. In future research, we plan to improve the robustness of the gaze-estimation model to extreme head poses and self-occlusion. We will explore the possibility of dynamically selecting the subject's left or right eye in conjunction with the subject's head pose to enhance the accuracy of gaze estimation.

Author Contributions: Conceptualization, K.S. and Y.L.; methodology, K.S. and Y.L.; data curation and writing—original draft, Y.L.; funding acquisition, validtion and project administration, Z.G.; visualization and investigation, J.G.; software and validation, Y.W.; writing—review and editing, K.S. All authors have read and agreed to the published version of the manuscript.

Funding: This study was supported by Liaoning Provincial Department of Education Project (LJKQZ2021082), China.

Institutional Review Board Statement: Not applicable.

Informed Consent Statement: All the participating authors have signed and given the informed consent statements.

Data Availability Statement: The data presented in this study are available on request from the corresponding author. The data are not publicly available due to privacy protection for data recorders.

Acknowledgments: This work was guided by insightful suggestions on research directions from our friend Yan Mu, and greatly assisted by our friends Zhandong Ge, Jinghui Tao, Xiaojun Wang, Shouda Wang, and Bangxuan Tang in data collection. We express our profound gratitude to them.

Conflicts of Interest: The authors declare no conflicts of interest.

References

1. Kar, A.; Corcoran, P. A review and analysis of eye-gaze estimation systems, algorithms and performance evaluation methods in consumer platforms. *IEEE Access* **2017**, *5*, 16495–16519. [CrossRef]
2. Chandra, S.; Sharma, G.; Malhotra, S.; Jha, D.; Mittal, A.P. Eye tracking based human computer interaction: Applications and their uses. In Proceedings of the 2015 International Conference on Man and Machine Interfacing (MAMI), Bhubaneswar, India, 17–19 December 2015; pp. 1–5. [CrossRef]
3. Kapp, S.; Barz, M.; Mukhametov, S.; Sonntag, D.; Kuhn, J. ARETT: Augmented reality eye tracking toolkit for head mounted displays. *Sensors* **2021**, *21*, 2234. [CrossRef] [PubMed]
4. Valtakari, N.V.; Hessels, R.S.; Niehorster, D.C.; Viktorsson, C.; Nyström, P.; Falck-Ytter, T.; Kemner, C.; Hooge, I.T.C. A field test of computer-vision-based gaze estimation in psychology. *Behav. Res. Methods* **2023**, 1–16. [CrossRef] [PubMed]
5. Nandini, M.; Singh, J. A review of various state of art eye gaze estimation techniques. *Adv. Comput. Intell. Commun. Technol. Proc. CICT* **2021**, *2019*, 501–510. [CrossRef]
6. Wen, Q.; Bradley, D.; Beeler, T.; Park, S.; Hilliges, O.; Yong, J.; Xu, F. Accurate Real-time 3D Gaze Tracking Using a Lightweight Eyeball Calibration. *Comput. Graph. Forum* **2020**, *39*, 475–485. [CrossRef]
7. Sharma, P.K.; Chakraborty, P. A Review of Driver Gaze Estimation and Application in Gaze Behavior Understanding. *arXiv* **2023**, arXiv:2307.01470.
8. Mora, K.A.F.; Odobez, J.-M. Gaze estimation from multimodal Kinect data. In Proceedings of the 2012 IEEE Computer Society Conference on Computer Vision and Pattern Recognition Workshops (CVPR Workshops), Providence, RI, USA, 16–21 June 2012; pp. 25–30.
9. William, W.E. Gaze Estimation with Graphics. Doctoral Dissertation, University of Cambridge, Cambridge, UK, 2017. [CrossRef]

10. Chen, J.; Ji, Q. 3D gaze estimation with a single camera without IR illumination. In Proceedings of the 2008 19th International Conference on Pattern Recognition (ICPR), Tampa, FL, USA, 8–11 December 2008; pp. 1–4. [CrossRef]
11. Li, J.; Shigang, L. Eye-model-based gaze estimation by RGB-D camera. In Proceedings of the IEEE Conference on Computer Vision and Pattern Recognition Workshops, Columbus, OH, USA, 23–28 June 2014.
12. Guestrin, E.; Eizenman, M. General theory of remote gaze estimation using the pupil center and corneal reflections. *IEEE Trans. Biomed. Eng.* **2006**, *53*, 1124–1133. [CrossRef] [PubMed]
13. Zhang, X.; Sugano, Y.; Fritz, M.; Bulling, A. Appearance-based gaze estimation in the wild. In Proceedings of the IEEE Conference on Computer Vision and Pattern Recognition, Boston, MA, USA, 7–12 June 2015.
14. Zhang, X.; Sugano, Y.; Fritz, M.; Bulling, A. MPIIGaze: Real-world dataset and deep appearance-based gaze estimation. *IEEE Trans. Pattern Anal. Mach. Intell.* **2017**, *41*, 162–175. [CrossRef] [PubMed]
15. Zhang, X.; Sugano, Y.; Fritz, M.; Bulling, A. It's written all over your face: Full-face appearance-based gaze estimation. In Proceedings of the IEEE Conference on Computer Vision and Pattern Recognition Workshops, Honolulu, HI, USA, 21–26 July 2017. arXiv:1611.08860v4.
16. Seonwook, P.; Spurr, A.; Hilliges, O. Deep pictorial gaze estimation. In Proceedings of the European Conference on Computer Vision (ECCV), Munich, Germany, 8–14 September 2018. arXiv:1807.10002v1.
17. Bace, M.; Becker, V.; Wang, C.; Bulling, A. Combining gaze estimation and optical flow for pursuits interaction. In Proceedings of the ETRA '20: 2020 Symposium on Eye Tracking Research and Applications, Stuttgart, Germany, 2–5 June 2020. [CrossRef]
18. Park, S.; De Mello, S.; Molchanov, P.; Iqbal, U.; Hilliges, O.; Kautz, J. Few-shot adaptive gaze estimation. In Proceedings of the IEEE/CVF International Conference on Computer Vision, Seoul, Republic of Korea, 27 October–2 November 2019.
19. Abdelrahman, A.A.; Hempel, T.; Khalifa, A.; Al-Hamadi, A.; Dinges, L. L2CS-Net: Fine-grained gaze estimation in unconstrained environments. In Proceedings of the 2023 8th International Conference on Frontiers of Signal Processing (ICFSP), Corfu, Greece, 23–25 October 2023; pp. 98–102.
20. Murthy, L.R.D.; Mukhopadhyay, A.; Biswas, P. Distraction detection in automotive environment using appearance-based gaze estimation. In Proceedings of the IUI '22: 27th International Conference on Intelligent User Interfaces, Helsinki, Finland, 22–25 March 2022. [CrossRef]
21. Vasli, B.; Martin, S.; Trivedi, M.M. On driver gaze estimation: Explorations and fusion of geometric and data driven approaches. In Proceedings of the 2016 IEEE 19th International Conference on Intelligent Transportation Systems (ITSC), Rio de Janeiro, Brazil, 1–4 November 2016; pp. 655–660. [CrossRef]
22. Vora, S.; Rangesh, A.; Trivedi, M.M. On generalizing driver gaze zone estimation using convolutional neural networks. In Proceedings of the 2017 IEEE Intelligent Vehicles Symposium (IV), Los Angeles, CA, USA, 11–14 June 2017; pp. 849–854. [CrossRef]
23. Shah, S.M.; Sun, Z.; Zaman, K.; Hussain, A.; Shoaib, M.; Pei, L. A driver gaze estimation method based on deep learning. *Sensors* **2022**, *22*, 3959. [CrossRef] [PubMed]
24. Vicente, F.; Huang, Z.; Xiong, X.; la Torre, D.F.; Zhang, W.; Levi, D. Driver gaze tracking and eyes off the road detection system. *IEEE Trans. Intell. Transp. Syst.* **2015**, *16*, 2014–2027. [CrossRef]
25. Wang, K.; Ji, Q. 3D gaze estimation without explicit personal calibration. *Pattern Recognit.* **2018**, *79*, 216–227. [CrossRef]
26. Sesma, L.; Villanueva, A.; Cabeza, R. Evaluation of pupil center-eye corner vector for gaze estimation using a web cam. In Proceedings of the ETRA '12: Eye Tracking Research and Applications, Stuttgart, Germany, 28 June 2012. [CrossRef]
27. Park, S.; Aksan, E.; Zhang, X.; Hilliges, O. Towards end-to-end video-based eye-tracking. Computer Vision. In Proceedings of the ECCV 2020: 16th European Conference, Glasgow, UK, 23–28 August 2020; Proceedings, Part XII 16. Springer International Publishing: Berlin/Heidelberg, Germany, 2020. [CrossRef]
28. Park, S.; Zhang, X.; Bulling, A.; Hilliges, O. Learning to find eye region landmarks for remote gaze estimation in unconstrained settings. In Proceedings of the ETRA '18: 2018 Symposium on Eye Tracking Research and Applications, Warsaw, Poland, 14–17 June 2018; p. 21. [CrossRef]
29. Odobez, J.-M.; Mora, K.F. Geometric Generative Gaze Estimation Model from RGB-D Sensors. 2022. Available online: https://www.idiap.ch/webarchives/sites/www.idiap.ch/project/g3e/index.html (accessed on 10 September 2022).
30. Tamura, K.; Choi, R.; Aoki, Y. Unconstrained and Calibration-free gaze estimation in a room-scale area using a monocular camera. *IEEE Access* **2017**, *6*, 10896–10908. [CrossRef]
31. Cristina, S.; Camilleri, K.P. Model-based head pose-free gaze estimation for assistive communication. *Comput. Vis. Image Underst.* **2016**, *149*, 157–170. [CrossRef]
32. Zhang, X.; Park, S.; Beeler, T.; Bradley, D.; Tang, S.; Hilliges, O. Eth-xgaze: A large scale dataset for gaze estimation under extreme head pose and gaze variation. In Proceedings of the Computer Vision–ECCV 2020: 16th European Conference, Glasgow, UK, 23–28 August 2020; Proceedings, Part V 16. Springer International Publishing: Berlin/Heidelberg, Germany, 2020. [CrossRef]
33. Yusuke, S.; Matsushita, Y.; Sato, Y. Learning-by-synthesis for appearance-based 3d gaze estimation. In Proceedings of the IEEE conference on Computer Vision and Pattern Recognition, San Juan, PR, USA, 17–19 June 2014.
34. Baltrusaitis, T.; Robinson, P.; Morency, L.-P. OpenFace: An open source facial behavior analysis toolkit. In Proceedings of the 2016 IEEE Winter Conference on Applications of Computer Vision (WACV), Lake Placid, NY, USA, 7–10 March 2016. [CrossRef]
35. Jocher, G. YOLOv8 Pose Estimation Model. 2023. Available online: https://docs.ultralytics.com/tasks/pose/ (accessed on 3 July 2023).

36. Use Non-Linear Least Squares to Fit a Function f to Data. 2022. Available online: https://docs.scipy.org/doc/scipy/reference/generated/scipy.optimize.curve_fit.html (accessed on 11 October 2022).
37. Siegfried, R.; Odobez, J.-M. Robust unsupervised gaze calibration using conversation and manipulation attention priors. *ACM Trans. Multimedia Comput. Commun. Appl.* **2022**, *18*, 1–27. [CrossRef]
38. Siegfried, R.; Aminian, B.; Odobez, J.-M. ManiGaze: A Dataset for Evaluating Remote Gaze Estimator in Object Manipulation Situations. In Proceedings of the ETRA '20: 2020 Symposium on Eye Tracking Research and Applications, Stuttgart, Germany, 2–5 June 2020. [CrossRef]
39. Mora, F.; Alberto, K.; Monay, F.; Odobez, J.-M. Eyediap: A database for the development and evaluation of gaze estimation algorithms from rgb and rgb-d cameras. In Proceedings of the Symposium on Eye Tracking Research and Applications, Safety Harbor, FL, USA, 26–28 March 2014. [CrossRef]
40. Kellnhofer, P.; Recasens, A.; Stent, S.; Matusik, W.; Torralba, A. Gaze360: Physically unconstrained gaze estimation in the wild. In Proceedings of the IEEE/CVF International Conference on Computer Vision, Seoul, Republic of Korea, 27 October–2 November 2019.
41. Smith, B.A.; Yin, Q.; Feiner, S.K.; Nayar, S.K. Gaze locking: Passive eye contact detection for human-object interaction. In Proceedings of the UIST'13: The 26th Annual ACM Symposium on User Interface Software and Technology, St. Andrews Scotland, UK, 8–11 October 2013; pp. 271–280. [CrossRef]
42. Krafka, K.; Khosla, A.; Kellnhofer, P.; Kannan, H.; Bhandarkar, S.; Matusik, W.; Torralba, A. Eye tracking for everyone. In Proceedings of the IEEE Conference on Computer Vision and Pattern Recognition, Las Vegas, NV, USA, 27–30 June 2016.
43. Wood, E.; Baltruaitis, T.; Zhang, X.; Sugano, Y.; Robinson, P.; Bulling, A. Rendering of eyes for eye-shape registration and gaze estimation. In Proceedings of the IEEE international Conference on Computer Vision, Santiago, Chile, 7–13 December 2015.
44. Wood, E.; Baltrušaitis, T.; Morency, L.-P.; Robinson, P.; Bulling, A. Learning an appearance-based gaze estimator from one million synthesised images. In Proceedings of the ETRA '16: 2016 Symposium on Eye Tracking Research and Applications, Charleston, CA, USA, 14–17 March 2016; pp. 131–138. [CrossRef]
45. Wang, X.; Zhang, J.; Zhang, H.; Zhao, S.; Liu, H. Vision-based gaze estimation: A review. *IEEE Trans. Cogn. Dev. Syst.* **2021**, *14*, 316–332. [CrossRef]
46. Mallick, S. Head Pose Estimation using OpenCV and Dlib. 2016. Available online: https://learnopencv.com/head-pose-estimation-using-opencv-and-dlib/ (accessed on 15 October 2023).
47. Case on OpenCV Camera Calibration and Human Head Pose Estimation, CSDN Blog. 2021. Available online: https://blog.csdn.net/zb1165048017/article/details/115553641 (accessed on 9 October 2023).
48. Hempel, T.; Abdelrahman, A.A.; Al-Hamadi, A. 6d Rotation representation for unconstrained head pose estimation. In Proceedings of the 2022 IEEE International Conference on Image Processing (ICIP), Bordeaux, France, 16–19 October 2022; pp. 2496–2500. [CrossRef]
49. Sadekar, K. Understanding Lens Distortion. 2020. Available online: https://learnopencv.com/understanding-lens-distortion/ (accessed on 8 October 2023).
50. Camera Calibration Using OpenCV-Python Toolkit. 2023. Available online: https://docs.opencv.org/4.x/dc/dbb/tutorial_py_calibration.html (accessed on 11 October 2023).
51. Baltrusaitis, T. Issue 969 of OpenFace Github. 2021. Available online: https://github.com/TadasBaltrusaitis/OpenFace/issues/969 (accessed on 29 September 2023).
52. Kendrick, C.; Tan, K.; Walker, K.; Yap, M.H. Towards real-time facial landmark detection in depth data using auxiliary information. *Symmetry* **2018**, *10*, 230. [CrossRef]
53. Venturelli, M.; Borghi, G.; Vezzani, R.; Cucchiara, R. From Depth Data to Head Pose Estimation: A Siamese Approach. In Proceedings of the International Conference on Computer Vision Theory and Applications, Setúbal, Portugal, 27 February–1 March 2017; pp. 194–201.

sensors

MDPI

Article

An Improved TransMVSNet Algorithm for Three-Dimensional Reconstruction in the Unmanned Aerial Vehicle Remote Sensing Domain

Jiawei Teng, Haijiang Sun *, Peixun Liu * and Shan Jiang

Changchun Institute of Optics, Fine Mechanics and Physics (CIOMP), Chinese Academy of Sciences, Changchun 130033, China; tengjiawei@ciomp.ac.cn (J.T.); jiangs@ciomp.ac.cn (S.J.)
* Correspondence: sunhaijiang@126.com (H.S.); liupx@ciomp.ac.cn (P.L.)

Abstract: It is important to achieve the 3D reconstruction of UAV remote sensing images in deep learning-based multi-view stereo (MVS) vision. The lack of obvious texture features and detailed edges in UAV remote sensing images leads to inaccurate feature point matching or depth estimation. To address this problem, this study improves the TransMVSNet algorithm in the field of 3D reconstruction by optimizing its feature extraction network and costumed body depth prediction network. The improvement is mainly achieved by extracting features with the Asymptotic Pyramidal Network (AFPN) and assigning weights to different levels of features through the ASFF module to increase the importance of key levels and also using the UNet structured network combined with an attention mechanism to predict the depth information, which also extracts the key area information. It aims to improve the performance and accuracy of the TransMVSNet algorithm's 3D reconstruction of UAV remote sensing images. In this work, we have performed comparative experiments and quantitative evaluation with other algorithms on the DTU dataset as well as on a large UAV remote sensing image dataset. After a large number of experimental studies, it is shown that our improved TransMVSNet algorithm has better performance and robustness, providing a valuable reference for research and application in the field of 3D reconstruction of UAV remote sensing images.

Keywords: reconstruction; deep learning; drone remote sensing; TransMVSNet; artificial intelligence

1. Introduction

In recent years, multi-view stereo (MVS) has become a research hotspot in the field of computer vision, with high potential value in computer-aided design [1], virtual reality [2], augmented reality [3], and robot navigation [4]. Prior to deep learning, conventional multi-view stereo vision involved first calibrating the camera [5], i.e., calculating the camera's image coordinate system in relation to the world coordinate system. Information from multiple 2D images was then used to reconstruct 3D information. Although great achievements have been made in the reconstruction of Lambertian surfaces [6], they are still affected by factors such as illumination variations or low texture leading to poor reconstruction results.

The three-dimensional reconstruction of remote sensing scenes by unmanned aerial vehicles (UAVs) is receiving increasing attention. However, there are still some challenges in the 3D reconstruction process, including the accuracy and efficiency of reconstruction, especially in complex and large-scale scenes. Therefore, the problem to be addressed in this study is the accuracy and efficiency of the 3D reconstruction of remotely sensed scenes using UAVs, especially in complex and large-scale scenes. The specific objective of this research is to improve the existing TransMVSNet 3D reconstruction algorithm with the aim of providing more accurate and detailed 3D models for various scenes. The importance of this work is that it has the potential to improve the adaptability of multi-view vision in the field of unmanned remote sensing and contribute to the development of better algorithms.

Related Work and Contribution

Among the traditional 3D reconstruction algorithms, the most representative of sparse reconstruction is the Structure from Motion (SFM) [7] algorithm, which takes a set of images as input and generates two pieces of information: the camera parameters of each image and a set of 3D points visible in the image, which are usually encoded as trajectories. A trajectory is defined as a list of the 3D coordinates of the reconstructed 3D points and the corresponding 2D coordinates in a subset of the input images. Dense reconstruction [8] is the process of finding points in space with photometric consistency [9] to stereo match the scene when the camera parameters are known. On these bases, OpenMVS [10] is a more classical multi-view stereo (MVS) open-source library that integrates the complete technical solution for 3D reconstruction, which includes camera modeling, multi-view stereo, dense reconstruction, surface reconstruction [11], point cloud fusion [12], and texture mapping [13].

In the era of deep learning, deep learning-based stereo vision uses deep CNNs to extract the depth map for each view, and the 3D model is finally obtained through multi-view fusion, which can effectively improve the accuracy of 3D reconstruction. In particular, MVSNet [14] proposed by Yao Yao et al. is the originator of multi-view stereo vision. In this approach, the algorithm mainly extracts the depth map for each view, and central to this is that each pixel of the reference image is searched along the antipodal line in all the projection-transformed source images to find the best depth with the lowest matching cost. Consequently, a depth map with high resolution and accuracy can be obtained. Then, in 2019, Prof. Long Quan's team at the Hong Kong University of Science and Technology improved MVSNet and proposed RMVSNet [15], which replaced 3D convolution with the GRU temporal network to reduce the model size, and then the loss was changed to cross-entropy loss for multi-classification.

In 2019, Chen et al. proposed PointMVSNet [16] based on MVSNet, which is an algorithm that predicts the depth information and then forms a 3D point cloud using the image. It then uses the algorithm of the 3D point cloud to optimize the regression of depth. Subsequently, in 2020, Hongwei Yi et al. proposed PVA-MVSNet [17], which is an algorithm that uses the attention mechanism to adaptively learn weights, such as the weights of different viewpoints. X. Gu et al. also proposed the Cascade-MVSNet [18] algorithm, which utilizes the strategy of chained costume construction to estimate the coarser depth values first and then further reduces the depth estimation range to improve the depth estimation accuracy, achieving higher resolution and higher accuracy depth maps with less GPU consumption. After dense reconstruction, the results of Cascade-MVSNet are also more complete than those of the previously mentioned methods. Meanwhile, in 2020, Jiayu Yang et al. proposed an unsupervised neural network, CVP-MVSNet [19]. This is a costume-based, small, and computationally efficient MVS deep inference network. The costume pyramid is constructed in a coarse-to-fine manner based on a detailed analysis of the relationship between the depth residual search range and image resolution; the framework can use less memory to process higher resolution images. It is six times faster than PointMVSNet.

More recently, Ding, Yikang et al. proposed the TransMVSNet [20] algorithm, which is the first attempt to use Transformer for MVS tasks. The authors utilize MVS due to its suitability for feature matching tasks and propose a powerful Feature Matching Transformer (FMT) [21] to leverage intra- (self-) and inter- (cross-)attention [22] to aggregate long-range context information within and across images. In this paper, to facilitate a better adaptation of the FMT, we leverage an Adaptive Receptive Field (ARF) [23] module to ensure smooth transfer in terms of the scope of features and bridge different stages with a feature pathway to transfer transformed features and gradients across different scales.

The algorithms mentioned above provide outstanding contributions to the field of multi-view stereo (MVS). Moreover, the application of 3D reconstruction technology in the field of UAV remote sensing [24] has been expanding, providing richer information and data for topographic surveying [25], urban planning [26], environmental monitoring [27], and other fields. By carrying photographic equipment for aerial photography using unmanned aircraft and processing and analyzing aerial images with 3D reconstruction algorithms, high-precision and high-resolution 3D maps [28] and models can be constructed, providing data support for other geographic information systems [29] and geoscientific research [30]. Compared with traditional multi-view stereo (MVS) vision datasets, the scenes in UAV remote sensing images are more complex, the image resolution is larger, and the impact of weather and other factors may lead to lower texture clarity in the image. The TransMVSNet network adopts the Transformer module, which is more suitable for this kind of scene, so our work is based on this.

In this work, we improve the TransMVSNet network, which uses a feature extraction module (FPN) [31] as its feature extraction network. In this paper, we use an asymptotic feature pyramid network (AFPN) [32] to support the direct interaction of non-adjacent layers. AFPN is initiated by fusing two neighboring low-level features and progressively incorporating high-level features into the fusion process. In this way, large semantic gaps between non-adjacent levels can be avoided. Considering the possibility of multi-target information conflicts during the feature fusion process at each spatial location, adaptive spatial fusion operations are further utilized to mitigate these inconsistencies. We use a network module based on the UNet structure [33] combined with an attention mechanism to improve the original network module in the construction of the cost volume, which can improve the quality and the accuracy and reliability of the generated depth map.

To summarize, our contributions are as follows:

(1) We improve the TransMVSNet neural network to estimate the depth map of UAV remote sensing images and solve the information conflict in the depth extraction process that results in unreliable depth maps.
(2) We adopt an asymptotic feature pyramid network (AFPN) that progressively integrates low-level, high-level, and top-level features in the bottom–up feature extraction process of the backbone network [34]. Meanwhile, different spatial weights are assigned to the features of different levels by ASFF [35], which enhances the importance of key levels and mitigates the effect of contradictory information from different targets.
(3) We use a UNet neural network to predict the depth while incorporating an attention mechanism to extract critical region information by adding weights.

2. Proposed Methods

2.1. Feature Extraction

TransMVSNet adopts the FPN feature pyramid structure, comprising a top–down path to achieve the fusion of features of different levels and a bottom–up path to make up for the lack of low-level feature details in high-level features. However, detailed information from low-level features may be lost or degraded during propagation and interaction. This leads to suboptimal extraction of detailed features from the original view.

In our work, we introduce a novel feature extraction pyramid (AFPN) with the structure shown in Figure 1. The bottom–up feature extraction process in the backbone begins by fusing two low-level features of different resolutions. In the later stages of feature extraction, the high-level features are incorporated into the fusion process to finally fuse the top-level features of the backbone. This type of fusion avoids large semantic gaps between non-adjacent levels.

In this process, low-level features are fused with semantic information from high-level features, and high-level features are fused with detailed information from low-level features. Due to this direct interaction, information loss or degradation in multi-level transmission can be avoided. This solves the above-mentioned limitations.

Based on the overall network architecture of the TransMVSNet network, the AFPN structure extracts three multi-scale depth image features with resolutions ranging from coarse to fine. In the overall feature extraction structure, the features are first coarsely extracted using a sequence of three simple network layers, the combination of which is a Conv2d network layer, a batchnormed normalization layer, and a Sigmoid Linear Unit (SiLU) [36] activation function. The SiLU activation function is smoother as it approaches 0, which can make the network output range between 0 and 1, which is more applicable in this structure. It is defined as follows:

$$silu = x * sigmoid(x) = \frac{x}{1 + e^{-x}} \quad (1)$$

Next, we input the features into the AFPN after changing the number of feature channels. In the AFPN structure, we used a 2 × 2 convolution with stride of 2 for 2-fold downsampling and a 4 × 4 convolution with stride of 4 for 4-fold downsampling; we used a similar structure for upsampling. This adapts the Adaptively Spatial Feature Fusion (ASFF) module. This is the most important aspect of our AFPN network, as it solves the problem of inconsistency within the feature pyramid by learning the links between different feature maps.

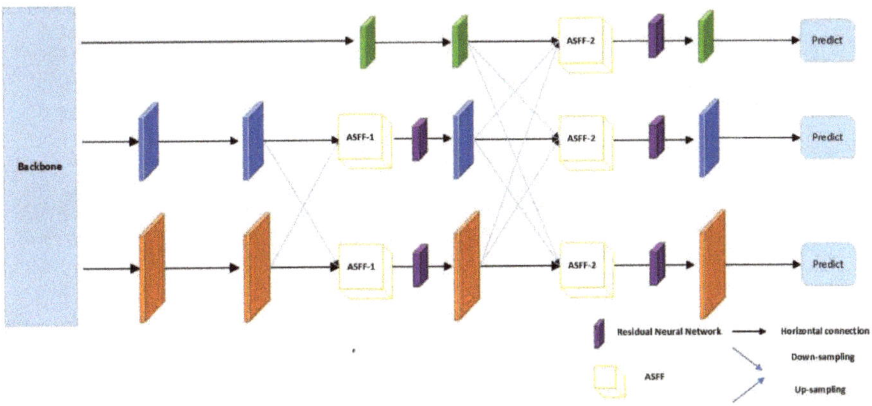

Figure 1. The architecture of the proposed asymptotic feature pyramid network (AFPN). AFPN is initiated by fusing two neighboring low-level features and progressively incorporating high-level features into the fusion process.

Next, we employ the ASFF [37] neural network model, which aims to improve the effectiveness of feature fusion and hence the accuracy of the deep costumers. The ASFF network model introduces an adaptive feature fusion module for fusing multiple feature maps at different levels. After the AFPN backbone network extracts the feature maps at different levels, it uses the adaptive attention mechanism to weight the fusion of these feature maps. In order to better retain the important feature information, compared to the feature extraction network without the ASFF network model, the multi-scale information can be better extracted after the addition, so that better results can be achieved in the next deep costal body construction.

In the ASFF module, for a certain level of features, the other levels are first adjusted to the same resolution and simply integrated, and then they are trained to find the best fusion. In Figure 1, we assume that before entering the ASFF-2 module, the feature levels are x1, x2, and x3. By multiplying the weight parameters α, β, and Y for the features from different layers and summing them up, the new fused features are obtained as shown in the following equation:

$$y_{ij}^{l} = \alpha_{ij}^{l} \cdot x_{ij}^{1 \to l} + \beta_{ij}^{l} \cdot x_{ij}^{2 \to l} + \gamma_{ij}^{l} \cdot x_{ij}^{3 \to l} \quad (2)$$

As can be seen from Equation (2), the ASFF module uses summation, which requires that the three level layers output the same-sized features and the same number of channels.

Therefore, it is necessary to perform upsampling or downsampling and adjust the number of channels for the features of different layers, as described above.

The weight parameters α, β, and Υ are then obtained by adjusting the feature maps of the different layers after a 1 × 1 convolution, followed by softmax after concat so that they are all in the range of [0, 1] and sum to one:

$$\alpha_{ij}^{l} = \frac{e^{\lambda_{\alpha_{ij}}^{l}}}{e^{\lambda_{\alpha_{ij}}^{l}} + e^{\lambda_{\beta_{ij}}^{l}} + e^{\lambda_{\gamma_{ij}}^{l}}} \tag{3}$$

The λ in Equation (3) represents the coefficients of the softmax function, meaning that the weight parameter can be used to adjust the size of the contribution of each feature map during the feature fusion.

Following the ASFF module, it is possible to enhance the importance of the critical level feature map and mitigate the impact of conflicting information from different targets. After feature fusion, we input each feature into the residual unit to continue learning features. As shown in Figure 1, we use a total of five residual units; each residual unit is similar to ResNet, including two 3 × 3 convolution modules, two batchnormed normalization layers, and a SiLU activation function. The residual unit maps the input and output to Equation (4), which allows for better feature learning and also optimizes the training of the neural network.

$$y = H(x, w_h) + x \tag{4}$$

In Equation (4), H(x, w_h) represents a residual unit, and x is the direct mapping component.

Through the above work, we can extract more detailed image features through the AFPN feature pyramid. After fusion with the Transformer model, its powerful self-attention mechanism and positional coding method can be used to extract and aggregate image features more accurately, laying a solid foundation for subsequent deep extraction.

2.2. Refinement of the Depth Forecast

The initial cost volume computed from the image feature maps is likely to contain noise, mainly due to problems related to the presence of non-Lambertian surfaces or line-of-sight occlusion.

Therefore, in order to predict the depth map, it is necessary to smooth the initial cost volume, optimize it, and refine the probability volume. In the original TransMVSNet network, a multi-scale 3D-CNN network is used for cost volume regularization. This network is similar to the 3D version of UNet, using an encoding–decoding architectural approach for neighborhood information aggregation over a large range of sensory fields at a relatively small cost volume.

Due to the fact that the global information is weighted on the same scale during the calculation process, it is not possible to suppress the information in regions of the image that are not related to the target object. The results predicted from each angle result in large errors at the edges and are smoother; thus, they fail to reflect the depth difference and make the reconstructed target hierarchy indistinct.

In order to solve this problem, the attention mechanism is added to the existing UNet structure in this work. The schematic is shown in Figure 2.

First, we applied the cross-attention module CCA [38]; the current level feature map and the previous level feature map are used as the first inputs into the CCA.

These two feature maps first travel to the AdaptiveAvgPool3d network layer, whose main role is to perform an adaptive average pooling operation on the input 3D data. Suppose the output data are N × h × w × d, where h is the height, w is the width, and d is the depth of the output data. The operation of the AdaptiveAvgPool3d module can be expressed as follows:

$$output[i, j, k] = 1/(h \times w \times d) * sum(input[p, q, r]) \tag{5}$$

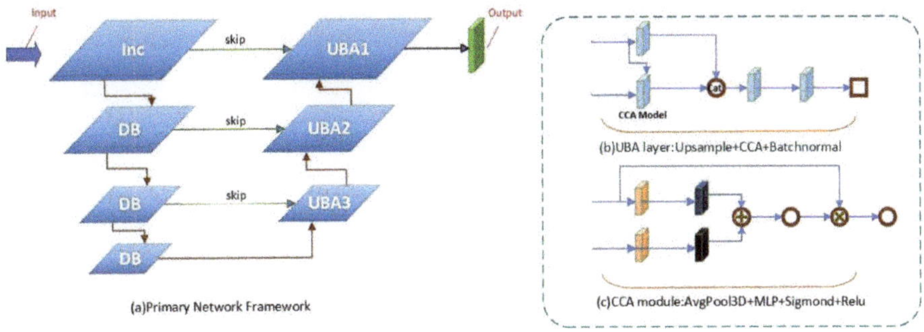

Figure 2. Cost volume regularization network: (**a**) the overall network, (**b**) the UBA layer, and (**c**) the CCA module in the UBA layer.

In Equation (5), the parameters satisfy the following conditions:

$$i = h/H \times p; j = w/W \times q; k = d/D \times r \tag{6}$$

After the AdaptiveAvgPool3d module adaptively tunes the features, they pass into the fully connected (FC) [39] network structure, which is shown in Figure 3.

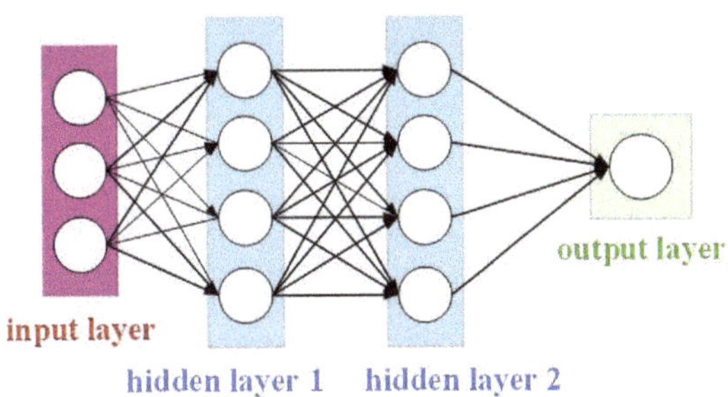

Figure 3. Fully connected (FC) network structure.

In the fully connected network, the input layer has n neurons, the hidden layer has m neurons, and the output layer has k neurons. The input of the input layer is denoted by x, the output of the hidden layer by h, the output of the output layer by y, the weight matrix by W, and the bias vector by b. Then, the computation process of the fully connected layer can be expressed as follows:

$$h = f(W_1 x + b_1) \tag{7}$$

$$y = g(W_2 h + b_2) \tag{8}$$

The computation of the hidden layer is shown in Equation (7), and the computation of the output layer is shown in Equation (8), F and g. The two formulas contain the activation functions; the dimensions of weight matrix W1 are (m, n), and the dimensions of W2 are (k, m); the dimensions of bias vector b1 are (m, 1), and the dimensions of b2 are (k, 1). So, by continuously iteratively adjusting the weights and biases, fully connected neural networks can learn complex nonlinear relationships between inputs and outputs.

Here, we assume that the input two feature maps are X and Y, and their dimensions are N × C and N × D, where N denotes the size of the feature map, and C and D denote the number of channels of the feature map, respectively. First, we compute the attentional weight matrices of X and Y, denoted as AX and AY, respectively. These weights are obtained by calculating the correlation between the two feature maps. Specifically, we can calculate the attentional weights between X and Y using the following formula:

$$AX = soft\,max(XW\_qY\hat{}T) \tag{9}$$

$$AY = soft\,max(YW\_qX\hat{}T) \tag{10}$$

In Equations (9) and (10), W_q is the query weight matrix. In this way, the CCA module can obtain the spatial location correlation on the feature map, and finally the spatial location correlation weight scale can be obtained via the Sigmoid activation operation.

The overall network structure is similar to that of the UNet network, where features are first downsampled in 3D and then upsampled, and attention is computed with the features in the downsampling process to obtain the feature relevance weight scale. This suppresses irrelevant regional features in the image by changing the weights while highlighting the significant features of the feature regions, especially the depth information of the edge mutation regions. This makes the predicted depth results hierarchical and more accurate.

3. Experimental Results

The DTU dataset [40] and a self-built UAV ground loop shot and push–sweep dataset were used to evaluate and validate our approach.

The DTU was captured using a fixed camera track in a well-controlled laboratory environment and contains 128 scenes in 49 views under seven different lighting conditions. Referring to the MVSNet network setup, we categorized the dataset into 79 training scenes, 18 test scenes, and 22 evaluation scenes.

We trained the original TransMVSNet network with the DTU dataset as well as our improved TransMVSNet network, and we used both the Pytorch training framework and cuda version 11.1 to train the network. In the training phase, we set the number of input images to N = 5 and the image resolution to 512 × 640. For coarse-to-fine regularization, the depth hypotheses were sampled from 425 mm to 935 mm; the number of depth hypotheses for each stage was 48, 32, and 8, respectively. The corresponding depth intervals were attenuated from the coarsest stage to the finest stage by 0.25 and 0.5, respectively.

Then, we tested the optimal weights of the training results separately on the test dataset. A comparison of the depth maps of the images in the Scan1 scene is shown in Figure 4.

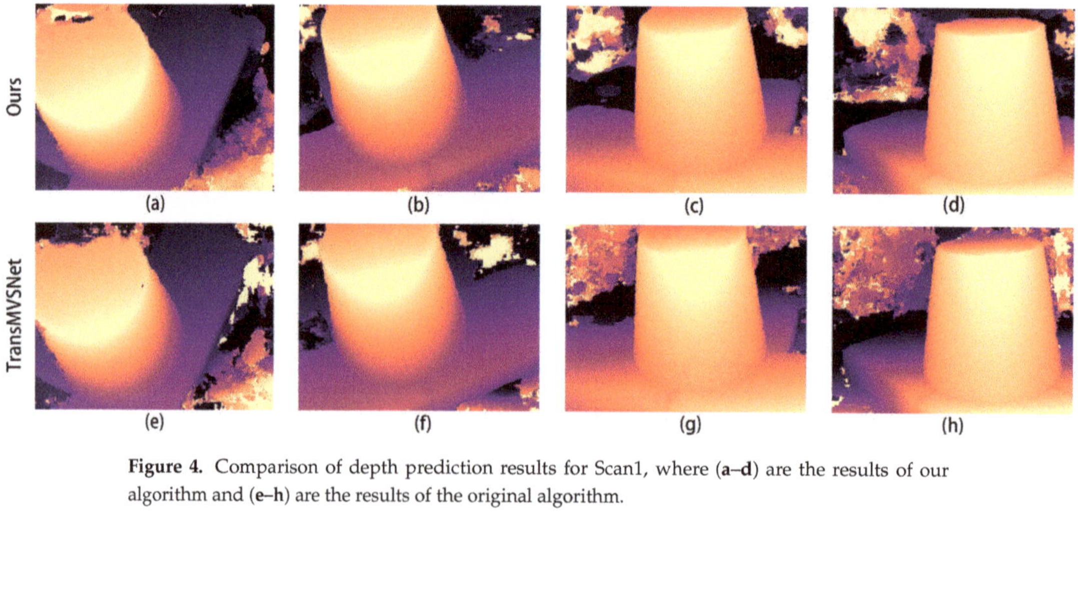

Figure 4. Comparison of depth prediction results for Scan1, where (**a–d**) are the results of our algorithm and (**e–h**) are the results of the original algorithm.

In the images in Figure 4a,e, it can be seen that the improved algorithm extracts more complete edges of the depth image and has less clutter in the background. The other results from b to g also show a more distinct and complete hierarchy in places in the mutated region at the edge of the depth map.

The comparison graphs of the Scan4, Scan9, and Scan10 scenes in the DTU dataset are shown in Figures 5–7.

In Figures 5–7, (a) to (d) are the depth prediction results of our improved algorithm, and (e) to (h) are the depth prediction results of the original algorithm. From the comparison results, the improved algorithm can be seen to outperform the original algorithm in terms of the accuracy, completeness, and detail of depth prediction. This is mainly due to the optimization of the improved algorithm in terms of feature extraction and depth prediction.

In the feature extraction stage, the AFPN structure can adaptively fuse features of different scales, which enhances the feature representation. In the depth prediction stage, large-scale depth variation and detail information can be better handled by introducing a coarse-to-fine regularization strategy.

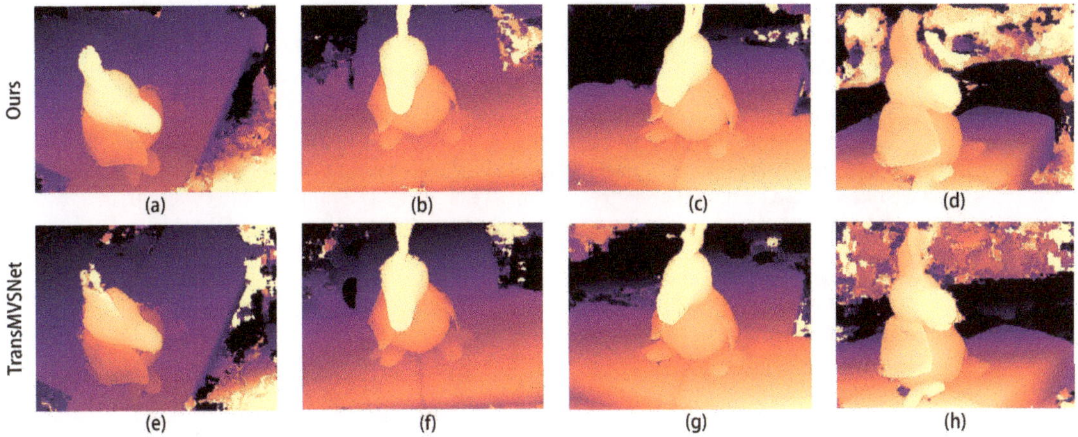

Figure 5. Comparison of depth prediction results for Scan4, where (**a–d**) are the results of our algorithm and (**e–h**) are the results of the original algorithm.

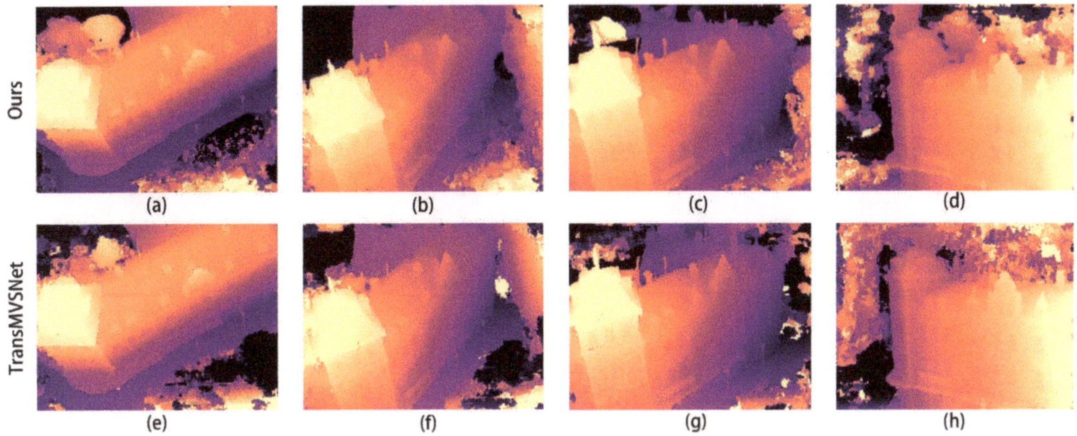

Figure 6. Comparison of depth prediction results for Scan9, where (**a–d**) are the results of our algorithm and (**e–h**) are the results of the original algorithm.

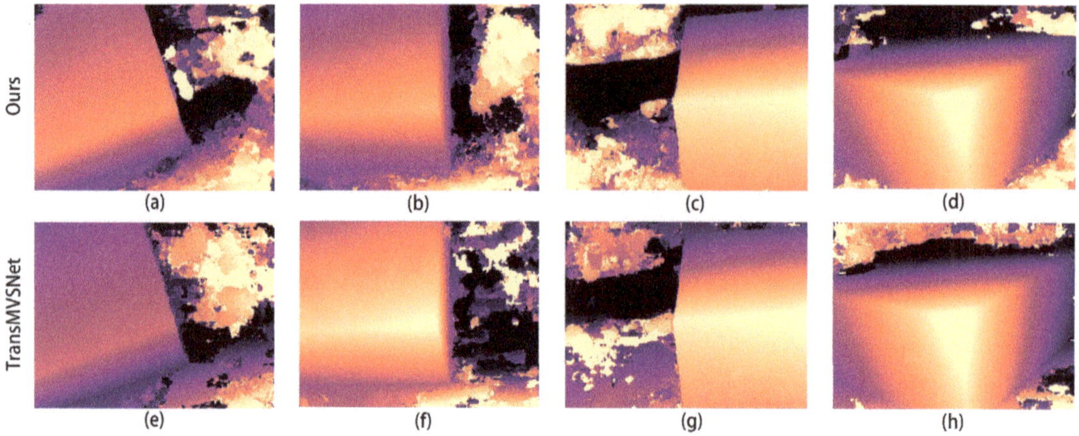

Figure 7. Comparison of depth prediction results for Scan10, where (**a–d**) are the results of our algorithm and (**e–h**) are the results of the original algorithm.

To evaluate the application of our model in the field of UAV remote sensing, we also performed the corresponding test in the main scene reconstruction of buildings, as shown in Figure 8. Here, the image of Scene 1 was obtained from a public dataset provided by the well-known UAV photogrammetry company PIX4D [41]. The camera model was DJI FC6310, the world coordinates were selected as WGS84/UTM zone 17N, and the image resolution was 5472 × 3478. The image for Scene 2 was captured with an AV-900 model drone with a Sony NEX-5T camera model; the world coordinate system was also selected as WGS84/UTM zone 17N, the average ground sampling distance (GSD) was 1.66 cm/0.65 in, and the image resolution was 4912 × 3264.

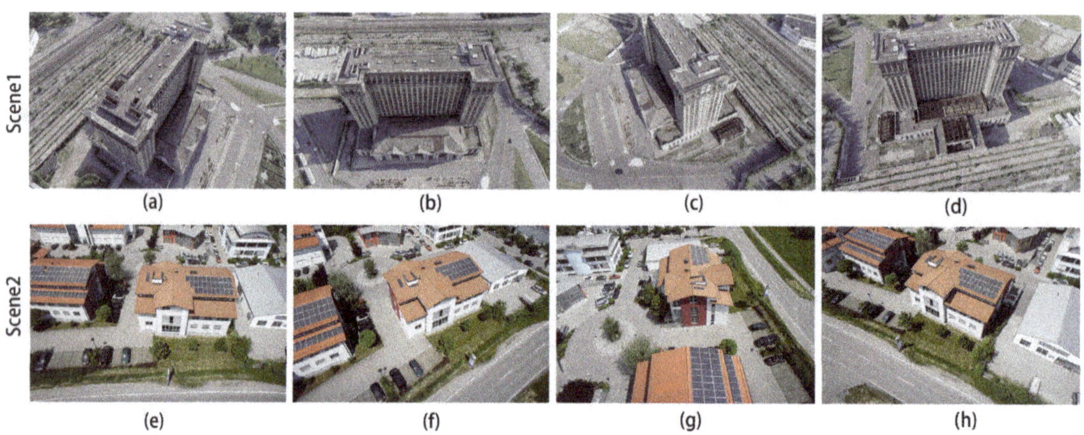

Figure 8. (**a–h**) are overhead drone images of buildings from the drone mapping dataset Pix4D. Scene 1 is an unfinished building and Scene 2 is a residential home in Chicago, IL, USA.

For both scene datasets, we extracted the internal and external camera parameters separately. After adjusting the format of the data to that of DTU, they were fed to both our improved algorithm as well as the original algorithm for depth extraction.

The corresponding depth map results for the two scenarios in Figure 8 are shown in Figures 9 and 10. In both figures, (a–d) show the depth prediction images of the improved algorithm and (e–h) show the depth prediction images of the original algorithm.

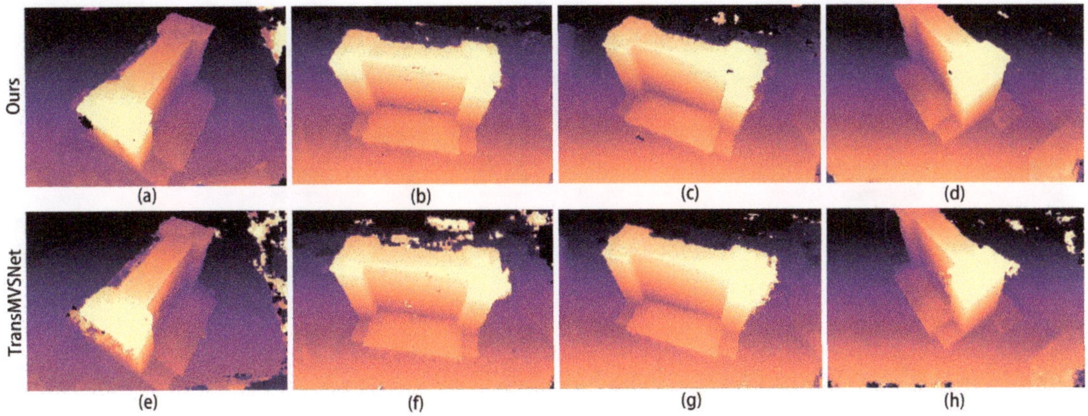

Figure 9. Depth map of the first scene in Figure 8: (**a–d**) are depth prediction images of our improved algorithm; (**e–h**) are depth prediction images of the original algorithm.

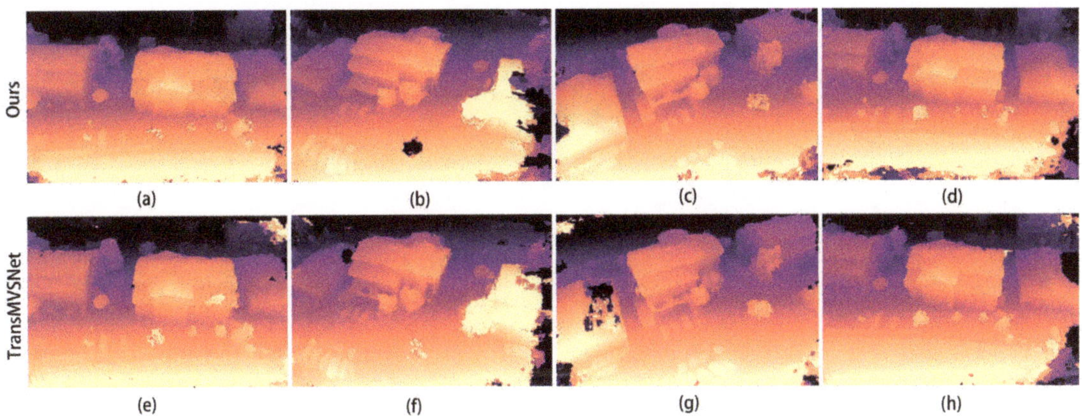

Figure 10. Depth map of the second scene in Figure 8: (**a–d**) are depth prediction images of our improved algorithm; (**e–h**) are depth prediction images of the original algorithm.

As can be seen from Figure 9a,e, the edges of the building in Figure 9e are not smooth and appear jagged. After employing our improved algorithm, the edges of the building are smoother, and the depth information of the mutated region is more accurate.

These two scenes belong to the UAV ring shot dataset. The camera is positioned at a fixed attitude angle around the scene, similar to the DTU dataset, and the reconstruction of such scenes is also good. The reconstruction results are shown in Figure 11, in which (a–c) are the reconstruction results of Scene 1, and (d–f) are the reconstruction results of Scene 2.

The 3D models in Figure 11a–d are the 3D reconstruction results of Scene 1 in Figure 8, and (e–h) are the 3D reconstruction results of Scene 2 in Figure 8. This 3D model was created with MeshLab v2022.02 [42] software, and we used a part of the model under different angles for illustration; the following 3D model also uses the same method.

We also built two of our own datasets to validate our algorithms, as shown in Figure 12. We prepared a sandbox demonstration system for ground targets, and we used a robotic arm to drive the camera around to capture the image. The camera's focal length is 26 mm, the aperture size is 1.5, and the resolution of the captured image is 1080 × 1920.

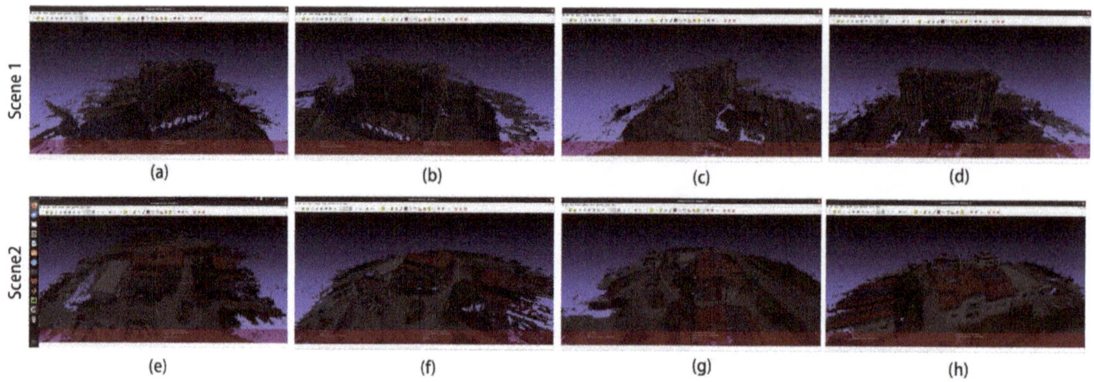

Figure 11. The 3D reconstruction results of the improved algorithm: (**a–d**) for Scene 1 and (**e–h**) for Scene 2 in Figure 8.

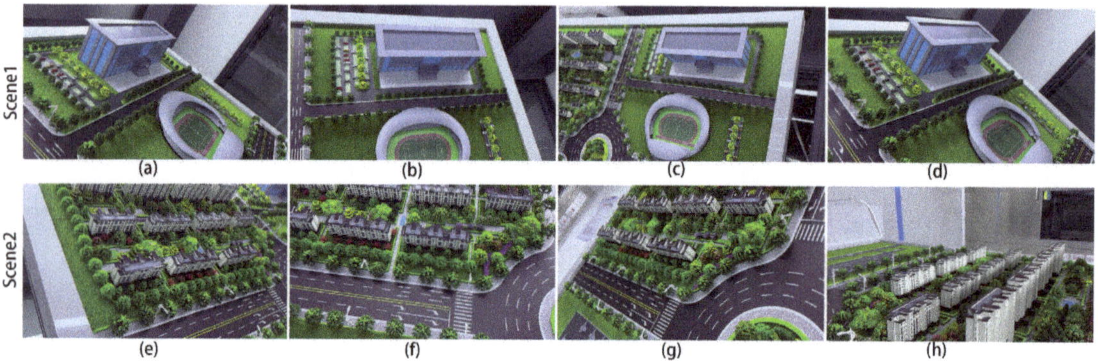

Figure 12. Self-constructed wrap-around robotic arm overhead shooting scene dataset: (**a–d**) are Scene 1, which mainly includes schools and stadiums; (**e–h**) are Scene 2, which mainly includes residential areas.

The results for the two scenes in Figure 12 are shown in Figure 13, and it can be seen clearly that the edges of the building are clearer and there is less depth loss in the improved algorithm between Figures 13b and 13e. From Figure 13b,e, it can be clearly seen that the edges of the building are clearer, and less depth is missing in the results of the improved algorithm. Similarly, the comparison between Figures 13i and 13l shows the same effect. Figure 16 shows the 3D reconstruction model produced using our improved algorithm.

Next, we acquired a dataset of push–sweep photography captured with a drone and a publicly available dataset from the photogrammetric company Pix4d, whose camera model is the Canon IXUS 127 HS, and selected the world coordinate system as WGS84/UTM zone 32N. Because the ground sampling resolution is small and the scene as a whole is very large, we selected a few images to be displayed in Figure 15.

The depth maps in Figure 16 contain the more iconic buildings in this scene. From the comparison of Figure 16c,g, for example, the edges of the buildings in Figure 17c are smoother and the layers are clearer, while the depth of the buildings in Figure 16g is more pronounced, which can also show that our improved algorithm is very effective in improving the results. Figure 17 shows the 3D reconstruction model created using our improved algorithm.

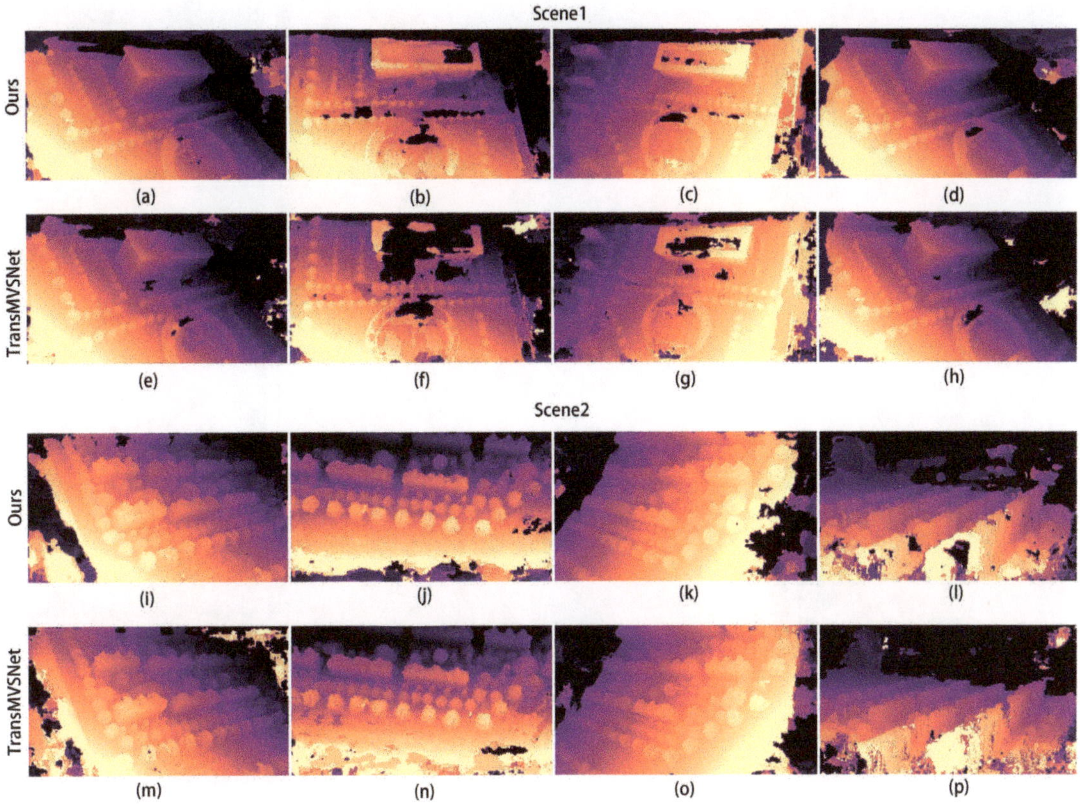

Figure 13. (**a**–**p**) contain the comparison of the depth maps of the two self-built scenario datasets: Scene 1 is the result of Figure 13, and Scene 2 is the result of Figure 14.

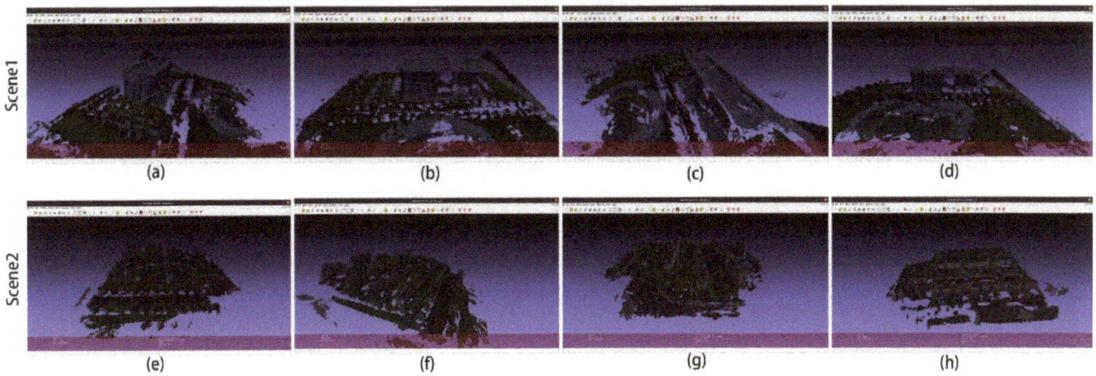

Figure 14. (**a**–**h**) are the three-dimensional reconstruction modeling diagram of the two scenes in Figure 12.

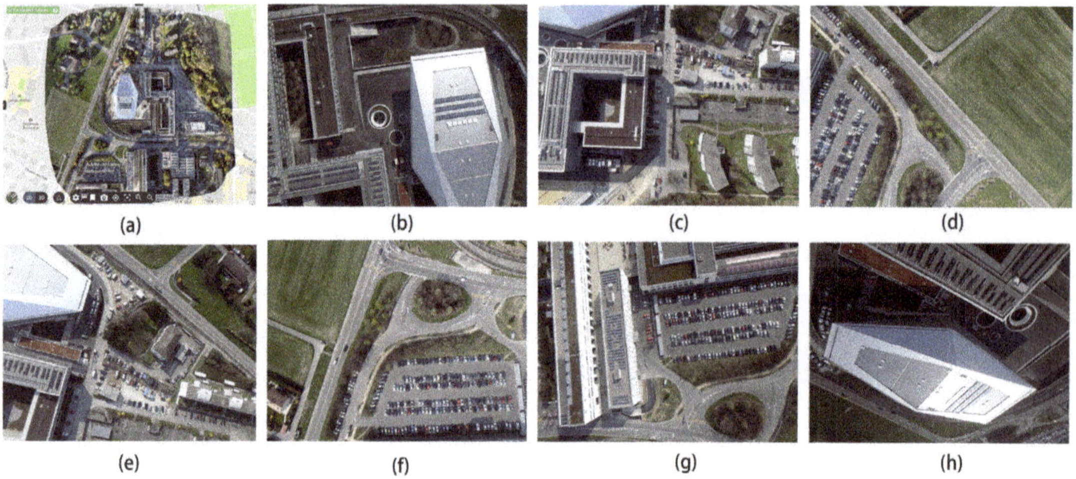

Figure 15. (**a–h**) are iconic site in Lausanne, showcasing the city's beauty and history. It is the capital of the canton of Vaud, Switzerland, from the unmanned remote sensing dataset Pix4D.

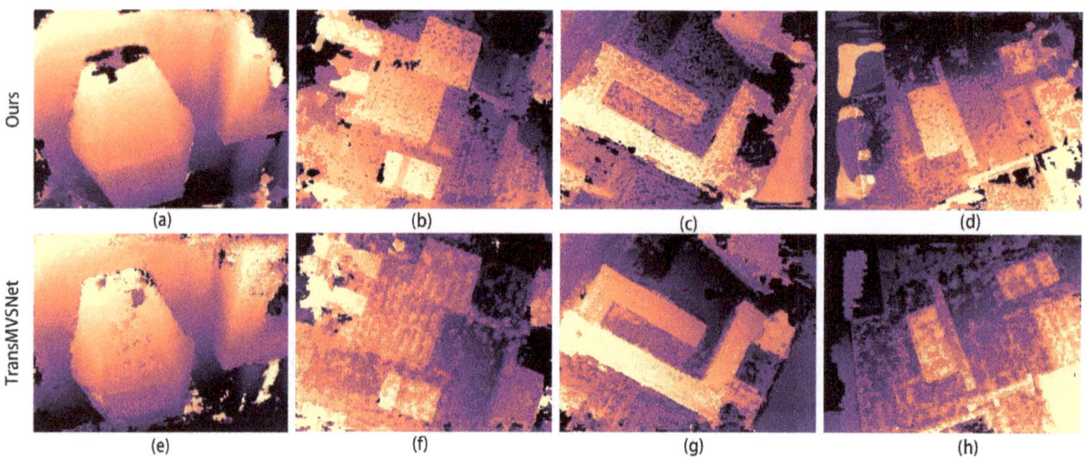

Figure 16. Depth prediction image of the scene in Figure 15, comparing our improved algorithm with TransMVSNet, where (**a–d**) are the results of our algorithm and (**e–h**) are the results of the TransMVSNet.

The scenes in Figure 15 are mainly urban scenes. We then found an image of a scene with a mountain village and a natural landscape, located in the capital of the canton of Vaud, district of Lausanne, Swiss Confederation. This dataset was obtained with the camera model senseFly S.O.D.A, and the coordinate system used is CH1903+/LV95. The full view of the scene in the dataset is shown in Figure 18a; b–e are the parts of the images that were fed into the neural network, which have a resolution of 3648 × 5472.

Figure 19 shows the computed depth image and the results of the 3D reconstruction are shown in Figure 20 for each of the four views of the model.

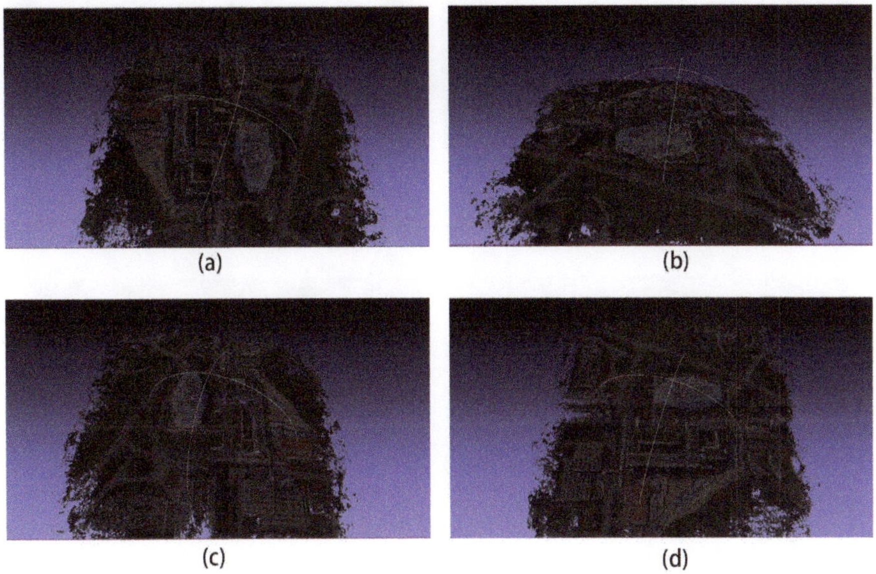

Figure 17. (**a–d**) are the three-dimensional reconstructed model view of the scene in Figure 15.

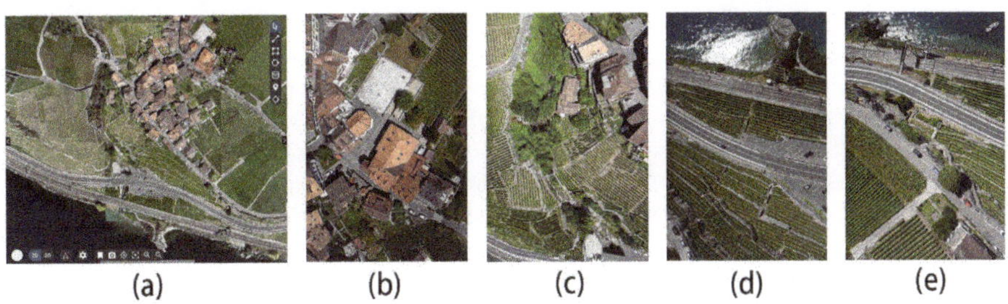

Figure 18. (**a–e**) show coastal mountain village in the capital of the canton of Vaud, district of Lausanne, Switzerland, photographed on Pix4D.

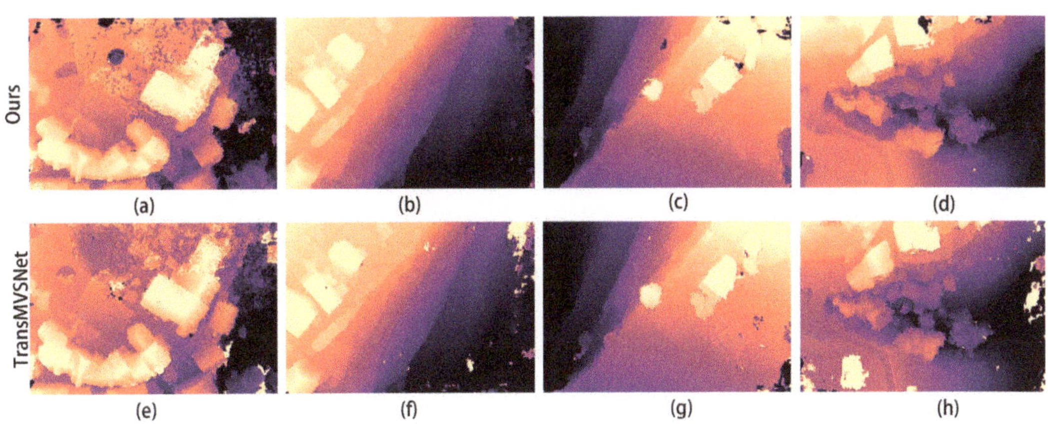

Figure 19. Depth map of the scene in Figure 18: (**a–d**) are depth prediction images of our improved algorithm; (**e–h**) are depth prediction images of the original algorithm.

Figure 20. (a–d) are the three-dimensional reconstruction model view of the scene in Figure 18.

4. Discussion

4.1. Comparison on the DTU Dataset

The main difference between our algorithm and TransMVSNet is the use of the multi-scale feature extraction network, which can provide multi-scale features for the Transformer to better compute inter-image and intra-image attention and, at the same time, change the global information weights when predicting the depth information. This can effectively inhibit the irrelevant regions in the image with the target, making the prediction results more accurate. We also compare it with the MVS algorithm mentioned in the Introduction section.

In the DTU dataset, there are two metrics to evaluate the accuracy of the point cloud: Acc and Comp. The Acc metric is used to find the points in the reconstructed point cloud according to the points in the reconstructed point cloud and evaluate the accuracy of the point cloud by the distance between the points in the reconstructed point cloud and the points in the reconstructed point cloud. And the Comp metric is used to find out whether there are any corresponding points in the reconstructed point cloud based on the points in the true value of the point cloud and to evaluate the integrity of the point cloud by the number of corresponding points. The lower the values of the metrics, the better, as this means that the distance between the reconstructed resultant point cloud and the true value of the point cloud is smaller and thus means that the recovered point cloud is more accurate. The comparison of our algorithm with several other algorithms is shown in Figure 21.

In Table 1, the comparison of the accuracy of these algorithms on the DTU dataset is shown. From the data in the table, it can be seen that our algorithm is ranked second in Acc and first in Comp. The overall value is the average of the first two metrics; so, based on this comparison, our algorithm performs better than the other algorithms on the DTU dataset.

In Table 2, it can be seen that for the same input size, our algorithm and TransMVSNet have reduced inference speed while requiring more GPU memory for training. This is what we need to optimize in subsequent neural networks.

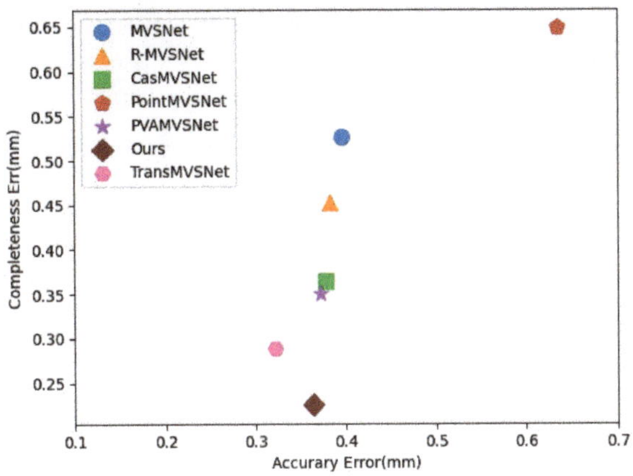

Figure 21. Comparison with state-of-the-art deep learning-based MVS methods on DTU dataset (lower is better).

Table 1. Comparison of reconstruction quality on DTU dataset.

Method	Acc. (mm)	Comp. (mm)	Overall
MVSNet	0.396	0.527	0.462
R-MVSNet	0.383	0.452	0.417
CasMVSNet	0.3779	0.3645	0.371
PointMVSNet	0.6344	0.6481	0.391
PVA-MVSNet	0.372	0.350	0.361
TransMVSNet	**0.321**	0.289	0.305
Ours	0.3643	**0.225**	**0.295**

Bolded data indicates current best results.

Table 2. Comparison of GPU memory usage and runtime on DTU dataset for different input sizes. GPU memory usage and runtime are obtained by running the official evaluation code of baselines on the same machine with an NVIDIA GeForce RTX 3090 laptop graphics card.

Method	Input Size	Depth Map Size	GPU Mem (MB)	Runtime
MVSNet	1600 × 1152	400 × 288	22,511	2.76
R-MVSNet	1600 × 1152	400 × 288	6915	5.09
CasMVSNet	1600 × 1152	640 × 512	5345	0.492
PointMVSNet	1600 × 1152	800 × 576	13,081	3.04
PVA-MVSNet	1600 × 1152	800 × 576	24,870	4.36
TransMVSNet	1600 × 1152	1152 × 864	23,008	0.65
Ours	1600 × 1152	1152 × 864	23,150	1.49

4.2. Comparison on UAV Remote Sensing Datasets

The main reasons for why we chose to improve TransMVSNet are the shortcomings related to the weak texture, repetitive texture, and non-Lambertian surfaces of UAV remote sensing images, which have a large impact on the results in the multi-view stereo (MVS) process. Moreover, the process of multi-view stereo (MVS) is a one-to-many feature matching process, which uses convolution to take local features. The localization of convolutional features hinders the perception of global information, which is crucial for robust depth estimation in regions with the above-mentioned shortcomings. TransMVSNet combines Transformer with multi-view stereo (MVS), and our work improves the feature extraction and depth prediction part of Transformer by considering the global feature information and discarding the feature information in the useless region, which makes the depth prediction result more accurate.

Meanwhile, our algorithms are very sensitive to the settings of hyperparameters, which include numdepth, depth hypotheses, and depth interval. In the DTU dataset, these three hyperparameters are set the same as in TransMVSNet to make it convenient to compare the results. In the dataset of remote sensing images from UAVs, we needed to adjust the hyperparameters to ensure that it achieved the best depth prediction. The numdepth was set to 192 in almost all MVS series algorithms. Therefore, we also used 192, followed by the depth interval hyperparameter (4, 1, 0.5), and finally set the depth hypotheses; this hyperparameter represents the number of plane scanning depth hypotheses for each stage and is generally set to three stages. After the first stage, with the maximum number of hypotheses, it can subsequently become smaller because the larger the setting, the smaller the depth interval. The initial stage requires strong supervision to be able to output more details and later becomes smaller to make the details smoother. Therefore, this is also a factor that can determine whether the depth prediction is accurate.

To set the hyperparameter depth hypotheses, we carried out quantitative experiments. First, we set the number of small two-plane scans in the three phases to a fixed value (32, 8) and changed the maximum number of plane scans x, which was set to 48, 64, 96, and 128. Then, we changed the number of second-plane scans y, which was set to 8, 16, 32, and 40, and set the other two phases to a fixed value (48, 8). Finally, we changed the number of third-plane scans in the three phases, which was set to 8, 16, 24, and 30, and set the other two phases to fixed values (48, 32). The results are shown in Figure 22.

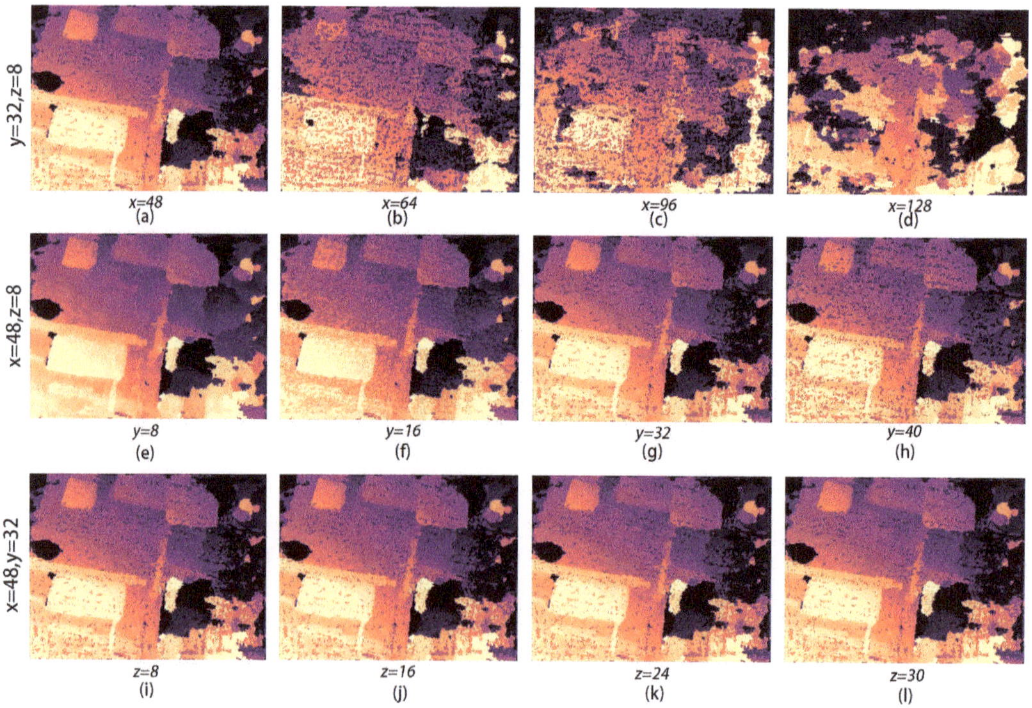

Figure 22. Quantitative experiments: (**a**–**d**) are the first to quantify the number of scans in three planes, (**e**–**h**) are the second to quantify the number of scans in three planes, and (**i**–**l**) are the third to quantify the number of scans in three planes.

The results of the quantitative experiments are shown in Figure 22. When y = 32 and z = 8, the first phase of the plane scanning depth x is 48. Here, the depth prediction result is the best; its depth error is small, and the edge of the object is smoother. Then, we set x = 48 and z = 8, and the best results are obtained when the second phase of the scanning depth y is 32, as shown in Figure 22g. When y = 8, the depth is not very obvious, but it is slightly better than at y = 16, and there is still a large part of the image missing. Finally, when we set x = 48 and y = 32, the best result is obtained when the third phase of the plane scanning depth z is 8. In the four images in Figure 22i–l, it does not look like the difference is very large because the third phase of the plane scanning depth is small, resulting in large depth intervals and less detailed information. So, although the difference is not very large, based on the smoothness of the object edges, z = 8 can be judged to be the best parameter setting. Therefore, the super parameter depth hypothesis is set to 48, 32, 8.

4.3. Constraints or Challenges

When we improved the feature extraction network model, first of all, the complexity of the AFPN network model was much larger than that of the FPN, so the parameters of each network layer needed to be constantly debugged to obtain the optimal collocation. Meanwhile, considering that after extracting multi-scale features, we need to assign weights to the key features to achieve the optimal feature extraction, we adopted the ASFF network model.

During the algorithmic research, after replacing the FPN feature extraction network model using the AFPN combined with the ASFF feature extraction network model, considering updating the FMT feature matching module of the original network, after checking the related literature, we found that the local feature transform LoFTR [43] network model can satisfy our needs, and this network model also uses the self- and cross-attention layer. This network model also uses a Transformer with self- and cross-attention layers to handle the dense local features extracted from the backbone network. After our modification, we found that there is not much difference in the idea and algorithm structure with the original network, so there is no big improvement, so we discarded this improvement.

In the final stage of designing the costume regularized network model, we continuously optimize the network structure and hyperparameter combinations and finally determine the best network design scheme to incorporate the cross-attention module CCA into the UNet network model, and at the same time, in order to optimize the training process of the model, we use two NVIDIA 3090 graphics cards for distributed training to improve the training efficiency.

All of the above are challenges and limitations that we encountered during the design and research phase of the algorithm, and we eventually overcame them to ensure the stability and reliability of the research model.

5. Conclusions

In this paper, we improve the TransMVSNet network by first extracting the cascade features using the AFPN feature extraction network and then improving the regularized costumed body network by incorporating an attention mechanism to make the overall network suitable for the 3D reconstruction of images captured by UAVs in the field of remote sensing. We combined the characteristics of the remote sensing images taken by UAVs, i.e., the image features are richer, the field of view is wider, and the ground buildings occupy fewer pixels in the image; therefore, our improved network was better able to extract the image features, highlight the information of the feature area, and make the edges of the objects more hierarchical.

In previous 3D reconstruction work, researchers have focused mainly on close-up object reconstruction and urban outdoor scene reconstruction. Three-dimensional reconstruction in the field of remote sensing is also a research focus. Our reconstruction method can completely restore the whole image of an area, which can provide valuable help for remote sensing measurements and other subsequent work.

Our algorithm also has limitations in the field of UAV remote sensing 3D reconstruction. First of all, the input image sequence must be continuous and comprehensive; if there are many missing images, it will lead to missing depth prediction, resulting in an incomplete reconstructed model. Meanwhile, the algorithm is very strict on the camera position; if the camera position is deviated, it will lead to wrong depth prediction. In addition, compared with the original algorithm, the computational speed will be slower, and these problems need to be solved in the future.

In the future, to address the above limitations, we would like to combine other algorithms such as the Superpoint feature point matching algorithm to find the bitmap, and we can complement the sequence image by the neural radiation field of Nerf series. At the same time, we can improve the algorithm to speed up the single-frame processing and add a real-time rendering function to realize a real-time reconstruction and rendering function. We hope to apply the algorithm to more fields of 3D reconstruction.

Author Contributions: Conceptualization, J.T.; methodology, J.T.; software, J.T.; validation, P.L., H.S. and S.J.; formal analysis, P.L.; investigation, H.S. and P.L.; resources, S.J.; data curation, P.L.; writing—original draft preparation, J.T.; writing—review and editing, H.S. and P.L.; visualization, S.J.; supervision, J.T.; project administration, H.S. and P.L.; funding acquisition, H.S. All authors have read and agreed to the published version of the manuscript.

Funding: This research was funded by the Jilin Provincial Science and Technology Development Program Key R&D Project, grant number No. 20220201148GX, and the Changchun Science and Technology Development Program Projects, grant number No. 23JQ01, 23YQ14.

Institutional Review Board Statement: Not applicable.

Informed Consent Statement: Not applicable.

Data Availability Statement: The DTU is a large dataset containing 128 scenes from controlled laboratory environments modeled with models captured using a structured light scanner (https://roboimagedata.compute.dtu.dk/, accessed on 1 January 2024). The dataset from the leading photogrammetry company Pix4d is publicly available (https://cloud.pix4d.com/demo, accessed on 1 January 2024).

Acknowledgments: The authors thank the anonymous reviewers for their constructive comments and suggestions that greatly improved this paper.

Conflicts of Interest: The authors declare no conflicts of interest.

References

1. Peng, Q.; Fei, L. Research and Development of Computer Aided Product Innovation Design System. In Proceedings of the 2020 5th International Conference on Mechanical, Control and Computer Engineering (ICMCCE), Harbin, China, 25–27 December 2020; pp. 1398–1401.
2. Yastikli, N.; Özerdem, Ö.Z. Architectural Heritage Documentation by Using Low Cost Uav with Fisheye Lens: Otag-I Humayun in Istanbul as a Case Study. *ISPRS Ann. Photogramm. Remote Sens. Spat. Inf. Sci.* **2017**, *IV-4/W4*, 415–418. [CrossRef]
3. Balci, D.; Kirimker, E.O.; Raptis, D.A.; Gao, Y.; Kow, A.W.C. Uses of a dedicated 3D reconstruction software with augmented and mixed reality in planning and performing advanced liver surgery and living donor liver transplantation (with videos). *Hepatobiliary Pancreat. Dis. Int.* **2022**, *21*, 455–461. [CrossRef]
4. Ann, N.Q.; Achmad, M.S.H.; Bayuaji, L.; Daud, M.R.; Pebrianti, D. Study on 3D scene reconstruction in robot navigation using stereo vision. In Proceedings of the 2016 IEEE International Conference on Automatic Control and Intelligent Systems (I2CACIS), Selangor, Malaysia, 22 October 2016; pp. 72–77.
5. Lu, Z.; Lv, Y.; Ai, Z.; Suo, K.; Gong, X.; Wang, Y. Calibration of a Catadioptric System and 3D Reconstruction Based on Surface Structured Light. *Sensors* **2022**, *22*, 7385. [CrossRef] [PubMed]
6. Langguth, F.; Sunkavalli, K.; Hadap, S.; Goesele, M. *Shading-Aware Multi-View Stereo*; Springer: Cham, Switzerland, 2016; pp. 469–485.
7. Um, D.; Lee, S. Microscopic Structure from Motion (SfM) for Microscale 3D Surface Reconstruction. *Sensors* **2020**, *20*, 5599. [CrossRef]
8. Yao, Y.; Li, S.; Zhu, S.; Deng, H.; Fang, T.; Quan, L. Relative Camera Refinement for Accurate Dense Reconstruction. In Proceedings of the 2017 International Conference on 3D Vision (3DV), Qingdao, China, 10–12 October 2017; pp. 185–194.

9. Hasson, Y.; Tekin, B.; Bogo, F.; Laptev, I.; Pollefeys, M.; Schmid, C. Leveraging Photometric Consistency Over Time for Sparsely Supervised Hand-Object Reconstruction. In Proceedings of the 2020 IEEE/CVF Conference on Computer Vision and Pattern Recognition (CVPR), Seattle, WA, USA, 13–19 June 2020; pp. 568–577.
10. Li, S.; Xiao, X.; Guo, B.; Zhang, L. A Novel OpenMVS-Based Texture Reconstruction Method Based on the Fully Automatic Plane Segmentation for 3D Mesh Models. *Remote Sens.* **2020**, *12*, 3908. [CrossRef]
11. Ruchay, A.; Dorofeev, K.; Kalschikov, V.; Kober, A. Accuracy analysis of surface reconstruction from point clouds. In Proceedings of the 2020 International Conference on Information Technology and Nanotechnology (ITNT), Samara, Russia, 26–29 May 2020; pp. 1–4.
12. Ai, L.; Xie, Z.; Yao, R.; Li, L. R-VPCG: RGB image feature fusion-based virtual point cloud generation for 3D car detection. *Displays* **2023**, *77*, 102390. [CrossRef]
13. Wu, X.; Zhou, D.; Wen, P. A MVS based automatic 3D model reconstruction system from turntable image sequence. In Proceedings of the 2016 IEEE International Conference on Information and Automation (ICIA), Ningbo, China, 1–3 August 2016; pp. 166–171.
14. Yao, Y.; Luo, Z.; Li, S.; Fang, T.; Quan, L. *MVSNet: Depth Inference for Unstructured Multi-View Stereo*; Springer: Cham, Switzerland, 2018; pp. 785–801.
15. Yao, Y.; Luo, Z.; Li, S.; Shen, T.; Fang, T.; Quan, L. Recurrent MVSNet for High-Resolution Multi-View Stereo Depth Inference. In Proceedings of the 2019 IEEE/CVF Conference on Computer Vision and Pattern Recognition (CVPR), Long Beach, CA, USA, 15–20 June 2019; pp. 5520–5529.
16. Chen, R.; Han, S.; Xu, J.; Su, H. Point-Based Multi-View Stereo Network. In Proceedings of the 2019 IEEE/CVF International Conference on Computer Vision (ICCV), Seoul, Republic of Korea, 27 October–2 November 2019; pp. 1538–1547.
17. Yi, H.; Wei, Z.; Ding, M.; Zhang, R.; Chen, Y.; Wang, G.; Tai, Y.-W. Pyramid Multi-view Stereo Net with Self-adaptive View Aggregation. *arXiv* **2019**, arXiv:1912.03001. [CrossRef]
18. Liu, W.; Wang, J.; Qu, H.; Shen, L. Hierarchical MVSNet with cost volume separation and fusion based on U-shape feature extraction. *Multimed. Syst.* **2023**, *29*, 377–387. [CrossRef]
19. Yang, J.; Mao, W.; Alvarez, J.M.; Liu, M. Cost Volume Pyramid Based Depth Inference for Multi-View Stereo. *arXiv* **2019**, arXiv:1912.08329. [CrossRef]
20. Ding, Y.; Yuan, W.; Zhu, Q.; Zhang, H.; Liu, X.; Wang, Y.; Liu, X. TransMVSNet: Global Context-aware Multi-view Stereo Network with Transformers. In Proceedings of the 2022 IEEE/CVF Conference on Computer Vision and Pattern Recognition (CVPR), New Orleans, LA, USA, 18–24 June 2022; pp. 8575–8584.
21. Wu, Z.-Z.; Zou, C.; Wang, Y.; Tan, M.; Weise, T. Rotation-aware representation learning for remote sensing image retrieval. *Inf. Sci.* **2021**, *572*, 404–423. [CrossRef]
22. Sun, L.; Liu, B.; Tao, J.; Lian, Z. Multimodal Cross- and Self-Attention Network for Speech Emotion Recognition. In Proceedings of the ICASSP 2021—2021 IEEE International Conference on Acoustics, Speech and Signal Processing (ICASSP), Toronto, ON, Canada, 6–11 June 2021; pp. 4275–4279.
23. Xu, C.; Qi, Y.; Wang, Y.; Lou, M.; Pi, J.; Ma, Y. ARF-Net: An Adaptive Receptive Field Network for breast mass segmentation in whole mammograms and ultrasound images. *Biomed. Signal Process. Control* **2022**, *71*, 103178. [CrossRef]
24. Chen, X.; Li, Q.; Li, R.; Cai, X.; Wei, J.; Zhao, H. UAV Network Path Planning and Optimization Using a Vehicle Routing Model. *Remote Sens.* **2023**, *15*, 2227. [CrossRef]
25. Du, M.; Li, H.; Roshanianfard, A. Design and Experimental Study on an Innovative UAV-LiDAR Topographic Mapping System for Precision Land Levelling. *Drones* **2022**, *6*, 403. [CrossRef]
26. Pan, L.; Gu, L.; Ren, R.; Yang, S. *Land Cover Classification Based on Machine Learning Using UAV Multi-Spectral Images*; SPIE: Bellingham, WA, USA, 2020; Volume 11501.
27. Eskandari, R.; Mahdianpari, M.; Mohammadimanesh, F.; Salehi, B.; Brisco, B.; Homayouni, S. Meta-analysis of Unmanned Aerial Vehicle (UAV) Imagery for Agro-environmental Monitoring Using Machine Learning and Statistical Models. *Remote Sens.* **2020**, *12*, 3511. [CrossRef]
28. Goulas, D.; Georgopoulos, A.; Sarakenos, A.; Paraschou, C. *3D Mapping from High Resolution Satellite Images*; SPIE: Bellingham, WA, USA, 2013; Volume 8795.
29. Fan, Y.-W.; Zhu, W.-J.; Ban, S.-H. Mimic Geographic Information System. In *E3S Web of Conferences, Proceedings of 2018 International Seminar on Food Safety and Environmental Engineering (FSEE 2018), Guangzhou, China, 30 November–2 December 2018*; EDP Sciences: Les Ulis, France, 2019; p. 03005.
30. Bittmann, F.; Bungenstock, F.; Wehrmann, A. Drowned palaeo-landscapes: Archaeological and geoscientific research at the southern North Sea coast. *Neth. J. Geosci.* **2022**, *101*, e3. [CrossRef]
31. Li, Z.; Li, E.; Xu, T.; Samat, A.; Liu, W. Feature Alignment FPN for Oriented Object Detection in Remote Sensing Images. *IEEE Geosci. Remote Sens. Lett.* **2023**, *20*, 6001705. [CrossRef]
32. Yang, G.; Lei, J.; Zhu, Z.; Cheng, S.; Feng, Z.; Liang, R. AFPN: Asymptotic Feature Pyramid Network for Object Detection. *arXiv* **2023**, arXiv:2306.15988. [CrossRef]
33. Feng, X.; Wang, T.; Yang, X.; Zhang, M.; Guo, W.; Wang, W. ConvWin-UNet: UNet-like hierarchical vision Transformer combined with convolution for medical image segmentation. *Math. Biosci. Eng.* **2023**, *20*, 128–144. [CrossRef]
34. Rajeh, S.; Savonnet, M.; Leclercq, E.; Cherifi, H. *Modularity-Based Backbone Extraction in Weighted Complex Networks*; Springer: Cham, Switzerland, 2022; pp. 67–79.

35. Qiu, M.; Huang, L.; Tang, B.-H. ASFF-YOLOv5: Multielement Detection Method for Road Traffic in UAV Images Based on Multiscale Feature Fusion. *Remote Sens.* **2022**, *14*, 3498. [CrossRef]
36. Elfwing, S.; Uchibe, E.; Doya, K. Sigmoid-weighted linear units for neural network function approximation in reinforcement learning. *Neural Netw.* **2018**, *107*, 3–11. [CrossRef]
37. Zhang, D.-Y.; Zhang, W.; Cheng, T.; Zhou, X.-G.; Yan, Z.; Wu, Y.; Zhang, G.; Yang, X. Detection of wheat scab fungus spores utilizing the Yolov5-ECA-ASFF network structure. *Comput. Electron. Agric.* **2023**, *210*, 107953. [CrossRef]
38. Wang, B.; Teng, Y.; Lau, V.; Han, Z. CCA-Net: A Lightweight Network Using Criss-Cross Attention for CSI Feedback. *IEEE Commun. Lett.* **2023**, *27*, 1879–1883. [CrossRef]
39. Zheng, T.; Wang, Q.; Shen, Y.; Lin, X. Gradient rectified parameter unit of the fully connected layer in convolutional neural networks. *Knowl.-Based Syst.* **2022**, *248*, 108797. [CrossRef]
40. Aanæs, H.; Jensen, R.R.; Vogiatzis, G.; Tola, E.; Dahl, A.B. Large-Scale Data for Multiple-View Stereopsis. *Int. J. Comput. Vis.* **2016**, *120*, 153–168. [CrossRef]
41. Caputo, T.; Bellucci Sessa, E.; Marotta, E.; Caputo, A.; Belviso, P.; Avvisati, G.; Peluso, R.; Carandente, A. Estimation of the Uncertainties Introduced in Thermal Map Mosaic: A Case of Study with PIX4D Mapper Software. *Remote Sens.* **2023**, *15*, 4385. [CrossRef]
42. Cignoni, P.; Callieri, M.; Corsini, M.; Dellepiane, M.; Ganovelli, F.; Ranzuglia, G. MeshLab: An Open-Source Mesh Processing Tool. In Proceedings of the European Interdisciplinary Cybersecurity Conference, Salerno, Italy, 2–4 July 2008.
43. Zhao, L.; Zhang, H.; Mbachu, J. Multi-Sensor Data Fusion for 3D Reconstruction of Complex Structures: A Case Study on a Real High Formwork Project. *Remote Sens.* **2023**, *15*, 1264. [CrossRef]

sensors

MDPI

Article

Phase Error Reduction for a Structured-Light 3D System Based on a Texture-Modulated Reprojection Method

Chenbo Shi [1], Zheng Qin [1], Xiaowei Hu [2], Changsheng Zhu [1], Yuanzheng Mo [1], Zelong Li [1], Shaojia Yan [1], Yue Yu [1], Xiangteng Zang [1] and Chun Zhang [1,*]

1 College of Intelligent Equipment, Shandong University of Science and Technology, Tai'an 271019, China; shichenbo@gmail.com (C.S.); qinz0304@163.com (Z.Q.); cs.zhu@sdust.edu.cn (C.Z.); 202283230023@sdust.edu.cn (Y.M.); 202383230007@sdust.edu.cn (Z.L.); 202383230010@sdust.edu.cn (S.Y.); 202383230013@sdust.edu.cn (Y.Y.); zangxt@sdust.edu.cn (X.Z.)
2 Department of Electronic Engineering, Tsinghua University, Beijing 100084, China; xiaoweihu1020@163.com
* Correspondence: 13811989049@163.com

Abstract: Fringe projection profilometry (FPP), with benefits such as high precision and a large depth of field, is a popular 3D optical measurement method widely used in precision reconstruction scenarios. However, the pixel brightness at reflective edges does not satisfy the conditions of the ideal pixel-wise phase-shifting model due to the influence of scene texture and system defocus, resulting in severe phase errors. To address this problem, we theoretically analyze the non-pixel-wise phase propagation model for texture edges and propose a reprojection strategy based on scene texture modulation. The strategy first obtains the reprojection weight mask by projecting typical FPP patterns and calculating the scene texture reflection ratio, then reprojects stripe patterns modulated by the weight mask to eliminate texture edge effects, and finally fuses coarse and refined phase maps to generate an accurate phase map. We validated the proposed method on various texture scenes, including a smooth plane, depth surface, and curved surface. Experimental results show that the root mean square error (RMSE) of the phase at the texture edge decreased by 53.32%, proving the effectiveness of the reprojection strategy in eliminating depth errors at texture edges.

Keywords: phase-shifting method; phase error; texture edge; reprojecting; scene modulation

1. Introduction

As a non-contact 3D measurement technology, FPP [1] has been widely used in cultural relics protection, manufacturing, and other fields [2–4]. However, due to the influence of scene texture and imaging system defocus, the scene brightness does not meet the conditions of the ideal pixel-wise model at the edge of the reflectivity change, causing phase estimation errors, as shown in Figure 1. Figure 1a represents a smooth plane with texture, and Figure 1b is a depth image calculated using the traditional FPP method. As shown in Figure 1b, the brightness of the edge pixels is affected by the surrounding pixels due to the defocus of the image collected by the camera at the edge of the black-and-white texture, resulting in phase estimation errors. Therefore, improving the depth estimation accuracy at the texture edge is a difficult problem faced by the FPP method.

Defocus and the overall measurement accuracy of the system are the leading causes of discontinuity-induced measurement artifacts (DMAs). The generation of DMA errors can be slowed by improving the accuracy of the system measurement and the degree of defocus. To improve accuracy, Zhang et al. [5] regarded the projector as an inverse camera to achieve high-precision measurement. Li et al. [6] used a distortion model to create distortion stripe patterns for projection, thereby reducing the measurement error caused by distortion. Peter et al. [7] located the error pixels and directly deleted them. Pan et al. [8] proposed a method to optimize the phase error by using harmonics iteratively. Wu et al. [9] and Burke et al. [10] used mathematical models and post-processing algorithms to eliminate the impact of DMA errors. Although the above method can improve the overall measurement accuracy, it could be more effective in eliminating measurement errors caused by sudden changes in reflectivity.

Figure 1. Measurement effect of traditional FPP method. (**a**) Smooth texture plane; (**b**) traditional FPP method measurement results.

In reducing the degree of defocus, the error is generally reduced by estimating the blur kernel. Li et al. [11] and Drouin et al. [12] reduced measurement errors by calculating the point spread function. Yue et al. [13] estimated the error pixel value based on the phase values around the error pixel. Wu et al. [14,15] estimated the phase error caused by the PSF through deconvolution. Brakhage et al. [16] used intensity gradients to measure the possible locations of artifacts and then used Gaussian curves to eliminate phase errors. Wang et al. [17] proposed a method to modify the projection intensity and exposure time at the pixel level by estimating the object's surface reflectance and ambient light. Although the above methods have improved results for simple scenes, they cannot adapt to complex textures due to the difficulty in accurately estimating the blur kernel. These methods are not able to sufficiently distinguish between texture edges and actual depth edges.

In industrial measurement, FPP technology can quickly obtain the surface topography of objects. However, phase errors can occur during the measurement process because of the object's surface texture interference. Therefore, this paper eliminates texture errors by modulating the intensity of the scene texture captured by the camera.

This paper theoretically analyzes the phase model and proposes a brightness equalization strategy based on scene modulation. First, the modulation intensity image of the scene is calculated using the actual scene image, and the modulation mask image is made using the coarse phase map. Then, the mask image is fused with the original stripe image to obtain the reprojected image. Finally, the coarse and reprojected phases are fused to obtain the refined phase map. The proposed method significantly improved depth error estimation at texture edges.

The remainder of this paper is organized as follows. Section 2 explains the FPP decoding model under non-pixel-wise ideal imaging. Section 3 describes the system framework of the feedback modulation projection method. Section 4 shows the experimental results. Section 5 discusses the experiments, and finally, Section 6 summarizes this paper.

2. Principle

This study used a monocular structured-light system to perform a 3D reconstruction of a scene. The system comprises a camera, a projector, a computer, and other equipment. Gray code and phase-shifting patterns are combined to perform the 3D reconstruction, not only retaining the advantages of the phase-shifting method but also alleviating the drawbacks, improving the 3D reconstruction accuracy of the scene.

Three-dimensional phase-shifting structured light generally uses M-bit Gray code patterns to obtain the phase period and N-step phase-shifting stripe patterns to obtain the wrapped phase. Subsequently, the wrapped phase is unwrapped to obtain a continuous phase. The N-step phase-shifting lighting model [18] projected by the projector can be expressed by Equation (1),

$$I_n(p) = A(p) + B(p)\cos[\varphi(p) + 2n\pi/N] \tag{1}$$

where p represents the pixel position, $A(p)$ represents the background light intensity, $B(p)$ represents the modulated light intensity, $\varphi(p)$ represents the wrapped phase of position p, N represents the number of phase-shifting steps, and n represents the nth phase-shifting fringe image.

However, during the measurement process, the local intensity of the target can change because of interference from factors such as camera defocus or sudden reflectivity changes, as shown in Figure 2.

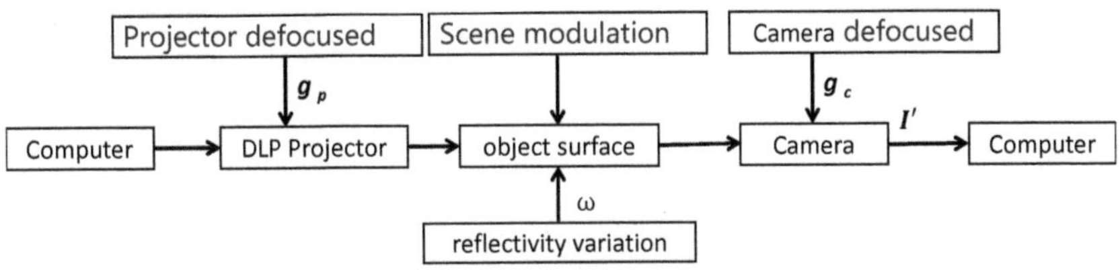

Figure 2. The process of capturing the intensity change in the stripe image by the camera.

According to Figure 2, when the camera is out of focus, the reflectivity of the measured surface changes. The light received by the camera will be affected, causing the intensity signal of a single pixel to be spatially averaged. Such pixels are called pixels affected by the non-pulse point spread function (PSF). The blur caused by defocus in the measurement system is similar to the Gaussian blur kernel [16]. Therefore, the defocus blur kernel g_c can be expressed in the form of Equation (2),

$$g_c(x) = \frac{1}{\sqrt{2\pi}\sigma} e^{-\frac{(x^2)}{2\sigma^2}} \tag{2}$$

where x represents the pixel position, and σ represents the Gaussian blur coefficient determined by the depth of the scene point. During the structured-light pattern's projection, modulation, and collection process, the pattern experiences multiple interferences and conversions. Meanwhile, the image projected by the projector onto the target experiences interference, e.g., camera defocus and projector defocus. The image is also disturbed by sudden changes in the reflectivity of the object's surface. Since the projector is out of focus, it does not directly affect the measured phase, but the sudden change in reflectivity will affect the measured scene. Assuming that point q is located in the neighborhood D of p, the actual brightness $I_n'(p)$ of point p captured by the camera can be expressed in the form of Equation (3),

$$\begin{aligned} I_n'(p) &= \sum_{q\in D} I_n(q,p)\cdot g_c(q,p) = \sum_{q\in D} A(p)\cdot g_c(q,p) \\ &+ \sum_{q\in D} B(q)\cdot \omega(q)\cdot g_c(q,p)cos\left(\varphi(p) + \frac{2\pi n}{N}\right) \end{aligned} \tag{3}$$

where $B(q)$ represents the projection intensity of point q, $w(q)$ represents the reflectivity of point q, and n represents the nth phase-shifting fringe pattern. The first term represents the influence of background light intensity; its value remains unchanged. Here, note $A'(p) = \sum_{q\in D} A(p)\cdot g_c(q,p)$.

For the second term in Equation (3), two points on the left and right sides of point p are picked in the scene in Figure 3a and are denoted by q_l and q_r, respectively. Assuming that the formula in Equation (4) is established,

$$B(q_l)\cdot\omega(q_l) \approx B(q_r)\cdot\omega(q_r) \tag{4}$$

and due to the symmetry properties of the Gaussian kernel in the local neighborhood, $g_c(q_l, p) \approx g_c(q_r, p)$ in Figure 3b. The relationship between the phases on point p's left and right sides can be expressed in the form of Equation (5):

$$\begin{aligned} &\cos\left(\varphi(q_l) + \frac{2\pi n}{N}\right) + \cos\left(\varphi(q_r) + \frac{2\pi n}{N}\right) = \\ &2\cos\frac{\varphi(q_r) - \varphi(q_l)}{2}\cos\left(\frac{\varphi(q_r) + \varphi(q_l)}{2} + \frac{2\pi n}{N}\right) \end{aligned} \tag{5}$$

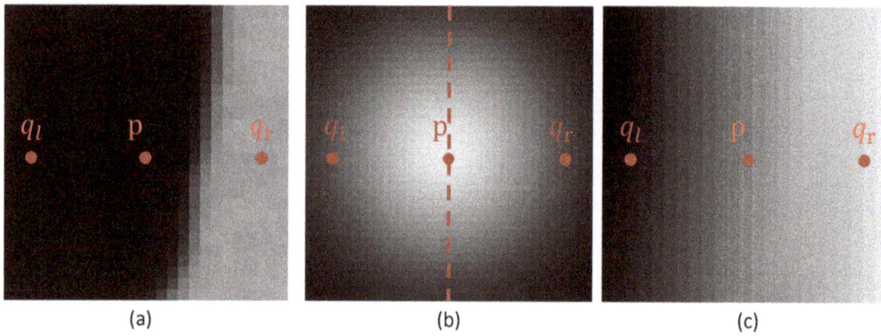

Figure 3. The relationship between camera defocus and phase in the scene. (**a**) The camera captures scene intensity; (**b**) the two-dimensional Gaussian distribution; (**c**) the phase value of (**a**).

Because of the smoothness of the phase in Figure 3c, assuming $\varphi(q_l) + \varphi(q_r) \approx 2\varphi(p)$, we can obtain Equation (6):

$$\cos\left(\frac{\varphi(q_r) + \varphi(q_l)}{2} + \frac{2\pi n}{N}\right) \approx \cos\left(\varphi(p) + \frac{2\pi n}{N}\right) \tag{6}$$

By combining Equations (3) and (6), the light intensity formula in the actual scene captured by the camera can be expressed as Equation (7):

$$\begin{aligned} I'_n(p) = A'(p) + &\sum_{q \in \frac{D}{2}} B(q) \cdot \omega(q) \cdot g_c(q, p) \\ &\cdot \cos\frac{\varphi(q_r) - \varphi(q_l)}{2}\cos\left(\varphi(p) + \frac{2\pi n}{N}\right) \end{aligned} \tag{7}$$

Since the value of $\varphi(q_r) - \varphi(q_l)$ is only related to depth changes in local scene points, it is irrelevant for $\varphi(p)$. Therefore, the factors independent of n in the second term of Equation (7) can be recorded in the form of Equation (8):

$$B'(p) = \sum_{q' \in \frac{D}{2}} B(q') \cdot \omega(q') \cdot g_c(q', p) \cos\varphi(q') \tag{8}$$

Hence, Equation (7) can be simplified to Equation (9):

$$I'_n(p) = A'(p) + B'(p)\cos[\varphi(p) + 2n\pi/N] \tag{9}$$

A more accurate phase decoding result can be obtained by adopting the form of Equation (1).

$$\varphi(p) = arctan\frac{\sum_{n=0}^{n=N-1} I'_n(p)\sin\frac{2\pi n}{N}}{\sum_{n=0}^{n=N-1} I'_n(p)\cos\frac{2\pi n}{N}} \tag{10}$$

The brightness model Equation (9) and the ideal phase model Equation (10) are based on the assumption of Equation (4). Therefore, to achieve brightness equalization for the scene, this paper proposes a feedback modulation projection strategy based on scene modulation to reduce the phase error at the texture edge.

3. Method

An anti-texture interference method based on feedback modulation projection is designed to correct measurement errors caused by a sudden change in reflectivity in the 3D reconstruction of structured light. Due to interference from the surface texture of the measured object, the pixels at the edge of the texture are disturbed by the pixels in the local neighborhood, which changes the ω value of the pixel and causes measurement errors. Inspired by this idea, this paper attempts to reduce the change degree of the ω value in a local neighborhood to reduce measurement errors.

3.1. Framework

The framework of the proposed method is shown in Figure 4. A typical method is used to obtain the original coarse phase value. The camera captures the most powerful illumination-modulated images to generate intensity-modulated images γ. According to the original coarse phase, the pixel positioning of the intensity-modulated image from the camera coordinate system to the projector coordinate system is realized, and the modulation mask image M is generated. M is combined with the original fringe to generate a reprojection pattern projected onto the scene to calculate the modulated absolute phase. The original coarse and modulated phases are fused to obtain the phase image with reduced error.

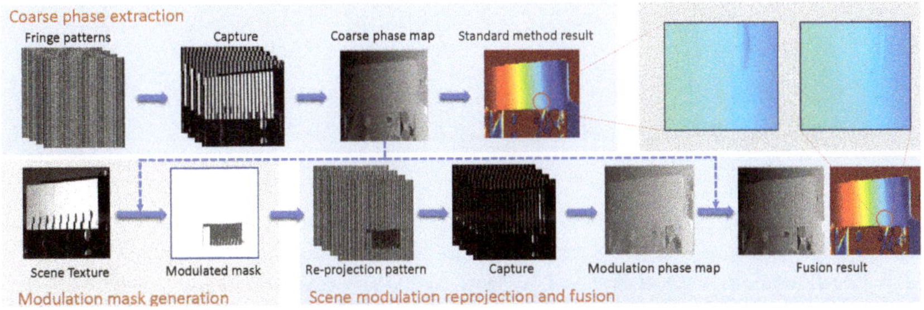

Figure 4. Computational framework of our proposed method.

3.2. Modulation Mask Generation

To reduce the impact of reflectivity changes on structured-light 3D measurement, it is necessary to reduce the change in reflectivity at the edge of the texture. Hence, the illumination intensity of the scene captured by the camera becomes consistent and achieves uniform reflectivity, thus reducing measurement errors caused by sudden changes in reflectivity.

Regarding the distribution of error pixels in the original error image, this paper locates the error pixel position $I_e(p)$ through the edge intensity characteristics of the texture position in the maximum light modulation pattern. For the modulation strategy, the measurement system parameters, or light source intensity, are modified to reduce the projection intensity of pixels in high-reflectivity areas so that the reflectivity at the position of the sudden change tends to be uniform. That is, the intensities of the bright and dark areas captured by the camera are the same. Since this paper uses the maximum light intensity modulation pattern to calculate the modulation intensity, the modulation strategy is as shown in Equation (11):

$$\gamma(p) = \frac{cI'_k(p)}{255 \times \max(I_{l,i}(p), t)} \tag{11}$$

where $\gamma(p)$ represents the modulation intensity that the pixel needs to be projected, $I_k'(p)$ represents the intensity value of point p in the pattern modulated by pure white light, and t represents a customized modulation intensity parameter. The purpose is to adjust the modulation intensity. $I_{l,i}(p)$ represents the lowest camera capture intensity, and c represents the self-set intensity modulation threshold. Such a modulation strategy can adjust the intensity of the projection parameters of the light source to meet the control requirements for sudden changes in reflectivity at the edge of the texture.

The projection modulation intensity information γ based on the camera pixel plane can be obtained by measuring changes in the scene surface reflectance. We also establish the mapping relationship between the camera and projector pixel coordinates. The texture edge correspondence during reprojection is achieved. According to the coarse phase, we can match the corresponding positions of the camera and the projector planes to obtain the modulated mask image M.

3.3. Scene Modulation Reprojection

By locating the error area and using the modulation strategy proposed in this paper, the ROI area scene shown in Figure 5a is intensity-modulated according to Equation (11). Image M is projected onto the surface of the measurement scene, as shown in Figure 5b. Before projecting image M, a rough estimate of the depth is required. When the depth estimate is inaccurate, it will cause a mismatch between the size of M and the texture of the scene. Image M's size can be changed through morphological operations, such as expansion and erosion, during image processing.

The comparison in Figure 5d shows that image M can slow down the brightness change in the texture's edge area. According to the comparison of the curves corresponding to the red line position in the image in Figure 5a–c, as shown in Figure 5d, the phase error peak appears on the darker side of the texture edge and gradient edge. Then, we used Equation (12) to add M to the original phase-shifting fringe pattern to obtain a new set of scene-modulated fringe patterns:

$$I_r(i) = I_o(i) \cdot M \tag{12}$$

where $I_o(i)$ and $I_r(i)$, respectively, represent the ith original stripe pattern and the ith modulated stripe pattern in the projection sequence. After adding mask modulation, the change in the $\omega(p)$ value at the texture's edge is reduced.

The generated stripe image with M is projected and collected. At this time, the reflectivity at the texture's edge in the scene tends to be uniform. The camera obtains a scene image with uniform brightness when capturing the image. We decoded the reprojected image and calculated the new absolute phase value Φ_r.

The phase error at the texture edge is reduced by fusing the original phase information with the modulated phase information. It can be seen from the comparison in Figure 5d that the error peak in the texture from the light to dark area appears on the dark side, with the peak value of the absolute gradient value as the divider; the error peak in the texture from the dark to light area is the same. Therefore, the average of absolute gradient values $G(p)$ in the local neighborhood is calculated using Equation (13) based on the pattern's texture characteristics under the strongest illumination modulation and the gradient edge characteristics:

$$G(p) = \frac{\sum\limits_{k=-m}^{m} |g(p+k)|}{2m+1} \tag{13}$$

where $g(p)$ represents the gradient value at position p, and m represents the neighborhood range for calculating the average of absolute gradient values.

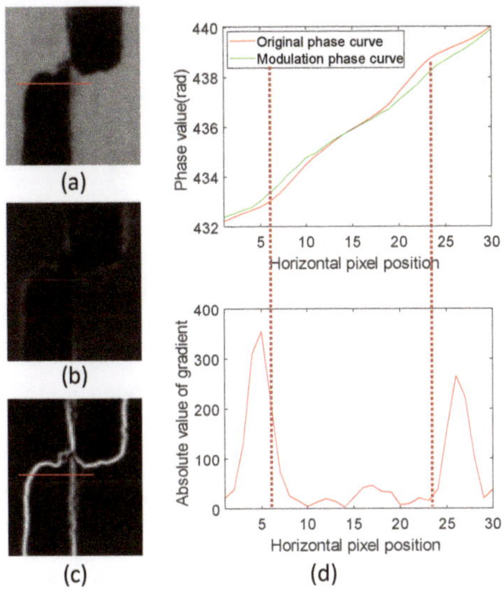

Figure 5. Modulation mask. (**a**) Maximum light modulation pattern; (**b**) scene image after adding mask; (**c**) gradient absolute value image; (**d**) absolute gradient value and phase comparison of line drawing positions.

We search for the depth peak in the original depth map following the position where the larger $G(p)$ occurs in the dark area's local neighborhood and find the position of the error pixel point $I_e(p)$. Phase fusion is performed according to the error pixel positioning. If a particular pixel is an error pixel, the modulated phase value is used as the fusion phase value. Otherwise, the original phase value is used, as shown in Equation (14):

$$\Phi_f(p) = \begin{cases} \Phi_o(p) & \text{if } I_e(p) = 255, \\ \Phi_r(p) & \text{if } I_e(p) = 0. \end{cases} \tag{14}$$

where Φ_o represents the original absolute phase map, and Φ_f represents the fused absolute phase map. Finally, the fused phase map is converted into height to obtain a depth map with reduced error.

To better analyze the phase error caused by texture, we utilized a fitting method to conduct phase error analysis. The phase error map is calculated by performing plane fitting on the acquired phase map using a nonlinear polynomial fitting method. Figure 6 depicts where the phase error occurs during reconstruction with the traditional structured-light method. Figure 6a compares the overall brightness of the original and modulated scenes. The brightness of the modulated scene is more uniform than that of the original scene.

Figure 6b shows the phase error map of the scene in Figure 6a, which is calculated using the traditional structured-light method and the proposed method. A conclusion can be drawn that the position where the phase error occurs in the scene is at the texture edge where the reflectivity changes. The modulated scene's phase error is greatly reduced, as shown in the button of Figure 6b. Figure 6c compares the original phase error at the line drawing position in the scene with the modulated phase error. The phase error at the edge position is greatly reduced. The original phase error is 0.056 rad, and the phase error after modulation is 0.016 rad, decreasing by 71.43% compared to the original phase error. Although the error elimination effect of this method is relatively good, it will still produce considerable noise when the overall brightness of the scene is very dark.

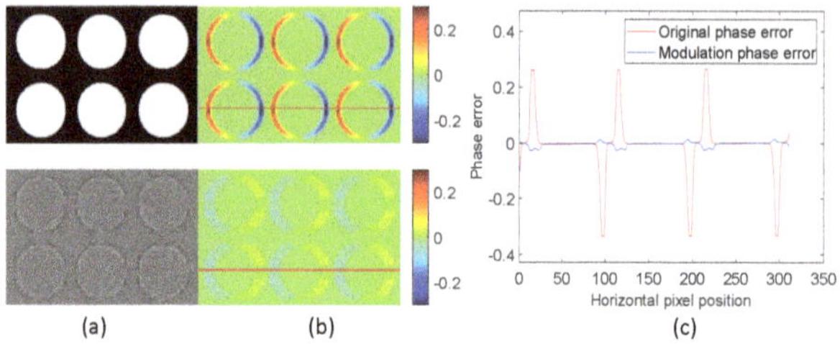

Figure 6. Phase error analysis of simulated modulated scene. (**a**) Simulation of original and modulated measurement scene pictures; (**b**) original phase error and modulated phase error; (**c**) comparison of the phase error.

4. Experiment

This study used an industrial camera (resolution 2448 × 2048) and a optical machine (resolution 912 × 1140) to build a structured-light 3D reconstruction system, as shown in Figure 7. The phase-shifting fringe patterns and Gray code patterns in the horizontal and vertical directions were photographed, decoded, and reconstructed as the original control data. We then used the maximum light intensity modulation pattern to create a modulation projection mask pattern, added the modulation projection mask pattern to the phase-shifting stripe pattern, and added the modulation pattern to re-shoot the projection. The actual measurement scene is shown in Figure 8. Figure 8a,c are two scenes affected only by texture edges. Figure 8b shows a scene affected by both depth and texture edges. The white 'MOUTAI' words stand out, particularly in the background. Figure 8d depicts a cylindrical container used to verify the measurement effect under different depths of field.

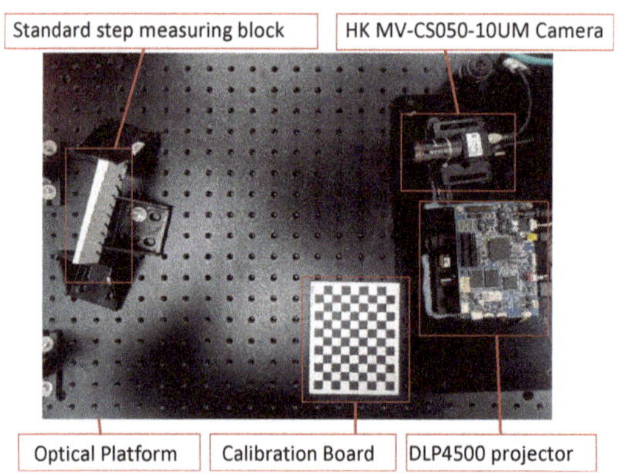

Figure 7. Structured-light 3D reconstruction system platform.

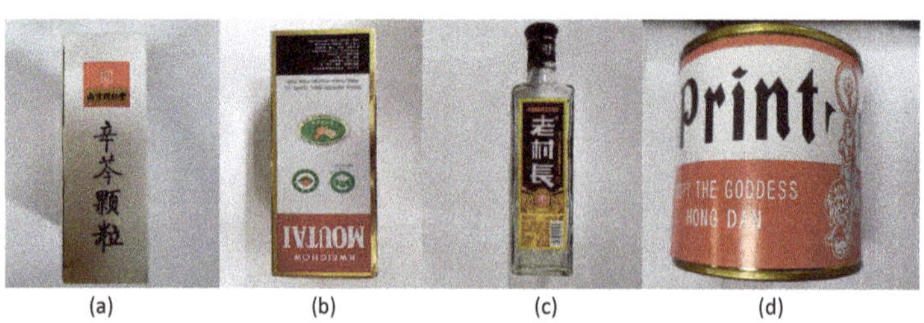

Figure 8. Actual measurement objects. (**a**) Smooth scene with only texture edges; (**b**) Scenes affected by both depth edges and texture edges; (**c**) Smooth surfaces affected by only texture edges; (**d**) Scenes with different depths of field.

4.1. Standard Step Measuring Block

First, we tested the performance of the proposed scene modulation method on a standard step measuring block with texture. The height difference between every two steps of the standard step block increases by 0.1mm from left to right, and the height difference increases from 0.1mm to 0.9mm, as shown in Figure 9a.

We applied black paint at the edges of varying depths to create measured scenes affected by depth and texture. The depth map shown in Figure 9b was calculated using the traditional structured-light phase-shifting method. The proposed method performs feedback modulation on the measurement scene, as shown in Figure 9d. After scene modulation, the brightness difference among different reflectivities at the texture edge becomes smaller. The phase fusion method generates the fused depth map, as shown in Figure 9e. The depth error at the edge position of the black–white texture of the fused depth map is greatly reduced.

Figure 9c shows the local ROI comparison of the original scene, original depth map, modulated scene, and fused depth map from top to bottom. The brightness of the modulated scene changes slowly relative to the original scene at texture edge positions. Compared with the original depth map, the depth value of the fused depth map is improved at the edge positions where texture and depth are jointly affected. The depth is compared on a straight line from the exact position of the original and fused depth maps. The fused blue depth curve is closer to the actual black depth curve than the original red depth curve, as shown in Figure 9f. Comparing the magnified positions of A and B in Figure 9d and Figure 9f, it can be seen that the brightness change at the texture edge after modulation is less at position A than at position B. Therefore, the fusion effect at position A is much better.

The experiments show that the proposed method reduces the measurement error of edge positions affected by depth and texture in actual standard step measuring block scene modulation. Table 1 provides statistics on edge errors at different depths. The RMSE of the original measurement scene is 0.274 mm, and the RMSE after fusion is 0.114 mm, dropping by 58.39%.

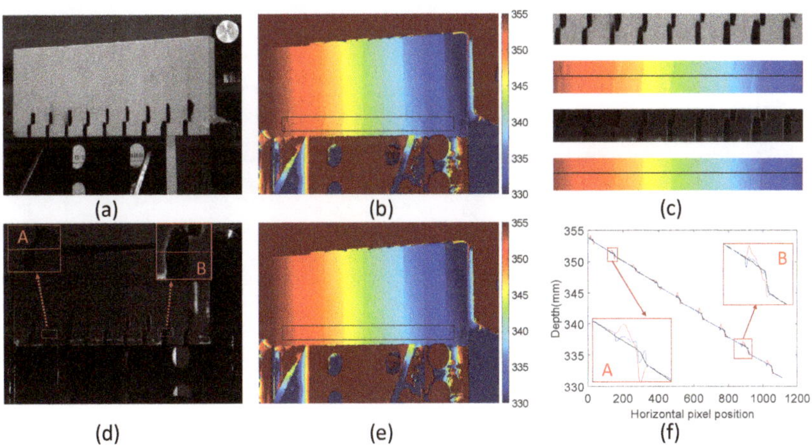

Figure 9. Comparison of measurement results for different depth differences. (**a**) Original scene image; (**b**) original depth map; (**c**) comparison of local ROI regions; (**d**) modulated scene image; (**e**) fusion depth map; (**f**) comparison of original depth curve (red), fusion depth curve (blue), and ground truth (black).

Table 1. RMSE comparison of standard ladder blocks with different depth differences.

Depth Difference/(mm)	0.1	0.2	0.3	0.4	0.5	0.6	0.7	0.8	0.9
Original RMSE (mm)	0.256	0.279	0.189	0.206	0.307	0.329	0.319	0.294	0.287
Fusion RMSE (mm)	0.116	0.114	0.104	0.124	0.102	0.099	0.111	0.117	0.141
Improvement	54.69%	59.14%	44.97%	39.81%	66.78%	69.91%	65.20%	60.20%	50.87%

4.2. Scene with Only Texture Edges

This study performed a structured-light 3D reconstruction of a measurement scene that is only affected by texture edges. The effectiveness of the proposed method is shown in Figure 10a. The scene has a black foreground and a white background. The proposed method was used for deep fusion, and the results are in Figure 10c. According to the comparison between the original depth map in Figure 10b and Figure 10c, a conclusion can be drawn that the method can significantly reduce the measurement error of texture edges.

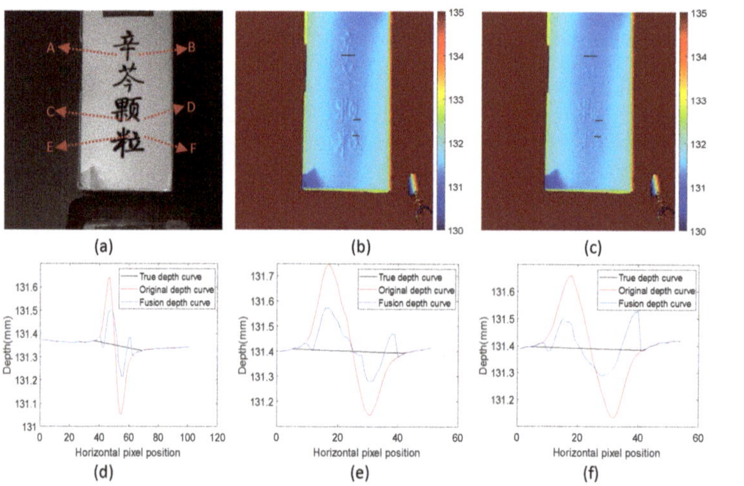

Figure 10. Comparison of measurement scenes only modulated by texture. (**a**) Original measurement scene; (**b**) original depth map; (**c**) fusion depth map; (**d**) depth comparison between position A and position B; (**e**) depth comparison between position C and position D; (**f**) depth comparison between position E and position F.

The six original depth curves, fused depth curves, and actual reference values with different directional texture characteristics, as shown in Figure 10a, are compared in Figure 10d–f. Scenes A, C, and E represent black–white edges, and the remaining positions represent white–black edges. By comparison, it is found that the proposed method has similar effects when processing black–white textures and white–black textures and can reduce measurement errors at both edge positions. Since Figure 10d shows the texture change effect in the horizontal direction, and Figure 10e,f show the texture changes with different tilt degrees, the analysis of the curves shows that the proposed method is suitable for eliminating texture edge errors with different tilt degrees.

The data in Table 2 show that the proposed method is adaptable to both black–white and white–black types of edges, and the error compensation values for the two types are similar. The experimental results show that the proposed method can improve the accuracy of 3D measurements of scene surfaces modulated only by texture edges. According to the statistical analysis in Table 2, the original RMSE of this scene is 0.084 mm, and the fused RMSE is 0.039 mm. The error is reduced by 53.57%.

Table 2. RMSE comparison of scenes modulated only by texture.

Number	A	B	C	D	E	F
Original RMSE (mm)	0.058	0.063	0.091	0.086	0.120	0.086
Fusion RMSE (mm)	0.032	0.025	0.034	0.047	0.056	0.038
Improvement	44.83%	60.32%	62.64%	45.35%	53.33%	55.81%

4.3. Scenes with Both Depth and Texture Edges

This study performed a structured-light 3D reconstruction of a scene with both depth and texture edges, as shown in Figure 11a. The white 'MOUTAI' words stand out in this scene with a non-ideal step depth, particularly in the background. Figure 11b represents the original depth map. The original scene is intensity-modulated to obtain the modulated mask scene image, as shown in Figure 11d. In this image, the brightness change at the texture edge position is reduced relative to the change in the original scene.

Figure 11e depicts the results of the proposed fusion method. The depth error is significantly reduced at edge locations that are co-affected by depth and texture. The same ROI area is intercepted from the original scene image in Figure 11a, the modulated scene image in Figure 11d, the original depth map in Figure 11b, and the fused depth map in Figure 11e for comparison, as shown in Figure 11c. It can be seen that the brightness of 'MOUTAI' in the modulated scene became dark and that the scene's contrast was reduced, and we can see the change in the depth value.

This paper analyzes the depth information of the original depth map and the fused depth map at the position of the black line. As shown in Figure 11f, it can be intuitively seen that the error of the fused depth curve is significantly reduced compared to the original curve. The original RMSE of the scene jointly affected by depth and texture is 0.011 mm, and the fused RMSE is 0.006 mm, with the error reduced by 45.45%. The experiments show that the fused depth map can significantly reduce the measurement error of edges jointly affected by depth and texture.

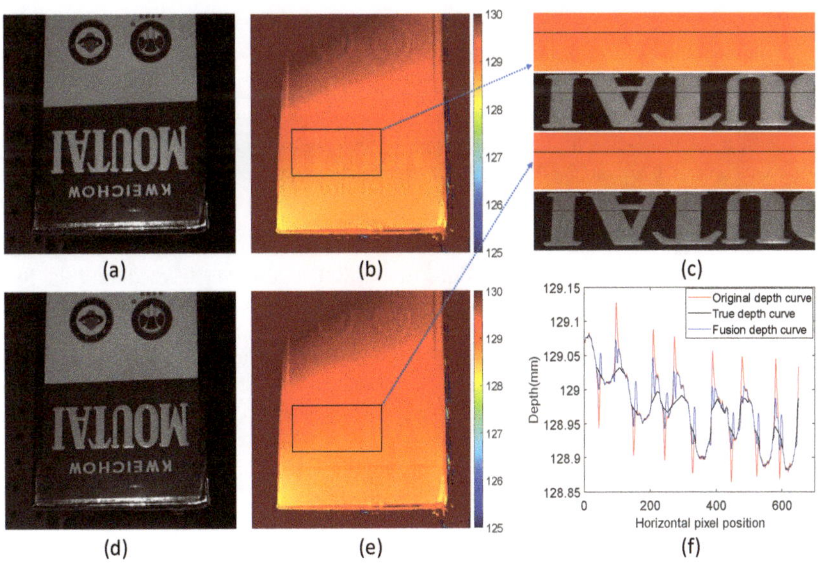

Figure 11. Comparison of measured effects on scenes modulated by depth and texture. (**a**) Original scene image; (**b**) original depth map; (**c**) comparison of local ROI regions; (**d**) modulated scene image; (**e**) fusion depth map; (**f**) comparison of original depth curve, modulated depth curve, and true depth curve.

4.4. Scenes with Textures of Different Widths

This study performed a structured-light 3D reconstruction of a scene with texture characteristics of different widths, as shown in Figure 12a. The scene is a measurement surface with a white foreground and a dark background, only affected by texture edges. After scene modulation in Figure 12b, the pixel intensities at texture edge positions with different widths in the scene are well modulated. The traditional method and the proposed method were each used for the depth calculation, as shown in Figure 12c,d. The comparison shows that the proposed method is also suitable for the scene measurement of different widths.

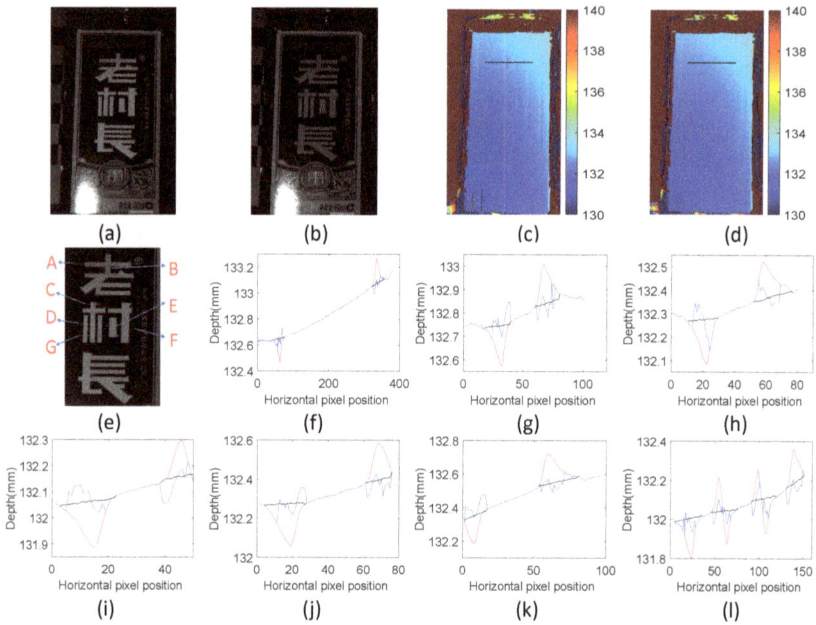

Figure 12. Comparison of measurements of different texture widths. (**a**) Original measurement scene; (**b**) modulated scene image; (**c**) original depth map; (**d**) fusion depth map; (**e**) ROI of original measurement scene; (**f–l**) original depth (red), fusion depth (blue), and actual value (black) comparison at positions A–G in (**e**).

The original depth curves, fused depth curves, and corresponding actual reference values of different line drawing positions in the ROI area were analyzed, and the ROI image is shown in Figure 12e. Positions (f)–(l) in Figure 12 are the positions represented by A–G in Figure 12e. The texture widths at these positions are different. Among them, positions A–F contain only one texture in the background. There is no interference from other textures near the texture, so these positions are less affected by textures at other positions. Therefore, the fusion effect at these locations is relatively ideal. The edge of the texture at position G is compact and is significantly interfered with by surrounding pixels compared to positions A–F.

Table 3 compares the RMSE values of the seven positions (f)–(l) in Figure 12. The original RMSE of the measurement scene is 0.068 mm, and the fused RMSE is 0.030 mm, decreasing by 55.88% on average. The experiments show that the proposed method is effective in the surface measurement of objects with texture edges of different widths.

Table 3. RMSE comparison of scenes with different texture characteristics.

Number	A	B	C	D	E	F	G
Original RMSE (mm)	0.037	0.062	0.070	0.073	0.088	0.065	0.081
Fusion RMSE (mm)	0.015	0.027	0.034	0.035	0.033	0.032	0.036
Improvement	59.46%	56.45%	51.43 %	52.05%	62.50%	50.77%	55.56%

4.5. Analysis of Different Depths of Field

This study used the scene shown in Figure 13a for an experimental comparison, and the traditional method was applied to calculate the depth map shown in Figure 13b. Since the object's surface is cylindrical, different camera defocus blur kernels will affect different positions during the measurement process. The proposed method was used to perform feedback modulation projection of the scene, as shown in Figure 13d. After scene modulation, the intensity of the white portion captured by the camera became darker. The depth map shown in Figure 13e was calculated using the proposed method in this paper.

Figure 13c compares the depth curves at position A in the original and fused scenes. In Figure 13c, A represents the texture ROI area in the original scene, and B represents the ROI area in the modulated scene. Since the camera on the left side of the scene has the most accurate focus, the left side is less affected by the camera's out-of-focus PSF, thus making the fusion effect more accurate. Figure 13f compares the depth curves of position B in the original and fused depth maps. Since position B is closer to the camera and projector than position A in the scene, the light intensity received by position B is stronger. The modulation effect at position B captured by the camera is not relative to the original scene A, so the fusion effect at position A is better than that at position B.

The experimental results show that the proposed method is suitable for scene measurement with different depths of field. However, the greater the camera defocus, the stronger the interference from the scene PSF. Therefore, the more accurately the camera focuses on the scene, the more pronounced the error elimination effect.

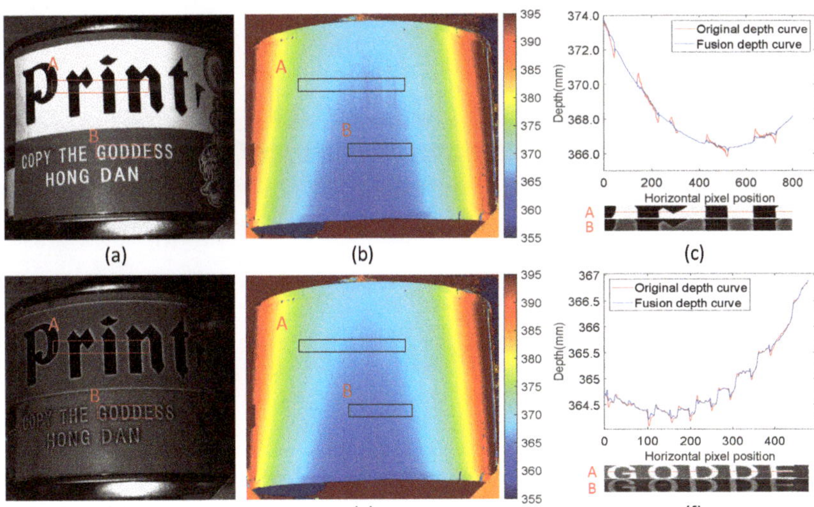

Figure 13. Measurement experiments under different depths of field. (**a**) The original scene image; (**b**) the original depth map; (**c**) the original depth map compared with the depth curve of position A in the fusion depth map; (**d**) the modulated scene image; (**e**) the fusion depth map; (**f**) the original depth map compared with the depth curve of position B in the fused depth map.

5. Discussion

This paper proposes a feedback modulation projection strategy based on scene intensity modulation to address the error problem at texture edges. Projectors of different intensities produce different effects. Figure 14 compares the scene effects after different intensity modulations. Figure 14a shows the measurement results obtained with the standard measurement method. From top to bottom, the figure shows the camera-captured light intensity, the depth map under the current intensity, and the depth curve of the line drawing positions. When the projector projects a light intensity of 220, as shown in Figure 14b, the contrast between light and dark edges does not change significantly. Thus, the measurement effect is poor when the projected light intensity is 90, as shown in Figure 14c. Depth errors at texture edges are greatly reduced when the projection intensity is 50, as shown in Figure 14d. There is considerable noise in the calculated depth map due to the dimming of the light intensity in the entire scene. Therefore, the light projected by the projector must meet the condition that the intensity on both sides of the texture edge captured by the camera be even to achieve the best fusion effect.

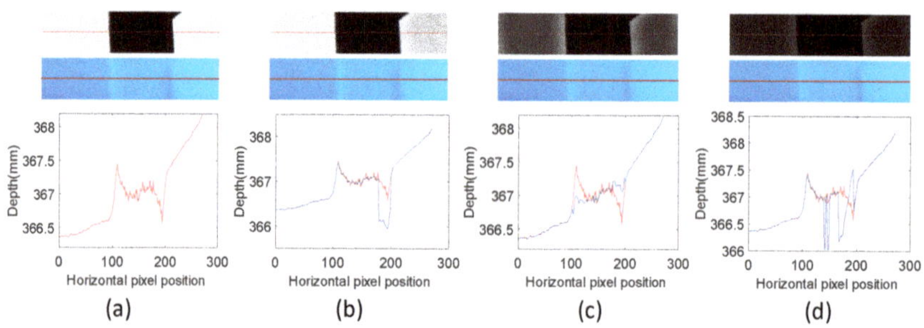

Figure 14. Comparison of the modulation effects of different light intensities. (**a**) The reconstruction effect of the traditional method; (**b–d**) the reconstruction result when the modulated light intensity is 220, 90, and 50.

Although the method proposed in this article can effectively reduce the phase errors at texture edge positions, the method still needs improvement in many aspects. First of all, the measurement method proposed in this article has many system parameters, and some parameters need to be adjusted manually, making the parameter adjustment process cumbersome. Secondly, during the fusion process, the fusion method proposed in this article still has inaccurate positioning for the error pixel position. Finally, due to differences in camera projector resolution, there are errors in texture edge positioning when making reprojected patterns.

6. Conclusions

This paper proposes a 3D reconstruction method to mitigate texture interference based on feedback modulation projection. This method eliminates phase errors caused by defocus and sudden changes in reflectivity at the edge of texture. According to the change in the reflectivity coefficient in the measurement scene, consistent reflectivity is achieved by changing the projection intensity and eliminating the measurement error caused by a sudden change in the reflectivity of the texture edge. The experimental results show that the error of the edge position is reduced by optimizing the feedback modulation projection strategy on the measured surface, which is only affected by the texture edge. Plenty of experimental data prove that the root mean square error of the proposed method can be reduced by 53.32% on average.

Author Contributions: Conceptualization, C.S. and Z.Q.; formal analysis, X.Z.; investigation, Z.L., S.Y. and Y.Y.; methodology, X.H.; supervision, C.Z. (Chun Zhang); validation, C.Z. (Changsheng Zhu) and Y.M.; visualization, Z.Q. and Y.M.; writing—original draft preparation, Z.Q.; writing—review and editing, C.S., Z.Q. and C.Z. (Chun Zhang). All authors have read and agreed to the published version of the manuscript.

Funding: This research was funded by the Shandong Province Science and Technology SMEs Innovation Capability Enhancement Project (No. 2023TATSGC051 and No. 2023TATSGC014).

Data Availability Statement: Data are contained within the article.

Conflicts of Interest: The authors declare no conflicts of interest.

References

1. Liberadzki, P.; Adamczyk, M.; Witkowski, M.; Sitnik, R. Structured-Light-Based System for Shape Measurement of the Human Body in Motion. *Sensors* **2018**, *18*, 2827. [CrossRef]
2. Xu, J.; Wang, P.; Yao, Y.; Liu, S.; Zhang, G. 3D multi-directional sensor with pyramid mirror and structured light. *Opt. Lasers Eng.* **2017**, *93*, 156–163. [CrossRef]
3. Hu, X.; Wang, G.; Hyun, J.; Zhang, Y.; Yang, H.; Zhang, S. Autofocusing method for high-resolution three-dimensional profilometry. *Opt. Lett.* **2020**, *45*, 375–378. [CrossRef]
4. Hu, X.; Zhang, S.; Zhang, Y.; Liu, Y.; Wang, G. Large depth-of-field three-dimensional shape measurement with the focal sweep technique. *Opt. Express* **2020**, *28*, 31197–31208. [CrossRef] [PubMed]
5. Zhang, S.; Huang, P. Novel method for structured light system calibration. *Opt. Lasers Eng.* **2006**, *45*, 083601.
6. Li, K.; Bu, J.; Zhang, D. Lens distortion elimination for improving measurement accuracy of fringe projection profilometry. *Opt. Lasers Eng.* **2016**, *85*, 53–64. [CrossRef]
7. Peter, B.; Matthias, H.; Gunther, N.; Richard, K. Influence of the pixel size of the camera on 3D measurements with fringe projection. In *Optical Measurement Systems for Industrial Inspection III*; SPIE: Bellingham, WA, USA, 2003; pp. 478–483.
8. Pan, B.; Qian, K.; Huang, L.; Asundi, A. Phase error analysis and compensation for nonsinusoidal waveforms in phase-shifting digital fringe projection profilometry. *Opt. Lett.* **2009**, *34*, 416–418. [CrossRef] [PubMed]
9. Wu, Y.; Dantanarayana, H.; Yue, H.; Huntley, J. Accurate characterisation of hole size and location by projected fringe profilometry. *Meas. Sci. Technol.* **2018**, *29*, 065010. [CrossRef]
10. Burke, J.; Zhong, L. Suppression of contrast-related artefacts in phase-measuring structured light techniques. In *Optical Measurement Systems for Industrial Inspection X*; SPIE: Bellingham, WA, USA, 2017; Volume 10329, pp. 32–58.
11. Li, R.; Da F. Local blur analysis and phase error correction method for fringe projection profilometry systems. *Appl. Opt.* **2018**, *57*, 4267–4276.
12. Drouin, M.; Godin, G.; Blais, F. Efficient representation of the variant PSF of structured light system. In *2010 IEEE International Conference on Image Processing*; IEEE: Piscataway, NJ, USA, 2010; pp. 1693–1696.
13. Yue, H.; Dantanarayana, H.; Wu, Y.; Huntley, J. Reduction of systematic errors in structured light metrology at discontinuities in surface reflectivity. *Opt. Lasers Eng.* **2019**, *112*, 68–76. [CrossRef]
14. Wu, Y.; Cai, X.; Zhu, J.; Yue, H.; Shao, X. Analysis and reduction of the phase error caused by the non-impulse system psf in fringe projection profilometry. *Opt. Lasers Eng.* **2020**, *127*, 105987. [CrossRef]
15. Wu, Y.; Cai, X.; Zhu, J.; Shao, X. Discontinuity-induced measurement artifact reduction of structured light system based on a deconvolution method. In *Optical Metrology and Inspection for Industrial Applications VI*; SPIE: Bellingham, WA, USA, 2019; Volume 11189, pp. 127–133.
16. Blanchard, C.; Zhang, S. Removal of phase artifacts from high-contrast texture for 3D fringe projection system. In *Dimensional Optical Metrology and Inspection for Practical Applications XI*; SPIE: Bellingham, WA, USA, 2022; Volume 12098, pp. 19–30.
17. Wang, J.; Yang, Y.; Zhou, Y. 3-D shape reconstruction of non-uniform reflectance surface based on pixel intensity, pixel color and camera exposure time adaptive adjustment. *Sci. Rep.* **2021**, *11*, 4700. [CrossRef] [PubMed]
18. Chen, B.; Zhang, S. High-quality 3D shape measurement using saturated fringe patterns. *Opt. Lasers Eng.* **2016**, *87*, 83–89. [CrossRef]

sensors

MDPI

Article

DSOMF: A Dynamic Environment Simultaneous Localization and Mapping Technique Based on Machine Learning

Shengzhe Yue, Zhengjie Wang * and Xiaoning Zhang

School of Electromechanical Engineering, Beijing Institute of Technology, Beijing 100081, China; 3120215111@bit.edu.cn (S.Y.); xnzhang@bit.edu.cn (X.Z.)
* Correspondence: wangzhengjie@bit.edu.cn

Abstract: To address the challenges of reduced localization accuracy and incomplete map construction demonstrated using classical semantic simultaneous localization and mapping (SLAM) algorithms in dynamic environments, this study introduces a dynamic scene SLAM technique that builds upon direct sparse odometry (DSO) and incorporates instance segmentation and video completion algorithms. While prioritizing the algorithm's real-time performance, we leverage the rapid matching capabilities of Direct Sparse Odometry (DSO) to link identical dynamic objects in consecutive frames. This association is achieved through merging semantic and geometric data, thereby enhancing the matching accuracy during image tracking through the inclusion of semantic probability. Furthermore, we incorporate a loop closure module based on video inpainting algorithms into our mapping thread. This allows our algorithm to rely on the completed static background for loop closure detection, further enhancing the localization accuracy of our algorithm. The efficacy of this approach is validated using the TUM and KITTI public datasets and the unmanned platform experiment. Experimental results show that, in various dynamic scenes, our method achieves an improvement exceeding 85% in terms of localization accuracy compared with the DSO system.

Keywords: dynamic scene; simultaneous localization and mapping; direct method; instance segmentation; video inpainting

1. Introduction

Simultaneous localization and mapping (SLAM) technology facilitates the acquisition of location and environmental information through pose estimation and map construction [1]. In recent years, visual SLAM technology, as a subject of extensive research, has advanced significantly [2]. Sophisticated visual SLAM algorithms have been developed to achieve localization precision at the centimeter level and can be used to successfully construct large-scale three-dimensional (3D) maps [3–8]. However, these advanced visual SLAM algorithms operate predominantly under the strong assumption of rigid scenes, which substantially limits their applicability to dynamic environments.

With the development of deep learning technologies, an increasing number of researchers have integrated object detection and semantic segmentation algorithms with classical SLAM algorithms to enhance their robustness in dynamic scenarios. Dyna-SLAM [9] combines semantic segmentation algorithms with geometric methods to identify and remove dynamic objects from images. Dm-SLAM [10] utilizes instance segmentation information and optical flow data to mitigate the effects of dynamic objects in a scene. Detect-SLAM [11] employs object detection algorithms to identify dynamic feature points and uses the motion probability to convey the motion information of these points. However, these algorithms were improved using feature-based SLAM systems. When most of the selected feature points originate from dynamic objects, the localization accuracy of the SLAM algorithm can decrease significantly because of the reduced number of usable feature points. By contrast, a more flexible selection mechanism for photometric gradient points can prevent the selection of points from being overly concentrated. Moreover, the frame-to-frame matching speed of the SLAM algorithms based on direct methods is higher.

Direct Sparse Odometry (DSO) is a visual odometry algorithm that estimates the camera motion in a sparse and direct manner [6]. Unlike traditional feature-based methods, which extract and match key-points across images, DSO operates directly on pixel intensities. This method significantly enhances the flexibility of map point selection, effectively avoiding the decrease in positioning accuracy caused by an excessive number of feature points from dynamic objects. While DSO primarily focuses on static scenes, the authors also mentioned in his paper that direct methods have a greater advantage when dealing with dynamic objects. During our practical applications, we have also observed that DSO exhibits greater robustness compared to ORB-SLAM2 when dynamic objects are present in the environment.

Although the DSO algorithm holds significant advantages over feature-based SLAM algorithms when it comes to handling dynamic environments, its adoption for further research and improvement is limited due to its low code readability and the challenging nature of modifying its direct method-based optimization approach. In this work, we not only integrate the DSO algorithm with semantic segmentation and video inpainting algorithms but also restructure its algorithmic framework. We introduce a SLAM method tailored for rigid dynamic scenes, named DSOMF. This method employs instance segmentation and video inpainting algorithms to mitigate the impact of dynamic objects, thereby enhancing the localization precision and mapping performance of the DSO algorithm. The principal contributions of this study are as follows:

1. We refine the region segmentation approach within the DSO algorithm, accelerating the motion recognition speed of the algorithm through dynamic region segmentation and the direct selection of optical flow points.
2. We propose a method that utilizes inter-frame semantic information to identify and remove dynamic objects. This approach effectively reduces the interference caused by noise introduced by dynamic objects, enhancing the system's robustness in dynamic environments. Furthermore, we also improve the matching accuracy of pixel intensities points by adding semantic probability, so that our algorithm can make full use of semantic information.
3. We synergize video inpainting algorithms with the map-building thread of the DSO algorithm, compensating for static background gaps caused by the removal of moving objects, thereby optimizing the map construction performance of the DSO algorithm in dynamic environments.
4. We integrate a loop closure detection module, thus rendering the DSO algorithm framework more comprehensive. Moreover, by associating loop closure detection with video inpainting algorithms, we enhance the efficiency of this module in identifying loop closures within dynamic environments.

In the following, we discuss the related studies in Section 2, providing a comprehensive introduction to its methodology in Section 3, followed by a detailed elaboration on motion object segmentation, semantic data association, motion object recognition, and static background completion, and a comparative analysis of the positioning accuracy between our algorithm and existing ones conducted using indoor and outdoor datasets in Section 4. The real-scene experiments based on the unmanned aerial vehicle and unmanned vehicle platforms is in Section 5 and we conclude the paper in Section 6.

2. Related Works

In recent years, SLAM algorithms for dynamic environments have received considerable attention from the research community, thus resulting in the proposal of a multitude of dynamic environment SLAM algorithms. Based on the different approaches for managing dynamic objects in the environment, the solutions reported in the literature can be categorized into two types, which are detailed in the next subsections.

2.1. Eliminating Dynamic Objects

In one of the SLAM algorithm types, dynamic objects in images are typically classified as outliers for removal. Facilitated using machine learning algorithms, the primary approach of such SLAM algorithms is to use semantic segmentation or object detection to identify objects in images that can potentially move. Subsequently, the motion states of these potentially movable objects are assessed using geometric methods [12–14]. Finally, the dynamic features of the moving objects are eliminated using an improved RANSAC algorithm [15–17]. Detect-SLAM [11] combines ORB-SLAM2 with the SSD object detection algorithm, where motion probabilities are used to convey the dynamic information of feature points and remove dynamic points that reach a certain threshold. DS-SLAM [18] employs the SgeNet semantic segmentation algorithm to delineate dynamic object regions and delete all feature points within an area if dynamic features are detected. Moreover, DS-SLAM builds an octree map using semantic information and filters unstable voxels using a logarithmic scoring method. RDS-SLAM [19] utilizes a Bayesian filter to identify and remove dynamic objects and has been used to design a novel semantic segmentation thread execution to reduce the effect of semantic segmentation algorithms on the real-time performance of the SLAM system. Alcantarilla et al. [20] employed scene flows to remove dynamic objects from an environment. Although these SLAM methods discard dynamic objects in images, thereby enhancing the system robustness and estimation accuracy, they also reduce the ability of the SLAM system to capture static environmental information. Consequently, some SLAM algorithms that target dynamic scenes complete an incomplete static background after removing dynamic objects. Dyna-SLAM [9] removes dynamic objects using a combination of semantic segmentation and geometric methods and then applies multi-view geometry information to color and complete the missing background.

2.2. Constructing Dynamic Objects

In another type of SLAM method, the SLAM algorithm is primarily integrated with moving object tracking (MOT) algorithms. Thorpe et al. [21] performed SLAM and MOT in separate threads, where the MOT thread was isolated to detect and track dynamic objects, thus ensuring the real-time performance of the SLAM system. Reddy et al. [22] not only combined MOT with structure from motion to construct maps that included both the structure of static objects and the trajectories of dynamic objects but also introduced semantic constraints to achieve more precise results of 3D reconstruction. Owing to advancements in technologies such as 3D object detection, researchers have begun using simple geometric shapes to represent dynamic objects, thus facilitating their incorporation into static maps. Salas-Moreno et al. [23] first proposed an object-specific SLAM algorithm incorporating both object and camera poses into backend optimization. Subsequently, Tateno et al. [24] combined SLAM with 3D object detection incrementally and in the real-time segmentation of a 3D scene during map reconstruction, thus enhancing the robustness of the object-recognition system. Node-SLAM [25] introduced multiple classes of learning objects and a new probabilistic and differential rendering engine to derive complete object shapes from one or more RGB-D inputs. Hosseinzadeh et al. [26] was the first to use ellipsoids to envelope dynamic objects for the parametric representation of their size and pose. Building upon this concept, researchers proposed quadric-SLAM [27], where the geometric parameters of dynamic objects were integrated into the factor graph of the SLAM system for joint optimization. Additionally, researchers introduced Dyna-SLAM II [28], where dynamic objects were enveloped using 3D object detection frameworks and proposed a formula for estimating the size and pose of dynamic objects, thus allowing the system to simultaneously estimate the camera pose, map, and trajectory of moving objects.

Taking into account the two approaches outlined above, while the concept of constructing dynamic objects is more advanced, the current target tracking and 3D object detection technologies both require significant computational resources. Furthermore, existing SLAM algorithms do not accurately calculate the speed of dynamic objects. Therefore, we still adopt the approach of excluding dynamic objects to maximize the positioning accuracy of our SLAM system in dynamic environments.

3. Algorithm Design

In this section, we first introduce the overall algorithmic framework of the proposed SLAM system, followed by a detailed discussion of the methods introduced herein. This study addresses the problem of localization and mapping in dynamic environments and proposes an algorithm framework based on DSO, as illustrated in Figure 1. Within this framework, the regions highlighted in blue represent programs that have been added or modified, whereas those in green indicate the original programs.

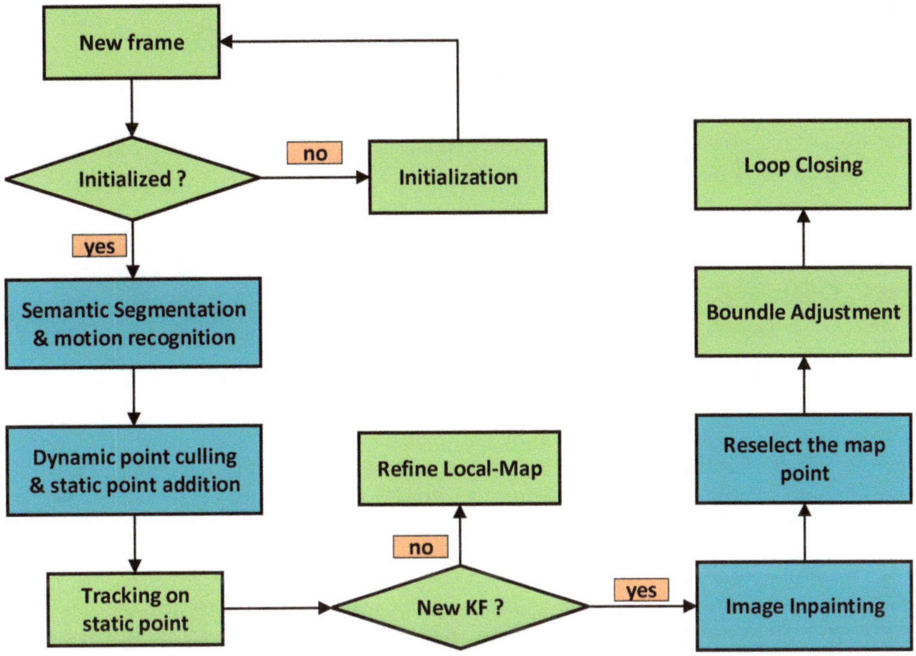

Figure 1. Algorithm framework.

Firstly, we employed an instance segmentation network, i.e., mask R-CNN [29], to extract all prior instances of dynamic objects. Subsequently, we utilized an enhanced PARSAC algorithm [30] for the motion recognition of dynamic object instances and for eliminating photometric gradient points within the dynamic object regions. Once elimination was completed, photometric gradient points were supplemented from static regions to increase the number of trackable points for the algorithm. After selecting the keyframes, we applied the flow-guided video completion (FGVC) algorithm [31] to replenish the static background occluded by dynamic objects in the keyframes. Finally, we re-supplemented photometric gradient points from the replenished portions of the keyframes and input them into the mapping thread for loop closing. The image processing procedure is depicted in Figure 2 below, with the tracking thread enclosed in blue and the mapping thread in orange.

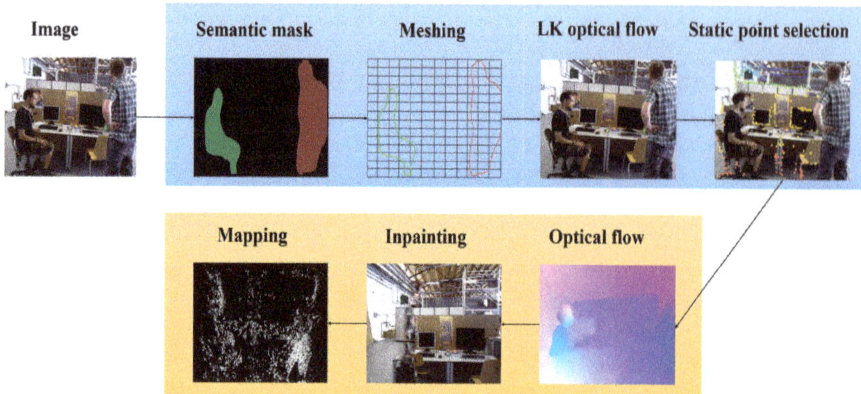

Figure 2. Image processing workflow (The blue box in the diagram represents the tracking thread, while the orange box represents the mapping thread).

3.1. Segmentation of Potential Dynamic Objects

To detect objects within an image that possesses the potential for motion, we employed a mask R-CNN instance segmentation network to segment the input image. The mask R-CNN network is a widely used instance segmentation technique that enables the acquisition of pixel-level semantic segmentation outcomes, along with instance-level object labels. Current semantic SLAM algorithms designed for dynamic environments typically utilize only semantic segmentation information and directly eliminate objects that are likely to move. This approach inadvertently removes objects that are potentially mobile yet stationary, thus diminishing the number of static feature points available for the algorithm and affecting the precision of SLAM localization. This study innovatively integrates semantic segmentation information with instance label data, thereby refining the identification of moving objects to the level of individual instances, to preserve as many static points in the image as possible.

The input for the mask R-CNN is the raw image captured using the camera, as shown in Figure 3a. In this study, the mask R-CNN network was exclusively utilized to segment the categories of objects that exhibit the potential for dynamics, including but not limited to movable humans, bicycles, cars, cats and dogs. These categories are posited to encompass the most dynamic objects likely to appear in most scenes. If additional object categories must be identified, then one can retrain the mask R-CNN network using the COCO dataset [32] and then fine-tune its weight files accordingly.

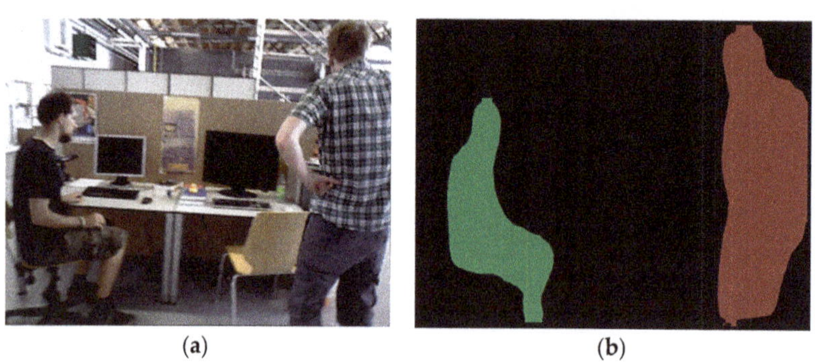

Figure 3. Dynamic object instance segmentation results. (**a**) Original image; (**b**) mask image.

For the output results of the mask R-CNN, we assumed that the input image size was $s \times h \times 3$. During processing, the network generated an $s \times h \times w$ matrix, where w represents the number of dynamic objects in an image. Each output channel ($c \in w$) generates a binary mask image for a specific object instance. Stacking these w images yielded a segmented result that encompassed all instances of dynamic objects, as illustrated in Figure 3b.

3.2. Region Segmentation and Data Association

The DSO performs tracking by selecting points with photometric gradients within an image. To achieve a more uniform point distribution, the DSO segments the image into n square regions, each with a side length of d, and selects photometric gradient points within each region. To further conserve computational resources, this study enhances the original algorithm by redefining the partitioning of regions based on the number and size of potentially moving objects in an image, thereby facilitating motion detection. An analysis of semantic segmentation labels across multiple datasets revealed that when the labels indicating potential motion exceeded 30% of the total label count, the image was likely to contain a higher number and larger projection area of moving objects. Consequently, when the proportion of labels for potentially moving objects exceeded 30%, the image was partitioned into square regions with a side length of 6d. Otherwise, the regions were defined as having a side length of 4d. Upon completing the partitioning of regions, the central point of each region was identified, and the Kanade–Lucas–Tomasi method was applied to track their optical flow f: $(u, v) \rightarrow (u + \Delta u, v + \Delta v)$. Thus, the correspondence between the segmentation regions of the two frames was identified, as illustrated in Figure 4.

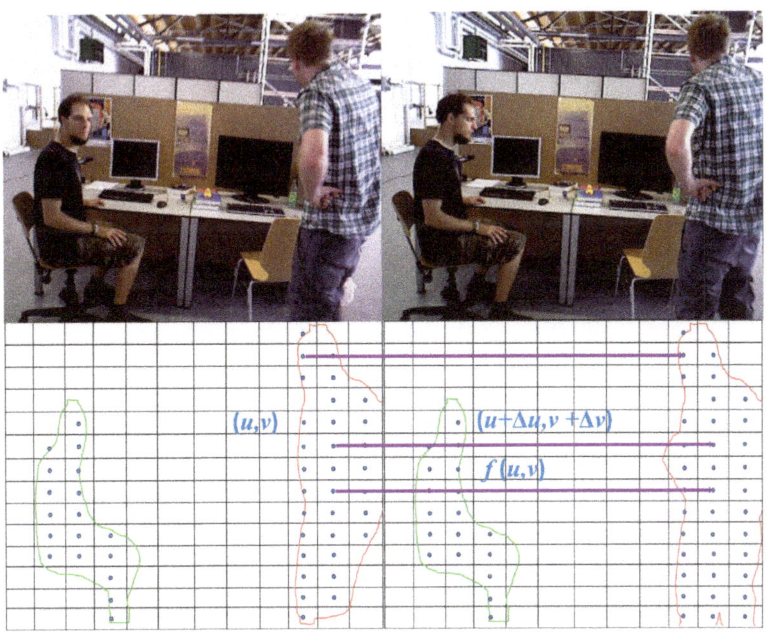

Figure 4. Optical flow tracking of regional centroids.

The association degree between segmentation regions of successive frames can be represented as follows:

$$\varphi_f(C_a^{t-1}, C_b^t | Z, f_{t-1\to t}) = \frac{\sum_{k=1}^{N} [Loc(f(z_i), C_b^t) \times Loc(z_i, C_a^{t-1})]}{\sum_{k=1}^{N} Loc(z_i, C_a^{t-1})}, \tag{1}$$

where φ_f denotes the association degree of regional centroids, Z the observation function, z_i the observation point, a and b the semantic tag and C_a^t, C_b^t the semantic label clustering of central points at time t. By defining the spatial association of segment clustering, we can represent the overlap between segmented regions across two frames [33]. Specifically, it can be articulated as:

$$\varphi_s(C_a^{t-1}, C_b^{t-1}) = \frac{\left\| C_a^{t-1} \cap C_b^t \right\|}{\sum_{k=0}^{N} C_k^{t-1}}, \tag{2}$$

where, φ_s denotes the spatial association of segmentation clustering. By considering both the spatial and centroid associations, the probability that (C_a^{t-1}, C_b^t) belongs to the same category can be expressed as:

$$P = (l_i^t = j | C_{t-1}, C_t, L_{t-1}, Z, f_{t-1\to t}) = \frac{\varphi_s(C_i^{t-1}, C_j^t) + \alpha \times \varphi_f(C_i^{t-1}, C_j^t)}{\sum_{m=0}^{N} \sum_{n=0}^{N} [\varphi_s(C_m^{t-1}, C_n^t) + \alpha \times \varphi_f(C_m^{t-1}, C_n^t)]}, \tag{3}$$

where, l_i^t denotes the object label. Consequently, the label of C_i^t can be expressed as:

$$l_i^t = \text{argmax} P(l_i^t = j | C_{t-1}, C_t, L_{t-1}, Z, f_{t-1\to t}), \tag{4}$$

The equation above clearly indicates, that when $l_i^t = l_0^{t-1}$ and $i \neq 0$, a new object label emerges in the scene, thus incrementing the label count. Using this approach, the association between the segmentation results of potential moving objects across successive frames can be established based on both centroid matching and the overlap of segmentation regions.

3.3. *Dynamic Object Recognition and Determination of Dynamic Regions*

Because the methodology used in this study was adapted from DSO, using the photometric error-based matching approach, which is computationally efficient, may compromise the accuracy of point matching. Consequently, this study incorporates a motion recognition method based on semantic probability [34], which is expressed as follows:

$$\varepsilon^2(x, x'F) = \frac{(\overline{x}' F \overline{x})^2}{(F\overline{x})_1^2 + (F\overline{x})_2^2 + (F^T\overline{x}')_1^2 + (F^T\overline{x}')_2^2}, \tag{5}$$

where x denotes the coordinates of the regional centroid in the previous frame, x' the coordinates of the regional centroid in the current frame, $\overline{x}$ the coordinates in homogeneous form, and F the fundamental matrix between two adjacent frames. Consequently, for each label cluster, a parameter $D = \{d_i | i = 1, 2, \cdots, N\}$ can be obtained to evaluate whether the matching of the centroid of the cluster region adheres to geometric constraints. This can be expressed as follows:

$$D(Z, C_i^t, F, f_{t-1\to t}) = \frac{\sum_{k=1}^{N} [\varepsilon^2(z_k, f(z_k), F \times Loc(z_k, C_i^t))]}{\sum_{k=1}^{N} Loc(z_k, C_i^t)}, \tag{6}$$

$$d_i = D(Z, C_i^t, F, f_{t-1 \to t}), \tag{7}$$

When d_i surpasses a specified threshold τ_{dyn}, we assume that motion has occurred within the associated segmentation cluster.

After determining the motion status of the segmentation clusters, regions whose centroids are dynamic cluster points are marked as dynamic areas. Additionally, there are regions where the centroid is not a dynamic cluster point but the extremities are defined as edge areas. The dynamism of the edge areas is ascertained based on the distance from the centroid to the segmentation cluster. The distance from the centroid of an edge area to the segmentation cluster is expressed as:

$$dist(x_k, C_j) = \min\|x_k - x_i\|_2, x_k \in \overline{C}_j, x_j \in C_j, \tag{8}$$

In the equation, $\overline{C}_j$ represents the set of edge centroids of segmentation cluster C_j . Therefore, the semantic probability that the edge centroid x_k belongs to C_j can be expressed using binomial logistic regression as follows:

$$P = \frac{1}{\exp(-\lambda \times dist(x_k, C_j)) + 1}, \tag{9}$$

When P exceeds P_{dyn}, the edge area becomes dynamic. Following the determination of the dynamic areas, these regions are marked as occupied (as illustrated in Figure 5), and all photometric gradient points selected using the DSO algorithm within these areas are excluded. Subsequently, based on the proportion of dynamic areas to the total area, the threshold for selecting the photometric gradient points in the static areas is reduced appropriately to compensate for the number of points selected in unoccupied areas.

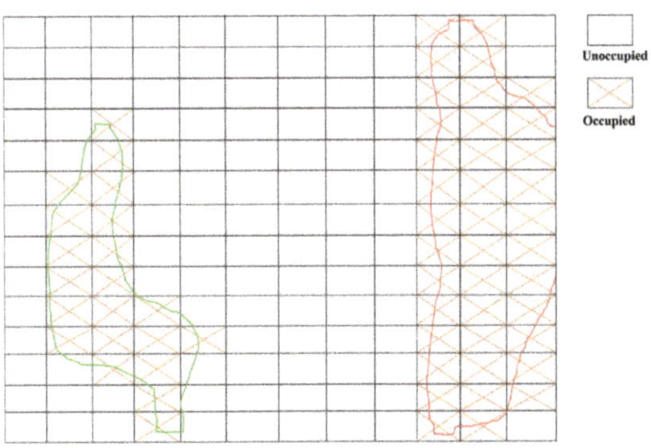

Figure 5. Delineation of dynamic and static regions.

3.4. Completion of Static Background in Keyframes and Loop Closure

After instance segmentation and motion-consistency verification are performed to eliminate dynamic objects, the constructed static background map may exhibit gaps, as illustrated in Figure 6. In the DSO framework, non-keyframes participate only in localization and tracking, whereas map construction relies on keyframes. Consequently, we utilized pixels from non-keyframes to fill in the static background voids caused by dynamic objects obstructing the keyframes. Thus, the keyframes can be used to synthesize more realistic static environment images after the removal of dynamic objects. This type of composite image, which includes static structures, can not only further optimize and enhance the accuracy of camera pose estimation but also contribute significantly to virtual and augmented reality applications.

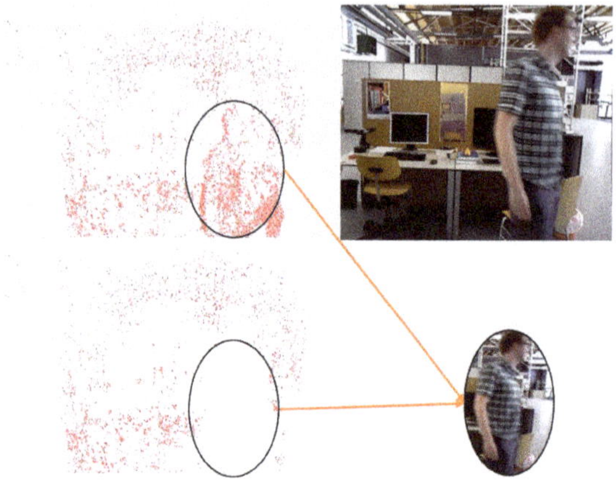

Figure 6. Comparative analysis of mapping outcomes pre and post dynamic object elimination.

For missing regions in an image, computing the optical flow field of the area is easier than direct pixel filling, and optical flow-guided pixel propagation can naturally maintain temporal coherence [35]. Additionally, owing to the tracking of object movement in non-key frames, their optical flow can be more readily obtained. Therefore, we adopted the FGVC algorithm, which is guided using optical flow edges. After the tracking thread identifies dynamic objects, it sends the keyframe images and dynamic object labels to the video completion thread. The FGVC video completion algorithm primarily comprises three steps (as shown in Figure 7): (1) Flow completion, where the forward and backward optical flows between adjacent frames are calculated; (2) temporal propagation, where the trajectory of the optical flow is followed to identify a set of candidate pixels for each missing pixel, and a confidence score as well as a binary validity indicator are estimated for each candidate frame; (3) fusion, where confidence-weighted averaging is employed to fuse each missing candidate pixel with at least one valid candidate pixel. Single-image completion techniques are used to fill areas devoid of candidate pixels. To ensure the effectiveness of the map completion thread, the tracking thread saves 20 frames of non-keyframes for achieving completion. After completing the missing areas, photometric gradient points are selected within the completed areas and integrated into the backend optimization thread to enhance the localization accuracy and mapping outcomes.

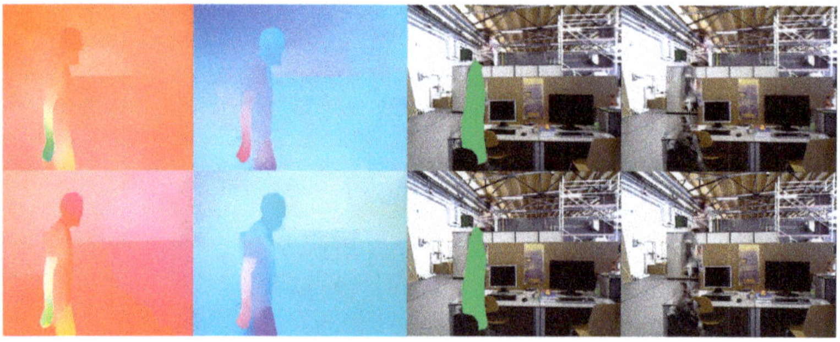

Figure 7. FGVC optical flow completion process.

After completing the video inpainting, we re-selected some photometric gradient points on the incorporated static background into the mapping thread. Subsequently, we detected loop closure candidates using the Bag of Words (BoW) model, computing the Sim(3) transformation between the candidate frames and the current frame, and we applied these constraints to pose a graph optimization to enhance the overall map accuracy. This method effectively avoids failures in the Bag of Words model detection caused by occlusions from dynamic objects, thereby improving the efficiency of loop closure detection in dynamic environments.

4. Simulation Testing

To verify the effectiveness of the proposed method, we conducted tests using a publicly available indoor dynamic TUM dataset [36] and the outdoor dynamic KITTI dataset [37]. Because the proposed method modifies the existing stable open-source DSO algorithm, it primarily serves as a benchmark for comparison. Additionally, we compared the proposed method with a similar Dyna-SLAM algorithm, which utilizes the mask R-CNN algorithm for segmenting dynamic objects. To evaluate the effect of map completion on the localization accuracy, we used an algorithm that removes dynamic objects but does not perform map completion (named DSOM) and an algorithm that removes dynamic objects and performs map completion (named DSOMF). Additionally, we employed the absolute trajectory error (ATE) and relative pose error (RPE) for a quantitative evaluation of the algorithms' localization accuracy. The ATE metric represents the global consistency of the trajectory, whereas the RPE metric reflects the drift in translation and rotation. All the experiments were conducted on a notebook computer equipped with an Intel Core i9-14900H CPU, RTX 4090 GPU with 16GB of graphics memory, and 64GB of RAM in a dual 32GB configuration.

4.1. Simulation Testing on TUM Dataset

The TUM dataset captures data for various task types in indoor environments using RGB-D cameras. Moreover, the dataset provides the ground truth for camera poses and comparison tools, thus rendering it highly suitable for SLAM researchers to evaluate the performance of their algorithms.

In this study, three sets of data from the dynamic object module of the dataset were used for simulation testing: fr3_sitting_static, fr3_walking_static, and fr3_walking_xyz. The first dataset represents a static environment, whereas the latter two are dynamic environments. The results yielded using the algorithm are shown in Table 1, where the first column lists the dataset names and the second to fourth columns are the names of the algorithms. From left to right, the second, third, and fourth columns present the root mean square error (RMSE) and standard deviation (STD), which effectively reflects the stability and robustness of the algorithm. In dynamic environments, the improvement in the localization accuracy of the proposed method relative to the other two algorithms is expressed as:

$$\delta = \frac{\alpha - \beta}{\alpha} \times 100\%, \tag{10}$$

where δ represents the improvement rate, α the data from the other two algorithms, and β the data from the proposed algorithm.

Table 1. Comparison of absolute trajectory errors in TUM datasets.

Identifier	DSO		Dyna-SLAM		DSOM		DSOMF	
	RMSE	STD	RMSE	STD	RMSE	STD	RMSE	STD
sitting_static	0.009	0.004	0.006	0.003	0.006	0.003	0.006	0.003
walking_static	0.307	0.113	0.037	0.043	0.035	0.039	0.029	0.032
walking_xyz	0.889	0.419	0.091	0.057	0.081	0.047	0.072	0.043

Based on the data shown in Table 1, one can observe that in the fr3_sitting_static data scenario, the RMSE and STD of DSOM improved by 37% and 24%, respectively, compared with those of DSO, whereas they did not improve significantly with respect to those of Dyna-SLAM2. The RMSE and STD of DSOMF improved by 45% and 27%, respectively, compared with those of the DSO, whereas they did not improve significantly with respect to those of Dyna-SLAM2. In the fr3_walking_static data scenario, the RMSE and STD of DSOM improved by 88.5% and 65.4%, respectively, compared to DSO, and by 5.4% and 9.3%, respectively, compared with those of Dyna-SLAM. The RMSE and STD of DSOM improved by 90.6% and 71.6%, respectively, compared with those of DSO, and by 21.6% and 25.5%, respectively, compared with those of Dyna-SLAM. In the fr3_walking_xyz data scenario, the RMSE and STD of DSOM improved by 90.8% and 87.8%, respectively, compared with those of DSO, and by 10.9% and 17.5%, respectively, compared with those of Dyna-SLAM. The RMSE and STD of DSOMF improved by 92% and 89.7%, respectively, compared with those of DSO, and by 20.8% and 24.6%, respectively, compared with those of Dyna-SLAM.

To further analyze the test results, Figure 8 shows a comparison of the ATEs among DSO, Dyna-SLAM, and the methods presented here in this study, i.e., DSOM and DSOMF, across the three scenarios of fr3_sitting_static, fr3_walking_static, and fr3_walking_xyz. One can intuitively observe that as the dynamic nature of the scenes increases, the improvement effect of the methods on the localization accuracy intensifies gradually. In environments with higher dynamics, the localization effect of the methods presents a clear enhancement compared with that of DSO. However, the improvement effect of DSOMF was slightly weaker relative to that of Dyna-SLAM, which is attributed to the deteriorating image completion effect owing to the increased number of dynamic objects in the image.

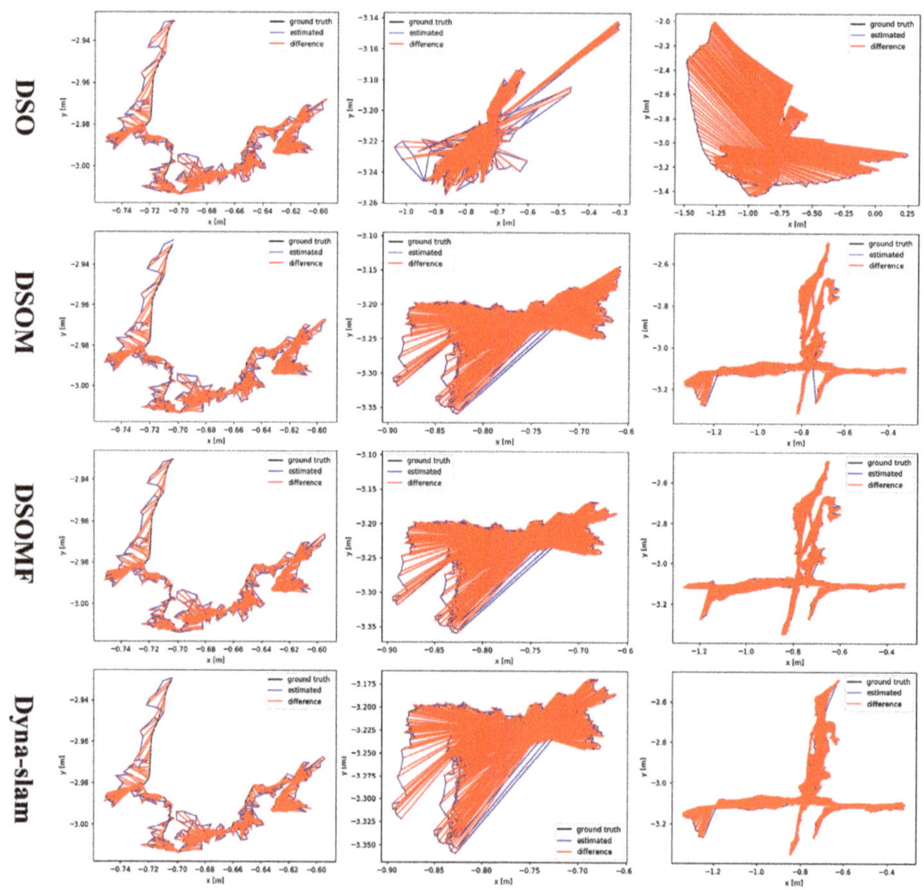

Figure 8. Comparison of absolute trajectory error for the camera on the TUM dataset.

To further enhance the real-time performance of our method, we drew inspiration from RDS-SLAM [19] and incorporated the selection of semantic keyframes into our algorithm. Therefore, in addition to comparing the localization accuracy, we quantitatively compared the runtime overhead and GPU memory consumption of several methods on the TUM dataset, as listed in Table 2. As shown, the per-frame processing time of DSOM was lower than that of Dyna-SLAM. After the video completion thread was incorporated, the per-frame processing time of DSOMF was slightly longer than that of Dyna-SLAM.

Table 2. Execution time and GPU memory cost on KITTI dataset based on several methods.

Algorithm Name	Time (ms/Frame)	GPU Memory Usage/GB
DSO	19	-
DSOM	240	5.2
DSOMF	312	6.5
Dyna-SLAM	300	5.7

Additionally, Table 3 shows the time overhead of the main modules of the proposed method on the TUM dataset. Clearly, the semantic segmentation module was the most time-consuming. In this study, instance segmentation is executed as a separate, independent thread, thus allowing for the substitution with a less time-consuming instance segmentation algorithm (if necessary) to further enhance the real-time performance of the proposed method. Moreover, through efficient parallel operations, the incorporation of instance segmentation and video completion modules, in addition to DSO, results in frame rates and memory usage that are comparable to those of Dyna-SLAM.

Table 3. Execution time cost of our method's main modules.

Algorithm Name	Time (ms/Frame)
Semantic Segmentation	70
Tracking	10
Data Association	5
Image Completion	55

4.2. Simulation Testing on KITTI Dataset

The KITTI dataset is widely recognized and utilized in the field of computer vision algorithms for testing an autonomous driving scenario. It encompasses various dynamic outdoor scenarios, including urban, rural, and highway environments. The images that captured the most dynamic objects include 15 vehicles and 30 pedestrians, thus indicating a high level of scene dynamism. Sequences 00-10 from the dataset were used to validate the DSOM and DSOMF algorithms proposed herein. The comparisons were performed made with the DSO and Dyna-SLAM algorithms using the EVO evaluation tool.

To analyze the positioning performance of DSOMF in outdoor dynamic environments, we present a comparison of the absolute pose errors between the DSOMF and DSO algorithms for dataset sequences 01, 02, 04, and 06 in Table 4. The data in the table include the corresponding RMSE, mean, max and min values. The data in the table indicate that, for sequences 01 and 02, the absolute pose error of DSOMF is significantly lower than that of DSO. For sequences 04 and 06, the absolute pose error of the method presented herein is comparable to that of DSO. This is because sequences 01 and 02 contain many dynamic vehicles and pedestrians, whereas sequences 04 and 06 contain primarily stationary vehicles.

To analyze the effect of the video completion module on the localization accuracy in outdoor environments, we present a comparison of the APEs among the DSOM, DSOMF, and Dyna-SLAM algorithms across dataset sequences 00–10 in Table 5. As shown in the table, in outdoor environments, both DSOM and DSOMF exhibited slight improvements in terms of pose-estimation accuracy across various dataset sequences compared with Dyna-SLAM. However, the inclusion of the video completion thread in DSOMF did not significantly enhance its performance compared with those of the first two methods. This is because in large outdoor scenes, dynamic objects typically occupy a relatively small area in images, and images completed thereafter fail to provide additional map information for backend optimization.

Table 4. Comparison of absolute pose errors in KITTI dataset.

Sequence	DSO				DSOMF			
	RMSE	Mean	Max	Min	RMSE	Mean	Max	Min
01	9.478	7.969	16.756	4.125	5.987	6.028	11.763	1.485
02	6.561	5.212	15.608	0.199	5.626	3.697	10.438	0.286
04	1.131	1.759	1.745	0.541	1.067	1.172	2.251	0.318
06	0.886	0.739	1.241	0.433	0.568	0.786	1.081	0.306

Table 5. Comparison of absolute pose errors of same-type algorithms.

Sequence	Dyna-SLAM	DSOM	DSOMF
00	3.505	2.937	2.521
01	9.003	7.607	6.420
02	5.219	4.213	4.238
03	1.299	1.054	0.966
04	1.591	1.256	1.214
05	1.779	1.289	1.372
06	0.824	0.672	0.604
07	2.489	2.036	1.880
08	3.291	2.778	2.473
09	2.564	2.101	1.966
10	2.743	2.259	2.375

Figure 9 shows the process of dynamic object removal using a video completion thread in the KITTI-04 dataset. In this figure, a white vehicle moving at a constant speed in the same direction is identified as a static object, whereas a black vehicle moving in the opposite direction is recognized as a dynamic object and thus removed and completed. The map-construction effect, as presented in Figure 10, shows that DSOMF excluded the interference of the black vehicle during map construction, thus resulting in a complete, linear road point cloud map.

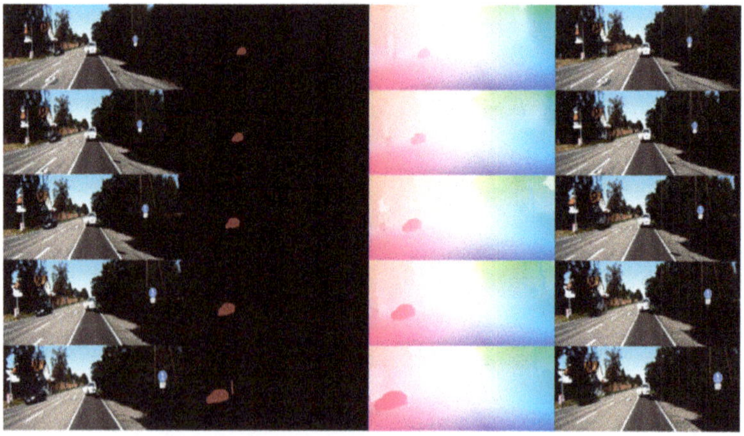

Figure 9. Video completion process in KITTI-04 dataset.

Figure 10. Map construction effect of DSOMF in the KITTI-04 dataset.

5. Unmanned Platform Experiment

5.1. Drone Experiment

Given the absence of distinct loops in the datasets utilized above, to verify the effectiveness of the loop closure detection module, we conducted real-world loop closure detection experiments using the quadcopter drone depicted in Figure 11. The drone is equipped with an Intel Realsense D435 image sensor (Santa Clara, CA, USA) and a micro-computer developed on the Jetson AGX Orin platform (2048-core NVIDIA Ampere architecture GPU (Santa Clara, CA, USA) featuring 64 Tensor Cores, 12-core ARM Cortex-A78AE v8.2 64-bit CPU, PVA v2 visual processing accelerator, 64 GB of 256-bit LPDDR5 memory).

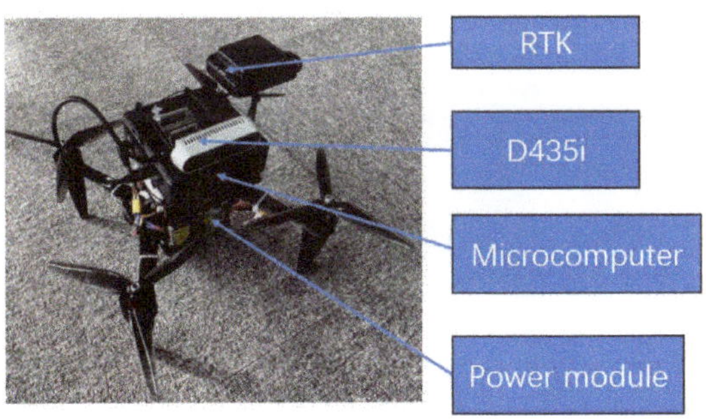

Figure 11. Unmanned flight platform SLAM algorithm test system.

In this experiment, we operated the drone to circle around the fixed-wing aircraft shown in Figure 12. By observing whether the semi-dense point clouds constructed at the starting and ending points overlap, we assessed the effectiveness of the loop closure detection module of our algorithm in a real-world setting. Figure 13a and Figure 13b, respectively, represent the semi-dense point cloud maps of the fixed-wing aircraft with and without loop closure detection. The red boxes indicate the semi-dense point cloud maps at the starting and ending points of the drone's flight. As shown in the red box in Figure 13a, with loop closure detection enabled, the drone successfully triggered loop closure at the starting and ending points, correcting the cumulative trajectory error and allowing the point cloud maps of these points to overlap effectively. In contrast, as illustrated in the red box in Figure 13b, without loop closure detection, the drone could not trigger loop closure at the endpoint, resulting in the inability to eliminate the cumulative trajectory error, which prevented the point cloud maps at the starting and ending points from overlapping. This experiment successfully validated the effectiveness of real-world loop closure detection on the same drone platform.

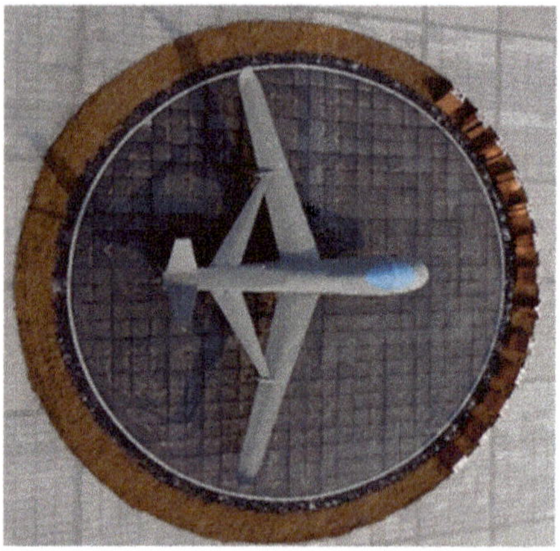

Figure 12. Top view of fixed wing aircraft.

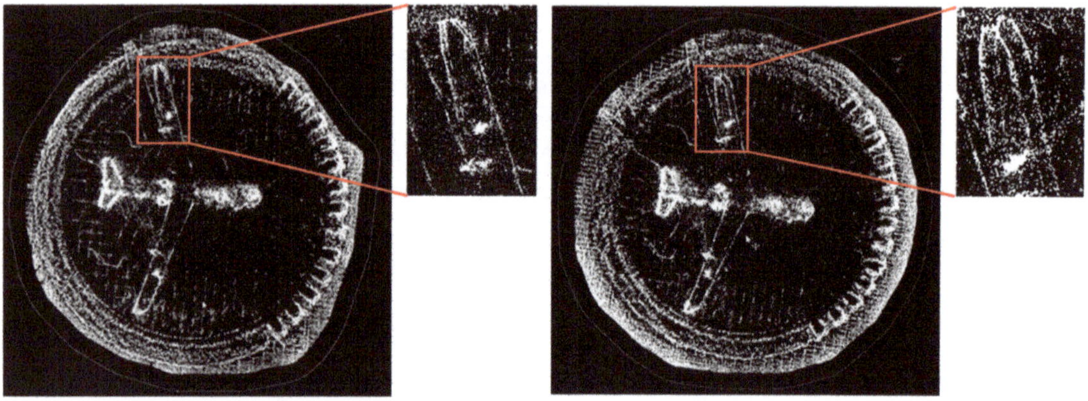

(**a**) (**b**)

Figure 13. Loop closure detection experiment. (**a**) The loop closure detection module runs; (**b**) the loop closure detection not runs.

5.2. Driverless Car Experiment

To further verify the effectiveness of the algorithm presented in this paper in handling dynamic objects, we conducted a localization and mapping experiment in an outdoor environment using a ground unmanned platform, as shown in Figure 14 below. To ensure the safety of the experiment, the unmanned platform was placed on the left side of the road, moving forward close to the edge of the road. The image sensor was oriented towards the center of the road to capture dynamic objects on the road. This experiment utilized the monocular mode of the Intel Realsense D435i image sensor mounted on the robot to collect environmental information and the same model of microcomputer as the drone. Due to the limited computing power of the computing platform carried by the unmanned vehicle, the collected image information was sent to a high-performance laptop computer by the unmanned vehicle for instance segmentation and video completion.

Figure 14. SLAM algorithm test system for unmanned ground platform.

We conducted tests on the algorithm proposed in this study by deploying unmanned vehicles to navigate around the site for one round, using DSO and DSOMF. The trajectories formed using the two algorithms are compared in Figure 15 below. In the site schematic, the green trajectory includes a section where a pedestrian is walking slowly (as shown in Figure 16a), while the white trajectory incorporates a segment with an electric truck moving at a higher speed (as shown in Figure 16b). The comparative observation of the trajectories generated using the two algorithms reveals that the algorithm proposed in this study demonstrates a notable improvement in positioning accuracy in both the white trajectory segments and the sections where loops occur. Upon calculation, it was determined that the processing time per frame for the algorithm discussed in this study was 49.6 milliseconds during the experimental process. Although the dynamic settings of this experiment were somewhat simplified due to hardware limitations, it has nonetheless validated the feasibility of the algorithm presented in this study in real-world scenarios to a certain extent.

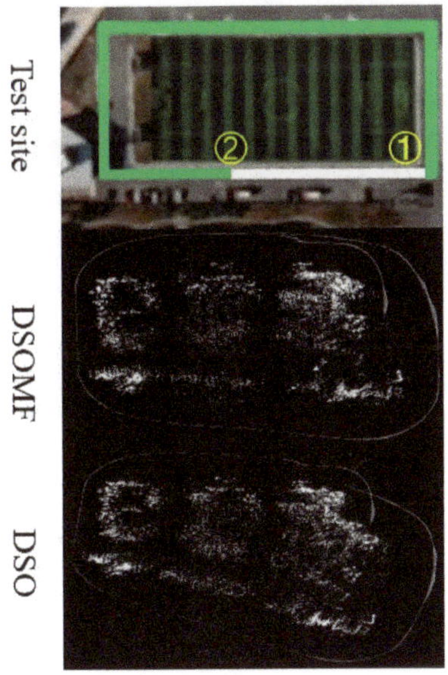

Figure 15. Comparison of outdoor dynamic environment trajectories (In the real-life scenario, the outlined boxes represent the trajectories of dynamic objects. Route one denotes the path of vehicles, while route two signifies pedestrian pathways).

(a)

(b)

Figure 16. Environment image. (**a**) Pedestrian environment image; (**b**) electric vehicle environment image.

6. Conclusions

This study addressed the need for high-precision navigation and positioning for unmanned platforms in dynamic environments by introducing instance segmentation and completion into the DSO algorithm framework, proposing a machine learning-based dynamic environment SLAM algorithm. Initially, the algorithm utilizes instance segmentation to divide the scene into objects with potential for motion. Subsequently, it combines semantic and geometric information to identify and eliminate moving objects. After the removal of dynamic objects, a video inpainting algorithm fills in the static background obscured by these moving entities, enhancing the algorithm's loop closure detection and improving pose alignment accuracy in dynamic environments. Finally, the methodology is validated using the TUM dataset, KITTI dataset, and real-world scenarios. The results demonstrate that in dynamic settings, the positioning accuracy of the proposed algorithm significantly surpasses that of DSO. In our future research, we aim to enhance the real-time performance of the proposed algorithm by improving keyframe selection strategies and data association methods, thereby reducing the computational resource consumption of semantic segmentation and optical flow completion algorithms. Additionally, dynamic objects in the environment hold significant value, and we plan to incorporate them into map construction in our subsequent studies.

Author Contributions: S.Y. conceived the idea; S.Y designed the software; S.Y., X.Z. and Z.W. collected the test data of real environment; S.Y. and X.Z. collected the related resources and supervised the experiment; X.Z. and Z.W. proposed the comment for the paper and experiment. All authors have read and agreed to the published version of the manuscript.

Funding: This work was supported by the National Natural Science Foundation of China (41971306).

Institutional Review Board Statement: This study does not involve research on human or animal subjects.

Informed Consent Statement: Written informed consent has been obtained from the patient(s) to publish this paper.

Data Availability Statement: The COCO dataset is obtained from http://images.cocodataset.org/zips/train2014.zip (accessed on 6 August 2023). TUM dataset is obtained from https://vision.in.tum.de/data/datasets/rgbd-dataset/download (accessed on 7 August 2023). KITTI dataset is obtained from http://www.cvlibs.net/datasets/kitti/eval_object.php?obj_benchmark=2d (accessed on 9 August 2023). Our real-world test data are available upon request from the corresponding author.

Conflicts of Interest: The authors declare no conflicts of interest.

References

1. Tourani, A.; Bavle, H.; Sanchez-Lopez, J.L.; Voos, H. Visual SLAM: What Are the Current Trends and What to Expect? *Sensors* **2022**, *22*, 9297. [CrossRef]
2. Zhu, Z.; Peng, S.; Larsson, V.; Xu, W.; Bao, H.; Cui, Z.; Oswald, M.R.; Pollefeys, M. NICE-SLAM: Neural Implicit Scalable Encoding for SLAM. In Proceedings of the 2022 IEEE/CVF Conference on Computer Vision and Pattern Recognition (CVPR), New Orleans, LA, USA, 18–24 June 2022; pp. 12776–12786.
3. Wang, H.; Wang, J.; Agapito, L. Co-SLAM: Joint Coordinate and Sparse Parametric Encodings for Neural Real-Time SLAM. In Proceedings of the 2023 IEEE/CVF Conference on Computer Vision and Pattern Recognition (CVPR), Vancouver, BC, Canada, 17–24 June 2023; pp. 13293–13302.
4. Mur-Artal, R.; Tardos, J.D. ORB-SLAM2: An Open-Source SLAM System for Monocular, Stereo, and RGB-D Cameras. *IEEE Trans. Robot.* **2017**, *33*, 1255–1262. [CrossRef]
5. Campos, C.; Elvira, R.; Rodríguez, J.J.G.; Montiel, J.M.; Tardós, J.D. ORB-SLAM3: An Accurate Open-Source Library for Visual, Visual–Inertial, and Multimap SLAM. *IEEE Trans. Robot.* **2021**, *37*, 1874–1890. [CrossRef]
6. Engel, J.; Koltun, V.; Cremers, D. Direct Sparse Odometry. *IEEE Trans. Pattern Anal. Mach. Intell.* **2018**, *40*, 611–625. [CrossRef]
7. El Ghazouali, S.; Mhirit, Y.; Oukhrid, A.; Michelucci, U.; Nouira, H. FusionVision: A Comprehensive Approach of 3D Object Reconstruction and Segmentation from RGB-D Cameras Using YOLO and Fast Segment Anything. *Sensors* **2024**, *24*, 2889. [CrossRef]
8. Yugay, V.; Li, Y.; Gevers, T.; Oswald, M.R. Gaussian-SLAM: Photo-Realistic Dense SLAM with Gaussian Splatting. *arXiv* **2023**, arXiv:2312.10070. [CrossRef]
9. Bescos, B.; Facil, J.M.; Civera, J.; Neira, J. DynaSLAM: Tracking, Mapping, and Inpainting in Dynamic Scenes. *IEEE Robot. Autom. Lett.* **2018**, *3*, 4076–4083. [CrossRef]
10. Cheng, J.; Wang, Z.; Zhou, H.; Li, L.; Yao, J. DM-SLAM: A Feature-Based SLAM System for Rigid Dynamic Scenes. *ISPRS Int. J. Geo-Inf.* **2020**, *9*, 202. [CrossRef]
11. Zhong, F.; Wang, S.; Zhang, Z.; Chen, C.; Wang, Y. Detect-SLAM: Making Object Detection and SLAM Mutually Beneficial. In Proceedings of the 2018 IEEE Winter Conference on Applications of Computer Vision (WACV), Lake Tahoe, NV, USA, 12–15 March 2018; pp. 1001–1010.
12. Sun, Y.; Liu, M.; Meng, M.Q.-H. Improving RGB-D SLAM in Dynamic Environments: A Motion Removal Approach. *Robot. Auton. Syst.* **2017**, *89*, 110–122. [CrossRef]
13. Li, S.; Lee, D. RGB-D SLAM in Dynamic Environments Using Static Point Weighting. *IEEE Robot. Autom. Lett.* **2017**, *2*, 2263–2270. [CrossRef]
14. Wang, Y.; Huang, S. Towards Dense Moving Object Segmentation Based Robust Dense RGB-D SLAM in Dynamic Scenarios. In Proceedings of the 2014 13th International Conference on Control Automation Robotics & Vision (ICARCV), Singapore, 10–12 December 2014; pp. 1841–1846.
15. Fischler, M.A.; Bolles, R.C. Random Sample Consensus: A Paradigm for Model Fitting with Applications to Image Analysis and Automated Cartography. *Commun. ACM* **1981**, *24*, 381–395. [CrossRef]
16. Tan, W.; Dong, Z.; Zhang, G.; Bao, H. Robust Monocular SLAM in Dynamic Environments. In Proceedings of the 2013 IEEE International Symposium on Mixed and Augmented Reality (ISMAR), Adelaide, Australia, 1–4 October 2013; pp. 209–218.
17. Ferrera, M.; Moras, J.; Trouvé-Peloux, P.; Creuze, V. Real-Time Monocular Visual Odometry for Turbid and Dynamic Underwater Environments. *arXiv* **2018**, arXiv:1806.05842. [CrossRef]
18. Yu, C.; Liu, Z.; Liu, X.-J.; Xie, F.; Yang, Y.; Wei, Q.; Fei, Q. DS-SLAM: A Semantic Visual SLAM towards Dynamic Environments. In Proceedings of the 2018 IEEE/RSJ International Conference on Intelligent Robots and Systems (IROS), Madrid, Spain, 1–5 October 2018; pp. 1168–1174.
19. Liu, Y.; Miura, J. RDS-SLAM: Real-Time Dynamic SLAM Using Semantic Segmentation Methods. *IEEE Access* **2021**, *9*, 23772–23785. [CrossRef]
20. Alcantarilla, P.F.; Yebes, J.J.; Almazan, J.; Bergasa, L.M. On Combining Visual SLAM and Dense Scene Flow to Increase the Robustness of Localization and Mapping in Dynamic Environments. In Proceedings of the 2012 IEEE International Conference on Robotics and Automation, St. Paul, MN, USA, 14–18 May 2012; pp. 1290–1297.
21. Wang, C.-C.; Thorpe, C.; Thrun, S.; Hebert, M.; Durrant-Whyte, H. Simultaneous Localization, Mapping and Moving Object Tracking. *Int. J. Robot. Res.* **2007**, *26*, 889–916. [CrossRef]
22. Reddy, N.D.; Singhal, P.; Chari, V.; Krishna, K.M. Dynamic Body VSLAM with Semantic Constraints. In Proceedings of the 2015 IEEE/RSJ International Conference on Intelligent Robots and Systems (IROS), Hamburg, Germany, 28 September–3 October 2015; pp. 1897–1904.
23. Salas-Moreno, R.F.; Newcombe, R.A.; Strasdat, H.; Kelly, P.H.J.; Davison, A.J. SLAM++: Simultaneous Localisation and Mapping at the Level of Objects. In Proceedings of the 2013 IEEE Conference on Computer Vision and Pattern Recognition, Portland, OR, USA, 23–28 June 2013; pp. 1352–1359.

24. Tateno, K.; Tombari, F.; Navab, N. When 2.5D Is Not Enough: Simultaneous Reconstruction, Segmentation and Recognition on Dense SLAM. In Proceedings of the 2016 IEEE International Conference on Robotics and Automation (ICRA), Stockholm, Sweden, 16–21 May 2016; pp. 2295–2302.
25. Sucar, E.; Wada, K.; Davison, A. NodeSLAM: Neural Object Descriptors for Multi-View Shape Reconstruction. In Proceedings of the 2020 International Conference on 3D Vision (3DV), Fukuoka, Japan, 25–28 November 2020; pp. 949–958.
26. Hosseinzadeh, M.; Li, K.; Latif, Y.; Reid, I. Real-Time Monocular Object-Model Aware Sparse SLAM. In Proceedings of the 2019 International Conference on Robotics and Automation (ICRA), Montreal, QC, Canada, 20–24 May 2019; IEEE: Piscataway, NJ, USA, 2019; pp. 7123–7129.
27. Nicholson, L.; Milford, M.; Sunderhauf, N. QuadricSLAM: Dual Quadrics From Object Detections as Landmarks in Object-Oriented SLAM. *IEEE Robot. Autom. Lett.* **2019**, *4*, 1–8. [CrossRef]
28. Bescos, B.; Campos, C.; Tardós, J.D.; Neira, J. DynaSLAM II: Tightly-Coupled Multi-Object Tracking and SLAM. *arXiv* **2020**, arXiv:2010.07820. [CrossRef]
29. He, K.; Gkioxari, G.; Dollar, P.; Girshick, R. Mask R-CNN. In Proceedings of the 2017 IEEE International Conference on Computer Vision (ICCV), Venice, Italy, 22–29 October 2017; pp. 2980–2988.
30. Kluger, F.; Rosenhahn, B. PARSAC: Accelerating Robust Multi-Model Fitting with Parallel Sample Consensus. *Proc. AAAI Conf. Artif. Intell.* **2024**, *38*, 2804–2812. [CrossRef]
31. Gao, C.; Saraf, A.; Huang, J.-B.; Kopf, J. Flow-Edge Guided Video Completion. *arXiv* **2020**, arXiv:2009.01835. [CrossRef]
32. Lin, T.-Y.; Maire, M.; Belongie, S.; Bourdev, L.; Girshick, R.; Hays, J.; Perona, P.; Ramanan, D.; Zitnick, C.L.; Dollár, P. Microsoft COCO: Common Objects in Context. *arXiv* **2014**, arXiv:1405.0312. [CrossRef]
33. Runz, M.; Buffier, M.; Agapito, L. MaskFusion: Real-Time Recognition, Tracking and Reconstruction of Multiple Moving Objects. In Proceedings of the 2018 IEEE International Symposium on Mixed and Augmented Reality (ISMAR), Munich, Germany, 16–20 October 2018; pp. 10–20.
34. Pan, X.; Liu, H.; Fang, M.; Wang, Z.; Zhang, Y.; Zhang, G. Dynamic 3D Scenario-Oriented Monocular SLAM Based on Semantic Probability Prediction. *J. Image Graph.* **2023**, *28*, 2151–2166. [CrossRef]
35. Xu, R.; Li, X.; Zhou, B.; Loy, C.C. Deep Flow-Guided Video Inpainting. In Proceedings of the 2019 IEEE/CVF Conference on Computer Vision and Pattern Recognition (CVPR), Long Beach, CA, USA, 15–20 June 2019; pp. 3718–3727.
36. Sturm, J.; Engelhard, N.; Endres, F.; Burgard, W.; Cremers, D. A Benchmark for the Evaluation of RGB-D SLAM Systems. In Proceedings of the 2012 IEEE/RSJ International Conference on Intelligent Robots and Systems, Vilamoura-Algarve, Portugal, 7–12 October 2012; pp. 573–580.
37. Geiger, A.; Lenz, P.; Stiller, C.; Urtasun, R. Vision Meets Robotics: The KITTI Dataset. *Int. J. Robot. Res.* **2013**, *32*, 1231–1237. [CrossRef]

buildings

MDPI

Article

A 3D Parameterized BIM-Modeling Method for Complex Engineering Structures in Building Construction Projects

Lijun Yang [1,2], Xuexiang Gao [2], Song Chen [2], Qianyao Li [3] and Shuo Bai [1,*]

1 School of Civil Engineering and Architecture, Wuhan University of Technology, Wuhan 430070, China
2 Shenzhen Nanshan District Construction and Works Department, Shenzhen 518000, China
3 School of Accounting, Wuhan Textile University, Wuhan 430200, China
* Correspondence: shuobai@whut.edu.cn; Tel.: +177-3738-3498

Abstract: The structural components of large-scale public construction projects are more complex than those of ordinary residential buildings, with irregular and diverse components, as well as a large number of repetitive structural elements, which increase the difficulty of BIM-modeling operations. Additionally, there is a significant amount of inherent parameter information in the construction process, which puts forward higher requirements for the application and management capabilities of BIM technology. However, the current BIM software still has deficiencies in the parameterization of complex and irregular structural components, fine modeling, and project management information. To address these issues, this paper takes Grasshopper as the core parametric tool and Revit as the carrier of component attribute information. It investigates the parametric modeling logic of Grasshopper and combines the concepts of parameterization, modularization, standardization, and engineering practicality to create a series of parametric programs for complex structural components in building projects. This approach mainly addresses intricate challenges pertaining to the parametric structural shapes (including batch processing) and parametric structural attributes (including the batch processing of diverse attribute parameters), thereby ensuring the efficiency in BIM modeling throughout the design and construction phases of complex building projects.

Keywords: building information modeling (BIM); common structure; Grasshopper; parametric modeling

1. Introduction

With the improvement in construction standards, large and complex public buildings are constantly emerging, each with its own unique structural shapes. While the Autodesk Revit modeling system typically comes with commonly used families such as beams, slabs, and columns, for structures with slightly more complex shapes, new families need to be created, increasing the workload of modeling. Additionally, the parameterization in the Revit modeling system often relies on reference planes to drive shape variations, resulting in limited flexibility. This exposes the shortcomings of Revit's parametric modeling system, particularly for complex, repetitive, curved, and procedural parameterization. The research objective of this paper is to establish a three-dimensional (3D) parametric BIM-modeling method for complex engineering structures in architectural engineering through Grasshopper visual programming, so as to improve design efficiency.

"Parameter" originates from a mathematical concept, referring to a complex system or function where the parameterized object of a quantity maintains an invariant relationship. Parameterization is the process of abstracting the internal organizational order (i.e., parameter relationships) between various parts of a system, and then using the relevant computer technology to describe it, obtaining a parameter model. In a parameter model, the relationships between components are dynamic, and making changes to any component will affect the components associated with it, thereby affecting the entire complex system. Engineering structural design has typical characteristics of complex systems. In the design process, various problems and contradictions are intertwined, forming a dynamic system containing many relationships. In the realm of engineering design, parametric design represents an advanced approach that incorporates a comprehensive consideration of various influencing factors. Through the utilization of computer languages, it delineates the intrinsic logical relationships and constructs parametric models on a digital platform. This methodology enables the acquisition of physical forms by controlling the input values of variables. In parametric design, parameters reflect the logical relationships between various influencing factors in architectural design. These parameters are not fixed and can vary depending on changes in design conditions. However, the variation of parameters differs from the variation of variables, as the former represents a qualitative change, while the latter signifies a quantitative change.

Building information modeling (BIM) technology is a data-driven tool that combines architectural data models with information models, which are applied to engineering design, construction, and management. The parameterization function is integrated into BIM software, such as the typical BIM software (version 2019), Autodesk Revit (version 2019). It enables Revit to provide co-ordination and change management capabilities, for instance, the process of specifying and controlling the properties, characteristics, and behavior of elements in the Revit model [1,2]. BIM modeling for engineering structures serves as an essential foundation for structural analysis and construction. The parametric 3D modeling of architectural structures has a significant impact on the entire structural engineering process, including conceptual design, structural analysis, layout plans, detailed drawings, and construction, as well as on structural engineering design practices. However, there exists a certain contradiction between complex model data and modeling automation, which leads to a waste of time on basic modeling tasks. BIM parametric modeling is a set of modeling methods that utilize professional knowledge and rules (rather than geometric rules to determine the method of generating graphics) to determine parameters and constraints. Therefore, numerous researchers have conducted extensive research on parametric modeling methods for engineering structures.

Singh et al. [3] integrated domain-specific knowledge into modeling tools by modeling rule-based BIM objects, parametric constraints, and visual programming tools, thereby reducing the time and effort invested by designers in the design process. Bai et al. [4] introduced IFC into BIM and proposed a digital graphic medium mapping model to address common design issues in prefabricated buildings. Lee et al. [5] proposes a comprehensive framework for parametric semi-automatic BIM and bridge member segmentation, generate BIM bridge models by automatically extracting shape information from each parameter. Zhao et al. [6] focused on hydraulic and hydroelectric engineering and established a hydraulic engineering information model based on existing BIM parametric design software. In the modeling of irregular architectural structures, Niu et al. [7] have opted for a method for the parametric generation of irregular architectural surfaces using Dynamo-Revit, and developed an integrated program of "logic–parameter–model–information" for architectural components. Considering the complexity of special structures in residential projects, Zhang et al. [8] reported a theory and method for the parametric modeling of irregular curved surfaces in residential buildings based on the combined parametric modeling capability of Rhino + Grasshopper. In the modeling of prefabricated structures, Tong [9] proposed a parametric BIM-modeling method for prefabricated buildings based on Dynamo-Python, improving modeling efficiency and reducing rework probability. Bianconi et al. [10] used the BIM tools Rhinoceros + Grasshopper to realize the parametric design and modeling of large-scale prefabricated houses. However, the parameterization in Grasshopper is not specific to individual components, and information integration and transmission are limited. Deng et al. [11] proposed a method that uses PBR and parametric modeling to construct woven textured materials with centimeter and millimeter level 3D structures. The design can be directly applied to mainstream 3D modeling software for virtual presentations in different applications. Zhang et al. [12] found that the introduction of modularized BIM design can simultaneously consider the diversity of architectural forms, but this method is also faced with the problem of component information integration and transmission. To improve modeling efficiency, scholars have also researched the development of component libraries. Wei et al. [13] adopted an architecture component library based on the IFC and the Part Library (PLIB) standards. In this study, IFC was used for the open data representation of building products, presenting product model data in the form of generic models, functional models, and functional view models, and providing a useful framework for the concept of a household. Bai et al. [14] developed a locally parametric BIM component database for prefabricated structural components and templates based on application programming interfaces (APIs) and custom component databases. Lu et al. [15] designed an open-access BIM object library by conceptualizing the ontology structure of components, defining BIM parameters, and implementing the object processing modules. However, this family library does not support IFC-based information sharing. Compared with geological structure modeling, engineering structure modeling is more flexible and its methods are more diversified.

Compared with conventional structures such as beams, slabs, and columns, they have been integrated into modeling software and can be directly accessed and used. However, in housing construction projects, there are still many other structures that cannot be integrated into modeling software and require efforts to recreate. Through the analysis of typical complex structural forms in residential construction projects, the objective setting of structural parametric control points is established using visual programming languages. This method addresses issues such as the parametrization of structural shapes, including batch processing, realizes the coupling of geometric data and attribute data, and forms a digital link design approach that integrates the "numerical" and "geometric" aspects.

2. Engineering Structural Graphical Parameterization Theory Method

Parameterization is a practical technology established in the field of computer-aided design (CAD), which has gradually evolved into the parametric technology seen today through continuous updates and optimizations. The term "parameter" refers to the mathematical concept of a "quantity" that maintains the invariant mapping relationship of a system or function. However, in the context of building information modeling (BIM) technology, parameters not only refer to the geometric parameters that constrain graphics, but also include non-geometric parameters such as physical and social attributes related to the model system. Therefore, a significant concept of BIM technology is parametric design.

"Graphics" are widely used to express complex relationships between various engineering entities, because they can intuitively reflect the relationships between engineering objects [16]. Graphics generally consists of two parts: the complete geometric information of the building (the external contours) and the topological information of the building (the relationship formed by the graphic elements). Initial drawings often lack depth in engineering representation, favoring functionality over clarity, resulting in a suboptimal reuse potential and obstacles to accommodating changing design intentions. Conversely, parametric graphics seamlessly integrate a diverse array of data throughout the lifecycle of a building, facilitating the precise alignment of digital representations with actual or prospective structures in the physical world. Through the graphical and digital abstraction of engineering knowledge, parametric modeling significantly diminishes the intricacy of engineering design, hastens the design process, and enhances design efficiency. BIM's parametric digital graphics can be aptly described as:

$$G = \{E, C, P, I, T\} \tag{1}$$

In the equation, G represents the parametric digital graph (overall graphic), E represents the elements involved in this parametric graph, C represents the set of parametric constraints, P represents the set of parameters attached to the graph, I represents the dimensionality of information, and T represents the transfer of information. As shown in Figure 1, this is an illustrative representation of the parametric digital graph in BIM.

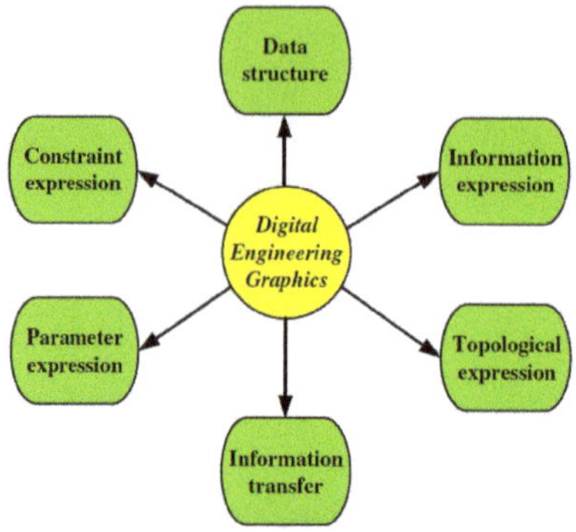

Figure 1. BIM parameterized digital graphic representation.

The parameterization of BIM digital graphics primarily encompasses two aspects: the model dimension and the information dimension. This model is a parametric-driven digital model. Primary modeling and secondary modeling constitute the two primary geometric models of BIM digital graphics. Primary modeling can be achieved through conventional methods such as extrusion, rotation, scanning, and lofting. Secondary modeling involves refinement operations such as punching, chamfering, and mold extraction, with their mathematical models described jointly by convex geometric models and rotational extrusion body geometric models [17]. Their mathematical expression is shown in Equations (2)–(6). Model parameters are divided into graphics-driven parameters (geometric properties) and custom parameters (non-geometric properties), which can be represented by numbers, expressions, or complex functions compiled by the program. The information dimension of BIM digital graphics mainly includes topological information, parametric information, material information, section information, prefabrication information, construction installation information, and other construction process content.

(1) The mathematical model of convex geometric models can typically be expressed as follows:

$$S_1(u,v) = \{x_1(u,v), y_1(u,v), z_1(u,v)\} \tag{2}$$

$$S(u,v) = \{x(u,v), y(u,v), z(u,v)\} \tag{3}$$

Among them, $u_1 \le u \le u_2, v_1 \le v \le v_2$; the convex geometric model is a generalized region enclosed by $S_1(u, v)$ and $S(u, v)$.

(2) The mathematical model of rotating and scanning geometric models can usually be expressed as follows.

$$r(m) = \{x(m), y(m), z(m)\} \tag{4}$$

$$S_1(u,v,r) = \{x_1(u,v,r), y_1(u,v,r), z_1(u,v,r)\} \tag{5}$$

$$S(u,v,r) = \{x(u,v,r), y(u,v,r), z(u,v,r)\} \tag{6}$$

When $0 \le m \le 1$, the geometric model of the rotational scanned geometric body is the generalized region enclosed by $S(u,v,r)$ and $S_1(u,v,r)$.

3. Grasshopper Parameterized Modeling Logic

Algorithms and data constitute the fundamental building blocks of all parametric design solutions. However, modeling software capable of handling their intricate interplay with agility is rare. The evolution of the Grasshopper (GH) visual programming language has profoundly strengthened the nexus between algorithms, data, and models. GH stands apart from other parametric tools in its ability to comprehensively document the modeling journey from inception to completion in the form of batteries or nodes [18]. This process enables the parametrization and modification of any nodal parameter or overarching logic, thereby bridging design concepts with the modeling process, streamlining repetitive tasks, and, ultimately, shaping the desired outcomes of the model. The modeling logic of this study is as follows: First, the geometric composition of complex structures is analyzed to find out their common features. Then, based on the operators in the Grasshopper visualization programming, the geometric description methods of these common features are summarized. For the missing operators, they need to be developed and obtained by oneself. Finally, the parametric closed loop of complex common structures is achieved by the point constraint parameterization method.

3.1. Parametric Modeling Vector Method

A vector is a quantity that combines both "direction" and "magnitude", such as velocity, force, etc. In a two-dimensional co-ordinate system, a vector is represented by two real numbers, for example, $v = \langle a_1, a_2 \rangle$. Similarly, in a 3D environment, an additional real number a_3 can be added to represent $v = \langle a_1, a_2, a_3 \rangle$. The availability of vector data manipulation in Grasshopper is a concept rarely found in other BIM-modeling software (version 2019). This functionality offers programming capabilities to flexibly move, array, and control components and models. It allows designers to input data and programs for automatic calculations, thus freeing them from manually defining distances and directions repeatedly. For instance, within the Vector tab of Grasshopper, you can find the Vector 2Pt tool, which is the standard tool for defining vector objects in Grasshopper. For instance, within the Rhino environment, you can position two point objects: Point 1 and Point 2. Subsequently, in Grasshopper, you would employ two point components to retrieve these two points from Rhino. Link these point components to the respective A and B terminals of the Vector 2Pt tool in Grasshopper. This integration will spawn a vector in Grasshopper, oriented from Point 1 to Point 2, with its magnitude equivalent to the distance between the two points, as depicted in Figure 2.

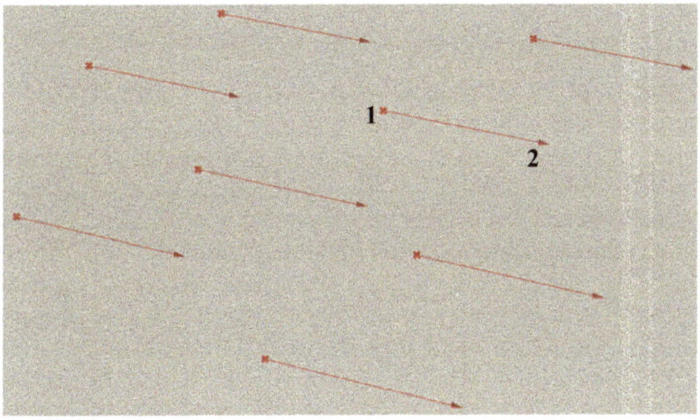

Figure 2. Vector representation in Grasshopper.

3.2. Data Structures and Data Matching in Parametric Modeling

Algorithms and data structures are closely related. A data structure refers to the organization of data, and an algorithm is the steps taken to operate on that data. The parametric modeling process in Grasshopper visual programming involves the processing of data, that is, compiling a series of input parameters into logical operations to generate a new set of output data that meets the expected requirements. The data needs to be stored in the appropriate data structures in order to play a role in process handling. This allows for the faster manipulation and application of the data. The design of data structures determines whether the parametric modeling program can run successfully and smoothly.

Tree data, list data, and single data represent three pivotal data structure types that underlie the programmatic flow within Grasshopper. Collectively, these data structures orchestrate the logical progression of the program. GH components perform diverse operations contingent upon the configuration of the input data; thus, a profound understanding of the data structures prior to their application is imperative. GH manifests varying outcomes dependent on the specific data structure. For example, when utilizing the Mass Addition component to manipulate single data and list data, the data-processing paradigm amalgamates all numerals to yield a solitary numerical outcome as the output. However, the processing of tree data is different. The results are presented in the form of a list, generating a summing list of numbers, with each numeric result mapping to the sum of each numeric branch. Visualization tools in GH show the differences in the form of single data, list data, and tree data, as well as the results of their operations, as shown in Figure 3.

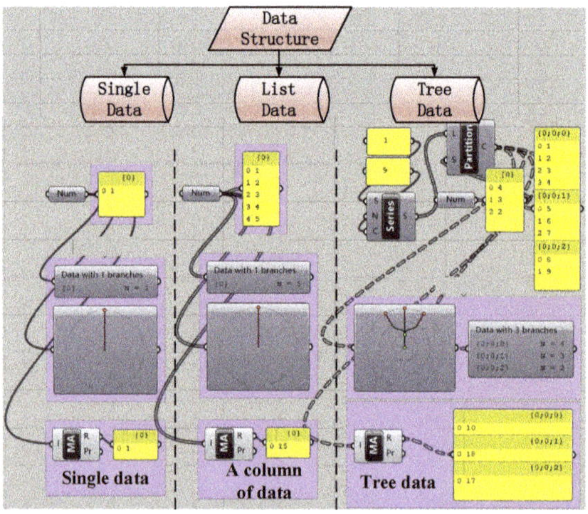

Figure 3. Differences in different types of data structures and operations.

In architectural engineering, many components exhibit various patterns and common characteristics in terms of shape, such as stairs, railings, retaining walls, and so on. Based on this, it is often necessary to perform the batch processing of components or graphical elements in Grasshopper, such as making mass modifications to meshes, levels, component positions, or quantities. In such scenarios, it is essential to store these variables in lists and convert them into the aforementioned data structures when required. Index numbers are used to index and call the data in the list, with the index order increasing from 0. During data processing, multiple sets of data are often paired, which means that multiple lists are paired. In Grasshopper, you can modify or manipulate the pairing mode of the data. The matching data paradigms encompass the longest list, shortest list, and cross-reference, each representing a distinct connection method for amalgamating the longest list, integrating the shortest list, and interlinking lists through cross-referencing. These three matching modalities offer immense versatility in data manipulation. Now, I shall elaborate on these three matching data paradigms in a visually intuitive manner.

The Longest List node operator performs calculations based on the length of the longest list. When matching between two data lists of varying lengths, the match is first made according to the corresponding index in the shorter list. After the short list data are matched, the last data in the short list are matched with all the remaining data in the long list. This process is represented by operators in Grasshopper, as shown in Figure 4a.

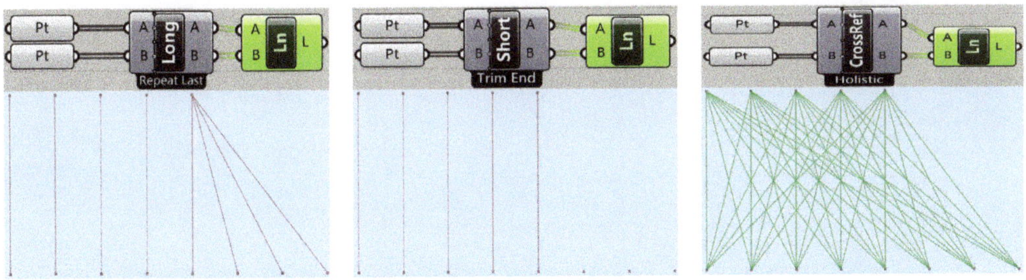

(a) (b) (c)

Figure 4. The three matching modes: (**a**) Matching with Longest List; (**b**) Matching with Shortest List; and (**c**) Cross-List Data Matching.

The shortest list node operator conducts computations according to the length of the shortest list. During the matching of two data lists with varying lengths, it aligns the shortest list with corresponding data from the other list. Upon the successful matching of the short list data flow, the matching mode ceases. At this point, any remaining data from the longer list are discarded. This operation is denoted by an operator in Grasshopper, as shown in Figure 4b.

The Cross Reference node operator is relatively complex. It performs a cross-matching of data between two lists, which means that all data are involved in the process. This process involves matching each piece of data from one list with all the data in the other list. After this matching is completed, the process is repeated in the opposite way, meaning that each piece of data in the second list is also matched with all the data in the first list. This establishes mutual connections between the two lists. This process is represented in Grasshopper through operators, as shown in Figure 4c.

In Grasshopper, the flexibility and effectiveness of building the required data structures to handle model variations by changing the types of operators is a unique characteristic that is not found in other BIM parametric modeling software such as Revit 2019, MicroStation V8i, and CATIA V5. This facilitates subsequent parametric modeling in methodological terms.

3.3. Line and Surface Processing and Geometric Transformations in Parametric Modeling

In the parametric modeling environment based on Rhino and Grasshopper, the point, line, surface, volume, and various attributes in the structure are driven by various battery nodes to realize parametric modeling. Compared with other BIM-modeling software that is based on reference planes, the parametric control in Grasshopper is more refined and comprehensive. It allows the precise control of the position of the lines and the shape of surfaces by inputting co-ordinate points, thus driving the deformation of components. For example, three co-ordinate points (x, y, and z) can be input to control the position of a point and form a closed cross-section with multiple points. The initial data points can be directly controlled by parameters, and the process of forming points, lines, and surfaces is shown in Figure 5.

After the model is formed in Grasshopper, various transformations can be made to the model such as Euclidean transformations, affine transformations, similar transformations, and deformation transformations. More intricate transformations can be executed through the integration of these transformations or specific operators. Euclidean transformation issues can be reduced to transformations between co-ordinate origins. Given that both local and absolute co-ordinates adhere to a right-handed co-ordinate system, this facilitates their mutual transformations. Typically, Euclidean transformations are implemented via a series of combined transformations employing translation and rotation matrices [19]. In a BIM system, if there is a component with co-ordinates $P_0(x_0, y_0, z_0)$ and it is desired to move the local co-ordinate origin of that component to an absolute co-ordinate position $P(x, y, z)$, it would require converting the absolute co-ordinates to a Cartesian co-ordinate system. This is because co-ordinate P_0 needs to undergo rotation and translation to transform it to point P. Let the local co-ordinates Z and Y be perpendicular to the ground and point to true north, and let $\theta_x, \theta_y, \theta_z$ represent the rotation angles with respect to the x, y, and z axes of the spatial co-ordinates. The rotation matrix of each spatial co-ordinate axis R_x, R_y, R_z can be expressed by a homogeneous matrix. Then, the component can be translated to a specified position using the translation matrix T.

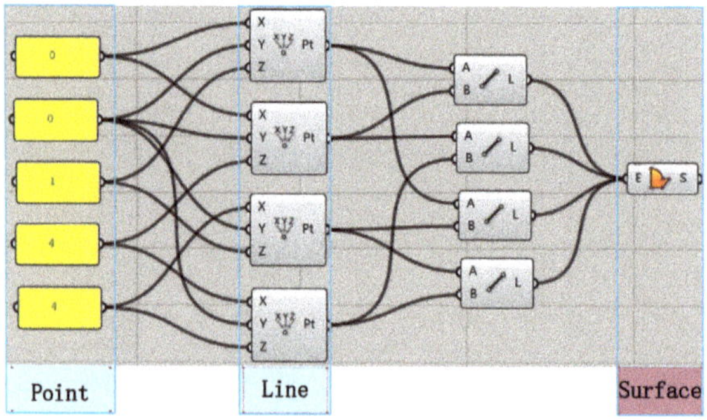

Figure 5. The process of forming points, lines, and surfaces.

According to the aforementioned rules, if a component needs to be translated in Grasshopper, it is necessary to define a unit direction Vector that indicates the direction of movement within the system. Then, the encapsulated translation command is utilized to achieve the translation along this unit direction. The translation process is illustrated in Figure 6a; if the component needs to be rotated, the axis of rotation must be defined around the line and then moved around the axis using the move command. The rotation process is shown in Figure 6b.

Certainly, Grasshopper also provides many other operators to achieve object affine transformations, graph mapping, solid deformations, and other operations. These operators or battery nodes can be logically combined to achieve the parametric modeling of structures.

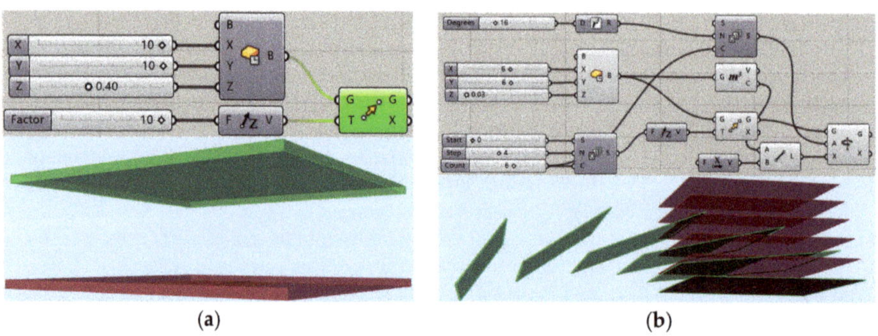

Figure 6. Diversified movement methods of components: (**a**) object translation along direction; and (**b**) object rotation around axis.

4. Parametric Modeling Method for Engineering Structures Based on Grasshopper

Parametric modeling in building projects encounters challenges beyond complex geological structures, such as specialized structures like retaining walls, railings, and irregular surfaces. These structures exhibit a high degree of variability, require precision, and involve complex relationships in parametric control. The conventional parametric BIM-modeling methods based on Revit may have limitations in handling these structures, particularly in terms of parametric flexibility and logic in dealing with complex structures. In general, it still requires manual adjustments to the spatial position and attribute parameters of components, making it difficult to achieve the detailed parametric modeling of complex structures, logical processing of batch components, and precise surface parameterization. Therefore, this study proposes to utilize Grasshopper as a parametric programming tool and Rhino as the modeling data kernel; by defining the shape-driving parameters within the unified Grasshopper operator, a parametric modeling method for complex engineering structures in building projects is established.

4.1. Method for Parameterized Creation of Irregular Structures

In addition to a large number of regularly shaped structures with singular functions, such as beams, slabs, and columns, building projects also involve many other irregular structures influenced by factors like irregular forces, irregular shapes, irregular lateral stiffness, local discontinuities in beams and slabs, and sudden changes in the load-bearing capacity at special locations. These irregular structures include landscape retaining wall structures, irregular column structures, irregular floor slab structures, and architectural facade structures. It is difficult for conventional parameterization methods to achieve the refinement and constraint of these structures. In order to achieve parametric sustainability, it is necessary to identify commonalities among them, implying that a single or a few parametric models can generate many other similar structures. Below, we will take the retaining wall structure in the construction project as an example to illustrate the parameterization.

The foundation conditions for building projects are not always ideal. The construction foundation conditions vary widely, sometimes involving soft soil, expansive soil, collapsible loess, and sometimes even liquefied soil, permafrost, or other special structures in specific areas. Retaining walls can serve as a typical load-bearing structure to prevent the instability of fill or soil due to deformation. In this case, the retaining wall structure model becomes the modeling target [20–22]. In the building projects, according to the needs of the project, the retaining wall has many types, such as inclined, inclined-backfill, vertical, counterweight, and reinforced concrete cantilever retaining walls, as shown in Figure 7. Its uses mainly include public retaining walls, vehicle ramp retaining walls, riverbank retaining walls, and landscape ecological retaining walls. While these retaining walls vary in structural forms, their common structural characteristics can be summarized, thereby developing a standardized retaining wall design method based on building information modeling (BIM).

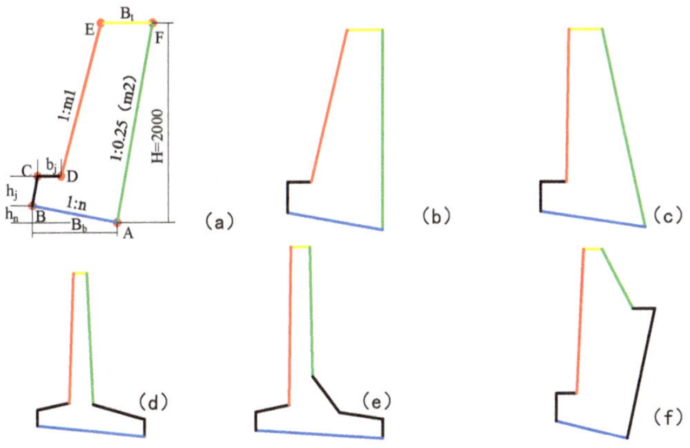

Figure 7. Type and section of retaining wall: (**a**) Type a; (**b**) Type b; (**c**) Type c; (**d**) Type d; (**e**) Type e; (**f**) Type f.

Due to the widespread use of BIM software such as Revit 2019 in building projects, the creation of parametric models is typically driven by reference planes and is better suited to regular structures. However, for retaining wall structures with varying slopes and angles, it is inconvenient to use a reference plane to control the structure flexibility. Therefore, a more refined parametric mode driven by point constraints is required. Meanwhile, although there are many types of retaining wall structures with various cross-sectional sizes, they always maintain a narrow top and wide bottom structure topology, as shown in Figure 8. Structures with the same color lines can be represented in Grasshopper using generic parameterization. Additionally, because it is necessary to calculate the dimensions of other parts of the structure based on the slope information in the structure, the slope information can be encapsulated and defined in the operation nodes in Grasshopper. Most importantly, this parametric program can encapsulate the parameters that need to be adjusted into its own operator. In other words, the parameters in the model creation process can be externalized and freely adjusted according to needs, facilitating their use in similar projects in the future.

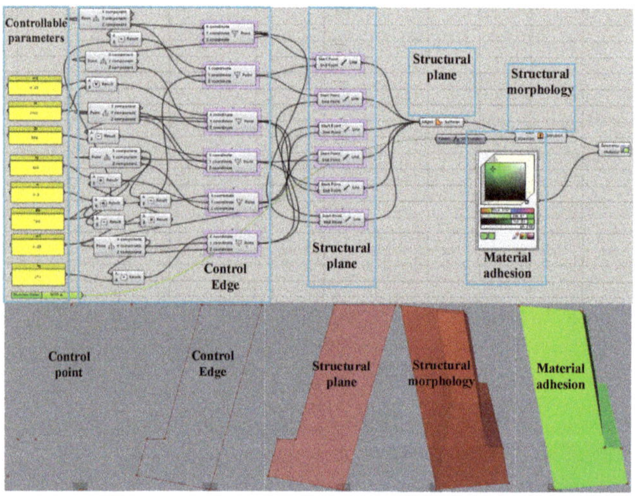

Figure 8. The parameterization process of GH for retaining walls.

In Grasshopper, the parameterized model can be created through process-based modeling approaches. Firstly, the point is used as the basic parameterized unit, as shown in Figure 7a. Starting from point *A* (0, 0) or the base point, the first step is the $A \rightarrow B$ segment. Here, as long as any two of the three parameters B_b, *hn*, and *n* are known, the position co-ordinates of point *B* can be expressed as GH by an operator and can be set to adjustable parameters; because there are currently not enough parameters in section $B \rightarrow C$ to locate point C, it is necessary to infer from $A \rightarrow F$. In general, the slope surface of a retaining wall is fixed, and the position of point F can be obtained in GH by the parameter operator based on the height of the retaining wall. The width of $F \rightarrow E$ is a variable, and the position of point E can be directly set in GH through co-ordinates; If h_n and h_j are known, the vertical height of $E \rightarrow D$ can be obtained through (H-h_n h_j) and the slope information, and the position co-ordinates of point *D* can be obtained through the slope parameter information; because $D \rightarrow C$ is horizontal, the position information of point C can be directly located, forming a closed-loop cross-section. The data from this process can be parameterized in Grasshopper (GH), and the GH process for forming control points is illustrated in Figure 9. Then, using the line operator in GH, the control points are connected to form a closed-loop boundary line. The boundary line needs to be generated through a boundary surface command, and, subsequently, based on the structural surface, a structure is created through commands such as extrusion, lofting, or extrusion. Here, the extrude command in GH is used, and the extrusion direction can be controlled by vectors. We use the unit Z direction as the extrusion unit and direction, and connect controllable parameters to control the extrusion length. At this point, the model has been created, and, finally, the parameterized model is added with the required color or material through "Colour Picker" or "Colour Swatch". The entire process is shown in Figure 8. The yellow icon on the left represents a modifiable parameter. Through this parameterized retaining wall model, many other types of retaining wall structures can be deformed. In the future, these operators shown in Figure 8 can be encapsulated into one operator, retaining only the input parameters and output model.

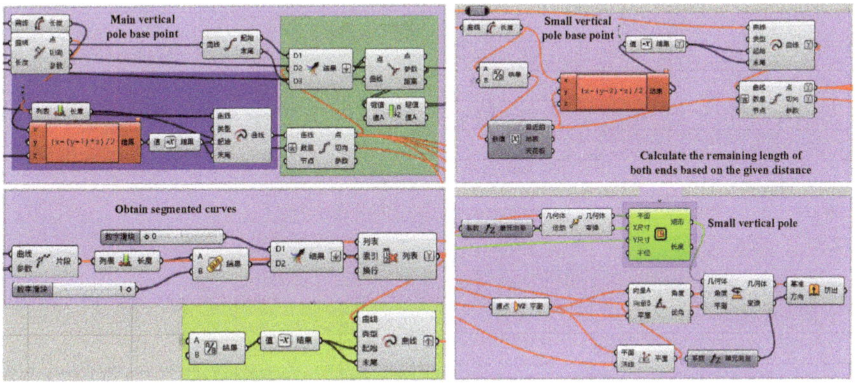

Figure 9. Implementation process of structural positioning.

4.2. Common Structural Parameterized Array Creation Method

In addition to conventional structures, there are many structures with common characteristics in housing construction projects, such as railings, stairs, curtain walls, floor tiles, etc. Traditionally, the creation method of these structures is usually performed manually via arrays. When compared to the manual creation of individual components, this approach offers a significantly greater efficiency. Nonetheless, integrating parameterization with array modeling can further elevate the modeling efficiency to an even higher level. Because the shape, spacing, height, etc. of common structures have strong regularity, they follow certain principles, so it is more suitable to program these principles and patterns through Grasshopper visual programming. The user can quickly create the desired model by simply providing the placement path of the structure. The parameterization creation method of common structures is similar, which will be explained in detail in the following example of railings in construction projects.

The railing is a common structure in construction engineering, and the conventional modeling method is relatively cumbersome. A single modification to the model may result in a complete rework and rebuild. Therefore, based on Grasshopper visual programming, a railing modeling method with wide applicability and controllable parameters is designed. Firstly, it is evident that the ultimate goal is to achieve the arrayed drawing of railings by drawing a line (including straight lines, broken lines, curves, etc.) in which the linear dimensions of the railing are defined. In GH, the base points of the main posts are primarily determined by the length operator based on the drawn curve. Since the main vertical pole is not a single line, the resulting base points of the main vertical pole form a numerical sequence, as shown in Figure 10. Then, the shatter operator is mainly used, and a series of operations are combined to obtain the segmented curve. Similarly, the remaining length of the two ends is obtained from the given distance, and the base point and segmented curve of the small vertical pole are obtained. Then, the segmented curves are obtained by the unit direction vector, geometric transformation, and extrusion. When obtaining a parameterized model of a small vertical pole by combining commands, it should be noted that this is not limited to a straight line here, so more curvy operators are used. The process of these steps is shown in Figure 9.

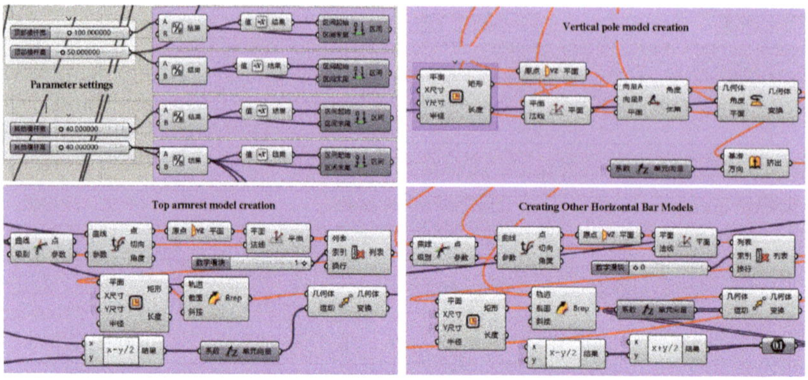

Figure 10. Parameter settings and model parameterization creation.

Once the structure is determined, parameters need to be set to enable the parameterized creation of each component. The main parameters include dimensions for the upper handrail, main baluster, vertical baluster, total railing height, and cross-section parameters for the horizontal railing. These parameters can be adjusted through parameter tuning. Due to the constraints among them, there are range limitations when applying these parameters. Therefore, the constructor operator is used to construct the corresponding interval for each parameter type. Then, utilizing discontinuous operators, the positions of different components along a curve are determined, and the modeling plane of the components is adjusted based on the normal direction of the curve. Since these components have a rectangular structure, the rectangle operator is used in the program to construct the corresponding cross-sections. The cross-section is then extruded or swept to create the corresponding geometry. Finally, the merge operator is used to merge these structures together. The key parameter settings and the process of parametric model creation are illustrated in Figure 10.

Furthermore, stair structures in architectural engineering are also a common type of structure similar to railing structures. However, achieving the flexible parametrization of stair structures in general BIM software such as Revit 2019 is challenging due to the limited controllable parameters available in Revit, which cannot provide an adequate solution. To achieve the parameterized creation of staircase structures, it is necessary to control a series of key parameters that determine the staircase's characteristics, such as height, tread height, width, stringer dimensions, segment lengths, railing height, handrail height, and number of steps. This paper defines these parameters in a unified Grasshopper package. The shape of the staircase is formed by picking or drawing straight lines or curves. Additionally, the geometric shape of the staircase can be changed arbitrarily by adjusting parameters such as the staircase height, tread height, and width. This process is illustrated in Figure 11.

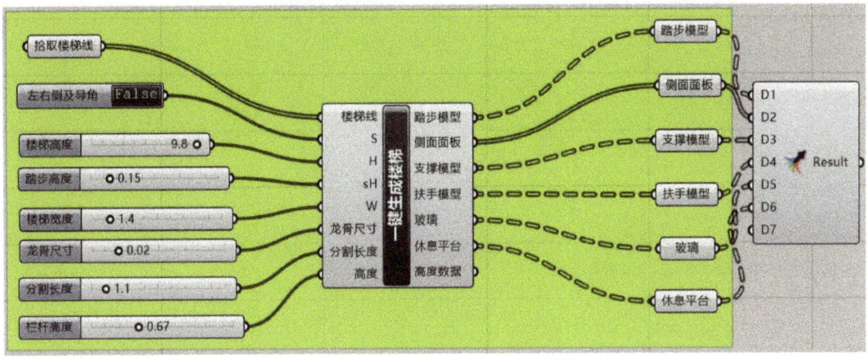

Figure 11. Parameterized variable display of staircase structure.

The study on the parameterization of stair structures begins with the stair projection line. By drawing the stair line, a parametric effect for stair creation is achieved. In this parameterization context, a series of logical operations are defined to associate parameters such as stair height, width, tread height, etc., with the stair projection line. Firstly, use the "Explore" operator to explode the drawn inner edge of the stairs. Then, calculate the lengths of these exploded curves and perform a cumulative calculation. Based on the preset step height, calculate the number of steps on the stairs. After that, create a step model that includes the height, direction, and movement distance of each step. The process is shown in Figure 12.

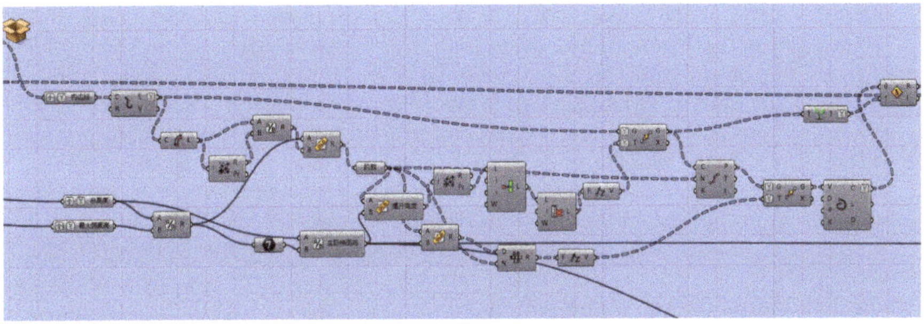

Figure 12. Parameterized node connection display of staircase structure.

Based on the compiled parametric battery, it is encapsulated into a structural module, as shown in Figure 11. The "One-Click Staircase Generation" battery module contains the core logical structure, which is generally fixed. The parametric part of the battery module can be adjusted externally, and the parameters on the left can be used to adjust the desired stair structure, as shown in Figure 13. By using these parameters, different shapes of stair structures can be formed based on the drawn stair projection line.

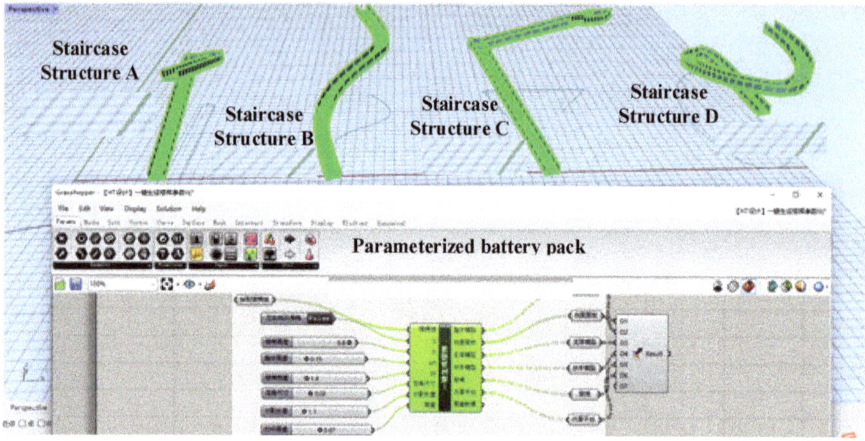

Figure 13. Draw parameterized staircase structure based on projection lines.

5. Discussion

Design institutes commonly consider design requirements based on intricate geometric relationships within a project. The fundamental nature of parametric design lies in achieving co-ordinated updates of the design entity through the variation of geometric shape variables driven by variables. Given the abundance of irregular structures in architectural engineering, traditional modeling methods are limited to one-to-one modeling. Therefore, by developing parameterized batteries (arithmetic units), a unique universal parametric model can be formed, which can achieve similar changes to the universal model. The system uses the Grasshopper visual programming language to connect the battery logic to some common structures in construction engineering, and stores each battery module in a visual interface to form a family library for design and construction personnel to choose from. Parametric modeling is considered a "propagation" system, which expresses the designer's design ideas through the constraints in the parametric model. This can simplify the design process of designers and improve production efficiency. For batch model operation and the creation of some irregular components, the BIM software Revit commonly used in building projects will show corresponding drawbacks. Generally, the software has a strong rule structural model parameterization function, and can flexibly deal with the parameterization within and between models. However, it can be cumbersome for irregular structures, such as creating surfaces and batch component arrays that require complex mathematical model parameterization.

Turrin and Brown et al. [23,24] applied parametric modeling to research related to building energy to achieve the benefits of a performance-oriented building design process. Xie et al. [25] proposed a parameterized segment library to achieve the information management and spatial constraints of shield tunnel lining segments. Andriasyan et al. [26] proposed a parameterized modeling method based on remote sensing point cloud data using the combination of Rhino + Grasshopper ArchiCAD. The above research has developed relevant parametric methods for different fields and purposes. The research purpose of this article is to implement parametric modeling methods for irregular buildings, repetitive structures, etc. in complex buildings. Therefore, the contribution of the visual programming language (Grasshopper) to this study is greater. Banihashemi et al. [27] studied modular co-ordination (MC) and parametric design. A generative algorithm is developed through the Rhinoceros 3D–Grasshopper platform, subject to MC rules. Two sets of horizontal and vertical modules are obtained from a prototype model, while an evolutionary solver function is applied in order to reduce the generated construction waste volume. This method may encounter some parameterization limitations when dealing with a large number of design constraints, but this study can accommodate enough architectural geometric logic

parameters to ensure a smooth parameterization operation; Yuan et al. [28] combined prefabricated building design with parameterized design in building information modeling (BIM) to develop a parametric design process for manufacturing and assembly design. The parametric process is based on Autodesk Revit, and the parametric method discussed in this article offers greater flexibility and finer parametric control, making it more suitable for complex architectural structures. Its application in the future prefabricated building design process will bring more advantages. Therefore, the method proposed in this paper can flexibly handle multiple models and improve the efficiency of model operation and parameterization in the architectural design process.

6. Conclusions

This study integrates the Grasshopper parametric modeling method with the complex structures in architectural projects, developing a process-oriented parametric modeling method that uniquely documents the entire modeling process from the initial model (point or box) to the final model. Compared with traditional parameterized design, by writing algorithm programs, mechanical repetitive operations and a large number of logical evolution processes can be replaced with computational loop calculations, effectively improving the efficiency of designers' work. Overall, this paper analyzes the technical difficulties in the process of 3D parametric modeling for special structures in construction engineering, and puts forward a method of developing component batteries (arithmetic units) through Grasshopper to realize a universal parametric modeling process of special structures. Firstly, a theoretical analysis is conducted on the vector method of parametric modeling in GH, data structure and data matching methods, line and surface processing, and geometric transformation methods. Then, in view of common structures such as complex retaining walls, irregular structures, and balustrades in construction projects, the ideas of a parametric battery connection are sorted out and logical battery nodes are established to realize the parametric modeling process of BIM for engineering structures of construction projects.

The Grasshopper algorithm developed in this research has limitations. There are many types of irregular structures in building projects, such as various irregular steel structures, curtain wall structures, landscape models, etc., all of which are non-standardized customization. In the future, Grasshopper algorithms should be further expanded to develop more and more comprehensive parameterized component templates suitable for the structural modeling of building projects, improving the quality and efficiency of BIM design; this may also provide methodological support for the future development of BIM.

Author Contributions: Conceptualization, L.Y. and X.G.; data curation, S.C.; writing—original draft preparation, S.C.; writing—review and editing, L.Y.; resources, software, visualization, and supervision, Q.L.; methodology, validation, and funding acquisition, S.B. All authors have read and agreed to the published version of the manuscript.

Funding: This research was funded by The State Key Research Development Program of China, grant number 2021YFC3100801.

Data Availability Statement: The original contributions presented in the study are included in the article, further inquiries can be directed to the corresponding authors.

Conflicts of Interest: The authors declare no conflict of interest.

References

1. Borkowski, S.A. A Literature Review of BIM Definitions: Narrow and Broad Views. *Technologies* **2023**, *11*, 176. [CrossRef]
2. Kochański, Ł.; Szymon, A.B. Automating the conceptual design of residental areas using visual and generative programming. *J. Eng. Des.* **2024**, *35*, 195–216. [CrossRef]
3. Singh, M.M.; Sawhney, A.; Borrmann, A. Modular coordination and BIM: Development of rule based smart building components. *Procedia Eng.* **2015**, *123*, 519–527. [CrossRef]
4. Bai, S.; Li, M.C.; Song, L.G. Developing a Common Library of Prefabricated Structure Components through Graphic Media Mapping to Improve Design Efficiency. *J. Constr. Eng. Manag.* **2021**, *147*, 04020156. [CrossRef]

5. Lee, J.M.; Yang, H.D.; Lee, H.J. Development of parametric bridge BIM and PCD generation algorithms and PCD-based member segmentation. *Adv. Eng. Softw.* **2024**, *194*, 103673. [CrossRef]
6. Zhao, J.W.; Wei, Q.; Zhang, G.X. Construction and Application of Water Conservancy Engineering Information Model. *Water Resour. Hydropower Technol.* **2016**, *47*, 29–33.
7. Niu, Y.F. Research and Application of BIM Based Parametric Modeling Method for Irregular Buildings. Master's Thesis, Overseas Chinese University, Quanzhou, China, 2020.
8. Zhang, S.; Yin, P.F. Research on parameterized modeling of irregular surface structures based on Rhino + Grasshopper. *Civ. Eng. Inf. Technol.* **2015**, *7*, 102–106.
9. Tong, Z. Research on Parameterized Modeling and Application of Prefabricated Building BIM Based on Dynamo Python. Master's Thesis, China University of Mining and Technology, Xuzhou, China, 2021.
10. Bianconi, F.; Filippucci, M.; Buffi, A. Automated design and modeling for mass-customized housing. A web-based design space catalog for timber structures. *Autom. Constr.* **2019**, *103*, 13–25. [CrossRef]
11. Deng, W.; Ke, W.; Deng, Z. Virtual design of woven fabrics based on parametric modeling and physically based rendering. *Comput. -Aided Des.* **2024**, *173*, 103717.
12. Zhang, D.H.; Chen, N.; Han, J.Y. Application of modular design method based on BIM in prefabricated buildings. *Civ. Eng. Inf. Technol.* **2014**, *6*, 81–85.
13. Wei, G.Z.; Zhou, X.; Zhao, Y. Design of building component library based on IFC and PLIB standard. In Proceedings of the 2010 2nd International Conference on Computer Engineering and Technology, Chengdu, China, 16–18 April 2010; IEEE: New York, NY, USA, 2010.
14. Bai, Q.H.; Deng, S.H.; Li, C.G.; Ze, Q. Application of BIM in the creation of prefabricated structures local parameterized component database. *Archit. Eng.* **2019**, *4*, 13–21. [CrossRef]
15. Lu, W.; Chen, K.; Wang, J.; Xue, F. Developing an open access BIM objects library: A Hong Kong study. In *2017 Lean and Computing in Construction Congress (LC3): Volume I—Proceedings of the Joint Conference on Computing in Construction (JC3), Heraklion, Crete, Greece, 4–7 July 2017*; Edinburgh University Press: Edinburgh, UK, 2017; pp. 407–414.
16. Jäger, S.R.; Maschotta, T.; Jungebloud, A.; Zimmermann, A. Model-driven development of simulation-based system design tools. In Proceedings of the IEEE 14th International Conference on Software Engineering Research, Management and Applications (SERA), Towson, MD, USA, 8–10 June 2016; pp. 209–215.
17. Wang, L.S.; Tan, Z. A volumetric geometric model of 3D entities. *J. Comput. Sci.* **1999**, *7*, 777–780.
18. Bai, Y.S.; Gao, Y.H. *GRASSHOPPER Parameterized Nonlinear Design*; Huazhong University of Science and Technology Press: Wuhan, China, 2018.
19. Russell, G.J. HydroVision Preview: Overcoming Operations and Maintenance Challenges. *Hydro Rev.* **2010**, *29*, 58.
20. Khosravikia, F.; Mahsuli, M.; Ghannad, M.A. The Effect of Soil-Structure Interaction on the Seismic Risk to Buildings. *Bull. Earthq. Eng.* **2018**, *16*, 3653–3673. [CrossRef]
21. Forcellini, D.; Tarantino, A.M. Assessment of stone columns as a mitigation technique of liquefaction-induced effects during Italian earthquakes (May 2012). *Sci. World J.* **2014**, *2014*, 216278. [CrossRef] [PubMed]
22. Ghorbani, J.; Airey, D. Modelling stress-induced anisotropy in multi-phase granular soils. *Comput. Mech.* **2021**, *67*, 497–521. [CrossRef]
23. Turrin, M.; Von Buelow, P.; Stouffs, R. Design explorations of performance driven geometry in architectural design using parametric modeling and genetic algorithms. *Adv. Eng. Inform.* **2011**, *25*, 656–675. [CrossRef]
24. Brown, N.C.; Jusiega, V.; Mueller, C.T. Implementing data-driven parametric building design with a flexible toolbox. *Autom. Constr.* **2020**, *118*, 103252. [CrossRef]
25. Xie, P.; Chen, K.; Zhu, Y.; Luo, H. Dynamic parametric modeling of shield tunnel: A WebGL-based framework for assisting shield segment assembly point selection. *Tunn. Undergr. Space Technol.* **2023**, *142*, 105395. [CrossRef]
26. Andriasyan, M.; Moyano, J.; Nieto-Julián, J.E. From point cloud data to building information modelling: An automatic parametric workflow for heritage. *Remote Sens.* **2020**, *12*, 1094. [CrossRef]
27. Banihashemi, S.; Tabadkani, A.; Hosseini, R.M. Integration of parametric design into modular coordination: A construction waste reduction workflow. *Autom. Constr.* **2018**, *88*, 1–12. [CrossRef]
28. Yuan, Z.; Sun, C.; Wang, Y. Design for Manufacture and Assembly-oriented parametric design of prefabricated buildings. *Autom. Constr.* **2018**, *88*, 13–22. [CrossRef]

isprs International Journal of *Geo-Information*

MDPI

Article

Learning Effective Geometry Representation from Videos for Self-Supervised Monocular Depth Estimation

Hailiang Zhao †, Yongyi Kong †, Chonghao Zhang, Haoji Zhang and Jiansen Zhao *

Merchant Marine College, Shanghai Maritime University, Shanghai 200135, China;
202110111138@stu.shmtu.edu.cn (H.Z.); 202210621089@stu.shmtu.edu.cn (Y.K.);
202010413004@stu.shmtu.edu.cn (C.Z.); 202210121093@stu.shmtu.edu.cn (H.Z.)
* Correspondence: jszhao@shmtu.edu.cn
† These authors contributed equally to this work.

Abstract: Recent studies on self-supervised monocular depth estimation have achieved promising results, which are mainly based on the joint optimization of depth and pose estimation via high-level photometric loss. However, how to learn the latent and beneficial task-specific geometry representation from videos is still far from being explored. To tackle this issue, we propose two novel schemes to learn more effective representation from monocular videos: (i) an Inter-task Attention Model (IAM) to learn the geometric correlation representation between the depth and pose learning networks to make structure and motion information mutually beneficial; (ii) a Spatial-Temporal Memory Module (STMM) to exploit long-range geometric context representation among consecutive frames both spatially and temporally. Systematic ablation studies are conducted to demonstrate the effectiveness of each component. Evaluations on KITTI show that our method outperforms current state-of-the-art techniques.

Keywords: self-supervised learning; monocular depth estimation

1. Introduction

Understanding the 3D structure of scenes is an essential topic in machine perception, which plays a crucial part in applications such as autonomous driving, robot vision, visual reality and so on [1–4]. For most scenarios, there is vast latent geometric information existing in the input videos. One of the key challenges in this domain is how to acquire effective task-specific geometry representation from videos to help obtain more accurate and reliable depth information.

Recently, there have been some successful attempts [1,2,5] to execute monocular depth estimation and visual odometry prediction together in a self-supervised manner by giving full consideration of the transformation between consecutive frames. In this pipeline, two networks are generally used to predict the depth and camera pose separately, which are then jointly exploited to warp source frames to the target ones, converting the depth estimation problem to a reprojection error minimization process, as shown in Figure 1a.

Despite various extensions of the self-supervised pipeline by adding more penalty items [5–7] or joining with other tasks (optical flow or segmentation) [8,9], these methods only design various high-level loss functions to combine and regularize the network learning, neglecting to leverage valuable geometry representation from videos, e.g., inter-task geometric correlation learning, inter-frame long-range dependency learning, and 3D geometry consistency representation from continuous frames.

Intuitively, modeling the process of perceiving 3D structure from videos can be informed by our human experience. According to the research in biology and neuroscience [10], human brains process motion information during the inference of depth, and conversely, the perceived depth information can bring significant benefits to motion estimation [11]. Inspired by this biological mechanism, we present an Inter-task Attention Module (IAM) to guide the feature-level inter-task geometric correlation learning. It can enhance the interaction between the depth and pose estimation networks and is effective in making structure and motion information mutually beneficial for improving estimation accuracy.

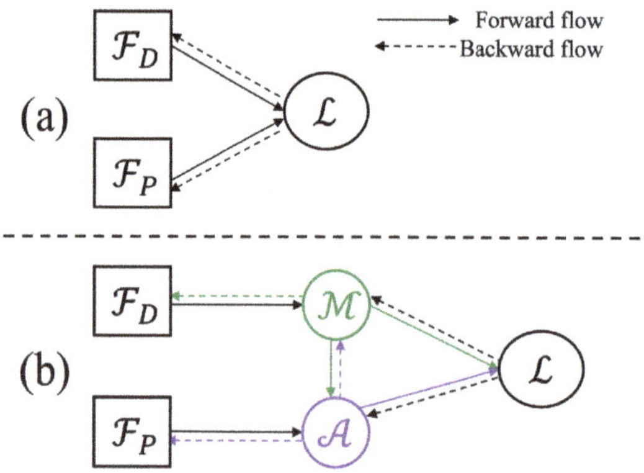

Figure 1. Comparison of the learning process of the general pipeline (**a**) and our method (**b**) for self-supervised monocular depth estimation. Different from the general pipeline that learns the depth feature F_D and the pose feature F_P separately using a 2D photometric loss L, we propose a new scheme for learning better representation from videos. A memory mechanism M is devised to exploit the long-range context from videos for depth feature learning. An inter-task attention mechanism A is devised to leverage depth information for helping pose feature learning, which inversely benefits depth feature learning as well via gradient back-propagation.

Furthermore, many psychologists believe that humans rely on not only immediate sensory feedback but also perception memories from the past for understanding an environment [12,13]. Similarly, it is significant to help networks learn a representation leveraging long-range context and memorizing historical information to disambiguate and realize more precise perception. Therefore, we introduce a Spatial-Temporal Memory Module (STMM) to learn spatial and temporal dependency from video clips and mimic the above perception mechanism of human beings. We embody an STMM based on the Non-local network [14], which is demonstrated to be effective in modeling long-range information, after exploring various attention structures.

In summary, the learning process of our method is shown in Figure 1b, and our main contributions are as follows:

- We devise an Inter-task Attention Module to exploit the inter-task geometric correlation between depth and pose estimation networks. It learns attention maps from depth information as guidance to help the pose network identify key regions to be targeted. To the best of our knowledge, this is the first attempt to propose this idea for exploiting the inter-task geometric correlation in self-supervised monocular depth estimation.
- We introduce a Spatial-Temporal Memory Module in a depth estimation network to leverage the spatial and temporal geometric context among consecutive frames, which is effective for utilizing historical information and improving estimation results.
- We conduct comprehensive empirical studies on the KITTI dataset, and the single-frame inference result of our method outperforms state-of-the-art methods by a relative gain of 6.6% based on the major evaluation metric.

2. Related Work

2.1. Inter-Task Monocular Video Learning

Ref. [1] proposed a fully unsupervised end-to-end network for training with monocular videos that can jointly predict the depth and pose transformation between consecutive frames. The core technique is a spatial transformer network [15] to synthesize target frames from source frames, which converts the depth estimation problem to a reprojection error

minimization process. This pipeline was then extended by plenty of researchers. Ref. [6] added a feature-based warping loss upon the original photometric loss and trained the networks with stereo image pairs to resolve the scale ambiguity. Ref. [2] further proposed an auto-masking strategy to handle situations where the camera is static or objects move at the same speed as the camera, yielding more accurate results. Moreover, some works combined depth and pose estimation with other tasks, e.g., normal, segmentation, and optical flow estimation. Ref. [7] implemented the estimation of normal in scenes and incorporated an edge-aware depth-normal consistency constraint. Ref. [16] used the Mask R-CNN [17] model to extract semantic information and obtain pre-computed object masks to filter out moving objects. Ref. [8] defined a cascaded network to jointly learn depth, pose, and optical flow for handling rigid motions and moving objects separately, using a forward-backward coherence loss. Ref. [18] also presented an architecture to simultaneously learn depth, ego-motion, and optical flow and focused on enforcing cross-task consensus between depth and optical flow. JPerceiver [19] jointly learn depth estimation, visual odometry, and Bird's-Eye-View segmentation. Despite the progress made by these methods, almost all of them follow the pipeline in [1] that uses separate networks to learn depth, pose, and other tasks without any interactions before being combined into the final loss. By contrast, we propose an IAM to learn geometry information from the depth network as guidance to help the pose network learn more valuable representation for pose estimation. Notably, the two tasks are joint-optimized via high-level photometric error, which enables an interaction between two networks via gradient back-propagation, meaning that depth tasks can also benefit from the IAM and learn more useful representation to improve the estimation results.

2.2. Long-Range Representation Learning

Taking videos instead of single images as input is extremely important for many applications, such as autonomous driving, robotic vision, and drones. However, the rich long-range dependency, including spatial and temporal correlations, is still far from being fully utilized to eliminate ambiguity and obtain more consistent estimation. UnDeepVO [20] was proposed as the first end-to-end visual odometry by combining CNNs and two stacking LSTMs to achieve simultaneous representation learning and sequential modelling of the monocular VO. Kumar et al. [21] proposed a convolutional LSTM-based network architecture for depth to capture inter-frame dependencies and variations. Wang et al. [22] also adopted ConvLSTM architecture, multi-view reprojection, and forward-backward consistency constraints to utilize the temporal information effectively. These research efforts demonstrated that utilizing long-range information from videos is helpful in learning more effective representation for both depth and pose networks and improving the estimation accuracy. However, convolutional and recurrent operations both process a local neighborhood, either in space or time [14]. And, all these RNN methods focused only on temporal dependency learning without long-range spatial context, which is not that useful for single image inference. Recently, Transformer-based methods [23–27] are attracting researcher's attention to use the stronger backbone to extract better visual representation. MonoViT [26] introduces a Vision Transformer-based encoder for self-supervised monocular depth estimation, leveraging both local and global reasoning capabilities to achieve state-of-the-art performance on the KITTI dataset. PixelFormer [25] was proposed as a novel pixel query refinement approach for monocular depth prediction, using a Skip Attention Module to effectively fuse global and local features. MonoFormer [27] was introduced as a deep analysis of self-supervised monocular depth estimation models, and the authors proposed methodological enhancements to improve their generalization across various environments. These Transformer-based methods achieve impressive performance but require larger network structures and consume more computational resources. In this paper, aligning with our lightweight network design, we introduce an STMM module to learn long-range geometric relationships both spatially and temporally among pixels in consecutive frames. We embody STMM based on the Non-local network [14] after exploring various attention structures. STMM is demonstrated to be beneficial for both multi-frame training and single-frame inference.

3. Method

3.1. Problem Definition

A typical self-supervised monocular depth estimation pipeline is mainly built upon the perspective projection among consecutive frames. Taking $<I_t, I_{t+1}, \ldots, I_{t+n}>$ as a training video within time window N, once the depth D_{t+n} and camera transformation $T_{t+n \to t}$ are obtained, we can warp the source frame I_{t+n} to reconstruct the target frame $\hat{I}_{t+n \to t}$ using the differentiable bilinear sampling approach [15], which can be formulated as

$$D_t^{ij} I_t^{ij} = KRK^{-1} D_{t+n}^{ij} I_{t+n}^{ij} + Kt, \tag{1}$$

where I_{t+n}^{ij} is the homogeneous coordinate given image I_{t+n} and D_{t+n}^{ij} denotes the depth value of the view I_{t+n}. Given a rotation matrix R, translation vector t, and camera intrinsics K, the transformed homogeneous coordinate I_t^{ij} and depth D_t^{ij} can be obtained. Thus, the reprojected image coordinate $\hat{I}_{t+n \to t}$ can be acquired by dehomogenization of $D_t^{ij} I_t^{ij}$.

Then, the self-supervised learning is conducted based on the difference between the synthetic view $\hat{I}_{t+n \to t}$ and the original view I_t:

$$L_e = L_r(I_t, \hat{I}_{t+n \to t}). \tag{2}$$

Here, L_r denotes a consistency measurement loss.

3.2. Network Architecture

As shown in Figure 2a, our network is composed of two main networks for depth estimation and pose estimation, respectively. Meanwhile, the pose network is split into two branches for the estimation of rotation and translation. The proposed IAM is used to address the importance of geometric correlation representation between the depth and pose tasks, while the proposed STMM is used to exploit the long-range geometric relevance among continuous frames. The details of IAM and STMM are presented later.

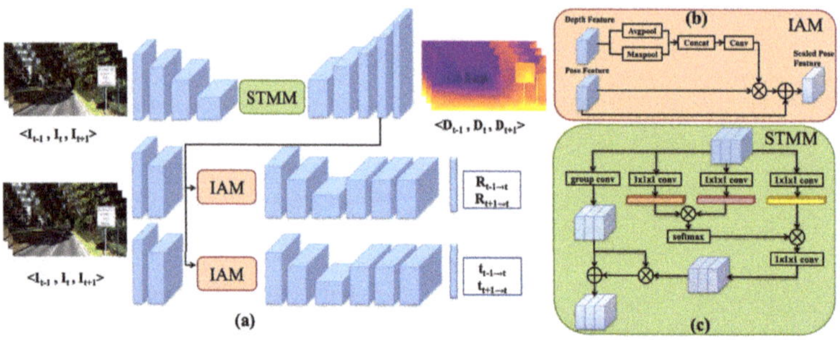

Figure 2. Illustration of our network framework (**a**) and the architecture of the IAM (**b**) and the STMM (**c**). The network takes three consecutive frames as input to learn the long-range geometric correlation representation by introducing STMM after the encoder. The pose network is split into two branches to predict rotation R and translation t separately. The IAM is applied after the second convolution layer of both R and t branches, learning valuable geometry information to assist R and t branches in leveraging inter-task correlation representation.

The depth network adopts an encoder–decoder architecture in a U-shape with skip connections similar to DispNet [28]. The encoder is a Resnet18 [29] network pre-trained on ImageNet [30]. Our depth decoder is similar to that of [2], using sigmoid activation functions in multi-scale side outputs and ELU nonlinear functions [31] otherwise. Most importantly, we take a three-frame snippet as the sequential input and stack the encoded features as the input of the STMM to learn the temporal and spatial geometric correlations among video sequences during training. The outputs are then decoded into a three-frame depth sequence.

The pose network takes two consecutive frames as input at each time and outputs the corresponding pose transformation based on an encoder–decoder structure as well. To generate more accurate estimations, the network is divided into two branches to calculate R and t, respectively. In the feature encoding phase, the IAM is employed to produce the attention from depth features as guidance for the R and t branches.

3.2.1. Inter-Task Attention Module

The IAM aims to leverage the latent geometric correlation between depth and pose estimation tasks during learning. To exploit geometry information, features from the penultimate layer of the depth decoder are first stacked in the same order as the input sequence of the IAM. In the IAM, the features are first processed by an average pooling layer and a max pooling layer along the channel axis and then concatenated together as a compact representation, as previous studies [32,33] show that pooling layers can help highlight features. Furthermore, a subsequent convolution layer is used to obtain the attention maps.

The varying weights regarding different pixels in the learned attention maps guide the R and t branches in deciding what feature should be the focus and prioritized. Therefore, we use the attention maps to obtain scaled pose features by element-wise multiplication, which are then added to the original pose features as a residual item. A schematic diagram of the IAM is provided in Figure 2b, which can be formulated as

$$F'_p = F_p(W_c[AVP(F_{mn}); MAP(F_{mn})]) + F_p. \tag{3}$$

Here, F_{mn} represents the stacked depth features encoded from continuous frames I_m and I_n by the depth network, while F_p and F'_p denote the original pose feature and the attended one, respectively. The average and max pooling layers are represented by AVP and MAP, respectively, while W_c denotes the learnable weight of the convolution layer.

Intuitively, the geometric patterns of learned attention maps for the two branches should be different or even opposite, as nearby regions tend to matter more to translation, while distant pixels may play a more important role in deciding the rotation. The ablation study and visualization results demonstrate that the IAM does learn different attention patterns for the R and t branches from geometry information. They are utilized to guide the pose network to learn more valuable and effective representation, improving estimation accuracy for both tasks via joint optimization.

3.2.2. Spatial-Temporal Memory Module

Instead of learning representation from each frame individually [1,2,5] in the depth network, we introduce an STMM to leverage and aggregate long-range geometric correlation from both a spatial context and a temporal context to obtain a more representative feature embedding for depth estimation. To this end, various attention structures can be leveraged, including SE [34], CBAM [32], and Non-local attention [14]. After a comparison study, we found that Non-local attention is more effective at capturing long-range context. Thereby, we chose it to embody STMM in this work. First, the encoded depth features from several consecutive frames are concatenated together and used as the input of the Non-local block. Then, the attention map for each frame is obtained, which is multiplied and added to the original depth features after a group convolution layer. The group number is the same as the number of input frames. As shown in Figure 2c, in STMM, the aggregated depth feature F'_D is calculated as follows:

$$F'_D = NL(F_D)W_\delta F_D + W_\delta F_D, \tag{4}$$

where F_D is the input depth feature and NL means the operation of Non-local block. W_δ is the learnable weight of the group convolution layer.

4. Experiments

4.1. Depth Estimation Result

Although our method is trained with three-frame snippet input, it can infer single image depth during inference by stacking the same encoded features three times before being fed into the STMM. Following the common evaluation protocol [1], we report the single-frame inference results in the following experiments, although better results can be achieved by leveraging multiple frames. The extensive experimental results on KITTI are presented in Table 1, from which it is clear that our method outperforms all prior works trained with monocular and even stereo videos in a self-supervised manner. The visual results shown in Figure 3 demonstrate our method can generate more accurate and sharper depth maps, especially for challenging situations, such as moving objects, distant objects, and fine structures. More experiment results for both depth and pose estimation can be found in Supplementary Materials.

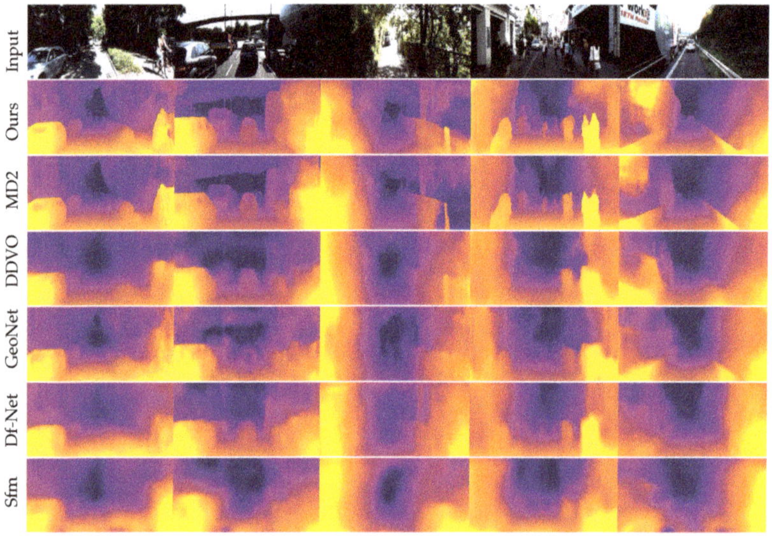

Figure 3. Qualitative results on KITTI test set. Our method produces more accurate depth maps with low-texture regions, moving vehicles, delicate structures, and object boundaries.

Table 1. Quantitative performance of single depth estimation over KITTI test set [35]. For a fair comparison, all the results are evaluated, taking 80 m as the maximum depth threshold. The "S" and "M" in the train column mean stereo and monocular inputs for training, while "R18" and "R50" denote the used Resnet [29] version. "†" means updated result after publication. We train our models using only KITTI without any post-processing. The best results are illustrated with bold text.

Methods	Train	Error Metric ↓				Accuracy Metric ↑		
		Abs Rel	**Sq Rel**	**RMSE**	**RMSE log**	$\delta < 1.25$	$\delta < 1.25^2$	$\delta < 1.25^3$
[36] †	S	0.152	1.226	5.849	0.246	0.784	0.921	0.967
MD (R50) † [37]	S	0.133	1.142	5.533	0.230	0.830	0.936	0.970
SuperDepth [38]	S	0.112	0.875	4.958	0.207	0.852	0.947	0.977
MD2 [2]	S	0.107	0.849	4.764	0.201	0.874	0.953	0.977
[1] †	M	0.183	1.595	6.709	0.270	0.734	0.902	0.959
[5]	M	0.163	1.240	6.220	0.250	0.762	0.916	0.968
GeoNet † [8]	M	0.149	1.060	5.567	0.226	0.796	0.935	0.975
DDVO [39]	M	0.151	1.257	5.583	0.228	0.810	0.936	0.974
DF-Net [18]	M	0.150	1.124	5.507	0.223	0.806	0.933	0.973

Table 1. *Cont.*

Methods	Train	Error Metric ↓				Accuracy Metric ↑		
		Abs Rel	Sq Rel	RMSE	RMSE log	$\delta < 1.25$	$\delta < 1.25^2$	$\delta < 1.25^3$
Struct2depth [16]	M	0.141	1.026	5.142	0.210	0.845	0.845	0.948
CC [9]	M	0.140	1.070	5.326	0.217	0.826	0.941	0.975
SC-SFMLearner [40]	M	0.137	1.089	5.439	0.217	0.830	0.942	0.975
HR [41]	M	0.121	0.873	4.945	0.197	0.853	0.955	0.982
MD2(R18) [2]	M	0.115	0.882	4.701	0.190	0.879	0.961	0.982
DeFeat [42]	M	0.126	0.925	5.035	0.200	0.862	0.954	0.980
[43]	M	0.113	**0.704**	4.581	0.184	0.871	0.961	**0.984**
Ours (R18)	M	**0.106**	0.761	**4.545**	**0.182**	**0.890**	**0.965**	0.983
Ours (R50)	M	**0.105**	0.731	**4.412**	**0.181**	**0.891**	**0.965**	0.983

4.2. Evaluation of Generalization Ability

Though our models were only trained on KITTI [44], competitive results can be achieved on unseen datasets without any fine-tuning. We evaluated our method on two outdoor datasets: Make3D [45] and Cityscapes [46]. In Table 2, our model outperforms other self-supervised methods on the Make3D test protocol, showing good domain adaptation ability. The qualitative comparison in Figure 4 on Cityscapes provides additional intuitive evidence on the generalization ability. More test results can be found in Supplementary Materials.

Table 2. Quantitative results on the Make3D dataset. The best results are illustrated with bold text.

Methods	Train	Abs Rel	Sq Rel	RMSE	log10
[47]	D	0.475	6.562	10.05	0.165
[37]	S	0.544	10.94	11.760	0.193
[1]	M	0.383	5.321	10.470	0.478
DDVO [39]	M	0.387	4.720	8.090	0.204
MD2 [2]	M	0.322	3.589	7.417	0.163
Ours	M	**0.316**	**3.200**	**7.095**	**0.158**

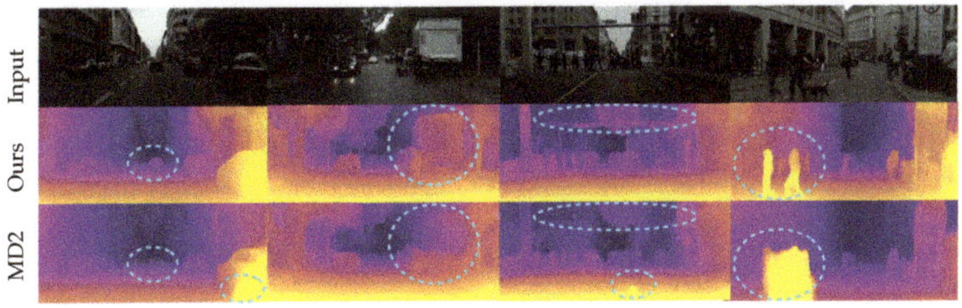

Figure 4. Visual results evaluated on the Cityscapes dataset. The evaluation uses models trained on KITTI without any refinement. Compared with the methods in [2], our method generates higher-quality depth maps and captures moving and slim objects better. The difference is highlighted with the dashed circles.

4.3. Ablation Study

The ablation study was conducted on KITTI to highlight the effects of individual components of our model. Table 3 shows the detailed results by removing specific component(s) from our model. The in-depth analysis of each part is given in corresponding sections. Moreover, we conducted systematic experiments to test the performance under various training conditions, listed in Table 3, including input resolution (1024 × 320 vs. 640 × 192), backbone networks (Resnet18 vs. Resnet50), and with/without pretraining.

Table 3. Ablation results on KITTI with each individual component removed and using backbone networks (Resnet18 or Resnet50) and different resolutions of input videos during training. The term "plain" means removing all components, while "pre" means pretraining on ImageNet. The best results are illustrated with bold text.

	Resolution	Net	IAM	STMM	Abs Rel	Sq Rel	RMSE	RMSE Log
Ours (full)	1024 × 320	R50	√	√	**0.105**	**0.731**	**4.412**	**0.181**
Ours (full)	1024 × 320	R18	√	√	**0.106**	**0.761**	**4.545**	**0.182**
Ours w/o IAM	1024 × 320	R18		√	0.112	0.844	4.815	0.190
Ours w/o STMM	1024 × 320	R18	√		0.111	0.829	4.799	0.190
Ours w/o STMM	1024 × 320	R18	√	CBAM	0.109	0.778	4.591	0.186
Ours w/o STMM	1024 × 320	R18	√	SE	0.111	0.799	4.704	0.187
Ours (plain)	1024 × 320	R18			0.120	0.915	4.972	0.196
Ours (full) smaller	640 × 192	R18	√	√	0.110	0.809	4.616	0.185
Ours (full) w/o pre	640 × 192	R18	√	√	0.124	0.847	4.713	0.196

Effect of Inter-Task Attention Module

As mentioned before, when predicting the pose from two consecutive frames, we believe that different geometry information has a different impact on the estimation of rotation and translation. Thus, we introduce valuable attention guidance learned by the IAM into the prediction of R and t. The attention maps learned for the two branches during training are visualized in Figure 5, with color variation denoting different weight values. The attention maps indicate that the two branches did learn different geometric priorities from the depth information to help with their own estimation and conversely improve the depth estimation result, as shown in Table 3. The learned geometric patterns demonstrate that the estimation of R attaches more importance to farther regions and corner places, while the t branch values closer areas more. Our IAM adopts an attention mechanism and works in a generalized representation learning manner to utilize the geometric correlation between depth and pose, which can also be useful in other similar tasks to improve estimation quality.

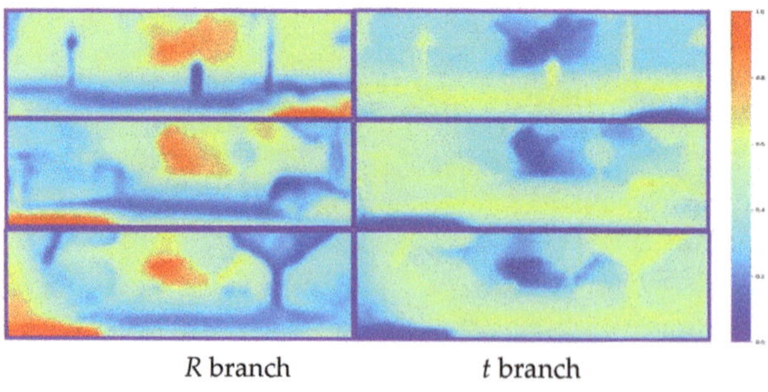

Figure 5. The visualization of learned attention maps in the IAM. It indicates the IAM places distinct emphasis on different regions for two branches to improve their estimation.

Effects of STMM on distant objects. The motivation of the STMM is to leverage the rich temporal and spatial geometric dependency among continuous frames. By exploiting the temporal information of depth features from three consecutive frames as input, The STMM is helpful for utilizing historical knowledge within the time window and enhancing the estimation of distant objects. During inference, the input of networks is a single image, and our STMM can exploit only spatial correlations from the pixels within the single image. The ablation study results shown in Table 3 demonstrate the benefit of STMM compared with the models replacing STMM with other attention structures (CBAM and SE). To better evaluate our model's performance on estimating distant objects, we segmented each scene into two groups of pixels according to a distance of 20 m, following [41] to ensure fairness. We conducted an ablation test for the estimation of distant objects, and the results are listed in Table 4. The results show that removing the STMM severely decreases the performance of our model for distant objects, which demonstrates the effectiveness of STMM in distant scenes.

Table 4. Ablation study and comparison for distant objects.

Methods	Dist	Abs Rel	Sq Rel	RMSE	RMSE Log
HR [41]	≤20	0.102	0.391	1.959	0.146
Ours	≤20	**0.076**	**0.189**	**1.410**	**0.123**
HR [41]	>20	0.187	**2.430**	9.695	0.305
Ours	>20	**0.152**	2.556	**9.226**	**0.211**
Ours w/o STMM	>20	0.179	2.803	9.667	0.291
Ours w/o IAM	>20	0.158	2.643	9.346	0.234

4.4. Evaluation with Improved Ground Truth

The main evaluation method proposed by Eigen [35] uses the reprojected raw LIDAR points as ground truth, which brings severe effects on the estimation of tricky cases, such as occlusion, object motion, and so on. To conduct a fair comparison with [2], we also adopted the annotated depth map from the official KITTI website as ground truth to evaluate methods. These annotated depth maps introduced by [48] tackle the above-mentioned tough cases to improve ground truth using stereo pair. We compared our models with other self-supervised methods, as shown in Table 5. The results demonstrate that our method outperforms all previous methods, including both monocular and stereo training approaches.

Table 5. Quantitative performance of a single depth estimation using an annotated depth map [48] as ground truth. For a fair comparison, all the results are evaluated, taking 80 m as the maximum depth threshold. The resolution column indicates the size of input images during training. We trained our network using only KITTI without any post-processing. The best results are illustrated with bold text. "†" means updated result after publication.

Methods	Train	Resolution	Error Metric ↓				Accuracy Metric ↑		
			Abs Rel	Sq Rel	RMSE	RMSE log	$\delta < 1.25$	$\delta < 1.25^2$	$\delta < 1.25^3$
MD R50 † [37]	S	512 × 256	0.109	0.811	4.568	0.166	0.877	0.967	0.988
3Net (VGG) [49]	S	512 × 256	0.119	0.920	4.824	0.182	0.856	0.957	0.985
3Net (R50) [49]	S	512 × 256	0.102	0.675	4.293	0.159	0.881	0.969	0.991
SuperDepth [38]	S	1024 × 382	0.090	0.542	3.967	0.144	0.901	0.976	0.993
MD2 [2]	S	1024 × 320	0.085	0.537	3.868	0.139	0.912	0.979	0.993
Zhou et al. † [1]	M	416 × 128	0.176	1.532	6.129	0.244	0.758	0.921	0.971
Mahjourian et al. [5]	M	416 × 128	0.134	0.983	5.501	0.203	0.827	0.944	0.981
GeoNet [8]	M	416 × 128	0.132	0.994	5.240	0.193	0.833	0.953	0.985
DDVO [39]	M	416 × 128	0.126	0.866	4.932	0.185	0.851	0.958	0.986
CC [9]	M	832 × 256	0.123	0.881	4.834	0.181	0.860	0.959	0.985
MD2 (R18) [2]	M	1024 × 320	0.090	0.545	3.942	0.137	0.914	0.983	0.995
Ours (R18)	M	1024 × 320	**0.083**	**0.447**	**3.667**	**0.126**	**0.924**	**0.986**	**0.997**

4.5. Single-Scale Evaluation

Monocular training methods usually need a scaling step during evaluation because monocular solutions do not have a certain metric scale during training. For evaluation, ref. [1] calculated the median of each predicted depth map and the ground truth as the scaling factor. However, using a distinct scaling factor for every frame may cause an unfair advantage in contrast to stereo methods, which use a certain scale for all images, according to [2].

In [2], the authors changed this evaluation protocol by taking the median of all the scaling ratios of the depth maps on the test set as a constant scale for all test images. To conduct a fair comparison, we adopted this modified protocol to validate our methods. The quantitative comparison can be found in Table 6, in which our method still outperforms all previous approaches. The standard deviation σ_{scale} of our method is also lower than other methods, which indicates our approach can generate more consistent depth map scales.

Table 6. Quantitative performance using single scale on KITTI Eigen test set [35]. "†" means updated result after publication.

Methods	σ_{scale}	Error Metric ↓				Accuracy Metric ↑		
		Abs Rel	Sq Rel	RMSE	RMSE log	$\delta < 1.25$	$\delta < 1.25^2$	$\delta < 1.25^3$
Zhou et al. † [1]	0.210	0.258	2.338	7.040	0.309	0.601	0.853	0.940
Mahjourian et al. [5]	0.189	0.221	1.663	6.220	0.265	0.665	0.892	0.962
GeoNet [8]	0.172	0.202	1.521	5.829	0.244	0.707	0.913	0.970
DDVO [39]	0.108	0.147	1.014	5.183	0.204	0.808	0.946	0.983
CC [9]	0.162	0.188	1.298	5.467	0.232	0.724	0.927	0.974
MD2 (R18) [2]	0.093	0.109	0.623	4.136	0.154	0.873	0.977	0.994
Ours (R18)	**0.082**	**0.096**	**0.507**	**3.828**	**0.139**	**0.898**	**0.983**	**0.996**

4.6. Results with Post-Processing

To finish the comprehensive comparison with the previous state-of-the-art work [2], we also evaluated our method with post-processing. This technique was proposed by [37] to improve stereo-based methods, but it has proved effective for monocular training methods as well. As shown in Table 7, this post-processing step did improve the result of our methods. In addition, the performance of our models exceeds the post-processed results of [2] even without post-processing.

Table 7. Evaluation results with post-processing compared with MD2 [2].

Methods	Resolution	Error Metric ↓				Accuracy Metric ↑		
		Abs Rel	Sq Rel	RMSE	RMSE log	$\delta < 1.25$	$\delta < 1.25^2$	$\delta < 1.25^3$
MD2 [2]	1024 × 320	0.115	0.882	4.701	0.190	0.879	0.961	0.982
MD2 (pp) [2]	1024 × 320	0.112	0.838	4.607	0.187	0.883	0.962	0.982
Ours (R18)	1024 × 320	**0.106**	**0.761**	**4.545**	**0.182**	**0.890**	**0.965**	**0.983**
Ours (R18 + pp)	1024 × 320	**0.104**	**0.726**	**4.457**	**0.180**	**0.893**	**0.965**	**0.984**
Ours (R50)	1024 × 320	**0.105**	**0.731**	**4.412**	**0.181**	**0.891**	**0.965**	**0.983**
Ours (R50 + pp)	1024 × 320	**0.104**	**0.709**	**4.352**	**0.179**	**0.894**	**0.966**	**0.984**

4.7. Inference Speed

The depth inference task usually plays an important role in autonomous driving and robotic vision. In these fields, there generally are strict requirements for calculation speed. To test the practicability of models, we calculated the inference speed of our models under the condition with a GPU or CPU device. In Table 8, we list the average time cost for testing 697 frames of Eigen's test set [35].

Table 8. Inference speed on Eigen's test set [35]. "Time" means the total time required for the inference for 697 frames.

Device	Time (s)	Speed (f/s)
GPU	60.9	11.5
CPU	8721.1	0.08

The inference speeds of our model on the GPU and CPU devices are significantly different. Frames of the KITTI [44] dataset were collected at 10 Hz, and our inference speed on the GPU device is over 10 fps, which indicates the practicability of our method on the GPU device. However, the speed on the CPU device is much lower, which will be improved in our future work.

5. Visual Odometry

Trajectory estimation is also very important for environment perception [1,50]. Since the accuracies of the pose and depth estimations are correlated, our proposed method not only produces a high-quality depth estimation but also improves the accuracy of the pose estimation. We used the 00-08 sequences of the KITTI odometry split for training and the 09-10 sequences for the evaluation, as in [1]. We compared the absolute trajectory errors calculated in overlapping five-frame and three-frame snippets with various methods. In Table 9, our results are clearly superior to the latest self-supervised monocular training methods and also close to the traditional ORB-SLAM method with the loop closure step. The estimated trajectories by our models and other methods are shown in Figure 6 for comparison purposes.

Table 9. Results of the visual odometry on the KITTI Odometry dataset. "Frame" means the number of frames used when calculating absolute trajectory error. "†" means updated result after publication. The best results are illustrated with bold text.

Methods	Sequence09	Sequence10	Frame
ORB-SLAM	0.014 ± 0.008	0.012 ± 0.011	
ORB-SLAM (short)	0.064 ± 0.141	0.064 ± 0.130	
[1]	0.021 ± 0.017	0.020 ± 0.015	5
Zhou et al. †	0.016 ± 0.009	0.013 ± 0.009	5
DDVO [39]	0.045 ± 0.108	0.033 ± 0.074	5
DF-Net [18]	0.017 ± 0.007	0.015 ± 0.009	5
[2]	0.017 ± 0.008	0.015 ± 0.010	5
Ours	$\mathbf{0.015 \pm 0.007}$	$\mathbf{0.015 \pm 0.009}$	5
[5] (no ICP)	0.014 ± 0.010	0.013 ± 0.011	3
[5] (with ICP)	0.013 ± 0.010	0.012 ± 0.011	3
[5]	0.013 ± 0.010	0.012 ± 0.011	3
[2]	0.013 ± 0.007	0.011 ± 0.008	3
Ours	$\mathbf{0.009 \pm 0.005}$	$\mathbf{0.010 \pm 0.007}$	3

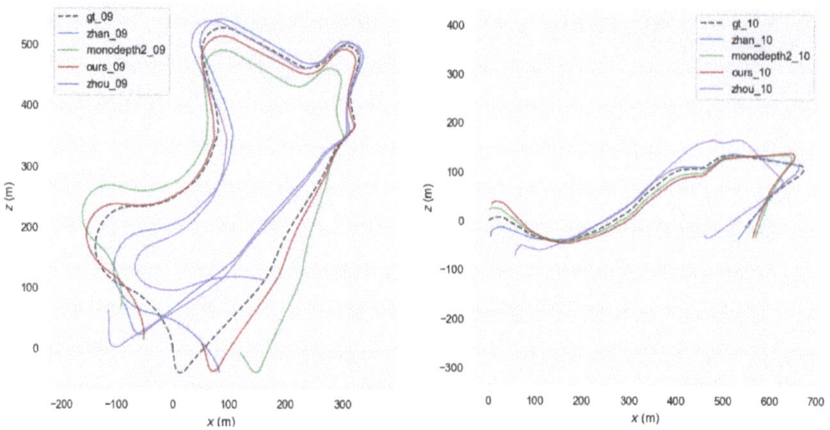

Figure 6. Visual comparison of the visual odometry trajectories. Full trajectories are plotted using the Evo visualization tool [51].

6. Conclusions

Our work is dedicated to the self-supervised monocular depth estimation problem with a focus on learning more effective task-specific representation during learning. In our method, the IAM can actively explore the geometric correlation between depth- and pose-estimation tasks by learning attentive representation from depth to guide the pose network to highlight and leverage more valuable geometry information, which improves the estimation quality of depth and pose. We also introduce an STMM to learn the spatial and temporal geometric dependencies among sequential frames, which are helpful for utilizing long-range historical knowledge within the time window to perceive distant objects. Experimental results demonstrated that our method is superior to existing state-of-the-art approaches and can generate higher-quality depth maps. In our future work, we will explore more powerful network architectures, such as Transformers and their corresponding attention mechanisms.

Author Contributions: Conceptualization, Hailiang Zhao and Jiansen Zhao; data curation, Hailiang Zhao; experiments, Hailiang Zhao and Yongyi Kong; funding acquisition, Hailiang Zhao and Jiansen Zhao; investigation, Chonghao Zhang and Haoji Zhang. All authors have read and agreed to the published version of the manuscript.

Funding: This research is supported by the National Key Research and Development Program, China (Grant no. 2021YFC2801004), National Natural Science Foundation of China (Grant no. 51709167), National Natural Science Foundation of China (Grant No. 52331012).

Data Availability Statement: The data presented in this study are available in the KITTI dataset at https://www.cvlibs.net/datasets/kitti/, reference number [44].

Conflicts of Interest: The funders had no role in the design of the study; in the collection, analyses, or interpretation of data; in the writing of the manuscript; or in the decision to publish the results.

References

1. Zhou, T.; Brown, M.; Snavely, N.; Lowe, D.G. Unsupervised learning of depth and ego-motion from video. In Proceedings of the IEEE Conference on Computer Vision and Pattern Recognition, Honolulu, HI, USA, 21–26 July 2017.
2. Godard, C.; MacAodha, O.; Firman, M.; Brostow, G.J. Digging into self-supervised monocular depth estimation. In Proceedings of the IEEE International Conference on Computer Vision, Seoul, Republic of Korea, 27 October–2 November 2019; pp. 3828–3838.
3. Zhao, H.; Zhang, Q.; Zhao, S.; Chen, Z.; Zhang, J.; Tao, D. Simdistill: Simulated multi-modal distillation for bev 3d object detection. In Proceedings of the AAAI Conference on Artificial Intelligence, Vancouver, BC, Canada, 18–22 November 2024.
4. Shu, Y.; Hu, A.; Zheng, Y.; Gan, L.; Xiao, G.; Zhou, C.; Song, L. Evaluation of ship emission intensity and the inaccuracy of exhaust emission estimation model. *Ocean. Eng.* **2023**, *287*, 115723. [CrossRef]

5. Mahjourian, R.; Wicke, M.; Angelova, A. Unsupervised learning of depth and ego-motion from monocular video using 3d geometric constraints. In Proceedings of the IEEE Conference on Computer Vision and Pattern Recognition, Salt Lake City, UT, USA, 18–22 June 2018; pp. 5667–5675.
6. Zhan, H.; Garg, R.; Weerasekera, C.S.; Li, K.; Agarwal, H.; Reid, I. Unsupervised learning of monocular depth estimation and visual odometry with deep feature reconstruction. In Proceedings of the IEEE Conference on Computer Vision and Pattern Recognition, Salt Lake City, UT, USA, 18–22 June 2018.
7. Yang, Z.; Wang, P.; Xu, W.; Zhao, L.; Nevatia, R. Unsupervised learning of geometry with edge-aware depth-normal consistency. *arXiv* **2017**, arXiv:1711.03665.
8. Yin, Z.; Shi, J. Geonet: Unsupervised learning of dense depth, optical flow and camera pose. In Proceedings of the IEEE Conference on Computer Vision and Pattern Recognition, Salt Lake City, UT, USA, 18–22 June 2018; pp. 1983–1992.
9. Ranjan, A.; Jampani, V.; Balles, L.; Kim, K.; Sun, D.; Wulff, J.; Black, M.J. Competitive Collaboration: Joint Unsupervised Learning of Depth, Camera Motion, Optical Flow and Motion Segmentation. In Proceedings of the IEEE Conference on Computer Vision and Pattern Recognition, Long Beach, CA, USA, 15–20 June 2019; pp. 12240–12249.
10. Kim, H.R.; Angelaki, D.E.; DeAngelis, G.C. The neural basis of depth perception from motion parallax. *Philos. Trans. R. Soc. B Biol. Sci.* **2016**, *371*, 20150256. [CrossRef] [PubMed]
11. Colby, C. Perception of Extrapersonal Space: Psychological and Neural Aspects. *Int. Encycl. Soc. Behav. Sci.* **2001**, 11205–11209. [CrossRef]
12. Gieseking, J.J.; Mangold, W.; Katz, C.; Low, S.; Saegert, S. *The People, Place, and Space Reader*; Routledge: London, UK, 2014.
13. Gregory, R.L. Knowledge in perception and illusion. *Philos. Trans. R. Soc. Lond. Ser. B Biol. Sci.* **1997**, *352*, 1121–1127. [CrossRef] [PubMed]
14. Wang, X.; Girshick, R.; Gupta, A.; He, K. Non-local neural networks. In Proceedings of the IEEE Conference on Computer Vision and Pattern Recognition, Salt Lake City, UT, USA, 18–22 June 2018; pp. 7794–7803.
15. Jaderberg, M.; Simonyan, K.; Zisserman, A. Spatial transformer networks. In *Advances in Neural Information Processing Systems*; Curran Associates, Inc.: Glasgow, UK, 2015.
16. Casser, V.; Pirk, S.; Mahjourian, R.; Angelova, A. Depth prediction without the sensors: Leveraging structure for unsupervised learning from monocular videos. In Proceedings of the AAAI Conference on Artificial Intelligence, Honolulu, HI, USA, 27 January–1 February 2019; Volume 33, pp. 8001–8008.
17. He, K.; Gkioxari, G.; Dollár, P.; Girshick, R. Mask r-cnn. In Proceedings of the IEEE International Conference on Computer Vision, Venice, Italy, 22–29 October 2017; pp. 2961–2969.
18. Zou, Y.; Luo, Z.; Huang, J.-B. Df-net: Unsupervised joint learning of depth and flow using cross-task consistency. In Proceedings of the European Conference on Computer Vision, Munich, Germany, 8–14 September 2018; pp. 36–53.
19. Zhao, H.; Zhang, J.; Zhang, S.; Tao, D. Jperceiver: Joint perception network for depth, pose and layout estimation in driving scenes. In Proceedings of the European Conference on Computer Vision, Tel Aviv, Israel, 23–27 October 2022.
20. Li, R.; Wang, S.; Long, Z.; Gu, D. Undeepvo: Monocular visual odometry through unsupervised deep learning. In Proceedings of the IEEE International Conference on Robotics and Automation, Brisbane, Australia, 21–25 May 2018; pp. 7286–7291.
21. CS Kumar, A.; Bhandarkar, S.M.; Prasad, M. Depthnet: A recurrent neural network architecture for monocular depth prediction. In Proceedings of the IEEE Conference on Computer Vision and Pattern Recognition Workshops, Salt Lake City, UT, USA, 18–22 June 2018; pp. 283–291.
22. Wang, R.; Pizer, S.M.; Frahm, J.-M. Recurrent neural network for (un-) supervised learning of monocular video visual odometry and depth. In Proceedings of the IEEE Conference on Computer Vision and Pattern Recognition, Long Beach, CA, USA, 15–20 June 2019; pp. 5555–5564.
23. Dosovitskiy, A.; Beyer, L.; Kolesnikov, A.; Weissenborn, D.; Zhai, X.; Unterthiner, T.; Dehghani, M.; Minderer, M.; Heigold, G.; Gelly, S.; et al. An image is worth 16x16 words: Transformers for image recognition at scale. In Proceedings of the International Conference on Learning Representations, Addis Ababa, Ethiopia, 26–30 April 2020.
24. Zhao, H.; Zhang, J.; Chen, Z.; Yuan, B.; Tao, D. On Robust Cross-view Consistency in Self-supervised Monocular Depth Estimation. *Mach. Intell. Res.* **2024**, *21*, 495–513. [CrossRef]
25. Agarwal, A.; Arora, C. Attention attention everywhere: Monocular depth prediction with skip attention. In Proceedings of the IEEE/CVF Winter Conference on Applications of Computer Vision, Waikoloa, HI, USA, 2–7 January 2023.
26. Zhao, C.; Zhang, Y.; Poggi, M.; Tosi, F.; Guo, X.; Zhu, Z.; Huang, G.; Tang, Y.; Mattoccia, S. Monovit: Self-supervised monocular depth estimation with a vision transformer. In Proceedings of the International Conference on 3D Vision, Prague, Czechia, 12–15 September 2022.
27. Bae, J.; Moon, S.; Im, S. Deep digging into the generalization of self-supervised monocular depth estimation. In Proceedings of the AAAI Conference on Artificial Intelligence, Washington, DC, USA, 7–14 February 2023.
28. Mayer, N.; Ilg, E.; Hausser, P.; Fischer, P.; Cremers, D.; Dosovitskiy, A.; Brox, T. A large dataset to train convolutional networks for disparity, optical flow, and scene flow estimation. In Proceedings of the IEEE Conference on Computer Vision and Pattern Recognition, Las Vegas, NV, USA, 27–30 June 2016.
29. He, K.; Zhang, X.; Ren, S.; Sun, J. Deep residual learning for image recognition. In Proceedings of the IEEE Conference on Computer Vision and Pattern Recognition, Las Vegas, NV, USA, 27–30 June 2016; pp. 770–778.

30. Russakovsky, O.; Deng, J.; Su, H.; Krause, J.; Satheesh, S.; Ma, S.; Huang, Z.; Karpathy, A.; Khosla, A.; Bernstein, M.; et al. Imagenet large scale visual recognition challenge. *Int. J. Comput. Vis.* **2015**, *115*, 211–252. [CrossRef]
31. Clevert, D.-A.; Unterthiner, T.; Hochreiter, S. Fast and accurate deep network learning by exponential linear units(elus). *arXiv* **2015**, arXiv:1511.07289.
32. Woo, S.; Park, J.; Lee, J.-Y.; So Kweon, I. Cbam: Convolutional block attention module. In Proceedings of the European Conference on Computer Vision, Munich, Germany, 8–14 September 2018; pp. 3–19.
33. Zagoruyko, S.; Komodakis, N. Paying more attention to attention: Improving the performance of convolutional neural networks via attention transfer. *arXiv* **2016**, arXiv:1612.03928.
34. Hu, J.; Shen, L.; Sun, G. Squeeze-and-excitation networks. In Proceedings of the IEEE Conference on Computer Vision and Pattern Recognition, Salt Lake City, UT, USA, 18–22 June 2018; pp. 7132–7141.
35. Eigen, D.; Puhrsch, C.; Fergus, R. Depth map prediction from a single image using a multi-scale deep network. In Proceedings of the NIPS'14: Proceedings of the 27th International Conference on Neural Information Processing Systems, Montreal, QC, Canada, 8–13 December 2014; pp. 2366–2374.
36. Garg, R.; BG, V.K.; Carneiro, G.; Reid, I. Unsupervised cnn for single view depth estimation: Geometry to the rescue. In *Proceedings of the European Conference on Computer Vision*; Springer: Berlin/Heidelberg, Germany, 2016; pp. 740–756.
37. Godard, C.; MacAodha, O.; Brostow, G.J. Unsupervised monocular depth estimation with left-right consistency. In Proceedings of the IEEE Conference on Computer Vision and Pattern Recognition, Honolulu, HI, USA, 21–26 July 2017.
38. Pillai, S.; Ambruş, R.; Gaidon, A. Superdepth: Self-supervised, super-resolved monocular depth estimation. In Proceedings of the IEEE International Conference on Robotics and Automation, Montreal, QC, Canada, 20–24 May 2019; pp. 9250–9256.
39. Wang, C.; Buenaposada, J.M.; Zhu, R.; Lucey, S. Learning depth from monocular videos using direct methods. In Proceedings of the IEEE Conference on Computer Vision and Pattern Recognition, Salt Lake City, UT, USA, 18–22 June 2018; pp. 2022–2030.
40. Bian, J.-W.; Li, Z.; Wang, N.; Zhan, H.; Shen, C.; Cheng, M.-M.; Reid, I. Unsupervised scale-consistent depth and ego-motion learning from monocular video. In *Advances in Neural Information Processing Systems;* Curran Associates, Inc.: Glasgow, UK, 2019.
41. Zhou, J.; Wang, Y.; Qin, K.; Zeng, W. Unsupervised high-resolution depth learning from videos with dual networks. In Proceedings of the IEEE International Conference on Computer Vision, Seoul, Republic of Korea, 27 October–2 November 2019.
42. Spencer, J.; Bowden, R.; Hadfield, S. DeFeat-Net: General Monocular Depth via Simultaneous Unsupervised Representation Learning. In Proceedings of the IEEE Conference on Computer Vision and Pattern Recognition, Seattle, WA, USA, 14–19 June 2020; pp. 14402–14413.
43. Zhao, W.; Liu, S.; Shu, Y.; Liu, Y.-J. Towards better generalization: Joint depth-pose learning without posenet. In Proceedings of the IEEE Conference on Computer Vision and Pattern Recognition, Seattle, WA, USA, 14–19 June 2020.
44. Geiger, A.; Lenz, P.; Urtasun, R. Are we ready for autonomous driving? the kitti vision benchmark suite. In Proceedings of the IEEE Conference on Computer Vision and Pattern Recognition, Providence, RI, USA, 16–21 June 2012.
45. Saxena, A.; Sun, M.; Ng, A.Y. Make3D: Learning 3D Scene Structure from a single still image. *IEEE Trans. Pattern Anal. Mach. Intell.* **2008**, *31*, 824–840. [CrossRef] [PubMed]
46. Cordts, M.; Omran, M.; Ramos, S.; Rehfeld, T.; Enzweiler, M.; Benenson, R.; Franke, U.; Roth, S.; Schiele, B. The cityscapes dataset for semantic urban scene understandin. In Proceedings of the IEEE Conference on Computer Vision and Pattern Recognition, Las Vegas, NV, USA, 27–30 June 2016.
47. Liu, F.; Shen, C.; Lin, G.; Reid, I. Learning depth from single monocular images using deep convolutional neural fields. *IEEE Trans. Pattern Anal. Mach. Intell.* **2015**, *38*, 2024–2039. [CrossRef]
48. Uhrig, J.; Schneider, N.; Schneider, L.; Franke, U.; Brox, T.; Geiger, A. Sparsity invariant cnns. In Proceedings of the 2017 International Conference on 3D Vision (3DV), Qingdao, China, 10–12 October 2017.
49. Poggi, M.; Tosi, F.; Mattoccia, S. Learning monocular depth estimation with unsupervised trinocular assumptions. In Proceedings of the International Conference on 3D Vision, Verona, Italy, 5–8 September 2018.
50. Zhao, J.; Yan, Z.; Zhou, Z.; Chen, X.; Wu, B.; Wang, S. A ship trajectory prediction method based on GAT and LSTM. *Ocean. Eng.* **2023**, *289*, 116159. [CrossRef]
51. Grupp, M. evo: Python Package for the Evaluation of Odometry and SLAM. 2017. Available online: https://github.com/MichaelGrupp/evo (accessed on 5 May 2023).

sustainability

MDPI

Article

Synergistic Landscape Design Strategies to Renew Thermal Environment: A Case Study of a Cfa-Climate Urban Community in Central Komatsu City, Japan

Jing Xiao [1,*], Takaya Yuizono [2] and Ruixuan Li [3]

1 School of Design and Innovation, Zhejiang Normal University, Jinhua 321004, China
2 School of Advanced Science and Technology, Japan Advanced Institute of Science and Technology, 1-1 Asahidai, Nomi 923-1292, Ishikawa, Japan; yuizono@jaist.ac.jp
3 School of Art and Design, Dalian Polytechnic University, Dalian 116034, China; lirx@dlpu.edu.cn
* Correspondence: jingxiao@zjnu.edu.cn

Abstract: An effective community landscape design consistently impacts thermally comfortable outdoor conditions and climate adaptation. Therefore, constructing sustainable communities requires a resilience assessment of existing built environments for optimal design mechanisms, especially the renewal of thermally resilient communities in densely populated cities. However, the current community only involves green space design and lacks synergistic landscape design for renewing the central community. The main contribution of this study is that it reveals a three-level optimization method to validate the Synergistic Landscape Design Strategies (SLDS) (i.e., planting, green building envelope, water body, and urban trees) for renewing urban communities. A typical Japanese community in central Komatsu City was selected to illustrate the simulation-based design strategies. The microclimate model ENVI-met reproduces communities involving 38 case implementations to evaluate the physiologically equivalent temperature (PET) and microclimate condition as a measure of the thermal environments in humid subtropical climates. The simulation results indicated that the single-family buildings and real estate flats were adapted to the summer thermal mitigation strategy of water bodies and green roofs (W). In small-scale and large-scale models, the mean PET was lowered by 1.4–5.0 °C (0.9–2.3 °C), and the cooling effect reduced mean air temperature by 0.4–2.3 °C (0.5–0.8 °C) and improved humidification by 3.7–15.2% (3.7–5.3%). The successful SLDS provides precise alternatives for realizing Sustainable Development Goals (SDGs) in the renewal of urban communities.

Keywords: thermal environment renewal; urban community; ENVI-met V5; urban microclimate; synergistic landscape design strategies (SLDS); humid subtropical climate (Cfa)

1. Introduction

1.1. Background

With climate change and heat waves worldwide, urban heat islands (UHI) deteriorate the urban thermal environment and microclimate conditions, which increases the potential health risks of inhabitants. Balancing the energy consumption of buildings and urban resilience has become a critical challenge for sustainable urban planning [1]. In the Revised Integrated Energy Statistics Report (2019), the Agency for Natural Resources and Energy (ANRE) stated that global warming has increased the mean air temperature in Japan by 1 °C, and deaths due to heatstroke are increasing among the elderly population. The literature about community-related microclimate and thermal environment focuses on energy consumption and air quality [2–7], while less attention has been paid to the synergistic landscape design to reduce thermal stress. The mitigation strategies in subtropical cities have focused on green space layout and tree design in microclimatic simulation for thermal comfort improvement [6–10], ignoring mechanisms verification and comparative studies in synergistic landscape strategies.

1.2. Synergistic Landscape Design Strategies (SLDS) for Improving Thermal Environment

Synergistic Landscape Design Strategies (SLDS) are important approaches to urban cooling that integrate design elements in vegetation, water conditions, albedo of materials, and urban form. Previous mitigation strategies in the thermal environment have shown that SLDS can reduce cooling energy demand and greenhouse gas emissions [4,11–14]. Planting design in the SLDS involves complex factors such as vegetation structure, layout, tree species, type, and number on the microclimate and thermal environment [6,7]. Multi-layered vegetation structures have been validated for cooling and humidifying effects on thermal environments, especially in summer, where air temperature (T_a) is reduced by 2.14–5.15 °C and relative humidity (RH) is increased by 6.21–8.30% [15]. Optimal vegetation configuration coupled with the building form of the block, studies have shown that vegetation in low-rise building blocks has a high cooling potential [16]. Research on improving thermal environments found that increasing the albedo of urban fabric material and developing green roofs can deal with subtropical UHI in Osaka, Japan [8]. A study in a residential area of Nanjing [5] found that increasing green quantity improves outdoor thermal comfort by using a mean radiant temperature (T_{mrt}) and the mean voting index (PMV) as the evaluation criteria. Moreover, the vertical cooling performance (T_a and T_{mrt}) of the residential environment benefits from urban trees [10].

In other studies on cooling community strategies of SDLS, green building envelopes (GBE) retrofits play an important role in the thermal stress attenuation of residential buildings [4,17]. Green roofs reduce thermal radiation flux through evapotranspiration to increase surface albedo and reduce shortwave radiation [18–20]. Knaus and Haase [19] have shown that green roofs improve the temperature of residential roofs during the day and reduce physiologically equivalent temperatures (PET) by an estimated 9 k. Furthermore, some studies have indicated that green facade systems can be used in different climates with significant cooling and humidification effects [21–27]. In contrast, installing a single green facade has limitations in mitigating the ambient temperature [28,29]. The SLDS integrated planting design [6,30–32], urban trees [6,7,10], GBE design [33,34], and water body design [35] significantly contribute to balancing thermal comfort. Feitosa and Wilkinson [36] verified that green roofs and walls contribute to better thermal insulation of the building envelope and effectively reduce the thermal index. Lai et al. [37] found that PET was reduced by 13.0 K and 4.6 K in vegetation and water bodies design. However, synergistic landscape interventions ignore a mix of more than three design strategies to alleviate urban climate change and UHI-induced thermal perturbation.

1.3. Microclimate Simulation in the Urban Community

Microclimate simulation can reproduce specific urban spaces on a system of physical environments to simulate urban surface-plant-air interaction by computational fluid dynamics (CFD) models [38–40]. Most microclimate studies examined CFD-integrated thermal indices to investigate the influencing factors and strategies to mitigate the thermal environment. The ENVI-met V5.0.1 simulation software is applicable for simultaneous cross-simulations and comparative studies of microclimatic conditions and thermal environments by adopting SLDS [41–45]. In Egypt, ENVI-met 4.4.5 simulated canyons in urban residential communities and showed that hybrid landscape design scenarios can improve summer thermal comfort by reducing PET and T_a [46]. In a previous ENVI-met study on Nanjing City, the quantity of trees effectively relieves the heat stress of a residential district [5]. Another ENVI-met study in a residential district in Tabriz, Iran, validated that tree coverage and species can improve the cooling effect (reduction of T_a, T_{mrt}, and PET) [32]. To date, the major challenges of these simulation models are related to inadequate modeling of a synergistic landscape strategy optimization mechanism and limited support for the practical design of multifactorial improvements with parameter complexity [47].

1.4. Motivation

As mentioned in previous studies, there are some research gaps in the existing studies. First, it is unclear how to develop an optimization mechanism to assess the thermal and microclimatic environments in humid subtropical cities to renew the urban communities. Second, there is limited research on microclimate simulation for SLDS integrating the design of planting, GBE, water bodies, and urban trees [15,33,48]. Third, some research is scarce on applying SLDS consistent with the multifactorial improvements in building form, landscape design, climatic characteristics, scale change, and time mitigation [5,8,10]. Therefore, an optimization method is proposed, coupling a renewal experience and microclimate simulation mechanism. The aim is to comprehensively assess the potential for summer mitigation thermal performance and cooling effect on urban communities.

To address these gaps, the detailed purposes and novelty of this study are as follows:

(i) To develop a three-level optimization method to systematically verify the SLDS alternatives in a pre-renew stage of the central city for both summer outdoor thermal comfort and microclimate improvement.

(ii) To apply to quantify which the SLDS alternatives can affect the small-scale and the large-scale optimization community cooling demand and the summer thermal comfort more effectively multifactor improvements strategy following the optimal criteria (i.e., improvement of T_a, RH, WS, T_{mrt}, and PET).

(iii) To investigate the effect application of urban trees in the microclimate simulation ENVI-met of sustainable Japanese communities project and resilience assessment in the Cfa-climate by comparing analysis if the hypotheses do not reach the multifactorial improvements.

For these purposes, typical Japanese urban communities in central Komatsu City are selected as a case study for renewal planning for the Sustainable Development Goals. The potential SLDS in the pre-renewal stages are systemically verified on a small and large scale. The summer thermal comfort and community cooling demand prior to and after the application mechanism of the SLDS interventions are compared. The thermal sensation range of PET, specifically for humid subtropical cities, as detailed in Section 2.5, is applied to analyze the thermal environment improvement in this study. Finally, ideal SLDS are presented, considering thermal comfort and microclimate effects, which can serve as a practical guideline and method for urban designers.

2. Materials and Methods

This study combined field measurements with ENVI-met simulations in SLDS to assess the microclimatic conditions and thermal comfort in the urban community. The workflow can be divided into four steps (Figure 1): (1) Select three Japanese communities in Komatsu City as sample sites; (2) Investigate and monitor local meteorological data via weather stations to simulate the base model (L1 AC, L1 HC, and Ga BC); (3) Use numerical simulations and ArcGIS 10.8 created an accurate 3D environment model for microclimate simulation of the communities; (4) Validate the base model and develop the new SLDS simulations for comparative studies in renewal mechanism, as detailed in Section 3.

2.1. Study Area

Komatsu City is located at the center of the southwest Kaga Plain, and it has 106,292 inhabitants as of 2020 (Figure 2). This study area was identified as a future city for the Sustainable Development Goals (SDGs), which seek synergistic development with multiple goals in the areas of energy, climate change, and health. This study area was selected due to the Komatsu City Renewal and Maintenance Plan project, which implemented a specific plan to renew the city to a sustainable and resilient urban form starting in 2020 [49].

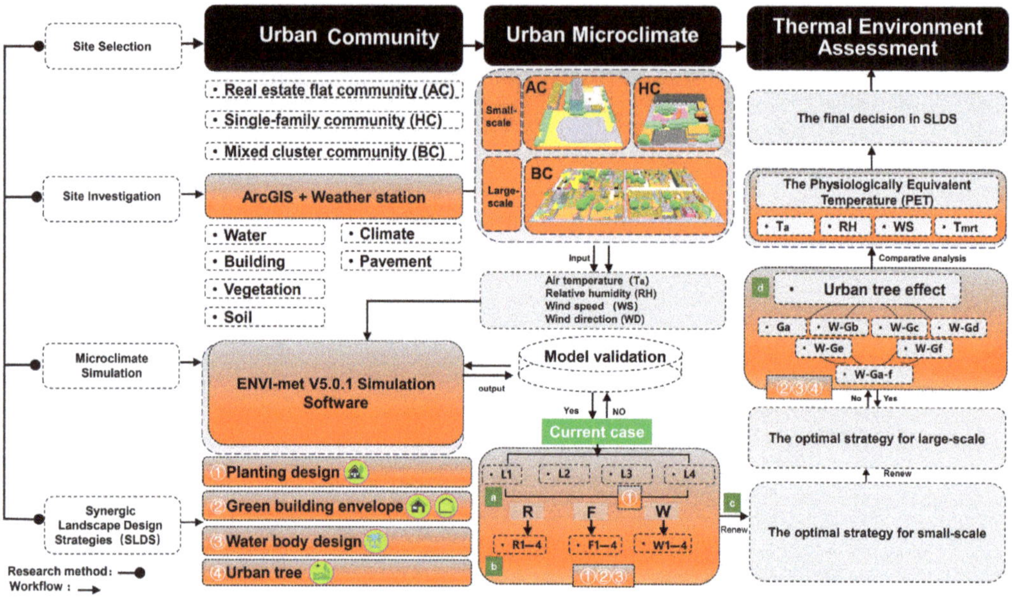

Figure 1. The methodology for microclimate simulation sets an optimization mechanism (from a to d) in the Synergistic Landscape Design Strategies (SLDS) to renew the thermal environment in urban communities.

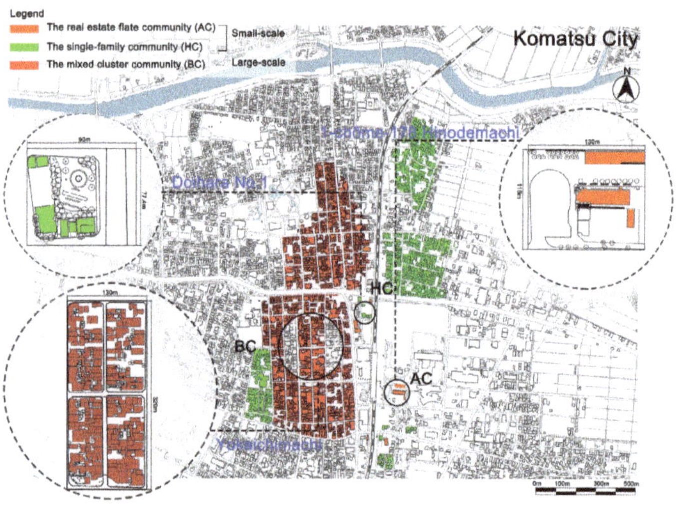

Figure 2. Local sample communities include the single-family building community (HC), the real estate flat community (AC), and the mixed cluster community (BC).

The local community was represented at the small scale by the single-family community (HC) of Doihara No. 1 (34.41° N, 136.45° E) and the real estate flat community (AC) at 1-chōme-178 Hinodemachi (36.40° N, 136.45° E) (Figure 2). The large scale was represented by the mixed cluster community (BC) of Yokaichimachi (36.24° N, 136.26° E). Japanese-style houses were present in the HC area with a civic square in the center, and the AC area formed an asymmetrical canyon with station hotels. The BC area was formed by the single-family (H type) and real estate flat buildings (A type). Moreover, the HC area is approximately 6536 m^2, and the tallest low-rise building is 12 m. The AC area had an overall area of 14,950 m^2 around the high-rise building in 30 m. The BC had an applied area of approximately 46,200 m^2, with the tallest building being 24 m. Among the landscape designs in the sample area, the HC and AC areas are populated with a mixture of trees, shrubs, and grasses, while the BC area is planted with a private garden landscape. A common feature is the distribution of functional spaces with parking lots, parks, and plazas within the urban communities.

2.2. Climate Condition

Komatsu City is located in the humid subtropical climate zone (Cfa) of Köppen's climate classification system [50] (Figure 3a). Summer in Komatsu City is studied in this paper, which is generally characterized by heat, high temperature, and rain humidity, with high mean air temperatures of 30 °C. The hottest times are between 12:00 and 16:00; the hot season lasts for 2.8 months, from June to September [51]. In the GISS of global surface temperature analysis for 2019–2021 in Japan, the surface temperatures increased by 1–2 °C in August [52] (Figure 3b). Local weather data are provided in real-time by the Japan Meteorological Agency (JMA). The agency shows that air temperatures in August may reach a maximum of 38 °C based on the maximum air temperatures of the last three years [53] (Figure 3c). August is the hottest month based on the annual mean air temperature in Komatsu City (Figure 3d). Inhabitants are exposed to high air temperatures for long periods, which can potentially lead to health risks associated with discomfort, especially in elderly communities [54]. So, selecting August as a typical simulation period allows people to provide timely feedback on discomfort sensations during the summer months. The measured meteorological data also provided evidence to simulate an effective SLDS in urban communities.

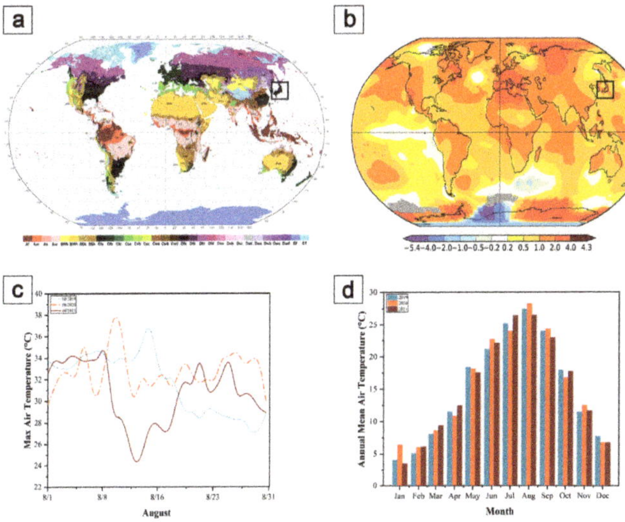

Figure 3. (**a**) Köppen-Geiger climate classification of Cfa, in Japan (with black square area); (**b**) surface temperature change in Japan from 2019 to 2021 for August warming; (**c**) maximum air temperature (T_a) in August from 2019 to 2021; and (**d**) annual mean air temperature (T_a) in Komatsu City from 2019 to 2021.

2.3. Meteorological Monitoring

The meteorological data were monitored by the Komatsu City Weather Station and Komatsu Airport Station [51,53]. Weather stations monitored microclimate parameters, including T_a, RH, wind direction (WD), and wind speed (WS). Based on the climate data for

2021, August was the hottest month, with a daily maximum T_a of up to 35 °C (Figure 3c). In the visible meteorological data for evaluating thermal comfort in specific environments, the thermal perception of the inhabitants was most pronounced in terms of discomfort. Therefore, this study chose the monitoring date of 22 August 2021 as a typical summer day, representing extremely hot days for examining the SLDS in a Cfa-climate urban community. The monitoring time is setting 24 h at 1 h intervals. Recorded meteorological parameters are presented in Table 1.

Table 1. Meteorological parameters (T_a, RH, WD, and WS) on 22 August 2021.

Time	T_a (°C)	RH (%)	WD (°)	WS (m/s)
00:00	26.5	74.0	112.5	0.8
01:00	28.7	62.0	180.0	3.2
02:00	27.1	70.0	247.5	1.1
03:00	28.5	66.0	180.0	3.0
04:00	28.3	66.0	180.0	2.9
05:00	27.6	66.0	180.0	1.2
06:00	26.9	70.0	135.0	1.6
07:00	29.3	62.0	180.0	2.0
08:00	29.7	58.0	202.5	2.4
09:00	31.4	58.0	180.0	2.9
10:00	32.5	52.0	180.0	4.6
11:00	33.0	55.0	180.0	4.4
12:00	34.1	52.0	202.5	3.5
13:00	33.6	55.0	202.5	4.2
14:00	32.2	59.0	202.5	3.3
15:00	31.8	62.0	202.5	3.7
16:00	31.3	62.0	202.5	2.1
17:00	28.2	79.0	202.5	2.2
18:00	27.2	84.0	202.5	2.0
19:00	27.0	84.0	202.5	0.7
20:00	27.0	84.0	225.0	0.3
21:00	27.0	84.0	157.5	0.3
22:00	25.7	94.0	270.0	1.2
23:00	25.8	89.0	135.0	1.2

2.4. *ENVI-Met and ArcGIS*

Urban microclimate reveals the behavior of microclimate in urban areas and between buildings, which helps researchers better understand the impact on the outdoor thermal environment and human health in a specific urban environment [55]. The ENVI-met model has been used for the numerical simulation of real scenes and a comparative study of strategic cases that affect thermal comfort and microclimate regulation. The ENVI-met software is widely used for multiscale microclimate simulations in humid subtropical climates [8,45,48]. This software is a grid-based model with fine resolution (0.5–10 m) based on the standard κ–ε turbulence model and Reynolds Averaged Navier-Stokes (RANS) equations [10,45]. ENVI-met V5.0.1 converted the vegetation model from geometric blocks to actual trunk and leaf shapes. The contour of the 3D tree model is more accurate and extends to new tree species in the DB database. The operation mode was selected in the ENVI-guide sub-tool, including full force and simple force [56]. The Bio-met in ENVI-met is used to evaluate the thermal index (PET). In this study, the simple force mode was selected, and the simulated height was set to a pedestrian height of 1.8 m. The X, Y, and Z gride dimensions in three sample models (HC, AC, and BC areas) based on the scale of the study areas were set to 38 × 43 × 15, 63 × 69 × 45, and 160 × 75 × 36; and the grid size is 2 × 2 × 2 m. The fundamental parameter settings in the ENVI-met models and the setting of the wall material are shown in Figure 4 and Tables 1 and 2. Figure 5 shows that the urban building land is used for residential and commercial purposes, so Komatsu City forms a highly built-up central area. The central urban area is covered with low and medium vegetation and distributed the UHI phenomenon in ArcGIS analysis for Komatsu City.

	The building form of the AC area in Sketchup	Building material in ENVI-met model
A	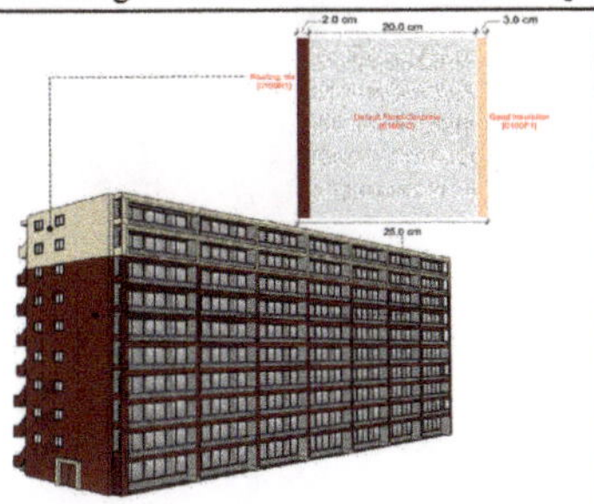	Type: Real estate flat building
		Outside layer in a wall: Roofing-tile [0100R1]
		Media layer in a wall: Default Ferro-Concrete [0100FC]
		Inside layer in a wall: Good insulation [0100F1]
		Building height:30 m
		Building thickness:25 cm
		Window: Plexiglass [0200G2]
		Simulation area: 14,950 m^2
		Roof: Wetroof [0100WR]
	The building form of the HC area in Sketchup	Building material in ENVI-met model
H	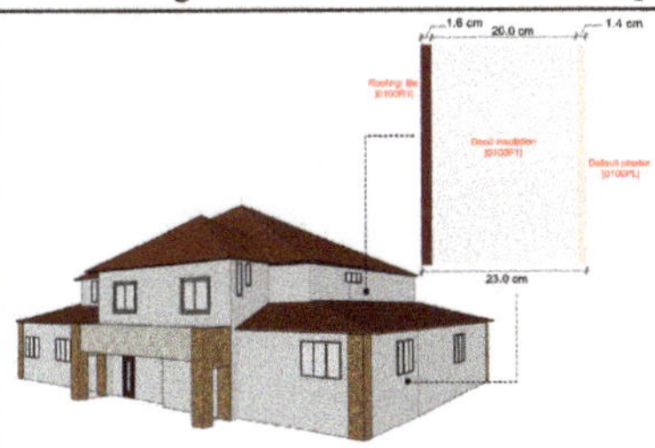	Type: Single-family building
		Outside layer in a wall: Roofing-tile [0100R1]
		Media layer in a wall: Good insulation [0100F1]
		Inside layer in a wall: Default plaster [0100PL]
		Building height:12 m
		Building thickness:23 cm
		Window: Plexiglass [0200G2]
		Simulation area: 6,536 m^2
		Roof: Terracotta [0000R2]

Figure 4. Japanese community is in two building forms (A and H types) and wall material settings in the ENVI-met.

Table 2. Fundamental parameter settings in the ENVI-met.

	Sample Site/Setting	HC	AC	BC
Time setting	Total simulation time (h)		24	
	Output time interval (min)		60	
	Start of simulation date and time		On 22 August 2021; at 00:00	
Create model	Model dimensions (X × Y × Z) (m)	38 × 43 × 15	63 × 69 × 45	160 × 75 × 36
	Grid size (m)	2 × 2 × 2	2 × 2 × 2	2 × 2 × 2
	Telescoping factor (%)	6%	-	-
	Start telescoping after height (m)	7	-	-
	Number of nested grids	5	-	-
Meteorological parameters	Minimum–maximum air temperature (°C)		25.7–34.1	
	Minimum–maximum relative humidity in 2 m (%)		52–94	
	Wind speed measured at 10 m height (m/s)		2.3	
	Wind direction (°)		189	
	Roughness length at the measurement site		0.01	
Soil	Soil layer (0–200 cm) humidity (%) and temperature (°C)		65, 20 70, 20 75, 19	
Cloud	Fraction of cloud (x/8)		6	
Force mode	Simple force/Full force		Simple force	

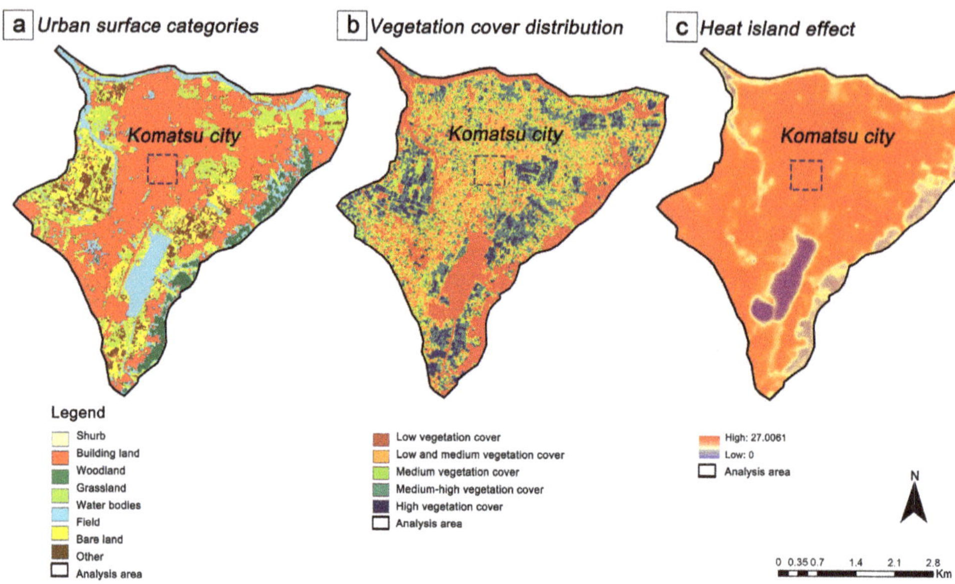

Figure 5. (**a**) ArcGIS analysis of Komatsu City using urban surface categories, (**b**) vegetation cover distribution, and (**c**) urban heat island (UHI) effect.

Airflow field turbulence in ENVI-met is given by RANS equations, as shown in Equation (1) [10]:

$$\begin{aligned} \tfrac{\partial u}{\partial t} + u_i \tfrac{\partial u}{\partial} &= -\tfrac{\partial u}{\partial x} + K_m\left(\tfrac{\partial^2 u}{\partial x_i{}^2}\right) + f(V - V_g) - S_u \\ \tfrac{\partial u}{\partial t} + u_i \tfrac{\partial u}{\partial} &= -\tfrac{\partial u}{\partial x} + K_m\left(\tfrac{\partial^2 u}{\partial x_i{}^2}\right) + f(u - V_g) - S_V \\ \tfrac{\partial w}{\partial t} + u_i \tfrac{\partial u}{\partial x_i} &= -\tfrac{\partial p'}{\partial z} + K_m\left(\tfrac{\partial^2 w}{\partial x_i{}^2}\right) + g\left(\tfrac{\theta(z)}{\partial x_i{}^2}\right) - S_w \end{aligned} \tag{1}$$

$$\frac{\partial u}{\partial x} + \frac{\partial v}{\partial y} + \frac{\partial w}{\partial y} = 0 \tag{2}$$

where f = 10^4 sce^{-1} is the Coriolis parameter, p′ is the local pressure perturbation, θ is the potential temperature at level z, and the reference temperature θ_{ref} should be recognized as average mesoscale conditions and are provided by a one-dimensional model running parallel to the primary model. Equation (2) is used to keep the model mass conserving for each time step.

T_a and RH in ENVI-met is given by advection-diffusion equations, as shown in Equations (3) and (4) [57]:

$$\frac{\partial \theta}{\partial t} + u_i \frac{\partial \theta}{\partial x_i} = K_h\left(\frac{\partial^2 u}{\partial x_i{}^2}\right) + Q_h \tag{3}$$

$$\frac{\partial \theta}{\partial t} + u_i \frac{\partial \theta}{\partial x_i} = K_q\left(\frac{\partial^2 q}{\partial x_i{}^2}\right) + Q_q \tag{4}$$

Similar to the momentum equations, Q_h and Q_q are used to link heat and vapor exchange at the plant surface with the atmospheric model.

2.5. The Human Thermal Comfort Index

Urban thermal environments have been assessed based on meteorological elements. PET is a general thermobioclimatic index used to characterize all climate zones. PET was developed by Hoppe in the 1990s based on the Munich Personal Energy Balance Model, which is the most widely used index for assessing outdoor thermal environments in humid subtropical climates [58]. This index considers all thermal bioclimatic factors using the Munich Energy-balance Model for Individuals (MENI) for individuals. The model assumes that the body reaches thermal equilibrium, where the equation of state Equation (5) [59].

$$M + W + R + C + ED + E_{VC} + E_{SE} + S = 0 \quad (5)$$

In Equation (5), M is the metabolic rate, W is the physical output, R is the net radiation of the physical body, C is the convective heat flow, ED is the skin diffusion of the latent heat flow, E_{VC} is the total latent heat flow, E_{SE} is the heat flow from sweat evaporation, and S is the heat that cools the body to store heat. The individual heat flow in Equation (5) is directly affected by the following microclimate parameters: T_a, RH, WS, and T_{mrt}. Moreover, the ENVI-met calculates the PET in Bio-met by personal setting (default male, summer clothing).

The evaluation criteria of PET were based on the classification of thermal perception in previous studies of humid subtropical cities in Taiwan and Kyoto [58,60]. Specifically, very cold (<14 °C), cold (14–18 °C), cool (18–22 °C), slightly cool (22–26 °C), comfortable (26–30 °C), slightly warm (30–34 °C), warm (34–38 °C), hot (38–42 °C), and very hot (>42 °C).

3. Synergistic Landscape Design Strategies (SLDS) in Japanese Communities

Based on the current case, the SLDS (planting design, GBE design, water body design, and urban trees) were compared in terms of their performance in improving the thermal environment. This study predicts the effect of thermal comfort improvement by vegetation structure (mixed in trees-grass-shrubs, no plant, trees and grass, shrubs and grass), number of urban trees, and planting layout (current layout, hard pavement layout, enclosed layout, and semi-enclosed layout) in the design of small-scale models (HC and AC areas). This SLDS establishes a mechanism divided into four steps (from a to d) to find an optimal strategy for improving thermal environment renewal. The details are as follows: (a) Testing the planting design ("L") to improve the thermal environment on a small scale. The vegetation structure and layout are integrated into various tree numbers representing: "L1"—mixed structure in the current layout, "L2"—no plant in hard pavement layout, "L3"—trees and grass in an enclosed layout, and "L4" shrub and grass structure in a semi-enclosed layout. (b) Adopting the GBE design was divided into an "R" strategy for the green roof, an "F" strategy for the green facade and the green roof, and a "W" strategy for water bodies and green roofs and the GBE design ("R, F, W") integrated planting design code cases in R1–4, F1–4, and W1–4. (c) Obtaining the output of the SLDS optimization simulated in small-scale communities. (d) Identifying optimization strategies for BC large-scale models based on small-scale results, particularly the thermal mitigation of urban tree types and numbers (Gb, Gc, Gd, Ge, and Gf) combined with pavement material. The community design cases for synergizing landscape design strategies are listed in Table 3. Based on the current cases (L1 HC, L1 AC, and Ga BC), 35 design cases were established to investigate the performance of the new SLDS to optimize the thermal environment in the three sample communities. Among them, the small scale involves 16 SLDS cases for comparative study, including L1–4, R1–4, F1–4, and W1–4 cases. It crosses two sample communities with various building forms (AC and HC), forming 32 cases of small-scale alternatives. The large-scale model is based on small-scale optimal SLDS for six cases (i.e., Ga, W-Gb, W-Gc, W-Gd, W-Ge, W-Gf). The performance of comparative strategies for thermal environment improvement is verified through hierarchical SLDS and the thermal benefits of deleting optimal design decisions for renewing sustainable communities in a homogeneous building context (Figure 6).

Table 3. All design cases using the Synergistic Landscape design strategies (SLDS) were conducted in three sample communities (HC, AC, and BC areas) (Note: "◎"indicates that SLDS cross-codes form different renewal cases).

SDLS	Code	Case	Tree Number (T_n)	Tree Number (T_n)	Planting Design				Adding GBE Design			Adding Urban Tree					
			HC/BC	AC	L1	L2	L3	L4	R	F	W	Ga	Gb	Gc	Gd	Ge	Gf
Current cases/ Planting design cases	L1–4	L1	34	54	◎												
		L2	0	0		◎											
		L3	32	76			◎										
		L4	0	0				◎									
Renewal small-scale cases	R1–4	R1	34	54	◎				◎								
		R2	0	0		◎			◎								
		R3	32	76			◎		◎								
		R4	0	0				◎	◎								
	F1–4	F1	34	54	◎					◎							
		F2	0	0		◎				◎							
		F3	32	76			◎			◎							
		F4	0	0				◎		◎							
	W1–4	W1	34	54	◎						◎						
		W2	0	0		◎					◎						
		W3	32	76			◎				◎						
		W4	0	0				◎			◎						
Current cases/ Renewal large-scale cases	W-Ga-f	Ga	126		◎							◎					
		W-Gb	126		◎						◎		◎				
		W-Gc	208		◎						◎			◎			
		W-Gd	208		◎						◎				◎		
		W-Ge	208		◎						◎					◎	
		W-Gf	208		◎						◎						◎

3.1. Planting Design (L) at a Small-Scale

At the small scale of the HC and AC models, the vegetation configuration was based on the layout of the existing plaza and parking lot for perimeter planting, with the tree types being mainly deciduous in combination with a small number of evergreens and conifers. Typical evergreen trees in the local area are Camphorwood and Cyclobalanopsis glauca, coniferous trees are planted pine, and deciduous trees are mainly planted with Cornus florida, Acer rubrum, and Zelkova serrata. The renewal planting design involved vegetation structure, landscape layout, and tree numbers in horizontal and vertical dimensions formed by integrating the reconfiguration cases (L1–4) shown in Figure 7.

3.2. Green Roof (R)

Green roofs respond to urban environmental challenges as a multifunctional greening strategy. Green roofs have five basic layers: Vegetation, growing substrate, drainage layer, root barrier, and waterproof membrane [61]. The cooling performance of green roofs depends on the roof material and vegetation characteristics in the context of the urban microclimate [62]. This study systematically investigated the degree of thermal mitigation provided by extensive green roofs based on planting designs (R1–4) at a small scale.

3.3. Green Facade and Green Roof (F)

Green facade components cover the green facade using climbing vegetation [63]. Green facades improve the urban microclimate by absorbing, evaporating, and insulating solar radiation to comply with a climate-adaptative design. In the ENVI-met microclimate model, green roofs and facades were classified as default greenings with or without air gaps. This study used default greenings with air gaps to model the GBE designs based on planting designs (F1–4) in HC and AC areas. The planting thickness (0.3 m) and substrate thickness (15 cm) were specified, with the vegetation layer consisting of 25 cm of grass for the green roof and ivy for the green facade.

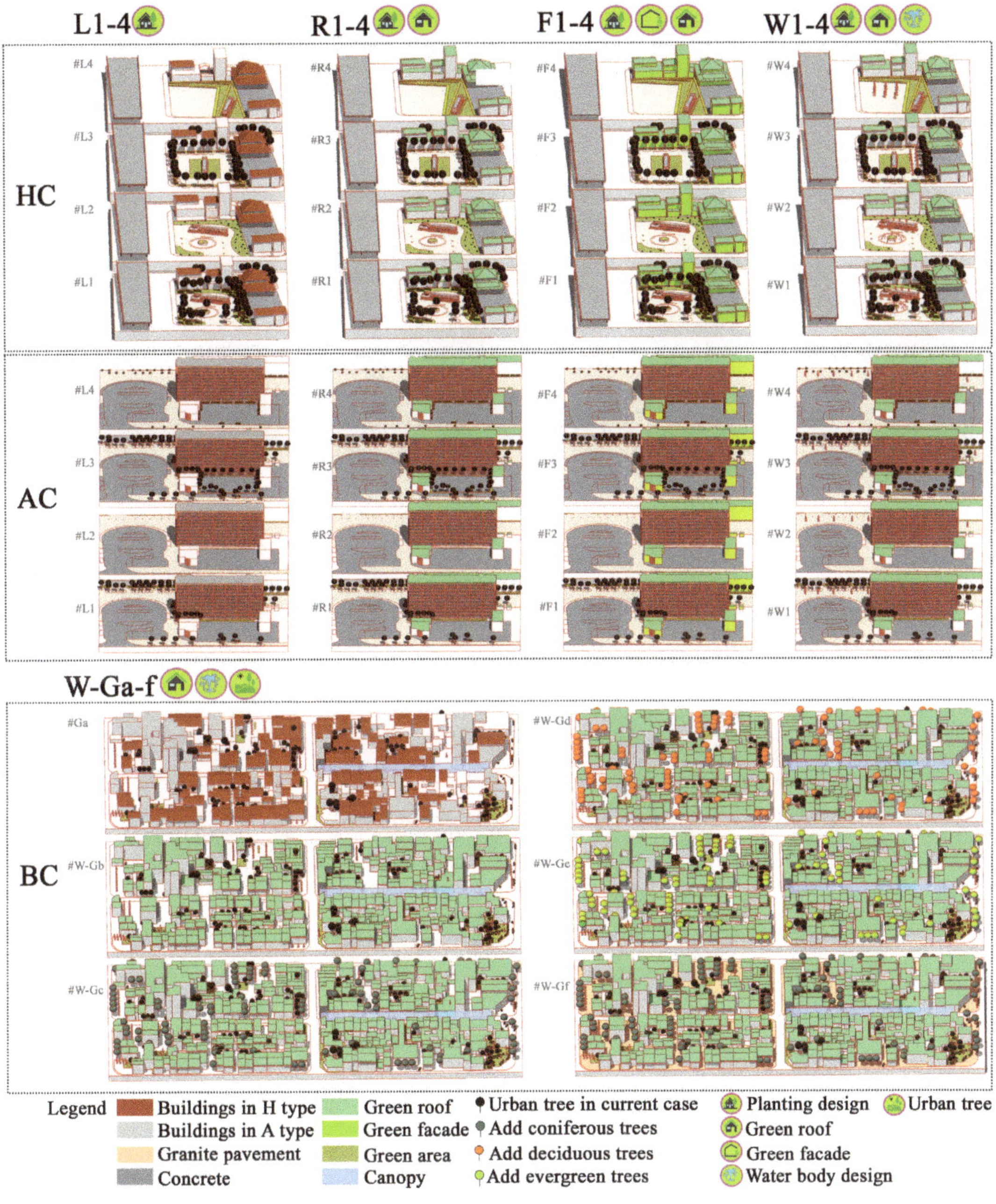

Figure 6. Axonometric diagrams for all design cases using the Synergistic Landscape design strategies (SLDS) in three sample communities (HC, AC, and BC areas).

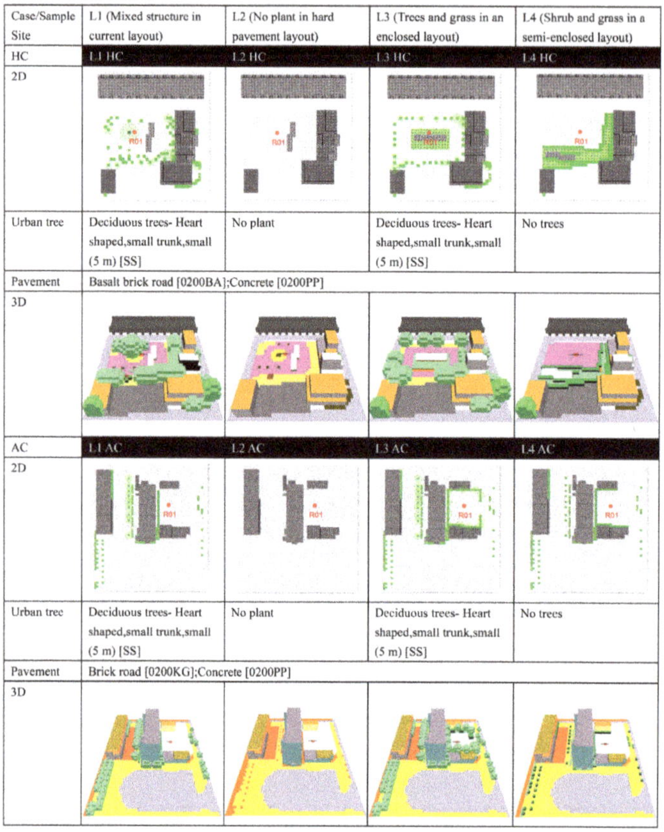

Figure 7. Planting design cases for small-scale models (HC and AC areas) with the position of receptors in ENVI-met.

3.4. *Water Body and Green Roof (W)*

Traditional community buildings in Japan have been maintained as front and back yards, with a courtyard landscape in the center. The design of water bodies in ENVI-met was via discharge fountains at the street green space of the study area to present traditional garden design techniques such as chōzubachi, bamboo bucket fountains, spiral sprays, and rain chains, including the main community activity areas and backyards of the communities. Water bodies and green roofs as SLDS are considered for validating the effect on a small scale (W1–4).

3.5. *Large-Scale Synergistic Landscape Design Strategies (W-Ga-f)*

Based on the evaluation of small-scale SLDS, an optimal strategy was applied to the BC area to investigate the mitigation performance and cooling effect on UHI at a large scale (W-Ga-f). For the Leaf Area Density Index (LAD) values of typical local tree species, an increase of 82 urban trees is used for placement in the large-scale cases (W-Gc-f); the corresponding case codes are Ga, W-Gb, W-Gc, W-Gd, W-Ge, and W-Gf. Ga represents the current case in the large-scale model, while W-Gb optimizes the "W" strategy based on the Ga case. W-Gc-e is the introduction of coniferous (conic, small trunk, dense, medium, 15 m), deciduous (middle American sweet gum), and evergreen (Camphorwood was set to change LAD by coniferous tree) types as the main urban trees to replacement based on W-Gb. W-Gf is a renewal of the granite pavement (single tone) (0100GS) based on the W-Gc case (Figure 8).

Figure 8. Synergistic landscape design cases for large-scale models (BC area) in ENVI-met.

4. Results

4.1. ENVI-Met Model Validation

A precise ENVI-met model can be validated by fitting measured results against simulated results. Statistical evaluation metrics are used to validate simulation results for microclimate parameters. Typical evaluation metrics include the coefficient of determination (R^2) and root-mean-square error (RMSE) [64]. The reliability model in the ENVI-met related to the evaluation criteria for the simulation and monitor parameters: R^2 close to 1, RMSE close to 0 [45]. Following previous studies, we focus on validating the T_a and RH combined with the evaluation metrics of R^2 in this study [45,46]. On-site monitoring of T_a and RH was performed on 22 August 2021, from 00:00 to 24:00 (Table 1). The monitored and simulated meteorological data were used to validate the current cases in the ENVI-met models for local sample communities.

For validating T_a and RH in three sample communities, R^2 in T_a was 0.87, 0.88, and 0.81; R^2 in RH was 0.87, 0.85, and 0.85 (Figure 9). The evaluation metrics performed reasonably, with R^2 close to 1. In this regard, the ENVI-met models in current cases were valid and reliable for compliance with the criteria in R^2. Based on validated current cases, this study develops the SLDS to renew models and improve the local thermal environment.

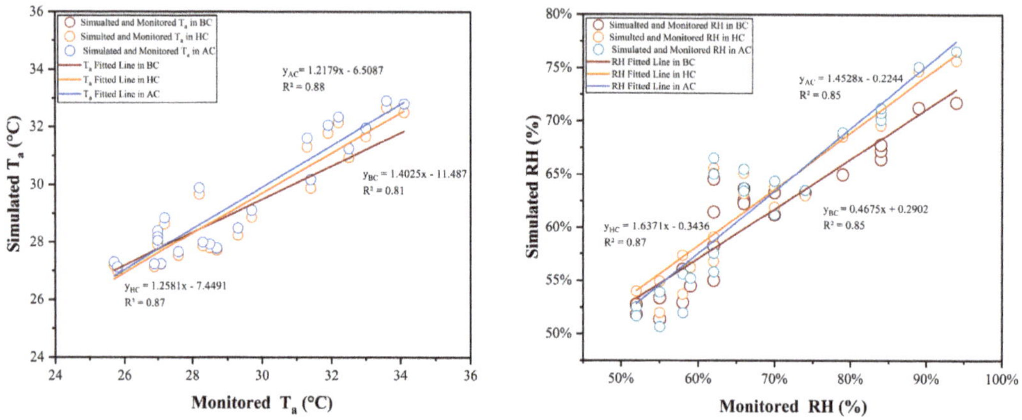

Figure 9. Validation of linear fit for monitored and modeled air temperature (T_a) and relative humidity (RH) in local sample communities (HC, AC, and BC areas) at small and large scales.

4.2. Microclimate Conditions in Renewal Strategies

4.2.1. Air Temperature (T_a)

In Figure 10, the maximum T_a simulated in the current cases was up to 33 °C; the minimum simulated T_a was about 26.9 °C. For all cases, see microclimate results in the Appendix A, the planting design cases (L1, L2, L3, and L4) are similar under the T_n, the optimal reduction of 0.2 °C in the HC area (Table A1). In Table A2, T_a is reduced by 0.3 °C in the HC area and increased to 0.7 °C in the AC area. These results indicated that the combination of landscape layout and vegetation structure had a minor cooling effect in HC area under similar tree numbers [48]. Planting design involved mitigation strategies ("R, F, W"), and T_a significant reduction occurred in the "W" series of renewal cases (Figure 10). In the HC area, the W1 case had the lowest mean T_a of 2.3 °C compared to the L1 case. In the AC area, the W1 and W3 cases effectively reduce the heat transmission by up to 0.4 °C (Table A1). At 14:00, W1 and W4 cases were maximum reduced by 1.9 °C in the HC area (Table A2). Therefore, the cooling effect was more significantly observed in the HC area. In the large-scale strategies ("W-Ga-f") (Tables A3 and A4), the W-Gc and W-Gf cases effectively compared to the Ga case, decreased mean T_a by 0.8 °C and reduced the T_a by up to 1.1 °C at 14:00. Accordingly, the W-Gb case was only 0.5 °C lower than the Ga case at 14:00, further indicating that adding the urban trees positively affects cooling air temperatures than only used "W" strategy at large-scale (Table A4). The simulation results showed that the cooling effect of introducing quantitative trees with the same "W" strategy followed the order of coniferous trees > evergreen trees > deciduous trees.

4.2.2. Relative Humidity (RH)

In Table A1, the mean RH increased by up to 0.7–1.0% in the HC and AC areas. At 14:00, the L3 case was effectively increased by 1.4% in the HC area, in contrast to a 1.7% reduction of RH in the AC area. The simulation results of RH further prove that the planting design has a minor effect on humidification. However, the W-series cases were also highly effective in increasing humidification (Figure 10). The W1 case yielded the best humidification effect compared to the current cases in HC and AC areas, with a mean humidification increase of 3.7–15.2% and an improvement RH of 0.7–12.1% at 14:00 (Tables A1 and A2). In Tables A3 and A4, the mean RH increases by 5.3% and 7.2% at 14:00 in W-Gc and W-Gf cases. The large-scale simulated results indicated synergistic landscape design strategies can help regulate community humidification.

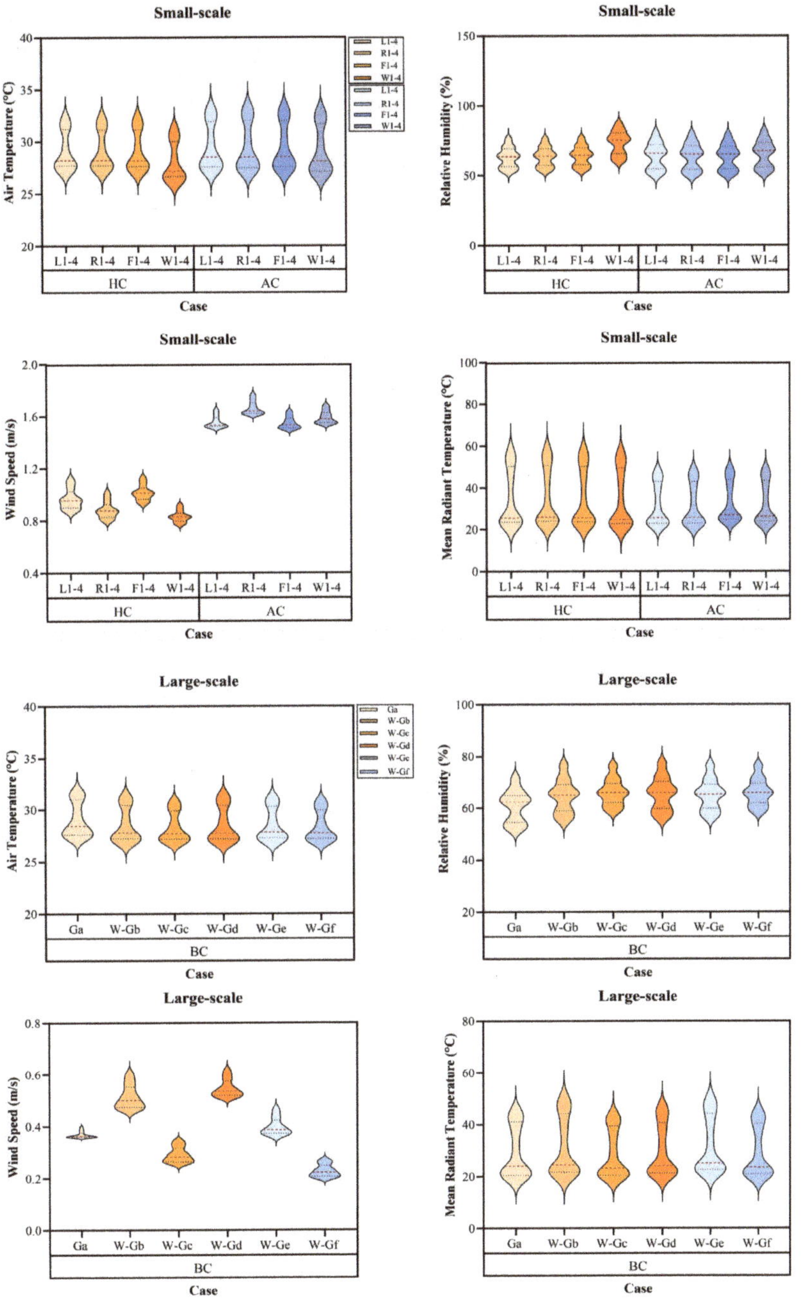

Figure 10. Simulation results of the microclimate variations in sample communities at small-large scales.

4.2.3. Wind Speed (WS)

In the microclimate simulation, the mean WS of the current case reached 0.9 m/s in the HC and AC areas. In comparison, the mean WS of the BC area with dense buildings was only 0.4 m/s (Tables A1 and A3). The small-scale models simulated WS without vegetation obstruction (T_n = 0) can maximize the improvement of 1.0 m/s in the AC area (Tables A1 and A2). The AC area formed an urban canyon, which realizes optimal summer ventilation in the absence of vegetation at the L2 case. Under the "W" strategy, the mean WS can maximize ventilation improvement up to 0.4–1.0 m/s in small-scale communities (Table A1). The well ventilation focused on the green roof and water body design (Figure 10). On this basis, the large-scale cases improve mean WS to 0.1 m/s, validated here to accommodate scale variations.

4.2.4. Mean Radiation Temperature (T_{mrt})

The AC and BC areas have the lowest simulated T_{mrt} for the current case. The shadows of the high-rise buildings reduce the reflections (Figure 10). In contrast, the HC area has the highest mean T_{mrt}, reaching a maximum of 38.0 °C in the L1 case (Table A1). With the intervention in the L3 case, the mean T_{mrt} decreased by 4.9 °C in the HC area. In comparison, it increased by 1.2 °C in the AC area. At 14:00, it also reduced by 6.9 °C in HC and increased by 3.2 °C in AC (Table A2). The thermal radiation temperature in the planting design fails to synergize the two community building forms to optimize the thermal environment. In Table A1, the W2 case decreased the mean T_{mrt} by 5.3 °C in the HC area, while the R2 case decreased the mean T_{mrt} by 0.2 °C in the AC area. Compared to the Ga case, the W-Gc case was able to reduce the mean T_{mrt} up to 0.9 °C (Table A3). Introducing more coniferous trees based on the "W" strategy has a positive effect on thermal radiation resistance under a fixed number of urban trees.

4.3. Mitigation Performance in Community Thermal Environments

The thermal environment is improved by reducing the thermal index and mitigation time. In Figure 11, renewal cases with a mean PET below 38–42 °C (in a hot state) are predominantly found in the "W" serie simulations, with an overall mitigation time of 18–24 h, except for the W-Gd case.

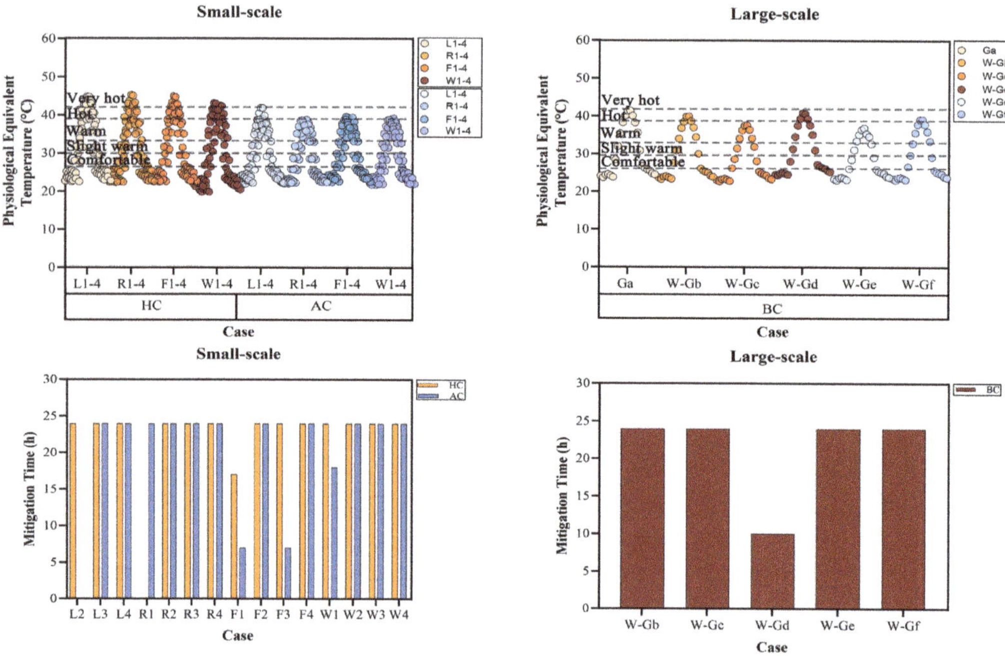

Figure 11. ENVI-met Simulation results on the physiologically equivalent temperature (PET) distribution and the mitigation time at a pedestrian height of 1.8 m.

4.3.1. Planting Design Effects on Sample Communities

Table 4a shows that the mean PET is 29.7–32.1 °C in the HC area and 28.1–30.5 °C in the AC area. The HC area was significantly observed with PET values of 40.5–43.0 °C at 14:00 (in the hot and very hot state). In the AC area, the PET was 37.5–39.9 °C at 14:00 (in a hot state) (Table 4b). The thermal comfort was poorer in the HC area than in the AC area, and extremely poor weather conditions were more likely to lower the PET to 2.4 °C (Table 4a). However, the thermal comfort performance failed to significantly alleviate the heat stress conditions on a small scale. On thermal maps in Figure 12, the overall level distribution still keeps hot and very hot states.

Table 4. Daily mean PET (**a**) and hourly PET (at 14:00) distribution (**b**) relative to current case (L1) for the small-scale community simulations with planting design (L1–4).

(**a**)

Simulation runs in a small-scale	Code	Case	Mean PET in HC (°C)	Mean deviation relative to L1 (ΔPET) in HC (°C)	Mean PET in AC (°C)	Mean deviation relative to L1 (ΔPET) in AC (°C)
Current case	L1–4	L1	32.1	-	29.2	-
Planting design cases		L2	32.1	0.0	30.5	1.3
		L3	30.4	−1.7	28.7	−0.5
		L4	29.7	−2.4	28.1	−1.1

(**b**)

Simulation runs in a small-scale	Code	Case	Mean PET in HC (°C)	Mean deviation relative to L1 (ΔPET) in HC (°C)	Mean PET in AC (°C)	Mean deviation relative to L1 (ΔPET) in AC (°C)
Current case	L1–4	L1	43.0	-	37.9	-
Planting design cases		L2	41.4	−1.6	39.9	2.0
		L3	41.1	−1.9	37.5	−0.4
		L4	40.5	−2.5	37.5	−0.4

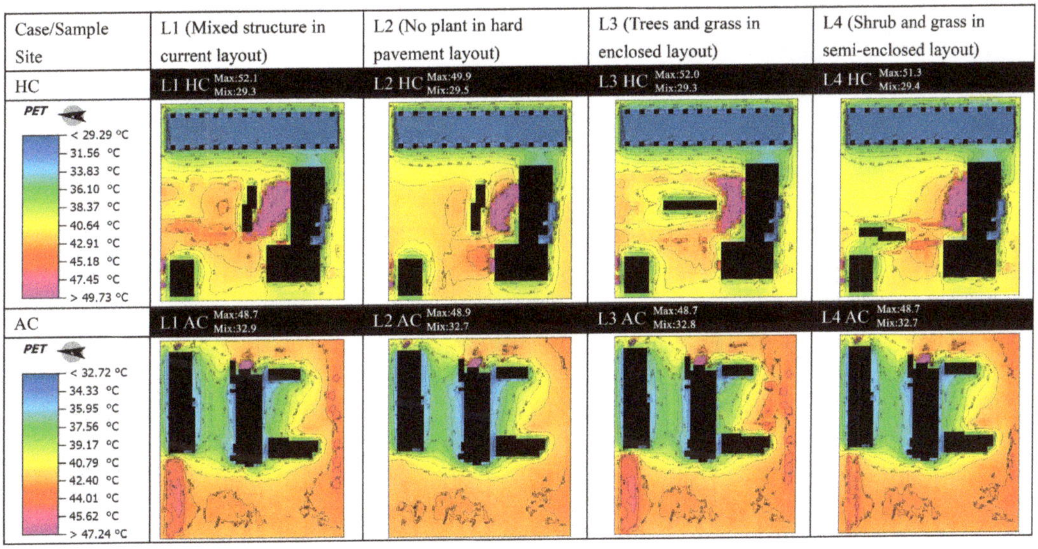

Figure 12. Distribution maps of the PET thermal index at 14:00 simulated with planting design strategies (L1, L2, L3, and L4) in two small-scale communities.

4.3.2. Green Building Envelope (GBE) Design Effects on Small-Scale Communities

The renewal cases (R1–4) compared the L1 case in the HC and AC areas. The mean PET can be reduced by 0.2–3.7 °C. R2 and R3 cases can lower the mean PET by 1.0–5.5 °C at 14:00. In the F1–4 cases, the maximum reduction in mean PET was 0.8–2.4 °C. The F3 and F4 cases reduced PET by 1.4–2.9 °C at 14:00. In the W1–4 cases, the mean PET was reduced by up to 1.4–5.0 °C, and the hot hour (at 14:00) was also reduced by 0.8–5.1 °C (Table 5). In Figure 13, the mitigation thermal comfort of the HC area was better than that of the AC area. Compared to the planted design cases (L1–4) (Figure 12), the W2 and W3 cases reduce the thermal index significantly to improve the thermal environment (ΔPET = 1.4–5.0 °C) (Figure 13 and Table 5). This result indicates that the water body and green roof realized a multiplicative effect on the thermal environment and the microclimate condition based on the planting design (Figures 10 and 13). At 14:00, the HC area varied from very hot (PET > 42 °C) to warm (PET = 34–38 °C) in W3 and R3 cases, and the AC area stayed to warm level in R1–4 and W2–4 cases (Figure 13 and Table 5b). The GBE design strategies in 92% of cases provided for adjusting the thermal environment to a comfortable state (PET = 26–30 °C) (Table 5a). So the introduced water body and green roof effectively reduce the risk of summer exposure and facilitate thermoregulation.

Table 5. Daily mean PET (**a**) and hourly PET (at 14:00) distribution (**b**) relative to current case (L1) for the small-scale community simulations with GBE design cases (R1–4, F1–4, W1–4) based planting design (L1–4).

(**a**)

Simulation runs in a small-scale	Code	Case	Mean PET in HC (°C)	Mean deviation relative to L1 (ΔPET) in HC (°C)	Mean PET in AC (°C)	Mean deviation relative to L1 (ΔPET) in AC (°C)
Renewal of the small-scale cases	R1–4	R1	32.4	0.3	28.2	−1.0
		R2	30.0	−2.1	28.0	−0.2
		R3	28.4	−3.7	28.5	−0.8
		R4	29.6	−2.5	28.2	−1.0
	F1–4	F1	31.9	−0.2	29.3	0.1
		F2	29.8	−2.2	28.4	−0.8
		F3	29.9	−2.2	29.4	0.2
		F4	29.7	−2.4	28.4	−0.8
	W1–4	W1	29.9	−2.1	29.0	−0.2
		W2	29.0	−3.1	27.8	−1.4
		W3	27.1	−5.0	29.1	−0.1
		W4	28.6	−3.5	27.9	−1.3

(**b**)

Simulation runs in a small-scale	Code	Case	Mean PET in HC (°C)	Mean deviation relative to L1 (ΔPET) in HC (°C)	Mean PET in AC (°C)	Mean deviation relative to L1 (ΔPET) in AC (°C)
Renewal of the small-scale cases	R1–4	R1	43.4	0.4	37.4	−0.5
		R2	41.1	−1.9	36.9	−1.0
		R3	37.5	−5.5	37.6	−0.3
		R4	40.4	−2.6	37.5	−0.4
	F1–4	F1	42.9	−0.1	38.4	0.5
		F2	40.9	−2.1	37.6	−0.3
		F3	40.1	−2.9	38.3	0.4
		F4	40.4	−2.6	36.5	−1.4
	W1–4	W1	41.4	−1.6	38.1	0.2
		W2	40.4	−2.6	37.1	−0.8
		W3	37.9	−5.1	37.7	−0.2
		W4	39.5	−3.5	37.2	−0.7

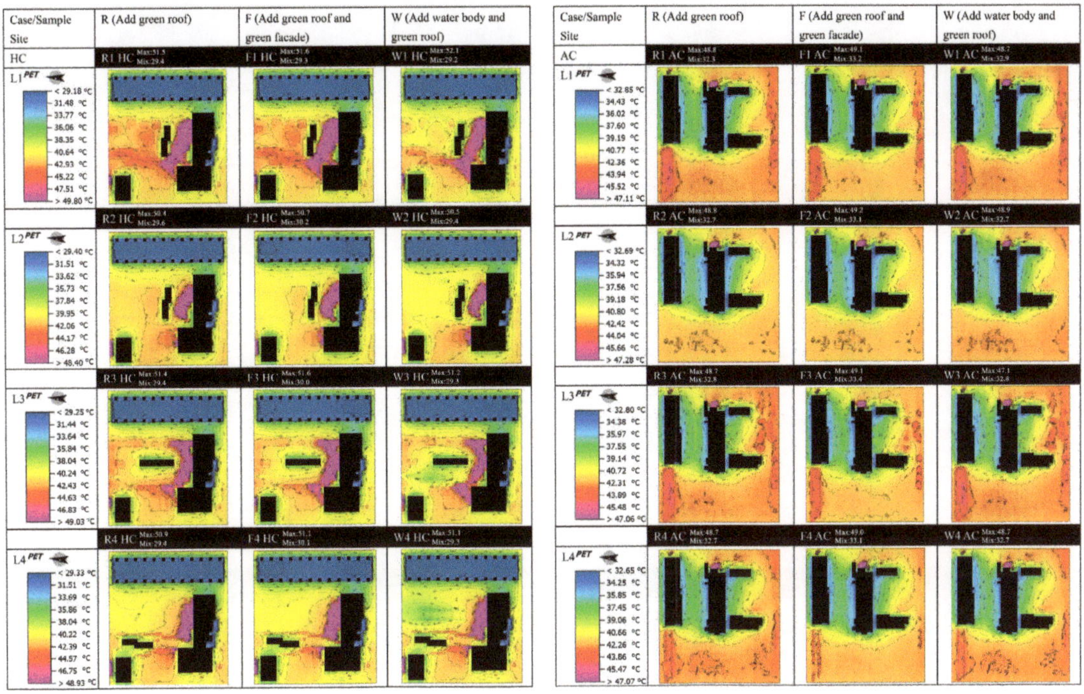

Figure 13. Distribution maps of the PET thermal index at 14:00 under green building envelope (GBE) design strategies ("R, F, and W") renewed in the HC and AC areas based on planting design (L1–4).

4.3.3. Urban Tree Effects on Large-Scale Community

In Table 6a, the W-Gc and W-Ge cases effectively reduce the mean PET by 2.2–2.3 °C compared to the Ga case. However, W-Gb was only reduced by 0.9 °C. The W-Ge case reduced PET by 4.7 °C but only by a reduction of 1.5 °C in the W-Gb case at 14:00. The results indicate that adding coniferous or evergreen trees combined with the "W" strategy resulted in multiple effects on mitigating the thermal environment (Figures 11 and 14). Adding water bodies and green roofs provides less thermal stress mitigation for the large-scale community. Still, it introduces a proportionate number of coniferous or evergreen trees that can adapt to the thermal conditions from hot to warm at 14:00 (Table 6b). Compared to the results of Tables 5 and 6, this research found that the difficulty of thermal mitigation is greater on a large scale than on a small scale. The nature-based case is to reintroduce urban trees, where the mitigation thermal index performance (ΔPET) is in the order of coniferous trees > evergreen trees > deciduous trees (Table 6a). With the synergistic GBE, urban trees, and pavement material, the mean PET was changed from slightly warm (PET = 30–34 °C) to a comfortable standard (Table 6a). Thus, holistic blue-green infrastructure contributes to the climatic resilience and sustainability of Komatsu's traditional residential and flat houses.

Table 6. Daily mean PET (**a**) and hourly PET (at 14:00) distribution (**b**) relative to current case (Ga) for the large-scale community simulations under urban tree effect (W-Ga-f) based water body and green roof design.

(a)

Simulation runs in a large-scale	Code	Case	Mean PET in BC (°C)	Mean deviation relative to Ga (ΔPET) in BC (°C)

Table 6. *Cont.*

Current case		Ga	30.4	-
Renewal of large-scale cases	W-Ga-f	W-Gb	29.5	−0.9
		W-Gc	28.1	−2.3
		W-Gd	30.5	0.1
		W-Ge	28.2	−2.2
		W-Gf	29.0	−1.5

(**b**)

Simulation runs in a large-scale	Code	Case	Mean PET inBC (°C)	Mean deviation relative to Ga (ΔPET) in BC (°C)
Current case		Ga	40.1	-
Renewal of large-scale cases	W-Ga-f	W-Gb	38.6	−1.5
		W-Gc	36.4	−3.7
		W-Gd	39.3	−0.8
		W-Ge	35.4	−4.7
		W-Gf	37.8	−2.3

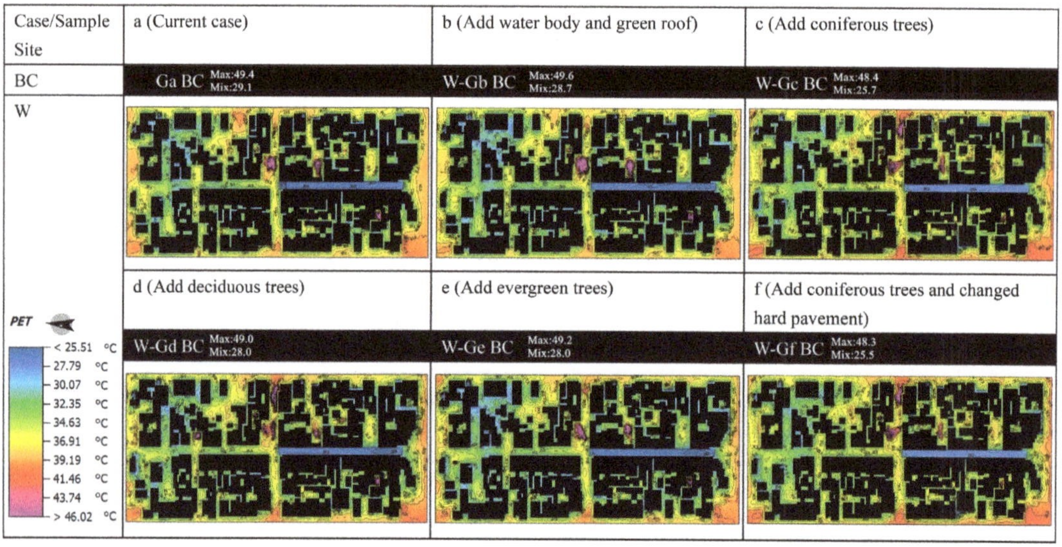

Figure 14. Distribution maps of the PET thermal index at 14:00 under urban tree effect (W-Ga-f) based water body and green roof (W) design of the BC area.

5. Discussion

Synergistic landscape design strategies were used to regulate microclimate and thermal stress in Japanese communities. This study validated that sample communities are more suitable for SDLS adopting water bodies and green roofs to improve daytime and nighttime thermal regulation. In addition, more coniferous or evergreen trees as urban trees in large-scale communities capture the overall building form, landscaping, climatic characteristics, scale, and time mitigation. Simultaneously, the synergy of more than three landscape design strategies is more conducive to the renewal plan of the central urban community.

5.1. Implications for the Planting Design

The simulation results in this paper show that planting design has a small effect on improving the thermal environment in Japanese communities under the SLDS condition (a).

This result is confirmed in some subtropical cities [48,65], especially changing landscape layout and vegetation structure under similar tree numbers. In this study, L2 and L4 cases result in similar microclimate conditions under $T_n = 0$. The reduction of the thermal index is strongly affected in the L4 case (ΔPET = −2.5 °C) (Table 4). The reduction of thermal radiation in the neighborhood was mainly concentrated in the HC area by planting trees and grass in an enclosed layout (L3) (Table A1). This finding further indicated that urban trees reflect and absorb via irradiance, obtaining transpiration and shade cooling for the local microclimate. However, thermal comfort was still in the hot level state at 14:00. Compared to previous studies on community design in ENVI-met [41,42,44,45], this study found that the planting design fails to realize improvements in scale effect and the mitigation time for the HC and AC building form (Figures 10 and 12). Therefore, considering the planting design level alone will not achieve resilient community regeneration. Three or more strategies are sufficient to realize a wide range of environmental parameter improvements, especially the SLDS conditions (c) and (d) have significant positive effects (Figure 11).

5.2. *Advantages of Green Building Envelope (GBE) Design*

The GBE designs show that introducing water bodies and green roofs (W) has a strong cooling effect and leads to a more comfortable thermal environment (Figure 11 and Table 5). Within this strategy, 85% of the alternatives resulted in thermal mitigation during the summer day and night (Figure 11). Moreover, the community thermal conditions in the sample area were moderated to warm levels at 14:00, with an optimal PET reduction of 0.8–5.1 °C (Figure 13 and Table 5b). According to Lalošević et al. [66], green roofs at the pedestrian level achieve a maximum cooling effect of 0.9–1.6 °C when combined with high albedo cooling materials. However, in the present study, the water bodies and green roofs effectively reduced T_a to 0.4–2.3 °C and increased RH to 3.7–15.2% (Table A1). These results indicated that water body dispersion obtained the greatest cooling effect [14,67]. Previous studies on Cfa-climate design strategies [48,58,62,65,66] via one or two-level optimization methods, this study seeks a better thermal contribution under these three-level strategies (planting design, green roofs, and water body design) to mitigate the thermal environment producing positive cooling and humidifying effects.

Mitigation strategies in the green roof (R) at the pedestrian level significantly reduced the PET values in the HC area. In contrast, the AC area had a negative effect (Table 5). The AC area is modeled for building heights above 30 m; therefore, the effect of green roofs on air temperature at the pedestrian level becomes negligible for building heights of 10 m above [19]. There is very low microclimate regulation at pedestrian heights (Table A1), and these results are mostly influenced by the elevation between vertical buildings and green roofs [13,68,69]. The mitigation strategy of the green roof and green facade (F) is the least effective in cooling and improving thermal comfort at the pedestrian level (Table 5b), with 40% of the alternatives failing to provide thermal regulation during the day and night (Figure 11). The primary explanation for this result is that the time-spatial distribution during the night provides a passive warming effect by suppressing longwave radiation emitted from building facades and attenuating vegetation evaporation [13,43,70]. The HC area provides better cooling performance than the AC area in small-scale simulation with a green facade and green roof, validating the advantage of thermal mitigation for low-rise communities (Tables A1 and A2). This result is consistent with a previous study [4].

5.3. *Urban Tree Effect on Sample Communities*

Urban tree effects produced different effects on thermal performance due to wind speed, wind direction, and shade [13]. The L2 case has a maximum wind speed that improves thermal comfort in hot time, whereas the L3 and L4 cases significantly reduce the thermal index due to crown shade (Figure 12 and Table 4). The tree-planting design includes key attributes such as the number, type, layout, and arrangement of the trees [13,32,44,48]. In similar tree coverage and the GBE design, the cooling effect and thermal mitigation depend on planting design and building form in renewal cases such as R3, F3, and W3 cases on a small scale (Tables 5 and A1). The results suggest that the number of urban trees can provide more shade and thermal benefits, especially in an enclosed layout (a rectangular pattern) [48,65]. In this study of the renewal cases (L2, R2, F2, and W2) without plant trees, great wind speed has a lower thermal index among the green building envelope designs, especially with the green roofs and the water body design. Compared to previous studies that have improved colling potential by increasing the number of trees [6, 7], this study focuses on summer thermal mitigation synergizing multifaceted optimization of environmental criteria, with coniferous trees and evergreen trees implementing a co-optimized large-scale community design for microclimatic conditions (T_a, RH, WS, T_{mrt}) and thermal comfort (PET) in T_n = 208 (Tables 6 and A3). Previous studies on a higher tree coverage ratio have shown that it can lower T_a and PET and raise RH in the daytime [32]. Still, this study has effectively multifactor improvements (T_a, RH, WS, T_{mrt}, and PET) via green roof and water body design (W) via introducing coniferous or evergreen trees in sample communities can mitigate summer thermal comfort for all day, especially at large-scale community (Figures 10 and 11).

5.4. *Scale Adaptation for Microclimate and Thermal Comfort Mitigation*

5.4.1. Small-Scale Community Models

A strong synergistic cooling effect exists between green and blue infrastructure (GBI) [13]. Especially in small-scale models, T_a reduction reached a maximum of 2.3 °C in green roof and water body design. In contrast, a single green roof under intervention is less effective for cooling than the former at pedestrian heights (Table A1). The main reason is that water bodies have a strong microclimatic impact, especially the mitigation of summer temperatures and the openness of water bodies to increase arboricultural shading effects and to promote natural ventilation, where small-scale modeling ventilation is significant and responsive to scale requirements. The optimal performance of the planting design varies with the characteristics of the building form [65]. It forms an area of high-rise building canyons with weaker heat stress than the single-family building areas of the HC, where the building blocks are heat sources by conductive and convective heat fluxes to reduce the urban surface heat stress (Figures 13 and 14) [71]. In the renewal strategy of the small-scale model, the best results for the optimization of microclimate conditions and thermal comfort at the pedestrian level were in the following order: W > R > F > L (Tables 5 and A1). This study found that the GBE design contributed to improving the thermal environment more than the small-scale planting design with similar numbers of trees in terms of cooling and humidifying effects (Figure 10). In addition, the thermal comfort of the Japanese community in both scales was simultaneously optimized from very hot and hot levels to a warm condition at 14:00 (Figures 13 and 14). Referencing Zhang et al. [15], this study found that in subtropical urban parks with field measurements results of 15 small-scale vegetation communities, the cooling and humidification effect of the multi-layer vegetation structure (trees, shrubs, and grasses) is significant. Accordingly, this simulation experiment (W1–4 cases) found that the cooling and humidification effect is optimal under the mixed structure planting (W1 case) (Table A1). In contrast to Rui et al. [5], an increased green quantity results in a smaller improvement in the thermal environment. The SLDS in the present study was used to obtain a more significant thermal mitigation effect on a small scale, such as a mitigation time that can optimally reach 24 h. The optimal SLDS ("W") satisfies multifactorial improvements (T_a, RH, WS, T_{mrt}, and PET) (Table A1). Notably, the predominance of high-rise buildings in the AC area has a disadvantage in reducing thermal radiant temperatures than in the HC area. Similar to a previous study [16], the vegetation had the lowest impact on the community's mean T_{mrt}, and the low-rise community had a better cooling effect on the microclimate than the high-rise community.

5.4.2. Large-Scale Community Models

The large-scale models re-simulated the best optimization strategy "W" from the small-scale models, which showed an optimal reduction in ΔPET of 4.7 °C, and the thermal comfort level is assessed at a warm level at 14:00 (Table 6b). These results verified the effectiveness of small- and large-scale models in implementing the "W" renewal plan, especially regarding climate resilience. What's more, introducing tree types and numbers (Gb, Gc, Gd, Ge, Gf) (T_n = 208) based on the "W" strategy, the large-scale model thermal comfort states (ΔPET) are in order of improvement: Gc > Gf > Ge > Gb > Gd (Table 6). Therefore, coniferous trees in the Japanese community are more effective in reducing PET than other tree types. The cooling effect of trees by reducing mean T_a on the thermal environment in the order Gc ≥ Gf > Ge > Gb ≥ Gd (Table A3). Moreover, the coniferous tree is beneficial in reducing T_{mrt} and affecting PET levels in the W-Gc and W-Gf cases. According to Xiao and Yuizono [48], in the ENVI-met simulation for summer, planting more evergreen trees results in a more comfortable environment than planting deciduous trees, which is consistent with this finding. Compared to other studies that have improved cooling potential by urban tree effects [6,7,48], this study's contribution validated that urban tree strategies (Gc, Ge, and Gf) could mitigate thermal comfort during the day and night (Figure 11). Accordingly, the best strategy to promote the regeneration of the Komatsu community is to validate multiple thermal mitigation to capture urban physical features (i.e., scale, climatic characteristics, cooling, humidification, and time mitigation). The introduction of optimal strategies allows a more climate-responsive architectural design of the community for renewal, adapting to the summer characteristics of the Cfa climate.

5.5. Limitations

Here, this study selected two typical building types of Japanese communities in a hot-humid climate context and used the combination of numerical simulation and thermal index assessment to select a synergistic landscape design strategy. However, some limitations and areas for improvement in the simulation method and our outcomes are listed as follows. (i) In the synergistic landscape design strategy, implementations focused on natural solutions to mitigate the thermal environment regarding planting design with structure, layout, tree numbers, green roofs/facades, and water body design. The pavement material was only replaced in the W-Gf case, which lessened the consideration of the cooling ground material. Simultaneously, this model of the urban community focuses on improving the thermal environment in the summer and lacks an assessment of the overall renewal of the area in all seasons. (ii) In the ENVI-met simulation, no explicit microclimate sensitivity parameters were given for native trees and green roofs/facades. Instead, the default arbor types settings and LAD values were used in ENVI-met V5.0.1, which has some limitations on the model accuracy. Unlike other studies, most low LAD trees were replaced with different tree species. Among them, the practice of substituting coniferous trees for evergreen ones in this study is relatively less in reference cases [72]. (iii) There are some limitations in modeling water body design using fountain settings in ENVI-met, and most of the simulations investigating water body design replace the model with a fountain model, lacking specific parameter settings and iterations of model algorithms.

6. Conclusions

Synergistic landscape design strategies were proposed and assessed thermal environments in densely populated Japanese communities to guide anticipatory design decisions and guidance for urban renewal and resilience. Summer thermal comfort was analyzed using the PET thermal index and microclimatic parameters. ENVI-met V5 reproduced the current and alternative cases to simulate and apply the new design at a small and large scale. The community-based design strategies in a mechanism were systematically examined and compared. A three-level optimization method demonstrates its effectiveness. Key findings include:

(1) Applying a systematic SDLS mechanism to the urban community created an optimal strategy using a water body and green roof at two scales, which proved effective in microclimate and thermal improvement in summer during the day and night, optimizing outdoor comfort all day in 85% of cases.

(2) There are synergistic landscape design strategies that result from integrated water design, green roofs, and urban trees (i.e., three-level optimization method) on Japanese building-specific community forms to achieve better adaptive design for building form, landscape design, climatic characteristics, scale, and time mitigation that reduces occupant health risks in summer, especially improves thermal comfort from a very hot to warm level at 14:00.
(3) Regarding urban trees, adding evergreen or coniferous trees is more conducive to reducing the urban heat island phenomenon in a large-scale community. The optimal strategy "W" will be applied to the Komatsu City Renewal and Maintenance Plan project.

These planning strategies can guide a decision-making reference for landscape architects who design communities for the SDGs, including specific cases and other Japanese community areas characterized by Cfa-climates. Furthermore, our simulation results can provide design support for urban community planning and design to confirm the optimization of the thermal environment in hot summer, including the selection of urban trees.

Author Contributions: J.X.: Conceptualization, Methodology, Software, Validation, Formal analysis, Investigation, Data Curation, Writing—Original Draft, Writing—Review and Editing, Visualization; T.Y.: Resources, Software, Supervision, Writing—Review and Editing; R.L.: Conceptualization, Writing—Review and Editing. All authors have read and agreed to the published version of the manuscript.

Funding: This research received no external funding.

Institutional Review Board Statement: No applicable.

Informed Consent Statement: No applicable.

Data Availability Statement: The data presented in this study are available on request from corresponding author.

Acknowledgments: A very special thanks go to Zhao for his help in investigating the building environment in the study area. The authors also appreciate the anonymous reviewers who provided invaluable comments for this paper.

Conflicts of Interest: The authors declare no conflicts of interest.

Abbreviations

List of symbols

SLDS	Synergistic landscape design strategies
T_a	Air temperature
RH	Relative humidity
T_{mrt}	Mean radiant temperature
WD	Wind direction
WS	Wind speed
PMV	Predict mean voting index
PET	Physiologically equivalent temperature
UTCI	Universal thermal climate index
GBE	Green building envelopes
CFD	Computational fluid dynamics
EBM	Energy balance modeling
SDGs	Sustainable development goals
UHI	Urban heat island
HC	Single-family community
AC	Real estate flat community
BC	Mixed cluster community
JMA	Japan meteorological agency
LAD	Leaf area density index
R^2	Coefficient of determination

RMSE	Root-mean-square error
L	Planting design
R	Green roof
F	Green facade and green roof
W	Water body and green roof
GBE	Green building envelopes
T_n	Tree number
RANS	Reynolds Averaged Navier-Stokes

Appendix A

Table A1. Mean values of the simulation microclimate condition (at 1.8 m height) for the Synergistic Landscape Design Strategies (SLDS) (from a to c) on a small scale.

Simulation Runs in a Small-Scale	Code	Case	Mean T_a in HC (°C)	Mean RH in HC (%)	Mean WS in HC (m/s)	Mean T_{mrt} in HC (°C)	Mean T_a in AC (°C)	Mean RH in AC (%)	Mean WS in AC (m/s)	Mean T_{mrt} in AC (°C)
Current case		L1	29.2	62.5	0.9	38.0	29.4	62.2	0.9	30.9
Planting design case	L1–4	L2	29.1	62.3	1.1	35.2	29.4	62.6	1.9	31.4
		L3	29.0	63.5	0.7	33.1	29.5	62.8	1.7	32.1
		L4	29.1	62.5	1.1	35.0	29.5	62.9	1.7	31.5
Renewal small-scale cases	R1–4	R1	29.2	63.0	0.9	39.1	29.5	63.0	1.7	31.4
		R2	29.0	62.7	1.2	35.3	29.4	63.1	1.6	30.7
		R3	29.1	63.8	0.8	34.7	29.5	62.7	1.8	33.0
		R4	29.1	63.1	0.7	34.6	29.5	62.7	1.6	31.4
	F1–4	F1	29.1	63.3	0.6	37.3	29.5	62.6	1.6	33.5
		F2	29.1	63.8	1.1	35.2	29.5	62.8	1.9	32.3
		F3	29.0	64.5	1.2	34.4	29.5	62.9	1.7	32.3
		F4	29.1	63.1	1.2	35.2	29.4	62.7	0.9	34.2
	W1–4	W1	26.9	77.7	0.6	36.0	29.0	65.9	1.9	32.2
		W2	27.4	72.6	0.3	32.7	29.1	64.8	1.7	31.4
		W3	28.2	67.8	1.0	34.8	29.0	65.8	1.7	31.5
		W4	27.3	73.6	1.3	34.8	29.3	63.3	1.0	33.8

Table A2. Microclimate conditions at 14:00 (at 1.8 m height) for the Synergistic Landscape Design Strategies (SLDS) (from a to c) on a small scale.

Simulation Runs in a Small-Scale	Code	Case	Mean T_a in HC (°C)	Mean RH in HC (%)	Mean WS in HC (m/s)	Mean T_{mrt} in HC (°C)	Mean T_a in AC (°C)	Mean RH in AC (%)	Mean WS in AC (m/s)	Mean T_{mrt} in AC (°C)
Current case		L1	32.1	54.9	0.8	57.3	32.3	53.9	0.9	43.3
Planting design case	L1–4	L2	31.8	54.4	1.1	54.9	32.8	52.5	1.9	46.3
		L3	31.8	56.3	0.7	50.4	33.0	52.2	1.7	46.5
		L4	31.8	55.0	1.1	54.3	33.0	52.2	1.6	46.3
Renewal small-scale cases	R1–4	R1	32.1	55.6	0.8	57.3	33.0	52.4	1.7	45.7
		R2	31.8	54.9	1.2	55.0	32.9	52.5	1.5	45.0
		R3	31.9	56.6	0.7	53.3	33.0	52.2	1.8	47.7
		R4	31.8	55.9	0.7	53.3	32.9	52.3	1.6	45.9
	F1–4	F1	31.9	56.3	0.6	55.8	32.9	54.2	1.5	47.6
		F2	32.2	54.9	1.1	54.4	32.9	52.9	1.9	46.9
		F3	31.8	57.5	1.2	52.6	33.0	52.4	1.7	46.4
		F4	31.8	56.1	1.1	54.2	32.7	53.3	1.0	46.0
	W1–4	W1	30.2	67.0	0.6	55.4	32.5	54.6	1.9	47.3
		W2	30.3	63.0	0.3	49.9	32.6	53.7	1.7	46.4
		W3	31.0	60.4	1.0	53.7	32.5	54.6	1.7	46.0
		W4	30.2	63.8	1.3	54.1	32.5	53.5	1.1	45.9

Table A3. Mean values of the simulation microclimate condition (at 1.8 m height) for the Synergistic Landscape Design Strategies (SLDS) (from d) on a large scale.

Simulation Runs in a Large-Scale	Code	Case	Mean T_a in BC (°C)	Mean RH in BC (%)	Mean WS in BC (m/s)	Mean T_{mrt} in BC (°C)
Current case		Ga	29.1	60.8	0.4	29.6
Renewal large-scale cases	W-Ga-f	W-Gb	28.6	64.5	0.5	31.7
		W-Gc	28.3	66.1	0.3	28.7
		W-Gd	28.6	65.4	0.5	30.1
		W-Ge	28.5	64.9	0.4	32.0
		W-Gf	28.3	65.9	0.5	29.4

Table A4. Microclimate conditions at 14:00 (at 1.8 m height) for the Synergistic Landscape Design Strategies (SLDS) (from d) on a large scale.

Simulation Runs in a Large-Scale	Code	Case	Mean T_a in BC (°C)	Mean RH in BC (%)	Mean WS in BC (m/s)	Mean T_{mrt} in BC (°C)
Current case		Ga	31.7	53.4	0.4	43.6
Renewal large-scale cases	W-Ga-f	W-Gb	31.2	57.5	0.5	47.5
		W-Gc	30.6	60.1	0.3	41.9
		W-Gd	31.2	58.3	0.5	44.8
		W-Ge	31.0	58.5	0.4	47.3
		W-Gf	30.6	60.6	0.2	42.9

References

1. Zhang, Q. Residential Energy Consumption in China and Its Comparison with Japan, Canada, and USA. *Energy Build.* **2004**, *36*, 1217–1225. [CrossRef]
2. Rosenfeld, A.; Akbari, H.; Romm, J.; Pomerantz, M. Cool Communities: Strategies for Heat Island Mitigation and Smog Reduction. *Energy Build.* **1998**, *28*, 51–62. [CrossRef]
3. Peeters, L.; De Dear, R.; Hensen, J.; D'haeseleer, W. Thermal Comfort in Residential Buildings: Comfort Values and Scales for Building Energy Simulation. *Appl. Energy* **2009**, *86*, 772–780. [CrossRef]
4. Peng, L.L.H.; Jiang, Z.; Yang, X.; Wang, Q.; He, Y.; Chen, S.S. Energy Savings of Block-Scale Facade Greening for Different Urban Forms. *Appl. Energy* **2020**, *279*, 115844. [CrossRef]
5. Rui, L.; Buccolieri, R.; Gao, Z.; Gatto, E.; Ding, W. Study of the Effect of Green Quantity and Structure on Thermal Comfort and Air Quality in an Urban-like Residential District by ENVI-Met Modelling. *Build. Simul.* **2019**, *12*, 183–194. [CrossRef]
6. Rui, L.; Buccolieri, R.; Gao, Z.; Ding, W.; Shen, J. The Impact of Green Space Layouts on Microclimate and Air Quality in Residential Districts of Nanjing, China. *Forests* **2018**, *9*, 224. [CrossRef]
7. Zhang, L.; Zhan, Q.; Lan, Y. Effects of the Tree Distribution and Species on Outdoor Environment Conditions in a Hot Summer and Cold Winter Zone: A Case Study in Wuhan Residential Quarters. *Build. Environ.* **2018**, *130*, 27–39. [CrossRef]
8. Zheng, T.; Qu, K.; Darkwa, J.; Calautit, J.K. Evaluating Urban Heat Island Mitigation Strategies for a Subtropical City Centre (a Case Study in Osaka, Japan). *Energy* **2022**, *250*, 123721. [CrossRef]
9. Srivanit, M.; Jareemit, D. Modeling the Influences of Layouts of Residential Townhouses and Tree-Planting Patterns on Outdoor Thermal Comfort in Bangkok Suburb. *J. Build. Eng.* **2020**, *30*, 101262. [CrossRef]
10. Liao, J.; Tan, X.; Li, J. Evaluating the Vertical Cooling Performances of Urban Vegetation Scenarios in a Residential Environment. *J. Build. Eng.* **2021**, *39*, 102313. [CrossRef]
11. Xu, T.; Sathaye, J.; Akbari, H.; Garg, V.; Tetali, S. Quantifying the Direct Benefits of Cool Roofs in an Urban Setting: Reduced Cooling Energy Use and Lowered Greenhouse Gas Emissions. *Build. Environ.* **2012**, *48*, 1–6. [CrossRef]
12. Levinson, R.; Akbari, H.; Levinson, R.; Akbari, H. Potential Benefits of Cool Roofs on Commercial Buildings: Conserving Energy, Saving Money, and Reducing Emission of Greenhouse Gases and Air Pollutants. *Energy Effic.* **2010**, *3*, 53–109. [CrossRef]
13. Liu, Z.; Cheng, W.; Jim, C.Y.; Morakinyo, T.E.; Shi, Y.; Ng, E. Heat Mitigation Benefits of Urban Green and Blue Infrastructures: A Systematic Review of Modeling Techniques, Validation and Scenario Simulation in ENVI-Met V4. *Build. Environ.* **2021**, *200*, 107939. [CrossRef]
14. Kleerekoper, L.; Van Esch, M.; Salcedo, T.B. How to Make a City Climate-Proof, Addressing the Urban Heat Island Effect. *Resour. Conserv. Recycl.* **2012**, *64*, 30–38. [CrossRef]
15. Zhang, Z.; Lv, Y.; Pan, H. Cooling and Humidifying Effect of Plant Communities in Subtropical Urban Parks. *Urban For. Urban Green.* **2013**, *12*, 323–329. [CrossRef]
16. Ge, J.; Wang, Y.; Akbari, H.; Zhou, D.; Gu, Z.; Meng, X. Cooling Energy Saving by Vegetation Planting in High-Density Districts: Evaluation Using the Coupled Simulation. *Build. Environ.* **2023**, *232*, 110054. [CrossRef]

17. Castiglia Feitosa, R.; Wilkinson, S.J. Attenuating Heat Stress through Green Roof and Green Wall Retrofit. *Build. Environ.* **2018**, *140*, 11–22. [CrossRef]
18. Herath, H.; Halwatura, R.; Jayasinghe, G. Modeling a Tropical Urban Context with Green Walls and Green Roofs as an Urban Heat Island Adaptation Strategy. *Procedia Eng.* **2018**, *213*, 691–698. [CrossRef]
19. Knaus, M.; Haase, D. Green Roof Effects on Daytime Heat in a Prefabricated Residential Neighbourhood in Berlin, Germany. Urban For. *Urban Green.* **2020**, *53*, 126738. [CrossRef]
20. Kim, J.; Lee, S.; Kang, J. Temperature Reduction Effects of Rooftop Garden Arrangements: A Case Study of Seoul National University. *Sustainability* **2020**, *12*, 6032. [CrossRef]
21. Medl, A.; Stangl, R.; Florineth, F. Vertical Greening Systems–A Review on Recent Technologies and Research Advancement. *Build. Environ.* **2017**, *125*, 227–237. [CrossRef]
22. Eumorfopoulou, E.; Kontoleon, K. Experimental Approach to the Contribution of Plant-Covered Walls to the Thermal Behaviour of Building Envelopes. *Build. Environ.* **2009**, *44*, 1024–1038. [CrossRef]
23. Jim, C.Y. Thermal Performance of Climber Greenwalls: Effects of Solar Irradiance and Orientation. *Appl. Energy* **2015**, *154*, 631–643. [CrossRef]
24. Yang, F.; Yuan, F.; Qian, F.; Zhuang, Z.; Yao, J. Summertime Thermal and Energy Performance of a Double-Skin Green Facade: A Case Study in Shanghai. *Sustain. Cities Soc.* **2018**, *39*, 43–51. [CrossRef]
25. Pérez, G.; Coma, J.; Sol, S.; Cabeza, L. Green Facade for Energy Savings in Buildings: The Influence of Leaf Area Index and Facade Orientation on the Shadow Effect. *Appl. Energy* **2017**, *187*, 424–437. [CrossRef]
26. Cuce, E. Thermal Regulation Impact of Green Walls: An Experimental and Numerical Investigation. *Appl. Energy* **2017**, *194*, 247–254. [CrossRef]
27. Perez, G.; Rincon, L.; Vila, A.; Gonzalez, J.; Cabeza, L. Green Vertical Systems for Buildings as Passive Systems for Energy Savings. *Appl. Energy* **2011**, *88*, 4854–4859. [CrossRef]
28. Hoelscher, M.; Nehls, T.; Jänicke, B.; Wessolek, G. Quantifying Cooling Effects of Facade Greening: Shading, Transpiration and Insulation. *Energy Build.* **2016**, *114*, 283–290. [CrossRef]
29. Perini, K.; Ottelé, M.; Fraaij, A.; Haas, E. Vertical Greening Systems and the Effect on Air Flow and Temperature on the Building Envelope. *Build. Environ.* **2011**, *46*, 2287–2294. [CrossRef]
30. Salata, F.; Golasi, I.; Petitti, D.; de Lieto Vollaro, E.; Coppi, M.; de Lieto Vollaro, A. Relating Microclimate, Human Thermal Comfort and Health during Heat Waves: An Analysis of Heat Island Mitigation Strategies through a Case Study in an Urban Outdoor Environment. *Sustain. Cities Soc.* **2017**, *30*, 79–96. [CrossRef]
31. Tan, Z.; Lau, K.K.L.; Ng, E. Urban Tree Design Approaches for Mitigating Daytime Urban Heat Island Effects in a High-Density Urban Environment. *Energy Build.* **2016**, *114*, 265–274. [CrossRef]
32. Teshnehdel, S.; Akbari, H.; Di Giuseppe, E.; Brown, R.D. Effect of Tree Cover and Tree Species on Microclimate and Pedestrian Comfort in a Residential District in Iran. *Build. Environ.* **2020**, *178*, 106899. [CrossRef]
33. Zhang, A.; Bokel, R.; van den Dobbelsteen, A.; Sun, Y.; Huang, Q.; Zhang, Q. An Integrated School and Schoolyard Design Method for Summer Thermal Comfort and Energy Efficiency in Northern China. *Build. Environ.* **2017**, *124*, 369–387. [CrossRef]
34. Kim, J.; Hong, T.; Jeong, J.; Koo, C.; Jeong, K. An Optimization Model for Selecting the Optimal Green Systems by Considering the Thermal Comfort and Energy Consumption. *Appl. Energy* **2016**, *169*, 682–695. [CrossRef]
35. Ulpiani, G.; di Perna, C.; Zinzi, M. Water Nebulization to Counteract Urban Overheating: Development and Experimental Test of a Smart Logic to Maximize Energy Efficiency and Outdoor. *Appl. Energy* **2019**, *239*, 1091–1113. [CrossRef]
36. Feitosa, R.C.; Wilkinson, S. Retrofitted Green Roofs and Walls and Improvements in Thermal Comfort. *AIP Conf. Proc.* **2017**, *1856*, 020006.
37. Lai, D.; Liu, W.; Gan, T.; Liu, K.; Chen, Q. A Review of Mitigating Strategies to Improve the Thermal Environment and Thermal Comfort in Urban Outdoor Spaces. *Sci. Total Environ.* **2019**, *661*, 337–353. [CrossRef]
38. Yang, Y.; Gatto, E.; Gao, Z.; Buccolieri, R.; Morakinyo, T.E.; Lan, H. The "Plant Evaluation Model" for the Assessment of the Impact of Vegetation on Outdoor Microclimate in the Urban Environment. *Build. Environ.* **2019**, *159*, 106151. [CrossRef]
39. Potchter, O.; Cohen, P.; Lin, T.P.; Matzarakis, A. Outdoor Human Thermal Perception in Various Climates: A Comprehensive Review of Approaches, Methods and Quantification. *Sci. Total Environ.* **2018**, *631–632*, 390–406. [CrossRef]
40. De Dear, R.J.; Akimoto, T.; Arens, E.A.; Brager, G.; Candido, C.; Cheong, K.W.D.; Li, B.; Nishihara, N.; Sekhar, S.C.; Tanabe, S.; et al. Progress in Thermal Comfort Research over the Last Twenty Years. *Indoor Air* **2013**, *23*, 442–461. [CrossRef]
41. Crank, P.J.; Sailor, D.J.; Ban-Weiss, G.; Taleghani, M. Evaluating the ENVI-Met Microscale Model for Suitability in Analysis of Targeted Urban Heat Mitigation Strategies. *Urban Clim.* **2018**, *26*, 188–197. [CrossRef]
42. Lee, H.; Mayer, H.; Chen, L. Contribution of Trees and Grasslands to the Mitigation of Human Heat Stress in a Residential District of Freiburg, Southwest Germany. *Landsc. Urban Plan.* **2016**, *148*, 37–50. [CrossRef]
43. Herath, H.M.P.I.K.; Halwatura, R.U.; Jayasinghe, G.Y. Evaluation of Green Infrastructure Effects on Tropical Sri Lankan Urban Context as an Urban Heat Island Adaptation Strategy. *Urban For. Urban Green.* **2018**, *29*, 212–222. [CrossRef]
44. Wu, Z.; Chen, L. Optimizing the Spatial Arrangement of Trees in Residential Neighborhoods for Better Cooling Effects: Integrating Modeling with in-Situ Measurements. *Landsc. Urban Plan.* **2017**, *167*, 463–472. [CrossRef]
45. Ouyang, W.; Sinsel, T.; Simon, H.; Morakinyo, T.E.; Liu, H.; Ng, E. Evaluating the Thermal-Radiative Performance of ENVI-Met Model for Green Infrastructure Typologies: Experience from a Subtropical Climate. *Build. Environ.* **2022**, *207*, 108427. [CrossRef]

46. Abdallah, A.S.H.; Mahmoud, R.M.A. Urban Morphology as an Adaptation Strategy to Improve Outdoor Thermal Comfort in Urban Residential Community of New Assiut City, Egypt. *Sustain. Cities Soc.* **2022**, *78*, 103648. [CrossRef]
47. Liu, S.; Pan, W.; Zhang, H.; Cheng, X.; Long, Z.; Chen, Q. CFD Simulations of Wind Distribution in an Urban Community with a Full-Scale Geometrical Model. *Build. Environ.* **2017**, *117*, 11–23. [CrossRef]
48. Xiao, J.; Yuizono, T. Climate-Adaptive Landscape Design: Microclimate and Thermal Comfort Regulation of Station Square in the Hokuriku Region, Japan. *Build. Environ.* **2022**, *212*, 108813. [CrossRef]
49. Urban Design Vision Action Plan/Komatsu City Website. Available online: https://www.city.komatsu.lg.jp (accessed on 28 August 2022).
50. Kottek, M.; Grieser, J.; Beck, C.; Rudolf, B.; Rubel, F. World Map of the Köppen-Geiger Climate Classification Updated. *Meteorol. Z.* **2006**, *15*, 259–263. [CrossRef]
51. Magic, V. WeatherSpark Website. Available online: https://weatherspark.com (accessed on 7 April 2022).
52. Schmunk, R.B. Data.GISS: GISS Surface Temperature Analysis (v4): Global Maps. Available online: https://data.giss.nasa.gov/gistemp/maps/index_v4.html (accessed on 7 August 2022).
53. Japan Meteorological Agency (JMA). Available online: https://www.data.jma.go.jp/risk/obsdl/index.php (accessed on 7 April 2022).
54. Wu, H.W.; Kumar, P.; Cao, S.J. Implementation of Green Infrastructure for Improving the Building Environment of Elderly Care Centres. *J. Build. Eng.* **2022**, *54*, 104682. [CrossRef]
55. Shi, Y.; Ren, C.; Zheng, Y.; Ng, E. Mapping the Urban Microclimatic Spatial Distribution in a Sub-Tropical High-Density Urban Environment. *Archit. Sci. Rev.* **2016**, *59*, 370–384. [CrossRef]
56. Forouzandeh, A. Prediction of Surface Temperature of Building Surrounding Envelopes Using Holistic Microclimate ENVI-Met Model. *Sustain. Cities Soc.* **2021**, *70*, 102878. [CrossRef]
57. Bruse, M.; Fleer, H. Simulating Surface-Plant-Air Interactions inside Urban Environments with a Three Dimensional Numerical Model. *Environ. Model. Softw.* **1998**, *13*, 373–384. [CrossRef]
58. Cui, L.; Rupprecht, C.D.D.; Shibata, S. Climate-Responsive Green-Space Design Inspired by Traditional Gardens: Microclimate and Human Thermal Comfort of Japanese Gardens. *Sustainability* **2021**, *13*, 2736. [CrossRef]
59. Höppe, P. The Physiological Equivalent Temperature—A Universal Index for the Biometeorological Assessment of the Thermal Environment. *Int. J. Biometeorol.* **1999**, *43*, 71–75. [CrossRef] [PubMed]
60. Lin, T.P.; Matzarakis, A. Tourism Climate and Thermal Comfort in Sun Moon Lake, Taiwan. *Int. J. Biometeorol.* **2008**, *52*, 281–290. [CrossRef]
61. Getter, K.; Rowe, D. The Role of Extensive Green Roofs in Sustainable Development. *HortScience* **2006**, *41*, 1276–1285. [CrossRef]
62. Herrera-Gomez, S.; Quevedo-Nolasco, A. The Role of Green Roofs in Climate Change Mitigation. A Case Study in Seville (Spain). *Build. Environ.* **2017**, *123*, 575–584. [CrossRef]
63. Hunter, A.; Williams, N.; Rayner, J.; Aye, L.; Hes, D.; Livesley, S.J. Quantifying the Thermal Performance of Green Façades: A Critical Review. *Ecol. Eng.* **2014**, *63*, 102–113. [CrossRef]
64. Moriasi, D.N.; Arnold, J.G.; Van Liew, M.W.; Bingner, R.L.; Harmel, R.D.; Veith, T.L. Model Evaluation Guidelines for Systematic Quantification of Accuracy in Watershed Simulations. *Trans. ASABE* **1983**, *50*, 885–990. [CrossRef]
65. Hong, B.; Lin, B. Numerical Studies of the Outdoor Wind Environment and Thermal Comfort at Pedestrian Level in Housing Blocks with Different Building Layout Patterns and Trees Arrangement. *Renew. Energy* **2015**, *73*, 18–27. [CrossRef]
66. Lalošević, M.D.; Komatina, M.S.; Miloš, M.V.; Rudonja, N.R. Green Roofs and Cool Materials as Retrofitting Strategies for Urban Heat Island Mitigation: Case Study in Belgrade, Serbia. *Therm. Sci.* **2018**, *22*, 2309–2324. [CrossRef]
67. Nishimura, N.; Nomura, T.; Iyota, H.; Kimoto, S. Novel Water Facilities for Creation of Comfortable Urban Micrometeorology. *Sol. Energy* **1998**, *64*, 197–207. [CrossRef]
68. Zhang, G.; He, B.; Zhu, Z.; Dewancker, B. Impact of Morphological Characteristics of Green Roofs on Pedestrian Cooling in Subtropical Climates. *Int. J. Environ. Res. Public Health* **2016**, *16*, 179. [CrossRef] [PubMed]
69. Jin, C.; Bai, X.; Luo, T.; Zou, M. Effects of Green Roofs' Variations on the Regional Thermal Environment Using Measurements and Simulations in Chongqing, China. Urban For. *Urban Green.* **2018**, *29*, 223–237. [CrossRef]
70. Peng, L.L.H.; Jiang, Z.; Yang, X.; He, Y.; Xu, T.; Chen, S.S. Cooling Effects of Block-Scale Facade Greening and Their Relationship with Urban Form. *Build. Environ.* **2020**, *169*, 106552. [CrossRef]
71. Lobaccaro, G.; Acero, J.A. Comparative Analysis of Green Actions to Improve Outdoor Thermal Comfort inside Typical Urban Street Canyons. *Urban Clim.* **2015**, *14*, 251–267. [CrossRef]
72. Abdi, B.; Hami, A.; Zarehaghi, D. Impact of Small-Scale Tree Planting Patterns on Outdoor Cooling and Thermal Comfort. *Sustain. Cities Soc.* **2020**, *56*, 102085. [CrossRef]

International Journal of
Geo-Information

MDPI

Article

Globally Optimal Relative Pose and Scale Estimation from Only Image Correspondences with Known Vertical Direction

Zhenbao Yu [1], Shirong Ye [1,*], Changwei Liu [2], Ronghe Jin [3], Pengfei Xia [1] and Kang Yan [1]

1 Global Navigation Satellite System (GNSS) Research Center, Wuhan University, Wuhan 430072, China; zhenbaoyu@whu.edu.cn (Z.Y.); pfxia130@whu.edu.cn (P.X.); 2020106180011@whu.edu.cn (K.Y.)
2 School of Future Technology, South China University of Technology, Guangzhou 510641, China; liuchw01@pcl.ac.cn
3 School of Remote Sensing and Information Engineering, Wuhan University, Wuhan 430072, China; huanhexiao@whu.edu.cn
* Correspondence: srye@whu.edu.cn

Abstract: Installing multi-camera systems and inertial measurement units (IMUs) in self-driving cars, micro aerial vehicles, and robots is becoming increasingly common. An IMU provides the vertical direction, allowing coordinate frames to be aligned in a common direction. The degrees of freedom (DOFs) of the rotation matrix are reduced from 3 to 1. In this paper, we propose a globally optimal solver to calculate the relative poses and scale of generalized cameras with a known vertical direction. First, the cost function is established to minimize algebraic error in the least-squares sense. Then, the cost function is transformed into two polynomials with only two unknowns. Finally, the eigenvalue method is used to solve the relative rotation angle. The performance of the proposed method is verified on both simulated and KITTI datasets. Experiments show that our method is more accurate than the existing state-of-the-art solver in estimating the relative pose and scale. Compared to the best method among the comparison methods, the method proposed in this paper reduces the rotation matrix error, translation vector error, and scale error by 53%, 67%, and 90%, respectively.

Keywords: globally optimal solver; relative pose estimation; scale; known vertical direction; minimizing algebraic error

1. Introduction

Estimating the relative pose from two views is a cornerstone in multi-view geometry problems which has been applied in many fields, such as visual odometry (VO) [1,2], structure from motion (SfM) [3,4], and simultaneous localization and mapping (SLAM) [5–7]. In addition, the camera sensor for indoor positioning is also an application [8–10]. The multi-camera system consists of multiple individual cameras fixed on a system. It has the advantages of a large field of view and high precision in relative pose estimation. Therefore, a large number of scholars have studied how to improve the accuracy, robustness, and efficiency of the relative pose estimation algorithm.

Compared with the standard pinhole camera, the multi-camera system lacks a single projection center. To solve this problem, Plücker lines are proposed to represent the light rays that pass through the multi-camera system [8]. This model is called the generalized camera model (GCM) [11], which describes the relationship between the Plücker lines and the generalized essential matrix. Generalized cameras are widely used in fields such as autonomous driving, robotics, and micro aerial vehicles. Pless proposed calculating the relative poses of multiple cameras using 17-point correspondences. Some methods have been developed on multi-camera relative pose estimation using the generic camera model [12–17]. However, these algorithms can estimate multi-camera poses only if the distances between all camera centers are known. This assumption limits the use of the generic camera model. In this paper, we focus on estimating the relative poses and scales of the generic camera model.

The relative pose and scale of the multi-camera system consist of a total of 7 degrees of freedom (DOFs), including 3 DOFs of the rotation matrix, 3 DOFs of translation vectors, and 1 DOF for scale, as shown in Figure 1. To improve the relative pose estimation of the camera and reduce the minimum number of required feature point pairs, an auxiliary sensor, such as an IMU, is often added [13–15,18–20]. An IMU can provide the yaw, pitch, and roll angles. The pitch and roll angles are more accurate than the yaw angle [21]. Therefore, we can use the pitch and roll angle provided by the IMU to reduce the degrees of freedom of the rotation matrix from 3 to 1. In this case, the relative pose and scale of the multi-camera system consist of a total of 5 degrees of freedom (DOFs). Thus, only five feature point pairs are needed to estimate the relative poses and scales of the camera [22].

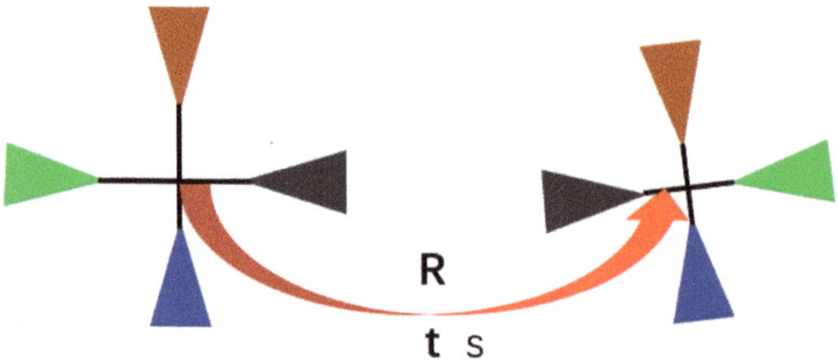

Figure 1. The rotation matrix, translation vector, and scale are **R**, **t**, and s, respectively.

Depending on the number of points required to solve the relative poses of a multi-camera system, solvers can be divided into minimum sample solvers and non-minimum sample solvers. When the distance between camera centers is known, a large number of scholars have used both minimum and non-minimum samples to solve for the relative poses of cameras. A constraint equation for the rotation matrix, translation vector, scale, and Plücker lines in the generic camera model is proposed in [22]. The minimum solution for a known vertical direction is also known. This method avoids 3D point noise in the calculation of relative poses and scale using the method with 2D-3D point correspondences. A simple heuristic global energy minimization scheme based on local minimum suppression is proposed in [23]. However, this method is not a closed-form solver.

This paper mainly focuses on globally optimal relative pose and scale estimation from 2D-2D point correspondences. Cameras and IMUs, such as mobile phones, unmanned aerial vehicles, and autonomous vehicles, are usually fixed together, so we assume the vertical direction is known. The main contributions of this paper are summarized below:

- A novel globally optimal solver to estimate relative pose and scale is proposed from N 2D-2D point correspondences ($N > 5$). This problem is transformed into a cost function based on the least-squares sense to minimize algebraic error.
- We transform the cost function to solve two unknowns in two equations, which are composed of the parameter of the relative rotation angle. The highest degree of rotation angle parameter is 16.
- We derive and provide a solver based on polynomial eigenvalues to calculate the relative rotation angle parameter. The translation vector and scale information are obtained from the corresponding eigenvectors.

The rest of this paper is organized as follows. We review the related work in Section 2. In Section 3, we introduce methodology, including the generalized epipolar constraint, problem description, and globally optional solver. We test the performance of the proposed method on synthetic and real-world data and discuss this in Section 4. The conclusions are presented in Section 5.

2. Related Work

Multi-camera relative pose estimation has received significant attention in academia and industry. The multi-camera model differs from the standard pinhole model due to the absence of a single center of projection in the multi-camera system.

Grossberg and Nayar introduced the generalized camera model [24]. To describe the lines sampled in space for each pixel in a multi-camera system, Pless proposed using Plücker lines to express light rays and provide the relationship between the Plücker vector, the rotation matrix, and the translation vector [11]. The generalized camera model proposed by Pless has been widely used in multi-cameras. Stewenius et al. proposed an estimation of the relative pose using six-point correspondences in a multi-camera system [12]. This solver generates 64 solutions using the Gröbner basis technique. However, this method runs slow when solving for relative pose. Li et al. proposed a linear solver using 17-point correspondences [16]. Based on this, Li et al. analyzed the degeneracy of the 17-point method and proposed a new solver [25]. Some solvers were proposed where the IMU provides the pitch angle and roll angle. Lee et al. proposed a solver to estimate the yaw angle by computing an eight-degree univariate polynomial using four-point correspondences [13]. Sweeney et al. transformed the relative pose estimation problem into a quadratic eigenvalue problem [15]. Liu also proposed the use of four-point correspondences to calculate the relative pose of the camera [14]. Guan et al. proposed four solutions using affine correspondences in a multi-camera system [26]. Kneip utilized the minimization of the algebraic error to build the objective function to solve the rotation matrix and then calculated the translation vector based on the eigenvalues and eigenvectors [17]. Zhao proposed a globally optimal solver by transforming the minimization of the sum of squares of residuals constructed from generalized epipolar constraints into quadratically constrained quadratic programming (QCQP) [27]. Ding proposed a novel globally optimal solver using polynomial eigenvalue when the vertical direction is known [18].

All of the above methods are based on the case where the internal scale between two multi-camera systems is known. However, the internal scale of each view is difficult to obtain or is ambiguous. So, it is necessary to estimate the scale information of the camera. Ventura et al. provided a minimal solver to estimate the absolute pose and scale of the generalized camera using four 2D-3D correspondences [24]. This solver produces eight solutions. Sweeney et al. proposed a globally optimal solver from four or more 2D-3D correspondences [28]. This method does not need iterations or initialization in the process of solving. The accuracy of pose and scale estimation using 2D-3D correspondence is greatly affected by the depth because this method relies on the accuracy of 3D. To reduce the influence of depth, some scholars propose using 2D-2D correspondence to calculate relative pose and scale.

Sweeney first proposed using 2D-2D correspondence to calculate the relative poses and scale between two generalized cameras. A constraint on the rotation matrix, translation vector, scale, and Plücker vector was presented. The authors provided two solvers (a quadratic eigenvalue solver and a closed-form solver) when the vertical direction is known based on five-point correspondences. Experiments showed that they are ill-conditioned and very unstable in quadratic eigenvalue solutions [22]. Kneip dropped the assumption of known vertical direction. Kneip transformed the relative pose and scale problem into a symmetric eigenvalue problem. The method computes the rotation matrix by direct search using a minimally suppressed heuristic global optimization method [23]. However, the method is not a closed-form solution. Recently, the solver of polynomial eigenvalue has been widely applied in the field of camera pose estimation [29–32].

3. Methodology

3.1. Epipolar Constraint

In a multi-camera system, we define a corresponding point pair $(\mathbf{x}_{ki}, \mathbf{x}_{k'j}, \mathbf{R}_{ki}, \mathbf{R}_{k'j}, \mathbf{t}_{ki}, \mathbf{t}_{k'j})$, where $\mathbf{x}_{ki}$ is the normalized homogeneous coordinate of the i-th camera capture image in the k frame and $\mathbf{x}_{k'j}$ is the normalized homogeneous coordinate of the j-th camera capture image in the $k+1$ frames. The rotation matrix and translation vector of the i-th camera in the k frame are $\mathbf{R}_{ki}$ and $\mathbf{t}_{ki}$. The rotation matrix and translation vector of the j-th camera in the $k+1$ frame are $\mathbf{R}_{k'j}$ and $\mathbf{t}_{k'j}$ in Figure 2. $\mathbf{I}_{ki}$ and $\mathbf{I}_{k'j}$ denote a pair of corresponding Plücker line vectors pointing at k and $k+1$ frames. The Plücker line vector is written as follows:

$$\mathbf{I}_{ki} = \begin{pmatrix} \mathbf{f}_{ki} \\ \mathbf{t}_{ki} \times \mathbf{f}_{ki} \end{pmatrix}, \ \mathbf{I}_{k'j} = \begin{pmatrix} \mathbf{f}_{k'j} \\ \mathbf{t}_{k'j} \times \mathbf{f}_{k'j} \end{pmatrix}, \tag{1}$$

where $\mathbf{f}_{ki}$ and $\mathbf{f}_{k'j}$ denote the direction vectors of the corresponding rays between the two generalized cameras. $\mathbf{f}_{ki}$ and $\mathbf{f}_{k'j}$ are written as follows:

$$\mathbf{f}_{ki} = \frac{(\mathbf{R}_{ki}\mathbf{x}_{ki})}{||\mathbf{R}_{ki}\mathbf{x}_{ki}||}, \ \mathbf{f}_{k'j} = \frac{(\mathbf{R}_{k'j}\mathbf{x}_{k'j})}{\left\|\mathbf{R}_{k'j}\mathbf{x}_{k'j}\right\|}. \tag{2}$$

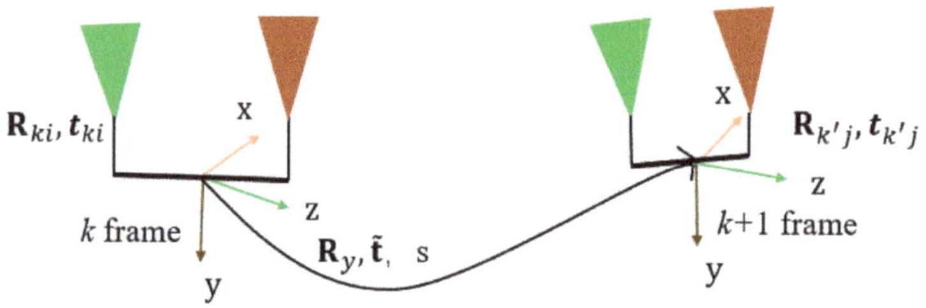

Figure 2. The rotation matrix and translation vector of the i-th camera in the k frame are $\mathbf{R}_{ki}$ and $\mathbf{t}_{ki}$. The rotation matrix and translation vector of the j-th camera in the $k+1$ frame are $\mathbf{R}_{k'j}$ and $\mathbf{t}_{k'j}$. The rotation matrix, translation vector, and scale vector between aligned k and $k+1$ are $\mathbf{R}_y$, $\tilde{\mathbf{t}}$, and s.

The generalized epipolar constraint is written as follows:

$$\mathbf{I}_{k'i}^T \begin{bmatrix} \mathbf{E} & \mathbf{R} \\ \mathbf{R} & 0 \end{bmatrix} \mathbf{I}_{ki} = 0, \tag{3}$$

where $\mathbf{R}$ and $\mathbf{t}$ represent the original rotation matrix and original translation vector, respectively. The essential matrix $\mathbf{E} = [\mathbf{t}]_\times \mathbf{R}$ and $[\mathbf{t}]_\times$ represents the antisymmetric matrix of $\mathbf{t}$.

$$\mathbf{f}_{k'j}^T \mathbf{E} \mathbf{f}_{ki} + \mathbf{f}_{k'j}^T (\mathbf{R}[\mathbf{t}_{k'j}]_\times - [\mathbf{t}_{ki}]_\times \mathbf{R}) \mathbf{f}_{ki} = 0. \tag{4}$$

A large number of solvers have been proposed for this problem. The premise of applying these methods is then based on the assumption that scale information has been reconciled. In the application, the scale information is fuzzy, so the above methods are not available. Therefore, we mainly focus on the relative pose estimation when the scale is unknown. Equation (5) can be easily obtained according to Equation (4).

$$\mathbf{f}_{k'j}^T \mathbf{E} \mathbf{f}_{ki} + \mathbf{f}_{k'j}^T (\mathbf{R}s[\mathbf{t}_{k'j}]_\times - [\mathbf{t}_{ki}]_\times \mathbf{R}) \mathbf{f}_{ki} = 0, \tag{5}$$

where s represents the scale. Similar to Equation (3), Equation (5) can be expressed as follows:

$$\mathbf{I}_{k'j}^T \begin{bmatrix} \mathbf{E} & \mathbf{R} \\ s\mathbf{R} & 0 \end{bmatrix} \mathbf{I}_{ki} = 0. \tag{6}$$

A multi-camera system is usually coupled with the IMU, which can provide the roll (θ_x) and pitch (θ_z) angles. We define the Y-axis of the camera coordinate system to be parallel to the vertical direction, and the X-Z plane is orthogonal to the Y-axis. $\mathbf{R}_{\text{imu}}$ and $\mathbf{R}'_{\text{imu}}$ are provided by the IMU at k and $k+1$ frame, respectively.

$$\mathbf{R}_{\text{imu}} = \mathbf{R}_x \mathbf{R}_z, \tag{7}$$

where $\mathbf{R}_x$ and $\mathbf{R}_z$ can be written as follows:

$$\mathbf{R}_x = \begin{bmatrix} 1 & 0 & 0 \\ 0 & \cos(\theta_x) & -\sin(\theta_x) \\ 0 & \sin(\theta_x) & \cos(\theta_x) \end{bmatrix}, \quad \mathbf{R}_z = \begin{bmatrix} \cos(\theta_z) & -\sin(\theta_z) & 0 \\ \sin(\theta_z) & \cos(\theta_z) & 0 \\ 0 & 0 & 1 \end{bmatrix}. \tag{8}$$

The rotation matrix and translation vector between the aligned frames k and $k+1$ are $\mathbf{R}_y$ and $\tilde{\mathbf{t}}$. The relationship between the original relative pose ($\mathbf{R}$ and $\mathbf{t}$) and the aligned relative pose ($\mathbf{R}_y$ and $\tilde{\mathbf{t}}$) can be expressed as follows:

$$\mathbf{R} = (\mathbf{R}'_{\text{imu}})^T \mathbf{R}_y \mathbf{R}_{\text{imu}}, \mathbf{t} = (\mathbf{R}'_{\text{imu}})^T \tilde{\mathbf{t}}, \tag{9}$$

where

$$\mathbf{R}_y = \begin{bmatrix} \cos(\theta_y) & 0 & \sin(\theta_y) \\ 0 & 1 & 0 \\ -\sin(\theta_y) & 0 & \cos(\theta_y) \end{bmatrix}, \tag{10}$$

where θ_y represents the rotation angle of the Y-axis. The rotation matrix $\mathbf{R}_y$ can be rewritten with the Cayley parameterization as follows:

$$\mathbf{R}_y = \frac{1}{1+y^2} \begin{bmatrix} 1-y^2 & 0 & 2y \\ 0 & 1 & 0 \\ -2y & 0 & 1-y^2 \end{bmatrix}, \tag{11}$$

where $y = \tan\frac{\theta_y}{2}$. In practical applications, $\theta_y = 180°$ is very rare [33].

By substituting Equation (9) into Equation (6), we can obtain

$$\left(\begin{bmatrix} \mathbf{R}'_{\text{imu}} & 0 \\ 0 & \mathbf{R}'_{\text{imu}} \end{bmatrix} \mathbf{I}_{k'j} \right)^T \cdot \begin{bmatrix} [\tilde{\mathbf{t}}]_\times \mathbf{R}_y & \mathbf{R}_y \\ s\mathbf{R}_y & 0 \end{bmatrix} \cdot \left(\begin{bmatrix} \mathbf{R}_{\text{imu}} & 0 \\ 0 & \mathbf{R}_{\text{imu}} \end{bmatrix} \mathbf{I}_{ki} \right) = 0. \tag{12}$$

By substituting Equation (1) into Equation (12), we can obtain

$$\begin{pmatrix} \mathbf{R}'_{\text{imu}} \mathbf{f}_{k'j} \\ \mathbf{R}'_{\text{imu}} (\mathbf{t}_{k'j} \times \mathbf{f}_{k'j}) \end{pmatrix}^T \cdot \begin{bmatrix} [\tilde{\mathbf{t}}]_\times \mathbf{R}_y & \mathbf{R}_y \\ s\mathbf{R}_y & 0 \end{bmatrix} \cdot \begin{pmatrix} \mathbf{R}_{\text{imu}} \mathbf{f}_{ki} \\ \mathbf{R}_{\text{imu}} (\mathbf{t}_{ki} \times \mathbf{f}_{ki}) \end{pmatrix} = 0. \tag{13}$$

3.2. Problem Description

Based on the constraint equation of Equation (13) in the previous section, Equation (13) can be rewritten as follows:

$$\underbrace{\begin{pmatrix} \mathbf{f}_{k'j} \times (\mathbf{R}'_{\text{imu}})^T \mathbf{R}_y \mathbf{R}_{\text{imu}} \mathbf{f}_{ki} \\ \mathbf{f}_{k'j}^T [\mathbf{t}_{k'j}]_\times (\mathbf{R}'_{\text{imu}})^T \mathbf{R}_y \mathbf{R}_{\text{imu}} \mathbf{f}_{ki} \\ -\mathbf{f}_{k'j}^T (\mathbf{R}'_{\text{imu}})^T \mathbf{R}_y \mathbf{R}_{\text{imu}} [\mathbf{t}_{ki}] \mathbf{f}_{ki} \end{pmatrix}^T}_{\mathbf{M}} \begin{pmatrix} \tilde{\mathbf{t}} \\ s \\ 1 \end{pmatrix} = 0, \tag{14}$$

where the size of M is 5×1. Suppose there are N point correspondences. If $N = 5$, Sweeney proposes the solver using 5-point correspondences in [22]. In this paper, we focus on non-minimal sample point correspondences ($N > 5$). We can stack the constraints in each correspondence

$$\mathbf{M}^T \begin{pmatrix} \tilde{\mathbf{t}} \\ s \\ 1 \end{pmatrix} = (\mathbf{m}_1 \dots \mathbf{m}_n)^T \begin{pmatrix} \tilde{\mathbf{t}} \\ s \\ 1 \end{pmatrix} = 0, \tag{15}$$

We minimize the algebraic error based on the least-squares sense and establish the cost function

$$\arg_{\mathbf{R}_y,\tilde{\mathbf{t}}}\min \hat{\mathbf{t}}^T \mathbf{C}\hat{\mathbf{t}}, \tag{16}$$

where $\hat{\mathbf{t}} = \begin{bmatrix} \tilde{\mathbf{t}} & s & 1 \end{bmatrix}^T$ and $\mathbf{C} = \mathbf{M} \times \mathbf{M}^T$. Matrix $\mathbf{C}$ can be expressed as follows:

$$\mathbf{C} = \begin{bmatrix} C_{11} & C_{12} & C_{13} & C_{14} & C_{15} \\ C_{12} & C_{22} & C_{23} & C_{24} & C_{25} \\ C_{13} & C_{23} & C_{33} & C_{34} & C_{35} \\ C_{14} & C_{24} & C_{34} & C_{44} & C_{45} \\ C_{15} & C_{25} & C_{35} & C_{45} & C_{55} \end{bmatrix}. \tag{17}$$

The only unknown in matrix $\mathbf{C}$ is y. Supposing $\lambda_{\mathbf{C},\min}$ is the smallest eigenvalue of matrix $\mathbf{C}$, the optimization problem is expressed by

$$\mathbf{R}_y = \operatorname{argmin}_{\mathbf{R}_y} \lambda_{\mathbf{C},\min}. \tag{18}$$

Based on the form of the eigenvalues, we can write

$$\det(\mathbf{C} - \lambda\mathbf{I}) = -\lambda^5 + f_1\lambda^4 + f_2\lambda^3 + f_3\lambda^2 + f_4\lambda + f_5, \tag{19}$$

where λ is the eigenvalue of matrix $\mathbf{C}$, and $\mathbf{I}$ is a 5×5 unit matrix. Specific expressions for f_0, f_1, f_2, f_3, and f_4 contain only the unknown y.

For convenience of narration, we use λ instead of $\lambda_{\mathbf{G},\min}$. Based on the properties of eigenvalues, Equation (19) can be rewritten as follows:

$$-\lambda^5 + f_1\lambda^4 + f_2\lambda^3 + f_3\lambda^2 + f_4\lambda + f_5 = 0. \tag{20}$$

$\frac{d\lambda}{ds} = 0$ is the necessary condition for λ to be the smallest eigenvalue of $\mathbf{C}$. We can obtain

$$\frac{df_1}{d\lambda}\lambda^4 + \frac{df_2}{d\lambda}\lambda^3 + \frac{df_3}{d\lambda}\lambda^2 + \frac{df_4}{d\lambda}\lambda + \frac{df_5}{d\lambda} = 0. \tag{21}$$

Define $\alpha = 1 + y^2$. Then, we can obtain

$$f_1 = \frac{g_1}{\delta^2}, f_2 = \frac{g_2}{\delta^4}, f_3 = \frac{g_3}{\delta^6}, f_4 = \frac{g_4}{\delta^7}, f_5 = \frac{g_5}{\delta^8}, \tag{22}$$

$$\frac{df_1}{dy} = \frac{h_1}{\delta^3}, \frac{df_2}{dy} = \frac{h_2}{\delta^5}, \frac{df_3}{dy} = \frac{h_3}{\delta^7}, \frac{df_4}{dy} = \frac{h_4}{\delta^8}, \frac{df_5}{dy} = \frac{h_5}{\delta^9}, \tag{23}$$

where g_1, g_2, g_3, g_4, g_5, h_1, h_2, h_3, h_4, and h_5 are only polynomials of y. The highest degree of y is shown in Table 1.

Table 1. Highest degree of variable y.

	g_1	g_2	g_3	g_4	g_5	h_1	h_2	h_3	h_4	h_5
Degree of y	4	8	12	14	16	4	8	12	14	16

Define $\beta = \delta\lambda$. Equations (20) and (21) can be rewritten as follows:

$$\begin{cases} -\delta^3\beta^5 + \delta^2\beta^4 g_1 + \delta\beta^3 g_2 + \beta^2 g_3 + \beta g_4 + g_5 = 0 \\ \delta^2\beta^4 h_1 + \delta\beta^3 h_2 + \beta^2 h_3 + \beta h_4 + h_5 = 0 \end{cases}. \tag{24}$$

We can rewrite Equation (24) as follows:

$$\begin{bmatrix} -\delta^3 & \delta^2 g_1 & \delta g_2 & g_3 & g_4 & g_5 \\ 0 & \delta^2 h_1 & \delta h_2 & h_3 & h_4 & h_5 \end{bmatrix} \begin{bmatrix} \beta^5 \\ \beta^4 \\ \beta^3 \\ \beta^2 \\ \beta \\ 1 \end{bmatrix} = 0. \tag{25}$$

3.3. Globally Optimal Solver

We can easily find two equations with 6 monomials in Equation (24). To equalize the number of equations and the number of monomials, the first equation of Equation (24) is equalized by β^3, β^2, and β, and the second equation is equalized by β^4, β^3, β^2, and β. We can obtain seven equations.

$$\begin{cases} -\delta^3\beta^6 + \delta^2\beta^5 g_1 + \delta\beta^4 g_2 + \beta^3 g_3 + \beta^2 g_4 + \beta g_5 = 0 \\ -\delta^3\beta^7 + \delta^2\beta^6 g_1 + \delta\beta^5 g_2 + \beta^4 g_3 + \beta^3 g_4 + \beta^2 g_5 = 0 \\ -\delta^3\beta^8 + \delta^2\beta^7 g_1 + \delta\beta^6 g_2 + \beta^5 g_3 + \beta^4 g_4 + \beta^3 g_5 = 0 \\ \delta^2\beta^5 h_1 + \delta\beta^4 h_2 + \beta^3 h_3 + \beta^2 h_4 + \beta h_5 = 0 \\ \delta^2\beta^6 h_1 + \delta\beta^5 h_2 + \beta^4 h_3 + \beta^3 h_4 + \beta^2 h_5 = 0 \\ \delta^2\beta^7 h_1 + \delta\beta^6 h_2 + \beta^5 h_3 + \beta^4 h_4 + \beta^3 h_5 = 0 \\ \delta^2\beta^8 h_1 + \delta\beta^7 h_2 + \beta^6 h_3 + \beta^5 h_4 + \beta^4 h_5 = 0 \end{cases}. \tag{26}$$

Based on Equations (24) and (26), we can easily obtain nine equations with nine monomials.

$$\mathbf{V}_{9\times 9}\mathbf{X}_{9\times 1} = \mathbf{0}, \tag{27}$$

where $\mathbf{V}$ is 9×9 and $\mathbf{X}$ is 9×1.

$$\mathbf{V} = \begin{pmatrix} 0 & 0 & 0 & -\delta^3 & \delta^2 g_4 & \delta g_3 & g_2 & g_1 & g_0 \\ 0 & 0 & -\delta^3 & \delta^2 g_4 & \delta g_3 & g_2 & g_1 & g_0 & 0 \\ 0 & -\delta^3 & \delta^2 g_4 & \delta g_3 & g_2 & g_1 & g_0 & 0 & 0 \\ -\delta^3 & \delta^2 g_4 & \delta g_3 & g_2 & g_1 & g_0 & 0 & 0 & 0 \\ 0 & 0 & 0 & 0 & \delta^2 h_4 & \delta h_3 & h_2 & h_1 & h_0 \\ 0 & 0 & 0 & \delta^2 h_4 & \delta h_3 & h_2 & h_1 & h_0 & 0 \\ 0 & 0 & \delta^2 h_4 & \delta h_3 & h_2 & h_1 & h_0 & 0 & 0 \\ 0 & \delta^2 h_4 & \delta h_3 & h_2 & h_1 & h_0 & 0 & 0 & 0 \\ \delta^2 h_4 & \delta h_3 & h_2 & h_1 & h_0 & 0 & 0 & 0 & 0 \end{pmatrix}, \tag{28}$$

$$\mathbf{X} = \begin{bmatrix} \beta^8 & \beta^7 & \beta^6 & \beta^5 & \beta^4 & \beta^3 & \beta^2 & \beta & 1 \end{bmatrix}^T. \tag{29}$$

The elements of $\mathbf{V}$ are univariate polynomials in y, and the highest degree of y is 16. Equation (27) can be rewritten as follows:

$$(\mathbf{V}_0 + y\mathbf{V}_1 + \ldots + y^{16}\mathbf{V}_{16})\mathbf{X} = 0. \tag{30}$$

We define the matrix $\mathbf{B}$, $\mathbf{J}$, $\mathbf{L}$.

$$\mathbf{B} = \begin{bmatrix} \mathbf{0} & \mathbf{I} & \ldots & \mathbf{0} \\ \mathbf{0} & \mathbf{0} & \ldots & \mathbf{0} \\ \ldots & \ldots & \ldots & \mathbf{I} \\ -\mathbf{V}_0 & -\mathbf{V}_1 & \ldots & -\mathbf{V}_{15} \end{bmatrix}, \mathbf{J} = \begin{bmatrix} \mathbf{I} & \mathbf{0} & \ldots & \mathbf{0} \\ \mathbf{0} & \mathbf{I} & \ldots & \mathbf{0} \\ \ldots & \ldots & \ldots & \mathbf{0} \\ \mathbf{0} & \mathbf{0} & \ldots & \mathbf{V}_{16} \end{bmatrix}, \mathbf{L} = \begin{bmatrix} \mathbf{X} \\ y\mathbf{X} \\ \ldots \\ y^{15}\mathbf{X} \end{bmatrix}. \tag{31}$$

Equation (30) can be rewritten as $\mathbf{BL} = y\mathbf{JL}$. The eigenvalue of $\mathbf{J}^{-1}\mathbf{B}$ is y. $\mathbf{J}^{-1}\mathbf{B}$ can be written as follows:

$$\mathbf{J}^{-1}\mathbf{B} = \begin{bmatrix} \mathbf{0} & \mathbf{I} & \dots & \mathbf{0} \\ \mathbf{0} & \mathbf{0} & \dots & \mathbf{0} \\ \dots & \dots & \dots & \mathbf{I} \\ -\mathbf{V}_{16}^{-1}\mathbf{V}_0 & -\mathbf{V}_{16}^{-1}\mathbf{V}_1 & \dots & -\mathbf{V}_{16}^{-1}\mathbf{V}_{15} \end{bmatrix}. \tag{32}$$

where $\mathbf{V_0}, \mathbf{V_1}, \dots, \mathbf{V_{15}}$ and $\mathbf{V_{16}}$ are 9×9 matrices.

It is found that the matrix $\mathbf{V}_{16}^{-1}$ is inaccurate because there are zero columns, resulting in $\mathbf{V}_{16}$ being a singular matrix. Since $\mathbf{V}_0$ is full rank, we define $z = \frac{1}{y}$, and Equation (30) can be rewritten as follows:

$$(z^{16}\mathbf{V}_0 + z^{15}\mathbf{V}_1 + z^{14}\mathbf{V}_2 + \dots + \mathbf{V}_{16})\mathbf{X} = 0 \tag{33}$$

where z is the eigenvalue of matrix $\mathbf{G}$.

$$\mathbf{G} = \begin{bmatrix} \mathbf{0} & \mathbf{I} & \dots & \mathbf{0} \\ \mathbf{0} & \mathbf{0} & \dots & \mathbf{0} \\ \dots & \dots & \dots & \mathbf{I} \\ -\mathbf{V}_0^{-1}\mathbf{V}_{16} & -\mathbf{V}_0^{-1}\mathbf{V}_{15} & \dots & -\mathbf{V}_0^{-1}\mathbf{V}_1 \end{bmatrix} \tag{34}$$

A method for reducing the size of the polynomial eigenvalue problem is proposed in [32]. Zero columns and corresponding zero rows of matrix $\mathbf{G}$ are removed. The eigenvalues of matrix $\mathbf{G}$ are calculated using Schur decomposition. The translation vector and scale can be obtained through Equation (15) when y is known. The algorithm flow chart is shown in Figure 3.

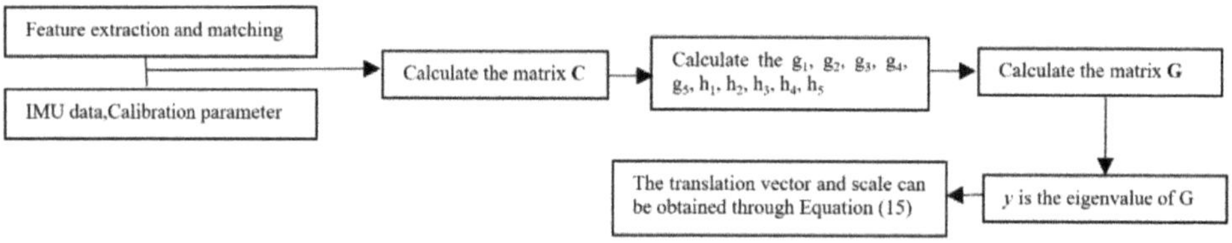

Figure 3. Algorithm flow chart.

The method proposed in this paper is suitable for cameras and IMUs that are fixedly connected together. The specific steps of the algorithm are as follows: (1) The data input to the algorithm include feature point pairs, pitch and roll angles provided by the IMU, and calibration parameters. (2) Based on the input data, calculate the coefficients of each element of matrix $\mathbf{C}$ in Equation (17) with respect to the variable y. (3) Calculate g_1, g_2, g_3, g_4, g_5, h_1, h_2, h_3, h_4, and h_5 according to Equations (20)–(23). (4) Calculate matrix $\mathbf{G}$ according to Equation (34). (5) The eigenvalue of matrix $\mathbf{G}$ is the rotation parameter y, thus obtaining the rotation matrix. (6) The translation vector and scale are obtained by bringing the rotation matrix into Equation (15).

4. Experiments

In this section, we test the accuracy of the rotation matrix, translation vector, and scale on synthetic and real-world data. Since the solver proposed in this paper is a global optimization solver with a known vertical direction, we chose *Sw* [22] for comparison. The method proposed in this paper is called *OURs*.

$$\varepsilon_{\mathbf{R}} = \arccos(\frac{\text{trace}(\mathbf{R}_{gt}\mathbf{R}^T) - 1}{2}) \tag{35}$$

$$\varepsilon_{\mathbf{t}} = 2\frac{||\mathbf{t}_{gt} - \mathbf{t}||}{(||\mathbf{t}_{gt}|| + ||\mathbf{t}||)} \tag{36}$$

$$\varepsilon_{\mathbf{t},\text{dir}} = \arccos\frac{\mathbf{t}_{gt}^{T}\mathbf{t}}{(\|\mathbf{t}_{gt}\| + \|\mathbf{t}\|)} \quad (37)$$

$$\varepsilon_{s} = \frac{|s - s_{gt}|}{s_{gt}} \quad (38)$$

where $\mathbf{R}_{gt}$, $\mathbf{t}_{gt}$, and s_{gt} are the truth of rotation, translation, and scale, respectively. $\mathbf{R}$, $\mathbf{t}$, and s are the evaluated values of rotation, translation, and scale, respectively.

4.1. Experiments on Synthetic Data

To demonstrate the performance of the method proposed in this paper, we first perform experiments on a synthetic dataset. We randomly generate five cameras in space. Three hundred random 3D points are generated within a range of −5 to 5 m (X-axis), −5 to 5 m (Y-axis), and 5–20 m (Z-axis). The resolution of the image is 640 × 480 pixels, and the focal length of the camera is 400 pixels. We assume that the principal point is located at the center of the image at (320, 240) pixels. The scale s is randomly generated in the range [0.5, 2]. Rotation matrices and translation vectors for the five cameras to the reference frame are randomly generated. We establish the frame of reference in the middle of the five cameras. The rotation angle between two adjacent reference frames ranges from -10° to 10°. The direction of the translation vector between two adjacent frames is also randomly generated, and the norm of the translation vector is between 1 and 2 m.

Parameter sensitivity analysis: Due to the fact that the solver proposed in this paper uses a non-minimum sample to estimate the relative pose of the camera and scale, we analyze the accuracy of the calculation by varying the number of points. We set the noise in the image to 1 pixel. The noise of the pitch angle and the noise of the roll angle are both zero degrees. Figure 4 shows the accuracy of rotation, translation, and scale estimation by *OURs* with different numbers of feature points. It is evident that as the number of points increases, the rotation error, translation error, and scale error estimated by the *OURs* method all decrease in Figure 4.

Noise resilience: The solvers of *Sw* and *OURs* are tested with added image noise under four motions: random motion ($\mathbf{t} = \begin{bmatrix} t_x & t_y & t_z \end{bmatrix}^T$), planar motion ($\mathbf{t} = \begin{bmatrix} t_x & 0 & t_z \end{bmatrix}^T$), forward motion ($\mathbf{t} = \begin{bmatrix} 0 & 0 & t_z \end{bmatrix}^T$), and sideways motion ($\mathbf{t} = \begin{bmatrix} t_x & 0 & 0 \end{bmatrix}^T$). We add image noise ranging from 0 to 1 pixel. We added noise to the pitch angle and roll angle when adding noise to the IMU in the synthetic data. The noise of the image is fixed to 1 pixel when noise is added to the roll angle and pitch angle. The maximum noise of the roll angle and pitch angle is 0.5 degrees. Figure 5 shows the error values of the rotation matrix, translation vector, and scale calculated by *OURs* and *Wu* when the image noise, pitch angle noise, and roll angle are added under random motion. Figure 6 shows the error values of the rotation matrix, translation vector, and scale calculated by *OURs* and *Wu* when the image noise, pitch angle noise, and roll angle are added under planar motion. Figure 7 shows the error values of the rotation matrix, translation vector, and scale calculated by *OURs* and *Wu* when the image noise, pitch angle noise, and roll angle are added under sideways motion. Figure 8 shows the error values of the rotation matrix, translation vector, and scale calculated by *OURs* and *Sw* when the image noise, pitch angle noise, and roll angle are added under forward motion. The second column shows the calculation results of adding pitch angle noise. The third column shows the calculation results of adding roll angle noise. The first row represents the rotation matrix error. The second and third rows represent translation vector errors. The fourth row represents scale error. From Figures 5–8, it can be observed that the method proposed in this paper yields rotation matrix errors, translation vector errors, and scale errors smaller than those estimated by the *Sw* method. The effectiveness of the proposed method is demonstrated through simulated data.

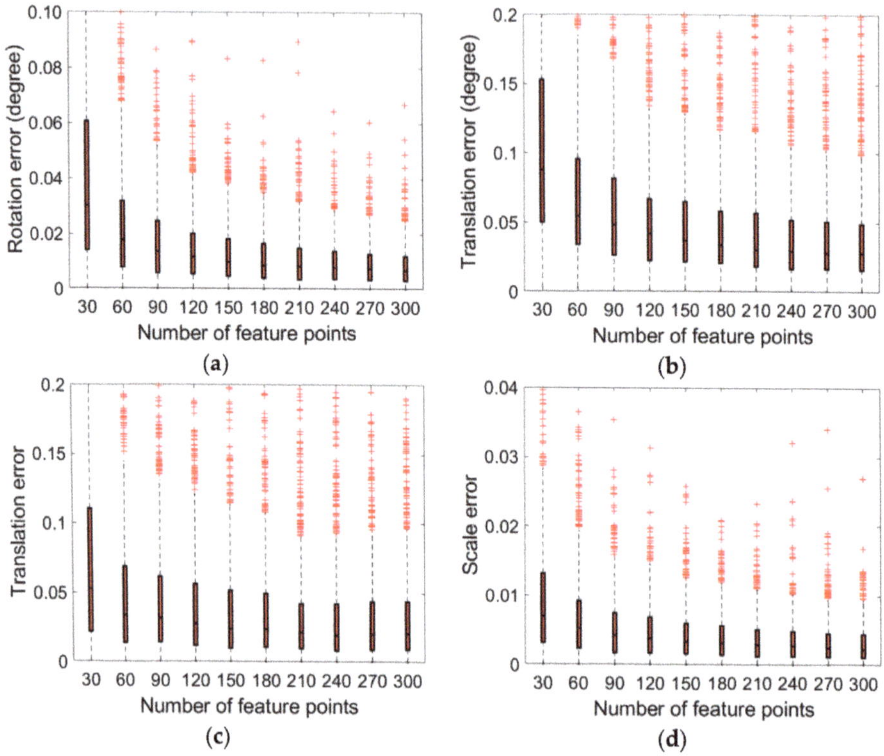

Figure 4. Effect of the number of feature points on the accuracy of rotation, translation, and scale estimation by the method proposed in this paper with different feature points. (**a**) Rotation error (degree); (**b**) translation error (degree); (**c**) translation error; (**d**) scale error.

Random motion: When the image noise is 1 pixel, the average rotation matrix error calculated by the *OURs* method is 0.011°, with a median of 0.008° and a standard deviation of 0.010. The average rotation matrix error calculated by the *Sw* method is 0.197°, with a median of 0.06° and a standard deviation of 0.559. The average translation vector error calculated by the *OURs* method is 0.249°, with a median of 0.156° and a standard deviation of 0.374. The average translation vector error calculated by the *Sw* method is 6.927°, with a median of 1.323° and a standard deviation of 14.908. The average scale error calculated by the *OURs* method is 0.005, with a median of 0.004 and a standard deviation of 0.005. The average scale error calculated by the *Sw* method is 0.031, with a median of 0.015 and a standard deviation of 0.050. When the pitch noise is 0.5°, the average rotation matrix error calculated by the *OURs* method is 0.164°, with a median of 0.089° and a standard deviation of 0.224. The average rotation matrix error calculated by the *Sw* method is 0.624°, with a median of 0.245° and a standard deviation of 1.321. The average translation vector error calculated by the *OURs* method is 1.397°, with a median of 0.196° and a standard deviation of 4.239. The average translation vector error calculated by the *Sw* method is 5.562°, with a median of 1.099° and a standard deviation of 12.152. The average scale error calculated by the *OURs* method is 0.010, with a median of 0.006 and a standard deviation of 0.014. The average scale error calculated by the *Sw* method is 0.045, with a median of 0.025 and a standard deviation of 0.068. When the roll noise is 0.5°, the average rotation matrix error calculated by the *OURs* method is 0.183°, with a median of 0.103° and a standard deviation of 0.230. The average rotation matrix error calculated by the *Sw* method is 0.591°, with a median of 0.253° and a standard deviation of 1.136. The average translation vector error calculated by the *OURs* method is 2.051°, with a median of 0.221° and a standard deviation of 8.799. The average translation vector error calculated by the *Sw* method is 5.595°, with a median of 1.021° and a standard deviation of 12.733. The average scale error calculated by the *OURs* method is 0.010, with a median of 0.006 and a standard deviation of 0.012. The average scale error calculated by the *Sw* method is 0.037, with a median of 0.019 and a standard deviation of 0.052.

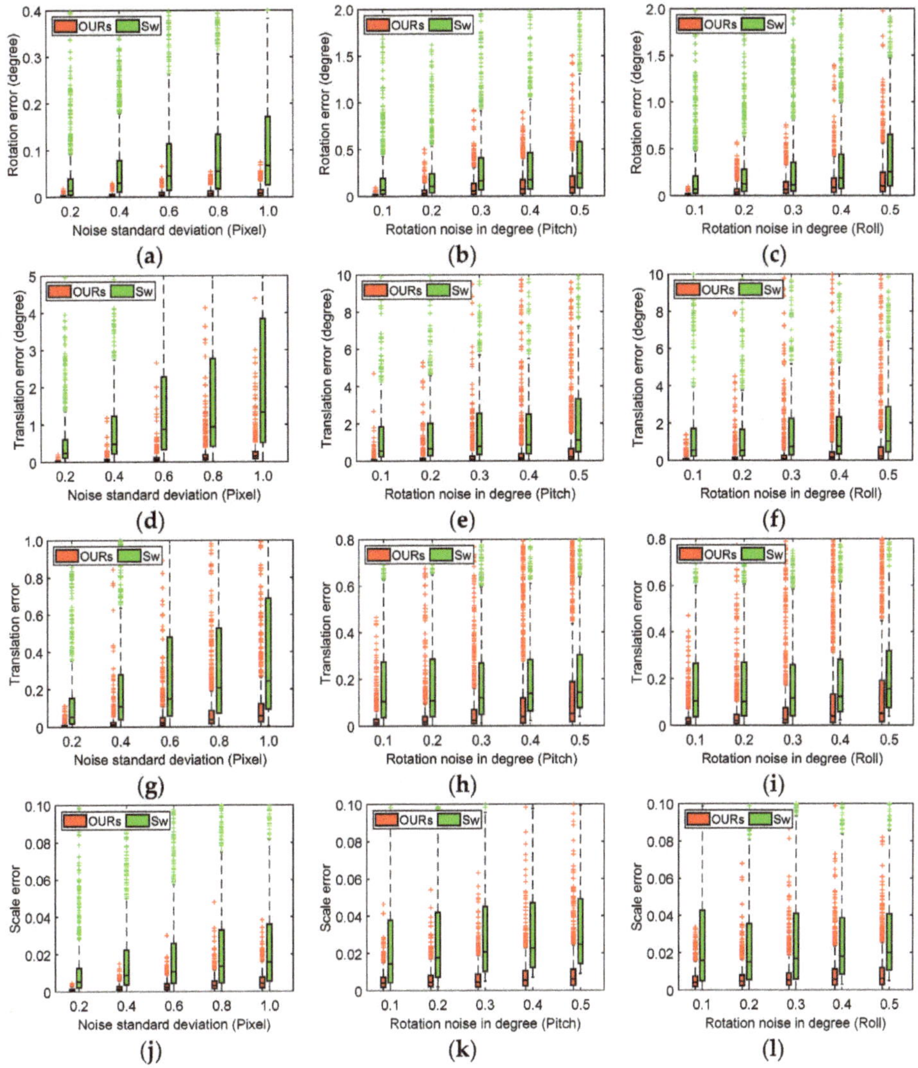

Figure 5. Estimating errors in the rotation matrix, translation vector, and scale information under random motion. The first column shows the calculation results of adding image noise. The second column shows the calculation results of adding pitch angle noise. The third column shows the calculation results of adding roll angle noise. The first, second, third and fourth rows represent the values of $\varepsilon_{\mathbf{R}}$, $\varepsilon_{\mathbf{t}}$, $\varepsilon_{\mathbf{t},\mathrm{dir}}$ and ε_s respectively.

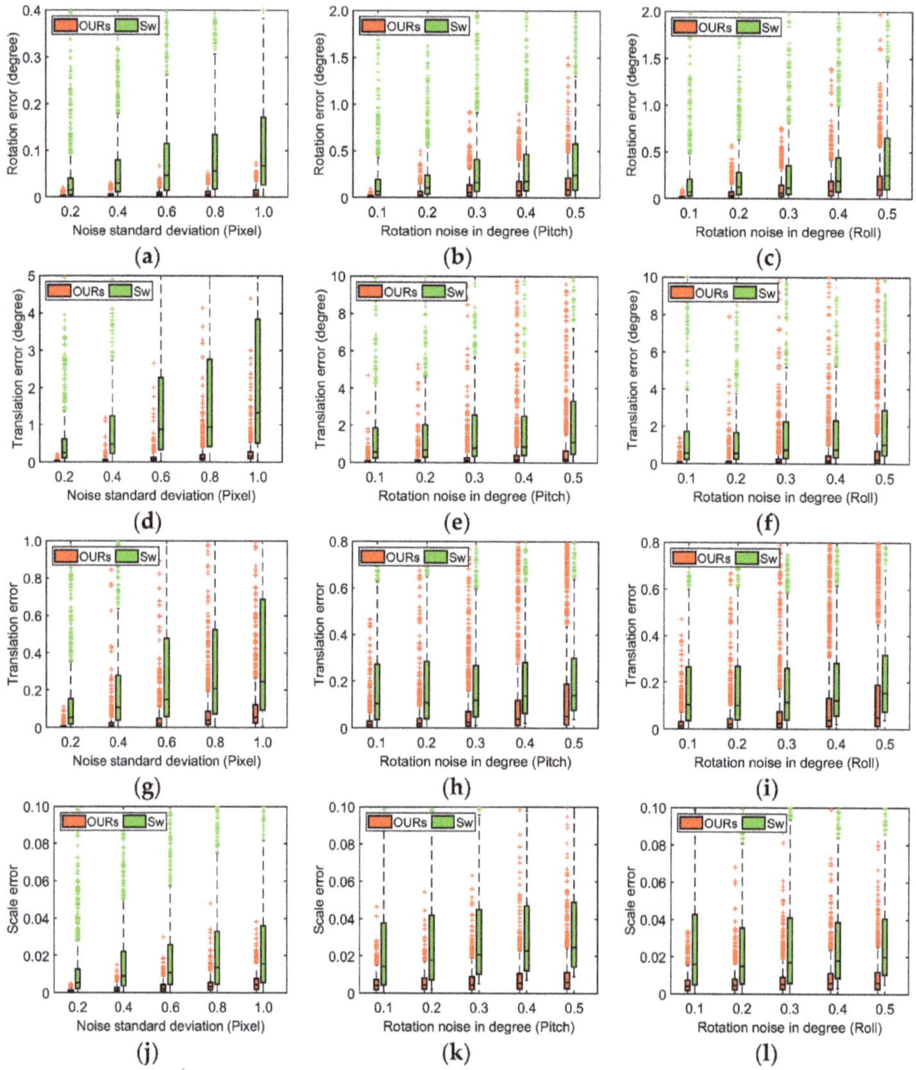

Figure 6. Estimating errors in the rotation matrix, translation vector, and scale information under planar motion. The first column shows the calculation results of adding image noise. The second column shows the calculation results of adding pitch angle noise. The third column shows the calculation results of adding roll angle noise. The first, second, third and fourth rows represent the values of $\varepsilon_{\mathbf{R}}$, $\varepsilon_{\mathbf{t}}$, $\varepsilon_{\mathbf{t},\mathrm{dir}}$ and ε_s respectively.

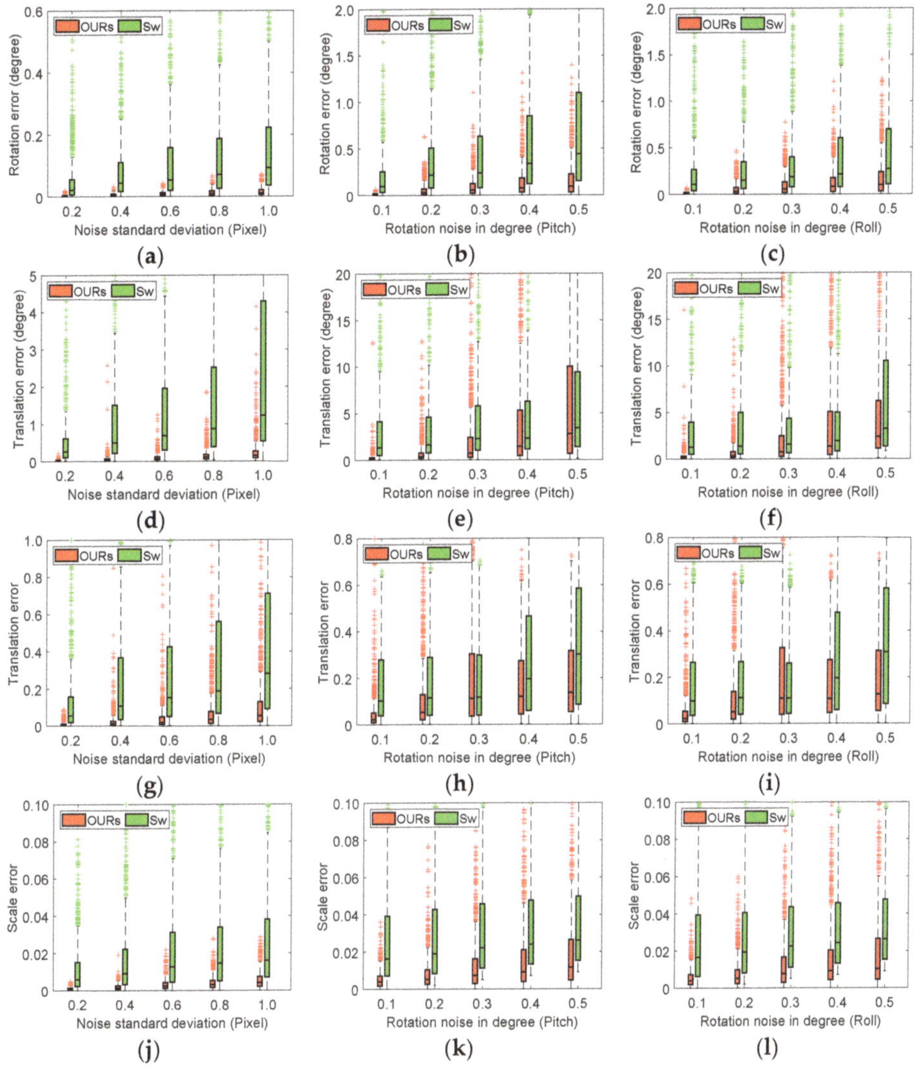

Figure 7. Estimating errors in the rotation matrix, translation vector, and scale information under sideways motion. The first column shows the calculation results of adding image noise. The second column shows the calculation results of adding pitch angle noise. The third column shows the calculation results of adding roll angle noise. The first, second, third and fourth rows represent the values of $\varepsilon_{\mathbf{R}}$, $\varepsilon_{\mathbf{t}}$, $\varepsilon_{\mathbf{t},\mathrm{dir}}$ and ε_s respectively.

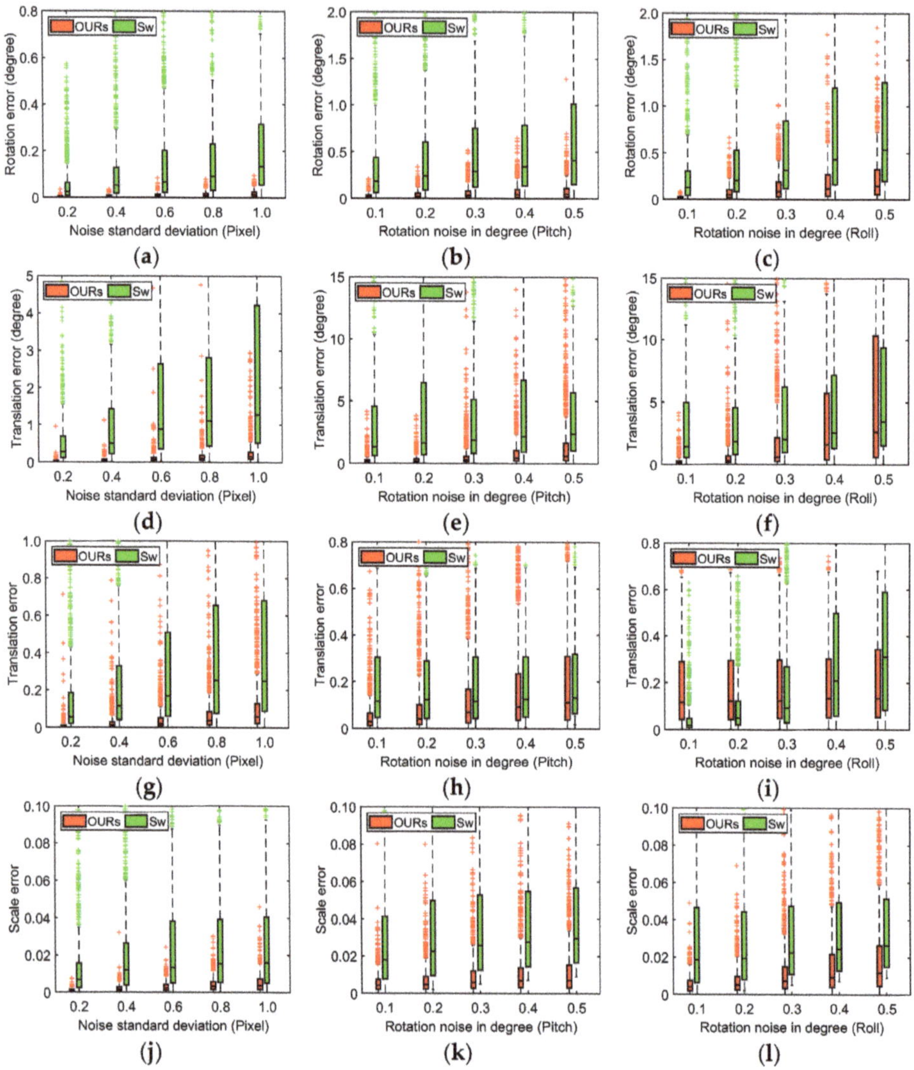

Figure 8. Estimating errors in the rotation matrix, translation vector, and scale information under forward motion. The first column shows the calculation results of adding image noise. The second column shows the calculation results of adding pitch angle noise. The third column shows the calculation results of adding roll angle noise. The first, second, third and fourth rows represent the values of $\varepsilon_{\mathbf{R}}$, $\varepsilon_{\mathbf{t}}$, $\varepsilon_{\mathbf{t},\mathrm{dir}}$ and ε_s respectively.

Planar motion: When the image noise is 1 pixel, the average rotation matrix error calculated by the *OURs* method is 0.015°, with a median of 0.012° and a standard deviation of 0.013. The average rotation matrix error calculated by the *Sw* method is 0.368°, with a median of 0.097° and a standard deviation of 1.134. The average translation vector error calculated by the *OURs* method is 0.194°, with a median of 0.093° and a standard deviation of 0.722. The average translation vector error calculated by the *Sw* method is 4.864°, with a median of 0.802° and a standard deviation of 12.211. The average scale error calculated by the *OURs* method is 0.005, with a median of 0.004 and a standard deviation of 0.005. The average scale error calculated by the *Sw* method is 0.0374, with a median of 0.016 and a standard deviation of 0.069. When the pitch noise is 0.5°, the average rotation matrix error calculated by the *OURs* method is 0.127°, with a median of 0.071° and a standard deviation of 0.156. The average rotation matrix error calculated by the *Sw* method is 0.883°, with a median of 0.357° and a standard deviation of 1.644. The average translation vector error calculated by the *OURs* method is 4.802°, with a median of 0.838° and a standard deviation of 11.473. The average translation vector error calculated by the *Sw* method is 7.813°, with a median of 1.847° and a standard deviation of 14.928. The average scale error calculated by the *OURs* method is 0.015, with a median of 0.008 and a standard deviation of 0.019. The average scale error calculated by the *Sw* method is 0.049, with a median of 0.030 and a standard deviation of 0.059. When the roll noise is 0.5°, the average rotation matrix error calculated by the *OURs* method is 0.156°, with a median of 0.090° and a standard deviation of 0.182. The average rotation matrix error calculated by the *Sw* method is 0.931°, with a median of 0.353° and a standard deviation of 1.897. The average translation vector error calculated by the *OURs* method is 5.271°, with a median of 1.006° and a standard deviation of 12.505. The average translation vector error calculated by the *Sw* method is 6.234°, with a median of 1.762° and a standard deviation of 12.573. The average scale error calculated by the *OURs* method is 0.019, with a median of 0.008 and a standard deviation of 0.020. The average scale error calculated by the *Sw* method is 0.046, with a median of 0.026 and a standard deviation of 0.065.

Sideways motion: When the image noise is 1 pixel, the average rotation matrix error calculated by the *OURs* method is 0.015°, with a median of 0.011° and a standard deviation of 0.012. The average rotation matrix error calculated by the *Sw* method is 0.295°, with a median of 0.093° and a standard deviation of 0.797. The average translation vector error calculated by the *OURs* method is 0.250°, with a median of 0.151° and a standard deviation of 0.373. The average translation vector error calculated by the *Sw* method is 6.638°, with a median of 1.231° and a standard deviation of 13.752. The average scale error calculated by the *OURs* method is 0.005, with a median of 0.004 and a standard deviation of 0.005. The average scale error calculated by the *Sw* method is 0.0374, with a median of 0.016 and a standard deviation of 0.076. When the pitch noise is 0.5°, the average rotation matrix error calculated by the *OURs* method is 0.160°, with a median of 0.094° and a standard deviation of 0.185. The average rotation matrix error calculated by the *Sw* method is 1.019°, with a median of 0.441° and a standard deviation of 1.708. The average translation vector error calculated by the *OURs* method is 9.559°, with a median of 2.765° and a standard deviation of 17.419. The average translation vector error calculated by the *Sw* method is 9.693°, with a median of 3.385° and a standard deviation of 15.701. The average scale error calculated by the *OURs* method is 0.020, with a median of 0.012 and a standard deviation of 0.024. The average scale error calculated by the *Sw* method is 0.044, with a median of 0.026 and a standard deviation of 0.058. When the roll noise is 0.5°, the average rotation matrix error calculated by the *OURs* method is 0.169°, with a median of 0.099° and a standard deviation of 0.198. The average rotation matrix error calculated by the *Sw* method is 0.732°, with a median of 0.274° and a standard deviation of 1.365. The average translation vector error calculated by the *OURs* method is 8.354°, with a median of 2.348° and a standard deviation of 12.123. The average translation vector error calculated by the *Sw* method is 10.764°, with a median of 3.230° and a standard deviation of 19.194. The average scale error calculated by the *OURs* method is 0.020, with a median of 0.010 and a standard deviation of 0.026. The average scale error calculated by the *Sw* method is 0.045, with a median of 0.026 and a standard deviation of 0.062.

Forward motion: When the image noise is 1 pixel, the average rotation matrix error calculated by the *OURs* method is 0.016°, with a median of 0.013° and a standard deviation of 0.015. The average rotation matrix error calculated by the *Sw* method is 0.421°, with a median of 0.135° and a standard deviation of 1.215. The average translation vector error calculated by the *OURs* method is 0.321°, with a median of 0.149° and a standard deviation of 1.325. The average translation vector error calculated by the *Sw* method is 7.156°, with a median of 1.27° and a standard deviation of 15.035. The average scale error calculated by the *OURs* method is 0.005, with a median of 0.004 and a standard deviation of 0.005. The average scale error calculated by the *Sw* method is 0.036, with a median of 0.016 and a standard deviation of 0.068. When the pitch noise is 0.5°, the average rotation matrix error calculated by the *OURs* method is 0.082°, with a median of 0.048° and a standard deviation of 0.104. The average rotation matrix error calculated by the *Sw* method is 0.965°, with a median of 0.411° and a standard deviation of 1.614. The average translation vector error calculated by the *OURs* method is 2.195°, with a median of 0.589° and a standard deviation of 5.921. The average translation vector error calculated by the *Sw* method is 9.442°, with a median of 2.364° and a standard deviation of 17.648. The average scale error calculated by the *OURs* method is 0.012, with a median of 0.007 and a standard deviation of 0.015. The average scale error calculated by the *Sw* method is 0.049, with a median of 0.029 and a standard deviation of 0.060. When the roll noise is 0.5°, the average rotation matrix error calculated by the *OURs* method is 0.229°, with a median of 0.141° and a standard deviation of 0.260. The average rotation matrix error calculated by the *Sw* method is 1.068°, with a median of 0.537° and a standard deviation of 1.639. The average translation vector error calculated by the *OURs* method is 11.024°, with a median of 2.628° and a standard deviation of 22.204. The average translation vector error calculated by the *Sw* method is 9.431°, with a median of 3.476° and a standard deviation of 14.699. The average scale error calculated by the *OURs* method is 0.020, with a median of 0.012 and a standard deviation of 0.024. The average scale error calculated by the *Sw* method is 0.046, with a median of 0.026 and a standard deviation of 0.068.

4.2. Experiments on Real-World Data

To further validate the effectiveness of the proposed method, the KITTI dataset was chosen for real data evaluation [31]. The KITTI dataset was jointly founded by the Karlsruhe Institute of Technology in Germany and the Toyota American Institute of Technology. It is currently the largest computer vision algorithm evaluation dataset in the world for autonomous driving scenarios. The raw dataset is divided into the categories 'Road', 'City', 'Residential', 'Person', and 'Campus'. The car is equipped with GPS, an IMU, one 64-line 3D LiDAR, and two grayscale cameras. The KITTI dataset provides ground truth for 11 sequences (00–10). The pitch angle and roll angle can be extracted from the IMU sensor data. The intrinsic parameters of the camera and the rotation and translation between two cameras from the reference frame are given in the data document [34]. We utilized the SIFT algorithm to obtain corresponding feature point pairs. Figure 8 shows the results of feature extraction and matching using SIFT in the KITTI dataset. We selected one out of every five pairs of points for display in Figure 9.

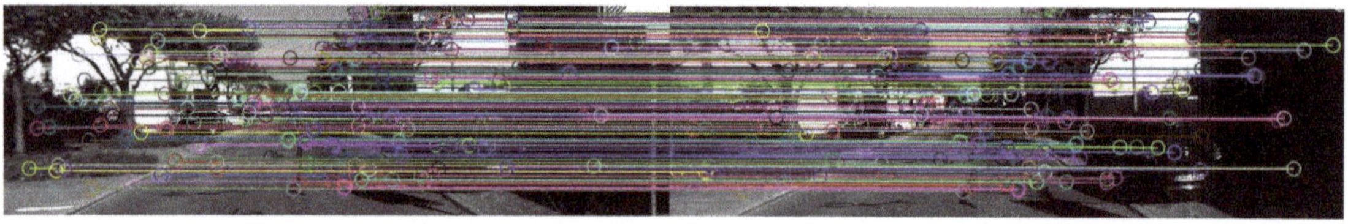

Figure 9. Test image pair from KITTI dataset with feature detection.

Table 2 shows the error results of the rotation matrix, translation vector, and scale estimated by the *OURs* method and the *Sw* method on the KITTI dataset. From Table 2, we can see that the accuracy of the rotation matrix, translation vector, and scale estimated by the *OURs* method is significantly better than that of the *Sw* method. Table 3 shows the percentage by which the error calculated by the *OURs* method is reduced compared to the error calculated by the *Sw* method. For the rotation matrix, the *OURs* method computes the error on average about 53% less than the *Sw* method. The maximum error of the *OURs* method decreased by 71%, and the minimum decreased by 32%. For the translation vector, the *OURs* method computes the error on average about 67% less than the *Sw* method. The maximum error of the *OURs* method decreased by 73%, and the minimum decreased by 61%. For the scale, the *OURs* method computes the error on average about 90% less than the *Sw* method. The maximum error of the *OURs* method decreased by 95%, and the minimum decreased by 80%. The standard deviation of the rotation matrix estimated by the *OURs* method is 65% less than that of the *Sw* method. The standard deviation of the translation vector estimated by the *OURs* method is 51% less than that of the *Sw* method. The standard deviation of the scale estimated by the *OURs* method is 94% less than that of the *Sw* method.

Table 2. Rotation, translation, and scale error on KITTI sequence by the *Sw* method and the *OURs* method.

Seq	Sw			OURs		
	ε_R (Degree)	$\varepsilon_{t,dir}$ (Degree)	ε_s	ε_R (Degree)	$\varepsilon_{t,dir}$ (Degree)	ε_s
00	0.1760	3.4598	0.0086	0.0847	1.3452	0.0012
01	0.2509	4.1682	0.0205	0.1042	1.5081	0.0008
02	0.1985	3.9163	0.0096	0.0965	1.2836	0.0010
03	0.1809	3.8168	0.0134	0.0754	1.0739	0.0009
04	0.1026	3.6274	0.0033	0.0590	1.0030	0.0003
05	0.2723	4.0362	0.0160	0.0801	1.2315	0.0008
06	0.1814	3.0784	0.0063	0.0664	1.0562	0.0003
07	0.0945	3.4602	0.0043	0.0452	1.1856	0.0008
08	0.1219	3.9419	0.0059	0.0833	1.0837	0.0012
09	0.2093	3.7111	0.0128	0.1133	1.2027	0.0011
10	0.1984	3.6022	0.0110	0.0864	1.3294	0.0008
AVG	0.1806	3.7107	0.0101	0.0813	1.2094	0.0008
MAX	0.2723	4.1682	0.0205	0.1133	1.5081	0.0012
MIN	0.0945	3.0784	0.0033	0.0452	1.0030	0.0003
SD	0.0537	0.2964	0.0050	0.0187	0.1443	0.0002
RMSE	0.1884	3.7225	0.0113	0.0835	1.2179	0.0008

Table 3. The percentage by which the error calculated by the *OURs* method is reduced compared to the error calculated by the *Sw* method.

Seq	Rotation (%)	Translation (%)	Scale (%)
00	52%	61%	86%
01	58%	64%	96%
02	51%	67%	90%
03	58%	72%	93%
04	42%	72%	91%
05	71%	69%	95%
06	63%	65%	95%
07	52%	66%	81%
08	32%	73%	80%
09	46%	68%	91%
10	56%	63%	93%
AVG	53%	67%	90%
MIN	32%	61%	80%
MAX	71%	73%	95%
SD	65%	51%	94%
RMSE	56%	67%	92%

To further verify the performance of the proposed method, we add the *Kneip* method [23], which is the latest method for estimating relative pose and scale from 2D-2D only without the use of an IMU. This method solves the relative pose and scale by using the non-minimum sample number. This method requires at least eight-point correspondences. The *Kneip* method transforms relative pose and scale estimation into a symmetric eigenvalue problem. A simple heuristic global energy minimization scheme based on local minimum suppression is used in the *Kneip* method. We added the *Peter* method [35], which requires a minimum of three 3D-3D correspondences to find the similarity. This is the orthogonal Procrustes approach. The 3D points are obtained by triangulating in each view.

Table 4. Rotation, translation, and scale error on KITTI sequence by the *Kneip* method and the *Peter* method.

Seq	Kneip			Peter		
	ε_R (Degree)	$\varepsilon_{t,dir}$ (Degree)	ε_s	ε_R (Degree)	$\varepsilon_{t,dir}$ (Degree)	ε_s
00	0.9147	6.4101	0.0204	1.9805	9.8001	0.0712
01	0.7057	5.0460	0.0913	1.7606	7.0888	0.1064
02	0.6269	4.9256	0.0258	1.8166	5.9685	0.0918
03	0.7856	4.9410	0.0835	1.8242	6.0235	0.1123
04	0.7901	4.7540	0.0298	1.7948	5.4217	0.0852
05	0.9512	6.0975	0.0957	1.9278	7.6275	0.1254
06	0.7506	4.2787	0.0277	1.9023	5.2621	0.0902
07	0.5956	5.0482	0.0157	1.7452	7.6125	0.0725
08	0.7816	5.1886	0.0130	1.8722	7.2626	0.0806
09	0.8919	5.2186	0.0816	1.9985	6.1282	0.1235
10	0.9643	4.9204	0.0758	2.0592	6.2176	0.1002
AVG	0.8052	5.1662	0.0509	1.8892	6.7648	0.0963
MAX	1.0643	6.4101	0.0957	2.0592	9.8001	0.1254
MIN	0.5956	4.2787	0.0131	1.7606	5.2621	0.0712
SD	0.1340	0.5699	0.0322	0.0894	1.2423	0.0180
RMSE	0.8163	5.1975	0.0603	1.8913	6.8779	0.0979

Table 4 shows the rotation matrix errors, translation vector errors, and scale errors calculated by the *Kneip* method and the *Peter* method. As can be seen from Table 4, the average value, maximum value, minimum value, standard deviation, and root mean square error of the rotation matrix error estimated by the *Kneip* method are 0.8052°, 1.0643°, 0.5956°, 0.1340, and 0.8163. The average value, maximum value, minimum value, standard deviation, and root mean square error of the translation vector error estimated by the *Kneip* method are 5.1662°, 6.4101°, 4.2787°, 0.5699, and 5.1975. The average value, maximum value, minimum value, standard deviation, and root mean square error of the scale error estimated by the *Kneip* method are 0.0509, 0.0957, 0.0131, 0.0322, and 0.0603. The average value, maximum value, minimum value, standard deviation, and root mean square error of the rotation matrix error estimated by the *Peter* method are 1.8892°, 2.0592°, 1.7606°, 0.0894, and 1.8913. The average value, maximum value, minimum value, standard deviation, and root mean square error of the translation vector error estimated by the *Peter* method are 6.7648°, 9.8001°, 5.2621°, 1.2423, and 6.8779. The average value, maximum value, minimum value, standard deviation, and root mean square error of the scale error estimated by the *Peter* method are 0.0963, 0.1254, 0.0712, 0.0180, and 0.0979.

4.3. Discussion

The method proposed in this paper estimates the relative pose (4 DOFs) and scale from image correspondences. Therefore, the *Sw* method was chosen as the comparison method for the simulation experiment. From Figures 4–7, it can be observed that the method proposed in this paper yields rotation matrix errors, translation vector errors, and scale errors smaller than those estimated by the *Sw* method. The effectiveness of the proposed method is demonstrated through simulated data. In the experiment on real data, to further verify the performance of the proposed method, we added the *Kneip* method and *Peter* method as comparison methods. The errors of the rotation matrix, translation vector, and scale calculated by our method are all smaller than those of the comparison method. The root mean square error of the rotation matrix estimated by the *OURs* method is 56% less than that of the *Sw* method. The root mean square error of the rotation matrix estimated by the *OURs* method is 90% less than that of the *Kneip* method. The root mean square error of the rotation matrix estimated by the *OURs* method is 96% less than that of the *Peter* method. The root mean square error of the translation vector estimated by the *OURs* method is 67% less than that of the *Sw* method. The root mean square error of the translation vector estimated by the *OURs* method is 77% less than that of the *Kneip* method. The root mean square error of the translation vector estimated by the *OURs* method is 82% less than that of the *Peter* method. The root mean square error of the scale estimated by the *OURs* method is 92% less than that of the *Sw* method. The root mean square error of the scale estimated by the *OURs* method is 98% less than that of the *Kneip* method. The root mean square error of the scale estimated by the *OURs* method is 99% less than that of the *Peter* method.

5. Conclusions

We propose a new globally optimal solver to estimate the relative pose and scale for a multi-camera system from only image correspondences with a known vertical direction. Firstly, we transformed the problem into a cost function based on the least-squares sense to minimize algebraic error. Based on the characteristic equation method and its first derivative equal to zero, two independent polynomial equations with two unknowns are provided. These two equations consist of the rotation angle parameter. We utilized the polynomial eigenvalue method to solve the rotation angle parameter. The translation vector and scale information were obtained based on the corresponding eigenvectors. We tested the superiority of the proposed method in relative pose and scale estimation on synthetic data and the KITTI dataset. Compared to the best method in the comparison methods, the method proposed in this paper reduced the rotation matrix error, translation vector error, and scale error by 53%, 67%, and 90%, respectively.

From Equation (14), it can be observed that the error sources of the proposed algorithm mainly come from the accuracy of feature extraction and matching, as well as the accuracy of the IMU. The measurement accuracy of the IMU is determined by the gyroscope. Our next task is to study how to enhance the accuracy of feature extraction and matching.

Author Contributions: Conceptualization, Zhenbao Yu and Shirong Ye; methodology, Zhenbao Yu and Pengfei Xia; software, Zhenbao Yu and Ronghe Jin; validation, Zhenbao Yu, Shirong Y, Kang Yan, and Ronghe Jin; formal analysis, Zhenbao Yu and Changwei Liu; investigation, Zhenbao Yu and Changwei Liu; resources, Zhenbao Yu, Shirong Ye, Kang Yan, and Changwei Liu; data curation, Shirong Ye and Changwei Liu; writing—original draft preparation, Zhenbao Yu and Ronghe Jin; writing—review and editing, Zhenbao Yu and Pengfei Xia; visualization, Zhenbao Yu, Changwei Liu, Kang Yan, and Pengfei Xia; supervision, Zhenbao Yu, Shirong Ye, and Ronghe Jin; project administration, Zhenbao Yu, Changwei Liu, Kang Yan, and Ronghe Jin; funding acquisition, Shirong Ye. All authors have read and agreed to the published version of the manuscript.

Funding: This research was funded by the National Natural Science Foundation of China (No. 41974031), the National Key Research and Development Program of China (No. 2019YFC1509603), and the Ministry of Industry and Information Technology of China through the High Precision Timing Service Project under Grant TC220A04A-80.

Data Availability Statement: The original contributions presented in this study are included in this article; further inquiries can be directed to the corresponding author.

Acknowledgments: We would like to thank the editor and anonymous reviewers for their constructive comments and suggestions for improving this manuscript.

Conflicts of Interest: The authors declare no conflicts of interest.

References

1. Zhang, J.; Xu, L.; Bao, C. An Adaptive Pose Fusion Method for Indoor Map Construction. *ISPRS Int. J. Geo-Inf.* **2021**, *10*, 800. [CrossRef]
2. Svärm, L.; Enqvist, O.; Kahl, F.; Oskarsson, M. City-scale localization for cameras with known vertical direction. *IEEE Trans. Pattern Anal. Mach. Intell.* **2016**, *39*, 1455–1461. [CrossRef] [PubMed]
3. Li, C.; Zhou, L.; Chen, W. Automatic Pose Estimation of Uncalibrated Multi-View Images Based on a Planar Object with a Predefined Contour Model. *ISPRS Int. J. Geo-Inf.* **2016**, *5*, 244. [CrossRef]
4. Raposo, C.; Barreto, J.P. Theory and practice of structure-from-motion using affine correspondences. In Proceedings of the IEEE Conference on Computer Vision and Pattern Recognition, Las Vegas, NV, USA, 27–30 June 2016; pp. 5470–5478.
5. Wang, Y.; Liu, X.; Zhao, M.; Xu, X. VIS-SLAM: A Real-Time Dynamic SLAM Algorithm Based on the Fusion of Visual, Inertial, and Semantic Information. *ISPRS Int. J. Geo-Inf.* **2024**, *13*, 163. [CrossRef]
6. Qin, J.; Li, M.; Liao, X.; Zhong, J. Accumulative Errors Optimization for Visual Odometry of ORB-SLAM2 Based on RGB-D Cameras. *ISPRS Int. J. Geo-Inf.* **2019**, *8*, 581. [CrossRef]
7. Mur-Artal, R.; Tardós, J.D. SLAM2: An open-source SLAM system for monocular, stereo, and RGB-D cameras. *IEEE Trans. Robot* **2017**, *33*, 1255–1262. [CrossRef]
8. Niu, Q.; Li, M.; He, S.; Gao, C.; Gary Chan, S.H.; Luo, X. Resource-efficient and Automated Image-based Indoor Localization. *ACM Trans. Sens. Netw.* **2019**, *15*, 19. [CrossRef]
9. Poulose, A.; Han, D.S. Hybrid Indoor Localization on Using IMU Sensors and Smartphone Camera. *Sensors* **2019**, *19*, 5084. [CrossRef] [PubMed]
10. Kawaji, H.; Hatada, K.; Yamasaki, T.; Aizawa, K. Image-based indoor positioning system: Fast image matching using omnidirectional panoramic images. In Proceedings of the 1st ACM International Workshop on Multimodal Pervasive Video Analysis, Firenze, Italy, 25–29 October 2010.
11. Pless, R. Using many cameras as one. In Proceedings of the IEEE Computer Society Conference on Computer Vision and Pattern Recognition, Madison, WI, USA, 18–20 June 2003; Volume 2, p. II-587.
12. HenrikStewénius, M.O.; Aström, K.; Nistér, D. Solutions to minimal generalized relative pose problems. In Proceedings of the Workshop on Omnidirectional Vision, Beijing, China, October 2005.
13. Hee Lee, G.; Pollefeys, M.; Fraundorfer, F. Relative pose estimation for a multi-camera system with known vertical direction. In Proceedings of the IEEE Conference on Computer Vision and Pattern Recognition, Columbus, OH, USA, 23–28 June 2014; pp. 540–547.
14. Liu, L.; Li, H.; Dai, Y.; Pan, Q. Robust and efficient relative pose with a multi-camera system for autonomous driving in highly dynamic environments. *IEEE Trans. Intell. Transp.* **2017**, *19*, 2432–2444. [CrossRef]
15. Sweeney, C.; Flynn, J.; Turk, M. Solving for relative pose with a partially known rotation is a quadratic eigenvalue problem. In Proceedings of the 2014 2nd International Conference on 3D Vision, Tokyo, Japan, 8–11 December 2014; Volume 1, pp. 483–490.
16. Li, H.; Hartley, R.; Kim, J. A linear approach to motion estimation using generalized camera models. In Proceedings of the IEEE Conference on Computer Vision and Pattern Recognition, Anchorage, AK, USA, 23–28 June 2008; pp. 1–8.
17. Kneip, L.; Li, H. Efficient computation of relative pose for multi-camera systems. In Proceedings of the IEEE Conference on Computer Vision and Pattern Recognition, Columbus, OH, USA, 23–28 June 2014; pp. 446–453.
18. Wu, Q.; Ding, Y.; Qi, X.; Xie, J.; Yang, J. Globally optimal relative pose estimation for multi-camera systems with known gravity direction. In Proceedings of the International Conference on Robotics and Automation, Philadelphia, PA, USA, 23–27 May 2022; pp. 2935–2941.
19. Guan, B.; Zhao, J.; Barath, D.; Fraundorfer, F. Minimal cases for computing the generalized relative pose using affine correspondences. In Proceedings of the IEEE/CVF International Conference on Computer Vision, Montreal, QC, Canada, 10–17 October 2021; pp. 6068–6077.
20. Guan, B.; Zhao, J.; Barath, D.; Fraundorfer, F. Relative pose estimation for multi-camera systems from affine correspondences. *arXiv* **2020**, arXiv:2007.10700v1.
21. Kukelova, Z.; Bujnak, M.; Pajdla, T. Closed-form solutions to minimal absolute pose problems with known vertical direction. In Proceedings of the Asian Conference on Computer Vision, Queenstown, New Zealand, 8–12 November 2010; pp. 216–229.
22. Sweeney, C.; Kneip, L.; Hollerer, T.; Turk, M. Computing similarity transformations from only image correspondences. In Proceedings of the TEEE Conference on Computer Vision and Pattern Recognition, Boston, MA, USA, 7–12 June 2015; pp. 3305–3313.
23. Kneip, L.; Sweeney, C.; Hartley, R. The generalized relative pose and scale problem: View-graph fusion via 2D-2D registration. In Proceedings of the 2016 IEEE Winter Conference on Applications of Computer Vision, Lake Placid, NY, USA, 7–10 March 2016; pp. 1–9.
24. Grossberg, M.D.; Nayar, S.K. A general imaging model and a method for finding its parameters. In Proceedings of the Eighth IEEE International Conference on Computer Vision, Vancouver, BC, Canada, 7–14 July 2001; Volume 2, pp. 108–115.
25. Kim, J.H.; Li, H.; Hartley, R. Motion estimation for nonoverlap multicamera rigs: Linear algebraic and $L\infty$ geometric solutions. *IEEE Trans. Pattern Anal. Mach. Intell.* **2009**, *32*, 1044–1059.
26. Guan, B.; Zhao, J.; Barath, D.; Fraundorfer, F. Minimal solvers for relative pose estimation of multi-camera systems using affine correspondences. *Int. J. Comput. Vision* **2023**, *131*, 324–345. [CrossRef]

27. Zhao, J.; Xu, W.; Kneip, L. A certifiably globally optimal solution to generalized essential matrix estimation. In Proceedings of the IEEE/CVF Conference on Computer Vision and Pattern Recognition, Seattle, WA, USA, 13–19 June 2020; pp. 12034–12043.
28. Sweeney, C.; Fragoso, V.; Höllerer, T.; Turk, M. gdls: A scalable solution to the generalized pose and scale problem. In Proceedings of the 13th European Conference, Zurich, Switzerland, 6–12 September 2014; pp. 16–31.
29. Bujnak, M.; Kukelova, Z.; Pajdla, T. 3d reconstruction from image collections with a single known focal length. In Proceedings of the IEEE 12th International Conference on Computer Vision, Kyoto, Japan, 29 September–2 October 2009; pp. 1803–1810.
30. Fitzgibbon, A.W. Simultaneous linear estimation of multiple view geometry and lens distortion. In Proceedings of the 2001 IEEE Computer Society Conference on Computer Vision and Pattern Recognition, Kauai, HI, USA, 8–14 December 2001; Volume 1, p. I.
31. Ding, Y.; Yang, J.; Kong, H. An efficient solution to the relative pose estimation with a common direction. In Proceedings of the 2020 IEEE International Conference on Robotics and Automation, Paris, France, 31 May–31 August 2020; pp. 11053–11059.
32. Kukelova, Z.; Bujnak, M.; Pajdla, T. Polynomial eigenvalue solutions to minimal problems in computer vision. *IEEE Trans. Pattern Anal. Mach. Intell.* **2011**, *34*, 1381–1393. [CrossRef]
33. Larsson, V.; Astrom, K.; Oskarsson, M. Efficient solvers for minimal problems by syzygy-based reduction. In Proceedings of the IEEE Conference on Computer Vision and Pattern Recognition, Honolulu, HI, USA, 21–26 July 2017; pp. 820–829.
34. Geiger, A.; Lenz, P.; Stiller, C.; Urtasun, R. Vision meets robotics: The kitti dataset. *Int. J. Robot Res.* **2013**, *32*, 1231–1237. [CrossRef]
35. Schonemann, P. A generalized solution of the orthogonal Procrustes problem. *Psychometrika* **1966**, *31*, 1–10. [CrossRef]

sensors

MDPI

Article

Numerical Simulation and Field Monitoring of Blasting Vibration for Tunnel In-Situ Expansion by a Non-Cut Blast Scheme

Zhenchang Guan, Lifu Xie, Dong Chen and Jingkang Shi *

College of Civil Engineering, Fuzhou University, Fuzhou 350108, China; zcguan@fzu.edu.cn (Z.G.); 220527193@fzu.edu.cn (L.X.); 220520109@fzu.edu.cn (D.C.)
* Correspondence: jkshi@fzu.edu.cn

Abstract: There have been ever more in-situ tunnel extension projects due to the growing demand for transportation. The traditional blast scheme requires a large quantity of explosive and the vibration effect is hard to control. In order to reduce explosive consumption and the vibration effect, an optimized non-cut blast scheme was proposed and applied to the in-situ expansion of the Gushan Tunnel. Refined numerical simulation was adopted to compare the traditional and optimized blast schemes. The vibration attenuation within the interlaid rock mass and the vibration effect on the adjacent tunnel were studied and compared. The simulation results were validated by the field monitoring of the vibration effect on the adjacent tunnel. Both the simulation and the monitoring results showed that the vibration velocity on the adjacent tunnel's back side was much smaller than its counterpart on the blast side, i.e., the presence of cavity reduced the blasting vibration effect significantly. The optimized non-cut blast scheme, which effectively utilized the existing free surface, could reduce the explosive consumption and vibration effect significantly, and might be preferred for in-situ tunnel expansion projects.

Keywords: in-situ tunnel expansion; non-cut blast scheme; numerical simulation; field monitoring; vibration effect

1. Introduction

Traffic volume has increased rapidly in past decades with rapid economic development in China, and a large number of existing infrastructures have become insufficient to cope with the growing traffic volume. As far as tunnels are concerned, reconstruction or in-situ expansion projects have become more and more popular in recent years (Figure 1) to meet the growing demand for traffic capacity. Similar tunnel expansion projects can also be seen outside China, such as the Lowari Tunnel in Pakistan [1], the Castellano tunnel in Italy [2] and the M2 Motorway tunnel in Sydney, Australia [3].

The drilling and blasting method still plays an important role in tunnel reconstruction or expansion projects due to its flexibility and cost-efficiency. However, blasting can lead to a great number of negative effects, including the cracking of concrete lining [4], the loosening of surrounding ground [5–10], and negative effects on adjacent structures, such as existing tunnels [11,12], pipelines [13–16], airports [17], and ground buildings [18–20]; the impact of tunnel blasting on adjacent existing tunnels is the focus of this paper.

The primary indicators utilized to assess the impact of tunnel blasting on adjacent tunnels are the response mechanism of the lining itself and the vibration variation law of surrounding rock mass. For the lining's response mechanism, Dang et al. [21] and Zhao et al. [22] studied the impact of new tunnel blasting on the safety of existing tunnels' lining using PPV and vibration frequency as safety evaluation indexes in combination with numerical simulation and field monitoring, and the research results can provide theoretical guidance for similar projects. Through a series of numerical simulations on LS-DYNA,

Han et al. [23] and Zhang [24] obtained the lining damage modes under different blast-load levels and the variation characteristics of the maximum principal stresses and PPV of adjacent tunnel linings during the excavation of existing tunnels, respectively. Wang et al. [25] used Sadovsky's empirical formula to determine the PPV attenuation law of old and new tunnel linings based on field monitoring data from an in-situ expansion project. Ma et al. [26] realized vibration signal extraction and analysis of tunnel linings and other structures in in-situ expansion projects by developing a CEEMD-MPE-HT time-frequency analysis model. Zhou et al. [27] conducted a study on the damage mechanism of tunnel lining structures under blasting loads during the excavation of an adjacent metro station using LS-DYNA. The study revealed that the lining structures experienced tensile damage when the blasting tensile stresses significantly exceeded their tensile strength. Utilizing the tunnel expansion project as an example, Zhang et al. [24] leveraged LS-DYNA to analyze the dynamic response of the adjacent tunnel lining during the blasting and excavation of an existing tunnel, using the maximum principal stresses and PPV as criteria. By combining field monitoring and numerical simulation for railway cross tunnels, Zhao et al. [28] presented a method for evaluating the blasting vibration response of existing tunnels with a full section. This method can serve as a guide for the blasting vibration control of similar projects. Utilizing hard rock tunnels as an engineering background, Zhou et al. [29] investigated the vibration effect of adjacent structures (tunnels, slopes, etc.) during tunnel blasting construction. Additionally, the blasting plan was refined by optimizing the blasting parameters, and field tests confirmed that the refined plan made sense.

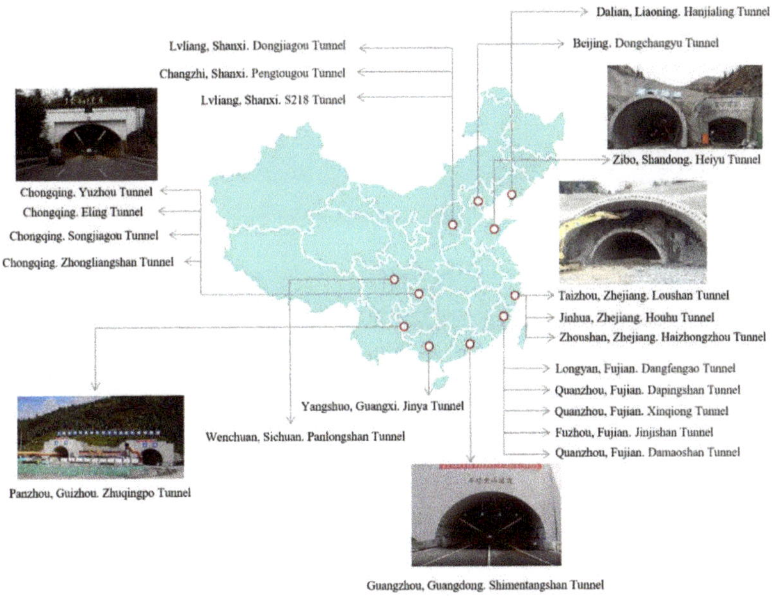

Figure 1. The engineering practices of tunnel reconstruction or expansion.

For the vibration variation law of surrounding rock mass, Dang et al. [21] concluded from 3D numerical simulation that the damage to surrounding rock mass was primarily concentrated around the new tunnel. An et al. [30] used a numerical simulation method that combined finite and discrete elements to study the rupture of surrounding rock and debris accumulation caused by blasting, and proved the superiority of the method through actual engineering monitoring data. Song et al. [31] designed a large-scale dimensional tunnel excavation simulation test system to explore the dynamic response of the interlayer surrounding rock during the excavation of a large cross-section tunnel with small clearance.

The results indicated that the blasting process during the backward tunnel excavation had a greater influence on the stability of the interlaid rock. Qiu et al. [32] derived the strain distribution on the model surface and the failure pattern of the surrounding rock under different blasting positions by conducting a series of model tests. Wang et al. [33] predicted the PPV on adjacent tunnel section considering the diffraction and reflection amplification effects of blast-induced vibration around the adjacent tunnel.

The two evaluation indicators above are closely related to the blast scheme design in underground excavation. Sharafat et al. [11] proposed an innovative approach to limit the range of explosion damage by incorporating critical particle velocity into the vibration attenuation model. Kang and Jang [34] evaluated the blast damage zone by considering both the rock mass condition and the blasting mechanism. Jia et al. [35] established three models to predict blast vibration velocity and enhance the explosion quantity by considering the free surface effect. Minh et al. [36] optimized the contour blasting parameters by numerical simulations and optimization algorithms. Iwano et al. [37] optimized the blast scheme by using advanced electronic detonators to reduce the vibration effect on the adjacent environment.

The traditional blast scheme in previous studies, however, required a large number of explosives, and it was difficult to control the vibration effects. Therefore, this paper proposed a non-cut blast scheme, aiming to reduce the explosives used in the blast and the vibration effect on the surrounding environments. The rest of this paper was structured as follows: first, the Gushan Tunnel was introduced as the engineering background for the whole; second, the traditional blast scheme and the non-cut blast scheme were analyzed and compared through refined numerical simulations; third, the non-cut blast scheme was selected and applied to engineering practice; fourth, field monitoring was carried out to assess the vibration effect on the adjacent environment and validate the efficiency of the non-cut blast scheme for an in-situ tunnel expansion project; finally, several conclusions were drawn.

2. Expansion of the Gushan Tunnel

2.1. General Situation

The Gushan Tunnel is located in the east district of Fuzhou city and serves as a significant part of the second ring road from 1987. It consists of two separate tunnels with lengths of 968 m and 936 m, respectively, and accommodates four lanes in two directions. Due to early construction and long-term heavy-duty operation, some problems appeared in the Gushan Tunnel, including insufficient thickness of the arch lining, incomplete arch back, and water seepage into the lining. At the same time, rapid economic development also led to the actual traffic volume far exceeding the design capacity of the tunnel after three decades. Therefore, the in-situ expansion project was carried out from March 2018 to June 2020 to accommodate eight lanes in two directions.

The typical cross-section of the Gushan tunnel before and after expansion (taking mileage K18+110 as an example) is shown in Figure 2. The expansion of the north tunnel was carried out first (from March 2018 to May 2019) and bidirectional transportation was temporarily shifted to the existing south tunnel with two lanes. It was succeeded by the expansion of the south tunnel (from May 2019 to June 2020) and bidirectional transportation was temporarily shifted to the expanded north tunnel with four lanes. The cross-section was extended to 16.75 m in width after expansion, and the distance between the two centerlines was extended to 37.97 m after expansion.

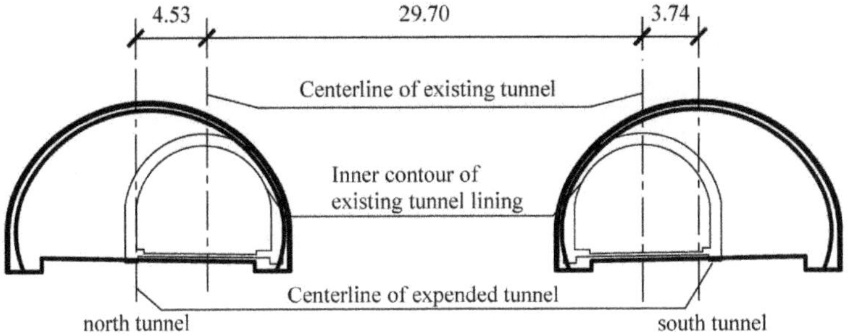

Figure 2. The typical cross-section of the Gushan tunnel before and after in-situ expansion (unit: m).

The surrounding ground mainly consisted of tuff lava (ranging from slightly weathered to strongly weathered) and was classified into grade II or grade III, according to relative specifications. The top-bench excavation method was adopted and the supporting system was designed according to the principle of the New Austrian Tunnelling Method (NATM). The shotcrete and foot-lock bolt were used as a primary lining, and the reinforced concrete was cast in place as a secondary lining. Taking mileage NK18+100~300 of the north tunnel as an example, the excavation sequence was schematically shown in Figure 3.

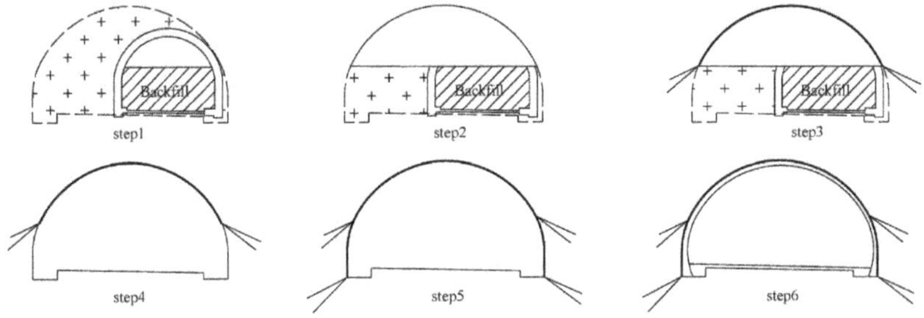

Figure 3. The excavation sequence for the in-situ expansion of the north tunnel. The dashed areas represents the lining profile after in-situ expansion and the "+" areas represent the unexcavated rock mass.

Step 1: The bench part of the existing tunnel was backfilled, which provided a work platform for the top part excavation.

Step 2: The rock mass, as well as the existing tunnel lining of the top part, was excavated.

Step 3: The primary lining of the top part was installed.

Step 4: The rock mass, the backfill, as well as the existing tunnel lining of the bench part, were excavated.

Step 5: The primary lining of the bench part was installed.

Step 6: The waterproof layer was installed and the reinforced concrete was cast in place as a secondary lining.

Controlling the vibration effect on the adjacent environment was the key issue in urban areas. According to design documents and municipal regulations, the maximum velocity of the adjacent tunnel (alternately accommodating two-direction transportation during construction) was restricted to 5 cm/s. Therefore, the traditional blast scheme, as well as the non-cut blast scheme, were both proposed in this article and described in detail as follows.

2.2. Traditional Blast Scheme

Taking mileage NK18+110 of the north tunnel as an example, the traditional blast scheme for the top part is illustrated in Figure 4, and the detailed parameters for blast holes are listed in Table 1. Each blast hole has the same diameter of 42 mm, and the designed cycle footage was 2.0 m. The depths of the auxiliary hole and peripheral hole were 2.1 m, and the depths of the "V"-type cutting hole was 2.3 m. A 2# emulsion explosive with diameter of 32 mm was used, which was initiated from the bottom by an electronic detonator. The explosive consumption for one standard cycle was 134.8 kg, and the explosive consumption per volume of rock mass was 1.35 kg/m^3.

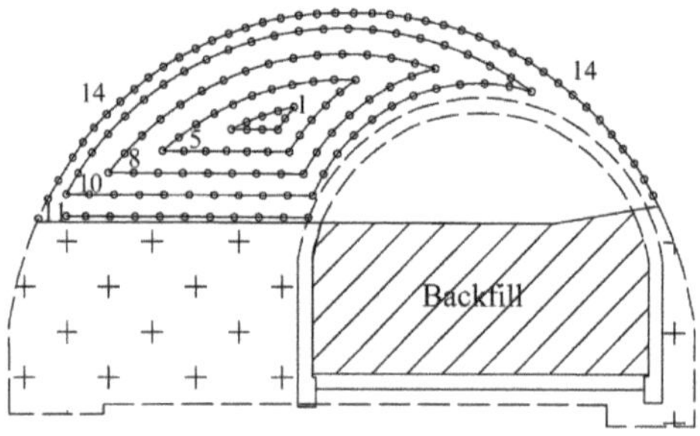

Figure 4. Traditional blast scheme for the top part of the north tunnel. Numbers represent detonator sequences. Plus sign represents unexcavated rock mass. Circles represent blast holes.

Table 1. Blast hole parameters for the traditional blast scheme.

	Detonator Sequence	Hole Distance	Number of Hole	Delayed Time	Charge Quantity per Hole	Axial Decoupling Coefficient K_l	Charge Quantity per Sequence
Cutting hole	1	0.5 m	9	0 ms	1.7 kg	1.3	15.5 kg
Auxiliary hole	5	0.6 m	19	110 ms	1.2 kg	1.8	23.2 kg
	8	0.6 m	28	250 ms	1.1 kg	2.0	30.8 kg
	10	0.6 m	30	380 ms	1.1 kg	2.0	33 kg
	11	0.6 m	11	460 ms	1.4 kg	1.6	15.1 kg
Peripheral hole	14	0.5 m	43	760 ms	0.4 kg	5.5	17.2 kg

2.3. Non-cut Blast Scheme

Considering the free surface of the existing tunnel, an optimized blast scheme without cutting hole was also proposed in this article, as illustrated in Figure 5. Instead of creating a free surface by cutting holes, the non-cut blast scheme took advantage of the existing free surface, and the arrangement of blast holes was basically parallel to the free surface (i.e., existing tunnel). The designed cycle footage and the depth of the blast hole were the same as in a traditional blast scheme, and the detailed parameters for blast holes were listed in Table 2.

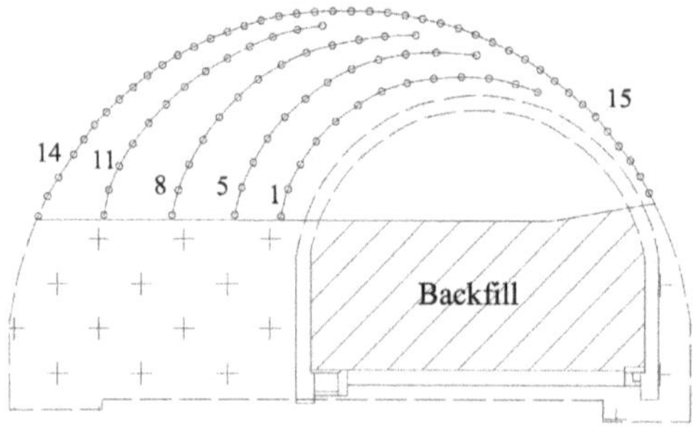

Figure 5. Non-cut blast scheme for the top part of the north tunnel.

Table 2. Blast hole parameters for non-cut blast scheme.

	Detonator Sequence	Hole Distance	Number of Hole	Delayed Time	Charge Quantity per Hole	Axial Decoupling Coefficient K_l	Charge Quantity per Sequence
Auxiliary hole	1	0.6 m	12	0 ms	1.0 kg	2.2	12.0 kg
	5	0.6 m	12	110 ms	1.0 kg	2.2	12.0 kg
	8	0.7 m	13	250 ms	1.0 kg	2.2	13.0 kg
	11	0.7 m	14	460 ms	1.0 kg	2.2	14.0 kg
Peripheral hole	14	0.5 m	20	760 ms	0.4 kg	5.5	8.0 kg
	15	0.5 m	20	880 ms	0.4 kg	5.5	8.0 kg

The maximum charge for one single sequence was reduced by 57.6%, the explosive consumption for one standard cycle was reduced by 50.3% (to 67.0 kg), and the explosive consumption per unit rock mass was reduced to 0.67 kg/m^3.

3. Numerical Simulation for the Millisecond Blasting of Tunnel Excavation

3.1. Dynamic Calculation in FLAC^{3D}

FLAC^{3D} is a fast Lagrange analysis program based on a 3D finite difference method developed by ITASCA. The program discretizes the solution domain based on a difference grid, and represents the differential equations required to be solved using finite and discrete difference equations. In the discretization process, the program uses the difference quotient approximation instead of the inverse in the differential equations to obtain the difference decomposition used to approximate the solution of the differential equations. The solution process of FLAC^{3D} adopts explicit methods, which effectively reduce memory and computation time consumption when solving large-scale problems.

The dynamic analysis module of FLAC^{3D} is also based on the explicit difference algorithm, which realizes the solution of all equations of motion by concentrating the surrounding mesh density over the mesh point mass. This method is capable of coupling rock-soil mass and structural units, making it highly suitable for analyzing soil structure-interaction issues induced by events such as earthquakes, blasting, and so on.

When performing a blast vibration analysis in FLAC, the equivalent blast load could be applied to the centerline of blasting contour (i.e., the expected excavation contour), as shown in Figure 6. The equivalent blast load was loaded as follows:

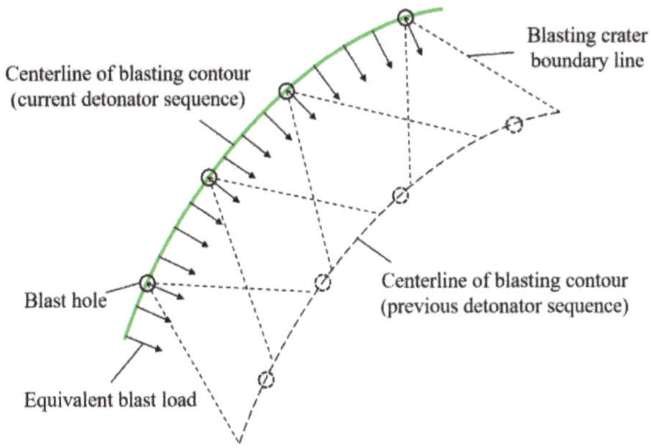

Figure 6. Loading boundary of equivalent blasting load.

Step 1: According to the position of the blast hole and the range of the rock mass to be blasted, the loading interface of explosion load was determined, and the palm face was divided into several pre-blasting areas.

Step 2: After an explosive blast in a section, the rock mass was considered to be perfectly flaked off from the area controlled by the blast hole in that section, and the grids of this area were deleted by the "Delete" command.

Step 3: The required equivalent blast loads were inputted using the "Table" command and applied to each of the reserved blast load loading interfaces using the "Apply" command.

3.2. Numerical Model

The numerical model for the Gushan tunnel was established in the FLAC^{3D} platform. The overall size of the numerical model was 250 m × 4 m × 117 m/190 m (width × depth × height left/right), as shown in Figure 7. The strata consisted of fully, strongly, moderately, and slightly weathered tuff lava, where the ground surface was slightly biased with an angle of 16°. The tunnel had an average overburden of 65 m and was mainly located in the stratum of slightly weathered tuff lava.

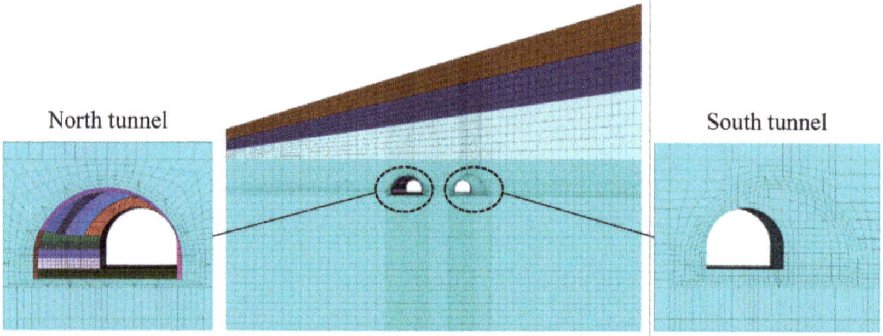

Figure 7. Numerical model for the Gushan tunnel.

The rock mass was simulated by hexahedral grids, with a total of 96,698 zones and 105,015 nodes. The Mohr-Coulomb constitutive model was adopted for each stratum, with the mechanical properties listed in Table 3. The existing tunnel lining was simulated by 3332 liner elements, with the mechanical properties also listed in Table 3.

Table 3. The mechanical properties of rock mass and existing tunnel lining.

	Density ρ (g·cm^{-3})	Young's Modulus E (GPa)	Poisson Ratio μ	Cohesive Forces c (kPa)	Friction Angle φ (°)	Thickness (m)
Strongly weathered	2.2	20.5	0.33	690	39.33	
Moderately weathered	2.5	24	0.31	1620	51.45	
Slightly weathered	2.6	26	0.3	1740	51.76	
Existing tunnel lining	2.7	32.2	0.2			0.35

The ground is typically regarded as an infinite medium when solving geotechnical engineering problems. The border far from the area of interest is generally configured as a fixed and elastic boundary in numerical simulation. In dynamic problems, however, the fixed and elastic boundary may cause the "unreal" reflection of vibration wave. The FLAC^{3D} platform provides a quiet boundary to absorb vibration energy and prevent "unreal" reflection, which can reasonably simulate the infinite rock mass.

The essence of a quiet boundary is to set a normal damper and a tangential damper on the boundary so that the vibration wave can be absorbed or canceled. The normal and tangential viscous forces (i.e., τ_n and τ_s) provided by the dampers could be calculated by [38].

$$\begin{cases} \tau_n = -\rho C_p v_n \\ \tau_s = -\rho C_s v_s \end{cases} \quad (1)$$

where, v_n and v_s were the normal and tangential velocities on the model boundary, respectively, ρ was the density of rock mass, and C_p and C_s were the compression and shear wave velocities of the stratum, respectively.

3.3. Equivalent Blasting Load for Two Blast Schemes

The instantaneous blasting process can be generally simplified as a triangular impulse load. For the ground classification of grade II and the 2# emulsion explosive, Guan et al. [39] provided an empirical formula to estimate the peak and the duration of the equivalent blasting load. The empirical formula, as shown in Equation (2), was fitted from the refined numerical simulations. The fluid–solid interaction algorithm performed on LS DYNA was used to simulate the transient process of blasting. The pressure–time history curve on the crushing zone boundary of blast hole was acquired, and the simplified triangular impulse load could be fitted for far-field vibration effect evaluation.

$$\begin{cases} P_{\max} = 187K_l^{-0.996} \\ t = 305K_l^{-0.587} \end{cases} \quad (2)$$

where, $P_{\max}$ (in MPa) and t_{dur} (in µs) were the peak pressure and the duration of equivalent blasting load, K_l (dimensionless) was the axial decoupling coefficient of the blast hole and indicated the charging quantity compared to blast hole length.

According to Equation (2) and Table 1, the equivalent blasting loads for every detonator sequence in a traditional blast scheme could be calculated and shown in Figure 8. It was notable that the time interval between adjacent detonator sequences (in milliseconds) was much larger than the duration of the equivalent blasting load (in microseconds). Therefore, the breaking in the horizontal axis (time axis) indicated the dull time without impulse load. Taking denotator sequence 8 as an example, the trigger time was 250 ms after detonation, and the peak and duration of the equivalent blasting load were 217.2 MPa and 110 µs, respectively.

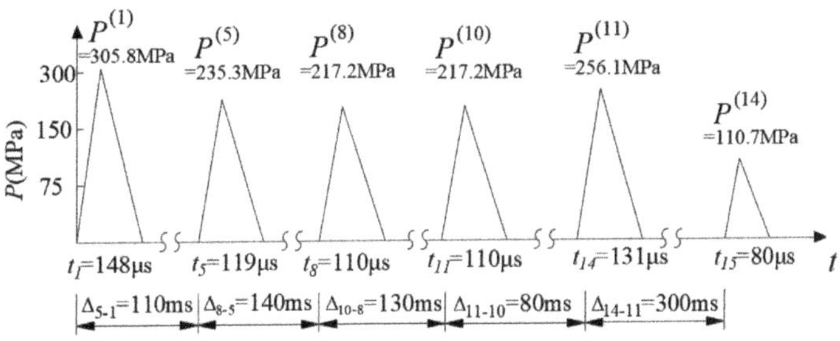

Figure 8. Equivalent blasting loads for every detonator sequence in a traditional blast scheme.

According to the excavation sequence shown in Figure 3, the bench part of the existing tunnel was backfilled first, and the top part of the existing tunnel lining was then removed from the numerical model. Subsequently, the equivalent blasting load of each detonator sequence (as shown in Figure 8) was applied to the centerline of the blasting contour (i.e., the centerline of the blast holes) in the numerical model according to the loading method in Section 3.1, chronologically. Taking detonator sequence 8 and sequence 14 as examples, the implementation of equivalent blasting loads in the traditional blast scheme was shown in Figure 9. The specific steps for implementing the equivalent blast load were as follows:

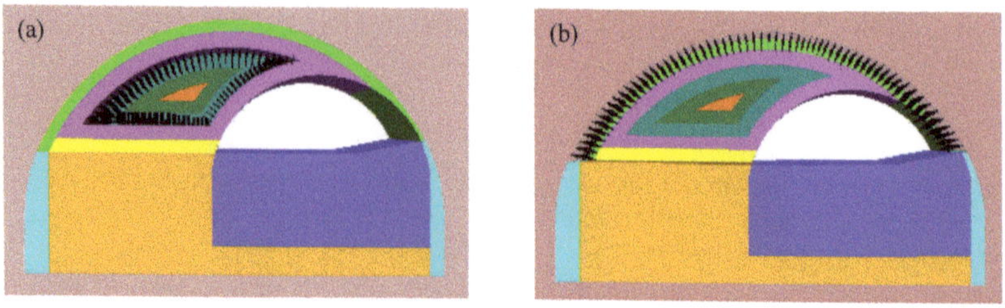

Figure 9. The implementation of equivalent blasting load for traditional blast scheme: (**a**) detonator sequence 8; (**b**) denotator sequence 14.

Step 1: Backfilled the bench part of the existing tunnel and then removed the existing lining of the top part.

Step 2: Cutting hole blasting (detonator sequence 1), removing the rock mass within the blasting contour line of the cutting hole, and loading the equivalent cutting hole blasting load on the centerline of the blasting contour.

Step 3: Auxiliary hole blasting (detonator sequences 5, 8, 10, and 11), deleting the rock mass within the blasting contour line of each auxiliary hole, and loading the equivalent blasting load of the corresponding segment on the centerline of the blasting contour.

Step 4: Peripheral hole blasting (detonator sequence 14), deleting the rock mass within the blasting contour line of the peripheral hole, and loading the peripheral hole equivalent blasting load on the centerline of the blasting contour.

The numerical model and the implementation of equivalent blasting loads for the non-cut blast scheme was basically the same as the traditional blast scheme. According to Equation (2) and Table 2, the equivalent blasting loads for every detonator sequence in the non-cut blast scheme were calculated and shown in Figure 10. For denotator sequence 8, the trigger time was 250 ms after detonation, the peak and duration of the equivalent blasting load were 104.1 MPa and 216 μs, respectively.

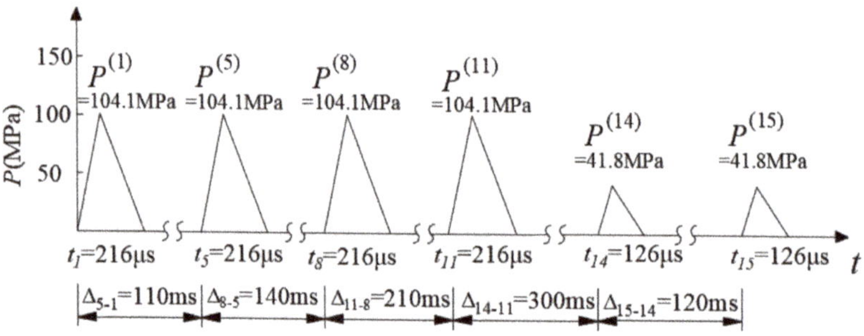

Figure 10. Equivalent blasting load for every detonator sequence in the non-cut blast scheme.

Similarly, the equivalent blasting loads shown in Figure 10 were applied chronologically upon the blasting contour (i.e., the centerline of blast holes) in the numerical model. As an example, the implementation of detonator sequence 8 and sequence 14 was shown in Figure 11. It could be seen from Figure 11 that, due to the change in the arrangement of the blast hole, the pre-division method of rock mass was also different, and the pre-excavation sections of each section were roughly distributed in strips along the outline of the existing tunnel.

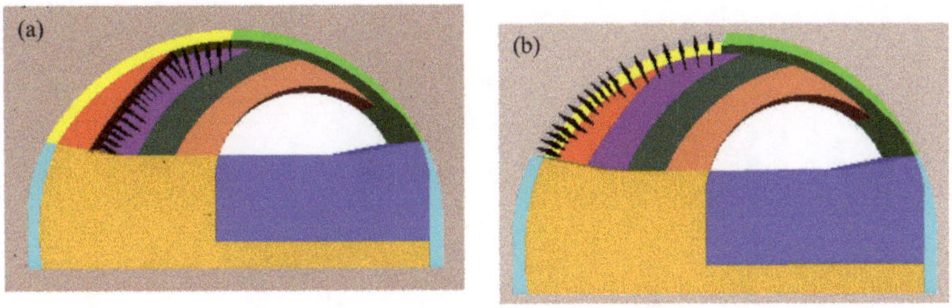

Figure 11. The implementation of equivalent blasting load for the non-cut blast scheme: (**a**) detonator sequence 8; (**b**) detonator sequence 14.

3.4. Arrangement of Numerical Monitoring Points

Monitoring points were set at key nodes in the numerical model by using the "model history" command to record the vibration response of rock mass and existing structures during the expansion blasting process. As shown in Figure 12, eight monitoring points denoted by M1~M8 were deployed on the adjacent tunnel, and sixteen monitoring points denoted by A0~A3, B0~B3, C0~C3, and D0~D3 were deployed within the interlaid rock mass. The velocity–time histories of every monitoring point during the whole blasting process were recorded, and the vibration effect on the adjacent tunnel and the vibration effect within the interlaid rock mass are carefully studied in the next section.

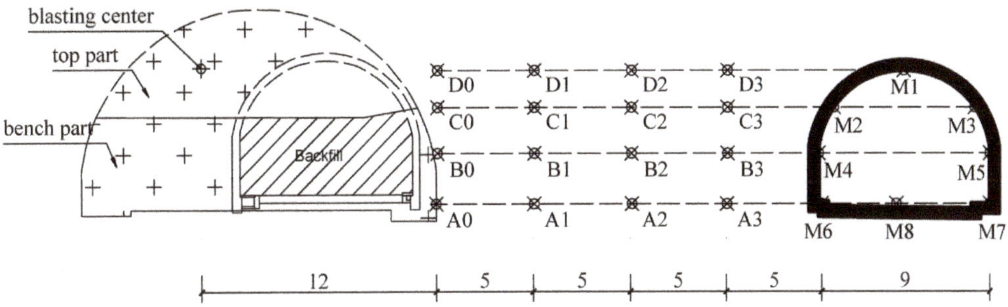

Figure 12. Arrangement of numerical monitoring points (unit: m).

4. Blasting Vibration Analyses Based on Numerical Simulations

4.1. Vibration Effect on Adjacent Tunnel

For the traditional blast scheme, the velocity–time histories of the M6 monitoring point were depicted in Figure 13 as examples. The time histories were characterized by multi-peaks, which roughly corresponded to the six detonator sequences in the traditional blast scheme. The maximum velocities occurred at detonator sequence 10#, with their values also being listed in Figure 13. The vibration effects in the X-direction and Z-direction were strongly correlated and kept changing synchronously. Fast Fourier Transform was used to obtain the frequency spectrum of the simulated vibration velocity, as shown in Figure 13b,d. The spectrum analysis showed that the velocity density was concentrated on the frequency range of 50 Hz~170 Hz for the X-direction, and the frequency range of 50 Hz~150 Hz for the Z-direction.

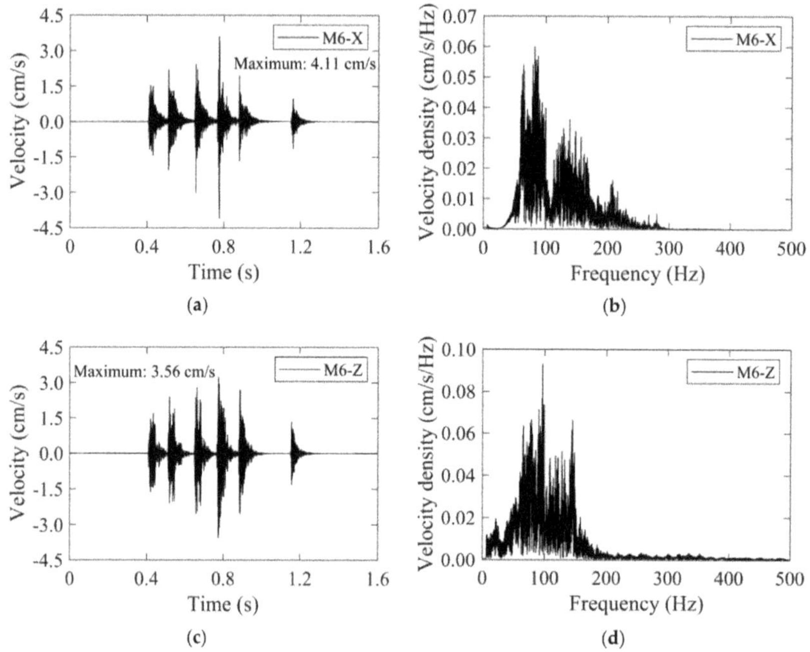

Figure 13. The velocity–time histories and frequency spectra of the M6 monitoring point for the traditional blast scheme: (**a**) time history in the X-direction, (**b**) frequency spectrum in the X-direction, (**c**) time history in the Z-direction, (**d**) frequency spectrum in the Z-direction.

Furthermore, the maximum velocities on the adjacent tunnel (i.e., M1~M8 monitoring points) were depicted in Figure 14. The maximum velocities on the left side (i.e., blast side) were much larger than their counterparts on the right side (i.e., back side). The maximum velocity occurred at point M2 (the left arch shoulder), with its value reaching 4.87 cm/s in the X-direction and 4.16 cm/s in the Z-direction, respectively, which were both very close to the safety threshold.

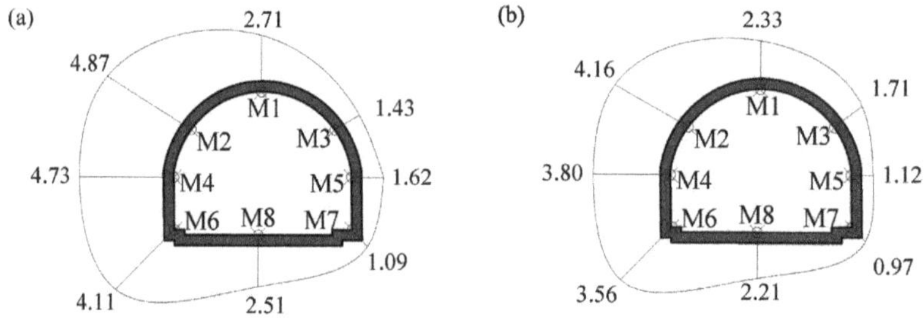

Figure 14. The maximum velocities on the adjacent tunnel for the traditional blast scheme: (**a**) the X-direction; (**b**) the Z-direction. Units: cm/s.

For the non-cut blast scheme, the velocity–time histories of the M6 monitoring point were also depicted in Figure 15. The time histories were also characterized by multi-peaks, and roughly corresponded to the six detonator sequences in the non-cut blast scheme. Due to the small charge quantity in peripheral holes and the short time interval between detonator sequences, the peaks of detonator sequences 14# and 15# were difficult to distinguish. The maximum velocities occurred at detonator sequence 1#, with their values also being listed in Figure 15. Similarly, the frequency spectrum analysis was conducted as shown in Figure 15b,d. The frequency spectrum had an identical concentrated range for velocity in the X-direction and the Z-direction, which was 50 Hz~120 Hz. The frequency spectrum of the traditional cut scheme was close to that of the non-cut scheme.

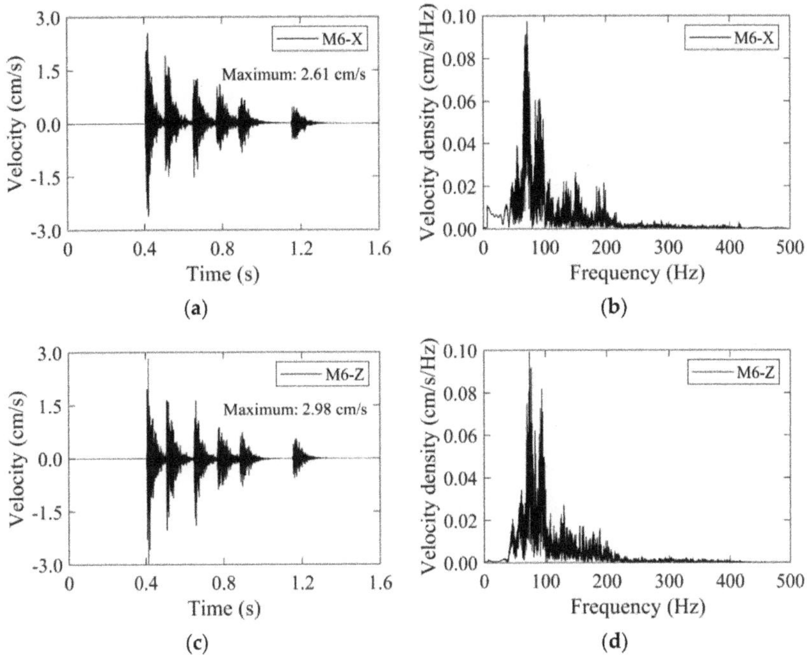

Figure 15. The velocity–time histories and frequency spectra of the M6 monitoring point for the non-cut blast scheme: (**a**) time history in the X-direction, (**b**) frequency spectrum in the X-direction, (**c**) time history in the Z-direction, (**d**) frequency spectrum in the Z-direction.

The maximum velocities on adjacent tunnel were also depicted in Figure 16, and the distribution of maximum velocities along the adjacent tunnel was similar to that in Figure 14. The maximum velocity also occurred at point M2, with its value reaching 3.48 cm/s in the X-direction and 3.63 cm/s in the Z-direction, respectively, with a large safety margin from the vibration velocity threshold. Compared to the traditional blast scheme, the vibration effect on the adjacent tunnel was roughly reduced by 30~40% by using the non-cut blast scheme, due to the face–parallel arrangement of blast holes and the lower consumption of explosives.

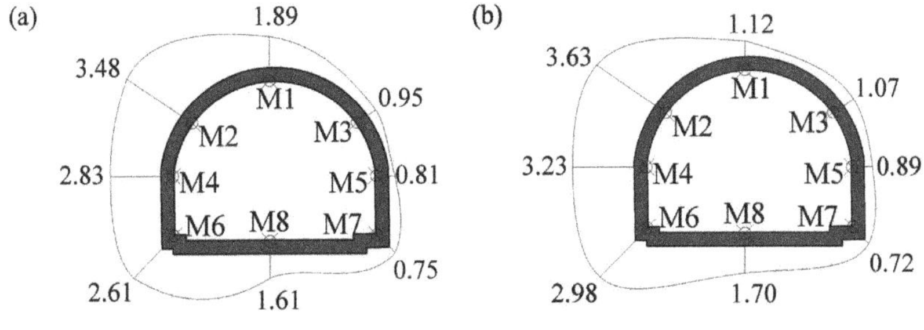

Figure 16. The maximum velocities on the adjacent tunnel for the non-cut blast scheme: (**a**) the X-direction; (**b**) the Z-direction; units: cm/s.

4.2. Vibration Effects within Interlaid Rock Mass

The maximum velocities of two blast schemes along four horizontal propagation paths were illustrated in Figures 17 and 18, respectively. Taking the traditional blast scheme as an example, the rock mass near to the blasting area vibrated significantly. The maximum velocity at the D0 measuring point reached 14.88 cm/s in the X-direction and 15.25 cm/s in the Z-direction. However, the maximum velocity declined rapidly within the propagation path of 0–5 m, where the average attenuation rate reached 1.083 cm/s (in the X-direction) and 1.422 cm/s (in the Z-direction) per meter. The attenuation rate decreased significantly within the propagation path of 5–20 m, and then increased slightly within the propagation path of 20–29 m (passing through the existing tunnel cavities). The case of the non-cut blast scheme was similar to that presented above, but not mentioned in detail. In a word, whether it was the traditional blast scheme or the non-cut blast scheme proposed in this paper, the attenuation law of vibration velocity of interlaid rock mass in the X-direction and the Z-direction showed a logarithmic form of rapid attenuation followed by slow attenuation, which also showed that the existing lining and cavity had a strong weakening effect on the vibration.

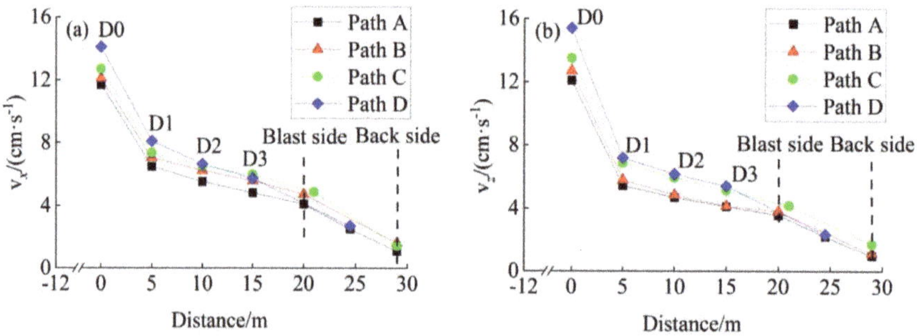

Figure 17. The maximum velocities within interlaid rock mass for the traditional blast scheme: (**a**) X-direction, (**b**) Z-direction.

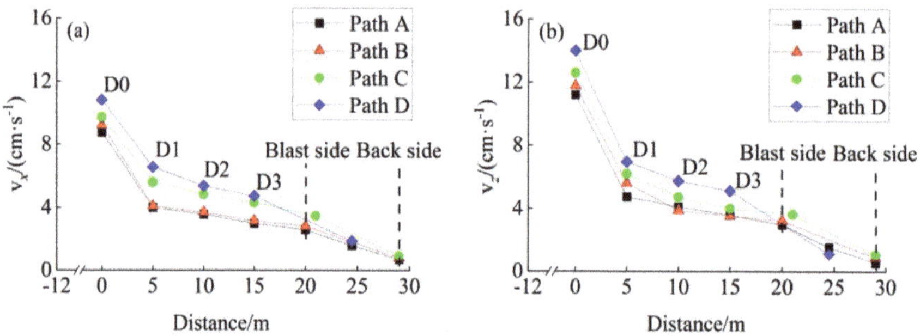

Figure 18. The maximum velocities within the interlaid rock mass for the non-cut blast scheme: (**a**) X-direction, (**b**) Z-direction.

Generally speaking, if the maximum velocity exhibited a logarithmic attenuation trend along the propagation path, then it could be fitted by Equation (3).

$$v = \alpha ln(d + \beta) + \gamma \tag{3}$$

where v denotes the maximum velocity, d denotes the horizontal distance of propagation, and α, β, and γ are fitting parameters. The fitting result of maximum velocity along path A (as shown in Figures 17 and 18) is shown in Table 4, where the Root Mean Square Error

(RMSE) and Determination Coefficient (R^2) are used as the fitting evaluation indicators. None of the RMSEs of the R^2 along path A exceeded 0.61 cm/s or 0.96, respectively. The fitting results for paths B, C, and D were similar to those of path A, which are not listed in Table 4.

Table 4. Fitting results for the peak vibration velocity attenuation on the propagation path.

Propagation Path		Fitting Equations	RMSE (cm·s^{-1})	R^2
Figure 17a	path A	$v_x = -3.521ln(d + 2.041) + 14.112$	0.606	0.96
Figure 17b	path A	$v_z = -2.473ln(d + 0.478) + 10.251$	0.553	0.97
Figure 18a	path A	$v_x = -1.876ln(d + 0.590) + 7.719$	0.416	0.97
Figure 18b	path A	$v_z = -2.373ln(d + 0.476) + 9.405$	0.552	0.97

4.3. Comparison and Summary of Two Blast Schemes

The main parameters and results of the traditional blast scheme and the non-cut blast scheme are summarized in Table 5. Among them, the non-cut blast scheme made full use of the existing tunnel-free surface and relied on the gravity of rock mass to achieve falling, which significantly reduced the amount of explosives needed. The total amount of explosives was reduced by about 50%, and the maximum amount of explosives in a single sequence was reduced by about 60%.

Table 5. Main parameters and results of the two blast schemes.

	Traditional Scheme	Optimized Scheme	Remark
Total charge (kg)	134.8	67.0	50.2% reduction
Maximum charge in single sequence (kg)	33.0	14.0	57.6% reduction
Maximum vibration velocity of monitoring points of adjacent tunnel lining (X-direction) (cm/s)	2.71 (M1) 4.87 (M2) 1.43 (M3) 4.73 (M4) 1.62 (M5) 4.11 (M6) 1.09 (M7) 2.51 (M8)	1.89 (M1) 3.48 (M2) 0.95 (M3) 2.83 (M4) 0.81 (M5) 2.61 (M6) 0.75 (M7) 1.61 (M8)	35.76% reduction in average
Maximum vibration velocity of monitoring points of adjacent tunnel lining (Z-direction) (cm/s)	2.33 (M1) 4.16 (M2) 1.71 (M3) 3.80 (M4) 1.12 (M5) 3.56 (M6) 0.97 (M7) 2.21 (M8)	1.12 (M1) 3.63 (M2) 1.07 (M3) 3.23 (M4) 0.89 (M5) 2.98 (M6) 0.72 (M7) 1.70 (M8)	25.35% reduction in average
Average attenuation rate of interlaid rock mass (X-direction) (cm·s^{-1}/m)	(0–5 m): 1.083 (5–20 m): 0.159 (20–29 m): 0.354	(0–5 m): 0.911 (5–20 m): 0.106 (20–29 m): 0.239	Basically consistent
Average attenuation rate of interlaid rock mass (Z-direction) (cm·s^{-1}/m)	(0–5 m): 1.422 (5–20 m): 0.146 (20–29 m): 0.286	(0–5 m): 1.305 (5–20 m): 0.149 (20–29 m): 0.271	Basically consistent

Based on the vibration velocity of the adjacent tunnel, the vibration intensity distribution of the two blast schemes on the lining was basically consistent, and the maximum vibration velocity was obtained at the arch shoulder of the blast side. Among them, the vibration of the non-cut blast scheme was reduced by approximately 28.54% in the X-direction and 12.74% in the Z-direction at the blast side's arch shoulder, and the average vibration reduction amplitudes of each point of the adjacent tunnel lining in the X- and Z-directions were approximately 35.76% and 25.35%, respectively. According to the average attenuation rate of interlaid rock mass in Table 5, it could be considered that the vibration attenuation velocity of the two blast schemes in the X-direction and Z-direction was basically consistent.

In general, the non-cut blast scheme was a simple blast hole arrangement, and could make full use of the existing free surface to enhance the rock-breaking effect and achieve the rock falling by its own gravity, which greatly saved the amount of explosives and made the blasting vibration lighter, so it was obviously more suitable for in situ expansion projects.

5. Blasting Vibration Analyses Based on Field Monitoring

According to the numerical simulations as presented above, the non-cut blast scheme was superior to the traditional blast scheme in terms of reducing explosive consumption and vibration effect. Therefore, the non-cut blast scheme was put into practice for the in-situ expansion project of the Gushan Tunnel, and the upper part of the NK18+110 section before and after expansion is illustrated in Figure 19.

Figure 19. The upper part of NK18+110 section before and after expansion.

To assess the vibration effect on the adjacent tunnel and validate the efficiency of the non-cut blast scheme, filed monitoring was also conducted during the in situ expansion of the north tunnel. Two blasting vibration meters were installed at the feet of the adjacent tunnel, as shown in Figure 20. The vibration meter was composed of a micro-computer and two sensors. Among the two sensors, one was the vibration sensor monitoring the velocity, and the other was the sound sensor monitoring the noise in the environment. The computer surrogated the monitoring of the two sensors and transferred the monitoring data to the remote platform wirelessly. The velocity sensing range was 0.0005~35 cm/s, and the frequency sensing range was 5~500 Hz. The two vibration meters corresponded to the M6 point (on the blast side) and M7 point (on the back side) in numerical simulations, respectively. The vibration meters followed up with the advancement of the north tunnel excavation face, as seen in Figure 21. A total of 136 cycles were carried out in the north tunnel excavation (from NK18+100 to NK+300 with ground classification of grade II). As far as 42 standard footage cycles in the upper part of north tunnel were concerned, 84 monitoring data (velocity–time histories) were recorded.

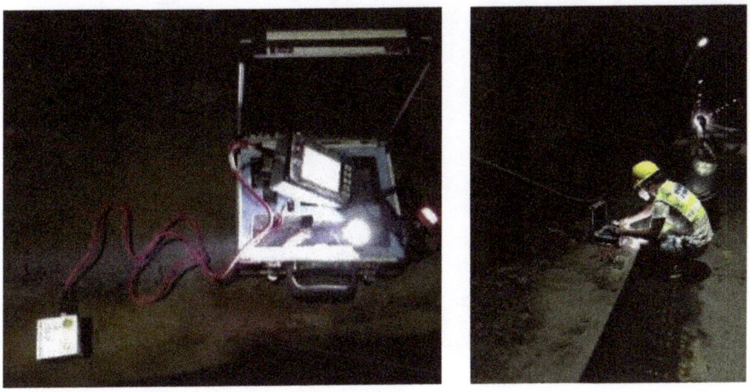

Figure 20. Field monitoring for blasting vibration.

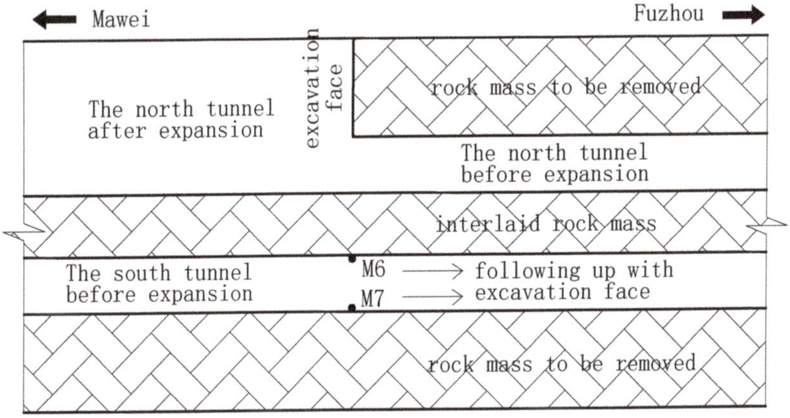

Figure 21. Arrangement of blasting vibration meters.

Taking the upper part of the NK18+110 section as an example, the velocity–time histories obtained from field monitoring are depicted in Figure 22. Similar to the simulation results, the time histories were also characterized by multi-peaks, and generally corresponded to five detonator sequences. The maximum velocities at the left foot (blast side) were 2.23 cm/s in the *xX*-direction and 2.52 cm/s in the *Z*-direction, and occurred at detonator sequence 1#. The maximum velocities at the right foot (back side) were 0.85 cm/s in the *X*-direction and 0.82 cm/s in the *Z*-direction, much smaller than their counterparts at the left foot.

The velocity–time histories corresponding to 42 standard footage cycles were all recorded in a similar way, with their maximum velocities being summarized in Table 6. The monitoring data showed that the maximum velocities of the south tunnel were all less than 3 cm/s and under the safety threshold of 5 cm/s, which implied that the non-cut blast scheme was more suitable for the in situ tunnel expansion projects.

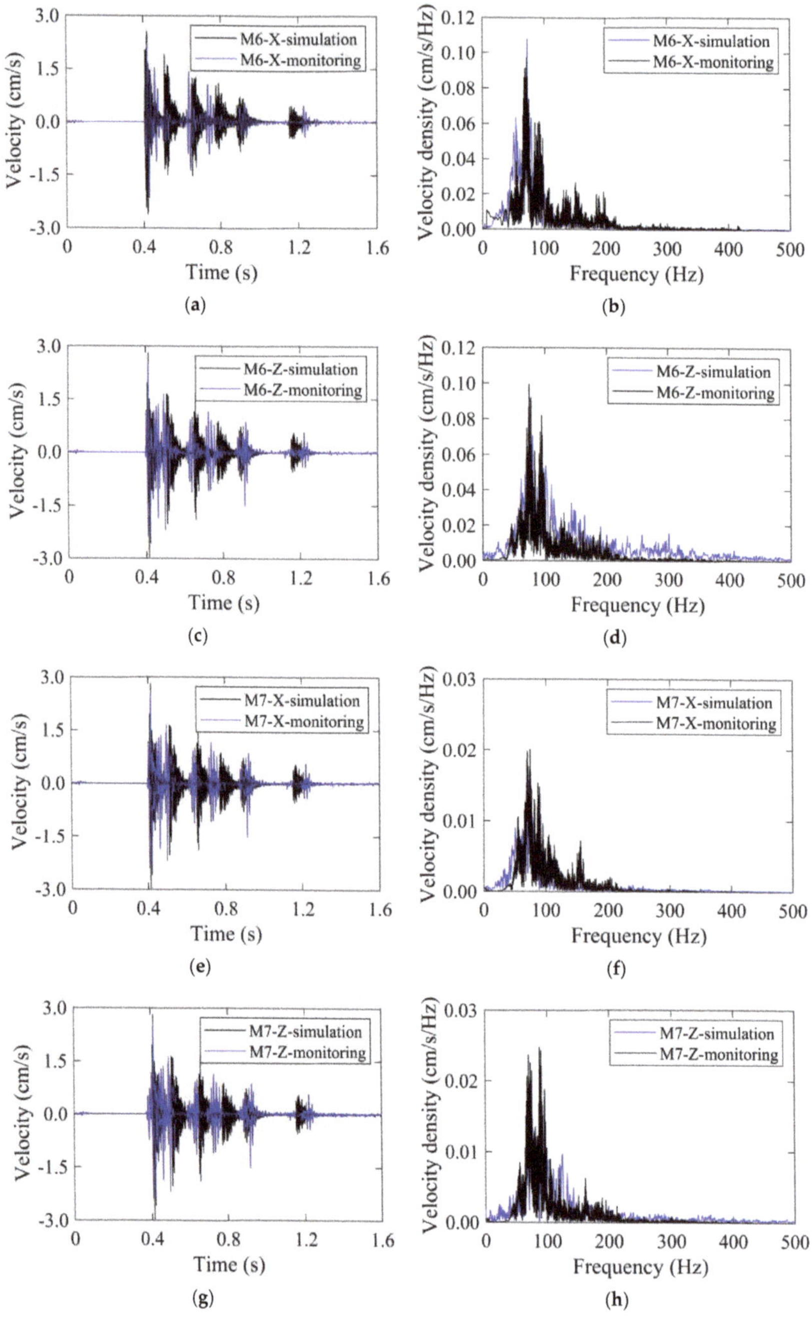

Figure 22. The velocity–time histories and frequency spectra recorded by field monitoring and compared with numerical simulation results: (**a**) time history of M6 in the *X*-direction, (**b**) frequency spectrum of M6 in the *X*-direction, (**c**) time history of M6 in the Z-direction, (**d**) frequency spectrum of M6 in the Z-direction, (**e**) time history of M7 in the *X*-direction, (**f**) frequency spectrum of M7 in the *X*-direction, (**g**) time history of M7 in the Z-direction, (**h**) frequency spectrum of M7 in the Z-direction.

Table 6. Maximum velocities of M6 and M7 monitoring points.

Monitoring Point	Mileage	In X-Direction ($cm \cdot s^{-1}$)	In Z-Direction ($cm \cdot s^{-1}$)
M6	NK18+104	2.44	2.61
	NK18+110	2.23	2.52
	NK18+214	2.52	2.98
	...	...	...
	averaged	2.44	2.51
M7	NK18+104	0.73	0.70
	NK18+110	0.85	0.82
	NK18+214	0.75	0.54
	...	...	...
	averaged	0.76	0.77

Furthermore, the maximum velocities recorded from 42 standard footage cycles were averaged to 2.44 cm/s (M6 in the X-direction), 2.51 cm/s (M6 in the Z-direction), 0.76 cm/s (M7 in the X-direction), and 0.77 cm/s (M7 in the Z-direction), respectively. The maximum velocities on the blast side being slightly overestimated by 7.0%. The simulated time histories of vibration velocity agreed well with the field monitoring results from Figure 22a,c,e,g. Furthermore, the simulated frequency spectrum also agreed with the field monitoring results. The concentrated frequency ranges for both monitored and simulated velocity were 50 Hz~120 Hz. The velocity spectrum density of point M6 was much higher than that of point M7. This observation was in accordance with time history analysis.

6. Conclusions

Based on the in situ expansion project of the Gushan Tunnel in Fuzhou, the traditional and optimized blast schemes were thoroughly compared through refined numerical simulations. The vibration attenuation within the interlaid rock mass and the vibration effect on the adjacent tunnel lining were investigated. The optimized non-cut blast scheme was then put into practice, and the vibration effect on the adjacent tunnel lining was monitored. Some conclusions could be drawn as follows:

(1) Applying equivalent blasting loads upon the blasting contour by detonator sequences could simulate the whole process of millisecond blasting, which could be used as an effective method for blast scheme optimization and vibration effect prediction.
(2) Both the simulation and the monitoring results showed that the vibration effect on the adjacent tunnel's back side was much smaller than its counterpart on the blast side. In particular, the presence of a cavity considerably reduced the blasting vibration effect.
(3) The non-cut blast scheme, which effectively utilized the existing free surface, could reduce the explosive consumption and vibration effect significantly, and might be preferred for the tunnel in situ expansion projects.

In a further study, the detailed layout of blast holes could be optimized through a series of numerical simulations, and the proposed non-cut construction method might be validated in more field cases.

Author Contributions: Conceptualization, Z.G. and J.S.; methodology, L.X.; software, L.X.; validation, Z.G. and L.X.; formal analysis, D.C.; investigation, D.C.; resources, Z.G.; data curation, L.X. and J.S.; writing—original draft preparation, L.X. and J.S.; writing—review and editing, Z.G. and J.S.; visualization, D.C.; supervision, Z.G.; project administration, Z.G.; funding acquisition, Z.G. All authors have read and agreed to the published version of the manuscript.

Funding: This research was funded by the Natural Science Foundation of China, grant number 52278399 and the Natural Science Foundation of Fujian Province, grant number 2021J01599.

Institutional Review Board Statement: Not applicable.

Informed Consent Statement: Not applicable.

Data Availability Statement: The data used to support the findings of this study are included within the article.

Conflicts of Interest: The authors declare no conflicts of interest.

References

1. Khan, B.; Jamil, S.M.; Jafri, T.H.; Akhtar, K. Effects of different empirical tunnel design approaches on rock mass behaviour during tunnel widening. *Heliyon* **2019**, *5*, e02944. [CrossRef] [PubMed]
2. Andrea, O. Design and excavation for the widening of a railway tunnel: The case of the Castellano tunnel in Italy. In Proceedings of the SEE Tunnel: Promoting Tunneling in SEE Region "ITA WTC 2015 Congress and 41st General Assembly, Dubrovnik, Croatia, 22–28 May 2015.
3. Bertuzzi, R. Back-analysing rock mass modulus from monitoring data of two tunnels in Sydney, Australia. *J. Rock Mech. Geotech. Eng.* **2017**, *9*, 877–891. [CrossRef]
4. Wu, L.M.; Wang, Z.J.; Chang, Y.Z.; Gao, F.; Zhang, B.; Wu, Y.; Fan, H.X. Vibration Performance of Steel Fiber Concrete Tunnel Lining by Adjacent Tunnel Blasting Construction. *Appl. Sci.* **2023**, *13*, 4201. [CrossRef]
5. Li, Y.; Zhu, J.; Han, D.; Zhao, R.; Ma, Y.; Zhou, T. Experimental study of the dynamic responses of surrounding jointed rock masses and adjacent underground openings and induced ground vibrations subjected to underground explosion. *Tunn. Undergr. Space Technol.* **2023**, 105060. [CrossRef]
6. Zhao, Y.; Feng, S.; Zhang, X.; Zheng, Q.; Cao, B. Numerical analysis of the impact of drill-and-blast tunneling on an overlying landfill. *Comput. Geotech.* **2024**, *170*, 106296. [CrossRef]
7. Ramulu, M.; Chakraborty, A.K.; Sitharam, T.G. Damage assessment of basaltic rock mass due to repeated blasting in a railway tunnelling project—A case study. *Tunn. Undergr. Space Technol.* **2009**, *24*, 208–221. [CrossRef]
8. Mesec, J.; Vrkljan, D.; Ester, Z. Allowed Quantity of Explosive Charge Depending on the Distance from the Blast. *Geotech. Geol. Eng.* **2009**, *27*, 431–438. [CrossRef]
9. Ishchenko, O.; Konoval, V.; Ishchenko, K. Physical and simulation modelling of solid media fracturing by means of explosive charges of different cross-sectional shapes. *Min. Miner. Depos.* **2022**, *16*, 122–131. [CrossRef]
10. Chakraborty, A.K.; Pal Roy, P.; Jethwa, J.L.; Gupta, R.N. Blast performance in small tunnels—A critical evaluation in underground metal mines. *Tunn. Undergr. Space Technol.* **1998**, *13*, 331–339. [CrossRef]
11. Sharafat, A.; Tanoli, W.A.; Raptis, G.; Seo, J.W. Controlled blasting in underground construction: A case study of a tunnel plug demolition in the Neelum Jhelum hydroelectric project. *Tunn. Undergr. Space Technol.* **2019**, *93*, 103098. [CrossRef]
12. Peng, Y.X.; Liu, G.J.; Wu, L.; Zuo, Q.J.; Liu, Y.S.; Zhang, C. Comparative study on tunnel blast-induced vibration for the underground cavern group. *Environ. Earth Sci.* **2021**, *80*, 68. [CrossRef]
13. Jiang, N.; Gao, T.; Zhou, C.B.; Luo, X.D. Effect of excavation blasting vibration on adjacent buried gas pipeline in a metro tunnel. *Tunn. Undergr. Space Technol.* **2018**, *81*, 590–601. [CrossRef]
14. Xia, Y.; Jiang, N.; Zhou, C.; Sun, J.; Luo, X.; Wu, T. Dynamic behaviors of buried reinforced concrete pipelines with gasketed bell-and-spigot joints subjected to tunnel blasting vibration. *Tunn. Undergr. Space Technol.* **2021**, *118*, 104172. [CrossRef]
15. Zhu, B.; Jiang, N.; Zhou, C.; Luo, X.; Li, H.; Chang, X.; Xia, Y. Dynamic interaction of the pipe-soil subject to underground blasting excavation vibration in an urban soil-rock stratum. *Tunn. Undergr. Space Technol.* **2022**, *129*, 104700. [CrossRef]
16. Guan, X.; Zhang, L.; Wang, Y.; Fu, H.; An, J. Velocity and stress response and damage mechanism of three types pipelines subjected to highway tunnel blasting vibration. *Eng. Fail. Anal.* **2020**, *118*, 104840. [CrossRef]
17. Lu, S.; Zhou, C.; Jiang, N.; Xu, X. Effect of Excavation Blasting in an Under-Cross Tunnel on Airport Runway. *Geotech. Geol. Eng.* **2015**, *33*, 973–981. [CrossRef]
18. Fan, H.; Yu, D.; Zhao, D.; Lai, J.; Xie, Y. Experimental and numerical investigation of blasting-induced ground vibration from tunnel undercrossing a village. *Civ. Eng. J.-Staveb. Obz.* **2017**, *26*, 404–417.
19. Shi, H.; Jiang, N.; Zhou, C.; Zhnag, Y.; Yao, Y.; Zhou, W.; Cai, Z. Safety assessment of ancient buddhist pagoda induced by underpass metro tunnel blasting vibration. *Eng. Fail. Anal.* **2023**, *145*, 107051. [CrossRef]
20. Ren, K.; Jiang, A.; Guo, X.; Min, Q. Research on Optimization Design of Tunnel Blasting Scheme Adjacent to Buildings. *Appl. Sci.* **2023**, *13*, 11509. [CrossRef]
21. Dang, V.K.; Dias, D.; Do, N.A.; Vo, T.H. Impact of blasting at tunnel face on an existing adjacent tunnel. *Int. J. GEOMATE* **2018**, *15*, 22–31. [CrossRef]
22. Zhao, H.; Long, Y.; Li, X.; Lu, L. Experimental and numerical investigation of the effect of blast-induced vibration from adjacent tunnel on existing tunnel. *KSCE J. Civ. Eng.* **2016**, *20*, 431–439. [CrossRef]
23. Han, Y.Z.; Liu, H.B. Failure of circular tunnel in saturated soil subjected to internal blast loading. *Geomech. Eng.* **2016**, *11*, 421–438. [CrossRef]
24. Zhang, M. Numerical analysis for dynamic response of in situ blasting expansion of large cross-section tunnel with small net distance. *Adv. Civ. Eng.* **2021**, *2021*, 2896782. [CrossRef]
25. Wang, Y.Q.; Gong, L.J.; An, N.N.; Peng, X.B.; Wang, W.; Wang, Z.F. Field investigation of blasting-induced vibration in concrete linings during expansion of old highway tunnel. *Adv. Civ. Eng.* **2021**, *2021*, 8820544. [CrossRef]

26. Ma, C.Y.; Wu, L.; Sun, M.; Yuan, Q. Time-frequency analysis and application of a vibration signal of tunnel excavation blasting based on CEEMD-MPE-HT. *Shock Vib.* **2021**, *2021*, 6672942. [CrossRef]
27. Zhou, J.; Shu, P.; Zhang, B.; Deng, B.; Wu, Y. A Finite Element Analysis of Tunnel Lining Demolition by Blasting for Subway Tunnel Expansion. *Appl. Sci.* **2022**, *12*, 9564. [CrossRef]
28. Zhao, Y.; Wang, H.; Shan, R. Blasting vibration effect and safety evaluation method of railway cross tunnels. *Tunn. Undergr. Space Technol.* **2024**, *145*, 105588. [CrossRef]
29. Zhou, J.; Gao, S.; Luo, P.; Fan, J.; Zhao, C. Optimization of Blasting Parameters Considering Both Vibration Reduction and Profile Control: A Case Study in a Mountain Hard Rock Tunnel. *Buildings* **2024**, *14*, 1421. [CrossRef]
30. An, H.M.; Liu, H.Y.; Han, H.; Zheng, X.; Wang, X.G. Hybrid finite-discrete element modelling of dynamic fracture and resultant fragment casting and muck-piling by rock blast. *Comput. Geotech.* **2017**, *81*, 322–345. [CrossRef]
31. Song, S.G.; Li, S.C.; Li, L.P.; Shi, S.S.; Zhou, Z.Q.; Liu, Z.H.; Shang, C.S.; Sun, H.Z. Model test study on vibration blasting of large cross-section tunnel with small clearance in horizontal stratified surrounding rock. *Tunn. Undergr. Space Technol.* **2019**, *92*, 103013. [CrossRef]
32. Qiu, J.D.; Li, X.B.; Li, D.Y.; Zhao, Y.Z.; Hu, C.W.; Liang, L.S. Physical Model Test on the Deformation Behavior of an Underground Tunnel Under Blasting Disturbance. *Rock Mech. Rock Eng.* **2021**, *54*, 91–108. [CrossRef]
33. Wang, X.; Li, J.; Zhao, X.; Liang, Y. Propagation characteristics and prediction of blast-induced vibration on closely spaced rock tunnels. *Tunn. Undergr. Space Technol.* **2022**, *123*, 104416. [CrossRef]
34. Kang, S.S.; Jang, H.A. case study on tunnel blasting design evaluation considering blast damage zone. *Sci. Technol. Energ. Mater* **2020**, *81*, 106–113.
35. Jia, B.X.; Zhou, L.L.; Cui, J.J.; Chen, H. Attenuation model of tunnel blast vibration velocity based on the influence of free surface. *Sci. Rep.* **2021**, *11*, 21077. [CrossRef] [PubMed]
36. Minh, N.N.; Cao, P.; Liu, Z.Z. Contour blasting parameters by using a tunnel blast design mode. *J. Cen. South Univ.* **2021**, *28*, 100–111. [CrossRef]
37. Iwano, K.; Hashiba, K.; Nagae, J.; Fukui, K. Reduction of tunnel blasting induced ground vibrations using advanced electronic detonators. *Tunn. Undergr. Space Technol.* **2020**, *105*, 103556. [CrossRef]
38. Lysmer, J.; Waas, G. Shear Waves in Plane Infinite Structures. *J. Eng. Mech. Div.* **1972**, *98*, 85–105. [CrossRef]
39. Guan, Z.; Zhu, L.; Yu, B. Fine numerical simulation of row-hole blasting in tunnel excavation. *J. Vib. Shock* **2021**, *40*, 154–162. (In Chinese)

buildings

Article

Automatic Generation of Standard Nursing Unit Floor Plan in General Hospital Based on Stable Diffusion

Zhuo Han and Yongquan Chen *

School of Architecture and Design, Beijing Jiaotong University, Beijing 100000, China; 21140609@bjtu.edu.cn
* Correspondence: chenyongquan@bjtu.edu.cn

Abstract: This study focuses on the automatic generation of architectural floor plans for standard nursing units in general hospitals based on Stable Diffusion. It aims at assisting architects in efficiently generating a variety of preliminary plan preview schemes and enhancing the efficiency of the pre-planning stage of medical buildings. It includes dataset processing, model training, model testing and generation. It enables the generation of well-organized, clear, and readable functional block floor plans with strong generalization capabilities by inputting the boundaries of the nursing unit's floor plan. Quantitative analysis demonstrated that 82% of the generated samples met the evaluation criteria for standard nursing units. Additionally, a comparative experiment was conducted using the same dataset to train a deep learning model based on Generative Adversarial Networks (GANs). The conclusion describes the strengths and limitations of the methodology, pointing out directions for improvement by future studies.

Keywords: standard nursing unit; automatic generation of floor plans; stable diffusion; LoRA fine-turning; generative adversarial network

1. Introduction

As artificial intelligence develops, using deep learning models for architectural floor plan generation has become a cutting-edge research hotspot in the field of architectural design. Relevant research has already made breakthroughs in the residential building type, producing relatively ideal results [1,2]. This can significantly reduce repetitive labor time for architects during the planning phase and even allow ordinary people to participate in the architectural design process. The success in using residential buildings as research subjects can be attributed to two main reasons: First, there is a large amount of floor plan data available, such as the open-source dataset RPLAN [3], which contains more than 80,000 residential floor plans that researchers can directly access for deep learning training. Secondly, the functional relationships in residential buildings are relatively simple, and the generated results have a high tolerance for errors, providing a relaxed premise for research. However, architects need to design a variety of building types, and due to data protection measures by different companies, it is often difficult to obtain large datasets for special types of buildings like those available for residential buildings. Therefore, research on floor plan generation based on small sample size data is highly necessary.

1.1. Nursing Units as Research Objects

After the COVID-19 pandemic, the demand for the construction of general hospitals in China has gradually increased. Choosing the standard nursing units of general hospitals as research objects has practical significance. In a general hospital, a standard nursing unit consists of a fully equipped team (doctors, nurses, and support staff), several patient beds, related diagnostic and treatment facilities, as well as associated medical, living, administrative, and circulation spaces. It operates with functional independence. It is typically connected to medical technology departments and outpatient departments via vertical circulation, ensuring horizontal independence [4–6]. The floor plans of these units have undergone many years of development, and their functional configurations and spatial organizations have become increasingly mature, highly standardized, and typified [4]. However, in nursing units, the various functions are highly interrelated. Taking the centralized nursing unit as an example, the nurse station must be positioned at the center of the unit to better serve patients. Patient rooms need to be situated on the southern side of the unit for better daylighting, and corridors must connect every space to avoid functional overlaps and intersections. These factors pose certain challenges for research.

A standard nursing unit typically encompasses wards for fundamental medical disciplines such as internal medicine, surgery, ENT, obstetrics and gynecology, and pediatrics. The required supporting facilities for these wards are generally similar. However, specialized nursing units such as infection wards and ICUs require unique workflow designs and are not included within the scope of this study.

1.2. Using SD + LoRA as the Generation Method

The emergence of the Diffusion model [7] has propelled the significant advancement of deep generative models, marking a new milestone for the AI industry as it transitions from the era of traditional deep learning to the era of Artificial Intelligence Generated Content (AIGC). The Stable Diffusion (SD) model [8], a large generative model based on a latent diffusion process, is a fully open-source project with a vast application community. Techniques like Low-Rank Adaptation (LoRA) [9] can be used for parameter-efficient fine-tuning, enabling personalized adjustments under conditions of small sample data to meet various generative task requirements. Additionally, the SD model supports multiple generation control methods, granting it substantial generative flexibility to satisfy diverse application needs. Notably, the SD model incorporates innovative modules such as self-attention and cross-attention mechanisms [10], significantly enhancing the model's generative quality and control precision.

1.3. Highlights

This study innovatively employed the SD model to generate floor plans for standard nursing units. The input consisted of bitmap images of the nursing unit boundaries, and the output was the functional layout of the nursing unit. Before the experiment, we first studied the layout composition of nursing units and created a dataset based on their characteristics. Subsequently, we fine-tuned the Stable Diffusion model using LoRA. Then, during the generation process, hyperparameter adjustments and the combination of various control methods were the focus of the research. Multiple control variable experiments were conducted for different hyperparameters and control methods. Additionally, the introduction of major control structures into the input conditions optimized the generation results and improved the qualification rate of the generated layouts. Ultimately, through quantitative analysis of the generated samples and real samples, the study demonstrated that the workflow of fine-tuning the SD model with LoRA can serve as a method for automatic floor plan generation for buildings with small sample sizes, and it established an automated workflow from parameter-controlled generation of nursing unit boundaries to functional layout generation by the SD model.

2. Related Work

Before 2022, research on architectural floor plan generation based on deep learning mainly employed Generative Adversarial Network (GAN) models [11]. GAN models consist of a generator and a discriminator. The generator is responsible for generating new data samples similar to the training data samples, while the discriminator determines whether the input data is real training data or fake data. The generator accepts random noise input and attempts to generate data that can deceive the discriminator, while the discriminator strives not to be deceived by the generator. The two form an adversarial training process, alternating optimization, ultimately achieving high-quality generated data that is difficult to distinguish from real data. The widespread application of GAN models in the field of architectural floor plan generation can be attributed to the pix2pix model, improved by Isola P. et al. (2017) from GAN, which realized Image-to-Image translation using paired data [12]. This was followed by the derivation of pix2pixHD, which can generate higher-resolution images [13].

In recent years, most research applying GAN models for architectural floor plan generation has employed the aforementioned Image-to-Image approach, predominantly focusing on residential buildings. Huang W. et al. (2018) used pix2pixHD for residential floor plan generation and first proposed the method of marking functional rooms in apartment floor plans with color blocks to construct training sets and generate results [14]. Chaillou S. (2019) trained a workflow with pix2pix to gradually generate and associate derivations from building contours to room segmentation to furniture layout, simulating the architect's design process [15]. At the CAADRIA conference in 2020, Zheng H. et al. demonstrated the use of apartment datasets from China and Japan to train the pix2pixHD model separately, achieving satisfactory generation results [16]. Pan Y. et al. (2021) first attempted to use the upgraded version of the pix2pixHD model, GauGAN, for generation experiments. They used data on roads, buildings, and other information from northern Chinese communities to train the GauGAN model to generate residential building layouts, aiming for higher resolution and more diverse generation results, as well as adapting to irregular contour conditions [17].

In 2021, Nelson N. et al. introduced the HouseGAN++ model, which improved the model network using relational GANs and conditional GANs, achieving iterative refinement by making the previous generation result a constraint condition for the next generation [2]. Luo Z. et al. (2022) proposed a GAN model framework that combines vector generation and raster image discrimination capable of directly generating vector floor plans, though limited to rectangular room blocks [18].

The use of GAN models for automatic architectural floor plan generation has formed a relatively common and effective methodology, namely dividing architectural floor plans into specific functional areas, establishing segmentation masks for rooms or different functional areas to form identifiable training data, thereby establishing a deep learning model for training and simulation. This approach reduces the complexity of machine recognition and learning of architectural floor plans and significantly improves generation efficiency.

From late 2022, the field gradually began to see research using diffusion models as the primary tool. Shabani et al. introduced a new method for generating vector floor plans using diffusion models, named HouseDiffusion [1]. The authors represented floor plans as one-dimensional polygonal rings, with each ring corresponding to a room or door. By denoising the two-dimensional coordinates of these two inference targets, vector graphic floor plans were directly generated. Qualitative and quantitative evaluations indicated that the proposed system outperformed the state-of-the-art technology House-GAN++ [2]. In other research directions, Fan Y. et al. (2023) enhanced indoor lighting ambiance by converting optimized shading patterns into landscape or animal patterns using customized LoRA models [19]. Wang L. et al. (2023) conducted generation experiments for shear wall layout in residential floor plans using the SD model, comparing the generation results with those of GAN and CNN models [20]. This study's methodology draws on the approaches used in the aforementioned research on residential floor plan generation [14–16]. However, it differs by focusing on nursing unit floor plans with small sample sizes, marking the first known attempt to use SD+LoRA for automatic floor plan generation of healthcare-type buildings.

3. Preliminary

Figure 1a depicts the architecture of the Latent Diffusion Model (LDM) [8], which forms the foundation of the SD model. Initially, the input image x is transformed into a latent representation $\mathcal{Z}$ via an encoder ε. In the latent space, the diffusion process starts from the initial noise $\mathcal{Z}_T$ and progressively denoises it using a Denoising U-Net ϵ_θ, resulting in the latent representation $\mathcal{Z}_0$. The Denoising U-Net incorporates conditional information (such as semantic maps, text descriptions, representations, and images) during the denoising process, integrating external conditions at each step through a cross-attention mechanism. Finally, the latent representation $\mathcal{Z}_0$ is converted back to pixel space by a decoder $\mathcal{D}$, yielding the reconstructed image $\tilde{\mathcal{X}}$. This approach allows for efficient denoising and generation in the latent space, while leveraging conditional information to control the generation outcomes. The SD model can generate high-quality images based on given text descriptions. Training foundational models requires substantial computational resources, which small research teams cannot independently manage. Researchers have developed cost-effective fine-tuning methods [9,21,22], making it possible to deploy SD models on consumer-grade GPUs. From the perspectives of generation quality, time efficiency, and the size of the required training dataset, LoRA is a superior choice [23].

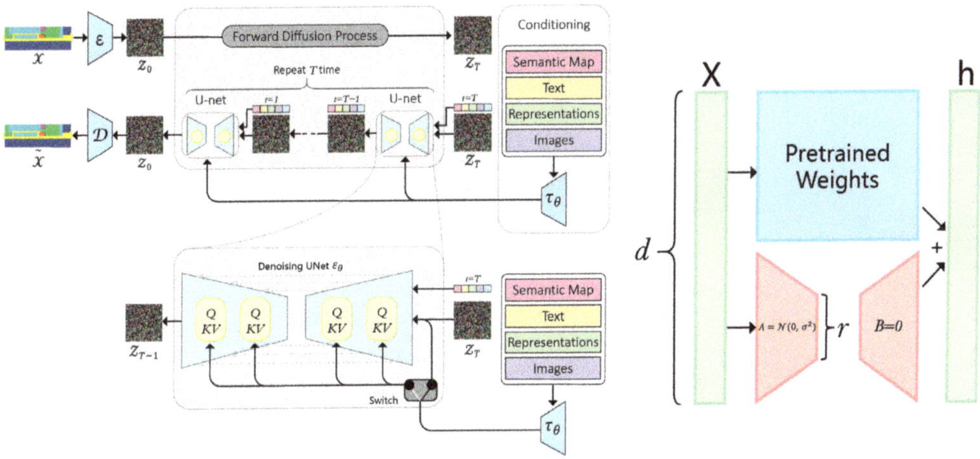

(a) (b)

Figure 1. (**a**) the basic architecture of the SD model: Latent Diffusion Model [8]; (**b**) LoRA [9].

LoRA (Low-Rank Adaptation) is a technique that reduces the complexity of large models by fitting their high-dimensional structures with low-dimensional ones. Instead of fine-tuning the entire model, LoRA focuses on training the "residual" part of the model (ΔW). The fine-tuned weights (W') are given by:

$$W' = W + \Delta W$$

The technical principle of LoRA is illustrated in Figure 1b. The input x has a dimension of d, with the left side representing the frozen pretrained weights of the original model (W) and the right side representing the newly added branch under the LoRA strategy (ΔW). First, through linear layer A, the data dimension is reduced from d to r, and after computation, it is restored from r to d through linear layer B. By fine-tuning the smaller matrices A and B instead of W, the hyperparameters that need to be fine-tuned are significantly reduced [9].

As a powerful generative AI model, SD can be applied to various generation tasks, with its main input control methods including Text-to-Image [8], Image-to-Image [8], and ControlNet [24]:

- Text-to-Image: Generates an image based on the input text.
- Image-to-Image: Adds a reference image as a condition to the Text-to-Image task.

- ControlNet: Adds structured condition signals (such as control_canny, control_depth, control_hed, control_mlsd, etc.) on top of the aforementioned tasks to finely control image content and layout [24].

The relationship among these three control conditions is as follows: a reference image can be added to the Text-to-Image task to transform it into an Image-to-Image task, and further adding ControlNet allows for more precise control of the image structure. Of course, ControlNet can also be directly added to the Text-to-Image task to perform image generation [25–29].

4. Methodology and Testing Process

The experimental process was carried out in three steps: dataset processing, model training, and model testing and generation, as shown in Figure 2.

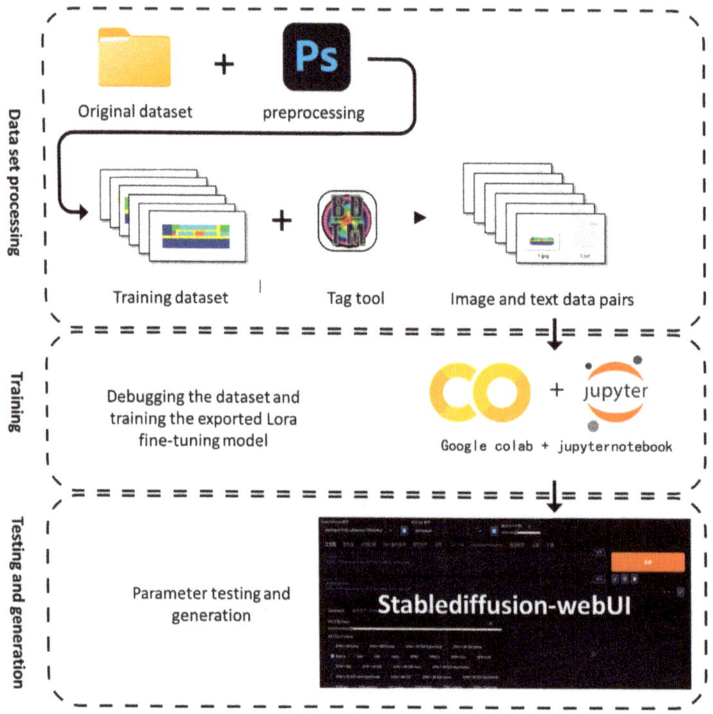

Figure 2. Methodological framework of the experiment.

The dataset processing involved manually labeling the collected floor plans to create functional space segmentation masks, thereby establishing the dataset. Unlike the application of GAN models, the SD is a text-prompt-guided image generation model. Therefore, we used a tagging tool [30] to attach corresponding descriptive text to each image, generating a corresponding .txt file. The image files and .txt files together form the final training dataset.

This experiment relied on the Google Colab platform, utilizing the interactive computing environment Jupyter Notebook for model training and dataset debugging.

Model testing and generation involved hyperparameter tuning and image output. This step was performed on the Stable Diffusion WebUI platform, a Python web UI framework suitable for showcasing deep learning tasks. It incorporates various common functionalities of the SD model and supports extensions such as ControlNet and LoRA [25–28].

4.1. Producing Datasets

4.1.1. Study on the Topology of Standard Nursing Units

The development of nursing units can be traced back to the late 19th and early 20th centuries, when the Nightingale ward layout was proposed and evolved. Its primary characteristics included an open elongated ward configuration, centralized nursing functions at the ward's terminus, and an emphasis on improving ventilation, daylighting, and other environmental conditions within the ward spaces [31]. This layout served as a significant milestone in the spatial evolution of hospital architecture. Entering the 1930s to 1950s, air conditioning technology saw widespread application in buildings, significantly reducing the need for natural ventilation. Concurrently, the need to optimize workflow efficiency for medical staff became increasingly pressing. In 1955, the Nuffield Hospital Study Group published the "Report on the Functions and Design of Hospitals", recommending the centralized placement of nurse stations within the core area of nursing units [32]. Subsequently, this centralized layout paradigm gained widespread popularity, spawning various derivative forms such as double-corridor, single-corridor, and radial configurations. Early scholarly studies compared the nursing efficiency across these layout variations [33]. To further enhance nursing efficiency, decentralized nurse station layouts emerged and were implemented, proving beneficial in improving patient safety and mitigating nurse fatigue [34–38].

In China, the development of modernized nursing units commenced in the late 1970s, predominantly adopting centralized nurse station layouts. These layouts evolved into single-corridor, double-corridor, and other composite forms. However, due to regulatory constraints and cultural norms, Chinese nursing units prioritized natural ventilation and daylighting, favoring south-facing patient rooms. The centralized nurse station layout remained predominant, while decentralized configurations were not widely adopted. In recent years, the single-corridor layout has gradually diminished due to its limited capacity and singular circulation organization. It has been supplanted by the main and sub-corridor typology, which ensured space for patient rooms on the south side while expanding the depth of medical support spaces to the north, thereby enhancing the auxiliary functions for medical care [39]. The nursing units of general hospitals typically feature two layout types: main and sub-corridor style and double-corridor style (Table 1). The primary differences between the two lie in the location of the vertical circulation, the accessibility of the corridors, and the depth of the north-side rooms. The double-corridor layout has a more complex functional topology, compared to the main and sub-corridor style.

Table 1. Functional partition and Functional Topology Extraction.

<table>
<tr><th></th><th>Main and Sub-Corridor Style</th><th>Double-Corridor Style</th></tr>
<tr><td>Functional partition</td><td>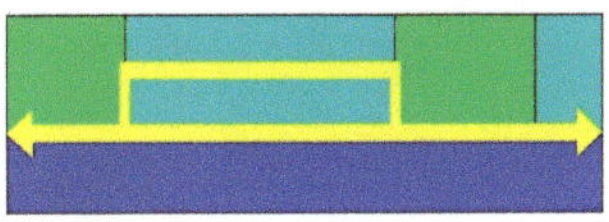</td><td>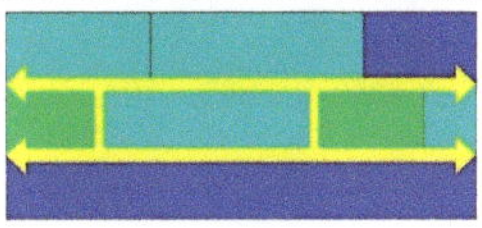</td></tr>
<tr><td>Topological map</td><td>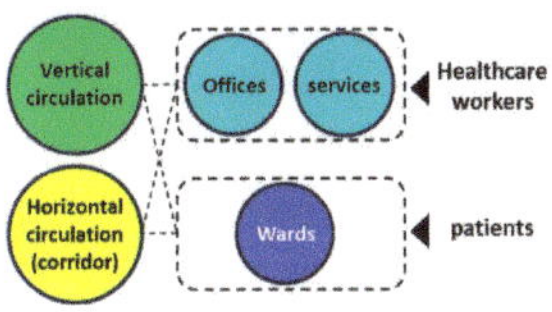
</td><td>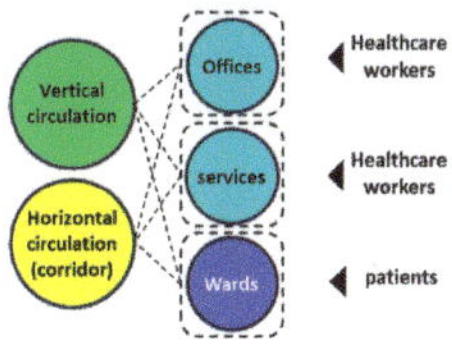
</td></tr>
</table>

4.1.2. Processing of the Dataset

For this experiment, 80 standard nursing unit cases from inpatient departments of general hospitals were collected, mostly from key general hospital projects across various provinces and cities in China, either completed, under construction, or in the bidding stage.

These cases represent the mainstream design approaches for standard nursing units in contemporary general hospitals.

The original drawings were simplified by marking each major function with color blocks [14–16], as shown in Table 2. To ensure that the bitmaps match the scale of the actual architectural drawings, a unified scale and annotation method were used: the dimensions marked on the floor plans served as the basis for converting to a unified scale. All samples were printed at a scale of 1:100 on 500 mm × 1000 mm white background images, with the image resolution set to 512 × 1024. A consistent image resolution also helped reduce the difficulty of training, allowing LoRA to more accurately extract image features. In addition, If a standard floor of an inpatient building comprises two or three nursing units, it should be subdivided into individual nursing units based on the following principles (Table 3).

Table 2. Correspondence between function and mask color.

Function	Color	RGB
Nurse Station		255, 0, 0
Medical and Auxiliary Rooms		0, 255, 255
Wards		0, 0, 255
Vertical Circulations		0, 255, 0
equipment rooms		255, 0, 255
corridor		255, 255, 0

Table 3. Nursing unit datasets processing.

Inpatient Building Floor Plan	A Single Nursing Unit after Division	Illustrate
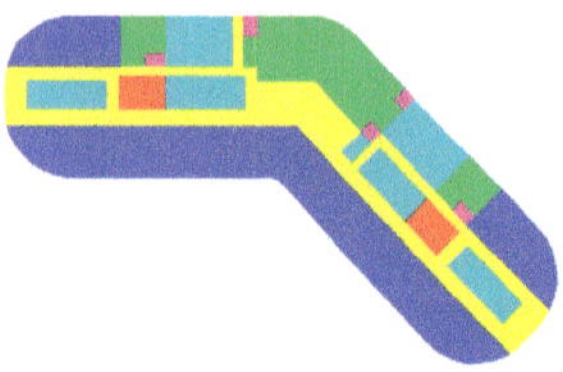	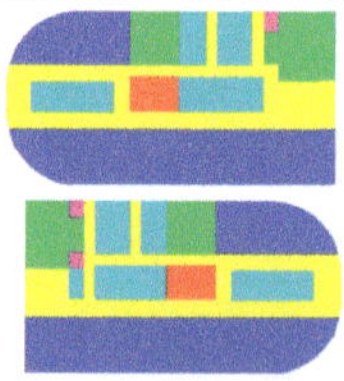	Complete the segmentation position into a rectangle.
	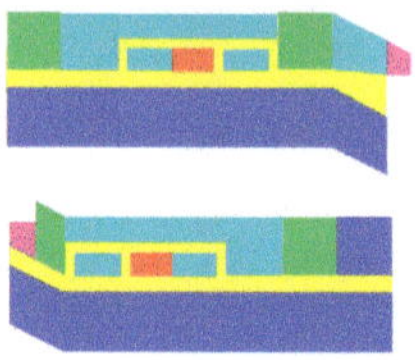	When two nursing units share a common vertical circulation, the entire area of the vertical circulation should be preserved during the subdivision into separate units.
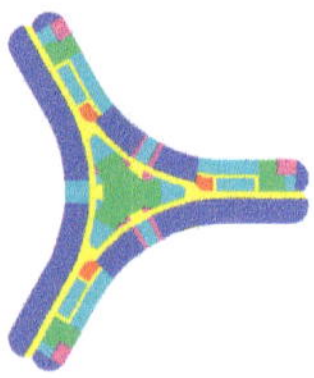	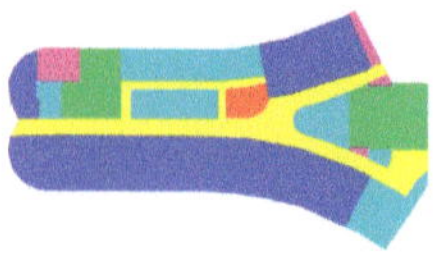	Rotate or mirror the divided nursing unit to a horizontal position so that most of the wards face south and patch the edges.
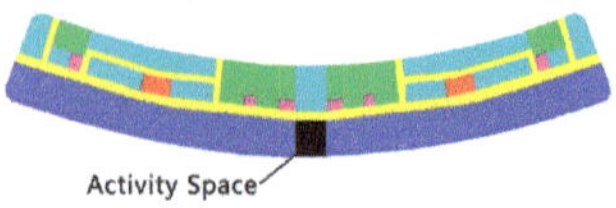		If the intersection is a public activity space, it will be divided into one nursing unit.

After removing highly similar images, we ended up with a dataset consisting of 110 floor plans of standard nursing units in a main and sub-corridor layout (Figure 3). Due to insufficient and inconsistent data collection for the double-corridor standard nursing unit, it was excluded from subsequent experiments. The experiment focused solely on main and sub-corridor nursing units.

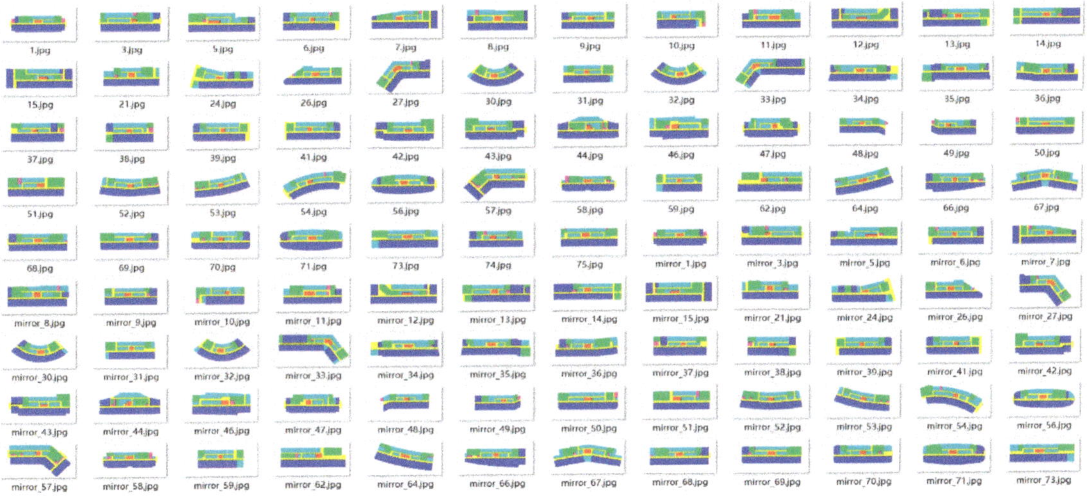

Figure 3. Main and sub-corridor style nursing units floor plan dataset (portion).

When fine-tuning a large model with LoRA, it is theoretically best to keep the labels as consistent with the official model as possible to achieve optimal generation performance. However, the subject of this study is rather unique, as it is an abstracted concept derived from reality, possessing a high degree of specificity. Therefore, when labeling the dataset, it is only necessary to ensure the use of uncommon words to describe the data, allowing the large model to learn from this dataset without interfering with the content of the original training set [25–28]. The objective of this training is to generate functional zoning diagrams for a specific typology of nursing units. Internal room-level information has been simplified, rendering the text prompt a non-decisive factor for layout variations. The text prompt serves solely as a trigger condition for the generation process. Consequently, the text prompt can remain consistent across instances, such as "a floor plan of a nursing unit" for this training. This approach reduces training complexity and enhances the efficiency and accuracy of the model generation [25–28].

4.2. LoRA Fine-Tuning

The training is based on Stable Diffusion V1.5, using the Adam8bit [40] optimizer with decoupled weight decay. The training consists of 22 k steps with a batch size of 1. The initial learning rate is 1×10^{-4}, and a single Tesla T4 GPU is used. The training is planned for 20 epochs, and a total of 5 LoRA fine-tuned models are recorded. The change in the loss function value (Loss) was also recorded. The loss function is an important metric for evaluating the training effectiveness of the model. Generally, as the number of training iterations increases, the loss function tends to converge, indicating that the model training has converged [24]. Figure 4 shows the trend of the loss function value changing with the increase in training iterations during the training process. It can be observed that, as the number of training iterations increases, the loss function value gradually decreases, indicating effective training [41]. However, if the training loss decreases too much, it may indicate overfitting. Therefore, it is necessary to monitor the model's performance using a validation set and test each set of fine-tuned model weights to ensure generalization. Finally, the model needs to be evaluated on an independent test set to ensure its effectiveness in practical applications [16].

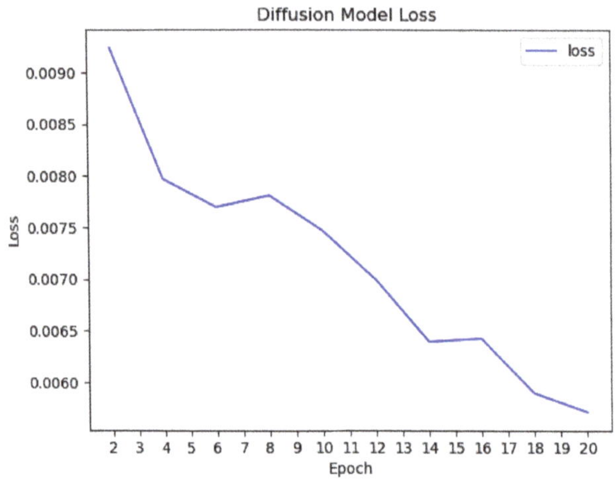

Figure 4. Stable Diffusion loss.

Without changing the main hyperparameters, the effects of each fine-tuned model were tested by varying the LoRA weight values (Table 4). The test results show that epochs 6 to 10 can produce relatively excellent LoRA models, characterized by well-defined functional partitions, clear boundaries, and accurate color values for functional blocks. Model 5, which is the tenth generation model, can be selected for subsequent generation experiments. The LoRA model weight value should be set in the range of 1 to 1.2.

Table 4. Testing the Results of LoRA Fine-Tuning.

Epoch	LoRA Weight				
	0.6	0.8	1	1.2	1.4
Model1 (epoch4)	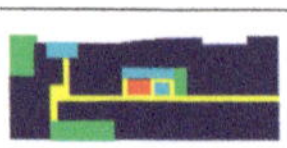	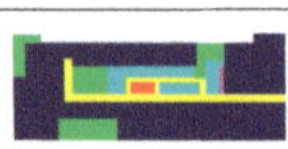		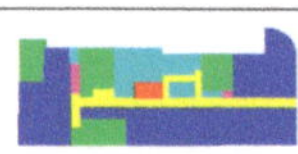	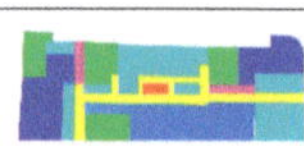
Model2 (epoch8)	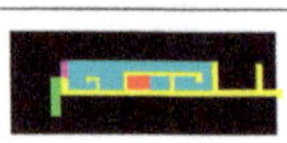	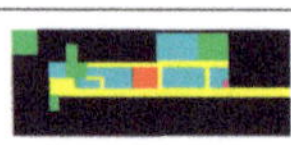	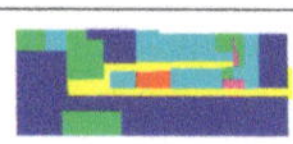	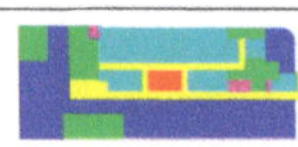	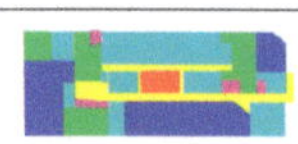
Model3 (epoch12)	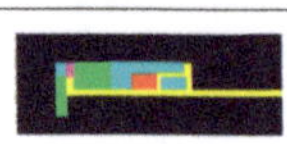	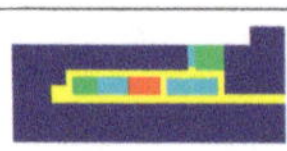	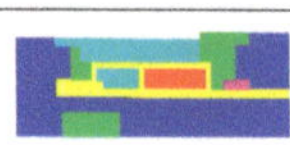	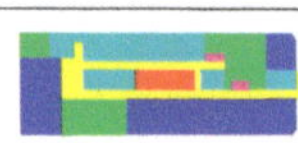	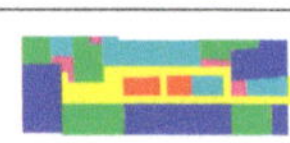
Model4 (epoch16)	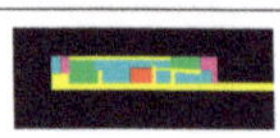		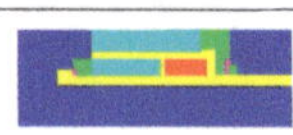	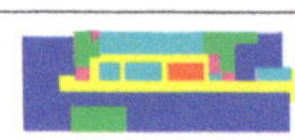	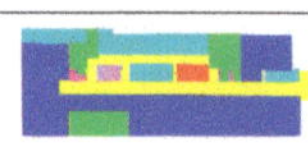
Model5 (epoch20)		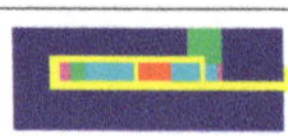	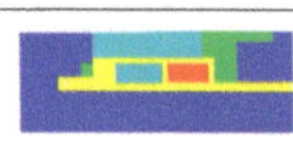	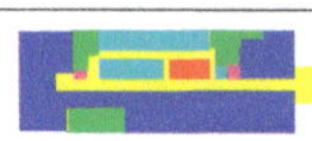	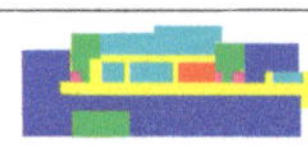

4.3. Testing Process

The hyperparameter settings of the SD model are crucial to the quality of the generated results, necessitating controlled variable experiments for generation testing. Given the determined version of the SD base model, the variables significantly impacting the results include: input boundaries, selection of the LoRA model, LoRA model weight values, sampling steps, sampler, classifier-free guidance (CFG) scale, random seed, and denoising strength (Table 5) [8,26].

Table 5. The descriptions of the hyperparameter settings [25–28].

Seting	Descriptions
Input image	This refers to the initial image used to generate a new image.
Sampling Steps	This refers to the number of sampling iterations performed during the image generation process
Sampler	This is a method used in the denoising process of diffusion models
Seed	This is used to set the initial value for random number generation
Denoising strength	This refers to the intensity of noise removal during the image generation process

The number of sampling steps affects the model's sampling efficiency. If the value is too low, the control exerted by the text on the image will be weak, resulting in high randomness. Conversely, if the value is too high, it will lead to low sampling efficiency and increased computational load on the GPU. The CFG scale serves a similar function to the number of sampling steps. Since a unified text description is used, the default value is adopted and is not included in the comparative test. The sampler is a method used in the denoising process of diffusion models. Currently, the Stable Diffusion web UI supports dozens of samplers. After preliminary testing, we will proceed with experiments using the "Euler a" sampler. The random seed determines the initial state of diffusion and is crucial for the generalizability of the generated floor plans. Denoising strength, a hyperparameter in Image-to-Image control, refers to the proportion of the reference image's features extracted by the model [7].

Draw the nursing unit boundaries on a blank image with a resolution of 512 × 1024, preprocess it into a mask image, set the text description to "a_floorplan_of_nurse_unit", add the LoRA model, and set the weight values. Design the following three test methods (Figure 5):

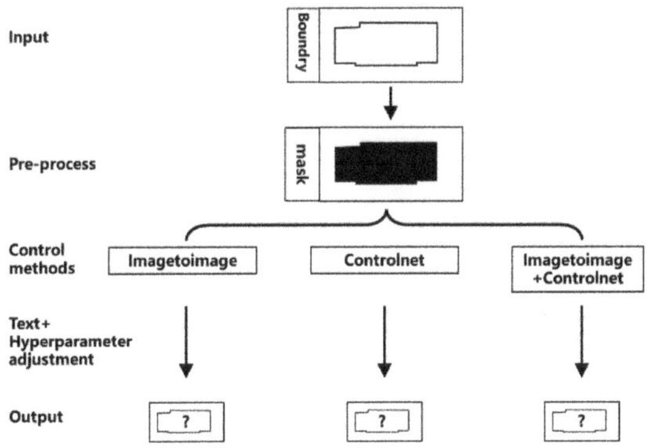

Figure 5. Testing and Generation Framework.

- Image-to-Image
    1. Add the preprocessed nursing unit boundary image in the Image-to-Image settings.
    2. Set various variables for image generation.
    3. Compare the generation effects of different hyperparameter values.
    4. Determine the optimal hyperparameter settings.
    5. Summarize the pros and cons of the method.

- ControlNet
    1. Add the preprocessed nursing unit boundary image in the ControlNet settings.
    2. Add the ControlNet preprocessor.
    3. Compare the generation effects of different preprocessors and hyperparameter values.
    4. Determine the optimal hyperparameter settings.
    5. Summarize the pros and cons of the method.
- Image-to-Image + ControlNet
    1. Add the preprocessed nursing unit boundary image in the Image-to-Image settings.
    2. Add the preprocessed nursing unit boundary image in the ControlNet settings.
    3. Test the best hyperparameters from previous tests.
    4. Determine the optimal hyperparameter settings.

The optimal values obtained from these three test paths can be used interchangeably to reduce repetitive testing.

4.3.1. Image-to-Image

Sampling steps and denoising strength: When other hyperparameters remain unchanged, changing the sampling steps and denoising strength produces the results shown in Figure 6. The following phenomena can be observed: when both the denoising strength and sampling steps are relatively low, the generated results show minimal changes compared to the input image. However, with higher denoising strength, the generated image boundaries slightly deviate from the input boundaries. Nevertheless, when the denoising strength exceeds 0.94, the image quality does not significantly improve. With sampling steps between 15 and 30, the generated images maintain a high quality, but further increasing the sampling steps may result in unclear boundaries of color blocks. Additionally, the higher the sampling steps, the greater the computational resource consumption. Therefore, to achieve clear functional zoning and accurate color values in the generated floor plan images, it is recommended to set the denoising strength between 0.94 and 0.95 and the sampling steps between 20 and 25. This ensures the balance between image quality, computational resource consumption, and processing efficiency.

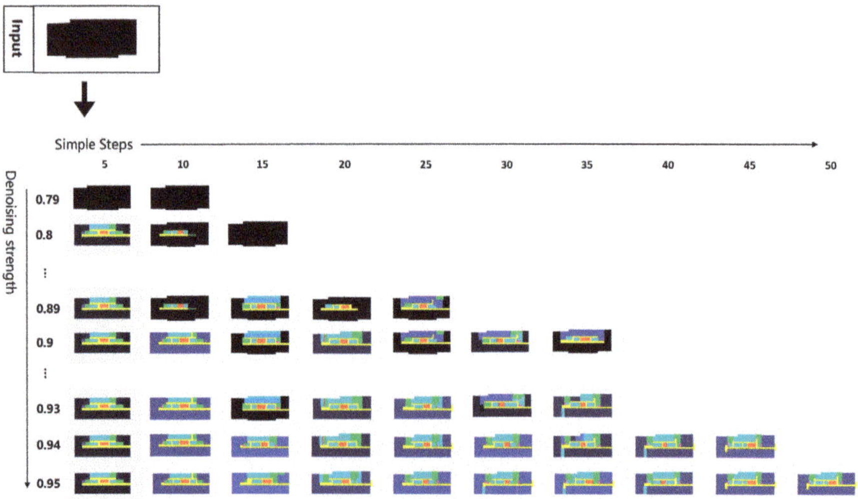

Figure 6. Sampling steps and denoising strength.

Input image and seed: The testing mentioned above represents the better outcomes achieved under the same random seed input. When other hyperparameters remain unchanged but different random seeds are used, the generated functional color blocks exhibit weaker regularity, and the area of each color block does not match the corresponding functional area of the nursing unit (Figure 7). By introducing a significant spatial organizational condition (in this case, a main corridor) to the input image, the generation results can be significantly improved (Figure 8). Under unchanged hyperparameters, this approach enables the generation of relatively ideal architectural floor plan color block images with clear functional block boundaries, reasonable layouts, and relatively reasonable shapes and area ratios of functional zones, regardless of the random seed used. However, the outer boundary of the nursing unit may change.

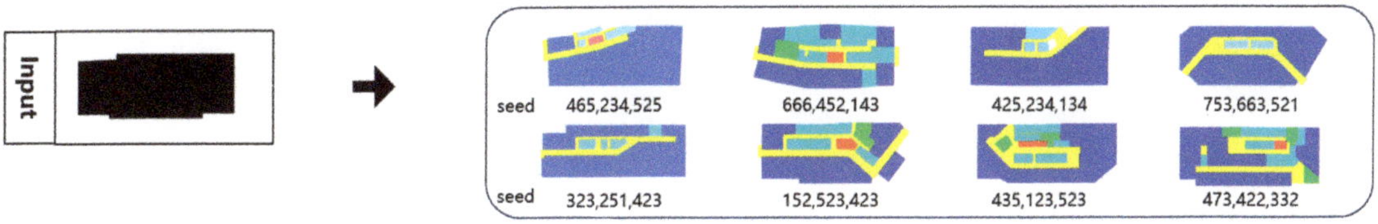

Figure 7. Other hyperparameters remain unchanged; the seed is changed.

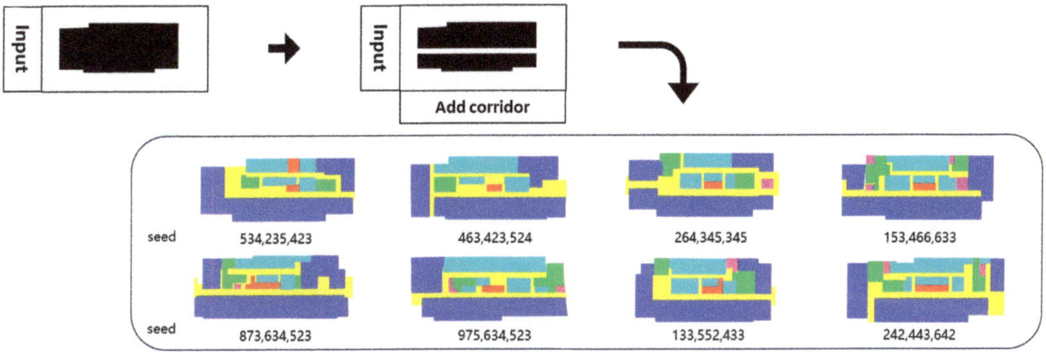

Figure 8. Other hyperparameters remain unchanged; the input image is added to the main corridor and the seed is changed.

Summarize: Under the Image-to-Image control, the denoising strength and sampling steps affect the boundaries and color values of the generated image blocks. When the color values are accurately represented, the boundaries of the output result may exhibit slight deformation, making them inconsistent with the input image. Adding control structures to the input image can effectively optimize the layout of various functions in the generated image. Under different random seed inputs, good results can be obtained.

4.3.2. ControlNet

This section of testing is conducted under the Text-to-Image option. The input images are processed directly by ControlNet in the SD-WebUI, bypassing the influence of the Image-to-Image section. The main factor affecting the results is the choice of the ControlNet preprocessor. Therefore, this section focuses on testing the output results of different preprocessors under different random seeds.

Figures 9 and 10 show the generated effects of four ControlNet preprocessors under the optimal hyperparameters determined in the previous sections. It can be seen that none of the preprocessors can generate images that meet the basic requirements (reasonable color block arrangement, accurate color values), and even the background color fails to generate as white. Placing a main corridor also yielded similar results. However, the advantage is that the boundaries of the output results from each preprocessor generally match the input boundaries.

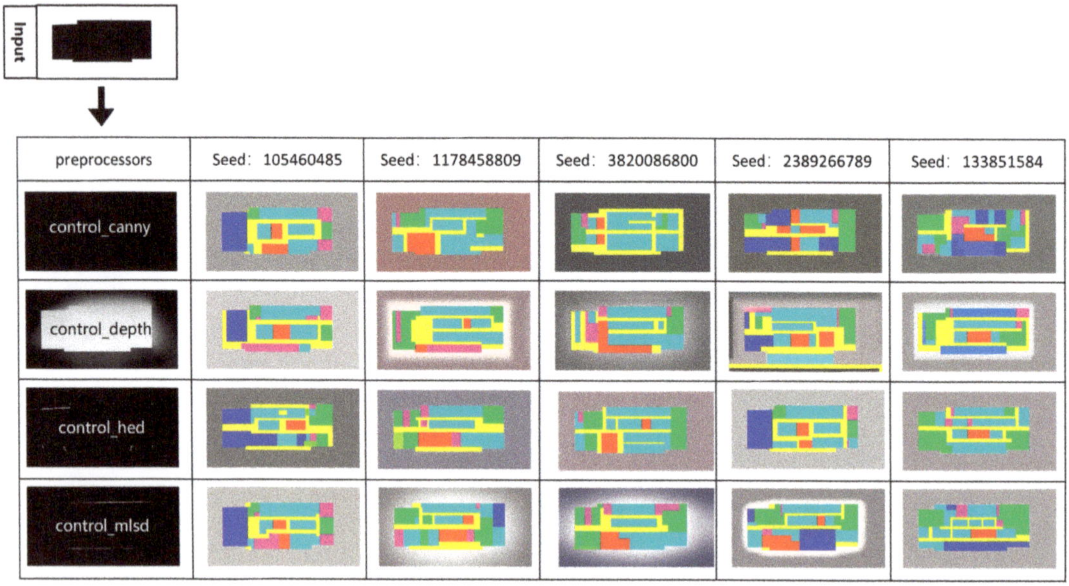

Figure 9. ControlNet preprocessors.

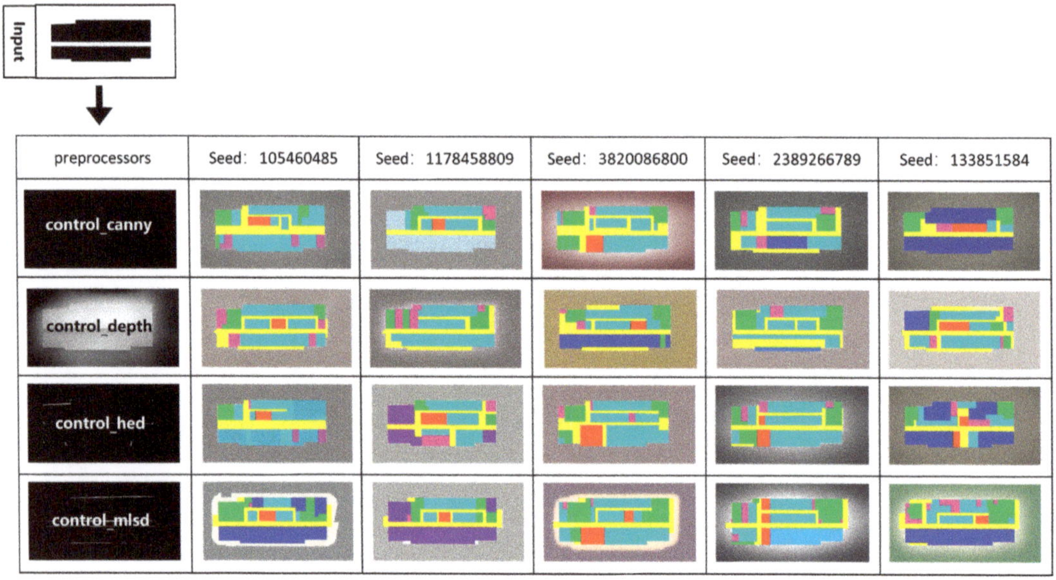

Figure 10. ControlNet preprocessors with the input image added to the main corridor.

4.3.3. Image-to-Image + ControlNet

Through separate testing of the Image-to-Image and ControlNet methods, it is evident that neither method alone can generate images that fully meet the requirements. However, it can be concluded that Image-to-Image control can produce more accurate color values, color block layouts, and a pure white background, while ControlNet can precisely control the boundaries of the generated layout. Therefore, the next step is to combine both methods for generation testing.

Since ControlNet is a post-processing extension of the Image-to-Image function, this test will set the optimal hyperparameters for Image-to-Image to control the boundaries of the generated image. In ControlNet controls, besides the preprocessor directly influencing the results, there are three other variables that can affect its degree of control over the Image-to-Image process: ControlNet weight, Guidance Start, and Guidance End.

Preprocessor, ControlNet weight, Guidance Start, and Guidance End: In this section of the test, we first selected Control_canny as the preprocessor and disabled the Guidance End time option to test the ControlNet weight and Guidance Start time. As shown in Figure 11, it can be seen that a ControlNet weight greater than 0.6 can exert significant boundary control on the image result. Increasing the value beyond this threshold does not have a noticeable impact on the results. The Guidance Start time must be set to the initial moment, as intervening at any intermediate point in the Image-to-Image process with ControlNet does not influence the outcome. With the aforementioned hyperparameters held constant, setting the ControlNet weight to 1.2 produced the results shown in Figure 12. The chart indicates that if ControlNet starts at time 0.0 in the Image-to-Image process, the Guidance End time has no significant effect on the final image. Regarding the choice of preprocessor, Control_canny and Control_hed demonstrated more stable performance, achieving reasonable boundary, color block layout, and area proportions.

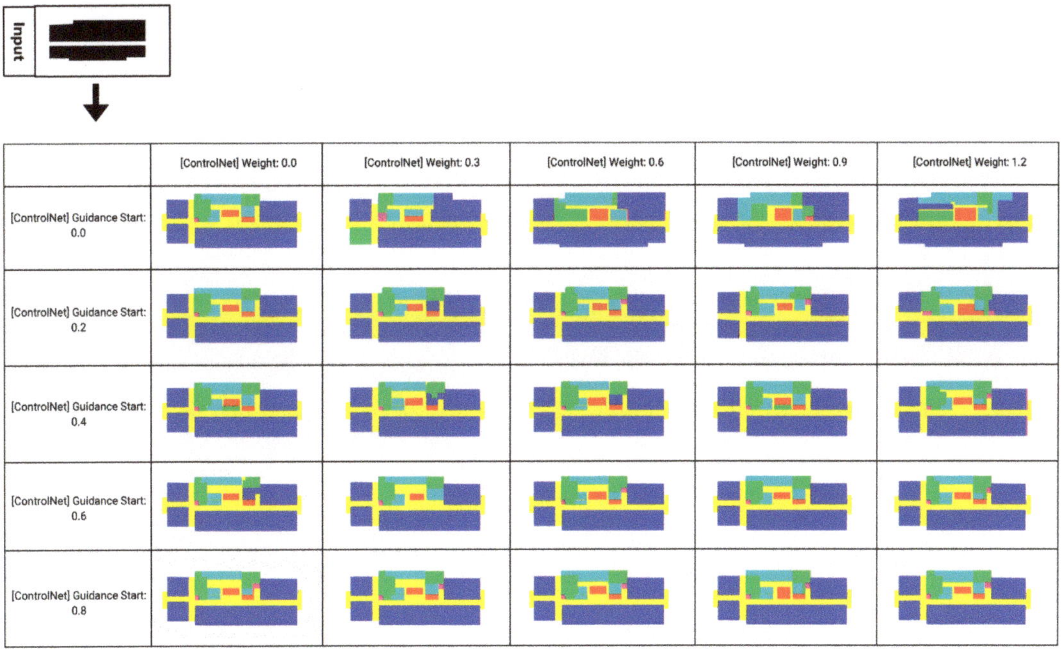

Figure 11. ControlNet Weight, Guidance Start.

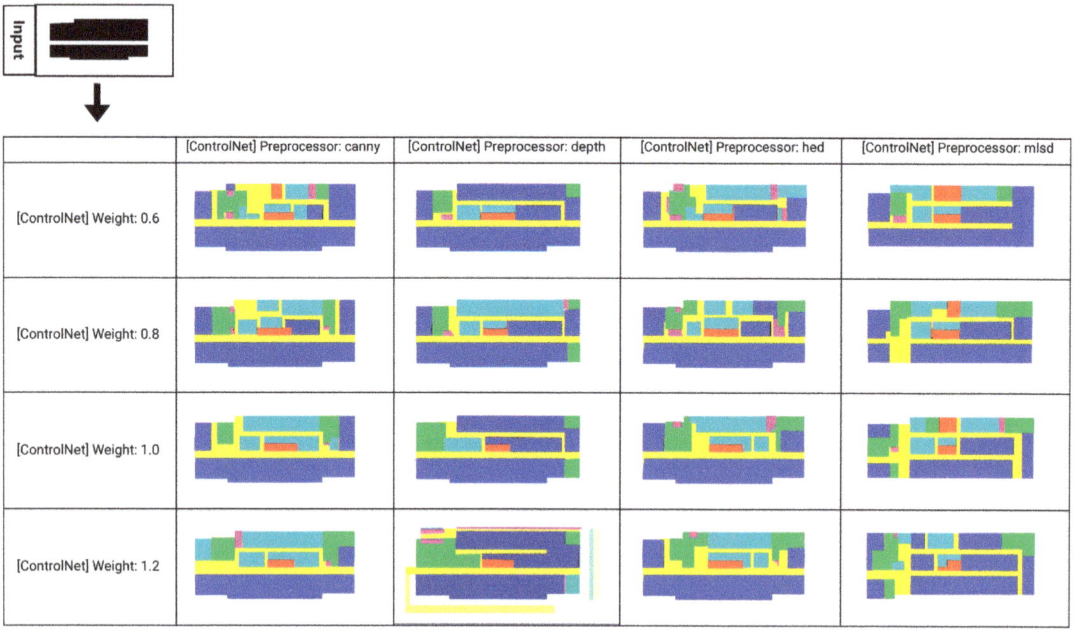

Figure 12. Preprocessor and Guidance End.

Seed: As previously mentioned, the random seed determines the generalization capability of the SD model. Each random seed represents the initial random state during image generation. If reasonable images can be generated under any random seed input, it demonstrates that the LoRA model trained in this hyperparameter combination can achieve the desired spatial layout for nursing units. Figure 13 shows images generated with different random seeds, covering five random intervals with a total of 25 outputs. Preliminary assessment indicates that approximately 20 of these results (highlighted with dashed lines) are reasonably valid. This demonstrates that the combination of Image-to-Image generation and ControlNet for spatial layout generation is feasible and capable of producing reasonably accurate results.

Summaries: The above tests prove that integrating ControlNet into the Image-to-Image process is feasible and can address the issue of weak boundary control in Image-to-Image generation. Under the recommended hyperparameter settings from previous tests, ControlNet's preprocessor should be set to Control-canny or Control-hed. The ControlNet weight should be above 0.6, ideally at 1.2. The guidance start time needs to be set at 0.0, while the guidance end time does not affect the final image. With these hyperparameter settings, any random seed input has about an 80% probability of generating results with accurate color values and reasonable layouts.

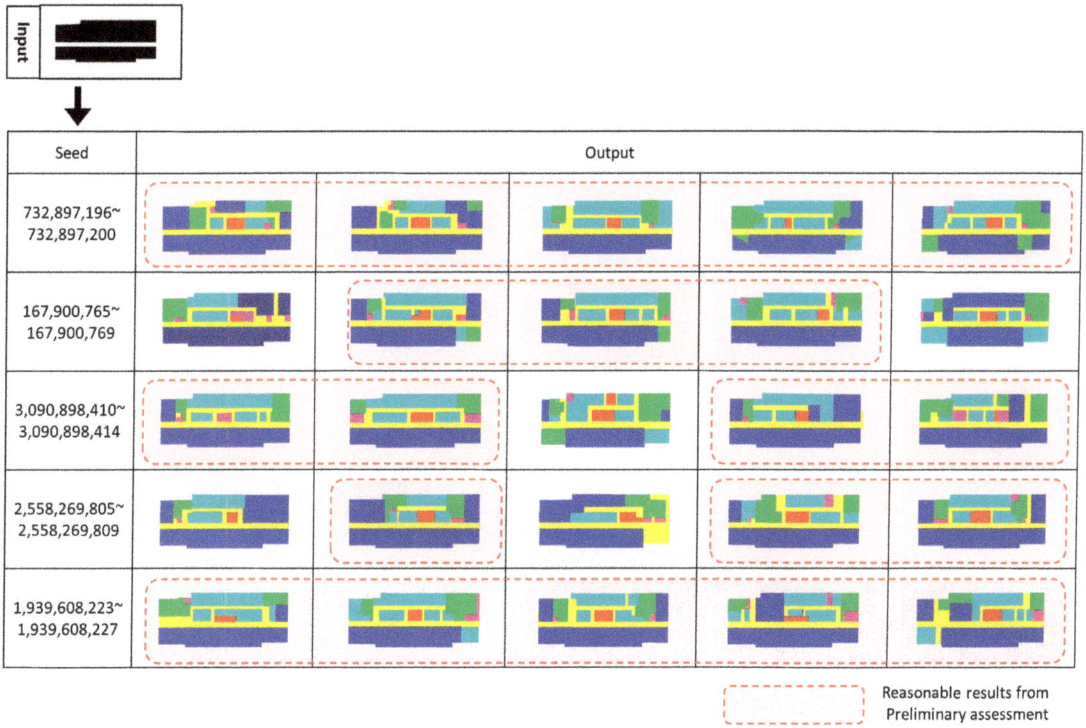

Figure 13. Image-to-Image + ControlNet, change the seed.

4.4. Baseline: Pix2pixHD

To evaluate whether the SD model-based method offers advantages over the GAN model-based method, this paper conducted a comparative experiment. The pix2pixHD model, a widely used and effective GAN-based model, is capable of generating images with a maximum resolution of 2048 × 1024. To ensure a fair comparison, this experiment used the same small sample dataset for training the pix2pixHD model.

The test data was derived from real floor plans. We selected the best results from pix2pixHD training for comparison. Table 6 shows five results generated by the SD model and the pix2pixHD model, along with their corresponding real floor plans. The qualitative evaluation of the results is based on the following three aspects:

1. Reasonableness of Functional Layout: Both models can generate relatively reasonable functional layouts. Pix2pixHD tends to conform closely to the training dataset, with few instances of layouts not present in the training data. The SD model, however, can control parameters such as iteration steps, denoising strength, and random seeds to generate reasonable layouts.
2. Generality of Functional Layout: Since pix2pixHD does not have extensive parameter inputs for generation, its generality is mainly reflected in generating different layouts under varying boundary conditions. The SD model, on the other hand, can generate desirable layouts under the same boundary conditions by controlling parameters and can produce a wide variety of derivative floor plans based on the existing dataset by controlling the random seed, offering more options.
3. Image Quality of Generated Floor Plans: This metric mainly reflects the clarity of the generated image boundaries and the accuracy of the color values for each functional block. If both values are ideal, the generated result can facilitate operations such as region recognition. From the generated results, the pix2pixHD model trained under

the same conditions as the SD model cannot produce very clear and straight functional block boundaries, although the color values for each block are generally correct. The SD model, however, can produce results with both clear functional block boundaries and accurate color values, making the generated images more suitable for subsequent processing and analysis.

Table 6. Test two deep learning models using a real-world planar validation set.

Input	Output		Dataset Simple
	SD + LoRA	Pix2PixHD (GAN)	
	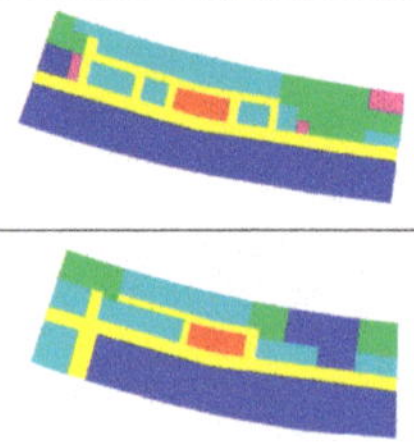	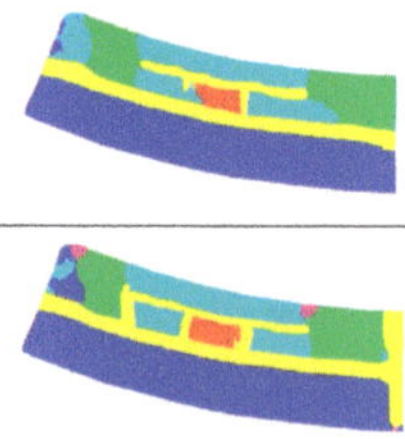	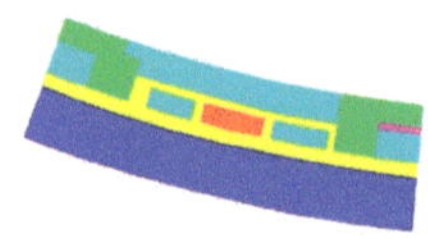
	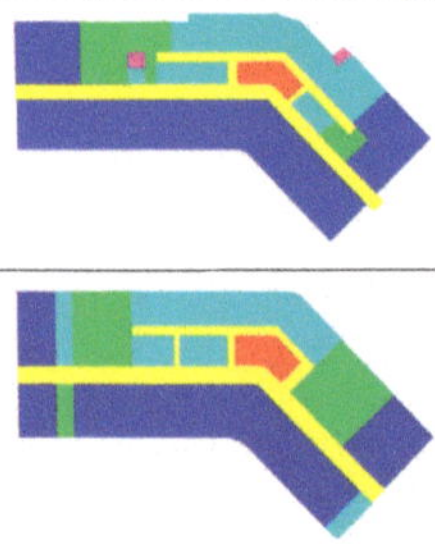	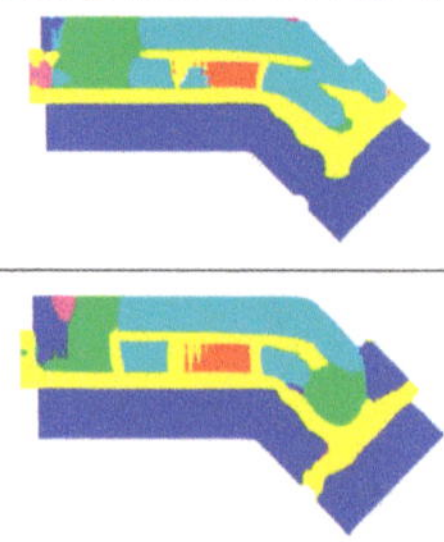	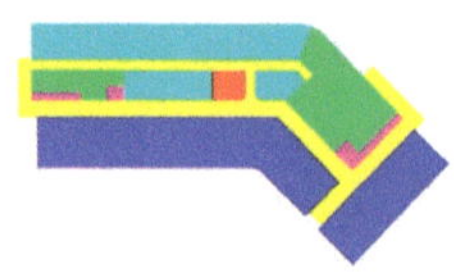
	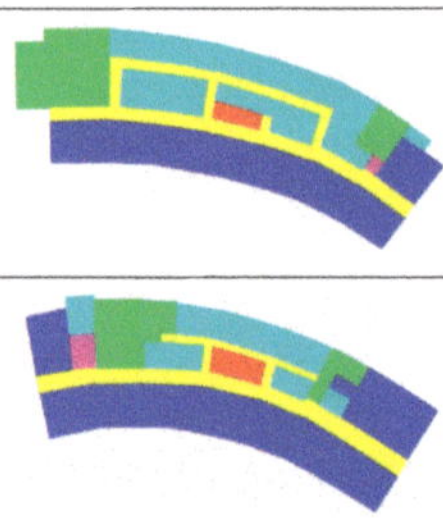	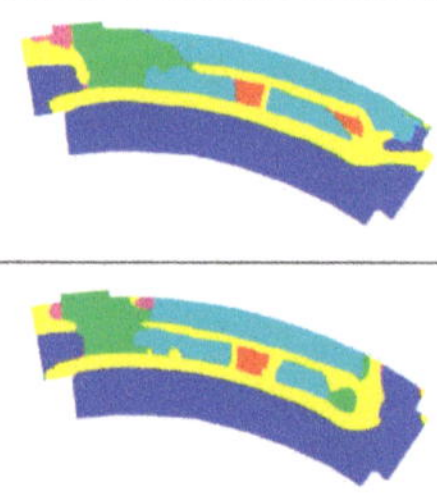	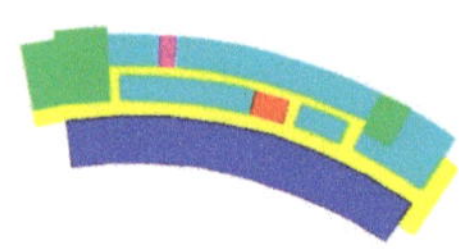
	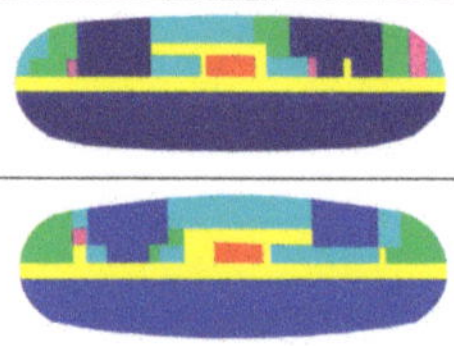	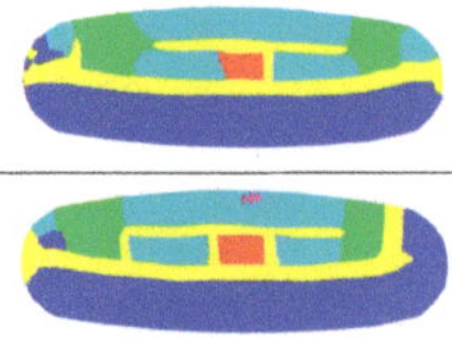	
	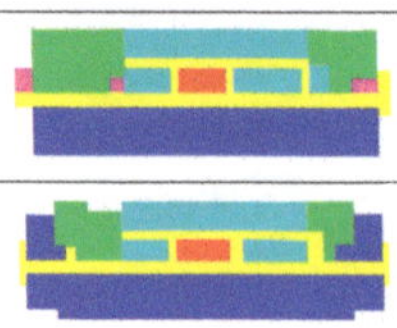	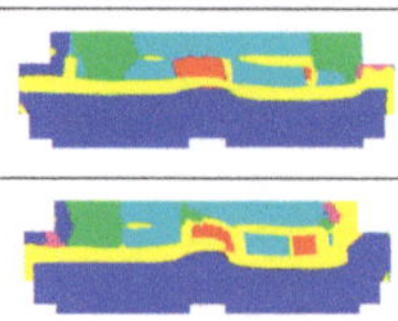	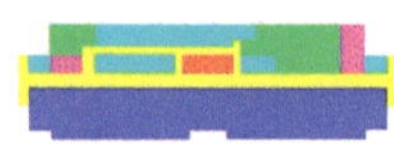

By comparing these aspects, it can be inferred that the SD model-based method shows certain advantages over the GAN model-based method, particularly in the clarity and accuracy of the generated images and the versatility in generating diverse layouts.

5. Experiment and Discussion

5.1. Combining Boundary Generation for Automation

After training and testing, we identified the optimal input conditions and hyperparameter configurations for generating the best results with the SD model. If boundary generation for nursing units can be controlled through parameter adjustments, further automation can be achieved. We use the Rhino and Grasshopper platform to implement this part, as illustrated in Figure 14. The primary variables include L (length of the nursing unit), a (depth of the patient rooms), b (width of the main corridor), and S (area of the nursing unit), which align with architectural practice. Additionally, we set variables to control shape variations to meet creative needs: L_1 and L_2 jointly control the position of the corner folds, R controls the angle of the folds, and c controls the radius of the chamfers. These variables can manage the generation of nursing unit boundaries in straight, cornered, and curved forms.

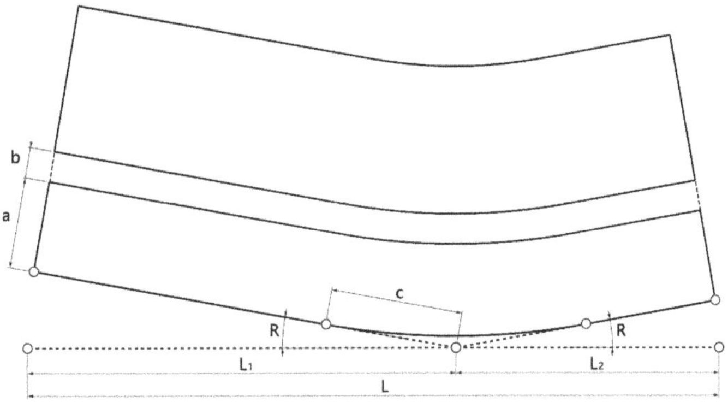

Figure 14. Parameter-controlled boundary generation.

Using the aforementioned method, we generated six nursing unit boundaries with different scales, corner positions, and curvatures. These boundaries were input into the SD model, and each boundary was used with different random seeds to produce 20 results, resulting in a total of 120 outputs.

5.2. Principal Component Analysis

We employed domain-specific feature extraction methods to assess the authenticity of the generated samples from an architectural perspective. In the design of nursing unit floor plans, the area ratios of functional zones are a crucial metric for evaluating design rationality. Thus, we computed the area ratios of each functional zone relative to the total area in the output samples and consolidated these ratios into a six-dimensional feature array to characterize the nursing unit areas. These features were then visualized using line charts for clarity.

Additionally, we compared these results with the corresponding metrics from the real data in the training set to perform an effective comparative analysis. We overlaid the line charts of the generated samples and real samples, as shown in Figure 15. The analysis reveals significant overlap between the generated and real samples in terms of functional zone area proportions, with only a few deviations from the main trend. This indicates that the generated samples exhibit a high degree of similarity to the real samples in terms of functional zone area ratios, demonstrating that the generation model performs well in this regard. This analysis not only validates the reasonableness of the generated samples but also provides a basis for further optimization and application.

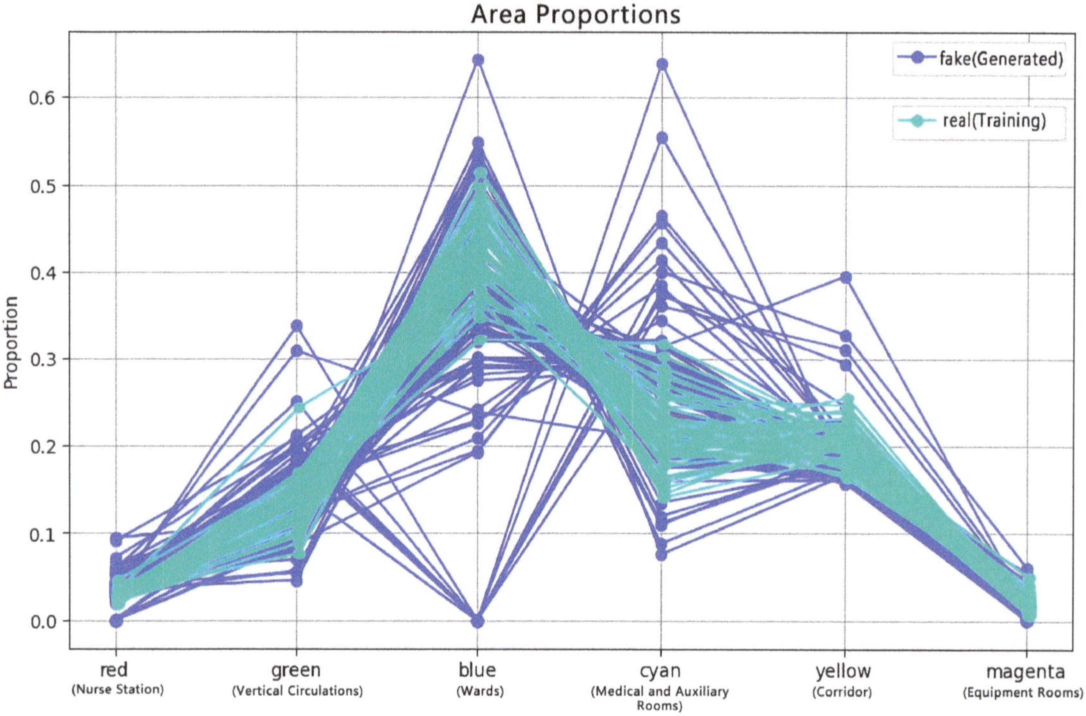

Figure 15. Area feature distribution.

5.3. User Study

Functional topology is also a critical factor in evaluating nursing unit floor plans. In residential floor plan generation studies, the Manhattan distance is often used to assess the spatial relationships between rooms. However, the relationships between functions in a nursing unit are more complex, and many samples feature non-right-angle coordinate planes, making this metric unsuitable. Therefore, we conducted a user study to analyze this aspect.

We used the functional topology of standard nursing units as a reference standard and invited 10 professionals to participate in the user study, including 5 medical architects and 5 graduate students in architecture. We constructed a dataset consisting of 230 samples by mixing 120 generated samples with 110 real samples. For each session, 30 samples were randomly selected from this dataset, and the participants were asked to evaluate the authenticity of these samples based on the functional topology of standard nursing units and their professional expertise, categorizing the samples accordingly. To ensure the accuracy of the experiment, the participants were not informed of the experimental objectives or the sample proportions beforehand.

We applied classification model performance evaluation methods to analyze the obtained data, with the statistical results shown in Table 7. The accuracy rate represents the proportion of real samples among all randomly selected samples, with a statistical result of 46%. Precision refers to the accuracy of the participants in predicting real samples, with a result of 55%, which is close to the accuracy rate. This indicates that the generated samples are sufficiently realistic and capable of deceiving the participants. The recall rate is 92%, indicating that the participants accurately identified real samples, and most of the samples classified as fake were generated samples. This finding is consistent with the previous analysis, where some generated samples failed to produce accurate results.

Table 7. Results of each subject in user study.

Subjects id	1	2	3	4	5	6	7	8	9	10	Avg.
TP	13	13	13	12	12	14	11	12	14	13	
FP	10	10	10	10	10	10	13	11	9	9	
TN	0	1	2	2	0	2	1	1	2	0	
FN	7	6	5	6	8	4	5	6	7	8	
Precision	0.57	0.57	0.57	0.55	0.55	0.58	0.46	0.52	0.61	0.59	0.55
Recall	1.00	0.93	0.87	0.86	1.00	0.88	0.92	0.92	0.88	1.00	0.92
Accuracy	0.43	0.47	0.50	0.47	0.40	0.53	0.40	0.43	0.50	0.43	0.46
Pass rate of generated samples	0.77	0.82	0.87	0.85	0.76	0.89	0.90	0.84	0.78	0.72	0.82

The probability of a generated sample being classified as real by the participants can be calculated using the following formula:

$$Pass\ rate\ of generated\ samples = \frac{1 - Precision}{1 - Accuracy}$$

The final statistical result shows that the probability of generated samples being classified as real by the participants is 82%.

In this experiment, participants not only compared the generated samples with the functional topology of standard nursing units but also considered the morphology and boundaries of the functional zones. The results of the user study indicate that, from a professional perspective, the generated nursing unit floor plans are also considered ideal.

5.4. Discussion

This study explored the automatic generation of architectural floor plans using SD models, focusing specifically on standard nursing units in general hospitals. The results indicate that deep learning models, particularly diffusion models, can effectively generate preliminary architectural layouts that align with established design principles and functional requirements. The generated layouts demonstrate potential for assisting architects in the early design stages, providing a foundation for more detailed and customized planning.

The main sections of this paper are concentrated in Sections 4 and 5. Section 4 extensively describes the generation process testing of the SD model, which is crucial for finding the optimal solution. It was ultimately discovered that incorporating the main-corridor into the input image and combining Image-to-Image generation with ControlNet methods is highly effective. By controlling different random seed inputs, diverse layouts meeting the requirements can be generated. Section 5 successfully completed the automated process from parameter-controlled boundary generation to SD-generated functional layouts, further controlling parameters such as area, main-corridor location, and length, making the study practically valuable. Additionally, the effectiveness of the method was demonstrated through a comparative analysis of a large number of generated samples against real samples.

Two methods were used in the analysis section. Firstly, area assessment is essential, as the proportion of functional areas determines whether the nursing unit meets the project specifications. Different RGB value intervals were set to distinguish color blocks, facilitating the calculation of area ratios. This step also identified results with inaccurate RGB values. Figure 15 shows that most results align with the real area features, though some results deviate significantly, reflecting the instability of the SD model. Further research is needed to improve control in this part. Secondly, user research was conducted on the topological relationships of the generated results, with statistical analysis using classification model performance evaluation methods. The final statistics showed that 82% of the generated samples met the evaluation criteria, consistent with preliminary conclusions from the testing chapter.

While the independence of the nursing unit avoids analyzing the relationship with other functions within the hospital system, the internal relationships among various functions are complex, such as accessibility analysis of the nurse station, visual analysis of the nurse station, the number of patient rooms, and the relationship between traffic flow and the number of serviced patients. This study does not delve into these aspects, but they can serve as interesting starting points for future work.

The analysis and discussion above indicate that AI-assisted generated floor plans for nursing units are comparable to traditional design methods in terms of spatial layout rationality and clarity of functional zones. At the same time, AI methods demonstrate significant advantages in reducing design time and improving design efficiency. However, since this study focuses on standard nursing units, further research is needed to assess the performance of AI tools when dealing with non-standardized building types and complex engineering conditions.

6. Conclusions and Future Work

This paper conducted an experiment on generating architectural floor plans for standard nursing units in general hospitals using the SD model. The experiment successfully demonstrated that clear, readable, and functionally reasonable floor plan images with colored functional blocks can be quickly and automatically generated by inputting a boundary range. The experiment validated the methods for dataset processing, model training, and the overall effectiveness of the entire workflow.

Under conditions with relatively few training samples, the SD model-based method for generating architectural floor plans exhibited advantages such as reasonable layout, strong generalizability, and clear, easily readable image boundaries. When the input conditions include significant spatial features of the floor plan type, the model's generalization capability is even more pronounced, resulting in better generation outcomes.

Using deep learning to generate architectural floor plans is not the only approach to floor plan generation, but it still demonstrates significant potential for research applications. Although the generated color block images do not represent traditional floor plans in a practical sense, they can provide valuable insights for architects during the building design phase.

The limitations of this experiment are quite evident. The only effective control parameters are the boundaries of the nursing unit and the main corridor. While LoRA can generate functionally coherent layouts, it also introduces randomness. Additionally, quantitative metrics such as room area, room scale, and room count, which are of great concern to architects, are difficult to represent at the functional layout level. This is inherently tied to the operational mode of the Stable Diffusion image-generation process. Future work in this research aims to explore the text-based control capabilities of the Stable Diffusion model to actively participate in the generation process. Furthermore, we will vectorize the output functional block images and automate the layout for each functional room, allowing the generated results to be quantitatively represented and more closely aligned with architects' workflows.

In the current study, we focus primarily on the application of AI tools in the architectural design process, particularly in the generation of standard floor plans for nursing units in general hospitals. However, if the scope of research were to be expanded to other complex building types, engineering design requirements such as structural safety and MEP (Mechanical, Electrical, and Plumbing) system configurations would also be crucial. Although the emphasis of this study is on architectural design, the proposed methods also hold potential for integration with engineering design. AI tools can learn from images of engineering design layouts to provide recommendations on aspects such as structural loads and system configurations, thereby optimizing the overall design. This approach can assist architects in anticipating and addressing potential engineering issues at the early design stage, enhancing the scientific basis and feasibility of the design. As AI technology in architectural design is still in its early stages, future research should further explore how to better integrate AI with engineering design needs to improve overall design quality and practicality.

Author Contributions: Conceptualization, Z.H. and Y.C.; Methodology, Y.C.; Validation, Y.C.; Resources, Z.H.; Data curation, Z.H.; Writing—original draft, Z.H.; Writing—review & editing, Z.H.; Supervision, Y.C.; Funding acquisition, Y.C. All authors have read and agreed to the published version of the manuscript.

Funding: This research was supported by Beijing Jiaotong University Horizontal Project of Social Sciences (No. A24SK00020): Big Data Management System Project for Medical Building Space.

Data Availability Statement: Data is contained within the article.

Conflicts of Interest: The authors declare no conflict of interest.

References

1. Shabani, M.A.; Hosseini, S.; Furukawa, Y. HouseDiffusion: Vector Floorplan Generation via a Diffusion Model with Discrete and Continuous Denoising. In Proceedings of the 2023 IEEE/CVF Conference on Computer Vision and Pattern Recognition (CVPR), IEEE, Vancouver, BC, Canada, 18–22 June 2023; pp. 5466–5475.
2. Nauata, N.; Hosseini, S.; Chang, K.-H.; Chu, H.; Cheng, C.-Y.; Furukawa, Y. House-GAN++: Generative Adversarial Layout Refinement Networks. *arXiv* **2021**, arXiv:2103.02574.
3. Wu, W.; Fu, X.-M.; Tang, R.; Wang, Y.; Qi, Y.-H.; Liu, L. Data-driven interior plan generation for residential buildings. *ACM Trans. Graph.* **2019**, *38*, 1–12. [CrossRef]
4. Zhou, L.Q. *Standardization Design of Nursing Unit Based on Open Building Theories. M.S.*; Harbin Institute of Technology: Harbin, China, 2019.
5. Jia, M.; Zhou, Y.M. The Design of Nursing Unit in Western Nursing Home and the Enlightenment to China. *Archit. Tech.* **2017**, 108–111. Available online: https://kns.cnki.net/kcms2/article/abstract?v=MBTPQIn9ZKG0NDfhk54ic1Feth2SLrZU0CoFC43LnTsStgl4iBRD16NRQaPqFch8tv_xY5M5cpLTKmkW9_s0kZhw1amFMgKQ_RVLWMDjDrZNUDnXVxEC0NhK1zfArHWzJbOScJpb6u-dosH2JBmnapA4YWIaYDH0T4IBYAUVe9k=&uniplatform=NZKPT (accessed on 18 July 2024).
6. Li, X. *The Research on the Evolution of PatientCare Unit for Hospital Buildings in China. M.S*; Chongqing University: Chongqing, China, 2017.
7. Ho, J.; Jain, A.; Abbeel, P. Denoising Diffusion Probabilistic Models. *Adv. Neural Inf. Process. Syst.* **2020**, *33*, 6840–6851.
8. Rombach, R.; Blattmann, A.; Lorenz, D.; Esser, P.; Ommer, B. High-Resolution Image Synthesis with Latent Diffusion Models. In Proceedings of the 2022 IEEE/CVF Conference on Computer Vision and Pattern Recognition (CVPR), IEEE, New Orleans, LA, USA, 19–21 June 2022; pp. 10674–10685.
9. Hu, E.J.; Shen, Y.; Wallis, P.; Allen-Zhu, Z.; Li, Y.; Wang, S.; Wang, L.; Chen, W. LoRA: Low-Rank Adaptation of Large Language Models. *arXiv* **2021**, arXiv:2106.09685.
10. Vaswani, A.; Shazeer, N.; Parmar, N.; Uszkoreit, J.; Jones, L.; Gomez, A.N.; Kaiser, L.; Polosukhin, I. Attention Is All You Need. *arXiv* **2023**, arXiv:1706.03762.
11. Goodfellow, I.; Pouget-Abadie, J.; Mirza, M.; Xu, B.; Warde-Farley, D.; Ozair, S.; Courville, A.; Bengio, Y. Generative Adversarial Networks. *Commun. ACM* **2020**, *63*, 139–144. [CrossRef]
12. Isola, P.; Zhu, J.-Y.; Zhou, T.; Efros, A.A. Image-to-Image Translation with Conditional Adversarial Networks. In Proceedings of the 2017 IEEE Conference on Computer Vision and Pattern Recognition (CVPR), IEEE, Honolulu, HI, USA, 21–26 July 2017; pp. 5967–5976.
13. Wang, T.-C.; Liu, M.-Y.; Zhu, J.-Y.; Tao, A.; Kautz, J.; Catanzaro, B. High-Resolution Image Synthesis and Semantic Manipulation with Conditional GANs. In Proceedings of the 2018 IEEE/CVF Conference on Computer Vision and Pattern Recognition, IEEE, Salt Lake City, UT, USA, 18–23 June 2018; pp. 8798–8807.
14. Huang, W.; Zheng, H. Architectural Drawings Recognition and Generation through Machine Learning. In Proceedings of the 38th Annual Conference of the Association for Computer Aided Design in Architecture, Mexico City, Mexico, 18–20 October 2018; pp. 156–165.
15. Chaillou, S. ArchiGAN: Artificial Intelligence x Architecture. In *Architectural Intelligence*; Yuan, P.F., Xie, M., Leach, N., Yao, J., Wang, X., Eds.; Springer: Singapore, 2020; pp. 117–127. ISBN 9789811565670.
16. Zheng, H.; An, K.; Wei, J.; Ren, Y. Apartment Floor Plans Generation via Generative Adversarial Networks. In Proceedings of the 25th International Conference of the Association for Computer-Aided Architectural Design Research in Asia (CAADRIA), Bangkok, Thailand, 5–8 August 2020; pp. 599–608.
17. Pan, Y.; Qian, J.; Hu, Y. A Preliminary Study on the Formation of the General Layouts on the Northern Neighborhood Community Based on GauGAN Diversity Output Generator. In *Proceedings of the 2020 DigitalFUTURES*; Yuan, P.F., Yao, J., Yan, C., Wang, X., Leach, N., Eds.; Springer: Singapore, 2021; pp. 179–188. ISBN 978-981-334-399-3.

18. Luo, Z.; Huang, W. FloorplanGAN: Vector Residential Floorplan Adversarial Generation. *Autom. Constr.* **2022**, *142*, 104470. [CrossRef]
19. Fan, Y.; Xue, J.; Zheng, H.; Lai, D. Draw to Shade: A Personalized Daylighting Regulation Method through User-Involved Paintings for Enhanced Indoor Visual Comfort and Aesthetics Experience. *J. Build. Eng.* **2023**, *80*, 108014. [CrossRef]
20. Wang, L.; Liu, J.; Cheng, G.; Liu, E.; Chen, W. Constructing a Personalized AI Assistant for Shear Wall Layout Using Stable Diffusion. *arXiv* **2023**, arXiv:2305.10830.
21. Ha, D.; Dai, A.; Le, Q.V. HyperNetworks. *arXiv* **2016**, arXiv:1609.09106.
22. Ruiz, N.; Li, Y.; Jampani, V.; Pritch, Y.; Rubinstein, M.; Aberman, K. DreamBooth: Fine Tuning Text-to-Image Diffusion Models for Subject-Driven Generation. *arXiv* **2023**, arXiv:2208.12242.
23. LoRA vs Dreambooth vs Textual Inversion vs Hypernetworks–YouTube. Available online: https://www.youtube.com/watch?v=dVjMiJsuR5o (accessed on 18 July 2024).
24. Zhang, L.; Rao, A.; Agrawala, M. Adding Conditional Control to Text-to-Image Diffusion Models. In Proceedings of the 2023 IEEE/CVF International Conference on Computer Vision (ICCV), IEEE, Paris, France, 1 October 2023; pp. 3813–3824.
25. Rombach, R. CompVis/Stable-Diffusion. 2024. Available online: https://github.com/CompVis/stable-diffusion (accessed on 18 July 2024).
26. AUTOMATIC1111 Stable Diffusion Web UI. 2022. Available online: https://github.com/AUTOMATIC1111/stable-diffusion-webui (accessed on 18 July 2024).
27. bmaltais GUI. 2024. Available online: https://github.com/bmaltais/kohya_ss (accessed on 18 July 2024).
28. Lora-Scripts/README-Zh.Md at Main Akegarasu/Lora-Scripts. Available online: https://github.com/Akegarasu/lora-scripts/blob/main/README-zh.md (accessed on 18 July 2024).
29. Ryu, S. Low-Rank Adaptation for Fast Text-to-Image Diffusion Fine-Tuning. 2024. Available online: https://github.com/cloneofsimo/lora (accessed on 18 July 2024).
30. starik222. Starik222/BooruDatasetTagManager. 2024. Available online: https://github.com/starik222/BooruDatasetTagManager (accessed on 18 July 2024).
31. Nightingale, F. *Notes on Nursing: What It Is, and What It Is Not*; J.B. Lippincott Company: Philadelphia, PA, USA, 1946.
32. Trust, N. Studies in the Functions and Design of Hospitals. Available online: https://www.nuffieldtrust.org.uk/research/studies-in-the-functions-and-design-of-hospitals (accessed on 18 July 2024).
33. Trites, D.K.; Galbraith, F.D.; Sturdavant, M.; Leckwart, J.F. Influence of Nursing-Unit Design on the Activities and Subjective Feelings of Nursing Personnel. *Environ. Behav.* **1970**, *2*, 303–334. [CrossRef]
34. Zborowsky, T.; Bunker-Hellmich, L.; Morelli, A.; O'Neill, M. Centralized vs. Decentralized Nursing Stations: Effects on Nurses' Functional Use of Space and Work Environment. *HERD Health Environ. Res. Des. J.* **2010**, *3*, 19–42. [CrossRef]
35. Becker, F. Nursing Unit Design and Communication Patterns: What Is "Real" Work? *HERD Health Environ. Res. Des. J.* **2007**, *1*, 58–62. [CrossRef]
36. Kalisch, B.J.; Russell, K.; Lee, K.H. Nursing Teamwork and Unit Size. *West. J. Nurs. Res.* **2013**, *35*, 214–225. [CrossRef] [PubMed]
37. Hua, Y.; Becker, F.; Wurmser, T.; Bliss-Holtz, J.; Hedges, C. Effects of Nursing Unit Spatial Layout on Nursing Team Communication Patterns, Quality of Care, and Patient Safety. *HERD Health Environ. Res. Des. J.* **2012**, *6*, 8–38. [CrossRef] [PubMed]
38. Pati, D.; Thomas, E. Harvey, J.; Redden, P.; Summers, B.; Pati, S. An Empirical Examination of the Impacts of Decentralized Nursing Unit Design. *HERD Health Environ. Res. Des. J.* **2015**, *8*, 56–70. [CrossRef] [PubMed]
39. Cui, H.W. *A Comparative Study of Hospital Careunits between China and UK. M.S.*; Harbin Institute of Technology: Harbin, China, 2018.
40. Kingma, D.P.; Ba, J. Adam: A Method for Stochastic Optimization. *arXiv* **2017**, arXiv:1412.6980.
41. Anzanello, M.J.; Fogliatto, F.S. Learning Curve Models and Applications: Literature Review and Research Directions. *Int. J. Ind. Ergon.* **2011**, *41*, 573–583. [CrossRef]

drones

MDPI

Article

A Minimal Solution Estimating the Position of Cameras with Unknown Focal Length with IMU Assistance

Kang Yan, Zhenbao Yu, Chengfang Song, Hongping Zhang * and Dezhong Chen

Global Navigation Satellite System (GNSS) Research Center, Wuhan University, 299 Bayi Road, Wuchang District, Wuhan 430072, China; 2020106180011@whu.edu.cn (K.Y.); zhenbaoyu@whu.edu.cn (Z.Y.); songchf@whu.edu.cn (C.S.); chendz@whu.edu.cn (D.C.)

* Correspondence: hpzhang@whu.edu.cn

Abstract: Drones are typically built with integrated cameras and inertial measurement units (IMUs). It is crucial to achieve drone attitude control through relative pose estimation using cameras. IMU drift can be ignored over short periods. Based on this premise, in this paper, four methods are proposed for estimating relative pose and focal length across various application scenarios: for scenarios where the camera's focal length varies between adjacent moments and is unknown, the relative pose and focal length can be computed from four-point correspondences; for planar motion scenarios where the camera's focal length varies between adjacent moments and is unknown, the relative pose and focal length can be determined from three-point correspondences; for instances of planar motion where the camera's focal length is equal between adjacent moments and is unknown, the relative pose and focal length can be calculated from two-point correspondences; finally, for scenarios where multiple cameras are employed for image acquisition but only one is calibrated, a method proposed for estimating the pose and focal length of uncalibrated cameras can be used. The numerical stability and performance of these methods are compared and analyzed under various noise conditions using simulated datasets. We also assessed the performance of these methods on real datasets captured by a drone in various scenes. The experimental results demonstrate that the method proposed in this paper achieves superior accuracy and stability to classical methods.

Keywords: relative pose estimation; IMU; focal length of camera; minimal solution

1. Introduction

With the continuous development in computer vision, research on using methods to estimate relative camera poses for achieving drone attitude control has become increasingly important. Accurately estimating camera relative poses is crucial for various practical applications in drones, such as visual odometry (VO) [1,2], simultaneous localization and mapping (SLAM) [3–5], and structure from motion (SFM) [6,7]. As a result, numerous scholars are focusing on estimating the relative pose of cameras, and algorithms for this are already publicly available.

The fundamental matrix is commonly employed to represent the relative position of an uncalibrated camera. Additionally, the essential matrix is utilized to depict the relative pose of a calibrated camera. Since scale information cannot be estimated using a single-camera system, relative pose for calibrated cameras has five degrees of freedom (DOFs), including three for rotation and two for translation [8]. Consequently, the relative pose of the camera can be estimated using five-point pairs. The intrinsic parameters include focal length, principal point, aspect ratio, and non-perspective distortion parameters. However, distortion is very weak when the field of view is narrow [9]. Moreover, modern cameras commonly feature square pixels, facilitating a straightforward determination of the aspect ratio [8]. Additionally, for the majority of cameras, the principal point is situated close to the center of the image. Thus, a reasonable approximation can be made.

In real-world scenarios, due to the presence of erroneous matching points in the feature matching process, it is common to combine Random Sample Consensus (RANSAC) with a solver [10]. Due to the inverse relationship between the outlier rate and the number of iterations in RANSAC, as well as the required number of points for the solver under a constant outlier rate, numerous scholars have explored methods to minimize the minimum required points needed to estimate pose. Usually, the required number of points can be reduced by using motion models and adding additional sensors. References [11,12] present a method of using planar motion. In [13–17], sensors including IMUs were used to achieve this goal. Utilizing IMUs can provide the pitch and roll angles, reducing the rotational degrees of freedom from three to one. Recent studies have also indicated that the drift of IMUs remains nearly constant over short durations, allowing us to compensate for using pre-observed IMU drift values. This enabled us to utilize IMUs to provide three rotation angles of the camera.

In this paper, we introduce a series of methods for estimating the relative pose of a camera with an unknown focal length. Thus, the main contributions of this paper are as follows:

- We propose a minimal solution, using auxiliary information provided by the IMU, to determine the relative pose and focal lengths for cameras with unknown and variable focal lengths during random and planar motions.
- We propose a degenerated model designed to address the situation where cameras with unknown and fixed focal lengths undergo planar motion.
- We provide a degenerated model for estimating the relative pose and focal length between a fully calibrated camera and a camera with an unknown focal length.

The rest of this article is organized as follows: In Section 2, a review of the existing literature is conducted. In Section 3, we introduce the fundamental principles of the epipolar constraint. Then, we propose a method for simultaneously estimating the translation vector and disparate focal lengths when IMU-provided rotation matrices are used, along with a degenerate model for planar motion. Furthermore, we present a method for estimating the focal length and translation vector when the focal length is unknown and fixed for cameras undergoing planar motion. Finally, we offer a method for estimating the focal length and translation vector when only one side of the camera's focal length is unknown and provide a degenerate model for planar motion in this scenario. In Section 4, we analyze the proposed algorithm using both simulated and real data and compare it with three classical algorithms. Finally, conclusions are drawn in Section 5.

2. Related Work

Numerous relative pose estimation algorithms exist for various application scenarios. The relative pose between adjacent moments can be represented for uncalibrated cameras using the fundamental matrix. The fundamental matrix is a 3×3 matrix consisting of nine elements, with one element being a constant factor, thus requiring eight corresponding point pairs to estimate the fundamental matrix [18]. Hartley et al. proposed a classical linear eight-point method to solve for the fundamental matrix F based on the epipolar constraint. This method is a linear solution with a relatively simple solving process. Additionally, due to the rank-2 property of the fundamental matrix F, Hartley et al. further introduced a seven-point method to solve for the fundamental matrix F. This method involves solving a third-degree polynomial to compute the fundamental matrix [18].

Numerous scholars have focused on computing the relative pose and focal length of a camera for which the focal length is the only unknown intrinsic parameter using the minimum number of sample points. Li et al. proposed a method based on implicit functions, in which they derived a polynomial up to the 15th order for the unknown focal length [19]. This method is relatively straightforward to implement. Building upon Li et al.'s work, Hartley et al. proposed an improved method based on a hidden variable, providing a detailed explanation of the technique [20]. This method is conceptually simple, involving the substitution of all monomials except one variable to simplify the problem into solving a system of linear equations and addressing polynomial eigenvalue problems. If two cameras have the same unknown focal length, six corresponding point pairs are required for the computation [21]. Stewénius et al. conducted a detailed analysis showing that using six points, when the focal length is unknown, allows for estimating both the camera's focal length and its relative pose [21]. They utilized the internal properties of the fundamental matrix, where the determinant equals 0, and the constraint equation of the trace of the essential matrix, formulating 10 equations with 33 monomials. Bujnak et al. proposed a new model for an unknown camera focal length, assuming one camera is fully calibrated while the other is partially calibrated [22]. The authors presented two methods, one utilizing eigenvalue polynomials and another employing a Gröbner solver. Torii et al. provided a comprehensive summary of previous algorithms and introduced a "4 + 1" method for estimating camera focal length and the essential matrix [23]. Here, "4 + 1" refers to using four coplanar feature point pairs and one off-plane pair. This algorithm improves upon the six-point algorithm proposed by Stewénius et al., increasing the quality of estimation.

When the camera's intrinsic parameters are known, the relative pose can be estimated using the classical five-point method [20,24,25]. The essential matrix represents the relative spatial relationship between two adjacent moments, with five degrees of freedom. In [20], numerical methods such as quotient-free Gaussian elimination and Levinson–Durbin iteration were employed to address polynomial eigenvalue problems during the solution process. In [24], a method based on a polynomial eigenvalue solver is proposed to transform a system of polynomial equations into polynomial eigenvalues. A comparison with the Gröbner basis method was conducted, demonstrating the accuracy and applicability of the proposed approach. Zuzana et al. proposed a method for solving the problem of computing relative camera poses for partially calibrated cameras by initially eliminating all unknowns that are not present in the linear equations and subsequently extending the solutions to encompass the remaining unknowns [26]. When there is a change in focal length, at least seven corresponding point pairs are required to compute the translation vector and focal length of cameras [27,28]. In [29], a relative pose estimation method was proposed for cameras with constant radial distortion based on a hidden variable. Jiang et al. analyzed methods for estimating the relative pose of cameras with unknown focal length and radial distortion and proposed a minimal solution [30]. Magnus et al. summarized the existing methods for estimating the relative pose of cameras with radial distortion and proposed a unified formulation to solve this [31].

Minimizing the number of points is crucial for estimating the relative pose of a camera, as this significantly reduces computational complexity, minimizes processing time, and fulfills the real-time demands of practical applications. To further reduce the number of feature points required for pose estimation, some scholars use IMUs. In [9], a method that uses IMUs was proposed. Using this method, the relative camera pose between two images can be solved with just three corresponding points. Fraundorfer et al. simplified traditional methods by using two known orientation angles, deriving three-point, four-point, and five-point algorithms [13]. Other scholars aligned one axis of the camera (e.g., the y-axis) with a common reference direction (e.g., the gravity vector), thereby reducing the degrees of freedom in camera pose estimation [14–17]. Marcus et al. proposed a method for estimating the full three-dimensional orientation of a camera using IMU data [32]. The authors of [32] analyzed IMU drift based on the slight variation in IMU drift biases, verifying that the observed biases can be compensated for in the remaining part of the sequence; by using IMU data, the system's rotation angles (pitch, roll, yaw) could be obtained, subsequently allowing them to derive the relative rotation matrix R of the camera. Therefore, when the camera has an unknown and fixed focal length, determining the focal length and the relative translation vector requires only three pairs of corresponding points.

Our method is based on the research presented in [32]. Firstly, we securely integrated the camera and IMU to utilize the IMU for calculating the camera's rotation angles. We referred to the method proposed by Savage [33], using the raw data observed by the IMU, and integrated them according to the navigation differential equations to calculate the IMU's relative attitude information by integrating the angular velocity measured by the gyroscope. Because the IMU was rigidly attached to the camera, we used the rotation angles provided by the IMU along with the pre-calibrated relative position between the IMU and the camera to calculate the camera's rotation matrix. Based on these conditions, we propose an algorithm and present a computational model for estimating the focal length and translation vector of a camera with unknown focal length (including both fixed and different focal lengths) under different motion conditions (random or planar motion). An overview of the different cases can be seen in Table 1. The solver for camera focal length was determined using Gröbner basis theory [34,35]. Finally, we validated the algorithm's performance using both simulated and real data, comparing it against other classical algorithms.

Table 1. Parameterization for the different relative pose cases.

Methods	Minimum Points Required	Estimated Parameters	Motion Model
Different $f_1 f_2$	4	$f_1 f_2 t$	Random motion
Different $f_1 f_2$ for planar motion	3	$f_1 f_2 t$	Planar motion
Single f	3	$f t$	Random motion
Single f for planar motion	2	$f t$	Planar motion
Unknown and fixed f for planar motion	2	$f t$	Planar motion

3. Minimal Solution Solver

At present, most cameras feature square pixels, and the principal point coincides with the image center. Hence, we can obtain

$$K_1^{-1} = \mathrm{diag}(1, 1, f_1), \quad (1)$$

$$K_2^{-1} = \mathrm{diag}(1, 1, f_2), \quad (2)$$

where f_1 and f_2 are the reciprocals of the camera focal length of the first and second cameras, respectively; K_1 and K_2 are the camera intrinsic matrices of the first and second cameras, respectively.

The relative pose of cameras is commonly computed based on the epipolar constraint. As shown in Figure 1, two corresponding image feature points from a pair of images satisfy the following relationship:

$$p_2^{\mathrm{T}} F p_1 = 0, \quad (3)$$

where F is the fundamental matrix, and p_1 and p_2 are pixel coordinates of feature points. In Figure 1, P denotes a feature point on the object, O_1 and O_2 represent the camera center, e_1 and e_2 indicate the epipoles, and l_1 and l_2 represent the epipolar lines.

The relationship between the fundamental matrix F and the essential matrix E can be expressed as

$$F = K_2^{-\mathrm{T}} E K_1^{-1}, \quad (4)$$

where K_1 and K_2 are the camera intrinsic matrices of the first and second cameras.

3.1. Different and Unknown Focal Lengths

In this section, two solvers are proposed for estimating the focal length and the relative pose when the focal length is unknown and variable, based on epipolar constraints. Additionally, a degenerate model is also provided for the scenario wherein the camera undergoes planar motion.

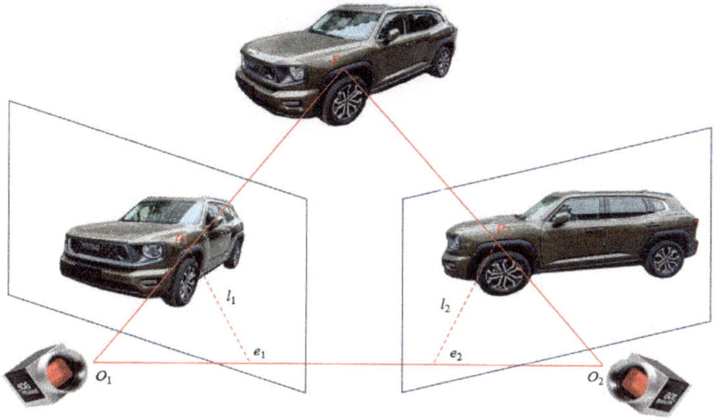

Figure 1. O_1 and O_2 represent the camera center; P denotes the target feature point; p_1 and p_2 are the pixel coordinates of the feature points; e_1 and e_2 are epipoles, which are the points where the line connecting O_1 and O_2 intersects with the image plane; O_1, O_2, and P forms the epipolar plane; and l_1 and l_2 are the epipolar lines, which are the lines where the epipolar plane intersects with the image plane.

3.1.1. Random Motion Model

When the camera undergoes random motion, the translation vector is given by

$$\boldsymbol{t} = \begin{bmatrix} t_x \\ t_y \\ t_z \end{bmatrix}. \tag{5}$$

Then, we can obtain the essential matrix as follows:

$$\boldsymbol{E} = [\boldsymbol{t}]_\times \boldsymbol{R}, \tag{6}$$

where $\boldsymbol{R}$ is the relative rotation matrix, and $[\boldsymbol{t}]_\times$ is the antisymmetric matrix of $\boldsymbol{t}$. For cameras with different and unknown focal lengths, their essential matrix is shown in Equation (4).

According to the epipolar constraint (Equation (3)), we can obtain an equation with five unknowns, including a translation matrix and two different focal lengths (f_1, f_2). In the case of single-camera displacement, scale information is absent, i.e., $t_x^2 + t_y^2 + t_z^2 = 1$. Hence, it is necessary to use four pairs of corresponding points to establish a system of equations that are linear in $\boldsymbol{t}$ for solving these unknowns. By substituting Equations (4)–(6) into the epipolar line constraint Equation (3), we can obtain

$$\boldsymbol{p}_2^{\mathrm{T}} \boldsymbol{K}_2{}^{-\mathrm{T}} [\boldsymbol{t}]_\times \boldsymbol{R} \boldsymbol{K}_1{}^{-1} \boldsymbol{p}_1 = 0, \tag{7}$$

By extracting the coefficients of t_x, t_y, and t_z from this equation to form the coefficient matrix, we can obtain

$$\boldsymbol{A}(f_1, f_2)\boldsymbol{t} = 0, \tag{8}$$

where $\boldsymbol{A}(f_1, f_2)$ is a 4×3 coefficient matrix and includes only f_1 and f_2. Since Equation (8) has non-trivial solutions, matrix $\boldsymbol{A}$ is not a full rank; thus, each of its 3×3 submatrices must satisfy a determinant equal to zero. We can obtain $\mathrm{C}_4^3 = 4$ different determinants. Each 3×3 determinant equal to zero represents an equation with the focal lengths f_1 and f_2, totaling four equations. Further extraction of the coefficients of f_1 and f_2 yields the following equation expressed in terms of f_1 and f_2:

$$Mv = M \begin{bmatrix} 1 \\ f_1 \\ f_2 \\ f_1 f_2 \\ f_1^2 \\ f_2^2 \\ f_1^2 f_2 \\ f_1 f_2^2 \\ f_1^2 f_2^2 \end{bmatrix} = 0, \tag{9}$$

where M is a 4×9 coefficient matrix, and v is a vector of all nine monomials in f_1 and f_2. Then, a Gröbner basis generator can be used to solve for f_1 and f_2 [36]. Finally, by substituting the obtained results into Equation (8) and finding the null space of the 3×3 submatrix of A, the translation vector t is obtained. Using the RANSAC algorithm to validate the estimated focal length and the translation vector, we selected the results that better conformed to the epipolar constraint as the final outcome [10].

3.1.2. Planar Motion Model

Planar motion is very common in practical applications such as removable suspension cameras; in this case, $t_y = 0$. This scenario is discussed separately, and the derivation is provided.

To provide a planar motion model for a camera, that is, $t_y = 0$, the translation vector can be obtained by

$$t' = \begin{bmatrix} t_x \\ 0 \\ t_z \end{bmatrix}. \tag{10}$$

Based on the epipolar constraint, we can also obtain an equation with four unknowns. Therefore, we only need three pairs of corresponding points to solve the camera parameters. The resulting system can be written as

$$A'(f_1, f_2)t = 0, \tag{11}$$

where $A'(f_1, f_2)$ is a 3×2 coefficient matrix. Similarly, we can also obtain a system of equations for f_1 and f_2:

$$M'v' = M' \begin{bmatrix} 1 \\ f_1 \\ f_2 \\ f_1 f_2 \\ f_1^2 \\ f_1^2 f_2 \end{bmatrix} = 0. \tag{12}$$

In this system, M' is a 3×6 coefficient matrix. Similar to the process described in Section 3.1.2, the solution for the focal lengths f_1 and f_2 can be obtained using a Gröbner basis generator, leading to the derivation of the translation vector t.

3.2. Fixed and Unknown Focal Lengths for Planar Motion

In practical applications, it is often the case that cameras with fixed focal lengths are used. In [23], the derivation of focal length and translation vector flow for a camera exhibiting a random motion model with unknown and fixed focal lengths is provided, so this will not be reiterated here. Therefore, based on the discussion in Section 3, a degenerate model is presented in this section for cameras with unknown and fixed focal lengths to estimate planar motion.

As previously described, by using the epipolar constraint, we can obtain a system of equations related to the focal length and translation vector as follows:

$$\boldsymbol{B}_1(f)\boldsymbol{t} = 0. \tag{13}$$

Since the camera has planar motion, $t_y = 0$; thus, $\boldsymbol{B}_1$ is a 2×2 coefficient matrix. By converting its determinant to an equation of focal length f, we can obtain

$$\boldsymbol{N}_1\boldsymbol{w} = 0. \tag{14}$$

Equation (14) is a cubic equation with one unknown focal length f. Since the coefficients of f are all real numbers, the solution can be obtained using the Cardan formula [37].

3.3. Unknown Focal Length for One Side

In certain scenarios, images can be captured by multiple cameras, but only one of them will be calibrated. This situation is quite common in the field of 3D reconstruction and other related areas, and there is currently some relevant research available [22]. This section introduces two degenerate models. Although there are multiple cameras in the system, due to the known focal length of one camera, the equations formulated with epipolar constraints involving the focal length and translation vector have only one unknown focal length and translation vector in three directions. Hence, solving them necessitates three corresponding pairs of feature points. The resulting system can be written as

$$\boldsymbol{B}_2(f)\boldsymbol{t} = 0, \tag{15}$$

and the determinant of $\boldsymbol{B}_2$ is an equation that depends only on the focal length f and can be written as

$$\boldsymbol{N}_2\boldsymbol{w} = 0. \tag{16}$$

In Equation (16), there is only one unknown variable with focal length f, and the equation is of second order. Therefore, the focal length f can be obtained through simple calculation.

When the cameras in the system lie in the same plane perpendicular to the y-axis, namely when the translation vector $\boldsymbol{t}$ is the same as in Equation (11), the problem can be further simplified. Similarly, through epipolar constraints, we can obtain equations related to the focal length and translation vector as follows:

$$\boldsymbol{B}_3(f)\boldsymbol{t} = 0. \tag{17}$$

Since $t_y = 0$, there are two degrees of freedom at this moment, requiring only two corresponding pairs of points. The determinant of $\boldsymbol{B}_3$, which depends only on focal length, can similarly be simplified into a linear equation. It can be written as

$$\boldsymbol{N}_3\boldsymbol{w} = 0. \tag{18}$$

Equation (18) is a linear equation with one unknown focal length f, so we can easily calculate it.

4. Experiments

We assessed the performance of our proposed method in comparison to that of current classical methods. We selected three classical algorithms for estimating camera relative pose to enable comparison with algorithms presented in the previous literature. These are labeled as Marcus [32], LHD [19], and Kukelova [24].

In order to more easily compare different algorithms, we provide the error calculation formulas for both the focal length f and the relative translation vector $\boldsymbol{t}$. The single-camera focal length error ξ_{f_i} is defined as follows:

$$\xi_{f_i} = \frac{|f_{ie} - f_{ig}|}{f_{ig}}, \tag{19}$$

where f_g denotes the ground-truth focal length, and f_e is the corresponding estimated focal length. For the different and unknown focal length problems, we computed the geometric mean of the focal length errors:

$$\xi_f = \sqrt{\xi_{f_1}\xi_{f_2}}. \tag{20}$$

The relative translation vector error ξ_t is defined as follows:

$$\xi_t = \arccos\frac{\boldsymbol{t}_g^T \boldsymbol{t}_e}{\|\boldsymbol{t}_g\|\|\boldsymbol{t}_e\|}, \tag{21}$$

where $\boldsymbol{t}_g$ denotes the ground-truth translation, and $\boldsymbol{t}_e$ is the corresponding estimated translation.

4.1. Synthetic Data

To obtain more realistic simulated data, we constructed a test scenario with randomly generated 3D points. Specifically, the scene points (X, Y, Z) were uniformly distributed with X, Z ∈ [−5, 5] m, the depth Y ∈ [10, 20] m, and the focal length f ∈ [100, 1000]. We set the resolution to 1000 × 700, and the principal point P_0 = (500, 350) pixels. The predefined three-dimensional points were projected onto the camera image to obtain their pixel coordinates. We conducted experiments with 10,000 sets of feature point coordinates and statistically analyzed the errors in the focal length f and translation vector $\boldsymbol{t}$ without noise. The results are presented in Figures 2 and 3. Figure 2 shows the focal length error probability density, while Figure 3 presents the translation vector error probability density.

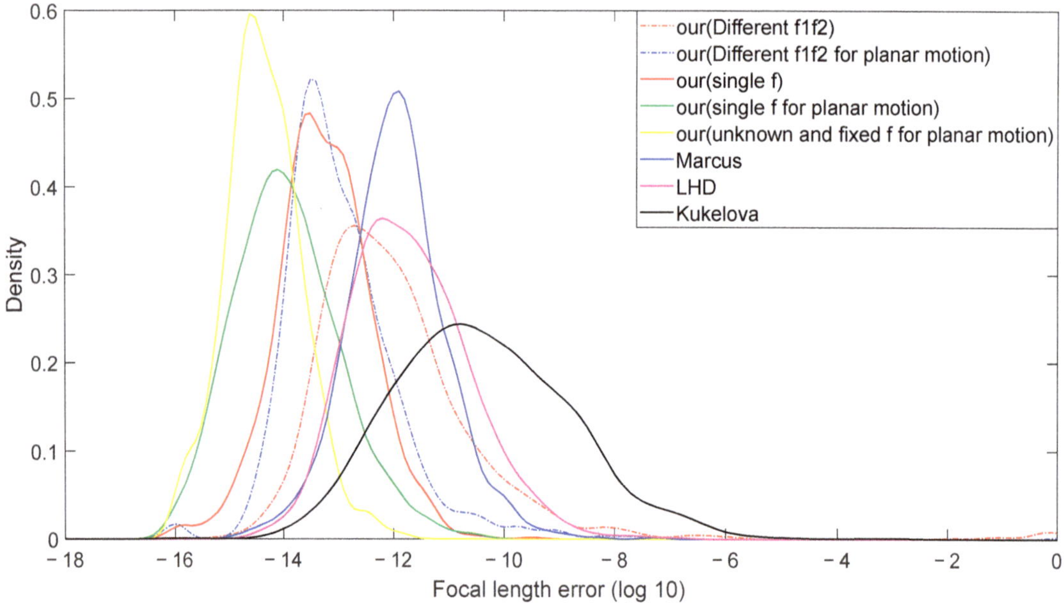

Figure 2. Focal length error probability density for 10,000 randomly generated problem instances.

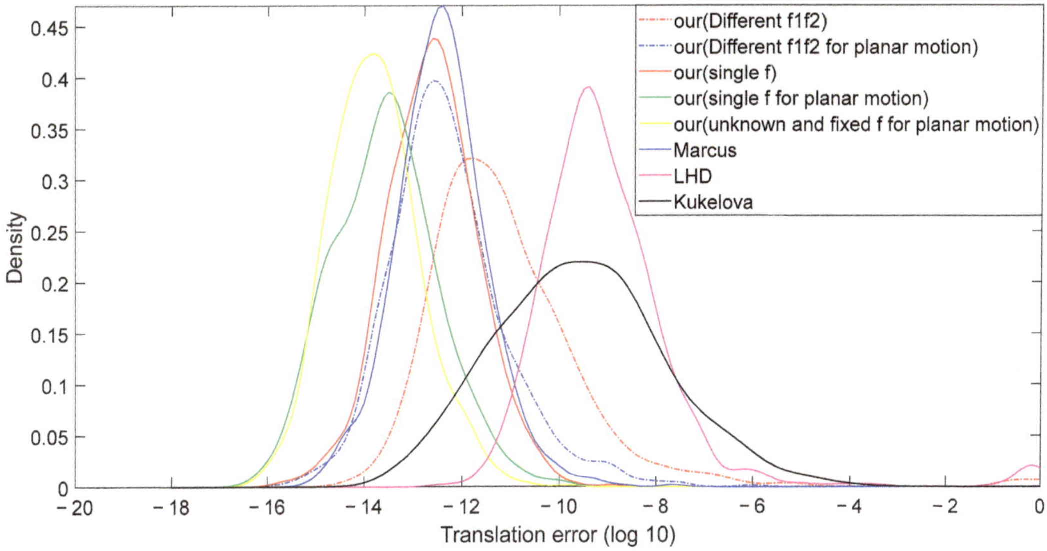

Figure 3. Translation matrix error probability density for 10,000 randomly generated problem instances.

In Figures 2 and 3, the horizontal axes represent the logarithmically transformed results for the estimated focal length error and translation vector error, respectively, while the vertical axis represents the probability density. In Figures 2 and 3, curves positioned farther to the left indicate smaller estimation errors, while higher peaks represent more concentrated estimation errors. It is evident from Figures 2 and 3 that although all the methods can accurately estimate relative pose, the algorithm proposed in this paper achieves higher accuracy than the reference algorithm. Table 2 presents the median estimation errors of the focal length and translation vector, which were calculated separately for the five proposed algorithms and the reference algorithm using the same dataset. The error is slightly larger when cameras with unknown and different focal lengths undergo random motion. This is attributed to the fact that, unlike the reference algorithm, the camera we used has a variable focal length, thereby adding an extra parameter that needs to be computed.

Table 2. The median estimation errors of the focal length f and translation vector $\boldsymbol{t}$ based on simulated data.

	ξ_f-Median/Pixel	ξ_t-Median/Deg
Marcus [32]	1.1023×10^{-13}	3.7090×10^{-13}
LHD [19]	1.6473×10^{-12}	5.3201×10^{-10}
Kukelova [24]	3.1238×10^{-11}	2.3635×10^{-10}
Different $f_1 f_2$	1.3707×10^{-13}	4.0739×10^{-13}
Different $f_1 f_2$ for planar motion	7.8180×10^{-15}	9.6702×10^{-14}
Unknown and fixed f for planar motion	1.3309×10^{-15}	3.6772×10^{-15}
Single f	9.8511×10^{-15}	3.0763×10^{-14}
Single f for planar motion	1.5763×10^{-15}	3.5108×10^{-16}

After estimating the values of the focal length and translation vector, three-dimensional coordinate points were generated using simulated data, and the reprojection coordinates in the pixel coordinate system were calculated based on these points and the estimated values. Subsequently, these reprojection coordinates were compared with those calculated using accurate focal lengths and translation vectors to compute the reprojection error.

Table 3 presents the mean reprojection error calculated over 10,000 experiments. From the table, it can be observed that the reprojection error obtained using the proposed algorithm for estimating the focal length and translation vector is smaller, indicating higher reprojection accuracy.

Table 3. The median reprojection errors with the eight algorithms.

	Reprojection Error/Pixel
Marcus [32]	8.1885×10^{-13}
LHD [19]	3.2519×10^{-12}
Kukelova [24]	5.8134×10^{-11}
Different $f_1 f_2$	7.8529×10^{-13}
Different $f_1 f_2$ for planar motion	5.2568×10^{-14}
Unknown and fixed f for planar motion	7.7419×10^{-15}
Single f	4.1573×10^{-14}
Single f for planar motion	6.8135×10^{-15}

In practical applications, when estimating the relative pose of cameras, the first step involves extracting feature point correspondences. However, errors are inevitable during the feature point extraction process. To validate the performance of the proposed algorithm in the presence of errors in feature point coordinates, we conducted additional experiments, building upon the previous ones. We introduced random noise with coefficients ranging from 0 to 1 into the pixel coordinates of simulated points. Each model underwent ten thousand experiments, and the median errors of the focal length f and the translation vector $\mathbf{t}$ were calculated separately. The results are presented in Figures 4 and 5.

In Figures 4 and 5, it can be seen that the algorithm proposed in this paper yielded a higher accuracy focal length and translation vector than the contrast algorithm. The improvement was particularly significant when the pixel coordinate errors were small.

Although we utilized the rotation angles provided by the IMU as prior information, in real-life scenarios, due to variations in the performance of the IMU itself, the calculated rotation angles may exhibit errors of different scales. To further verify the performance of the proposed algorithm in the presence of IMU errors, we set up control experiments. Random noise with coefficients ranging from $0°$ to $1°$ was introduced into the three rotation angles, and random noise with a coefficient of 1 pixel was added to the image noise. The resulting errors in camera focal length and the relative translation vector were then calculated. The experimental results are presented in Figure 6. The first row shows the curve graph of camera focal length errors calculated using the different algorithms after introducing errors into the three angles, while the second row illustrates the curve graph of errors in the relative rotation matrix of the camera. Figure 6a,d represent the cases where pitch angle rotation errors were introduced; Figure 6b,e represent the cases where yaw angle rotation errors were introduced; Figure 6c,f represent the cases where roll angle rotation errors were introduced. From the figures, it can be observed that the algorithm proposed in this paper achieves higher accuracy than the benchmark algorithms. Specifically, the calculation error of the roll angle has the least impact on the relative pose and focal length of the camera.

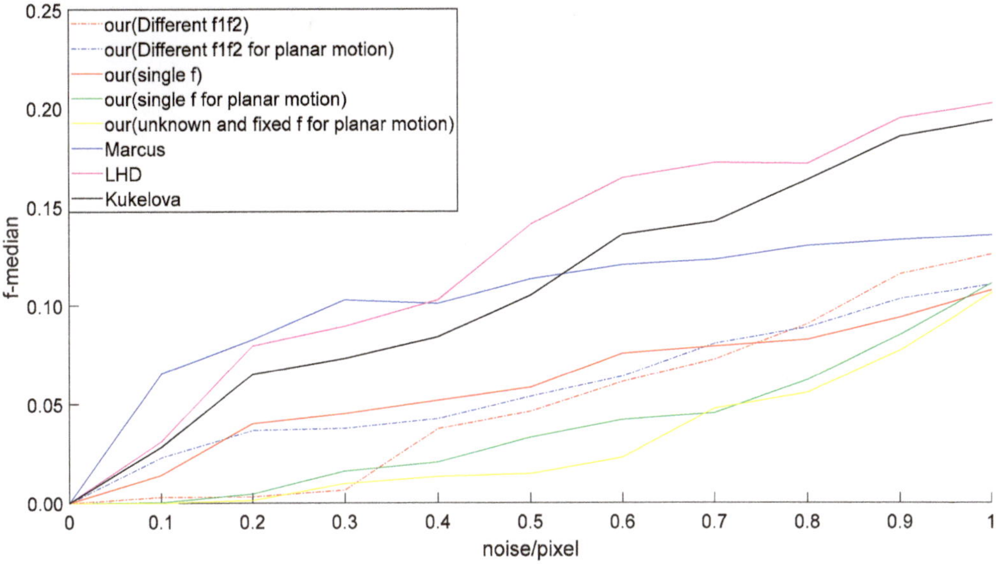

Figure 4. Error variation curve of focal length f with different scale errors in pixel coordinates.

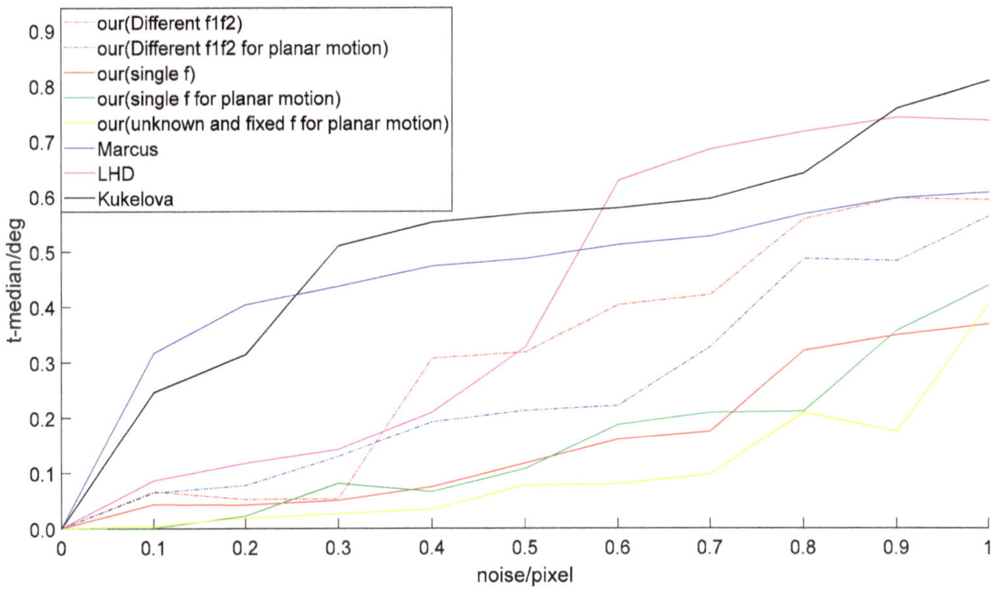

Figure 5. Error variation curve of translation vector $\boldsymbol{t}$ with different scale errors in pixel coordinates.

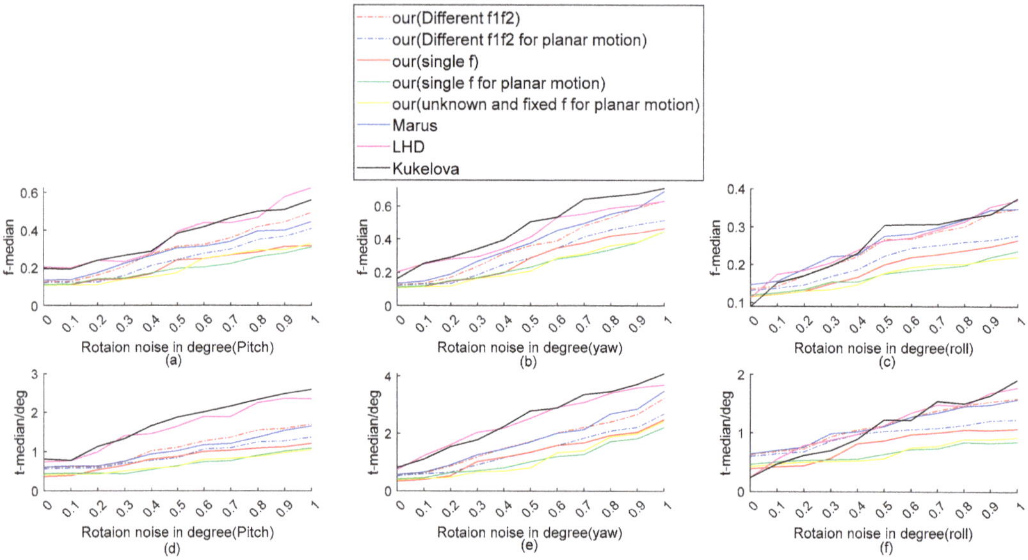

Figure 6. The error variation curves of eight methods when introducing different levels of noise into the three rotation angles with the IMU: (**a**) the median focal length error calculated after introducing pitch angle rotation errors; (**b**) the median focal length error calculated after introducing yaw angle rotation errors; (**c**) the median focal length error calculated after introducing roll angle rotation errors; (**d**) the median translation vector error calculated after introducing pitch angle rotation errors; (**e**) the median translation vector error calculated after introducing yaw angle rotation errors; (**f**) the median translation vector error calculated after introducing roll angle rotation errors.

4.2. Real Data

4.2.1. Data Description

In order to more comprehensively test the performance of the algorithm proposed in this paper, images were captured using a drone in three different scenarios: outdoor landscapes, urban buildings, and road vehicles. The drone was equipped with Basler acA2040-120uc color cameras to capture the images. The drone was also equipped with an IMU module to obtain the rotation angles in three directions, and the IMU module was rigidly attached to the camera. Table 4 lists the common parameters of the IMU mounted on the drone. Before operating the drone, we ensured it remained stationary on the ground for a period of time. This allowed us to perform the initial calibration of IMU drift using the information obtained from the IMU outputs. We collected a total of 30,000 images from three different scenes to serve as the validation dataset for the algorithm. The reference value for the camera focal length was obtained through pre-calibration using the calibration board, while the reference value for the translation vector was calculated using the GNSS module mounted on the drone. We show example images from the scenes in Figure 7.

We synchronized the timestamps of the two cameras mounted on the drone using a GNSS to capture images from different cameras at the same time. We also obtained the 3D coordinates of the drone from the GNSS at that same moment, thus allowing us to calculate the reference value for the translation vector. After obtaining a sufficient number of image data along with corresponding reference values for the camera focal lengths and translation vectors, we used the SIFT algorithm to extract the corresponding coordinates of feature point pairs from frames captured at the same moment by different cameras [38]. Subsequently, we employed the RANSAC algorithm to evaluate the extracted feature points and eliminate those with significant errors [37]. As shown in Figure 8, the SIFT algorithm was used to extract corresponding feature points from the images. In order to achieve a clearer visualization of the extracted feature point pairs, every 20th feature point is marked in the schematic.

Table 4. IMU parameters carried by drone.

	Parameter	Value
Gyroscope	Range	±300°/s
	Angular random walk	0.1 deg/$\sqrt{h}$
	In-run bias stability	0.5 deg/h
	Bias repeatability	0.5 deg/h
	Scale factor error	300 ppm
Accelerometer	Range	±10 g
	In-run bias stability	0.3 mg
	Bias repeatability	0.3 mg
	Scale factor error	300 ppm

Figure 7. Images captured by the drone: (**a**) outdoor landscapes; (**b**) urban buildings; (**c**) road vehicles.

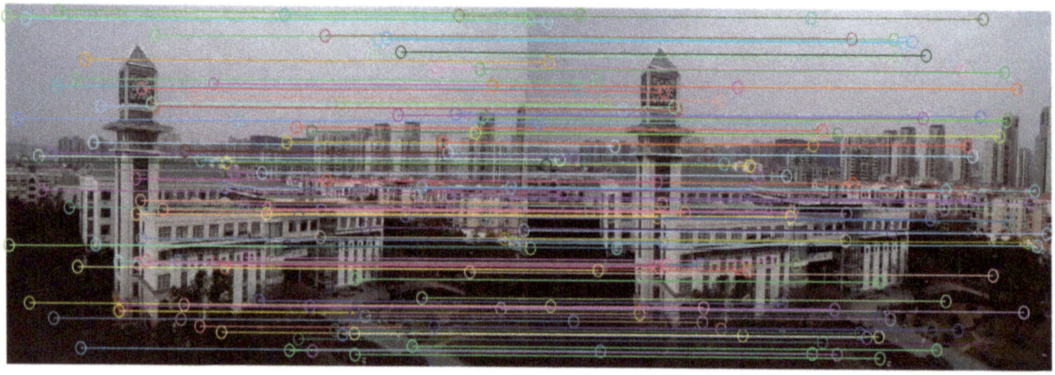

Figure 8. Schematic of feature point extraction using the SIFT algorithm.

4.2.2. Relative Pose Analysis

We divided the collected dataset into three groups based on different data collection scenarios: Group 1 represents outdoor landscapes, Group 2 represents urban buildings, and Group 3 represents road vehicles. Each group of data was processed separately. We conducted statistical analysis on the errors in the focal length and translation vector as calculated using the algorithm proposed in this paper to validate its applicability. The median and standard deviation of the calculation errors are shown in Table 5. As shown in the table, in any given scenario, it is evident that the errors in both the estimated focal length and translation vector using our algorithm were smaller, and they further decreased as the complexity of the model decreased. The standard deviation of the algorithm proposed in this paper is comparatively smaller than that of the reference algorithm, which demonstrates the superior stability of our algorithm. Comparing the computational results across the three scenarios, the focal length and translation vector precision calculated from images captured in urban scenes were the highest, followed by those determined for road vehicle scenes, with the lowest estimation accuracy calculated for outdoor landscapes. This is because, in urban scenes, there are more regular objects in the captured images, resulting in smaller errors when extracting feature points.

Table 5. The median estimation errors of the focal length f and translation vector $\boldsymbol{t}$ based on real data.

		1		**2**		**3**	
		ξ_f	ξ_t	ξ_f	ξ_t	ξ_f	ξ_t
Marcus [32]	Median	0.4423	1.2126	0.3845	0.9842	0.4352	1.1189
	SD	2.5118	4.6214	2.7978	4.3154	3.2684	4.9851
LHD [19]	Median	0.4947	1.2342	0.4153	1.0059	0.4585	1.1216
	SD	3.8273	5.1056	4.3158	6.6517	4.5627	8.6149
Kukelova [24]	Median	0.5253	1.4352	0.3975	0.9818	0.4737	1.1587
	SD	4.8628	7.5157	3.5159	8.3173	3.9791	5.9004
Different f_1f_2	Median	0.4707	1.1739	0.3809	0.9647	0.4336	1.1358
	SD	2.4891	3.4239	2.3513	2.9058	2.6125	3.2268
Different f_1f_2 for planar motion	Median	0.3173	1.0208	0.3047	0.9155	0.3159	0.9853
	SD	2.1041	2.8518	2.2318	2.6517	2.3361	3.0156
Unknown and fixed f for planar motion	Median	0.3058	0.6347	0.3114	0.5919	0.2931	0.6241
	SD	1.9194	2.1273	2.0181	2.3158	1.9180	2.2368
Single f	Median	0.3513	0.9766	0.3505	1.0183	0.3269	0.9186
	SD	1.8108	2.2539	1.9173	2.1586	1.7689	1.9627
Single f for planar motion	Median	0.2761	0.5706	0.2654	0.5286	0.2719	0.5697
	SD	1.4931	1.6817	1.4168	1.8817	1.5217	1.8136

In order to better understand the errors in the calculated focal lengths and translation vectors across all images in the dataset, the cumulative distribution functions of the errors are presented for different scenarios. In Figure 9, the curves positioned farther to the left indicate smaller errors estimated by the model, while steeper slopes suggest a more concentrated range of errors. From the graph, it is evident that the algorithm proposed in this paper yields smaller estimation errors than the reference algorithm. Larger errors only occurred when calculating parameters for cameras with different and unknown focal lengths, which is attributed to the increased complexity of calculating additional parameters, aligning with the experimental results using simulated data.

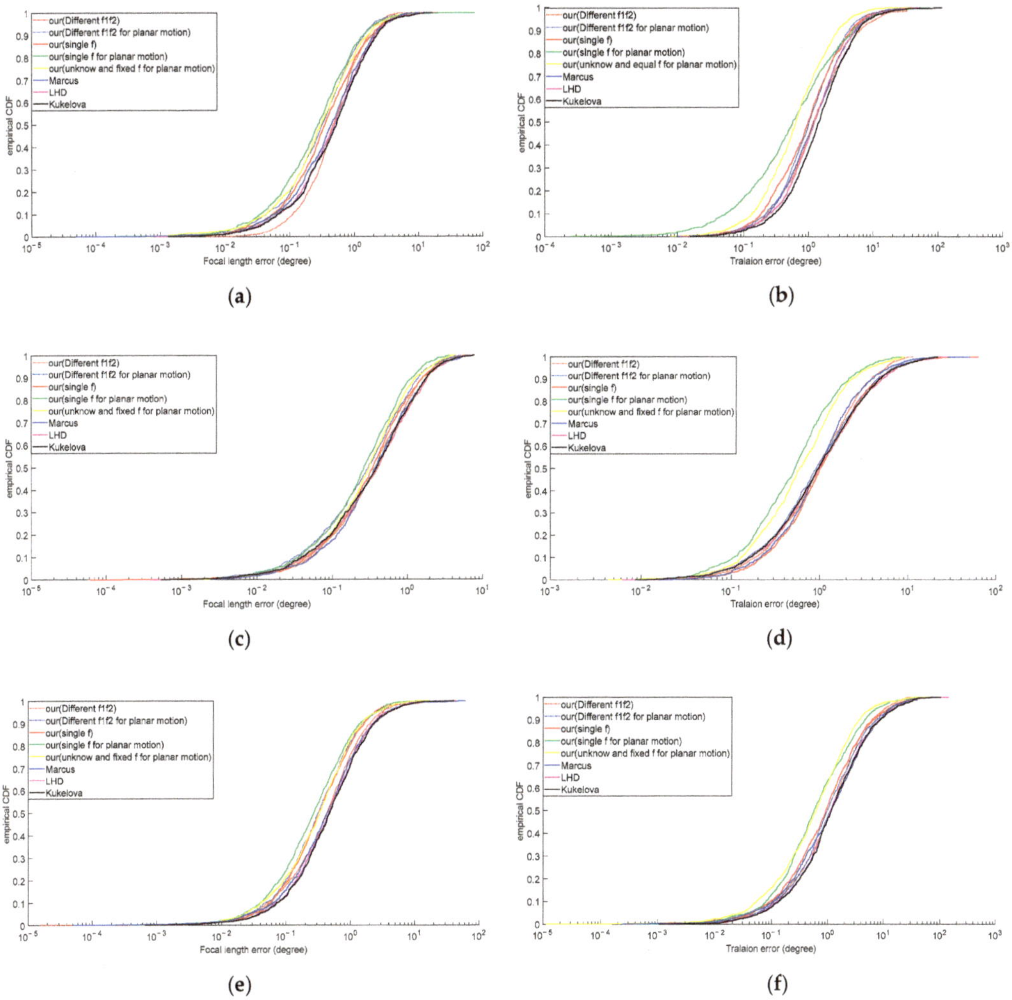

Figure 9. Cumulative distribution functions of the estimated errors in camera focal length and translation vector across three scenarios: (**a**) the camera focal length error of outdoor landscapes; (**b**) the translation vector error of outdoor landscapes; (**c**) the camera focal length error of urban buildings; (**d**) the translation vector error of urban buildings; (**e**) the camera focal length error of road vehicles; (**f**) the translation vector error of road vehicles.

4.2.3. Position Estimation Analysis

To visually assess the performance of various algorithms, two segments of data were extracted from the collected dataset and plotted on a trajectory graph. The trajectory graph uses GNSS positioning coordinates as reference ground truth. Since relative pose estimation lacks absolute positioning coordinates, the GNSS positioning result at the starting time was taken as the origin. Additionally, since none of the methods can estimate the scale correctly, the ground-truth scale was used to plot the trajectories. Since some of the algorithms proposed in this paper are based on planar motion, one segment of the trajectory consisted of data collected with the drone locked in the vertical direction. This segment was used to test the performance of algorithms based on planar motion. Figure 10 presents a 3D trajectory plot of random motion from measured data, while Figure 11 shows a 2D trajectory plot of planar motion. From the trajectory plots, it is evident that the algorithm proposed in this paper exhibited smaller errors than the reference algorithm when compared to the ground truth.

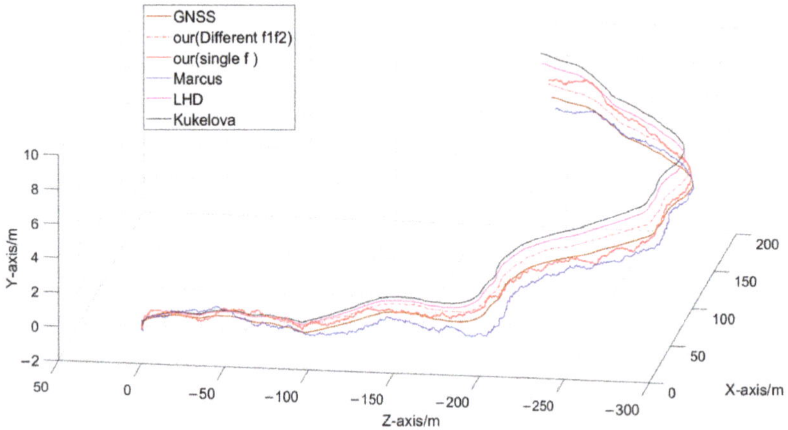

Figure 10. Three-dimensional trajectory plot of real data.

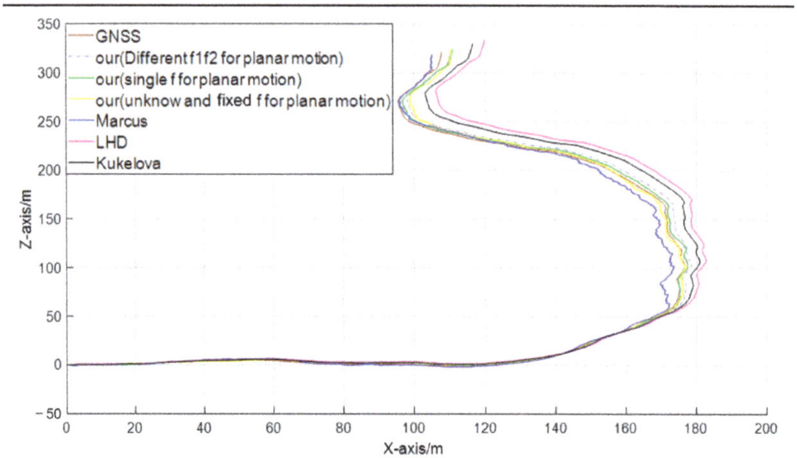

Figure 11. Two-dimensional trajectory plot of real data.

5. Conclusions

This paper presents four different methods of estimating relative pose and focal length in various application scenarios, aiming to enhance accuracy in addressing practical challenges. Given that the short-term drift of the IMU can be ignored, we calculated the rotation angles in three directions using IMU data. This reduces the number of feature point pairs required for relative pose and focal length estimation, thereby lowering the computational complexity of the relative pose estimation algorithm. The proposed algorithm was validated using both simulated data and real data collected from drones. The experiments demonstrated that, compared to the current state-of-the-art methods, the algorithm presented in this paper achieves higher accuracy in relative pose and focal length estimation, with gradual improvement as the model parameters are simplified.

Author Contributions: Conceptualization, K.Y. and H.Z.; methodology, K.Y. and Z.Y.; software, K.Y. and Z.Y.; validation, K.Y., C.S. and Z.Y.; formal analysis, D.C. and Z.Y.; investigation, K.Y. and Z.Y.; resources, Z.Y., D.C. and H.Z.; data curation, D.C. and C.S.; writing—original draft preparation, K.Y. and Z.Y.; writing—review and editing, K.Y. and Z.Y.; visualization, K.Y., C.S. and Z.Y.; supervision, D.C., H.Z. and C.S.; project administration, K.Y., Z.Y. and H.Z.; funding acquisition, H.Z. All authors have read and agreed to the published version of the manuscript.

Funding: This research was funded by the National Key Research and Development Program of China (No. 2021YFB2501104) and in part by the Ministry of Industry and Information Technology of China through the High-Precision Timing Service Project under grant TC220A04A-80 and in part by Major Program(JD) of Hubei Province(2023AA02604).

Data Availability Statement: The original contributions presented in the study are included in the article. Further inquiries can be directed to the corresponding author.

Acknowledgments: We would like to thank the editor and anonymous reviewers for their constructive comments and suggestions for improving the manuscript.

Conflicts of Interest: The authors declare no conflicts of interest.

References

1. Wang, H.; Ban, X.; Ding, F.; Xiao, Y.; Zhou, J. Monocular VO Based on Deep Siamese Convolutional Neural Network. *Complexity* **2020**, *2020*, 6367273. [CrossRef]
2. Wang, K.; Ma, S.; Chen, J.L.; Ren, F.; Lu, J.B. Approaches, Challenges, and Applications for Deep Visual Odometry: Toward Complicated and Emerging Areas. *IEEE Trans. Cogn. Dev. Syst.* **2022**, *14*, 35–49. [CrossRef]
3. Chen, J.; Xie, F.; Huang, L.; Yang, J.; Liu, X.; Shi, J. A Robot Pose Estimation Optimized Visual SLAM Algorithm Based on CO-HDC Instance Segmentation Network for Dynamic Scenes. *Remote Sens.* **2022**, *14*, 2114. [CrossRef]
4. Hao, G.T.; Du, X.P.; Song, J.J. Relative Pose Estimation of Space Tumbling Non cooperative Target Based on Vision only SLAM. *J. Astronaut.* **2015**, *36*, 706–714.
5. Yin, Z.; Wen, H.; Nie, W.; Zhou, M. Localization of Mobile Robots Based on Depth Camera. *Remote Sens.* **2023**, *15*, 4016. [CrossRef]
6. Barath, D.; Mishkin, D.; Eichhardt, I.; Shipachev, I.; Matas, J. Efficient Initial Pose-graph Generation for Global SfM. In Proceedings of the Computer Vision and Pattern Recognition, Nashville, TN, USA, 20–25 June 2021.
7. Liang, Y.; Yang, Y.; Mu, Y.; Cui, T. Robust Fusion of Multi-Source Images for Accurate 3D Reconstruction of Complex Urban Scenes. *Remote Sens.* **2023**, *15*, 5302. [CrossRef]
8. Kalantari, M.; Hashemi, A.; Jung, F.; Guedon, J.-P. A New Solution to the Relative Orientation Problem Using Only 3 Points and the Vertical Direction. *J. Math. Imaging Vis.* **2011**, *39*, 259–268. [CrossRef]
9. Barath, D.; Toth, T.; Hajder, L. A Minimal Solution for Two-view Focal-length Estimation using Two Affine Correspondences. In Proceedings of the IEEE Conference on Computer Vision and Pattern Recognition, Honolulu, HI, USA, 21–26 July 2017; IEEE: Piscataway, NJ, USA, 2017.
10. Mach, C.A.C. Random Sample Consensus: A paradigm for model fitting with application to image analysis and automated cartography. *Commun. ACM* **1981**, *24*, 381–395.
11. Hajder, L.; Barath, D. Relative planar motion for vehicle-mounted cameras from a single affine correspondence. In Proceedings of the 2020 IEEE International Conference on Robotics and Automation (ICRA), Paris, France, 31 May–31 August 2020.
12. Choi, S.-I.; Park, S.-Y. A new 2-point absolute pose estimation algorithm under planar motion. *Adv. Robot.* **2015**, *29*, 1005–1013. [CrossRef]
13. Fraundorfer, F.; Tanskanen, P.; Pollefeys, M. A Minimal Case Solution to the Calibrated Relative Pose Problem for the Case of Two Known Orientation Angles. In *European Conference on Computer Vision*; Springer: Berlin/Heidelberg, Germany, 2010.

14. Ding, Y.; Barath, D.; Yang, J.; Kong, H.; Kukelova, Z. Globally Optimal Relative Pose Estimation with Gravity Prior. In Proceedings of the IEEE/CVF Conference on Computer Vision and Pattern Recognition, Nashville, TN, USA, 20–25 June 2021.
15. Ding, Y.; Yang, J.; Kong, H. An efficient solution to the relative pose estimation with a common direction. In Proceedings of the 2020 IEEE International Conference on Robotics and Automation (ICRA), Paris, France, 31 May–31 August 2020.
16. Saurer, O.; Vasseur, P.; Boutteau, R.; Demonceaux, C.; Pollefeys, M.; Fraundorfer, F. Homography Based Egomotion Estimation with a Common Direction. *IEEE Trans. Pattern Anal. Mach. Intell.* **2017**, *39*, 327–341. [CrossRef] [PubMed]
17. Sweeney, C.; Flynn, J.; Turk, M. Solving for Relative Pose with a Partially Known Rotation is a Quadratic Eigenvalue Problem. In Proceedings of the 2014 2nd International Conference on 3D Vision, Tokyo, Japan, 8–11 December 2014; IEEE: Piscataway, NJ, USA, 2014.
18. Hartley, R.; Zisserman, A. *Multiple View Geometry in Computer Vision*, 2nd ed.; Cambridge University Press: Cambridge, UK, 2003.
19. Li, H. A simple solution to the six-point two-view focal-length problem. In *Computer Vision-ECCV 2006, Proceedings of the 9th European Conference on Computer Vision, Graz, Austria, 7–13 May 2006, Proceedings, Part IV 9*; Leonardis, A., Bischof, H., Pinz, A., Eds.; Lecture Notes in Computer Science; Springer: Berlin/Heidelberg, Germany, 2006; Volume 3954, pp. 200–213.
20. Hartley, R.; Li, H. An Efficient Hidden Variable Approach to Minimal-Case Camera Motion Estimation. *IEEE Trans. Pattern Anal. Mach. Intell.* **2012**, *34*, 2303–2314. [CrossRef] [PubMed]
21. Stewenius, H.; Nister, D.; Kahl, F.; Schaffalitzky, F. A minimal solution for relative pose with unknown focal length. In Proceedings of the IEEE Computer Society Conference on Computer Vision & Pattern Recognition, San Diego, CA, USA, 20–25 June 2005.
22. Bujnak, M.; Kukelova, Z.; Pajdla, T. 3D reconstruction from image collections with a single known focal length. In Proceedings of the IEEE International Conference on Computer Vision, Kyoto, Japan, 29 September–2 October 2009.
23. Torii, A.; Kukelova, Z.; Bujnak, M.; Pajdla, T. The Six Point Algorithm Revisited. In Proceedings of the Computer Vision–ACCV 2010 Workshops: ACCV 2010 International Workshops, Queenstown, New Zealand, 8–9 November 2010.
24. Kukelova, Z.; Bujnak, M.; Pajdla, T. Polynomial Eigenvalue Solutions to Minimal Problems in Computer Vision. *IEEE Trans. Pattern Anal. Mach. Intell.* **2012**, *34*, 1381–1393. [CrossRef] [PubMed]
25. Hedborg, J.; Felsberg, M. Fast iterative five point relative pose estimation. In Proceedings of the 2013 IEEE Workshop on Robot Vision (WORV), Clearwater Beach, FL, USA, 15–17 January 2013.
26. Kukelova, Z.; Kileel, J.; Sturmfels, B.; Pajdla, T. A clever elimination strategy for efficient minimal solvers. In Proceedings of the IEEE Conference on Computer Vision and Pattern Recognition, Honolulu, HI, USA, 21–26 July 2017.
27. Bougnoux, S. From projective to Euclidean space under any practical situation, a criticism of self-calibration. In Proceedings of the International Conference on Computer Vision, Bombay, India, 4–7 January 1998.
28. Hartley, R.I. Estimation of Relative Camera Positions for Uncalibrated Cameras. In *Computer Vision—ECCV'92: Second European Conference on Computer Vision Santa Margherita Ligure, Italy, May 19–22, 1992 Proceedings 2*; Springer: Berlin/Heidelberg, Germany, 1992.
29. Li, H.; Hartley, R. *A Non-Iterative Method for Correcting Lens Distortion from Nine Point Correspondences*; OMNIVIS: South San Francisco, CA, USA, 2009.
30. Jiang, F.; Kuang, Y.; Solem, J.E.; Åström, K. *A Minimal Solution to Relative Pose with Unknown Focal Length and Radial Distortion*; Springer International Publishing: Cham, Switzerland, 2015; pp. 443–456.
31. Oskarsson, M. Fast Solvers for Minimal Radial Distortion Relative Pose Problems. In Proceedings of the IEEE/CVF Conference on Computer Vision and Pattern Recognition, Virtual, 19–25 June 2021; pp. 3663–3672.
32. Rnhag, M.V.; Persson, P.; Wadenbck, M.; Strm, K.; Heyden, A. Trust Your IMU: Consequences of Ignoring the IMU Drift. In Proceedings of the IEEE/CVF Conference on Computer Vision and Pattern Recognition, New Orleans, LA, USA, 18–24 June 2022.
33. Savage, P.G. *Strapdown Analytics*; Strapdown Associates: Maple Plain, MN, USA, 2000.
34. Larsson, V.; Oskarsson, M.; Astrom, K.; Wallis, A.; Kukelova, Z. Beyond Grobner Bases: Basis Selection for Minimal Solvers. In Proceedings of the IEEE/CVF Conference on Computer Vision & Pattern Recognition, Salt Lake City, UT, USA, 18–23 June 2018.
35. Stewénius, H.; Engels, C.; Nistér, D. An Efficient Minimal Solution for Infinitesimal Camera Motion. In Proceedings of the IEEE Conference on Computer Vision & Pattern Recognition, Minneapolis, MN, USA, 17–22 June 2007.
36. Byrod, M.; Josephson, K.; Astrom, K. Fast and Stable Polynomial Equation Solving and Its Application to Computer Vision. *Int. J. Comput. Vis.* **2009**, *84*, 237–256. [CrossRef]
37. Cardano, G.; Witmer, T.R.; Ore, O. *The Great Art or the Rules of Algebra*; Dover Publications: New York, NY, USA, 1968.
38. Lowe, D.G. Distinctive Image Features from Scale-Invariant Key-points. *Int. J. Comput. Vis.* **2004**, *60*, 91–110. [CrossRef]

buildings

MDPI

Article

Research on Technological Innovation Capability of Yancheng Prefabricated Construction Industry Based on Patent Information Analysis

Renyan Lu [1], Feiting Shi [2] and Houchao Sun [2,*]

[1] Library, Yancheng Institute of Technology, Yancheng 224051, China; lurenyan@ycit.edu.cn
[2] School of Civil Engineering, Yancheng Institute of Technology, Yancheng 224051, China; shifeiting@ycit.cn
* Correspondence: sunhouchao@ycit.edu.cn

Abstract: In order to improve the innovation capabilities of Yancheng's prefabricated construction industry, the Dawei Innojoy patent database was used to search the prefabricated construction technology patent literature data of Yancheng and other major cities in the Yangtze River Delta region from 2012 to 2022, and the prefabricated construction patents in Yancheng were analyzed from the number of patent applications. Analysis and research were conducted on trends, application type composition, applicants, technical fields, patent legal status, etc. At the same time, the prefabricated building technology innovation capability evaluation system was constructed, and the factor analysis method was used to compare and analyze the prefabricated building technology patent indicators of Yancheng and major cities in the Yangtze River Delta region. The results show that Yancheng has a small number of patent applications, a small proportion of invention patents, a low patent authorization rate, and a low patent conversion rate, and the industry-university-research chain needs to be opened up. Among the cities in the Yangtze River Delta, Yancheng's comprehensive innovation ability in prefabricated building technology is medium to low, where it lags behind in terms of the scale and quality of technological innovation and ranks at the forefront of technological innovation operations. Based on this, the article puts forward countermeasures and suggestions for Yancheng's prefabricated building technology patent applications from three levels, macro, meso, and micro, in order to achieve efficient innovation and promote the high-quality development of Yancheng's new building industrialization.

Keywords: prefabricated buildings; innovation capabilities; patents; factor analysis; Yancheng City; Yangtze River Delta

1. Introduction

The report of the 20th National Congress of the Communist Party of China clearly stated that it is necessary to accelerate the construction of a new development pattern and strive to promote high-quality development. The report emphasizes that "promoting green and low-carbon economic and social development is a key link in achieving high-quality development". Prefabricated building is a green transformation method used in the construction industry. It is a method of building that produces prefabricated components in a factory and assembles the components on the construction site. It can not only ensure construction quality but also improve labor efficiency, shorten the construction period, reduce pollution, save energy, and have good development prospects [1,2].

Since the 13th Five-Year Plan, Chinese government departments at all levels have successively issued a series of policies to promote the development of prefabricated buildings and encourage local construction companies to transform in the direction of prefabricated buildings. At present, the construction industry in Yancheng City is in a critical period of transformation, upgrading, and accelerated development. Vigorously promoting prefabricated buildings has become an important starting point for the Yancheng City government to promote the development of the construction industry. In 2021, the Yancheng City government proposed in the "Yancheng City '14th Five-Year Plan' High-Quality Development Plan for Green Buildings" to accelerate the industrialization of new buildings and vigorously develop prefabricated buildings. However, insufficient technological innovation capabilities are an important factor restricting the vigorous development of prefabricated buildings in Yancheng City [3].

The key to the development of prefabricated buildings is to improve quality and efficiency through technological innovation. As one of the main manifestations of scientific and technological products, patents are considered in academia to be an important symbol for evaluating the level of technological innovation and progress. With the increased emphasis on intellectual property rights, research related to patent information has been expanded and improved. Combined with the development of modern Internet big data information, people can conduct a multi-angle and comprehensive measurement and data analysis of the output of patent documents. In the process of technology development, based on the research and analysis of prefabricated building technology patent information, we applied for prefabricated building technology patents, obtained authorization, and successfully realized technology transformation and applications, achieved efficient innovation, assisted the green and low-carbon development of the construction industry, and promoted new buildings in Yancheng City [4,5].

Prefabricated buildings are the direction of high-quality development in the construction industry. The number of applications and authorizations for prefabricated building technology patents is an important indicator of innovation capabilities. Realizing innovation in prefabricated building technology is conducive to the green and low-carbon development of the industry or region.

2. Literature Review

2.1. Current Status of Research on Technological Innovation of Prefabricated Buildings at Home and Abroad

In countries with advanced industrialization, the construction system, component standardization, technology integration, and large-scale production of prefabricated buildings are relatively mature. A large number of prefabricated buildings not only solve the housing problem for ordinary residential buildings but are also widely used in large buildings, hotels, etc., accelerating the transformation and upgrading of the construction industry. The development of new materials and construction techniques is sufficient to support the construction of more complex building structures, while also bringing overall economic and environmental benefits. Prefabricated buildings in the United States have basically formed a mature standard system. The *PCI Design Handbook* compiled by the Precast and Prestressed Concrete Institute (PCI) covers the design methods, construction technology, and construction quality control of prefabricated buildings, as well as other industry standards and specifications. It has a very important influence internationally [6]. Sweden has adopted the prefabricated technology system of large-scale concrete precast panels and has gradually incorporated the indicators required for the standardization of prefabricated building components into its industrial standard system [7]. In order to promote the standardization of components, connections, etc., the "Swedish Industrial Standard" (SIS) was formed based on module coordination. Japan has formed a complete prefabricated construction technology and standard system. After the introduction of the "PC" construction method from the United States, new materials and new application technologies have been continuously developed, and prefabricated housing has been vigorously developed through prefabricated components such as exterior wall panels, laminated floor panels, balconies, and stairs, with the componentization rate generally reaching 60% [8]. Germany focuses on the standardization and modularization of residential components, emphasizes building durability, promotes prefabricated product technology and environmentally friendly and energy-saving green assembly technology, and has formed a complete assembly and technology system. The proportion of residential prefabricated components has reached 94.5% [9].

The mature development of prefabricated buildings abroad is inseparable from the research and development of various parts and components, structural systems, and the support of information technology. Many foreign experts and scholars have conducted research from many perspectives. Kiruthika and Parthiban analyzed and explained the design of post-tensioned prestressed concrete beamless floors in precast prestressed concrete commercial buildings, and elaborated on the advantages of prefabricated structures over cast-in-situ concrete structures [10]. El-Sheikh et al. used the structural finite element analysis software OpenSees (version 1.0) to conduct numerical simulation research on a partially bonded prestressed concrete prefabricated frame structure and analyzed its seismic performance [11]. Ozturan et al. tested the connection performance of three types of precast concrete—cast-in-place, composite welding, and bolted connections—under the same loading mode and test configuration. By comparing the performance parameters, such as energy loss, it was shown that the improved bolted connection could be suitable for high seismic areas [12]. Thomas Olofsson's research shows that the use of VR (virtual reality) technology can create a virtual reality environment, which can better optimize design plans and guide on-site construction [13]. Li and Becerik-Gerber proposed that implanting radio frequency identification (RFID) chips into precast concrete (PC) components can help construction personnel better identify them, collect construction information, and monitor project progress [14].

However, the development level of China's prefabricated buildings lags behind that of other countries. Domestic research and development of prefabricated building technology started late, and the standard technology system is not yet mature. At present, core technologies from developed countries with mature prefabricated construction development are mostly introduced from abroad, and technological innovation is carried out based on the actual development situation of China's construction industry. Chinese experts and scholars have also been conducting relevant research in recent years. Qi and Li proposed the full life cycle of prefabricated buildings on the basis of the traditional building life cycle, including four stages: planning and design, production and manufacturing, construction and operation, and maintenance [15]. Zeng Qiang et al. proposed the "five-in-one" development idea of prefabricated buildings, namely design standardization, production industrialization, construction assembly, decoration integration, and management informatization [16]. In terms of component production, Sun Hong et al. proposed that large-scale intelligent PC component automated production lines are the direction of technological innovation in factory-based production in China [17]. In terms of construction technology, Du and Wang et al. conducted a detailed study on the node connection methods of prefabricated buildings and improved the seismic performance of prefabricated buildings [18]. Information technology such as BIM is also a focus of domestic scholars' attention. Zang used the BIM three-dimensional model as an information carrier to build a collaborative working platform for all project participants. All majors can work in the same model, which greatly improves efficiency [19].

2.2. Current Status of Patent Measurement Research at Home and Abroad

Research on patent measurement at home and abroad can be summarized into two aspects: patent indicator research and application research in specific technical fields. In terms of indicators, the patent measurement indicators used by foreign scholars mainly include the number of patents, average number of citations, impact factors, technical intensity, scientific intensity, and other indicators used to measure the patent level [20,21]. The academic community generally believes that the Dutch scholar Kunz was the first to use the time distribution of patent information quantity to study the value of patents [22]. With the development of patent measurement analysis methods, research on the application of patent measurement in various specific fields has gradually become richer, mainly reflected in two scenarios. The first is used to study the technological innovation or economic development of countries and regions. Narin conducted research and analysis on the GDP output value of the United Kingdom, Japan, Germany, and other countries and the number of authorized patents obtained in the United States, and found that there is a strong positive correlation between GDP output value and the number of patents [23]. The second scenario is applied to the study of a certain industry or specific technical field. For example, Ramani and Looze used patent statistical methods to study and analyze the patents of the United Kingdom, Germany, and France in the fields of biotechnology, such as genetic engineering, chemicals, and biocatalysis, and found that Germany is ahead of the United Kingdom and France in many fields [24]. Gemba and Tamada et al. applied patent measurement to corporate research and studied the patent activity tendencies of large Japanese electrical appliance manufacturers and the degree of corporate dependence on science [25].

China's patent measurement research started relatively late. Luo Shisheng's "Quantitative Analysis and Prediction of Patent Documents" in 1994 was the first domestic study on patent measurement. In terms of research on patent measurement indicators, Qiu gave a high-level overview of the theory of patent measurement. His point of view is to "apply mathematical and statistical methods to patent research to explore and tap its distribution structure, quantitative relationships, change patterns and other intrinsic values" [26,27]; Zhang and Liu et al. focused on patents combined with the theory of innovation, explored templates for innovation difficulties, focused on their institutional sources, and measured and evaluated the effectiveness of innovation capabilities with relevant indicators [28]. Some domestic scholars have used R language and Vosviewer and other methods to analyze the development trends and lifespan of patent applications over the years, as well as the geographical distribution of patented technologies. Based on the application trend, life cycle, and geographical distribution of technology, a visualization method is used to obtain a patent map reflecting this field [29]. In terms of technological innovation in specific fields, Zhang et al. used a spatial econometric model to study the relationship between China's patent innovation and regional economic growth based on the number of patent authorizations in 31 provinces and data reflecting regional economic growth indicators [30]. Luan et al. used the Derwent patent database to conduct a patent quantitative analysis in the fields of nanotechnology, biotechnology, and the electric vehicle industry, and researched the technical hot spots in each field [31–33]. Based on patent analysis, Zhang Guangping summarized the patents for prefabricated buildings, then focused on the patents related to structural systems, and summarized the current situation and future of patents related to prefabricated buildings in my country [34].

There are many statistical techniques used in patent trend analysis, including statistical analysis, time series analysis, technical index analysis, patent classification number analysis, technical theme analysis, and patent citation analysis, etc. These methods have their own characteristics and can be used in combination to complement each other to obtain more comprehensive and in-depth patent trend analysis results.

Through the literature review, we find that there is a lack of comparative analysis in research on the technological innovation of prefabricated buildings. There are studies on technological innovation in prefabricated buildings in the literature, but these studies focus on the methods of technological innovation and the research and development of specific technologies. They do not summarize and analyze the results of technological innovation in different regions or further analyze regional technological innovation capabilities. In addition, the innovation capability evaluation based on patent data is mainly concentrated in the industrial field. A large number of documents only focus on the research and evaluation of the traditional construction industry or corporate technological innovation, while focusing on the prefabricated construction industry in a targeted and specialized manner. There is a relative lack of research on technological innovation research and systematic evaluation.

3. Methodology

3.1. General Idea of Research

China's Yangtze River Delta region is the highland of China's economic development and technological innovation. Since patents are an important symbol of scientific and technological innovation capabilities, in order to study the innovation capabilities of prefabricated building technology in the Yancheng area, we first searched the patent database to study the status of patent applications for prefabricated building technology in the Yancheng area, and then used factor analysis to compare Yancheng and the Yangtze River Delta region. A comprehensive comparative analysis of the main indicators of prefabricated building patent applications in major cities was conducted, to find gaps in the technological innovation capabilities of prefabricated buildings and put forward improved countermeasures and suggestions.

3.2. Evaluation Method Selection and Evaluation Index Construction

3.2.1. Evaluation Method Selection

The factor analysis method is an important method in management research and has been widely used in management, economics, medicine, statistics, and other fields. The use of factor analysis to evaluate the level of technological innovation not only conforms to the scientific assessment of the level of technological innovation using methods such as the analytic hierarchy process and fuzzy evaluation methods, but can also reduce the inaccuracies caused by subjective factors such as expert scoring and issuing questionnaires, as well as limitations affecting the analysis and other issues. This method is simple to operate and easy to apply, and its scope of application does not have many restrictions. This study uses factor analysis to reduce multiple variables into a number of common factors with most of the information, and then reduces the dimensions and calculates the scores of the common factors by matching the relevant weights, thus achieving the goal of objective, scientific, quantitative judgments about technological innovation levels.

The steps of the factor analysis method are as follows:

(1) Correlation tests on variables through the KMO model are conducted to analyze whether the initial variable indicators are suitable for factor analysis. Only after matching verification can the next step of the process begin.
(2) Uncategorizing the variables. Since the variables may not be at the same latitude, this operation is performed in order to reduce the differences in the magnitude of the variables.
(3) The data processed in the previous step are then calculated through the correlation matrix to find the eigenvalues and eigenvectors of the data matrix, so that the correlation between different variables can be analyzed and classified.
(4) Calculating the variance contribution rate of each type of data. The cumulative variance contribution rate should be higher than 60% to scientifically explain and replace all initial variables.

3.2.2. Evaluation Index Construction

Regarding regional technological innovation capabilities, domestic and foreign scholars have proposed many evaluation indicators, and prefabricated buildings are a construction method that has developed rapidly in recent years and has certain particularities. At present, there is not much literature on the evaluation and research of technological innovation capabilities in regional prefabricated buildings. The index selection in this article is based on the literature [35] and combined with the actual situation of prefabricated buildings in the Yangtze River Delta in China. The indicators in the literature are screened and replaced, and work is added to form the final evaluation index system, as shown in Table 1.

Table 1. Patent indicators and calculation methods for evaluation.

First-Level Indicator	Secondary Indicators	Indicator Calculation	Variable Code
Scale of technological innovation	Number of patent applications	Number of patent applications	X1
	Effective number of patents	Number of valid patents	X2
	Amount of invention authorizations	Number of invention patents authorized	X3
Technology innovation operation	Average number of claims	Number of claims/total number of patents	X4
	Patent implementation rate	(Transfer + License + Number of Pledges)/Total Number of Patents	X5
	Patent efficiency	Number of effective patents/number of patent authorizations	X6
Technical innovation quality	Average number of patent IPCs	Total number of IPC categories/total number of patents	X7
	Average number of patent citations	Number of patent citations/total number of patents	X8

4. Results and Discussion

The Dawei Innojoy patent database was searched with "TAC = (prefabricated building or prefabricated house or prefabricated structure or prefabricated building or prefabricated structure or prefabricated frame or residential industrialization or 'prefabricated member' or 'prefabricated construction' or 'fabricated structure' or 'assembly building')" and AD = [20120101 to 20221231] and AR = Yancheng and IPC = E04" as the search formula, the patent applicant's address was set to Yancheng or a major city in the Yangtze River Delta region of China, and the search was for 2012~. Relevant patent data in 2022, a statistical analysis of Yancheng prefabricated building patent data, and comparative analysis with the prefabricated building patent data indicators of major cities in the Yangtze River Delta were explored to identify gaps in innovation capabilities and propose solutions to existing problems. The aims were to improve the quality of patents and achieve efficient innovation, thereby promoting the high-quality development of new building industrialization in Yancheng City.

4.1. Current Status of Yancheng Prefabricated Building Technology Patent Development

4.1.1. Number of Patent Applications and Application Trends

Patents are the most dynamic technological innovation achievements, and their application volume and trends reflect important indicators of technological innovation capabilities. As shown in Figure 1, overall, the patent application development process of Yancheng's prefabricated construction technology industry can be classified into three stages: (1) Slow development stage (2012~2016), during which the annual total volume is relatively smaller and develops slowly. The average annual number of applications does not exceed two, and the number of patent applications in 2015 was only three. (2) Rapid development stage (2017~2020). During this period, the number of annual patent applications is generally on a growing trend, exceeding 21 for the first time in 2019. (3) Steady development stage (2021~2022). At this stage, the annual number of relevant patent applications has grown steadily, reaching a peak of 23 in 2022. This is also consistent with the actual development of the prefabricated construction industry in Yancheng City to a certain extent. It has gone through a budding and nurturing period of slow development, a period of sustained rapid development, and a mature period of stable development. (It takes a certain amount of time from patent application to publication, and invention patents generally take about 18 months. Therefore, the data for 2020 have declined and are for reference only).

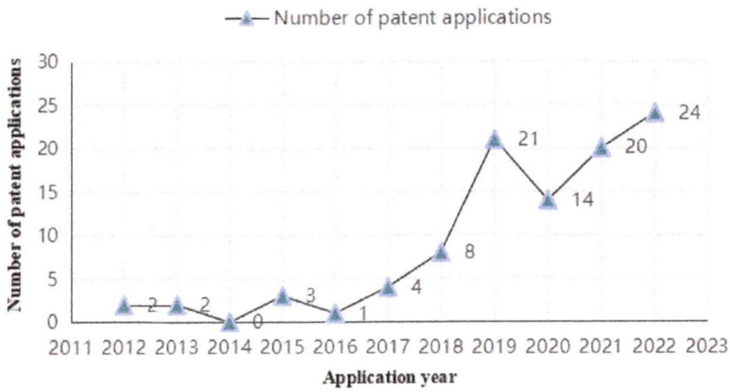

Figure 1. Number of patent applications in Yancheng City's prefabricated construction technology industry from 2012 to 2022.

4.1.2. Patent Application Type Composition

Patents in my country are divided into three types: invention patents, utility model patents and design patents. Figure 2 shows the composition of patent application types in Yancheng's prefabricated construction technology industry from 2012 to 2022. As can be seen from the figure that utility model patent applications account for the largest number, accounting for 62%, and invention patent applications and authorizations account for 26%. The protection period of utility model patents is only 10 years, but the technical and creative requirements for products are not as high as those for invention patents. After modification, the practical applicability of the products is more prominent, so the number of applications is the largest. Invention patents have a higher degree of legal protection and have the longest protection period, so their value is naturally higher. However, it is more difficult to apply for invention patents. The relative number of applications is much smaller than that for utility model patents, so the number of applications does not account for a high proportion. Comparing the number and proportion of different types of patent applications can represent the R&D strength and innovation capabilities of Yancheng's prefabricated building technology to a certain extent.

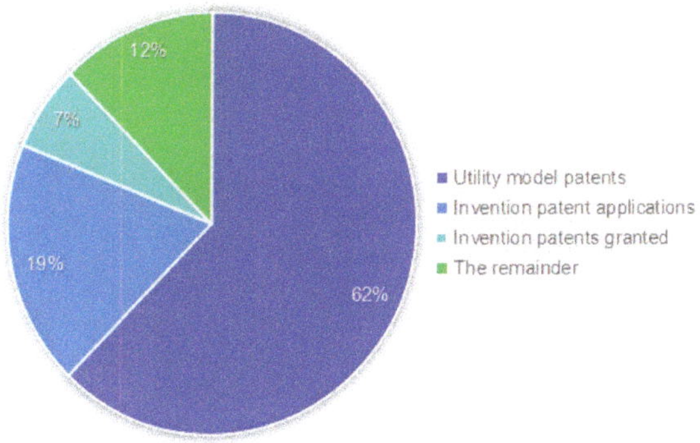

Figure 2. Composition of patent application types in Yancheng City's prefabricated construction technology industry.

4.1.3. Patent Application Subject

The composition of patent application subjects can analyze the identity composition of innovation subjects. Patent applicants can be divided into basic types such as enterprises, universities, scientific research institutes, and individuals.

Figure 3 shows the main applicants for patents in the prefabricated construction technology industry in Yancheng City. As can be seen from the above figure, the top

10 companies have applied for patents. The top two are the Yancheng Institute of Technology (nine pieces) and Jiangsu Jinmao Technology Development Co., Ltd. (Yancheng, china) companies (seven pieces). The total number of patent applications from these two companies is 16, accounting for about one-third of the total number of patent applications from these 10 units, of which the Yancheng Institute of Technology accounts for nearly 18.37%, and Jiangsu Jinmao Technology Development Co., Ltd. for 14.29%. This shows that Yancheng prefabricated construction technology patent applications are concentrated in Yancheng universities and key prefabricated construction enterprises. Strengthening the cooperation between enterprises and universities in industry, academia, and research is more conducive to the development of industry technology.

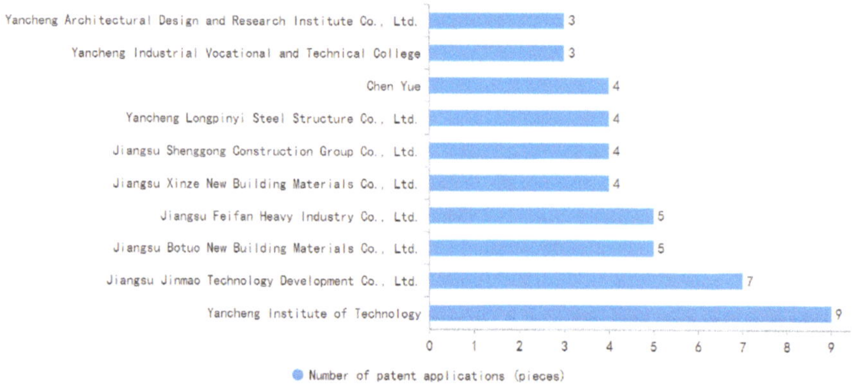

Figure 3. The main applicants for Yancheng's prefabricated construction technology industry patents.

4.1.4. Distribution of Patent Technology Fields

There is no specific classification of prefabricated construction technology in the international IPC patent classification table. With the help of the patent database platform and keyword search, the author found a total of 99 patent applications, and 73 were authorized, including 8 invention patents and utility model patents. The author found 65 pieces, among which the top 10 technology categories by number of patent authorizations are shown in Table 2.

It can be found from Table 2 that among the top ten patent categories, the number of patents in the E04B1 direction is far ahead of other technical fields, accounting for 60.27% of the patents, followed by the two fields of E04B2 and E04G21, respectively. The sum of these two fields, which account for 41.1% of the sample, can also be regarded as a technology-intensive area.

In the past five years, despite the impact of the epidemic, the number of patents for prefabricated building technology has grown rapidly. This is inseparable from the Yancheng City government's vigorous promotion of prefabricated building policies. From the perspective of patent technology branches, combined with domestic patent analysis, the research and development of prefabricated building technology focuses on construction technology, building structure systems, component connections, prefabricated components, and other technical directions. Therefore, studying these technology patents, one can accurately grasp the technical hot spots and development trends of Yancheng's prefabricated buildings, enhance the region's technological innovation capabilities in prefabricated buildings, and thereby promote the green and healthy development of Yancheng's construction industry.

Table 2. The top ten technical fields in Yancheng's patent authorization volume.

Serial Number	IPC Classification and Meaning	Number of Patents (Utility Model, Invention Patent)/Pieces	Percentage of Total Sample Patent Data/%
1	E04B1 General structure, not limited to walls, such as partition walls, or any structure in floor slabs, ceilings, or roofs	38, 6	60.27
2	E04B2 Building walls, such as partition walls and insulating walls, specifically for wall connections.	18, 1	26.03
3	E04G21 Preparation, handling, or processing of building materials or building components on site; other methods and equipment used in construction	8, 3	15.07
4	E04B5 Floor slab, used for insulated floor slab structures, and its special connectors	7, 0	9.59
5	E04C2 Thinner components for building house components, such as various thin plates, flat plates, or panels	7, 0	9.59
6	E04C5 Reinforcements, e.g., auxiliary members for concrete	7, 0	9.59
7	E04H9 A building or building complex or shelter that can withstand or protect against external anomalies, such as war, earthquakes, or abnormal weather effects	5, 2	9.59
8	E04C3 Long-strip structural members for load-bearing	6, 0	8.21
9	E04F13 Covering or lining, for example, for walls or ceilings	4, 0	5.48
10	E04H5 Industrial and agricultural buildings or building complexes	3, 0	4.11

4.1.5. Patent Legal Status Analysis

According to the relevant provisions of my country's Patent Law, only authorized patents are protected by law. According to Table 3 and Figure 4, we can see the following: (1) Yancheng City's prefabricated building technology industry applied for a total of 99 patents from 2012 to 2022, of which authorized patents accounted for 73%. (2) The total number of rejections reached nine, accounting for nearly 10%; four were in the substantive examination stage, accounting for 4%, and the number of authorized invention patents accounted for only 8.08%, which fully reflects that invention patents are one of three types of patents. Among the patent types, the application requirements are the highest, the review process is the most stringent, and the review time is the longest. (3) Currently, 65 utility model patents have been applied for and authorized, and 11 more have not paid the annual fee. The relative authorization rate of utility model patent applications in the field of construction technology is relatively high.

Table 3. Yancheng prefabricated construction technology industry patent application types and legal status.

Patent Type	Substantive Examination	Authorization	Withdrawal	Rejection	Disclosure	Annual Fee Not Paid	Total
invention patent	4	8	4	5	0	2	23
utility model patent	0	65	0	0	0	11	76

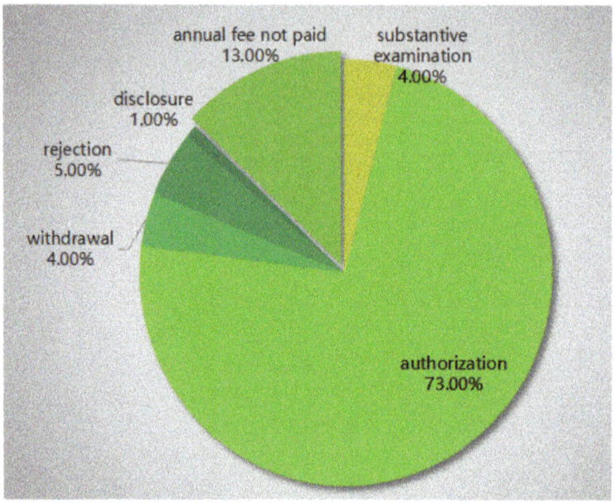

Figure 4. Legal status of patent applications for Yancheng prefabricated construction technology industry.

4.1.6. Analysis of Patent Development under Regional Collaboration

The integration of the Yangtze River Delta is the national strategy most closely related to Yancheng City, and it has a huge impact on the development of Yancheng's economy and industry. Connecting with the integrated development of the Yangtze River Delta region is a platform for the high-quality development of Yancheng's prefabricated construction technology industry, and it is also an important window period for Yancheng's prefabricated construction technology industry to "accelerate". Through the relevant patent search of the prefabricated construction technology industry in major cities in the Yangtze River Delta, the key cities for patent application and authorization in the prefabricated construction technology industry in the Yangtze River Delta region were obtained. The specific comparison is shown in Figures 5 and 6.

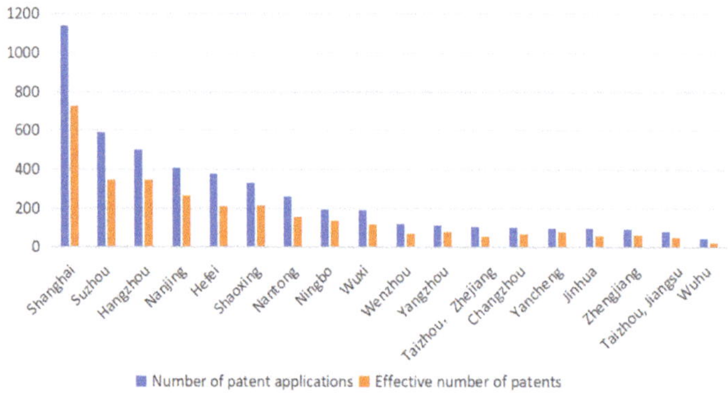

Figure 5. Comparison of the total number and effective number of patent applications in the prefabricated construction technology industry in major cities in the Yangtze River Delta.

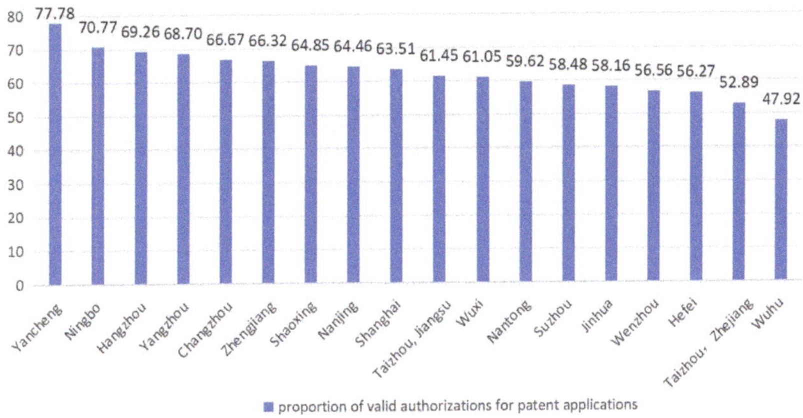

Figure 6. Comparison of the proportion of valid authorizations for patent applications in the prefabricated construction technology industry in major cities in the Yangtze River Delta.

According to Figures 5 and 6, the comparative situation of the total number and effective number of patent applications for the prefabricated construction technology industry in major cities in the Yangtze River Delta can be seen: (1) From the perspective of the total number of patent applications, the patents for the prefabricated construction technology industry in the Yangtze River Delta Applications are mainly concentrated in Shanghai, Southern Jiangsu, and Hangzhou and Ningbo. Because Shanghai benefits from its own abundant talent advantages and scientific research institutes, as well as its obviously advantageous financial investment environment, and at the same time relies on the mature and complete industrial chain foundation of the Yangtze River Delta, the total number of applications far exceeds that of other cities, ranking firmly in the list. First, Southern Jiangsu and the Hangzhou–Ningbo regions followed closely behind, relying on their geographical advantages and mature manufacturing base. (2) From the perspective of the total number of patent applications, there is still a certain gap in the development of the prefabricated construction technology industry in the major cities in the Yangtze River Delta, which can be roughly divided into three echelons: First, there are the patents in the four cities of Shanghai, Suzhou, Hangzhou, and Nanjing. The total number of patent applications in the four cities of Shaoxing, Hefei, Nantong, Ningbo, and Wuxi is more than 150 and they belong to the second tier. The total number of patent applications in ten cities including Jinhua, Zhenjiang, Taizhou, and Wuhu is less than 150, belonging to the third echelon. The total number of applications for Yancheng's prefabricated construction technology industry is 99, which is still far behind the second echelon. (3) From the perspective of the proportion of the number of valid patents to the total number of applications, the proportion of valid patents in the field of prefabricated construction technology industry in major cities in the Yangtze River Delta does not completely match the comparison trend between cities in the total number of patent applications. Figure 6 shows that the cities with effective proportions exceeding 60% include 11 cities: Yancheng, Ningbo, Hangzhou, Yangzhou, Changzhou, Zhenjiang, Shaoxing, Nanjing, Shanghai, Taizhou, Jiangsu, and Wuxi. Yancheng ranks first. It can be seen that, although Yancheng City does not have a clear advantage in the total number of patent applications, Yancheng City has a comparative advantage in the proportion of valid patents in the field of the prefabricated construction technology industry, which reflects Yancheng's leading position in prefabricated building technology in the Yangtze River Delta region. The quality potential for innovation in the field is huge.

4.2. Analysis of Technological Innovation Capabilities of Prefabricated Buildings in Yancheng and Other Major Cities in the Yangtze River Delta Based on Patent Information Analysis

This study conducts a comparative analysis of the technological innovation capabilities of the prefabricated construction industry in Yancheng and other major cities in the Yangtze River Delta region in China from the perspective of patents. The corresponding patent indicator data of the cities in the sample areas were obtained from patent reports such as Dawei Innojoy patent database, and the data were analyzed using factor analysis processing methods. In SPSS statistics 25, first, each variable indicator was dimensionless and variable significance was carried out in turn. Level analysis, etc., is used to clarify its reasonable weight, and finally the innovation factor score is obtained through expression operation.

4.2.1. Determination of Patent Indicators for Major Cities in the Yangtze River Delta of China

The initial variable data required for patent indicators come from the Dawei patent database. The results of various data in the Yangtze River Delta region after information extraction, integration, and calculation are shown in Table 4.

Table 4. Evaluation indicators of technological innovation capabilities of prefabricated buildings in the Yangtze River Delta region.

City	Number of Patent Applications	Effective Number of Patents	Amount of Invention Authorization	Average Number of Patent IPCs	Average Number of Claims	Patent Implementation Rate	Average Number of Patent Citations	Patent Efficiency
Yancheng	99	77	8	1.082	6.4	0.091	0.568	0.895
Shanghai	1140	724	121	1.115	6.785	0.083	0.721	0.887
Suzhou	590	345	29	1.154	7.465	0.052	0.22	0.91
Hangzhou	501	347	52	1.121	6.779	0.123	0.564	0.905
Nanjing	408	263	74	1.175	7.302	0.131	0.842	0.867
Shaoxing	330	214	25	1.075	8.208	0.153	0.818	0.871
Hefei	375	211	26	1.066	5.75	0.119	0.545	0.795
Nantong	260	155	35	1.091	8.543	0.195	0.73	0.771
Ningbo	195	138	20	1.086	6.419	0.072	0.795	0.891
Wuxi	190	116	25	1.103	6.156	0.096	0.56	0.833
Changzhou	102	68	9	1.088	5.968	0.106	0.471	0.898
Yangzhou	115	79	15	1.152	5.978	0.076	0.504	0.929
Zhenjiang	95	63	9	1.064	4.938	0.065	1.191	0.861
Wenzhou	122	69	25	1.043	6.207	0.246	0.783	0.945
Taizhou Zhejiang	104	55	16	1.055	6.224	0.145	0.618	0.809
Jinghua	98	57	13	1.211	5.813	0.439	0.386	0.731
Taizhou jiangsu	83	51	7	1.176	5.714	0.1	0.32	0.806
Wuhu	48	23	8	1.087	5.783	0.273	0.348	0.88

4.2.2. Data Processing of Patent Indicators in Major Cities in the Yangtze River Delta

In order to use the patent index data of major cities in the Yangtze River Delta region of China to evaluate the innovation capabilities of the prefabricated construction technology industry in Table 4, SPSS 25.0 software was used to conduct a factor analysis, test the reliability of the constraint system, and obtain the results reflecting the assembly performance of each city. Various scores and comprehensive scores and rankings of public factors of architectural technology innovation were considered. After completing the relevant settings in the SPSS 25.0 software, one has only to run it, and the software will automatically generate the relevant result data.

Suitability Test

KMO and Bartlett tests can measure whether a factor analysis is suitable. From Table 5 below, we can see that the value of the KMO statistic is 0.611 (greater than 0.5), and the SPSS test result shows that the p-value is 0 (less than 0.05), which reflects that the selected patent indicator variables can be used to study the relationship between variables using factor analysis. Combining the two experiments, the final result is more convincing.

Table 5. KMO and Bartlett test.

KMO and Bartlett Test		
KMO value		0.611
Bartlett's test of sphericity	approximate chi-square	115.738
	degrees of freedom	28
	significance	0.000

Variance Contribution Rate Analysis

According to the total variance explanation value in Table 6, it can be concluded that some and all of the first three causes are greater than 1, and they reach 3.306, 1.795, and 1.070, respectively, accounting for 41.322%, 22.441%, and 13.371% of the overall variance, respectively. The eigenvalues of the first three factors account for a total of 77.135% of the variance, so the system's selection of the first three common factors is in line with the requirements of the scientific characteristics of the factor analysis method. If you want to simplify the complexity of the original data, you can select these three indicators to compare. Appropriately, they replace almost all the basic information in the original indicator.

Table 6. Total variance explained value.

Element	**Initial Eigenvalue**		
	Eigenvalues	**Percentage of Variance**	**Cumulative Percentage**
1	3.306	41.322	41.322
2	1.795	22.441	63.764
3	1.070	13.371	77.135
4	0.747	9.334	86.469
5	0.549	6.856	93.325
6	0.462	5.779	99.104
7	0.069	0.867	99.972
8	0.002	0.028	100.000

Common Factor Naming

It can be seen from Table 7 that each starting factor can appropriately represent the original indicator, so there is no need to increase the process of factor rotation. Public factor 1 has relatively large loadings on the number of patent applications, the number of valid patents, the number of invention authorizations, and the average number of claims. Because the four indicators represent the scale and overall influence of patents, public factor 1 is represented by F1, that is, the technological innovation scale factor; public factor 2 has a relatively large load on the patent implementation rate and patent efficiency, because the two indicators indicate the patent operation situation, so public factor 2 is represented by F2, which is the technological innovation operation factor; public factor 3 has a relatively large load on the average number of patent IPCs and the average number of patent citations, because both indicators use patent coverage as the basis to show the strength of patent quality, so the author uses F3 to represent common factor 3, that is, the technology innovation quality factor.

Table 7. Factor loading coefficient matrix values.

Index	Factor Loading Coefficient		
	Factor1	Factor2	Factor3
Number of patent applications	0.940	0.233	0.101
Effective number of patents	0.943	0.251	0.089
Amount of invention authorizations	0.943	0.103	−0.019
Average number of claims	0.607	−0.178	−0.132
Patent implementation rate	−0.141	−0.804	0.151
Patent efficiency	0.056	0.838	−0.089
Average number of patent IPCs	0.208	−0.263	0.794
Average number of patent citations	0.173	0.023	−0.876

Factor Scores and Rankings

Table 8 shows the formulas of the three common factors, which can be edited as follows (relational expressions are established based on standardized data).

$$F1 = 0.288X1 + 0.287X2 + 0.312X3 + 0.068X4 + 0.239X5 + 0.050X6 + 0.099X7 - 0.087X8 \quad (1)$$

$$F2 = 0.063X1 + 0.073X2 - 0.053X3 - 0.072X4 - 0.233X5 - 0.534X6 - 0.166X7 + 0.581X8 \quad (2)$$

$$F3 = 0.071X1 + 0.065X2 - 0.041X3 + 0.521X4 - 0.158X5 - 0.030X6 - 0.643X7 + 0.085X8 \quad (3)$$

Table 8. Component score coefficient matrix.

Index	Element		
	Element 1	Element 2	Element 3
Number of patent applications	0.288	0.063	0.071
Effective number of patents	0.287	0.073	0.065
Amount of invention authorizations	0.312	−0.053	−0.041
Average number of patent IPCs	0.068	−0.072	0.521
Average number of claims	0.239	−0.233	−0.158
Patent implementation rate	0.050	−0.534	−0.030
Average number of patent citations	0.099	−0.166	−0.643
Patent efficiency	−0.087	0.581	0.085

The public factor score obtained above and its corresponding variance contribution rate are used to obtain the overall comprehensive score through a weighted algorithm: $F = (39.086F1 + 19.735F2 + 18.314F3)/77.135$ (where F represents the final index score).

The final calculation results are shown in Table 9.

Table 9. Comprehensive score table for technological innovation capabilities of prefabricated buildings in major cities in the Yangtze River Delta region.

City	Factor Score						Comprehensive Score	Comprehensive Ranking
	F_1		F_2		F_3			
	Score	Ranking	Score	Ranking	Score	Ranking		
Shanghai	2.932	1	0.706	4	0.094	8	1.689	1
Suzhou	0.677	5	1.117	2	1.669	1	1.025	2
Hangzhou	0.800	3	0.590	7	0.394	6	0.650	3
Nanjing	1.191	2	−0.352	14	−0.023	10	0.508	4
Yangzhou	−0.716	13	1.158	1	0.934	4	0.155	5
Taizhou, Jiangsu	−0.797	15	−0.070	11	1.550	2	−0.054	6
Shaoxing	0.583	6	−0.443	15	−1.172	17	−0.096	7
Hefei	−0.034	7	−0.189	12	−0.186	11	−0.110	8
Wuxi	−0.308	9	0.074	10	0.086	9	−0.117	9
Ningbo	−0.277	8	0.609	5	−0.683	13	−0.147	10
Changzhou	−0.858	17	0.803	3	0.276	7	−0.164	11
Yancheng	−0.727	14	0.595	6	−0.309	12	−0.290	12
Nantong	0.764	4	−1.800	17	−1.031	15	−0.318	13
Wuhu	−0.989	18	−0.200	13	0.528	5	−0.427	14
Wenzhou	−0.529	11	0.266	9	−1.106	16	−0.463	15
Jinhua	−0.311	10	−2.842	18	1.512	3	−0.526	16
Taizhou, Zhejiang	−0.564	12	−0.457	16	−0.692	14	−0.567	17
Zhenjiang	−0.837	16	0.435	8	−1.842	18	−0.750	18

Comprehensive Comparative Analysis of Innovation Capabilities between Yancheng and Other Major Cities in the Yangtze River Delta

From Table 8, we can see that there is a positive correlation between a city's comprehensive score, comprehensive ranking, and technological innovation capabilities. There are positive and negative signs for the three public factors and the comprehensive score. A positive value means that the technological innovation capability in this aspect is higher than the average level, and a negative value means that the technological innovation capability in this aspect is below the average level. From the observation of the comprehensive scores, we can see that there are differences between cities. The comprehensive scores of five cities, including Shanghai, Suzhou, Hangzhou, Nanjing, and Yangzhou, are above the average level, while the comprehensive scores of the remaining cities, including Yancheng, are below the average level. The range of comprehensive scores between most regions is not large, lying in the (−1, +2) interval.

Only two of the five cities with a comprehensive score above the average have a comprehensive score greater than 1, namely Shanghai and Suzhou. Their overall data scores are 1.689 and 1.025, indicating the technological innovation of prefabricated buildings among these five cities. There are also gaps in capabilities. In addition, among these cities, Shanghai ranks first in the technological innovation scale factor, Yangzhou ranks first in the technological innovation operation factor, and Suzhou ranks first in the technological innovation quality factor data score. Yancheng ranks sixth in the technological innovation operation factor data and is at the forefront of the cities in the Yangtze River Delta. The data scores of the technological innovation scale factor and technological innovation quality factor rank 14th and 12th, respectively, which is lower than the average position. This shows that the development of technological innovation capabilities for prefabricated buildings in cities in the Yangtze River Delta is unbalanced, and Yancheng City is generally in a backward position.

The technological innovation scale factor has the largest variance contribution rate after calculation, which is 41.322%. It is the main aspect that affects the technological innovation capability of the prefabricated construction industry. Only six regions scored above the average on this public factor. Among them, Shanghai, Nanjing, and Hangzhou scored the highest, with scores of 2.932, 1.191, and 0.800, respectively. The above means that these three regions are at the top of the overall data ranking. Yancheng's technological innovation scale score is −0.727, ranking 14th among the 18 cities in the Yangtze River Delta. Therefore, if we want to improve Yancheng's prefabricated building technological innovation capabilities, we should continue to increase the scale of patents and expand patented products.

The variance contribution rate of the technological innovation operation factor is 22.441%. There are 10 regions with scores above the average level on this common factor. Among them, Yangzhou and Suzhou scored high, 1.158 and 1.117, respectively. A higher ranking in the technological innovation operation factor also improves the overall ranking of these two regions. Yancheng's technological innovation operation factor score is 0.595, ranking sixth, which has improved the overall ranking of urban innovation. It can be seen that the operation of patents is important. However, many regions have ignored this point. For example, Nanjing and Shaoxing, which are ranked high in the comprehensive rankings, rank relatively low in terms of technological innovation operation factors. Therefore, regions need to strengthen technological innovation operation management.

The variance contribution rate of the technological innovation quality factor is 13.371%. There are nine cities whose scores on this common factor are above the average level. Among them, Suzhou, Taizhou, and Jinhua have the highest scores, with scores of 1.669, 1.550, and 1.512, respectively. It is obvious that Taizhou's high ranking in the technological innovation quality factor has also boosted the region's overall ranking, even though its scores on the other two factors are lagging behind. Yancheng's technological innovation quality factor score is −0.309, ranking low. Therefore, improving the quality of patents will help improve industrial technological innovation capabilities.

The successful implementation of prefabricated building patents requires not only an increase in the number of patent applications and authorizations, but also an improvement in the quality of patent technology innovation. Prefabricated building patent technology has innovative integrated design, ensures the safety and durability of building structures, simplifies the on-site assembly process, achieves the successful transformation of regional patent technology, forms economies of scale, significantly reduces construction costs, and improves the innovation capacity of regional prefabricated building technology. The protection and renovation project of Blythe House in London, UK, uses prefabricated building technology to solve the challenges of traditional building renovation, while preserving the cultural value of historic buildings. The "Sky City" prefabricated building of the Yuanda Technology Group in Changsha, China, has the advantages of prefabricated buildings in speed, cost-effectiveness, and sustainability. Yancheng should not only maintain the implementation rate and efficiency of prefabricated building patents, but also increase the scale and quality of prefabricated building technology innovation, and increase the transformation of patent technology achievements, so as to comprehensively improve the innovation capacity of prefabricated building technology in Yancheng and realize the green and sustainable development of the construction industry in Yancheng as soon as possible.

5. Conclusions and Suggestions

5.1. Main Conclusion

By analyzing the patent document data of the prefabricated construction technology industry in Yancheng City and major cities in the Yangtze River Delta from 2012 to 2022, the following conclusions can be drawn:

(1) Judging from the current development status of prefabricated building patents in Yancheng City, the number of patent applications in Yancheng City has been at a low level for a long time, the proportion of invention patents is relatively small, and the patent authorization rate is not high. After 2016, the number of patent applications increased significantly and entered a rapid climbing stage. In the prefabricated building technology branch, patent applications in Yancheng City focus on component, structure, and construction technology patents. Judging from the top 10 IPC classification numbers with patent authorizations, the E04B1 and E04B2 patents are the main ones, which is an advantage for Yancheng City's construction industry. In the field of prefabricated building technology industry, the number of patent applications in Yancheng City is stable. The top two applicants are in an absolutely dominant position. Their patent applications account for one-third of the applications of the top 10 applicants, of which the Yancheng Institute of Technology accounts for 18.37% and Jiangsu Jinmao Technology Development Co., Ltd. accounts for 14.29%. However, the major patent applicants are well-known enterprises or key universities in the city's industry. Small and medium-sized enterprises and high-tech enterprises have fewer patent applications, which limits the development space of small and medium-sized enterprises to a certain extent. The proportion of individual applications is slightly higher, and there is little cooperative research and development. In the long run, it will not be conducive to the integration and healthy development of the industry from the perspective of the legal status of patents. The number of utility model patent authorizations is relatively large, eight times that of invention patent authorizations. It is difficult to authorize invention patents, and there are problems such as a failure to pay annual fees after obtaining invention patent authorization. Invalidation, as well as the small number of invention patent transfers, and the integration of industry, academia, and research have not yet truly taken shape.

(2) From the perspective of major cities in the Yangtze River Delta, the number of patent applications and authorizations in the field of the prefabricated construction technology industry in Yancheng City is significantly lower, far behind the patent development level of Shanghai, Hangzhou, Nanjing, Hefei, Suzhou, Nantong, and other countries. Obviously, Yancheng City has a comparative advantage in the effective proportion of patent authorization applications in the field of prefabricated building technology industry, which to a certain extent reflects Yancheng City's great potential for innovation quality in the field of prefabricated building technology in the Yangtze River Delta.

(3) The authors have analyzed and studied the technological innovation capabilities of prefabricated buildings in Yancheng and major other cities in the Yangtze River Delta based on the perspective of patents. Drawing lessons from domestic and foreign patent index systems, we designed three first-level indicators and eight second-level indicators around patent information planning: technological innovation scale, technological innovation quality, and technological innovation operation. We combined the factor analysis method to build a model for rationality and correlation analysis, furthermore extracting three common factors. Through a comparative analysis of the technological innovation capabilities of prefabricated buildings in Yancheng and major cities in the Yangtze River Delta, the specific situation of Yancheng's technological innovation capabilities in prefabricated buildings among the cities in the Yangtze River Delta based on patent information analysis was obtained. Generally speaking, the technological innovation capabilities of prefabricated buildings are medium to low. Among them, the scale and quality of technological innovation are lagging behind, and technological innovation operations are at the forefront.

5.2. Suggestions

(1) In view of the current situation that Yancheng's prefabricated building technology innovation capabilities are not strong, government departments need to improve the

patent management system, such as by optimizing the patent application incentive system, establishing a patent application evaluation system, and strengthening the patent application supervision system. There needs to be a focus on the quality of patent applications and the transformation of the results, such as establishing a high-value patent cultivation demonstration center, conducting patent micro-navigation retrieval and analysis, and building a patent data-sharing service platform. In this way, we can strengthen the construction of prefabricated building technical talent teams and promote the cultivation and introduction of key prefabricated building enterprises.

(2) In the future, we can carry out research on how to effectively transform patents for prefabricated building construction, and the contribution of patent technology innovation to the high-quality development of the regional construction industry in order to enhance regional prefabricated building technology innovation capabilities.

Author Contributions: Conceptualization, H.S. and R.L.; methodology, R.L.; software, R.L.; validation, R.L., F.S. and H.S.; investigation, F.S.; resources, F.S.; data curation, R.L.; writing—original draft preparation, R.L.; writing—review and editing, H.S.; visualization, R.L.; supervision, F.S.; project administration, H.S.; funding acquisition, R.L. All authors have read and agreed to the published version of the manuscript.

Funding: This research was funded by the Yancheng Natural Science Soft Project Foundation of China, grant number yckxrkt2023-44.

Institutional Review Board Statement: Not applicable.

Informed Consent Statement: Not applicable.

Data Availability Statement: The original contributions presented in the study are included in the article, further inquiries can be directed to the corresponding author.

Acknowledgments: The authors gratefully acknowledge the financial support of YCIT.

Conflicts of Interest: The authors declare no conflicts of interest.

References

1. Yue, C. Research on the Bottleneck and Countermeasure of Assembled Building Development. *Archit. Pract.* **2017**, *37*, 106–108. (In Chinese)
2. Sun, H.; Bu, Y. Analysis of the Current Situation and Response Strategies of Assembly Building Development in Yancheng City under the Target of "Double Carbon". *Hous. Real Estate* **2022**, *35*, 59–62. (In Chinese)
3. Sun, H.; Fang, Y.; Yin, M.; Shi, F. Research on the Restrictive Factors of Vigorous Promotion of Prefabricated Buildings in Yancheng under the Background of "Double Carbon". *Sustainability* **2023**, *15*, 1737. [CrossRef]
4. Fan, Y. Reserach on the Countermeasures to Promote the Innovation Ability of Zhenjiang Medical Technology Industry from the Perspective of Patents. Master's Thesis, Jiangsu University, Zhenjiang, China, 2023. (In Chinese)
5. Ce, D.; Tong, Y.; Zhao, R. Research on the Technological Development Trend of Shanxi's New Energy Industry Based on Patent Perspective. *J. Libr. Inf. Sci.* **2022**, *7*, 71–77. (In Chinese)
6. Guo, D. Prefabricated Construction Plan and Cost Analysis. Master's Thesis, Zhengzhou University, Zhengzhou, China, 2017. (In Chinese)
7. Qi, B.; Zhang, Y. Prefabricated Construction Development Bottleneck and Countermeasures Research. *J. Shenyang Jianzhu Univ. (Soc. Sci.)* **2015**, *2*, 156–159. (In Chinese)
8. Tian, D. Research on the Application of BIM Technology Inprefabricated Concrete Housing Construction. Master's Thesis, Hubei University of Technology, Wuhan, China, 2017. (In Chinese)
9. Dai, H. Research on Constraints and Countermeasures for the Development of Assembly Building in Chengdu City. Master's Thesis, Southwest Petroleum University, Chengdu, China, 2017. (In Chinese)
10. Kiruthika, L.; Parthiban, S. Study on analysis and design of prefabricated building with precast post tensioned slab. *Int. J. Appl. Eng. Res.* **2015**, *10*, 11701–11706.
11. El-Sheikh, M.; Sause, R.; Pessiki, S.; Lu, L.W. Seismic behavior and design of unbonded post-tensioned precast concrete frames. *PCI J.* **1999**, *44*, 54–71. [CrossRef]
12. Ozturan, T.; Ozden, S.; Ertas, O. Ductile Connections in Precast Concrete Moment Resisting Frames. *PCI J. Prestress. Concr. Inst. J.* **2006**, *51*, 66–76.
13. Woksepp, S.; Olofsson, T. Credibility and applicability of virtual reality models in design and construction. *Adv. Eng. Inform.* **2008**, *22*, 520–528. [CrossRef]

14. Li, N.; Becerik-Gerber, B. Life-Cycle Approach for Implementing RFID Technology in Construction: Learning from Academic and Industry Use Cases. *J. Constr. Eng. Manag.* **2011**, *137*, 1089–1098. [CrossRef]
15. Qi, B.; Li, C. Research on the Whole Lifecycle of Prefabricated Construction Management Based on BIM Technology. *Constr. Technol.* **2014**, *15*, 25–29. (In Chinese)
16. Zeng, Q.; Gong, W.; Li, X.; Liu, W. Discussion on Structural Adjustment and Transformation Development of Construction Enterprise-Building an Industrialised General Engineering Contracting Enterprise with EPC as the Core and Five Integration. *Chongqing Archit.* **2017**, *16*, 33–35. (In Chinese)
17. Sun, H.; Sun, J.; Wu, Y.; Zhao, K. Introduction to large-scale intelligent PC component automated production line. *China Concr. Cem. Prod.* **2015**, *3*, 35–38. (In Chinese)
18. Du, F.; Wang, Q. Innovation of Technology for the new assembly frame structure. *Build. Technol. Dev.* **2014**, *41*, 1–3. (In Chinese)
19. Zang, L. BIM technology in assembly building application analysis. *Constr. Mater. Decor.* **2017**, *3*, 34–36. (In Chinese)
20. Francis, N.; Kimberly, S.; Dominic, O. The increasing linkage between U.S. technology and public science. *Res. Policy* **1997**, *26*, 317–330.
21. Francis, N.; Elliot, N.; Ross, P. Patents as Indicators of Corporate Technological Strength. *Res. Policy* **1987**, *16*, 143–155.
22. Kunz, M. Time distribution of patent information. *Scientometrics* **1979**, *1*, 275–282. [CrossRef]
23. Ji, L. Research on the method of prefabricated concrete structural design based on BIM technology. Master's Thesis, Shenyang Architecture University, Shenyang, China, 2014. (In Chinese).
24. Ramani, S.; Looze, M. Using patent statistics as knowledge base indicators in the biotechnology sectors: An application to France, Germany and the U.K. *Scientometrics* **2002**, *54*, 319–346. [CrossRef]
25. Suzuki, J.; Gemba, K.; Tamada, S.; Yasaki, Y.; Goto, A. Analysis of propensity to patent and science-dependence of large Japanese manufacturers of electrical machinery. *Scientometrics* **2006**, *68*, 265–288. [CrossRef]
26. Qiu, J.; Li, H. Comparative Analysis of Patent Quantitative Study in Library and Information Area at Home and Abroad. *Libr. Inf. Serv.* **2010**, *54*, 83–87. (In Chinese)
27. Luan, C.; Wang, X.; Liu, Z.; Hou, H. Quantitative studies on frontiers of international patentent bibliometrics. *Stud. Sci. Sci.* **2008**, *26*, 334–338. (In Chinese)
28. Zhang, Y.; Liu, H.; Chen, G.; Jin, Z. Are patents a good measure of innovation? *Foreign Econ. Manag.* **2018**, *40*, 3–16. (In Chinese)
29. Deng, X.; Gong, L.; Zhang, Z. Research of fabricated Building Technology development stuation Based on Patent Analysis. *Archit. Technol.* **2019**, *50*, 942–946. (In Chinese)
30. Zhang, J.; Wu, Y.; He, J. Spatial econometric analysis of the mechanism linking patent innovation and regional economic growth. *Sci. Sci. Manag. S&T* **2007**, *28*, 83–89. (In Chinese)
31. Luan, C.; Hou, H. Analysis of global patent metrics in the field of nanotechnology. In Proceedings of the 2008 Joint Annual Conference on Science and Technology and Science Theory and Discipline Building in China, Huangshan City, China, 31 July–3 August 2008; pp. 38–40. (In Chinese)
32. Luan, C.; Hou, H. World Patent Measurement Study in Biotechnology. *Sci. Technol. Manag. Res.* **2009**, *29*, 338–339. (In Chinese)
33. Luan, C. Patentometric on Global Electronic Vehicle Industry. *Technol. Innov. Manag.* **2011**, *32*, 114–116. (In Chinese)
34. Zhang, G.; Bian, Z. Preliminary analysis of patents for fabricated building structure systems. *Sichuan Build. Mater.* **2019**, *45*, 75–76 + 78. (In Chinese)
35. Liu, S. Research on Technological Innovation Capability of Assembly Building Industry Based on Patent Information Analysis. Master's Thesis, Fujian University of Technology, Fuzhou, China, 2022. (In Chinese)

buildings

MDPI

Article

Three-Dimensional Web-Based Client Presentation of Integrated BIM and GIS for Smart Cities

Abdullah Varlık [1,*] and İsmail Dursun [2]

1 Engineering Faculty, Geomatics Engineering, Necmettin Erbakan University, Konya 42140, Turkey
2 General Directorate of Land Registry and Cadastre, Ankara 06420, Turkey; dursuni@tkgm.gov.tr
* Correspondence: avarlik@erbakan.edu.tr

Abstract: Smart cities use technological solutions to reduce the drawbacks of urban living. The importance of BIM and GIS integration has increased with the popularity of smart city and 3D city concepts in recent years. In addition to 3D city models, Building Information Modeling (BIM) is an essential element of smart cities. The 3D city model web client in this study displays three-dimensional (3D) city models created using photogrammetric techniques, BIM, and campus infrastructure projects. The comparison and integration of the aforementioned systems were evaluated. A web-based 3D client framework and implementation for combined BIM and 3D city models are the goals of the submitted work. The Web is a very challenging platform for 3D data presentation. The Cesium engine based on HTML5 and WebGL is an open-source creation and the virtualcityMAP application using the Cesium infrastructure was used in this study.

Keywords: 3D city models; Cesium; virtualcityMAP; 3D web presentation; Building Information Modeling (BIM); GIS-BIM integration; level of details (LoD); LIDAR; HTML5; WebGL

1. Introduction

Smart cities use information technology to make life easier for people living in cities and to minimize the difficulties of living in cities. According to this definition, two of the essential elements of smart cities are geographic information systems (GIS) and Building Information Modeling (BIM).

GIS and BIM are constantly evolving with the contribution of information technologies and continue to benefit stakeholders. The effective use of BIM technology increases project quality and efficiency, reduces costs and project completion time [1], facilitates sustainable development at all stages of building, and facilitates building analysis [2]. In addition, GIS, which provides a 2D/3D digital and visual view of the physical world, offers many benefits in the management of cities [3].

In recent years, with the high popularity and necessity of smart city and 3D city concepts, the interoperability and integration of BIM and GIS have become much more important. By integrating the features of BIM that can parametrically describe the characteristics of building components and the macro geometric space of GIS, multiscale urban management from micro to macro can be realized. The emergence of GIS lays the foundation for smart development of the city, such as preventing fire hazards, mitigating earthquakes, and designing with minimal accidents [4]. Similarly, BIM aims to improve decision-making in cities by collecting information about buildings in the city [4]. ICM-CBS integration combines the heterogeneity of information models, enabling the effective management of information at all stages of a project life cycle. It ensures that the buildings are used effectively at all stages [5]. In addition, BIM and GIS have different applications, software formats, standards, and data representations [6]. These make the integration of BIM and GIS difficult due to the difficulty of data exchange. Although there are differences between these two systems that seem to be an obstacle to integration, if integration is achieved, it will provide convenience in many areas such as energy analysis, building management, disaster management, indoor navigation, and cost estimation [7]. Considering these benefits, these two systems should provide better data exchange and provide more information to each other for their integration as soon as possible. For example, during the data transfer process from BIM to GIS, it would be beneficial for GIS to provide more building attribute information. At the same time, BIM should receive more detailed 3D city objects in GIS.

Today, more and more cities around the world are providing their 3D city models using the CityGML standard published by the Open Geospatial Consortium (OGC). With CityGML 3.0, the data becomes more detailed and provides great convenience for BIM integration [8].

While the presentation and visualization of large 3D city models created in CityGML can be performed quickly with desktop applications such as Safe Software's FME (Feature Manipulation Engine) and Autodesk's InfraWorks, their presentation and interaction on the Web is still not at the desired level. This paper presents the framework and implementation of a 3D web client with the Cesium engine using HTML5 and WebGL for integrating and analyzing 3D city models with BIM data.

HTML5 is an open standard format that provides a common platform for developing and deploying applications on the Web [9]. HTML5 enables next-generation browsers to support multithreading, which allows different tasks to be executed in parallel on a single web page. WebGL is an extension of the most popular HTML5 canvas element for developers who want to create 3D visualizations on the Web [10]. By using such an approach, 3D capabilities are realized directly in all known web browsers running on all major operating systems, without any additional plug-ins or extensions. Another advantage of WebGL is that it uses the memory of the hardware graphics card to display and render 3D content, thus providing hardware-accelerated 3D functionality on the Web [11].

In general, our study consists of the following parts. First, information about 3D city models, Building Information Models, GIS/BIM integration, and presentation of 3D data on the Web is given. Then, the process of obtaining the study area and the data used in the study, creating BIM from these data, integrating the created BIM model with GIS, and presenting these data in a 3D web environment is explained. We used virtualcityMAP, which uses the virtual web globe Cesium as a visualization engine. Cesium is an open-source JavaScript package that provides all users with the ability to dynamically switch between 3D sphere visualization and 2D map projection and present it in 3D in a web browser. It uses WebGL to provide cross-browser and cross-platform functionality, plug-in independence, and hardware acceleration. The results of the system application are evaluated in the recommendations and conclusion.

2. Literature Review

2.1. 3D City Modeling

Three-dimensional city models, which are the most critical subcomponents of 3D GIS, consist of numerical representations of 3D spatial representations of buildings, land surfaces, trees, streets, and other earth objects located in cities [12]. They are also known by many names such as "Cybercity," "Virtual City," and "Digital City," the most popular being "Digital Twin" [13]. With technological developments, 3D city models aim to achieve the closest appearance to their physical reality and focus on decorating them with more realistic urban objects [12]. Many applications such as city and facility management, navigation, and urban objects are expected to contain semantic information in addition to their geometric data [14]. Suppose that 3D city models are produced for presentation purposes only and are devoid of topological, semantic, and thematic elements, although they may attract people visually. In this case, they are deprived of the information system function by being deprived of analysis and thematic queries [12]. CityGML proposes five different levels of detail (LoD) for 3D city models [15].

These levels of detail start at LoD0 and go up to LoD4, depending on how detailed the city objects are to be displayed (Figure 1). The simplest representation of the LoD0 level is the 2.5 D digital terrain model occupied by the orthophoto. LoD1 is a block model without any roof structure or texture. In contrast, a building in LoD2 presents models with distinguishable roof structure and texture and may contain vegetation objects. LoD3 architectural models feature detailed wall and roof structures and balconies, as well as detailed vegetation and traffic objects. LoD4 complements a LoD3 model by representing interior structures such as rooms, stairs, interior doors, and furniture [15].

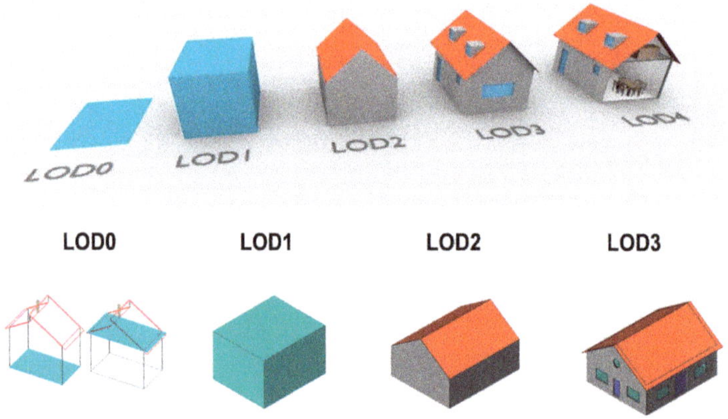

Figure 1. LoD representation is defined by CityGML 2.0 and CityGML 3.0 [16,17].

Although the LoD definition in CityGML 2.0 has been accepted and used by both industry stakeholders and academia due to its ease of sharing and use, the increasing diversity of applications makes the current LoD categorization inadequate. The main disadvantage is that this categorization assigns all indoor features to only one level by assigning them to the LoD4 level and also requires a detailed external representation [18]. Although LoD4 models are quite detailed, they are not usually used for simulations. It is common to use LoD4 models for a detailed internal architecture representation. Recently, LoD4 has also been removed from CityGML 3.0, and interior representation is allowed at all LoD levels [19]. Figure 1 gives an overview of the LoDs in CityGML.

2.2. BIM

The shared, digital, integrated, and multioperable Building Information Model is what makes the Building Information Modeling methodology unique. The Building Information Model is the foundation of Building Information Modeling, a process that creates a 3D model that is semantically enhanced [20]. It serves as the definition of Building Information Modeling and the process and compliance that provides information management. From the design phase to the operation of the building, BIM allows us to access the entire facility virtually at any time during its life cycle [21]. This use can be divided into four primary categories. These are:

1. Design Process
2. Environmental Analysis
3. Building Construction Process
4. Building Operation

The International Alliance for Interoperability (IAI), later known as "Building Smart," defines, disseminates, and publishes industry foundation classes (IFC) that serve as the basis for information exchange between different technical applications and disciplines during the life cycle of a building. IFC, which began the certification process after receiving ISO recognition in 2013, was released as an open international standard in 2018.

The American Institute of Architects (AIA) LoD definitions for the "G202-2013 Building Information Modeling Protocol Form" are used in the LoD specification. LoD definitions have been created to address some key issues in BIM-based project development. These issues typically begin with other stakeholders, other than the person who created the project, wanting to review and learn from the project, drawing incorrect conclusions about it, and often having to deal with complicated information that does not work (Figure 2).

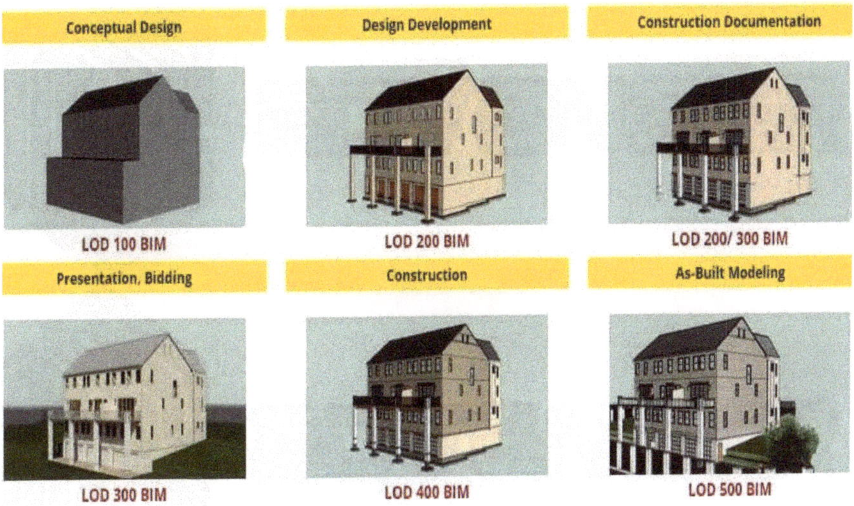

Figure 2. Relationship between the LoD and the degree of representativeness [22].

2.3. Integration of GIS-BIM

Indoor applications have not received much attention from GIS professionals until recently. This is due to the lack of spatial nature of the data. They are not related to a person or a place. Spatial data infrastructure guidelines do not directly define building interiors. As a result, the integration of Geographic Information System applications with BIM and other CAD-based construction, design, and planning applications has remained focused on the data transfer dimension, focusing on the interior in CAD and BIM and the exterior of the building boundary in GIS.

Automating a meaningful conversion of IFC data to CityGML data is quite challenging. Although both IFC and CityGML data are defined with a hierarchical data structure, the structure of IFC is significantly more complex because it contains more intermediate features than needed in the CityGML data set. This is because IFC data has a very complex geometric structure [23,24]. The representation of the building model and its structural components, such as walls, floors, and roofs, differs significantly between IFC and CityGML. In IFC, structural components are solid objects with attributes, connections, and often a volumetric geometry representation. The CityGML building model is not an object-oriented model and does not support representations of volumetric geometry.

On the other hand, it has explicit solid or surface geometry, as shown in Figure 3. Structural elements are modeled as bounding surfaces for buildings and spaces with no features or relationship to other bounding surfaces. To convert IFC to CityGML, volumetric representations of building elements must be converted to the boundary surfaces of the CityGML building or space [25].

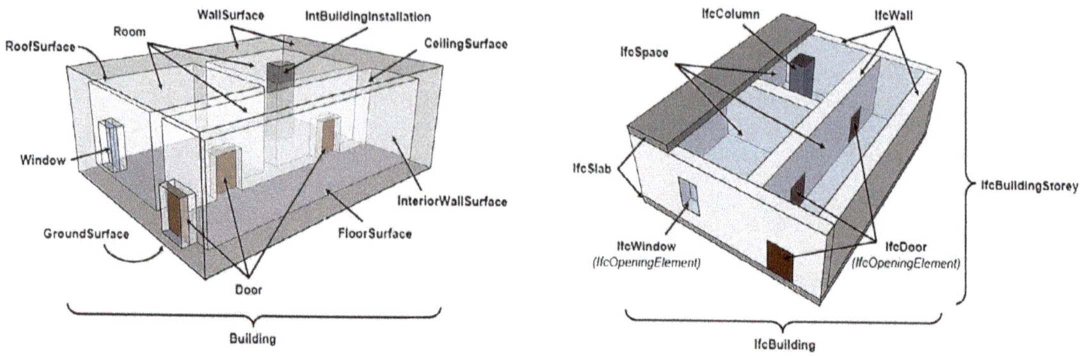

Figure 3. Snapshot of a building modeled in IFC (right side) and CityGML (left side) [26].

There is commercial software that allows conversion between IFC models and CityGML models at different levels of detail. These are FME Building Information Modelserver (FME 2022.2) and IFCExplorer (IFC 4). However, it is necessary to produce software according to the rules [25]. Finally, it would be most convenient to find a bidirectional method where not only a conversion from IFC to CityGML but also a conversion from CityGML to IFC would be possible. It is believed that a bidirectional approach will lead to the development of more applications and will provide benefits both operationally (integrated model with lower costs) and strategically (crisis management and enhanced analytical capabilities) [27].

To achieve a seamless and continuous whole level of detail specification for 3D building models, the outdoor and indoor scenes are treated separately and then combined, as shown in Figure 4.

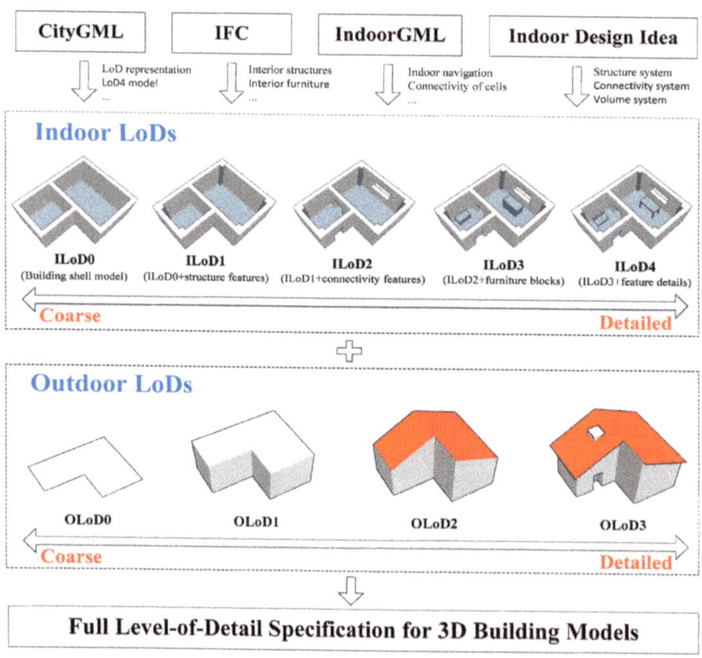

Figure 4. Research route of the full level of detail (LoD) specification for 3D building models. IFC, industry foundation classes; ILoD, indoor LoD; OLoD, outdoor LoD [18].

2.4. GIS-BIM Integration Challenges

BIM and GIS integration is a fundamental technique for a smart city and spatial digital twin, which requires integrating building models in BIM into a GIS environment for visualization and analysis [28,29]. For this purpose, BIM data needs to be converted to a format accessible by GIS [29].

During BIM/GIS data conversion, industry foundation classes (IFC) are used for BIM data, while CityGML and CityJSON format is used for 3D GIS data [30]. IFC is the primary open data schema created by buildingSMART for information exchange within the architecture, engineering, and construction (AEC) application domain [31]. CityGML is an open-standard data model and exchange format that is capable of storing 3D models of cities and their surroundings based on the Geography Markup Language (GML) defined by the OGC in the format of Extensible Markup Language (XML) [32]. BIM consists of geometric and semantic data. Geometry provides data about the shape, size, and location of objects, while semantics provides data about properties such as class type, material, and functions. Therefore, the transformation between BIM and GIS should include semantic transfer in addition to geometric transformation [29,33]. The geometric transformation between the two systems can be performed using some commercial software packages, such as FME [34], BIM Server, and Data Interoperability (DI), an extension of ArcGIS built on FME. However, none of these tools can successfully transform both geometric and semantic data in their entirety [32]. Therefore, new methods are needed. Recently, the integrated spatial information model (IGIM) approach based on semantic web technologies and resource description framework (RDF) has been used for BIM and GIS integration [35]. In addition, researchers have developed various data exchange formats to support the interoperability of BIM and GIS. The IFG (IFC for GIS) data model and the buildingSMART data dictionary (bSDD) are examples of studies on the integration of BIM with other engineering application areas such as GIS. The purpose of IFG is to enable the exchange of building and GIS data by importing or exporting a single data type. However, there are many heterogeneous classes for the representation of building and geographic information. Therefore, it is more logical to apply a different interoperability format for both building and GIS classes [36]. bSDD is an online service that hosts classifications and their properties, allowed values, units, and translations, as well as a data dictionary. bSDD enables the connection between all content within the database by providing a standardized workflow to ensure data quality and information consistency [37].

As mentioned above, there are still several challenges to fully implementing BIM and GIS integration.

- ***Semantic Transformation***

Semantic and geometric information are important for BIM integrity. The highest efficiency of interoperability is guaranteed by the semantic aspect of data integration. The key to semantic interoperability is to ensure that attributes and relationships between information management systems are preserved during data conversion [38]. Geometry forms the framework to which semantic information can be added, and it is semantics that enriches building models with additional information. Therefore, semantic data must be transferred correctly in addition to geometric data. Semantic data in BIM refers to the attributes and properties of building components, such as component type and materials used, and the relationships between these components [33]. Semantic transfer was carried out with the semantic mapping approach. Semantic mapping refers to the establishment of connections between classes in IFC and CityGML to ensure the correctness of the transferred semantics. Mapping of building elements involves mapping attributes and relationships [7]. Semantic mapping establishes a link between two classes so that information from the source class can be mapped to the target class [33]. However, due to the large number of classes in IFC and the fact that it is not necessary to transfer each data, various data classes were selected. A building in CityGML can have semantic properties for both the solid model and the surfaces of this solid model. IFC has a different structure to store semantics, and objects are interconnected through a network of relationships. In most cases, the IFC class and the type of the object are sufficient to extract CityGML semantics from an IFC object. However, understanding the relationships is also important for the most appropriate semantic mapping [23]. To solve problems such as the fact that the hierarchical structure of IFC is complex compared to CityGML (for example, doors belong to openings in walls in IFC, whereas doors belong directly to walls in CityGML) or that some building element parts in IFC are in different classes (for example, parts of windows and stairs are in the IfcMember class; however, when converted to CityGML, these parts must be in their parent classes, namely windows or stairs), it is necessary to find the descendants and ascendants of the objects in IFC. In the semantic mapping of IFC and CityGML, the classes to be mapped were determined by taking Donkers et al. [23] and Cecchini [39] (Figure 5) as basis and making additions. In CityJSON, IFC entities were mapped with various semantic surfaces under the "Building" class.

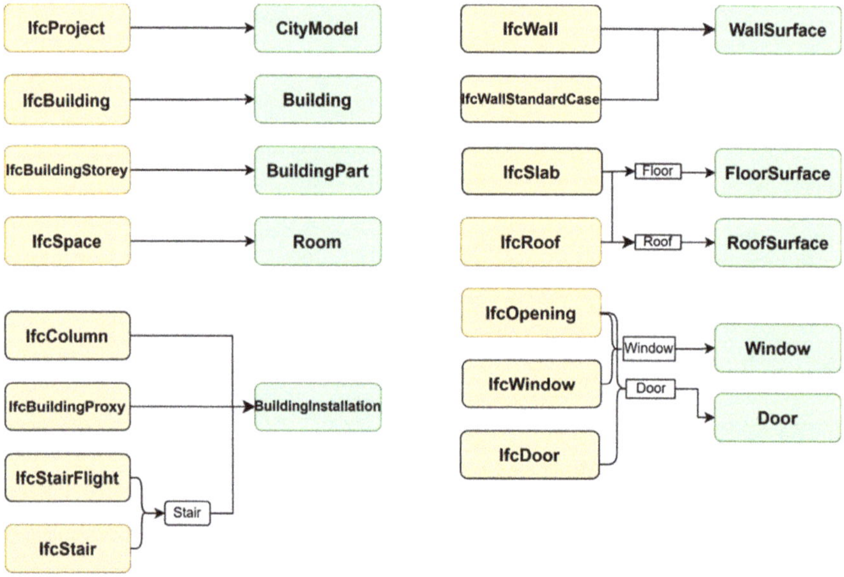

Figure 5. Semantic mapping of IFC and CityGML classes (yellow outline indicates IFC classes and green outline indicates CityGML classes. Classes in boxes without black outlines do not carry geometric information) [39].

- *Geometric Transformation*

Geometric transformation is the transformation of the geometry of building models into a form that can be used in GIS. Geometric transformation is necessary because BIM and GIS use different modeling paradigms. In this case, the three main issues that need to be addressed are the reference system, 3D geometry, and level of detail differences [7]. Therefore, geometric transformation consists of a series of subtasks such as coordinate system transformation, georeferencing, and representation transformation [33].

- *Representation Transformation*

One of the differences in the modeling paradigm is that 3D models can be explicit or implicit [33]. Representation conversion refers to the conversion of implicit models into explicit models. Implicit models are created with parametric modeling methods (CSG and SS) and are represented by a set of parameters, while explicit models are represented by explicit points such as B-rep. BIM can use both implicit models and explicit models [38], that is, IFC can use one or a combination of CSG, B-rep, and SS [40]. Since the shape, size, and position of parametric models can be easily adjusted, in other words, they are more flexible in geometry editing. IFC generally uses SS and CSG. IFC uses nonparametric B-Rep only when necessary. GIS, on the other hand, uses explicit models (solid models or surface models) because it is insufficient in parametric modeling. Conversion of CSG and SS to B-Rep allows these models to be used in GIS [33].

- *Georeferencing*

Georeferencing is a term originally used to refer to the process of associating a map or raster image with its corresponding location in geographic space. Georeferencing is necessary if building models are to be integrated with other spatial data in the GIS environment, such as a road network [29]. Georeferencing an object involves transforming its coordinates to place the object in the correct geographic location [41]. Georeferencing methods are available in GIS. Therefore, the problems in this integration arise from the IFC standards [33]. Georeferenced BIM can be integrated with other spatial data sets in GIS [42]. IFC versions before IFC4 do not have a clearly stated entity for defining spatial reference information and are considered inadequate for georeferencing. BIM and GIS use different coordinate systems in different ways [40]. BIM adopts the local positioning system in which objects are defined in the local planar coordinate system (3D Cartesian coordinate system). The local positioning system of an object is related to another object. For example, the local positioning system of a window can be related to the local positioning system of a wall. This mechanism facilitates model modification [7]. GIS generally uses a geographic coordinate system because it focuses on applications covering regions, countries, and even the entire world; each object in it has absolute coordinates in the form of latitude, longitude, and altitude [33,43]. GIS can also use a local planar coordinate system, but in most cases, it uses a geographic coordinate system [7]. Therefore, coordinate system transformation should be performed during geometric transformation [33]. It is recommended to use Equations (1) and (2) for reference system transformation. The matrix equation for calculating the coordinates of the corners of objects in the local coordinate system is shown in (1). Here, D is the sweep distance, and (Vx, Vy, Vz) is the direction vector of the sweep [44]. To transform the coordinates from the local system to the real-world system, (θx, θy, θz) in the matrix Equation (2) are the rotation angles around the X′ axis, Y′ axis, and Z′ axis to make the axes of the X, Y, Z coordinate system parallel to the X′, Y′, Z′ axes, respectively. (Δx, Δy, Δz) is the translation vector from the origin of the local coordinate system to the real-world coordinate system [32,45].

$$\begin{bmatrix} x' \\ y' \\ z' \end{bmatrix} = D.\begin{bmatrix} V_x \\ V_y \\ V_z \end{bmatrix} + \begin{bmatrix} x \\ y \\ z \end{bmatrix} \tag{1}$$

$$\begin{bmatrix} X_2 \\ Y_2 \\ Z_2 \end{bmatrix} = \begin{bmatrix} 1 & 0 & 0 \\ 0 & \cos\theta_x & \sin\theta_x \\ 0 & -\sin\theta_x & \cos\theta_x \end{bmatrix} \begin{bmatrix} \cos\theta_y & 0 & -\sin\theta_y \\ 0 & 1 & 0 \\ \sin\theta_y & 0 & \cos\theta_y \end{bmatrix} \begin{bmatrix} \cos\theta_z & \sin\theta_z & 0 \\ -\sin\theta_z & \cos\theta_z & 0 \\ 0 & 0 & 1 \end{bmatrix} \begin{bmatrix} X_1 \\ Y_1 \\ Z_1 \end{bmatrix} + \begin{bmatrix} \Delta x \\ \Delta y \\ \Delta z \end{bmatrix} \tag{2}$$

- ***Level of Detail Transformation***

Both BIM and GIS have a term that indicates the amount of information contained in building models [33]. The design and planning of structures are carried out step by step, starting with preliminary design and conceptual planning and ending with implementation planning. This is equally valid for GIS- and BIM-based planning in civil engineering and building construction. For this, digital models and therefore components initially require only rough detailing. With refined planning (submission of documents for planning application or planning approval, determination of masses or quantities, cost estimation, etc.), the demands for detailing for both geometric and semantic information increase. To meet the different requirements for detailing model objects in planning, the concept of LOD was developed. The concept of LOD should not be confused with the level of accuracy (LOA). LOA describes the geometric accuracy in measuring the current state of a component or the geometric accuracy of the model subsequently derived from the survey data [45]. CityGML uses the concept of LoD, which is partially different from LOD, to indicate the amount of information contained in the models [33,46]. Since LOD gradually becomes more detailed during the various planning stages in BIM, it is created to suit the various planning stages. On the other hand, since GIS already represents the existing real world, it is necessary to determine the real-world objects that need to be transferred to the system. The concept of LoD follows the principle of generalization. Low LoD means that small or less important building parts or elements are not modeled or simplified [45]. LoD focuses on the entire building model and specifies what the building model should contain. LOD focuses on the components of the building and what should be in the building components. Therefore, it is important to determine the building elements that should be present during the geometric transformation [47].

2.5. 3D Web Client

3D city models are now one of the most important services in metropolitan areas. As part of this evolution, development studies continue with numerous examples of 3D city models, urban planning, navigation services in cities, and solutions for businesses.

In recent years, 3D applications have increasingly moved to web-based platforms. Because they are applications that are easily accessible to many people and can be used without the need for additional licensed software downloads, web-based solutions are attracting a lot of attention. The creation of 3D presentations for the Web has accelerated the move from desktop 3D applications to browsers. This expansion has necessitated the standardization of 3D GIS applications and the introduction of uniform data formats. The most popular and well-known open-source options are CesiumJS, GeoServer, and 3DCityDB. Another important factor in 3D data presentation applications is whether they support common 3D data formats. Examples of formats include dense color point clouds (such as LAS and E57), large textured mesh models (such as OBJ, FBX, and glTF), city information models (such as CityGML and CityJSON), or building information models (IFC).

Another fundamental problem is that semantic 3D city models using CityGML can be presented in large data sizes. Presenting and managing large data on web-based clients can only be performed on processors and causes performance problems. This problem can be solved with good tiling strategies that break large data into small data.

CityGML data on the Web has created many practical applications that allow for better information sharing and dissemination. It also provides users with ease of navigation, query, and analysis of various virtual 3D city models on 3D city models. However, due to the large size and complexity of CityGML files, visualization in a web browser takes time. It can cause inefficiencies in terms of semantics and geometry. Consequently, visualization of CityGML files over the Web is important for both academia and industry and has become an important research area [48].

With technological developments, desktop-based GIS applications have started to move rapidly to the Web and the development of platform-independent web applications has emerged as an urgent need. HTML5, the fifth revision of HTML, marks a significant milestone in this direction. HTML5 is a common platform for applications developed on the Web and an open standard format [49]. The canvas, which can be used independently to develop robust GIS applications in a web browser, contains many valuable elements such as geolocation, web workers, web slots, and scalable vector graphics (SVG).

WebGL is an extension of the most popular HTML5 canvas element for developers who want to create 3D visualizations on the Web and is a 3D graphics API based on OpenGL ES 2.0 and a low-level language [10]. Today, many WebGL-based frameworks are being developed to facilitate development. The most important of these frameworks includes Three.js, a library written in JavaScript, a lightweight programming language commonly used by web developers to create more dynamic interactions when developing applications, web pages, even games, servers, and allows us to create 3D scenes that we can use on browsers and mobile devices; Scene.js, a library written in JavaScript that can render 3D objects in the web browser and render Canvas and SVG on them; and GLGE, which is a library written in JavaScript that takes low-level requests from the application and makes them meaningful [50]. Due to the technological infrastructure, existing 3D visualization solutions can currently only be used with specific browsers or when additional browser plugins are installed. This limitation can be overcome by combining visualization using HTML5 and WebGL. With the development of technological infrastructure and approach, 3D capabilities can now be built directly in the browser without the need for additional plugins or extensions [51].

Application program interface (API) support, web-based presentation, visualization capabilities, 3D geospatial information, data integration and management, usage and analysis capabilities (open data, level of interaction), and support for 3D data assets are all expected features when developing applications that use 3D city models (CityGML, IFC, mesh models, point clouds, etc.). Web-based platforms are becoming increasingly popular for 3D applications. Because they are applications that can be quickly accessed by a wide range of users and run without the need for additional licensed software downloads, web-based solutions are attracting a lot of attention. The creation of 3D presentations for the Web has accelerated the migration of 3D applications from the desktop to the browser. This growth has necessitated the standardization of 3D GIS applications and the development of common data format solutions.

As a result, the combination of HTML5 and WebGL is widely used by researchers to solve complex problems. Many virtual spheres have been developed using this combination. For example, the development of WebGL and HTLM5 sparked many developments such as Cesium.js [52], three.js [53], Unity3D [54], Unreal Engine [55], X3DOM [56], OSG.js [57]), O3D [58], WebGL Earth [59], WebGL Globe [60], etc. to visualize 2D/3D features and various geospatial functions [61,62]. Cesium is an open-source JavaScript library for rendering 3D web-based virtual spheres [63]. It uses WebGL for hardware acceleration and plugin independence and provides cross-platform and cross-browser functionality. Cesium is a robust, scalable, and secure 3D geospatial platform. The Cesium virtual world is based on the Scene.js JavaScript 3D-rendering engine.

Cesium, an open-source JavaScript library, has gained significant popularity in the 3D web visualization space. Its robust features, performance, and community support have made it a preferred choice for developers building interactive geospatial applications. The key factors that have contributed to the widespread adoption of Cesium in comparison to other leading 3D web viewers are listed as follows:

- Performance and Scalability: Cesium is known for its ability to handle large data sets efficiently, Cesium utilizes techniques like level-of-detail (LoD) and culling to optimize rendering performance [64], and while other 3D web presenters offer similar capabilities, Cesium often excels in terms of overall performance and scalability, especially when dealing with complex 3D scenes.
- Feature Richness: Cesium provides a comprehensive set of features, including support for various data formats (e.g., GeoJSON, KML, WMS), 3D terrain, real-time data visualization, and integration with popular mapping APIs (e.g., Google Maps, OpenStreetMap) [64]. While other viewers may offer comparable features, Cesium's feature set is often considered more extensive and well-integrated.
- Open-source Community and Ecosystem: As an open-source project, Cesium benefits from a large and active community of developers who contribute to its development and provide support. This community fosters innovation and ensures the library's continued growth [64]. While other viewers may support 3D Tiles to some extent, Cesium's implementation is often considered more robust and efficient.
- 3D Tiling Support: Cesium's native support for 3D Tiles, a standardized format for streaming massive geospatial data sets, makes it well-suited for large-scale 3D visualization projects [64], and while other viewers may support 3D Tiles to some extent, Cesium's implementation is often considered more robust and efficient.
- Integration with Other Technologies: Integrates seamlessly with other web technologies, including HTML5, WebGL, and JavaScript frameworks like React and Angular.

This flexibility allows developers to easily incorporate Cesium into existing web applications [64], while other viewers may have limitations in terms of integration with other technologies, making them less versatile for developers.

Based on the key factors, Cesium's combination of performance, feature richness, community support, 3D Tiles support, and integration capabilities make it an attractive choice for developers building 3D web applications, especially in the geospatial domain. While other alternatives are available, Cesium's strengths often outweigh the limitations of competing libraries, solidifying its position as a leading 3D web viewer.

2.6. Data Security

3D web-based clients in smart city applications often process large data sets to visualize and interact with complex urban environments. This presents unique challenges for data security as sensitive information must be protected while ensuring efficient performance and user experience. The most fundamental security considerations in 3D web-based clients are data encryption, access control, data masking, secure data transfer, input authentication, secure API design, regular updates and patching, and data backup and recovery [65]. 3D web-based clients that successfully solve these challenges will overcome them [66]. In addition, ensuring real-time data flows, data sharing and collaboration, and IoT integration are the most important challenges to be overcome for smart city applications in terms of data security [67,68]. To ensure adequate data security, the following items should be fulfilled so that they can effectively protect sensitive data, and guarantee confidentiality, integrity, and privacy in 3D web-based clients.

- Security by Design: Incorporate security into the development process from the beginning, rather than as an afterthought.
- Regular Security Audits: Conduct regular security audits to identify vulnerabilities and assess compliance with security standards.
- User Education: Educate users about security best practices, such as strong password management and avoiding phishing attempts.
- Incident Response Plan: Have a plan in place to respond to security incidents promptly and effectively [69].

3. Methodology

3.1. Working Area and Data Sets

To provide information for a GIS that will include interior spaces, this study created 3D models of a building using actual measurements and metrics. The result is a model that is adaptable to future developments and suitable for building components, architectural tools, and facility management. The Faculty of Social and Human Sciences (SBIF) building on the Köycegiz campus of Necmettin Erbakan University in Konya served as the test site for the application (Figure 6).

In this study, two different techniques were used to create a BIM model of the SBIF building. The first is a BIM model created from CAD data at the LOD 300 level. This method is called "CAD to BIM." BIM models created through CAD to BIM conversion offer improved visualization of layered information that was not clearly visible in 2D plans. Figure 7 shows the BIM model created by CAD to BIM conversion in detail.

The second is a BIM model created using point clouds and photographs from laser scanners and unmanned aerial vehicles. This process is called" scan to BIM." As a result of the photogrammetric processing of the images obtained with a DJI Phantom 4 RTK device, a point cloud of approximately 11 million points was created. Roof plans were generated from this data. In addition, orthophotos and digital terrain models of the entire campus were produced and used as a base map (Figure 8a,b).

Figure 6. Working area.

Figure 7. BIM model generated through CAD-to-BIM conversion.

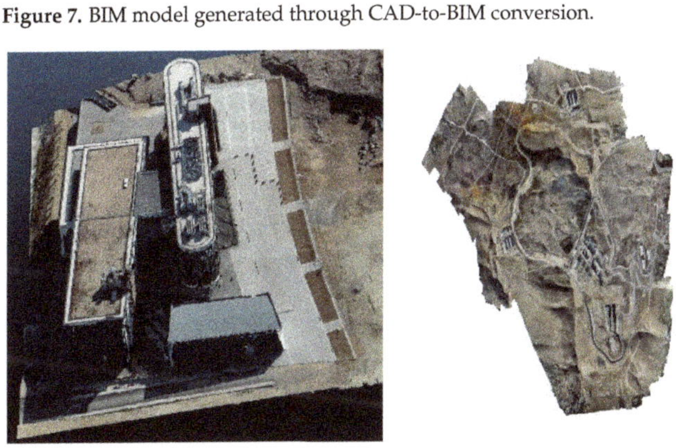

(a) (b)

Figure 8. (a) SBIF UAV data; (b) campus orthophoto.

TLS data was collected using the Zeb-Revo handheld laser scanner. These data, used to build the model at LoD 3 and LoD 4 levels, consist of six sessions and a point cloud of 217 million points (Figure 9).

Figure 9. SBIF LIDAR point cloud.

Digitization was performed from the scan data. To make the TLS point cloud data useful, floor plans were created by creating 2D CAD drawings by slicing the data into layers. Similarly, roof CAD drawings were created from the UAV point cloud data. These floor plans, attic plans, and conference room drawings were combined with BIM software to create a 3D model. As shown in Figure 10, a scan-to-BIM model of the entire building was created.

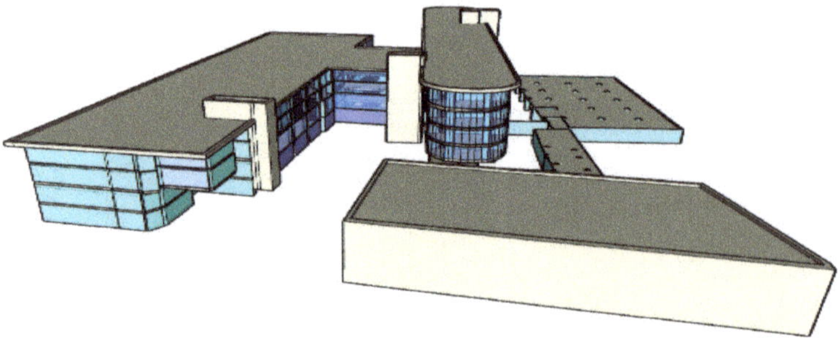

Figure 10. Scan-to-BIM model.

3.2. GIS/BIM Integration

Much theoretical information has been given about GIS-BIM integration. However, in practice, there are different software and applications for transferring BIM models to GIS software (ArcGIS Pro 3.1), combining them with spatial data, and performing spatial analysis commonly used in GIS. A decision must be made about which program to choose.

A formal semantic mapping procedure is introduced with the objective of facilitating the correspondence between individual instances belonging to the industry foundation classes (IFCs) and their counterparts within the CityGML class. This mapping process considers a number of different factors, including the interrelationships between entities and the attributes associated with them. The procedural framework is illustrated in Figure 11, which depicts the seamless integration of both IFC and CityGML entities into a unified modeling representation. This integration is often achieved through the application of Unified Modeling Language (UML) techniques. The region delineated by the dashed red lines encompasses a pivotal component, the bridge model. This model serves as an intermediary, establishing a cohesive link between entities originating from the IFC and

CityGML realms. Of note, this bridge model ensures comprehensive transformation of data between these entities through the use of intermediate objects, thus facilitating accurate and consistent information exchange.

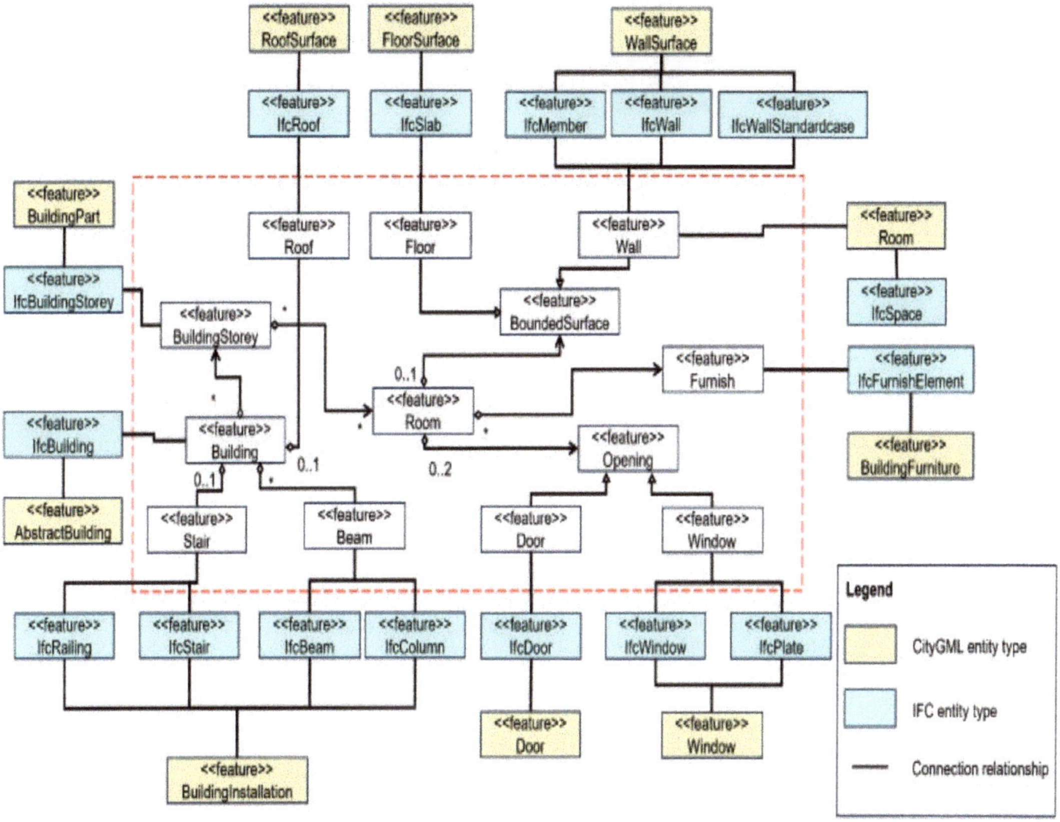

Figure 11. Integration of CityGML and IFC. Note: "*" UML notation used to representation the cardinal relationship among CityGML classes that shows the number of occurrence or possibilities and an intermediately model is shown inside the red box.

After that, additional software is needed to convert BIM models from IFC to CityGML. The most important aspect of converting from IFC to CityGML is that the IFC data are georeferenced. However, in this transformation, it is the ability to make changes to coordinate systems and spatial referencing between data sets that is important. In this context, FME is the only application that can meet all these requirements. FME is spatial data extraction, transformation, and loading software designed specifically for GIS, CAD, and raster graphics software.

Finally, the 3D GIS data presentation part is complete. Again, an application selection is required. When examining the world examples in this context, it was decided to use the Cesium engine for presentation, because it was understood that the open-source Cesium engine saw more cities and had better capabilities. However, the Cesium engine also works with its own format, "3D Tiles," when presenting 3D data. Since FME is the easiest method for this data transformation, a workflow diagram was revealed in terms of GIS-BIM integration. The workflow diagram is summarized in Figure 12.

Figure 12. 3D city model/BIM integration model.

According to the workflow diagram for GIS-BIM integration, BIM data should be created according to the CAD-to-BIM or scan-to-BIM data creation method. Then, the BIM data should be opened with the Revit or Sketch up application and georeferencing should be performed (Figure 13). Most models are modeled in a local coordinate system that does not exist in the real world. It is necessary to define the coordinates of the models based on the data-based spherical coordinate systems that represent the real position in the world.

The IFC transformation of the BIM model paired with the geospatial data is then performed. Once the IFC transformation is complete, the BIM data can be opened with the FME application and transformed according to the CityGML LoD level by arranging the necessary coordinate systems. Unnecessary geometry filtering is a transformation process that uses desired feature types from 2D and 3D models while ignoring unwanted features. FME provides conversion parameters for CityGML files at three different levels of detail on its website. These are:

- IFC LOD 100 to LoD 2 CityGML
- IFC LOD 200 to LoD 3 CityGML
- IFC LOD 300 to LoD 4 CityGML [70]

Figure 13. Georeferencing.

Many IFC classes are not needed in the CityGML conversion due to the definition and compatibility of the two formats. Therefore, geometries and semantic images that are not needed for different levels of detail are filtered out. Within the scope of the paper, a predefined FME workbench was used for the conversion from IFC LoD 300 to CityGML LoD 4 in FME, since the BIM model was created at the LoD 300 level [70]. The workspace used is shown in Figure 14. The conversion from an IFC model to a LoD4 CityGML file is a very advanced and comprehensive process. It also involves a significant number of different IFC attributes. By reading the IFC data type with the Revit reader in FME, the desired geometries can be easily used in CityGML or other GIS applications.

In addition, the scan-to-BIM model was created using the following GML architecture (Figure 15). This allows both models to be integrated with each other.

3.3. Web-Based Presentation

Finally, the CityGML format must be converted to the 3D Tiles format in order to present the data in the Cesium engine. Once the necessary transformations have been performed, there are no longer any barriers to presenting the data in a 3D GIS infrastructure and performing analysis. Numerous applications support CityGML, commercial or nonprofit international organizations, as already mentioned. Many CAD, BIM, and GIS formats are supported by Cesium (Table 1).

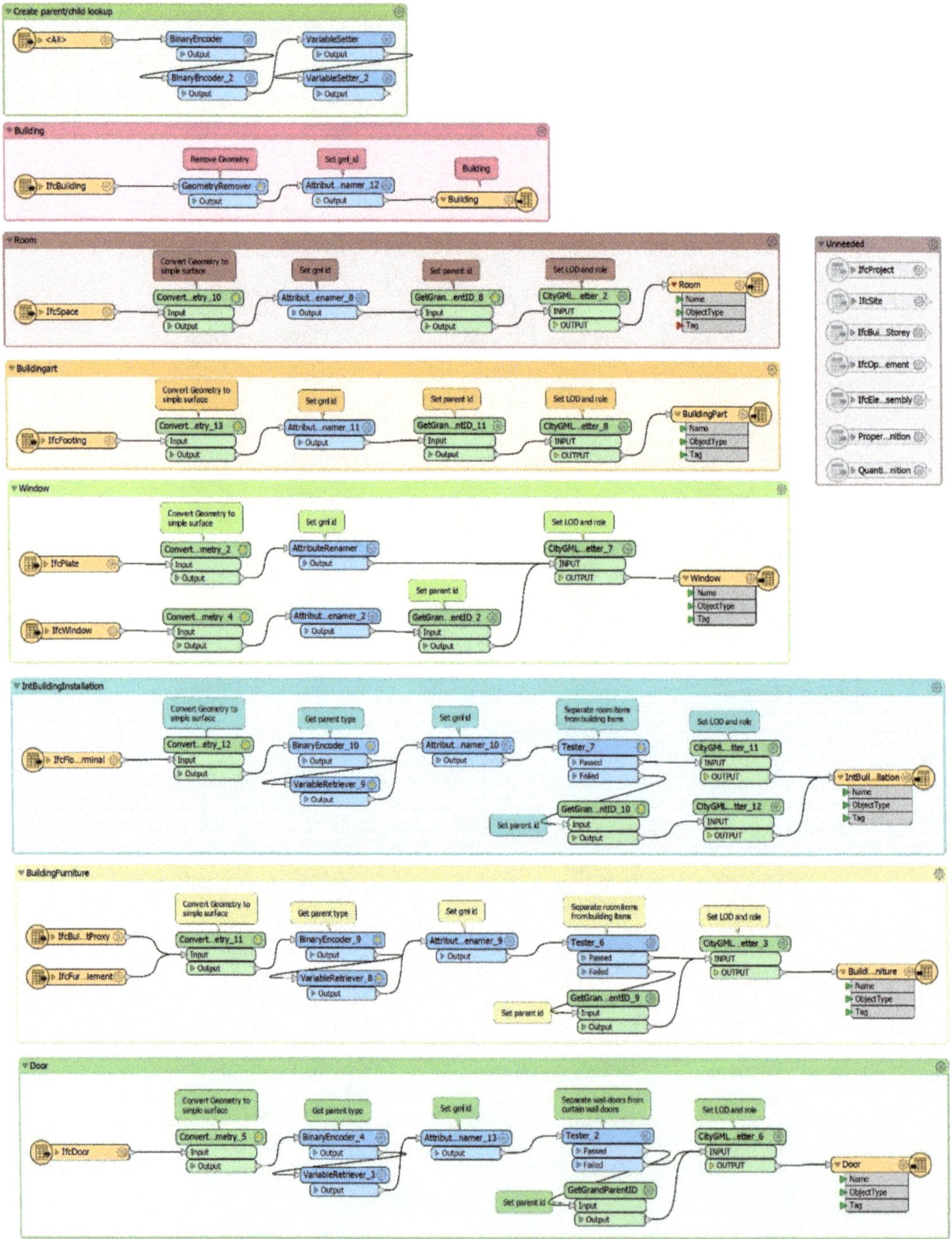

Figure 14. IFC to CityGML transformation FME workbench [70].

```
                                  PHOTOGRAMMETRIC BUILDING
<?xml version="1.0" encoding="utf-8"?>
<core: CityModel >
    <gml: boundedBy>
        <!--Envelope-->
        <gml: Envelope srsName="EPSG:5256" srsDimension="3">
            <gml: lowerCorner />
            <gml: upperCorner />
        </gml: Envelope>
    </gml: boundedBy>
    <core:cityObjectMember>
        <!--Fotogrametrik Bina-->
        <bldg:Building gml:id="FB_bb2989e3-5a7c-408c-8db3-02733c741e69">
                            <!--CityGML Attributes-->
            <gml:name>Fotogrametrik Bina_4111-4</gml:name>
            <bldg:class>FotogrametrikBina</bldg:class>
            <!--TKGM Attributes -->
            <gen:stringAttribute name="constructionID" />
            <gen:intAttribute name="buildingType" />
            <gen:doubleAttribute name="roofProjectionArea" />
            ...
            ...
            <!--Lod 0 Bina Çatı ve Taban İzdüşümü -->
            <bldg:lod0FootPrint />
            <bldg:lod0RoofEdge />
            <!--Lod 1 Bina Geometrisi -->
            <bldg:lod1Solid />
            <!--Lod 2 Bina Geometrisi -->
            <bldg:lod2MultiSurface />
            <!--Lod 2 TIC -->
            <bldg:lod2TerrainIntersection />
                <!--Bina cati ustu yapilasmalar -->
                <bldg:outherBuildingInstallation />
                        <bldg:BuildingInstallation />
                <!--Bina Gorunum -->
                             <app:appearance />
                <!--Bina Cati -->
                            <bldg: boundedBy />
                             <bldg: RoofSurface />
                <!--Bina Cati Teras-->
                            <bldg: boundedBy />
                             <bldg: OuterFloorSurface />
            <!--Duvarlar -->
            <!--Kuzey -->
            <bldg: boundedBy />
                <bldg: WallSurface />
            <!--Güney -->
            <bldg: boundedBy />
                <bldg: WallSurface />
            <!--Doğu -->
            <bldg: boundedBy />
                <bldg: WallSurface />
            <!--Batı -->
            <bldg: boundedBy />
                <bldg: WallSurface />
            <!--Zemin Yüzey -->
            <bldg: boundedBy />
                <bldg: GroundSurface />
    </core:cityObjectMember>
    <app:appearanceMember />
</core:CityModel>
```

Figure 15. Used CityGML structure encoded in GML.

In this context, some software that we have the opportunity to use both in theory and practice was examined. It was decided to use virtualcityMAP V5.0, one of the most stable applications working with HTML5 and WebGL, and the Cesium engine for the article.

VirtualcityMAP is a web-based application developed with long-term user experience that can be used in all cities or a specific region as a practical and cost-effective solution for creating and managing CityGML-based 3D city models. The virtualcityMAP software is developed by the Berlin-based multipartner virtualcitySYSTEMS GmbH. VirtualcitySYSTEMS GmbH is an innovative geographic information company specializing in real-time 3D visualization. It provides solutions for 3D city models with its product virtualcityMAP. It develops software for modeling, managing, and using 3D city models [71].

Table 1. Cesium-supported data formats [64].

Format	3D Tiles	Terrain	Imagery	glTF	Native
Zip Archive (.zip)	✔	✔	✔	✔	
glTF (.gltf, .glb)	✔			✔	
Filmbox (.fbx)	✔			✔	
CityGML (.citygml, .xml, .gml)	✔				
CZML(.czml)					✔
GeoJSON(.json, .geojson, .topojson)					✔
KML(.kml, .kmz)	✔				✔
Laser(.las, .laz)	✔				
COLLADA (.dae)	✔			✔	
Wavefront OBJ (.obj)	✔			✔	
Floating Point Raster (.flt)		✔	✔		
Arc/Info ASCII Grid (.asc)		✔	✔		
Source Map (.src)		✔	✔		
GeoTIFF (.tiff, .tif)		✔	✔		
Erdas İmagine (.img)		✔	✔		
USGS ASCII DEM and CDED (.dem)		✔	✔		
JPEG (.jpg, .jpeg)			✔		
PNG (.png)			✔		
Cesium Terrain Database (.terraindb)		✔			

The virtualcityMAP application includes an integrated viewer that uses the Cesium engine for tilted images, 2D maps, and 3D maps, depending on the configuration, and can be used with any browser that supports JavaScript and WebGL. Open source, developed by Mozilla, WebGL is an API for rendering 3D computer graphics in a browser without using any plugins.

4. Results

The virtualcityMAP application is published on http://212.174.59.122/ (accessed on 2 August 2024) with the title "Use and Integration of 3D City Models and Building Information Models for Smart Cities: Example of Köyceğiz Campus." There are three types of data in the application: main data, supplementary data, and base data. In addition, information about queries and analysis is given.

4.1. Main Data

The main data consists of CAD-to-BIM and scan-to-BIM data. As explained in the Integration of GIS-BIM section, the models created with BIM software were first converted to CityGML format and then to Cesium 3D Tiles format and uploaded to the system using FME (Figure 16).

4.2. Supplementary Data

Supplemental data; consists of campus infrastructure projects. Infrastructure projects related to electricity, fiber optics, high voltage, natural gas, wastewater, potable water, and storm water have been converted to the 3D Tiles format, uploaded into the system, and integrated. However, because they remain underground, they are not visible in the direct application. Thanks to the "Transparent Terrain Mode" of the application, the data can be seen under the ground, as shown in Figure 17.

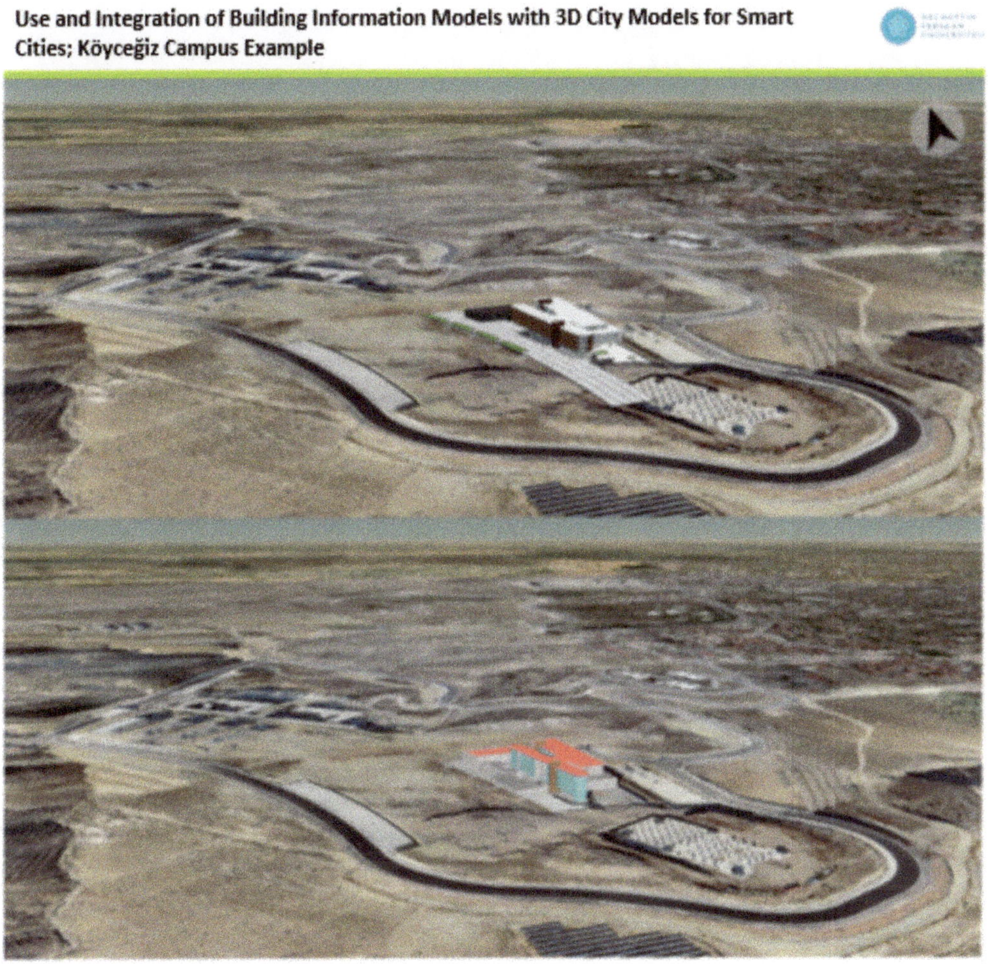

Figure 16. Main data.

There are also base maps as additional data. Base maps can be divided into three types: those included in the system, those provided by the WMS service, and those transferred to the system from outside. Ready-made base maps, satellite images, maps with OpenStreetMap, and 3D building floor models, etc., are available. In addition, base data can be integrated with WMS services that can be produced publicly or privately. In this paper, the orthophoto digital terrain model and cadastral data were integrated into the system as a base. Although it was desired to integrate the digital terrain model into the system, it could not be integrated. In fact, the system did not accept the produced digital terrain model because it was not of sufficient quality. In addition, NASA's public satellite images and OpenStreetMap's street maps are available as a base for the system.

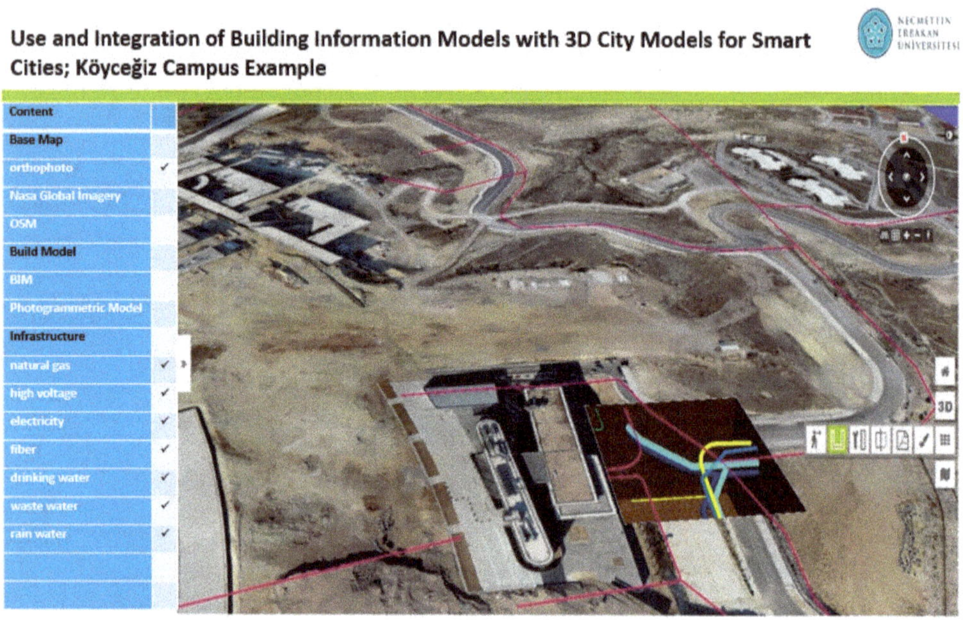

Figure 17. Supplementary data.

4.3. *Query and Analysis*

With the virtualcityMAP application, many query methods and analyses can be performed. First of all, the working area can be viewed from different perspectives with 2D and 3D viewers. In addition to 2D length and area queries, 3D horizontal and vertical length and area queries can be performed. In addition, horizontal and vertical slices of the models can be made using the clipping function. It is also possible to draw with points, lines, polygons, and their derivatives. New attachments can be added to the work and data import/export can be provided. Finally, the virtualcityMAP application can also perform some GIS analysis. The first one is the visibility and shadow analysis. Thanks to the application, the light and shadows falling on the models at different times of the day can be controlled, and solutions to issues such as energy efficiency can be produced. Another analysis is the proximity/distance analysis of the building to points of interest (POIs) thanks to OpenStreetMap maps. As a final analysis, the nonspatial attribute information contained in the GML data can be clicked on the relevant building to present this data with the balloon that opens.

5. Conclusions

The concept of the smart city will advance significantly with the integration of BIM, which specializes in building the smallest component of a city and has as much detail on buildings as GIS, which specializes in the city as a whole and has many details in general but does not deal with the details of the small components themselves. This is because virtual cities, integrated with the city as a whole, are built in their real locations in the world, reaching the most detailed levels of buildings and constructing their digital twins. In addition, analysis and management studies for smart cities can be carried out quickly with the help of fields such as artificial intelligence and machine learning, which are crucial components of technological breakthroughs.

The need for indoor models and building geometries in geographic information systems has been made clear by the growing complexity of cities and the efficient management of buildings and facilities. To this end, a study on 3D modeling and visualization for

GIS integration is provided. There are not many studies that automatically transform interior models called "LoD4" for GIS integration into the CityGML idea. There are usually semi-automatic conversion experiments like this one. Providing fully automatic integration between IFC and CityGML will come next.

Even if CityGML 3.0 makes provisions for BIM integration, it would be more beneficial for smart cities to have a common standard for BIM/GIS. That way, better solutions will be produced with a single software that conforms to the standard and a single expert who knows two subjects. Otherwise, the problem of integrating software from two different disciplines that are not integrated with each other and the need for experts from two different disciplines to understand each other will continue as it is today.

Although there are studies on the integration of BIM and GIS, it is still not at the desired level. The four different categories of barriers to a defined full integration are as follows: BIM usage and routines, detail differences, coordinate systems and georeferencing, and formats and software. In addition, in 3D city models, web-based clients cannot make the desired 3D geospatial analyst on BIM data.

This research has successfully tested the integration, visualization, and analysis functionality of 3D city models and BIM data over the Web in virtualcityMAP, which uses the open-source virtual web globe Cesium, which uses HTML5 and WebGL infrastructure. Cesium is an open-source project supported by a large user base and still needs improvements for both the gaming industry and 3D city models. In particular, the 3D Tiles format is still in a very early stage of development. It is expected to efficiently visualize the temporal dimension soon.

As a result, the web-based presentation of BIM models created in buildings and their integration with GIS has been explored. It has been demonstrated that semi-automated GIS-BIM integration is possible and that LIDAR data are an important source of information for both 3D city models and BIM data. It is expected to play a critical role in the creation of smart cities.

Author Contributions: Conceptualization, A.V. and İ.D.; methodology, A.V. and İ.D.; software, İ.D.; validation, A.V. and İ.D.; formal analysis, A.V. and İ.D.; investigation, A.V. and İ.D.; resources, İ.D.; data curation, İ.D.; writing—original draft preparation, İ.D.; writing—review and editing, A.V. and İ.D.; visualization, İ.D.; supervision, A.V.; project administration, A.V. All authors have read and agreed to the published version of the manuscript.

Funding: This research received no external funding.

Data Availability Statement: The original contributions presented in the study are included in the article, further inquiries can be directed to the corresponding author.

Conflicts of Interest: The authors declare no conflicts of interest.

References

1. Azhar, S. Building information modeling (BIM): Trends, benefits, risks, and challenges for the AEC industry. *Leadersh. Manag. Eng.* **2011**, *11*, 241–252. [CrossRef]
2. Lu, Y.; Wu, Z.; Chang, R.; Li, Y. Building Information Modeling (BIM) for green buildings: A critical review and future directions. *Autom. Constr.* **2017**, *83*, 134–148. [CrossRef]
3. Lü, G.; Batty, M.; Strobl, J.; Lin, H.; Zhu, A.X.; Chen, M. Reflections and speculations on the progress in Geographic Information Systems (GIS): A geographic perspective. *Int. J. Geogr. Inf. Sci.* **2019**, *33*, 346–367. [CrossRef]
4. Rai, H.S.; Goyal, L.K.; Chauhan, R.; Kumar, R. Use of BIM in Development of Smart Cities: A Review. *IOP Conf. Ser. Mater. Sci. Eng.* **2020**, *955*, 012010.
5. Bai, Y.; Zadeh, P.A.; Staub-French, S.; Pottinger, R. Integrating GIS and BIM for community-scale energy modeling. In Proceedings of the International Conference on Sustainable Infrastructure, New York, NY, USA, 26–28 October 2017; pp. 185–196.
6. Amirebrahimi, S.; Rajabifard, A.; Mendis, P.; Ngo, T. A Data Model for Integrating GIS and BIM for Assessment and 3D Visualization of Flood Damage to Building. *Locate* **2015**, *15*, 10–12.
7. Zhu, J.; Wright, G.; Wang, J.; Wang, X. A Critical Review of the Integration of Geographic Information System and Building Information Modelling at the Data Level. *ISPRS Int. J. Geo-Inf.* **2018**, *7*, 66. [CrossRef]
8. Open Geospatial Consortium. OGC Standards. Available online: https://www.ogc.org/standard/citygml/ (accessed on 23 June 2023).

9. W3C Recommendation. Extensible Markup Language (XML) 1.0 (Fifth Edition). 26 November 2008. Available online: http://www.w3.org/TR/REC-xml/#dt-cdsection (accessed on 10 June 2023).
10. Marrin, C. Webgl Specification. Version 1.0. 10 February 2011. Available online: https://registry.khronos.org/webgl/specs/1.0.0/ (accessed on 15 March 2023).
11. Taraldsvik, M. Exploring the Future: Is HTML5 the Solution for GIS Applications on the World Wide Web? Master's Thesis, Norwegian University of Science and Technology, Trondheim, Norway, 18 December 2011.
12. Döllner, J.; Kolbe, T.H.; Liecke, F.; Sgouros, T.; Teichmann, K. The Virtual 3D City Model of Berlin—Managing, Integrating, and Communicating Complex Urban Information. In Proceedings of the 25th International Symposiun on Urban Data Management, Aalborg, Denmark, 15–17 May 2006.
13. Sadek, M. The Design and Development of a Virtual 3D City Model. Available online: http://www.hitl.washington.edu/people/bdc/virtualcities.pdf (accessed on 11 March 2023).
14. Mao, B. Visualization and Generalization of 3D City Models. Ph.D. Thesis, KTH Royal Institute of Technology, Stockholm, Sweden, 2 December 2011.
15. Kolbe, T.H.; Gröger, G.; Plümer, L. CityGML: Interoperable Access to 3D City Models. In *Geo-Information for Disaster Management*; van Oosterom, P., Zlatanova, S., Fendel, E.M., Eds.; Springer: Berlin/Heidelberg, Germany, 2005.
16. Biljecki, F.; Ledoux, H.; Stoter, J. An improved LOD specification for 3D building models. *Comput. Environ. Urban Syst.* **2016**, *59*, 25–37. [CrossRef]
17. OGC City Geography Markup Language (CityGML) 3.0 Conceptual Model Users Guide. 2021. Available online: http://www.opengis.net/doc/UG/CityGML-user-guide/3.0 (accessed on 11 June 2023).
18. Tang, L.; Li, L.; Ying, S.; Lei, Y. A Full Level-of-Detail Specification for 3D Building Models Combining Indoor and Outdoor Scenes. *ISPRS Int. J. Geo-Inf.* **2018**, *7*, 419. [CrossRef]
19. Kutzner, T.; Chaturvedi, K.; Kolbe, T.H. CityGML 3.0: New Functions Open Up New Applications. *J. Photogramm. Remote Sens. Geoinf. Sci. PFG* **2020**, *88*, 43–61. [CrossRef]
20. Underwood, J.; Isikdag, U. *Handbook of Research on Building Information Modeling and Construction Informatics*; IGI Publishing: New York, NY, USA, 2010.
21. Volk, R.; Stengel, J.; Schultmann, F. Building Information Modeling (BIM) for existing buildings. *Autom. Constr.* **2014**, *38*, 109–127. [CrossRef]
22. TrueCADD. BIM LOD Definitions. 2024. Available online: https://www.truecadd.com/level-of-development-lod.php. (accessed on 21 May 2024).
23. Donkers, S.; Ledoux, H.; Zhao, J.J.; Stoter, J. Automatic conversion of IFC datasets to geometrically and semantically correct CityGML LOD3 buildings. *Trans. GIS* **2015**, *20*, 547–569. [CrossRef]
24. Sandeson, L.; BIM to GIS (Advanced) | IFC LOD 200 to LOD 3 CityGML. FME Support Center. 2024. Available online: https://support.safe.com/hc/en-us/articles/25407525412365-BIM-to-GIS-Advanced-IFC-LOD-200-to-LOD-3-CityGML (accessed on 12 June 2023).
25. Geiger, A.; Benner, J.; Haefele, K. Generalization of 3D IFC Building Models. In *3D Geoinformation Science*; Breunig, M., Al-Doori, M., Butwilowski, E., Kuper, P., Benner, J., Haefele, K., Eds.; Springer: Cham, Switzerland, 2015.
26. Amirebrahami, S.; Mendis, P.; Rajabifard, A.; Dug Ngo, T. A BIM-GIS integration method in support the assessment and 3D visualization of flood damage to a building. *Spat. Sci.* **2016**, *61*, 317–350. [CrossRef]
27. El-Mekawy, M. Integrating BIM and GIS for 3D City Modelling—The Case of IFC and CityGML. Licentiate Thesis, Royal Institute of Technology (KTH), Stockholm, Sweden, November 2010.
28. Xia, H.; Liu, Z.; Efremochkina, M.; Liu, X.; Lin, C. Study on city digital twin technologies for sustainable smart city design: A review and bibliometric analysis of geographic information system and building information modeling integration. *Sustain. Cities Soc.* **2022**, *84*, 104009. [CrossRef]
29. Zhu, J.; Wu, P. Towards effectiand BIM/GIS data integration for smart city by integrating computer graphics technique. *Remote Sens.* **2021**, *13*, 1889. [CrossRef]
30. Ohori, K.A.; Ledoux, H.; Peters, R. Chapter 10: Semantic 3D City Models. 3D Modeling of the Built Environment v.08 (Yayımlanmamış kitap). 2022, pp. 91–105. Available online: https://github.com/tudelft3d/3dbook/releases (accessed on 10 June 2023).
31. Herle, S.; Becker, R.; Wollenberg, R.; Blankenbach, J. GIM and BIM: How to obtain interoperability between geospatial and building information modelling? *PFG—J. Photogramm. Remote Sens. Geoinf. Sci.* **2020**, *88*, 33–42. [CrossRef]
32. Sani, M.J.; Rahman, A.A. GIS and BIM integration at data leandl: A review. *Int. Arch. Photogramm. Remote Sens. Spatial Inf. Sci.* **2018**, *XLII-4/W9*, 299–306. [CrossRef]
33. Zhu, J.; Wu, P. BIM/GIS data integration from the perspectiand of information flow. *Autom. Constr.* **2022**, *136*, 104166. [CrossRef]
34. Adouane, K.; Stouffs, R.; Janssen, P.; Domer, B. A model-based approach to conandrt a building BIM-IFC data set model into CityGML. *J. Spat. Sci.* **2020**, *65*, 257–280. [CrossRef]
35. Hor, A.H.; Jadidi, A.; Sohn, G. BIM-GIS integrated geospatial information model using semantic web and RDF graphs. *ISPRS Ann. Photogramm. Remote Sens. Spat. Inf. Sci.* **2016**, *III-4*, 73–79. [CrossRef]
36. Karan, E.P.; Irizarry, J.; Haymaker, J. BIM and GIS integration and interoperability based on semantic web technology. *J. Comput. Civ. Eng.* **2015**, *30*, 04015043. [CrossRef]

37. Costin, A.; Ouellette, J.W.; Beetz, J. Building product models, terminologies and object type libraries. In *Buildings and Semantics: Data Models and Web Technologies for the Built Environment*, 1st ed.; Pauwels, P., McGlinn, K., Eds.; CRC Press: London, UK, 2022.
38. Malinandrni, E.S.; Naticchia, B.; Lerma Garcia, J.L.; Gorreja, A.; Lopez Uriarte, J.; di Stefano, F. A semantic graph database for the interoperability of 3D GIS data. *Appl. Geomat.* **2022**, *14*, 53–66. [CrossRef]
39. Cecchini, C. From data to 3D digital archi and: A GIS-BIM spatial database for the historical centre of Pavia (Italy). *J. Inf. Technol. Constr.* **2019**, *24*, 459–471.
40. Ma, Z.; Ren, Y. Integrated application of BIM and GIS: An overview. *Procedia Eng.* **2017**, *196*, 1072–1079. [CrossRef]
41. Chen, L.C.; Wu, C.H.; Shen, T.S.; Chou, C.C. The application of geometric network models and building information models in geospatial environments for fire-fighting simulations. *Comput. Environ. Urban Syst.* **2014**, *45*, 1–12. [CrossRef]
42. Ingram, J. *Understanding BIM: The Past, Present and Future*; Routledge: London, UK, 2020. [CrossRef]
43. Deng, Y.; Cheng JC, P.; Anumba, C. Mapping between BIM and 3D GIS in different levels of detail using schema mediation and instance comparison. *Autom. Constr.* **2016**, *67*, 1–21. [CrossRef]
44. Blankenbach, J.; Becker, R. Building information modeling. In *Springer Handbook of Geographic Information*; Kresse, W., Danko, D., Eds.; Springer: Berlin/Heidelberg, Germany, 2022; pp. 613–628. [CrossRef]
45. Wu, I.C.; Hsieh, S.H. Transformation from IFC data model to GML data model: Methodology and tool deandlopment. *J. Chin. Inst. Eng.* **2007**, *30*, 1085–1090. [CrossRef]
46. Alhusban, M. Understanding BIM information management processes through international BIM standards. In *BIM Teaching and Learning Handbook—Implementation for Students and Educators*; Hosseini, R.M., Khosrowshahi, F., Aibinu, A.A., Abrishami, S., Eds.; Routledge: London, UK, 2021; pp. 169–183.
47. Zhu, J.; Wu, P. A common approach to geo-referencing building models in industry foundation classes for BIM/GIS integration. *ISPRS Int. J. Geo-Inf.* **2021**, *10*, 362. [CrossRef]
48. Prieto, I.; Izkara, J.L.; Delgado del Hoyo, F.J. Efficient Visualization of the Geometric Information of CityGML: Application for the Documentation of Built Heritage. In Proceedings of the Computational Science and Its Applications (ICCSA 2012), Salvador de Bahia, Brazil, 18–21 June 2012.
49. Hickson, I.; Hyatt, D. HTML5 A Vocabulary and Associated APIs for HTML and XHTML. W3C Working Draft. Available online: https://www.w3.org/TR/2010/WD-html5-20100304/Overview.html (accessed on 9 June 2023).
50. Brunt, P. GLGE WebGL Library/Framework. Available online: https://github.com/supereggbert/GLGE (accessed on 1 June 2023).
51. Iglesias, D.G. Design and Implementation of 3D Buildings Integration for a Webgl-Based Virtual Globe: A Case Study of Valencian Cadastre and Fide Building Mode. Master's Thesis, A Universidade NOVA de Lisboa (UNL) Information Management School (NIMS), Lisboa, Portugal, 2012.
52. Cesiumjs. Available online: https://cesium.com/platform/cesiumjs/ (accessed on 11 February 2023).
53. Three.js. Available online: https://threejs.org/ (accessed on 11 February 2023).
54. Unity 3D. Available online: https://unity3d.com/ (accessed on 10 February 2023).
55. Unreal Engine. Available online: https://www.unrealengine.com/en-US/blog (accessed on 1 February 2023).
56. X3dom. Available online: https://www.x3dom.org/ (accessed on 20 February 2023).
57. OSG.js. Available online: https://cedricpinson.github.io/osgjs-website/ (accessed on 21 February 2023).
58. O3D. WebGL Implementation of O3D. Available online: https://code.google.com/archive/p/o3d/ (accessed on 21 February 2023).
59. WebGL Earth. Available online: https://www.webglearth.com (accessed on 20 February 2023).
60. WebGL Globe. Available online: https://opensource.google.com/projects/webglglobe (accessed on 20 February 2023).
61. Brovelli, M.A.; Minghini, M.; Zamboni, G. New Generation Platforms for Exploration of Crowd-sourced Crowd-sourced Geo-Data. In *Earth Observation Open Science and Innovation*; ISSI Scientific Report Series; Springer: Bern, Switzerland, 2018; Volume 15.
62. Evangelidis, K.; Papadopoulos, T.; Papatheodorou, K.; Mastorokostas, P.; Hilas, C. 3D geospatial visualizations: Animation and motion effects on spatial objects. *Comput. Geosci.* **2018**, *111*, 200–212. [CrossRef]
63. Analytics Graphics, Inc. Cesium—WebGL Virtual Globe and Map Engine. Available online: http://cesium.agi.com/ (accessed on 21 February 2022).
64. Cesium. Cesium Supported Data Formats. 2022. Available online: https://cesium.com/learn/3d-tiling/tiler-data-formats/ (accessed on 20 February 2023).
65. Abdallah, A. Securing Online 3D Web-Based Models. In Proceedings of the Conference: ICT and Societal Challenges LAU Beirut, New York, NY, USA, 27–29 April 2017.
66. Limper, M.; Wanger, S.; Stein, C.; Jung, Y.; Strok, A.; IGD, F.; Darmstadt, T. Fast Delivery of 3D Web Content: A Case Study, Web3D. In Proceedings of the 18th International Conference on 3D Web Technology, San Sebastian, Spain, 20–22 June 2013; pp. 11–17.
67. Grasberger, H.; Shirazian, P.; Wyvill, B.; Greenberg, S. A Dataefficient Collaborative Modelling Method Using Websockets and the Blobtree for Over-the Air Networks. In Proceedings of the 18th International Conference on 3D Web Technology, San Sebastian, Spain, 20–22 June 2013; pp. 29–37.
68. Sons, K.; Klein, F.; Rubinstein, D.; Byelozyorov, S.; Slusallek, P. XML3D-Interactive 3D graphics for the Web. In Proceedings of the 15th International Conference on 3D Technology, Los Angeles, CA, USA, 24–25 July 2010; pp. 175–184.

69. Abdallah, A. 3D Web-Based Shape Modelling: Data Extraction and Delivery. In Proceedings of the FASSI 2017 the Third International Conference on Fundamentals and Advances in Software Systems Integration, Rome, Italy, 10–14 September 2017.
70. Sandeson, L. BIM to GIS (Intermediate) | IFC LOD 300 to LOD 4 CityGML. FME Support Center. 2024. Available online: https://support.safe.com/hc/en-us/articles/25407718003341-BIM-to-GIS-Intermediate-IFC-LOD-300-to-LOD-4-CityGML (accessed on 13 June 2023).
71. Virtual City System. Properties of VirtualCityMap. 2021. Available online: https://vc.systems/en/solutions/3d-city-models/ (accessed on 20 February 2023).

MDPI AG
Grosspeteranlage 5
4052 Basel
Switzerland
Tel.: +41 61 683 77 34

MDPI Books Editorial Office
E-mail: books@mdpi.com
www.mdpi.com/books

www.ingramcontent.com/pod-product-compliance
Lightning Source LLC
Chambersburg PA
CBHW061557220926
51850CB00005B/360